DATE DUE

The Deficit
and the Public Interest

The Deficit and the Public Interest

*The Search for Responsible Budgeting
in the 1980s*

Joseph White and Aaron Wildavsky

UNIVERSITY OF CALIFORNIA PRESS
Berkeley   Los Angeles   London
RUSSELL SAGE FOUNDATION
New York

University of California Press
Berkeley and Los Angeles, California

University of California Press, Ltd.
London, England

© 1989 by
The Russell Sage Foundation

Library of Congress Cataloging-in-Publication Data

White, Joseph, 1952–
   The deficit and the public interest : the search for responsible
budgeting in the 1980s / Joseph White and Aaron Wildavsky.
     p.   cm.
   Bibliography: p.
   Includes index.
   ISBN 0-520-06533-6 (alk. paper)
   1. Budget—United States. 2. Budget deficits—United States.
3. Government spending policy—United States. I. Wildavsky, Aaron
B. II.· Title.
HJ2051.W45   1989
336.3′9′0973—dc20   89-5122
                                                  CIP

Printed in the United States of America
1 2 3 4 5 6 7 8 9

For Michael J. White and Daniel K. Tenenberg

CONTENTS

LIST OF ACRONYMS
AND ABBREVIATIONS

AARP	American Association of Retired Persons
ACRS	Accelerated Cost Recovery System
AFDC	Aid to Families with Dependent Children
BA	Budget Authority
BRA	Budget Reconciliation Act
CBO	Congressional Budget Office
CCC	Commodity Credit Corporation
CDBG	Community Development Block Grant
CDF	Conservative Democratic Forum
CEA	Council of Economic Advisers
CETA	Comprehensive Employment and Training Act
CHAP	Child Health Assurance Program
COBRA	Consolidated Omnibus Budget Reconciliation Act
COLA	Cost of Living Adjustment
CPI	Consumer Price Index
CR	Continuing Resolution
CSR	Civil Service Retirement
DEFRA	Deficit Reduction Act
DNC	Democratic National Committee
DOD	Department of Defense
DRG	Diagnosis Related Group
DSG	Democratic Study Group
EAP	Energy Assistance Program

EITC	Earned Income Tax Credit
ERTA	Economic Recovery Tax Act
FAIR	Fund to Assure an Independent Retirement
FBI	Federal Bureau of Investigation
FICA	Federal Insurance Contributions Act
GAO	General Accounting Office
GNP	Gross National Product
GRH	Gramm-Rudman-Hollings
GRS	General Revenue Sharing
HBC	House Budget Committee
HHS	Health and Human Services
HI	Hospital Insurance
HPO&CS	House Post Office & Civil Service Committee
IDB	Industrial Development Bonds
IMF	International Monetary Fund
IRA	Individual Retirement Account
JTC	Joint Tax Committee
LIHEAP	Low-Income Housing Energy Assistance Program
LSC	Legal Services Corporation
MDA	Maximum Deficit Amount
NAM	National Association of Manufacturers
NEC	National Economic Commission
OASDHI	Old Age, Survivors, Disability and Health Insurance
OASI	Old Age and Survivors Insurance
OBRA	Omnibus Budget Reconciliation Act
OMB	Office of Management and Budget
PATCO	Professional Air Traffic Controllers' Organization
PPA	Program Project and Activity
PPBS	Planning, Programming, and Budgeting System
RDF	Rapid Deployment Force
SBA	Small Business Administration
SBC	Senate Budget Committee
SDI	Strategic Defense Initiative
SSI	Supplemental Security Income

TEFRA   Tax Equity & Fiscal Responsibility Act of 1982
TRAC   Tax Reform Action Coalition
UDAG   Urban Development Action Grants
UMTA   Urban Mass Transportation Agency
WIC   Women and Infant Children Nutrition Program

LIST OF TABLES

PREFACE:
THE ERA OF THE BUDGET

Political time is counted not in years but in issues; a political era is defined by the concerns that dominate debate and action, so that about other issues we ask: How does that affect————? Before the Civil War, all issues were subsumed by slavery; the tariff, internal improvements, territorial expansion were approved, opposed, or manipulated according to their perceived impact upon the battle between the "slave powers" and the free states. At the turn of the century, industrialization and the rise of giant corporations posed the challenge; conservation, antitrust legislation, and modernized government were part of the response. The Great Depression defined the 1930s; after 1945, the cold war cast its shadow over domestic politics as well as foreign affairs. The civil rights movement shaped the 1960s in ways too obvious to be seen at the time. Rights were expanded, grievances redressed, and authority, whether public or corporate, was continually called into account. Those themes carried over from the enfranchisement of blacks to the women's movement, the expansion of the welfare state, and even environmental concerns. Could institutions unable or unwilling to provide social justice, the reasoning went, be trusted to protect nature's bounty against dangers stemming from technology?

Now we are living in the era of the budget. The budget has been to our era what civil rights, communism, the depression, industrialization, and slavery were at other times. Nor does the day of the budget show signs of ending.

Budgeting has always been important; it is a process by which resources are acquired and allocated to the vast array of activities that make up our national government. Presidents and Congresses have had bitter clashes. Richard Nixon's tactic, impoundment, was considered as an article in the bill of impeachment. A horror of deficits is deeply rooted in American political rhetoric and belief, and blame for deficits has been a staple of political combat. Fights about the budget are not new.

What is new is their ubiquity. Year after year the key question has been, What will the president and Congress do about the deficit? Virtually all other issues are discussed and decided in terms of impacts on the deficit. Defense, for example, is discussed in terms not of strategy and needs but of the deficit and "fair shares" of the budget. For example, when Ferdinand Marcos was overthrown in the Philippines and replaced by Corazon Aquino, the new leader received a standing ovation from Congress, but her request for substantial aid was denied. The deficit mattered more.

That much is easy to see, but there is more. Budget worries shape the ways politicians make decisions. Congress and the president consider programs in terms of not only what they do or who they help but also when they spend the money. The appropriations committees meet targets for outlays by cutting quick-spending programs like military payroll instead of slow-spending ones like new aircraft carriers—even though both staff and committee members believe personnel and maintenance are more important than new procurement. As budget worries distort decisions, they combine with grave disagreement over priorities to distort procedure. More and more policy choices use two new, giant budgeting vehicles: the reconciliation act and the continuing resolution. Authorizers feel they are losing power to appropriators, who agree. Budget fights have "put things in such chaos," a House appropriations leader explains, "that in the end [the Appropriations Committee] is more powerful than before. Not by design but by dumb accident."

Not by design, but not quite by accident either, budget politics has shaped the wider conflict between the two political parties. Before Ronald Reagan took office, concern about the deficit's supposed effect on inflation and disagreement about military spending split and demoralized the Democratic party. Democrats lost both their rationale and their argument as to how spending programs, which served their constituents, were good for the whole nation. By 1984 Democratic presidential candidate Walter Mondale was campaigning on a promise to raise taxes so as to lower deficits. The strategy was so strange and unsuccessful that we might miss its significance: the Democrats were not sure what else to say. As for the Republicans, their problem has not so much been unpopularity; though they lost the Senate in 1986, they were better off than they had been for most of the postwar era. The Republicans' problem was guilt. After careers of inveighing against deficits, Republicans found themselves in charge of the worst deficits in history. A few, like Jack Kemp, didn't care. But most, like Bob Dole, did. As the budget bind wore on, Republicans in Congress grew more and more desperate for a way out.

The deficit became a crisis of confidence for political leaders. Members of Congress particularly saw it as a test of responsibility, of their ability to govern. Their own self-criticism was amplified by the establishment press and academic economists. The public agreed, but the public also objected to almost any action. After all, nothing terrible had happened yet. Why risk recession or savage welfare or undermine defense when no such drastic action appeared called for? The public was willing to cut "waste," but the politicians believed they had to cut programs or raise taxes. They bewailed deficits so loudly largely to convince the public to accept some pain in the interest of deficit reduction, but the public wasn't buying. Caught between their own rhetoric (and beliefs) and the limits of public support, politicians did things that made them feel even worse. Both president and Congress cheated in budget assumptions. They made fake cuts, such as changing a payment date from the last day of one fiscal year to the first day of the next. At the height of their panic, the politicians passed Gramm-Rudman-Hollings—a piece of legislation best described as budgetary terrorism, only this time the hostages were their own keepers.

Budget stalemate generated a desire to demonstrate a capacity to govern that led to radical changes in tax and expenditure processes. The main theme was the public interest in deficit reduction versus the nefarious private interests in self-aggrandizement. Our book issues a fundamental challenge to this "politicians-as-fools-and-cowards" thesis.

As we write, the budget battles have hit a bit of a lull. President Bush and Congress have called a cease-fire. Calm, however, is not comfort. On Capitol Hill the staff and members of the appropriations committees agonize more than ever about how they will produce bills that have enough programs but a small enough total to get through Congress. Off the Hill, in the cold shadow of the stock market's "Black Monday," economists, journalists, and other policy elites talk about the dangers of a financial crash if the deficit is not "fixed." These worries may be overstated, but they are pervasive enough to assure that the next few years will be as beset by budget difficulties as were the last year of President Carter and the eight years of President Reagan. And that is if there is not a recession. The era of the budget is not nearly over.

If Americans are going to live with the dominance of budget politics, they had better understand it. We write this book to help both citizens and politicians understand what has been going on, why it has happened, and therefore what we may reasonably expect to happen next. Part of our concern is with matters of fact. Who did what to whom? Why? What are the sides and the goals of the players? As best we can tell, what are the effects of the deficit? Where did it come from? These questions of fact then shade into questions of evaluation.

Evaluation can look like blame: Who is responsible for the deficit? But it is not just personal or partisan. Above all, we must understand what are reasonable demands of our political system. We agree with our politicians that the overarching question about deficit politics is whether our institutions and the people in them have behaved in a way that, given no democracy can satisfy everyone, is worthy of support. Ironically, we are more understanding of the politicians than they are of themselves.

The battle of the budget is a story of congressional horse-trading, partisan posturing, and technical tricks that affect billions of dollars. It is also a story of politicians operating within constraints set by both public opinion and political interpretations of economic reality. Throughout our story politicians were being told that the financial markets demanded one policy or another; as custodians of the economy, the government had to go along. We assess those claims, finding great reason for skepticism. Whether right or wrong, however, beliefs about how the budget affects the economy were and are a major part of budget politics. We therefore emphasize those beliefs—the "responsible opinion" represented in the pages of *Time,* the *Washington Post,* and other "powers that be" and stated with authority by "expert" economists. What these organs say is not simply "reporting" but a political fact. Politicians, like the rest of us, get opinions from experts and media stories; politicians, unlike the rest of us, have to worry about how the media will represent them to the public. For both reasons—the media as a source of opinion and as a shaper of it—the media view of what is required by the public interest influences political action.

Some of our facts will probably surprise most readers. Few people realize how much politicians, particularly members of Congress, have done about the deficit. They seem to have done little only because the problem was much larger than anyone realized. Each year's progress was diminished by each year's bad news. The budget cutting or defense buildup began not with Reagan but with Carter. And Reagan's victories in 1981 were primarily due to neither his great political skill nor positive public support. Far more important were the election of a much more conservative Congress than had existed before and a more negative desperation among the public, which made Democrats leery of seeming to obstruct. In these and other matters, we try to set the record straight.

Yet our evaluation may seem even more surprising. We see plenty of gimmicks, foolishness, and deception. But the crux of political understanding and practice is appreciating the many legitimate goals that people bring to a choice. Budgeting involves meeting obligations, keeping promises. It involves choices about values, about which purposes are of highest priority. It involves questions of power: How are we to be governed, and by whom? Most of all, tax and spending decisions involve real people with real pain and real benefits. What happens to any of us—the fate of farmers, the poor, or General Dynamics—may have meaning to others. In the rhetoric of deficit reduction, these other matters are either disparaged as "special interests" or, worse, ignored. Persistent deficits are blamed on a lack of courage or good will. Wrong. Deficits persist because all choices are bad. Choices are hard because important values are helped or hurt by all alternatives.

We admit to a prejudice in favor of understanding other people's values. Not only is that our business, but we two disagree on much. One voted for Ronald Reagan; the other would vote for any Democrat, the more liberal the better. We do not believe that understanding political differences requires downplaying conflict. Instead, we emphasize the real differences of interest and ideology behind the convenient rhetoric of "public" versus "special" interests. Naturally all sides think they are the public and the other guys are the selfish special interests.

Rather than clearly distinguishing between private and public interests, much of politics focuses on defining the relationship of the respective spheres. Thus the battle of the budget is largely about defining the role of the government and its relationship to the people: which responsibilities with what priorities—managing the economy, protecting the poor, defending the nation—are things "all good people" should support. All good people do not agree; that's part of the problem. Because people define their private interest as the public interest, they become self-righteous; yet political debate has to work that way.

At bottom, the budget battles are about what kind of country we want to be, expressed through what kind of government we will have. Whether the deficit will be diminished as a proportion of national product at high or low levels of taxing and spending will make a significant difference in the kind and quality of public life. Whether the struggle over the deficit leaves us with enhanced respect for the procedures and institutions through which we attempt self-rule or destroys our respect for government may well matter as much or more than the outcomes of specific issues. All of us have heard of extremists of the right or the left. Extremism of the center, defined as disregard and belittling of established procedures and institutions in the name of a transcendent goal, such as budget balance, is a new and troubling phenomenon we wish to bring to public attention, partly because everyone else sees it differently or not at all. Procedures are not considered a problem, but big deficits justify radical change.

This book is the story of how budgeting overwhelmed governing. We describe and discuss the ramifications of events in the economy, among the electorate, and in the policymaking processes of Washington, D. C. We hope to have captured the feel of events, the mood, because a growing frustration with budgeting became a factor in itself. Throughout we try to discern the real stakes behind the rhetoric. We emphasize why choices were so difficult.

In the end, we ask the big questions: What does this story tell us about our capacity to govern? Is ours a system, to quote Adlai Stevenson's definition of democracy, in which "the people get the government they deserve"? Can a government by the people and for the people have the authority to be a government of the people? Or does the budget impasse show that the more our government represents us, the less it can govern?

ACKNOWLEDGMENTS

Imagine that you are standing before an audience of students or of the general citizenry and you ask whether they think Congress has done a little or a lot to reduce the deficit. Virtually 100 percent say "Little or nothing." They are wrong, as the reader will see, but in this respect their reply is only a tiny part of the flood of misinformation about the deficit that we seek to correct here—misinformation joined to a kind of collective amnesia in which only a few of the major events of the past decades, and virtually none of the budgeting decisions except the tax cuts, survive in public consciousness.

We try to remedy the lack of public memory by providing detailed accounts of decisions and of how budgets were made and unmade. The errors in what is remembered have led us to exercise exceptional care in assembling the facts. Because of the attention paid to taxing and spending at the time, there is a considerable public record on which to rely, including many published interviews with leading participants. We cite reports in the major media not only to verify facts that could be obtained from numerous (and, some readers have told us, more respectable) sources but also to show what politicians were reading and saying to one another at the time.

In order to probe more deeply, we also conducted 112 interviews with people in the White House, the Office of Management and Budget, the executive departments, and Congress. These discussions, sometimes lasting several hours, took place on condition that we not attribute them to their sources. It seemed more important to us to get closer to the truth than to attach names to interviews. Nevertheless, we have followed certain precautions: where different interviews bear each other out, we have so indicated; where sources conflict, we have let the reader know. By and large, once given the essential clues, we have been able to track down the relevant information in published sources. Let us put the matter another way: there is much greater distance between the information available in numerous published sources and public discussion of the deficit than there is between different participants' versions of events.

We thank those participants who sought to enlighten us even at the risk of failing to persuade us of their interpretation of events. We are especially grateful to congressional staff members who devoted more time than we had a right to expect in order to explain the intricacies of budgeting matters as only they know them. We have tried to repay the gift of their time by providing an account that meets their standards.

Because we sought to recreate these events in lifelike detail, giving the reader the context as well as the facts themselves, our first draft was half again as large as this book. The reader must therefore sympathize with those who read the entire manuscript with a critical eye: Naomi Caiden, Donald W. Moran, Lawrence Malkin, Irene Rubin, Allen Schick, and anonymous reviewers from the Russell Sage Foundation and the University of California Press. A number of other people read selected chapters: Ron King, Theodore Marmor, William Niskanen, Richard Rose, and Murray Weidenbaum. They helped us improve our prose and straighten our line of argument. No one would dream of holding any of these responsible for a book that runs so strongly counter to the contemporary trend of finding fault with public officials, sometimes even excusing those who have faulted themselves.

Without the financial assistance of the Russell Sage Foundation, which gave a three-year grant to Aaron Wildavsky, the research for this book could not have been undertaken. Special thanks go to the presidents of the Foundation, Marshall Robinson, who helped get this project started, and Eric Wanner, who helped maintain it. When something happened that knowledgeable people believed could never occur, that is, tax reform, or never imagined might take place, namely, the Gramm-Rudman-Hollings Act, the Ford Foundation came to our rescue with a last-minute infusion of funds.

Aaron Wildavsky wishes to express his gratitude to the institutions at the University of California in Berkeley that sustained him during the years of research and writing a book of this kind requires: the Political Science Department, the Graduate School of Public Policy, and the Survey Research Center. They provided support for secretarial assistance, research, endless trips to the library, even longer telephone conversations; most of all, they accepted the not-always-self-evident proposition that something new could and should be said about federal budgeting.

There is no way to account for the innumerable conversations about budgets and deficits through which colleagues helped clarify our thoughts. John Gilmour, Duane Oldfield, and James Savage, then graduate students and now colleagues in the political science profession, went back and forth with us over numerous issues and read several chapters in the critical way that only those who are exceptionally knowledgeable and who are getting their own back can muster. Naomi Caiden gave us her friendship as well as her discerning comments about what was really happening in the world of budgeting. Our debt to colleagues in the study of budgeting and national politics will be evident from footnotes. Here we would like to single out the helpful and eminent group employed by Congress at the Congressional Research Service. Our counselors there included Stanley Bach, Louis Fisher, Robert Keith, and our late and dearly missed friend Charles Levine. Congress is well served.

Joseph White researched and wrote part of this book in Berkeley, but most of his work was done at the Brookings Institution in Washington, where he was first a student fellow and then a staff member. Thanks to the hospitality of the two directors of the Brookings Governmental Studies Program, Paul Peterson and Thomas Mann, the two authors were able to work together during Aaron Wildavsky's frequent visits to Washington to interview and to discuss the research with his coauthor. Above all, Brookings gave Joseph White a home within that remarkable community of scholars. Among the many advisers found there—whether the authors' questions involved defense or welfare, process or purpose— good ideas came in a constant stream from Edward M. Bernstein, Daniel Brill, Joshua M. Epstein, Robert Katzmann, James M. Lindsay, Lawrence Malkin, Ken Mayer, David Menefee-Libey, Joseph Pechman, Paul Pierson, Robert Reischauer, Alice Rivlin, Mark Rom, Yahya Sadowski, Steven S. Smith, R. Kent Weaver, Thomas Weko, and others who should be thanked. It is superfluous to say that neither they nor the Institution is responsible for the content of this book, if only because they did not agree with one another and the authors often did not agree with them even while benefiting from their association.

A personal word from Joseph White: My brother, Michael J. White, has more to do than anyone else with what good I have managed to accomplish. From the time he taught me to read and do math and play chess, through my 3:00 A.M. talks with him when he got home from driving a cab while he was in college, through my own rough years in college and after, as, finally, I perhaps figured out what to do with my life, my older brother has been a joy and support. Beyond everything else, his eagerness to see the world clearly is the greatest gift he has offered me, and I have tried to seize it.

A dedication from Aaron Wildavsky: I would like to dedicate my half of the book to Daniel K. Tenenberg for his friendship and wisdom. Dan has helped me see more clearly the difference between the versions of the public interest discussed here, from doing what other people think is good for them to doing what one thinks is good for others, especially when they don't like it. For an explanation of why that difference is central to understanding the battle of the budget, the dominant political issue of the 1980s, read on.

ONE

Madisonian Budgeting, or Why the Process Is So Complicated

The United States government's budget process is unique in its complexity. No other nation has a legislature so strong it actually dominates spending and taxing decisions, though, of course, without actually eliminating the important part played by the president and the executive branch. Congress itself is notoriously fragmented, partly by constitutional design and partly because its members and their constituents like it that way. Because majorities within Congress shift from election to election and program to program, winning coalitions often differ from month to month and issue to issue. Thus, the president's budget proposal—really his asking price—varies from being the center of negotiations to "dead on arrival." And Congress is quite capable of engaging in a series of exhausting votes that do not resolve matters.

There is more. In recent years, Congress has made many changes in budget procedures, partly to make up for its failure to follow past procedures. But nothing has been thrown out. Thus congressional supremacy coexists with the 1921 measures giving the president a bit more to say and the 1974 measures taking some of that back and trying to centralize consideration of the budget within Congress. Budget committees are loaded on top of appropriations and revenue committees; budget resolutions whose rules differ in each house are superimposed on the regular legislative processes. If one multiplies the number of independent actors times the number of different procedures times the variety of issues, bringing forth different alliances, no other national process can match the American for the sheer volume of considerations that must be taken into account.

We call this budget process Madisonian because it is designed not to secure efficiency but to prevent the abuse of power. Of course, we could argue that, because contemporary budgeting has not been designed by anyone, our ability to govern, not merely to prevent others from governing, is at stake. However one looks at this matter in the light of disputes over the deficit, the path of change leads through the same budget labyrinth. If you don't know the rules, you can't play the most important political game in America.

"Budget" is both a noun and a verb, both a thing and an action. According to one dictionary, to budget is "to determine in advance the expenditure of (time, money, etc.) over a period of time." We would add to this the common understanding that budgeting also involves assessing resources and relating them to expenditure. By another definition, the budget as a noun is a "comprehensive work plan," projecting the activities of an individual or organization.

The federal government does considerable budgeting, which means making commitments about future activity. Most of these commitments are in the form of either laws or agreements behind the laws between the executive and Congress. These are promises to society that government will do something: pay for medical care for the poor, buy some number of jet fighters, or employ so many people to test new pharmaceutical products.

The U.S. government does not, however, consider all these matters at once, creating a comprehensive work plan. The president's budget, issued with great fanfare each January, is indeed comprehensive. Yet it combines proposals for new commitments and estimates of old ones; it makes no commitments of its own. The obligations of the U.S. government are those mandated or permitted by law, and Congress passes no comprehensive budget law.

Instead, Congress (and the president by signing) makes commitments in a great many ways, at a great many times. "The budget" is not one decision but many.

Types of Budget Commitments

Laws that commit the government to spend money create *budget authority*. Budget authority (BA) is just what it sounds like: authority granted to some agent of the government to spend money. The money spent is called an *outlay*. Outlays cannot be made without budget authority; but some small amounts of BA may never be spent if the government buys something more cheaply than anticipated.

In a given year some appropriated funds may remain unspent. The acts provide budget authority, but each year's outlays (i.e., actual spending) combine this year's and previous years' authority. For example, an appropriation may allow the Urban Mass Transit Administration (UMTA) to commit $200 million for a rapid transit extension in Chicago. This BA allows UMTA to enter into an obligation (i.e., contract) to spend that money. The money actually will be outlaid (spent) over a period of years as the extension is built and material, labor, and design are paid for. In fiscal 1980, the year before our story begins, 17.9 percent of federal outlays were based on such prior year contracts and obligations;[1] a similar percentage of the budget authority obligated for fiscal 1980 would not be spent until later years.

This difference between budget authority and outlays is the primary source of confusion for people who follow federal budgeting. Congress votes on BA, but each year's spending—and thus fiscal policy and the deficit—depends on outlays. Congress has some idea how much outlay will result from its votes on BA, but the estimates can be controversial.

Budget authority itself takes a variety of forms, related mostly to the kind of activity being authorized. The major distinction is between *annual* and *permanent* appropriations.

Annual appropriations are enacted in the yearly appropriations acts, which allow agencies (e.g., the FBI or National Institutes of Health) to spend or contract to spend specific amounts of money. Annual appropriations acts are drafted and managed by special appropriations committees in the House and the Senate. Each committee in each house has the same thirteen subcommittees and identical jurisdiction over a group of federal agencies. Each subcommittee is supposed to produce a bill for its jurisdiction every year; thus there are thirteen annual appropriations acts.

Permanent appropriations generally are made by Congress in other legislation; the most important is the Social Security Act of 1935 with its numerous amendments. Almost all these are *entitlements;* the law says that a person or group is "entitled" to some payment if certain conditions are met.

Entitlements do not specify spending totals. Total spending under these programs is simply the sum of legislatively mandated payments applied for by recipients. Totals are not only not directly chosen, but they can also be known only in retrospect. One cannot know in advance either the number of unemployed or their previous base earnings, and therefore one cannot know the cost of unemployment insurance. Finally, while some entitlements are formally appropriated (for example, for food stamps, each year appropriations must be made so programs can draw funds from the Treasury), the government's obligations are created in the authorizing law. The appropriations committees cannot erase those obligations.

The differences between appropriation and entitlement spending mean that legal authority for spending is the product of decisions made by different committees at different times. Entitlements have been adopted and amended separately over the years. When one considers that over half the outlays comes from entitlements and that each year's appropriations create outlays over a period of years, it should be no surprise that only 27.3 percent of the outlays in the government's 1980 fiscal year resulted from that year's appropriations process.

What is true of spending is more true of taxing: tax law is an accretion of years of decisions. Like entitlement legislation, tax law is open-ended: individuals are obligated to contribute according to some criteria; the government is not guaranteed some specific sum of revenue. Revenue may be influenced and estimated but not decreed.

Tax legislation is considered by the House Committee on Ways and Means and the Senate Committee on Finance. These committees also control the many entitlement programs, such as unemployment compensation and the massive Old Age, Survivors, Disability and Health Insurance (OASDHI), that have special taxes to finance their benefits. OASDHI includes the old-age pensions we normally call social security, disability pensions, and medicare. Sometimes that system's taxes (FICA on your paycheck) are described as contributions earmarked for trust funds. They are still taxes: if you meet the criteria for paying them, do not pay them, and are caught, you may go to jail.

The tax committees have another type of jurisdiction that resembles spending in that it may allocate benefits among people and groups for social purposes: *tax preferences*. These provisions of the law can reduce a taxpayer's liability to the government so long as that person performs some act the government wishes to encourage. Tax preferences that benefit individuals greatly can yet be justified in wider social terms: the tax deduction for mortgage interest, for example, encourages both the construction industry and the social goal of widespread individual home ownership. Those who do not like a tax preference call it a loophole; the metaphor, suggesting money escaping or being diverted from its intended use, is misleading. Such loopholes, passed by Congress, are as intended as any other legislation.

Tax preferences and entitlements are similar in that people make commitments because of government policy—to invest under certain depreciation rules, to retire at a certain age given social security. Because people take action based on these promises, politicians are particularly reluctant to break them. The best-known entitlements and tax preferences are promises to huge numbers of people: the elderly (social security) or homeowners (the mortgage interest deduction). Both policies also increased substantially in the post–World War II era. On the spending side, which received the most attention, entitlements grew in part from keeping old promises; as more and more people reached retirement age, the promised social security or civil service retirement pensions cost the government more. Entitlements also grew from making new promises: medical care for the aged (medicare), nutrition for the impoverished (food stamps), or increases in the benefits of big, old programs (social security).

Entitlement spending rose from 35.2 percent of federal outlays in fiscal 1967 to 53.6 percent in 1974 to 55.7 percent in 1980.[2] Many commentators view this increase as an end-run by authorizing committees (spenders) around appropriations committees (guardians of the public purse). Yet the major entitlements would fit poorly into a system of annual appropriations. Medical care for the aged, for example, could be provided by annually funded government-run hospitals, but that is called socialized medicine, not considered politically feasible. Once the decision is made to reimburse patients for costs incurred in the private sector, spending cannot be planned in advance. In short, there are legitimate policy reasons for entitlement funding—efficiency or the political difficulty of alternatives or the desire to keep promises.

These good reasons should not obscure the consequences for government. First, more and more spending is not controlled by the institutions created for annual review of spending, the appropriations committees. Second, entitlement spending is subject to the vagaries of the economy; in providing certainty to the recipients, the government takes uncertainty upon itself. Third, the major entitlements are very difficult to cut.

A Madisonian Budget System

All modern governments are constrained in their budgeting by similar problems of budget composition. Most, however, have far simpler political systems. The main story of this book, the battle for control between Congress and the president, would make no sense in other nations. In England or Germany or Japan or Sweden the executive grows out of and dominates the legislature; an executive cannot exist without a legislative majority. If no majority exists, the government loses a vote of confidence, and a new election is held. In the United States the executive and the legislature may remain locked in bitter combat for years, each unable to remove the other.

This separation of the executive and the legislature is one of two distinguishing and, for budgeting, crucial aspects of the political system created by the Constitution. It is not just a structure but a value: we are taught in school James Madison's arguments that "separation of powers" and "checks and balances" prevent tyrannical government and protect minorities. What is less obvious may be even more important: a system of checks and balances means that the legislature is as strong as the executive.

In other countries the executive assembles a budget proposal, which is difficult enough, and presents it to the legislature, expecting it to pass, as designed, in one bill. There may be some small changes at the margins, but the legislature is in no position to extensively revise the executive's plan. After all, the prime minister leads the majority party or coalition. Even in American state governments, however, the legislature is much more active than elsewhere; and Congress is, beyond doubt, the most powerful legislature of all.[3]

Congress's unique role in budgeting is established by the Constitution, which states: "No Money may be drawn from the Treasury but in Consequence of Appropriations made by Law" (Article 1, Section 9). The president can only spend money if Congress lets him. This power of the purse was described by Madison, extrapolating from Parliament's battles with the king, as "the most complete and effectual weapon with which any constitution can arm the immediate representatives of the people, for obtaining a redress of every grievance, and for carrying into effect every just and salutary measure."[4] Congress may not feel its power of the purse is quite so effective, but if members of Congress as a group can ever be said to agree on anything it is that their power of the purse must be retained if they are to maintain their independence.

That means power over little as well as big things. Editorialists—and presidents—continually criticize Congress for attention to details that are beneath the dignity of a national legislature. In his 1988 State of the Union message, President Reagan cited "such items as cranberry research, blueberry research, the study of crawfish and the commercialization of wild flowers." From Congress's perspective, however, the issue is not whether there will be programs with local "pork-barrel" benefits. The Department of Agriculture is going to do research on *something, somewhere*.[5] The issue is who will decide which localities benefit. If the president decides, he has a substantial weapon to reward and punish legislators; if he can control the members, he can control Congress.[6]

We have, then, a Madisonian budget system, based on ambition opposing ambition, as part of our Madisonian government. After two hundred years we still have a powerful legislature, divided internally and checked externally. If anything, the system of checks and balances has grown more elaborate, both internally through the committee system and externally as Congress has given the president powers to do things Congress feels necessary but difficult for itself.

The Executive Budget

The president's budget is issued at the beginning of each year, shortly after the president's State of the Union address.[7] To this writing, it remains the only document that resembles our commonsense notion of a budget: a detailed summary of anticipated expenses and revenues, summed to totals that represent the fiscal policy of the U.S. government, a financial plan. The budget is produced by the entire executive branch in a process of planning and projection that begins more than a year before the president submits it to Congress. Its preparation is overseen by an elite executive agency of more than five hundred employees (once the Bureau of the Budget; now the Office of Management and Budget). The budget is a six-hundred-page book, accompanied by an appendix roughly as large as the Manhattan telephone directory. Agencies submit tens of thousands of pages of further documentation that are supposed to support presidential proposals and provide detailed plans for using the resources Congress agrees to provide. The president's program sets a standard; proponents of increases to one or another category have to explain not merely why that program needs more money but why it should be allowed to throw the whole budget out of whack. Agency heads must argue for the president's proposals even if they had originally requested greater spending.

The president's budget is only a proposal, without legal force, but it gives him a loud voice in the budget debate. It is the president's program, endorsed by the only official "elected by all the people." The effort expended in its preparation argues for its support; the executive claims to have assembled and considered far more information than Congress could ever manage. If the executive agencies behave and support the budget (a huge "if"), the president can claim that the people who run the programs have asked for these amounts. Because the president ultimately hires and fires, the agencies have reason to go along.

Until 1975, the president could also claim that only his set of choices was calibrated to the needs of fiscal policy, managing the economy through manipulating the deficit. He had economic specialists, in the Treasury Department and the Council of Economic Advisers, to justify his choices. Congress had no comparable set of experts to respond, no means to develop its own fiscal policy.

The president's budget-making powers stem from the Budget and Accounting Act of 1921. Before that act, agencies submitted their estimates directly to Congress. Although, like all legislation, it had multiple causes, the 1921 Act passed largely because, as Frederick C. Mosher explains, the First World War, "with its tremendous expenditures and

debt, magnified the enthusiasm among the public and particularly in the
Congress for any measures that promised reduction of alleged governmental extravagance and taxes, and this was exactly what supporters of
a budget system offered."[8] Reformers interested in making the government more businesslike had argued for several decades that the process
of review and coordination of a national budget would make the government more efficient. The idea had strong popular support, and apparently many members of Congress who objected to giving the
president new powers felt forced to go along.[9]

Congress, however, took steps to limit the grant. Most important,
Congress still had to pass the laws; it had the last word. The 1921 Act
also took the accounting oversight function away from the Treasury and
vested it in the General Accounting Office (GAO), under a comptroller
general appointed for a fifteen-year term with the advice and consent
of the Senate and explicitly not subject to removal by the president. GAO
was to be Congress's check on executive operations. Finally, in separate
action, Congress strengthened its appropriations committees, in form at
least, centralizing itself in response to the new central power within the
executive.

This new set of procedures had one major advantage for Congress:
it gave the president primary responsibility for proposing cuts, viewing
him as better equipped for such a task because he can impose priorities
within the executive branch far more easily than any group in Congress
can impose its will on colleagues. (The executive is in principle, and in
part in fact, a hierarchy; Congress is anything but a hierarchy.) Once
the president imposed priorities, members of Congress could then respond to the budget, changing it where it differed too much from their
own priorities or where constituency pressures were too great and leaving the president with the blame for other decisions.

In order to justify altering the president's budget, however, Congess
had to claim comparable knowledge and ability to look at the whole
picture. It opposed to the president's massive budget documents the
equally copious record of appropriations hearings. And the appropriations committees, while broadly decentralized in operation, somehow
always managed to stay within the president's totals.[10]

Appropriations: The Old Congressional Budget Process

Thirty years ago, the "power of the purse" and "budgetary process"
meant appropriations. Entitlements were smaller and, at any rate, they
were not in the mainstream of government. The real work—building
roads, testing drugs, forecasting the weather, defending our allies, paying salaries, and buying uniforms, tanks, and laboratory equipment—

all went through the appropriations committees. Because, as one current member puts it, "nothing happens without the money," those two committees were and remain among the most powerful and prestigious in Congress.

Their power and huge jurisdiction explains their structure. With fifty-seven members in the House and twenty-nine in the Senate, the two committees are easily the largest in Congress. They are big because they have so much work to do and because their members must have personal contacts throughout their houses. Appropriations committees have more subcommittees, which are particularly independent, because only the strongest of committee heads, with great knowledge and advantages in staffing, could hope to know enough to argue much with subcommittee leaders.

The heads of the thirteen appropriations subcommittees are known as the "College of Cardinals." The name testifies to the sense among other members of Congress that the Appropriations Committee is a priesthood of sorts, with its own rites and norms and with leaders wielding great power. That sense of appropriators as being different has always been much stronger in the House. Strength remains in the House because Appropriations is exclusive; a member of Appropriations cannot sit on any other House committee (except, under the new budget act, for five members who represent Appropriations on Budget). Before the vast expansion of congressional staff, members of House Appropriations did much of the budget review themselves. Time spent together and their involvement in a different kind of work built committee members' self-identification as appropriators, and nonmembers' view of them as forming an arcane priesthood. Even now the House committee, particularly its staff, remains an unusually unified and distinctive organization.[11]

The appropriations and authorizing committees are inherently in conflict. House rules distinguish appropriations from legislation and forbid legislation on an appropriations bill, but the separation is murky. Not funding an activity or funding it only under certain conditions (e.g., under what circumstances medicaid will pay for abortions) are policy decisions. If the military construction appropriation does not provide funds for housing American soldiers in the Sinai Peninsula of Egypt, then Congress is obstructing the Camp David agreement; an appropriation is legislating policy. Yet a military construction bill that says nothing about what will be built would be a bit skimpy.

In general, Congress expects the appropriators to make policy if, and only if, that is necessary to do their job; that is, no authoritative statement of current policy exists. An appropriations subcommittee chairman expressed the distinction: "Appropriations says the most efficient way to spend money . . . [authorizations] should say what the need is." Authorizations can provide limits on the need (e.g., a billion dollars for mass transit), and appropriations above those limits are not in order. Likewise, appropriations are not in order for a program that has not been authorized. These rules are weakened, however, by the fact that appropriations are laws like any other laws: they supersede older legislation. If Congress chooses to override its own rules about appropriations, it is within its rights.

Members of Congress frequently legislate on appropriations bills for various reasons. The authorizations committees may refuse to report legislation that would be supported on the floor. In cases of disagreement between the committee and chamber majorities, the latter can express its will through the appropriations. Thus U.S. aid to South Vietnam was ended in an appropriations bill. Opponents have extensively restricted federal funding for abortion through versions of the "Hyde amendment." Sometimes, authorizing legislation for a program has lapsed because of disagreement over some terms of its authorization. Everybody knows that the dispute will be settled but not on what terms or when. By funding the program (Housing, the Department of State, the Department of Justice) anyway, the appropriations committees technically legislate. Sometimes the appropriators just want some program change (rarely large) and can ram it through.

Appropriations, through which Congress exercises its power of the purse over the executive, can easily constitute a parallel legislative process for the president as well. A president who wants to kill programs would be crazy to push for new legislation; instead, a Nixon or Reagan proposes to zero out the appropriation. He can use his veto against appropriations, but he cannot force legislation.

Yet the veto is weakened for the same reason that members are tempted to use appropriations to legislate: the bills *must* pass. Almost every bill contains enough "must" items for enough members to make failure unthinkable.[12] Opponents of postal subsidies generally want to keep the IRS and Customs Service, all from the Treasury-Postal-General Government bill. Opponents of housing tend to like the National Aeronautics and Space Administration or the National Science Foundation and the Veterans Administration, all in the HUD (Housing and Urban Development)-Independent Agencies appropriations act. If those bills fail, parts of government important to many people may fail with them.

Appropriations bills are targets of extraneous "riders" precisely because the appropriations train is going to get through—maybe not on schedule, but eventually. Ultimately the norms that say appropriations should be matters of economy, good management of programs, and routine financing of existing obligations conflict with the opportunity that appropriations provide to get something done in a Madisonian system of checks and counterchecks.

The old system of House, Senate, president, authorizations, and appropriations was difficult enough to operate. Good times in the 1950s and 1960s helped, and so did a system of mutual expectations and roles that reflected substantial agreement (in retrospect) between Congress and the president on matters of budgetary priorities.[13] From 1966 to 1973, the system broke down in what Allen Schick called "The Seven-Year Budget War." Congress responded in the Budget Control and Impoundment Act of 1974.

Creating a New Budget Process

Like a family that expected good times and then was disappointed, the federal government in the early 1970s found itself without enough money to meet all its commitments. Entitlements grew faster, and the economy (and hence revenue) grew slower than expected. The deficit rose from 5.5 percent of federal outlays in fiscal year (FY) 1967 to 11 percent in FY71. The problem was more difficult than it sounds because the growth of entitlements meant that the old budget process of appropriations covered less of the budget. To eliminate the deficit through that system would have required cutting 8.4 percent of appropriations in 1967 but 19.6 percent in FY71.[14] The appropriators, and many other people, wanted some way to bring entitlements into the purview of annual budget choice.

Deficits alone, however, could not have united a broad bipartisan majority behind the Budget Act of 1974; for that, Congress needed Richard Nixon, who gave liberals reason to go along. Congress and the Nixon administration got into a vicious and enervating struggle over deficits and, more important, budget priorities. Nixon tried to slow the expansion of the welfare state and other functions by keeping budgets down, particularly for new programs. At the same time, he wanted to wind down ("Vietnamize") the war more slowly than did the war's critics and to employ any savings to remedy claimed military weaknesses that had been ignored while resources were poured into Indochina. Liberals particularly could not see why the military deserved a funding bill created for a war that was a mistake in the first place.

The story of these battles has been told extensively elsewhere.[15] For our purposes, three points are crucial:

1. Nixon blamed Congress for the deficit; members of Congress were embarrassed by the charge even if they did not believe it.
2. Nixon continually justified his restraint of domestic programs in

terms of the supposed inflationary impact of deficits. He had OMB, Treasury, and the Council of Economic Advisers (CEA) justifying his fiscal policy, but Congress had no fiscal policy at all. If Congress was to look good while opposing Nixon on the details, the leaders of the opposition needed some way to claim that they were attending to the totals.

3. Nixon kept getting beaten. After the 1972 election, he decided he could win only by changing the rules. Nixon impounded—simply refused to spend—billions of dollars in appropriations that he disliked.

Impoundment was an old device based on an understanding that if events changed, making an appropriation either no longer necessary or unserviceable, the executive did not have to spend it, so long as most concerned members of Congress agreed. It was supposed to be a tool for better management, and it presumed that the players agreed on policy. Instead, as Allen Schick wrote,

> far from administrative routine, Nixon's impoundments in late 1972 and 1973 were designed to rewrite national policy at the expense of congressional power and intent. Rather than the deferment of expenses, Nixon's aim was the cancellation of unwanted programs. . . . When Nixon impounded for policy reasons, he in effect told Congress, "I don't care what you appropriate; I will decide what will be spent."[16]

"The aim of impoundment was," Schick adds, "to change the mix, not merely the level, of expenditures."[17]

The policy stakes in Nixon's impoundments were striking enough, but the political stakes were decisive. Save during a major war, no president had ever so bluntly asserted his primacy over Congress. If Nixon could get away with massive impoundments, what could he not do? If the power of the purse could be defied, what was left for Congress?

The world had been stood on its head. Since the time of royal governors and their civil lists, the legislature's problem had been to restrain the executive by limiting its funds. Now it faced a chief executive who wanted to spend too little, who defied the legislature (which, as far as Congress was concerned, meant the people) by refusing funds for the bureaucracy.

The Budget Act of 1974

The 1974 Budget Act represented a wholly unprecedented approach to budgeting: the legislature itself, debating freely and openly and considering relevant information, would make programs fit fiscal policy; the parts would fit the whole. Congress would make a budget.

Republicans hoped that "spenders," forced into the glare of public scrutiny, would retreat from their nefarious schemes. Democrats hoped that the conservative priests of budget balance—forced to relate generalities about waste or states' rights to the body of programs that built the roads, fed the poor, and supported the farmers—would no longer be able to deceive the public with platitudes. Each believed that God, which in a democracy means the public, was on its side. The public, as our story will show, was on both sides and neither side.

A new procedure formalized and limited impoundment.[18] If Congress were to make fiscal policy, it needed its own economists. If it were to consider program costs, it needed neutral analysts, separate from its committee staffs, just as the executive had an OMB independent of the agencies. Therefore the Act created a new staff institution, the Congressional Budget Office (CBO). If CBO said a program would cost twice what its proponents claimed, the CBO could be believed. Its director, appointed jointly by the Speaker of the House and Senate president pro tem for a four-year term, has extensive authority over the office.

Under Dr. Alice Rivlin, CBO gained a reputation for both competence and neutrality. Because estimates of future spending cannot be known with certainty, CBO, like everybody else, errs. In regard to estimates of both the economy and individual program costs, however, CBO usually has less reason to compound lack of knowledge with a policy-political bias than do agencies or the OMB. In its first few years, especially, CBO's estimates proved the more accurate.

CBO and the impoundment-control process easily found their places in the congressional process. The budget committees and new budget resolutions fit far less well.

The Senate Budget Committee (SBC) was established with sixteen members (now twenty-two), chosen by party caucuses and serving indefinitely. The House Budget Committee (HBC) was structured in an unusual manner. Five of its members were to come from the Appropriations Committee and five from Ways and Means. One would be a member of the Democratic leadership, and one would come from the Republican leadership. The other thirteen members were appointed through the usual House procedures (and the numbers were increased as the committee grew more popular). The committee is a mixture, therefore, of regular members and those who represent power centers within the House. In addition, membership is rotating, rather than permanent; no member could serve on the Budget Committee for more than four (now six) years out of every ten. Rotation decreases the chance that committee members will become isolated or parochial in their viewpoints.

Rotation aids HBC in gaining information from other committees and also ensures that the committee's power is not hoarded by a small group of representatives. But rotation also weakens the committee, especially its head, because committee members, aware of the rotation, can afford to cross him.

The budget committees were to write a pair of budget resolutions. The *First Resolution* (to be passed by May 15) would set targets for other committees and Congress as a whole to meet; it is a formal counterpart to the president's budget. The resolution recommends totals for budget authority (BA), outlays, revenue, and thus the deficit and total public debt. It provides spending targets for each budget function (into which the president's budget is also divided), such as Function 150, International Affairs, or Function 350, Agriculture. Under Section 302(a) of the Act, after a resolution is passed, the budget committees report to every other committee the total outlays and new budget authority it could appropriately provide under the terms of that year's resolution. Under Section 302(b) each committee (most important, Appropriations) subdivides its 302(a) allocation among its subcommittees. The First Resolution was thus half a version of the president's budget. It divided spending into functions; 302(a) reports related the functional division to actual bills, and the Budget Committee staffs, at least, had a good idea of how much should be spent at the program and subcommittee levels. But the real allocation among programs was not in the budget resolution; it would be made by the other committees.

The budget committees used the president's budget, CBO analyses, views and estimates of need that other committees were required to submit by March 15, and their own extensive staff and hearings to develop the policy and political information needed to draft first resolutions. Procedures in passing that resolution were much like those for any other bill, except that, because it was a rule for Congress, it did not need the president's signature. Nor did it have the force of law or appropriate funds. The First Resolution was only a recommendation, less detailed than the president's budget but, as the product of a lengthy process of discussion and accommodation within Congress, more likely to reflect what Congress would actually do. And, like the president's budget, its estimates of revenue and debt and entitlement spending were as much wishful thinking as plan, dependent upon estimates of the future course of the economy.

By early September all relevant authorizations and appropriations were to have been passed. The budget committees were to review economic developments and legislative actions and then report out versions of the *Second Concurrent Resolution* on the budget. The Second Resolution had the same components as the First, except that its totals were supposedly binding. Thus, after passage of the Second Resolution, any legislation considered that would cause limits in that resolution to be breached could be objected to and ruled out of order. As the Act was written, if the limits in the Second Resolution would not be met as a result of legislation already passed, then *reconciliation* instructions could be included in that resolution. These would order the relevant committees to report legislation reconciling spending or taxing to the budget totals. The necessary legislation was supposed to be passed by September 25, in time for the new fiscal year to begin on October 1.

Special procedures expanded both the appropriations committees' ability to question entitlement growth and their control over various other types of backdoor spending. CBO's independent analysis was expected to restrain new entitlements by making their costs more prominent; no new entitlements could be created before the start of a new fiscal year; and the appropriations committees received a limited right to propose amendments to new entitlement legislation that exceeded the committee of jurisdiction's allocation under the First Resolution.

In form, therefore, the 1974 act created a real budget. Congress would choose totals, look at programs, and make the details conform. Entitlement spending would be confronted while totals were being considered. The process of adopting resolutions would draw attention to questions of the relative sizes of revenue and expenditures and their effects on the economy far more explicitly than had been possible in the past; and voting would force members of Congress to take stands in a way not previously required. Debate on the floor would inform legislators and the public about the choices made. The procedures that related taxing and spending to the size of the budget would force Congress to take the totals seriously.

How the New Process Worked

In 1980, as this book begins, Congress had been working within its new process for five years.[19] One cannot say the system was working as intended because its sponsors disagreed on the intent. A few developments, however, were worth noting.

The budget committees had developed very differently in the Senate and the House. Senate Budget Chairman Edmund Muskie (D–Maine) and ranking minority member Henry Bellmon (R–Okla.) worked to develop resolutions that could command substantial bipartisan support. In the House, by contrast, Republicans viewed the resolutions as the place to demonstrate the difference between the two parties. Because resolutions became partisan battles, the committee heads had to win majorities entirely within the Democratic party. Party leaders therefore became key actors in the House process. House resolutions tended to be more liberal than the Senate's, given the different coalitions needed to pass them.

First resolutions had not significantly constrained spending. If anything, they allowed liberal majorities in 1975 and 1976 to justify their opposition to President Ford's proposed spending cuts. The heavily Democratic majorities of 1975–1978, however, should not have been expected to want to limit spending. By 1979, in the wake of the Proposition 13 tax revolt in California, inflation fears, and a Democratic president's attempts to restrain spending, the First Resolution was assuming some spending cuts.

But the system had no teeth. Reconciliation was too late in the schedule; no one could expect committees to draft, debate, report, pass, and then confer on reconciliation bills in the ten days allowed—from September 15 to September 25. The big stick of the Second Resolution was the point of order against legislation that breached its totals, but this weapon was less than it seemed. The point of order could be waived; although HBC and SBC in different ways influenced that decision, the committees could be overridden on the floor. The proposals for increased spending could be virtually irresistible (e.g., food stamps running out of money or a Mount St. Helens blowing its top). Most important, even when a set of spending acts passed after the Second Resolution, the overall total was not likely to be exceeded until the last one or two bills. And that straggler was likely to be totally guiltless (like foreign aid, always late and always slashed before it reached the floor). It did not make much sense to savage one bill because of failings on others.

Although the new process was weak, it nonetheless was used in the battles over policy. Program opponents (or supporters) could claim that the First Resolution did not (or did) leave room in the budget for funding. Seeking to satisfy constituents, members could propose extra funding for pet programs in budget debate, where the results were not binding. Thus to the regular legislative process of authorizations and to the alternate legislative process of appropriations now was added a shadow legislative process of budget resolutions. We say "shadow" because its forms were produced by real bodies and real conflict, but themselves had no substance.

Whatever their effect, budget resolutions stood forth as visible statements about the direction of the nation. Therefore, the seven-year budget war did not end; only the field and weapons changed. Most Democrats and most Republicans, egalitarian liberals and individualist conservatives, fought over the size of government and, within that, over emphasis on military or social welfare spending. The budget resolution figures for spending and revenues, for defense and social functions, became battlegrounds even though they were not binding.

Coda: A Budget Is Many Things and One of Them Is a Performance

The budget is many different policies. It is fiscal policy, designed to stimulate or restrain the economy, to fight unemployment or inflation. The budget summarizes the balance of public and private sectors of the economy—the proportion of GNP taken by taxes or consisting of federal government spending—in short, "how much" federal government we have. The distribution of spending in very broad categories describes the kind of government we want: one that emphasizes military might or protects the middle class or helps the poor. The assumptions in budget resolutions, and action on appropriations or entitlements or tax expenditures, make the budget also a package of thousands of specific program policies: how much to invest in airport safety; which people, if any, should receive special nutrition benefits; how many F-16s the Air Force needs.

For partisans, particularly leaders, of the Democratic and Republican parties, the aggregates in the budget resolutions represent their party's influence on the course of American government; short of the actual organization of the two houses (election of the Speaker, committee assignments), no other action is potentially of as great import to the party leadership. The battle of the budget tests their generalship. The ability of the parties to stay together in the final encounter, apart from the vote to organize the houses along partisan lines, is now their ultimate test of cohesion.

To those members of Congress who identify with the institution—which, depending upon the issue and challenge, ranges from a few to all—budgeting tests Congress: Can Congress choose? Can it enforce its will? In short, can Congress govern? The president asks the same questions, slightly changed: Can I govern the agencies? Can I govern Congress? Can I govern responsibly and maintain public support? Finally, both president and Congress must ask: Do we control policy, or do the policies control us? Can any of us control events?

Republicans and Democrats alike had agreed that the great issues should be faced directly and without obfuscation. How the people they represent would fare under a budgetary process that compels great choices without agreement on what those choices should be is an integral part of the deficit problem, for it is one thing to agree that the deficit is too large and another to agree on how to reduce it.

TWO

Democrats in a Budget Trap

In 1980 the Democratic party lost control of the American government. The Democrats' defeat was most evident in the election. Incumbent Jimmy Carter got only 41 percent of the vote, with 51 percent going to Republican Ronald Reagan and 7 percent to independent John Anderson. In the House of Representatives, the Democratic majority was slashed by thirty-three seats, a change that, considering conservative southerners, made the Democratic majority fade away. Most dramatically, Democrats lost twelve Senate seats; their once solid majority now had melted to a forty-six to fifty-three minority. For the first time since 1954, Republicans would rule a house of Congress. For the first time in more than twenty years, a Republican president could more than dream of having legislative majorities to enact his program.

The election, however, only formalized the Democrats' loss of control. There is more to governing than simply holding office. In 1980 the Democrats could not govern because they could not agree on how to use the offices they held. Bitter divisions were revealed in Senator Edward M. Kennedy's (D–Mass.) challenge for the presidential nomination. But the nomination battle was only one phase of the strife within the governing coalition in Washington. Assailed from the left of his party in the campaign, Carter was attacked from the right in Congress. In either arena, conflict centered on the budget and the economy.

Internal conflict was hardly new to the Democratic party. As in any coalition, Democrats managed conflict by bargaining on some issues and, where agreement was impossible, ignoring others. Unfortunately for them, the Democrats could not finesse their 1980 disagreements over budget policy.

The Budgeting Dilemma

Budget resolutions (setting internal congressional targets for total spending and revenue) and appropriations could be delayed but eventually would have to be passed. When resolutions were considered, Democrats had to face the great divisive issues of defense spending and inflation. On defense, a large faction of Democrats, led by Senators Hollings of South Carolina and Nunn of Georgia, was enough alarmed by America's military position to join Republicans in fighting President Carter for a larger military buildup. And many Democrats, along with most Republicans, felt that inflation posed so great a threat that some action—probably budget balancing—was imperative.

Two contradictory pressures—higher defense spending and stopping inflation—originated in attitudes toward events beyond Capitol Hill. The Soviet Union's invasion of Afghanistan, the administration's reaction to a Soviet combat brigade in Cuba, and the taking of American hostages in Iran all helped generate a sense of American military weakness. Voters in their districts and commentators in the media informed politicians that people felt insecure about national defense.

Congress clamored for a big defense buildup. Speaker O'Neill declared:

> I think the mood out there is that we have to be prepared for conventional skirmishes, and the American people feel for the first time that we do not have that capability. I'm talking about the safety of the country, and you put that ahead of energy, inflation, balancing the budget and everything else.[1]

If Carter bowed to this pressure, yet wanted to balance the budget, he would have to raise taxes further or turn on the Democrats' own constituencies by taking from social programs to give to defense; if the president held down the defense buildup, he would come under fire for risking the nation's security.

But if the public felt insecure about defense, it reached near panic at the prospect of inflation. The polls were showing inflation as the major political issue, while financial markets gyrated wildly and the media clamored for action.

Consumer prices already had increased by 13 percent in 1979, and the trend was toward even faster increases. The inflation reduced individuals' real average gross weekly earnings by about 4 percent in 1979.[2] Consequently, the public's pain threatened to become the president's trouble. In mid-October 1979 a Gallup poll showed that only one-third of the respondents approved of Carter's job performance (with half disapproving) and that two-thirds listed inflation as the nation's most important problem.[3] Conventional wisdom said that one way to reduce inflation was to reduce the federal budget deficit.

Whether the deficit increased inflation or not, inflation did increase the deficit. Social security and the other pension programs were slated for large increases in fiscal 1981, mandated by law to compensate their beneficiaries for the 1979–1980 inflation. Costs of medical programs could be predicted to rise as the price of health care soared, along with fuel costs for the military and food costs for school lunches; in many such ways inflation would increase the cost of providing in FY81 the same services provided in FY80. Price increases were accompanied by (somewhat smaller) wage hikes, thereby increasing collections from income and other payroll taxes. The burden on many taxpayers increased as their nominal wages crept up into higher tax brackets but their real wages (what they could buy) remained steady or declined because prices rose more quickly. This automatic tax hike angered voters. Yet even higher tax payments from "bracket creep" could not make up for the automatic increases in entitlement funding and the desired jump in military spending.

The dilemma for Democrats was to reconcile the seemingly irreconcilable: cutting deficits caused by inflation in order to reduce inflation, while increasing defense spending and diminishing the tax burden. Something had to give; in 1981 the Reagan administration risked higher deficits to build the military up and keep taxes down. But in 1980 Jimmy Carter went the other way.

By all reports, Carter, who introduced the "zero base budgeting" reform system in Georgia, truly believed in the fiscal responsibility and control that a balanced budget represents.[4] This belief, moreover, was reinforced in the political-economic arena. His Republican challengers naturally were denouncing deficits, but so were Democrats: California Governor Edmund G. (Jerry) Brown, Jr., supported a constitutional amendment calling for a balanced budget; even Senator Edward Kennedy condemned deficits, announcing in late January that he favored "the steps that have been taken by the Congress to insure that we're going to achieve a balanced budget next year."[5] Most Americans agreed that a balanced budget was desirable; in March 1980, for example, a Gallup Poll reported respondents supporting by more than four to one a constitutional amendment requiring balanced budgets.[6]

In addition to the lasting symbolic power of a balanced budget in American political history—as a sign that things were right and government could govern—support for balanced budgets had two contemporary sources. One was a deep, widely held suspicion that the federal government wastes money—fifty-two cents on every dollar, according to the median respondent in a November 1979 Gallup Poll.[7] In the public mind, an unbalanced budget stands for and allows wastefulness. The second source was a widespread belief that government deficits fuel inflation. Although the link is neither direct nor predictable, and is possibly even mistaken when overwhelmed by other factors, most economists believe that deficits work more to increase than to decrease prices. The March 1980 Gallup Poll showed that the public, by more than a four to one margin, agreed that deficits were more likely to raise prices. In January 1980, government waste probably had not changed, but inflation was increasing dramatically. Politicians, therefore, seized on deficit reduction as something they could do about inflation.

The Politics of Recession

The difficulty with using the budget to attack inflation was that a recession might well result, bringing unemployment, lower profits, and bankruptcies. Recessions are not popular; neither, under normal circumstances, are presidents who go out of their way to start them.

Carter faced unique difficulties because he was a Democrat. Recessionary policies would attack his party's basic constituencies: labor and beneficiaries of social programs. In October, James Fallows reflected on Carter's plight:

> Ford and Nixon were Republicans, and therefore had some theoretical excuse for tolerating unemployment while fighting inflation. For a Democrat to do that is like an American fighter plane joining a kamikaze squad: no one can figure out what's in it for him.[8]

Because Democratic politicians were particularly opposed to unemployment, and because Republican politicians were particularly opposed to Democratic administrations, Carter could count on no one to support a recessionary budget. Beyond such short-term tactical difficulties, to pursue unemployment explicitly flew in the face of the mission and history of the Democratic party. Democrats had become the majority party because, in the Great Depression, they had worked to reduce unemployment and its miseries. Democrats built the modern welfare state so that fluctuations in the economy, the boom-and-bust business cycle, would not leave millions destitute. As the party of full employment, Democrats liked to portray Republicans as the party of unemployment. Even in January 1980, when the Carter administration's inability to control inflation caused Americans to feel that Republicans would be better at running the economy, the Republican party's own polls reported that Americans (by nearly two to one) still believed that Democrats were better at reducing unemployment, helping young people buy homes, and providing financial security for the elderly.[9] If they began to create unemployment, what were Democrats good for? If the public wanted to cut social programs, why not just hire some Republicans to do the job?

Caught in a double bind, the administration, like Goldilocks, wanted a recession that was "just right": one that would both reduce demand (one source of price pressure) and be *seen* to reduce demand (thereby reducing expectations of inflation, a major source, some thought, of the spiral), yet not hurt anyone very much. Ideally the recession would be long enough to convince the public but short enough to seemingly end by election day. By January 1980 it may well have been too late to accomplish any of those goals.

Carter's Goldilocks budget predicted an unemployment rate of 7.5 percent for 1980, inflation of 10.4 percent, and a FY81 deficit of $15.8 billion. Defense spending was up by choice; entitlements were up by inertia; and the remaining domestic budget was held constant or slightly decreased. The deficit would go down, in spite of higher unemployment, because taxes would go up. Inflationary effects on wages and legislation passed or in progress (e.g., the projected adoption of the windfall profits tax on oil companies and a January 1981 scheduled increase in the social security payroll tax) would increase revenues by 14.5 percent over the FY80 level, compared to a 9 percent spending increase.

Essentially, Carter was pushing the economy toward recession with higher taxes. His budget message promised to limit the pain of the unemployed. The deficit, he said, was only one cause of inflation. But the basic message remained that "by continuing a clear and consistent policy of restraint, the 1981 budget ensures that the federal budget will not be an inflationary force in the economy."[10] Another term for restraint was unemployment.

The president and his advisers had decided that to limit inflation—and to be seen as steadfast in this—was more important politically than to avoid tax increases. They believed that the public was willing to pay a high price to stop the inflationary spiral.[11] Yet accepting unemployment levels of more than 7 percent without countermeasures was extraordinary, especially for a Democratic administration. The administration could not have accepted such a grim prospect if its economic theory had offered any alternative.

The Economics of Recession

The administration's theory emphasized the impact of oil shocks on "core inflation." In mid-1979, the Organization of Petroleum Exporting Countries (OPEC) doubled oil prices. Oil was more expensive, so the nation would have either less oil or less of something else. In real terms (product per person), paying more for oil meant less personal income. As prices affected by oil rose, workers would try for proportionate pay increases in their wage bargaining. If workers succeeded, businesses that gave raises would immediately raise prices, hoping thereby to recapture profits. Then workers in other industries would react to these new prices by demanding higher wages from their employers. Wages and prices would chase each other at increasing speed, both spiraling upward, as employer and employee groups strove to stick the other with the cost of OPEC's oil. At worst, the spiral takes on its own life, as workers and managers expect it to continue, separate from its original cause.

This self-perpetuating spiral is called the core inflation rate. Administration economists believed that core inflation was up to 8 percent in 1979, and heading much higher, and their solution was to keep wages from chasing prices; the only reliable way to do this was through unemployment, which would pressure workers to accept smaller wage increases or lose their jobs to those already unemployed. Thus, as John Berry of the *Washington Post* reported the policy, "slower economic growth and higher unemployment [were] the key to both the short-run and the long-run attack on rising prices."[12] Chairman of the Council of Economic Advisers Charles Schultze said that "the Administration's greatest fear involves a further increase in inflation if workers try to recover some of the purchasing power lost last year to inflation and, particularly, to higher oil prices."[13]

While Carter's dilemma recalled Goldilocks, reactions to the budget reminded us of the classic Japanese story of Rashomon, in which the same event is reported entirely differently by various participants and witnesses. The *National Journal* titled its cover story, "A Campaign Budget for an Election Year," mentioning all the bows to defense, domestic programs, and anti-inflation pressures while somehow ignoring the electoral problems presented by tax increases. But *The Economist* proclaimed:

> The deficit is an infinitesimal part of a $3 trillion GNP and is dwarfed by the foreign tax imposed on the American economy by OPEC's increased oil prices. President Carter has presented a non-electioneering budget in an election year. Such courage deserves to succeed.[14]

Time described the galloping inflation and concluded that "the injection into the economy of new cold war defense spending, without any concomitant reduction in social expenditures, could be like hitting the gas pedal in a car already careening out of control down a hill."[15] *Newsweek*'s writers saw the exact opposite. "At bottom," they concluded, "the Carter budget obviously reflects the lessons learned in the late 1960s when Lyndon Johnson's pursuit of a guns-and-butter policy started the nation on a road to a disastrous inflation."[16]

These different judgments reflected the clashing perspectives about the economy that observers applied to Carter's set of choices. Each columnist wrote as if the analysis was self-evident but each analysis, of course, was not. The agreements and disagreements among competing schools of economists would, however, influence budget politics until the present time. We pause to describe the competing schools.

Economists and Budgets

In politics, though not in logic, there are three relevant schools of economists: Keynesians; an alliance of supply-siders and monetarists; and neoclassicists.

THE KEYNESIAN ORTHODOXY

However painful the conditions, classical economics claimed that government could do nothing to correct the problem of unemployment; instead, market conditions eventually would right themselves. Unemployment, for example, could lower wages to a point where hiring people would be more attractive. Looking at the 25 percent unemployment of the 1930s, Keynes pointed out that when times got rough enough no one would hire people because there would be no customers. Businesses needed to perceive a demand for their products. Without demand, even cheap labor would not be hired.

Keynes argued that the government could create demand, either by itself purchasing new goods and services (direct spending) or by increasing the money in people's pockets through a tax cut. Either way, a government deficit would result. But, by "priming the pump," government might get the economic well to again yield some water.

If a deficit would heat up the economy, a surplus, by reducing consumption (as the government took in money without spending it), would cool the economy down. Reduced demand would mean reduced inflation; in essence, a trade-off between limiting unemployment and limiting inflation could be managed through the government deficit.

Experience in the 1970s challenged Keynesian theory in two ways: First, over the decade, inflation and unemployment both rose; and inflation rose far more quickly than the level of employment seemed to warrant. Second, the United States faced a growing productivity crisis. Growth of GNP was slow—compared to both American experience in the previous two decades and the rate of growth in other industrialized nations, such as Japan.

THE SUPPLY-SIDE CHALLENGE

The supply-siders, as their name suggests, argued that by emphasizing demand Keynesians had neglected the factors that encourage investment. They claimed that productivity had slowed because government policies reduced the incentive to produce. Regulation had business owners filling out forms rather than doing business. High, progressive income taxes reduced the reward for working harder or investing more.

One version of this tendency, represented by the editors of the *Wall Street Journal,* emphasized reduction of what they deemed unproductive public spending:

> Income transfers conducted through the federal budget are seriously eroding savings and capital formation. . . . In other words, *it is money transferred from people who are working to people who are not, lowering the incentives of both for productive labor.*[17]

The *Journal's* editors believed that the welfare state had broken the link between work and reward. This side of the analysis was congenial to old-line Republicans who disapproved of nearly all government activity except maintaining public order and security. Another side, exemplified by Representative Jack Kemp, was willing to maintain most existing governmental activities (an important difference) while emphasizing the positive effects of tax cuts. Economist Arthur Laffer claimed that high taxes so discouraged economic activity that a large cut, by increasing incentives to work and invest, would generate much economic growth. In a reasonably short time, therefore, even the government would be better off because the smaller tax cut would come from a much larger economic pie. This was the (in)famous "Laffer Curve."

The supply-side analysis essentially ignored the demand problem that preoccupied Keynesians. Also it paid little attention to interest rates, which surely, if to an unknown degree, influenced rates of investment and economic growth. Yet, in spite of these analytic weaknesses, supply-side proponents had two practical advantages: in proposing tax cuts they were suggesting something that politicians like to do; they also were proposing to manipulate an instrument of policy—tax rates—that, unlike interest rates or personal consumption, the government could directly control.

Laffer used the Keynesians' tax cut during the Kennedy administration as an example of how lower taxes could increase economic growth. Keynesians, however, had argued that tax cuts stimulate demand and thus, potentially, inflation. With inflation already high, supply-siders needed a counterargument. They found it by allying with the monetarists, who held that monetary, not fiscal, policy affected prices.

MONEY AND MONETARISM

To monetarists, inflation came from too much money chasing too few goods. Prices rose when the banking system, meaning the Federal Reserve in its various ways of influencing banks, created money faster than the rest of the economy produced goods. If the Federal Reserve contracted the money supply, then prices would go down because there would be less money for goods. This deflation, monetarists believed (and Keynesians agreed), would slow down economic activity because it would make more sense to hold dollars, which would buy more goods later, than to invest or spend them, receiving fewer dollars later given price declines. Monetarists such as Nobel laureate Milton Friedman argued that, if the Federal Reserve maintained a steady, moderate rate of growth of the money supply, the economy would avoid both depression and inflation.

Perhaps this is true, but the Fed's actions also influenced interest rates, because the price of something depends on its supply. Rates depend as well on the demand for money, which brings us to the Federal Reserve's role in managing the federal debt.

Government bonds, "T-bills," and so on are the safest of all investments because the government can get money in ways that private industry cannot match and because, if the government went under, everything else would collapse with it anyway. The government will pay whatever interest is necessary to sell its bonds. If the government increases its sale of bonds (deficit) during an economic downturn, these sales will soak up idle cash and put it to (relatively) productive use. But if idle money is scarce, then the deficit must divert cash from other kinds of investments (crowd them out) and, in the competition for investment money, can drive interest rates upward. Keynesians and neoclassicists claim that less investment, lower profits from investment, and eventually lower economic growth result.

The Federal Reserve can intervene in this process by buying bonds from its member banks. When it buys a bond, it credits the seller's reserve account. Banks are allowed to lend an amount several times their reserves; therefore, expansion of reserves allows a proportionate expansion of lending. Some of that lending will come back into the banks as demand deposits (checking accounts), to be lent out again as the cycle repeats. Thus, when the Fed buys bonds, it increases demand deposits and bank reserves, the major bases of the money supply. It also increases bank lending, so interest rates should go down. Conversely, when the Fed sells bonds (debiting banks' reserve accounts), it contracts the money supply, thus driving interest rates higher.

The purchase of bonds is how the Federal Reserve "prints money" to pay for the government's expenses. The Fed's decision to purchase depends upon whether it is more concerned with steadying the money supply (then it will not buy bonds) or keeping interest rates low (then it will buy them).

If monetarists were right, the Federal Reserve could stop inflation by reducing the money supply. But the resultant higher interest rates might send the economy into a recession. Keynesians were nervous about using such potent measures. Because supply-siders believed interest rates mattered less and tax rates more to business interests, the supply-siders were more optimistic that a tax cut could be combined with monetary restraint to increase production and reduce inflation. To Keynesians the combination of tight money and large tax cuts guaranteed only high interest rates that would bring the economy down in a resounding crash.

THE NEOCLASSICISTS

The swing vote among economists was held by the neoclassicists, who shared the Keynesians' basic model of the economy but had the supply-siders' trust in markets and dislike of wage-setting unions. Representing a large segment of established academic economists, neoclassicists commanded the paraphernalia of authority (econometric models, chaired professorships at universities) needed to impress the nonexpert. These neoclassicists included some of the nation's most eminent mainstream economists, such as Paul McCracken, Herbert Stein, and Alan Greenspan, all former CEA chairmen. Their pronouncements would determine whether the supply-siders would seem irresponsible or respectable.

Neoclassicists shared the Keynesian concern with interest rates and the supply-sider dislike of taxes. Their ideal was low taxes and low spending, with occasional pump-priming if economic growth severely declined. The difference between Keynesians and neoclassicists was really a choice between inflation and unemployment, really a choice of whom to favor. Keynesians emphasized demand and employment, which favored employees. The neoclassical concern with steady prices served holders of wealth, the value of whose investments would be eroded by inflation.

Both mainstream schools, however, emphasized the need for investment to create growth. Members of each school worried because savings, and thus investment, were lower in the United States than in other industrial nations. They agreed that high interest rates and inflation created uncertainty that dampened the "Animal Spirits" (Keynes's term) of the entrepreneur. Both schools emphasized corporate investments rather than individual incentives, viewing capital investment more as the product of corporate choices than as the individual desire to make money. Unlike the supply-siders, therefore, neoclassicists (and Keynesians) preferred corporate tax cuts—particularly adjustments in the depreciation schedules for capital investment—to reduced personal levies.

ECONOMISTS AND THE ECONOMY

The reaction to Carter's January 1980 budget reflected these converging and diverging perspectives. To supply-siders, whose voice was the *Wall Street Journal,* a budget nearly balanced by tax hikes was totally unacceptable. *Newsweek* and *Time* differed because the more Keynesian *Newsweek,* caring more about unemployment, was impressed by the degree of restraint in the budget.

Yet there was also agreement, centering on the shared concern for business investment as the source of productivity. Keynesian Arthur Okun of the Brookings Institution called Carter's plan "a directionless, muddle-through budget of an election year." "I wish to hell," he added, "that there was some concrete policy you were buying with all that extra money, like a reduction in corporate depreciation rates to stimulate investment."[18] His colleague Joseph Pechman, similarly worried, felt that a tax cut was needed to stimulate investment; to allow for this, he wanted a spending cut.[19] Keynesians had begun to worry more about investment than consumption. The administration's economists were also working to restrain workers' consumption through recession. Democratic economists were deserting Democratic constituencies.

Ultimately, all economists emphasized the confidence of business interests. Keynesians wanted to manipulate demand in order to encourage entrepreneurs. Supply-siders wanted lower taxes. Neoclassicists wanted higher profits from lower wage increases and interest rates. All believed that if, for whatever reason, business lost confidence in the future, that future would be dismal. The crucial barometer of business confidence was the behavior of the financial markets. In February 1980, one major market, the market for bonds, collapsed; that collapse in turn killed Carter's budget.

Bonds and the Budget

Bonds are promises to pay interest at a fixed rate for a long period of time. Whether a bond is a good deal depends upon the ratio of the interest paid to the inflation rate. If prices are going up faster than the interest rate, the bondholder will have less purchasing power at the end than when she bought the bond. Prospective bondholders, therefore, demand a higher interest rate for their money if they expect high inflation. Conversely, the bond sellers (debtors) are more willing to offer those rates if they believe inflation will give them more dollars with which to pay off. In essence a 4 percent interest rate at 2 percent inflation is the same term of trade as 14 percent interest at 12 percent inflation: a real return ("real interest rate") of 2 percent per year.

On February 18, the Labor Department announced that in January wholesale prices had risen at an annual rate of 19.2 percent. Interest rates, *The Economist* reported, zoomed upward throughout the industrialized world "in hot pursuit of the inflation rate." High interest rates were bad for anyone who wanted to issue a new bond; they were terrible for anyone who owned an old bond.

A bond is an asset; its value depends on the income it provides. People want to be able to trade assets as well as hold them in their portfolios. The portfolio value of a bond is how much it can be sold for, which depends not on the original price but on its yield.

Take a $1,000 bond that yields $80 per year (8 percent). If 8 percent is a good return, the bond will sell for its original value (par). If new bonds or other comparable instruments yield 10 percent, however, it would be silly to pay $1,000 for the old bond. Someone who expected a 10 percent return would pay only $800 to get the $80 per year return. Inflation has the same effect on values.

As interest rates go up, therefore, the prices of old bonds and the value of portfolios of old bonds go down. In theory, bonds, promising a steady return over a long time, represent the ideal safe investment. If interest rates are volatile, however—especially if they and inflation head up—the last place to be is locked into a thirty-year contract for a devaluing asset. The bond market—not stocks—was the major source of capital investment. Conditions in 1980 threatened that "the notion of bonds as a safe harbor for prudent money managers . . . could become as archaic as gold at $35 an ounce."[20] Capital investment could dry up. Worse, losses on their bond portfolios could badly damage banks and other financial institutions, leading to a general contraction of credit.

The bond market collapse was noticed by only a small portion of Americans. But those who noticed mattered. Economic policymakers viewed it as evidence that Carter's budget was a disaster. Economists differed in the details of their explanation, but all agreed that, if investors had trusted Carter's policy to reduce inflation, then they would not have insisted on higher interest rates. And when economists used investors' behavior to show that the policy was insufficient, investors, hearing that the president's policy would not work, panicked further.

In October 1979 the new chairman of the Federal Reserve Board, Paul Volcker, announced that the board had adopted monetarist principles for a war against inflation. The Fed would tighten monetary policy and allow bank interest rates to rise accordingly. To attract buyers, long-term bond rates rose in tandem with the rates paid by banks. If market participants had believed that the tight money policy would reduce inflation, they might have tempered their predictions about inflation, therefore countering the short-term effects of higher interest rates. But that was not to be.

On January 29 interest rates on long-term Treasury bonds reached 11 percent, higher even than during the Civil War.[21] On February 5 professional bond traders, "faced with a prolonged buyers' strike," dumped a new thirty-year Treasury issue (maturing in 2009) on the market rather than waiting for buyers at face value (par). In response, the 2009 Treasury fell another 2.5 percent, and other bonds followed. The next day brought a flood of sell orders as bondholders tried to dispose of their devaluing portfolios. By Tuesday, February 19, the 2009 Treasuries had lost 20 percent of their value since the year's beginning. Issues from major companies like IBM were doing no better.[22]

A *Wall Street Journal* article on February 21 estimated portfolio losses since October at $400 billion. On that same day any hope of recovery was stifled when investment banking guru Henry Kaufman gave a speech to the American Banking Association in which, predicting continued high inflation, he called for declaring a national emergency. The markets were so jittery that Kaufman's speech immediately set them on their ear.[23]

There was no particularly good reason, under any economic theory, either to blame Carter's budget or even to panic. The bond market decline had begun before Carter announced his budget. A few voices did call for calm. Beryl Sprinkel of Harris Bank in Chicago, a leading monetarist, pointed out that Paul Volcker had only begun the Federal Reserve's monetarist fight against inflation in October, so the lack of immediate results was to be expected.[24] On February 19 and February 25, Volcker said the same in testimony to Congress, arguing that markets were overreacting to entirely predictable economic news, that is, the January wholesale price increase.[25]

By February 25 panic was replacing policy. The chairman of the Federal Reserve joined the chorus. "We have reached the point in this inflationary situation," Volcker declared, "where I believe decisive action is necessary."[26] The markets made no sense, but that did not reduce the need to calm them. He recommended the nation's all-purpose remedy, balancing the budget. On the same day, Jimmy Carter told a group of out-of-town newspaper editors that the inflation/energy problem had "reached a crisis stage."[27] His and Volcker's comments, of course, contributed to the fear. The balanced budget panic of 1980 had begun.

The great organs of the media fanned the flames of panic. On February 24, 1980, the *Washington Post* editorialized: "The latest inflation figures will set off another wild search for a quick solution." Joining in that search, the paper contended that "if President Carter wants to move fast on inflation, he has only one lever that will make much difference. He will have to start cutting his budget, rapidly and severely—not only next year's budget, but the current one."[28] The *New York Times* on February 28 added that "nobody any longer knows for sure" how to slow the inflation but that budget balance had to be part of the solution.[29]

For the next few months the key word would be "expectations." By expecting inflation, consumers and producers and borrowers and lenders might indeed make it come true; something had to be done to change those expectations. *Newsweek* reported,

> However it is achieved, a balanced budget would have almost magical significance. "The budget has raised inflationary expectations more than anything," says Leif Olsen of Citibank, "so cutting Federal spending is exactly what we need to do to restore confidence and cut those higher expectations."[30]

Balancing the budget supposedly would make everybody expect better times; I balance, Descartes might have said, therefore I am prosperous.

Politicians were scared. The administration felt the pressure. *Newsweek* reported that "the mood in the White House . . . seemed to verge on something close to panic. . . . 'Grown men, thoughtful men are scared,' said a top White House aide. 'It's time to be scared.' "[31] "When you have bank executives come in and say, 'We're getting close to bank lines,' people get frightened," reported Representative Richard Gephardt, a leader of the moderate Democrats. "If ever there was a time in recent history to balance the budget, this is it."[32]

Within the Keynesian logic, budget balance in that situation made little sense. Arthur Okun commented that $16 billion in cuts—enough, ostensibly, to balance the budget—"will reduce inflation by 0.3 percentage points and lower the gross national product by 1.3 percent . . . a minuscule effect on inflation and a significant, if not drastic, effect on employment."[33] The CBO issued a similar dampening prognosis.[34]

Policy makers, however, along with most commentators, had moved beyond reliance on input-output models of the economy. They had entered a land of speculation about the moods of economic actors in which the symbolic virtues of budget cutting exceeded any effects on demand. "The problem is psychological," one administration official declared. "That's where you really have to get results."[35]

The administration moved toward a policy of (a) balancing the FY81 budget so as to change inflationary expectations, and (b) finding more ways to ensure the recession that would have a real effect on inflation. On February 28 OMB ordered agencies to prepare cuts in their FY81 submissions. As a sign of resolve, the administration canceled plans for a $300-million farm policy initiative.[36] On the Hill cut lists were being devised by everybody, from liberals David Obey and William Brodhead to conservatives David Stockman and Phil Gramm.

New budget proposals would help only if they had a chance to pass. The administration therefore tried something unprecedented: the budget would be remade in negotiations with its party leaders in the House and the Senate. For forty-six hours, beginning March 6, administration and congressional Democratic leaders negotiated.[37] The meetings were chaired by Senate Majority Leader Robert Byrd, who explained that "this is an effort to develop unity, so we can all walk the plank together."[38]

There was a theme: it was a nasty job, but someone had to do it. Bargaining was painful because the negotiators included supporters of almost every threatened program.[39] Representative Brademas of Indiana protested education cuts; Jim Wright of Texas protected public works; Tom Foley of Washington fought for food stamps; and Senate Finance Chairman Russell Long resisted intrusions on the cherished jurisdiction of his Finance Committee.

The Democrats' internal negotiations foreshadowed later "big powwows"—the 1982 "Gang of 17," the 1984 negotiations, the 1987 summit. In theory, if the leaders all agreed, they could carry Congress with them. In practice, neither side wanted the blame for cutting cost-of-living adjustments (COLAs) to social security. Members of Congress thought a tax on imported oil might be fine, but they wanted Carter to impose it administratively so they wouldn't have to vote.[40] They were able to find many but not quite enough areas of agreement. Meanwhile, bad news piled up: CBO raised its FY80 deficit projection by $17 billion;[41] wholesale and retail prices went up 1.5 percent in February; Chase Manhattan raised its prime rate to a record 18.25 percent on March 13.[42]

On March 13 the negotiations ended with a rough sense of how cuts might be made and revenues raised, but no detailed package emerged. That left room for House, Senate, and president to fight over details. To respond to the panic, Carter felt he had to announce a new policy quickly. On March 14 Carter promised a balanced budget through roughly equal spending cuts and revenue increases. Though he specified only a few reductions from his January plan, including elimination of the states' portion of General Revenue Sharing (GRS), he promised to submit a total of $13 billion in cuts by the end of the month. To raise revenues, Carter proposed withholding taxes on dividend and interest income (a measure that was to have a long and controversial career over the following years) and an oil import fee (which was to have a very short, noncontroversial life).

Most important for the politics of the next few months—and nearly ignored—was a decision that did not reduce the ostensible deficit at all: Carter chose not to increase defense spending. Almost all analysts had been expecting defense spending to rise far above the January totals. The January budget included underestimated fuel costs and no reaction to the Soviet move into Afghanistan.[43] Now Carter decided that budget restraint required denying further increases for defense.[44] He stood with House liberals against the tide of defense spending demands.[45]

By his statement and subsequent actions, Carter hoped that the federal government would demonstrate "discipline," thereby calming the markets. Meanwhile, the Federal Reserve Board was called upon to force a recession. The Fed was asked to do its part by restraining credit. Chairman Volcker wanted to restrain business lending anyway. Aside from the generally tight money, the March 14 package added a "voluntary" program to restrain growth in loans by large banks, enforced by a hefty raise in the discount rate for any bank that borrowed from the Fed (used the discount window) too often.

Chairman Volcker was far less interested in directly limiting consumer credit. Carter, however, was interested. If consumer borrowing prevented recession, restrictions on that borrowing could bring on the slump. Volcker did not like controls in principle; he believed borrowing was already beginning to slow. Imposing controls became part of an implicit deal between the chairman and the president; in Charles Schultze's words, "Just as Carter was doing unpleasant things for himself . . . [alienating] the liberal constituencies, so he too, Volcker, would have to do some things he wasn't quite anxious to do."[46]

The controls focused on credit cards. Essentially, they worked by raising the costs for banks if they expanded total lending on those cards. Unenthusiastic about the idea, Fed officials allowed a lot of loopholes, expecting lenders and borrowers to find them.[47]

For mysterious reasons—the best source emphasizes the publicity attached to Carter's attacks on credit card debt and the imposition of controls, to which we might add the existing nervousness—the controls worked far better than intended. Consumer borrowing not only stopped growing but turned negative. The economy, which had already begun to falter, fell off the cliff.

THREE

"The Worst of All Worlds"

As the economy sank into a worse slump than the administration had been trying to engineer, all reasonable expectation of a balanced budget went out the window. More unemployment than planned would mean lower revenues (less income to tax) and higher spending (for unemployment insurance). Yet the increasing implausibility of budget balance would change nobody's behavior. The president and Democratic budget leaders in the House and the Senate acted as if, once they had set a target of budget balance to meet inflationary expectations, any retreat would only create further panic. At the least, the government would have to deliver the deficit reduction it had promised.

This was not exactly traditional Democratic economics, which called for spending to counter recessions. The entire enterprise was unpopular with a large segment of the Democrats' interest group constituency. Lane Kirkland, head of the AFL-CIO, led labor in continual blasts at the administration's "Hooverist" economic policies. Within Congress, the Black Caucus was particularly vocal in opposing the budget balancing craze. While the rest of the leadership was committed to budget balance, Speaker Thomas P. (Tip) O'Neill, Jr., remained ambivalent. A good party man, he wanted to follow his president and his colleagues, but his heart wasn't in it. The budget cuts attacked programs in which he, a self-styled New Deal liberal, believed strongly. In March O'Neill held aloof from budget negotiations and publicly aired his reservations.[1]

In line with neoclassicist and some Keynesian concerns about business investment, another faction of Democrats was most interested in "productivity-increasing" tax cuts; this group was led by Representative James Jones (Okla.) and Senator Lloyd Bentsen (Tex.). Jones, a member of the Budget and the Ways and Means committees, cosponsored with Republican Barber Conable (N. Y.) a very large business tax cut (to be discussed later) known as the "10–5–3" accelerated depreciation plan. In late February, Bentsen, chairman of the Joint Economic Committee, led that group as it endorsed a $25 billion tax cut designed to increase long-term productivity. Sentiment for such business tax cuts was particularly strong in the Senate.[2] Many of Jones's group were also budget balancers who wanted to cut more spending to pay for the tax cut. The budget chairmen would have a hard time getting the business-incentive group in the same coalition as liberals.

The first step would be a balanced First Budget Resolution. That would be hard enough given the discontented liberals and eager proponents of business tax cuts. The greatest difficulty, however, was not fiscal policy but priorities. How much would be spent on the military? The defense buildup associated with Ronald Reagan actually began in 1980, driven not by Reagan's ideology but by events (Afghanistan and Iran) and the mood within Congress. If defense exceeded Carter's plan, then social programs had to be cut further, taxes had to be raised (extremely unlikely), or the deficit had to go up. Pressure for more defense spending therefore put the budget committees in a bind.

Defense Spending

A guide to the politics of defense spending requires a guide to defense numbers; that is not easy to assemble. Edwin Dale, associate director of OMB for Public Affairs in the Reagan administration, comments that at one point the *New York Times* ran four stories in ten days, each with different figures—"and all were correct!"

Budget resolutions provide totals for the national defense budget function. Within that function most activities are funded through the Defense Department appropriation. Yet spending also shows up in other bills: a few billions for research and construction of some nuclear weapons are included in the Energy and Water appropriation because the Department of Energy does the work; another few billions go into the separate military construction appropriation; and a few more billions, the amount of the annual pay increase, is included each year in a supplemental appropriation. Because the budget resolutions' target for defense budget authority includes all these appropriations, "defense" authority amounts in the resolution will exceed funding as shown in the annual defense appropriation act.

The budget resolution, however—to further confuse—includes separate figures for outlays and authority. Outlays are the focus of attempts to cut this year's deficit. Authority, the legal right to buy things over time, is the amount appropriated; it matters most to the military. The relationship between outlays and budget authority (BA) is particularly tenuous in defense because contracts for development and purchase of large weapons systems spend very slowly.

The difference between BA and outlays encourages a game that favors slow-spending forms of defense: Congress and the president can vote for both a "strong defense" and "fiscal responsibility" by spending less for personnel and maintenance, which outlay immediately, while they increase weapons purchases. This game has the added dividend of delighting defense contractors. Unfortunately, buying new equipment without training people to run it is not the best defense policy; budgetary games can have perverse operational consequences.

Some defense budget disputes focused on actual operations. Raises for military personnel, creation of a system of MX nuclear missiles, or a "Rapid Deployment Force" to be used in third world crises—all could be discussed in terms of specific applications. But much of the dispute concerned the symbolism of defense spending totals as indicative of either the nation's will to resist the Soviets or the misplaced emphasis on military rather than social spending. Thus, comparisons were made between American and Soviet defense spending, between present and past American defense spending, and between defense and domestic spending, apart from what the money would actually buy.

The Vietnam war destroyed the policy consensus of the late 1950s and early 1960s, in which the two parties competed to show their dedication to the vision of the United States as deterring communist aggression. Much of the Democratic party came to see Vietnam as a hopeless effort, brutal in execution and brutalizing in effect (a description that fit the dispatches on the nightly news). Citizens protested in the streets, and issues about protest itself and national authority became tangled with controversy over foreign policy. The war was not only a bad idea, many felt, but also expensive, soaking up funds needed for Great Society social programs. Therefore controversy spilled over into budgeting. Ultimately, through ceasing appropriations Congress ended America's vestigial military assistance to South Vietnam.

The Republican right, and some segments of Democrats, insisted that intervention in Vietnam was proper. The lesson, they insisted, was only that we did not try hard enough—for which liberals were to blame.

At least temporarily, Vietnam increased congressional skepticism of both military involvements and expenditures. This antimilitary mood meant that military spending, as a proportion of federal spending or GNP, dropped steadily. Meanwhile, basic expenses increased. A volunteer army, requiring higher pay, replaced the draft. The Army had left much equipment in the jungles of Southeast Asia. Military equipment became steadily more expensive (we will return to this later). Restraint on defense spending meant a real decrease in military capacity. In the

1980s, when sentiment turned around, there was a long list of unmet defense needs.

Part of the change was due to a continuing Soviet military expansion, the size of which was widely disputed. It was not something the USSR was about to divulge, and American estimates heavily depended on the point the analyst wanted to support. But there was no doubt that the Soviets had deployed a new generation of nuclear missiles; these, it was argued, had the power and accuracy necessary to destroy the American Minuteman force. Whether such capability was important, even if true, was a matter of heated contention. But NATO allies' opinions mattered most. A new version of Soviet missiles aimed at Europe left NATO governments particularly nervous about whether Americans were willing to defend them against conventional attack and thus risk nuclear attack on the United States itself.

These (possible) changes in the nuclear balance ironically increased pressure for spending on conventional (nonnuclear, for example, tanks) weapons. No longer might we defend Europe cheaply by threatening to escalate to nuclear weapons; instead a conventional attack might require conventional response. But the Warsaw Pact had more of that stuff than did NATO. Therefore, the Carter administration in May 1978 joined with the other NATO nations in pledging a 3 percent annual increase in real (that is, inflation adjusted) defense spending. The administration also planned deployment within Europe of weapons, the Pershing II and Cruise missiles, that might balance the midrange Soviet missiles aimed at Europe. U.S. defense hawks thought 3 percent pitiably little.

Both the United States and the NATO nations had reasons beyond European defense for worrying about conventional forces; the main reason was oil. Europeans depended far more than Americans on oil supplies from the Persian Gulf. But Americans also—as we had discovered to our surprise during OPEC's 1973 embargo—could suffer from an interruption of Persian Gulf supplies. Fears about the Persian Gulf were, of course, greatly heightened by the 1978 revolution in Iran. Imprisonment of fifty-three hostages in the American embassy in Tehran (October 1979) further dramatized America's inability to intervene. Nobody knew what the United States could do if it had greater force available, but the dominant concern was defending Saudi Arabia against some sort of Iranian invasion. Carter, therefore, proposed creating a Rapid Deployment Force (RDF) of 100,000 men, with the airlift and sealift capability to move them into action quickly anywhere in the world. Although mostly a reorganization, it required more money for equipment and readiness.

Iran, and a preference for conventional over nuclear strategies of deterrence, led many fairly liberal Democrats, personified by Senator

Gary Hart (D-Colo.), to advocate stronger conventional forces. Throughout the 1970s, meanwhile, Republican and Democratic proponents of
greater preparedness, including Ronald Reagan, Senator Daniel Patrick
Moynihan (D-N.Y.), and Senator Henry Jackson (D-Wash.), and a group
of intellectuals calling themselves the Committee on the Present Danger
had lobbied for greater attempts to counter Soviet "expansionism." Many
of these hawks opposed the SALT II treaty with the Soviet Union; other
senators were particularly worried about the details of the treaty. Led
by Sam Nunn (D-Ga.), these senators bargained with the administration
throughout 1979, insisting they would support SALT II only if concerns
about American military strength outside SALT's purview were met. At
last that added pressure pushed the administration by October 1979 into
committing itself to a buildup greater than the 3 percent agreed with
the NATO allies. Thus, when the Soviets moved into Afghanistan, Congress was already moving toward a big defense buildup, most likely emphasizing conventional capabilities. But how much was enough? One
approach was looking at totals.

Defense advocates emphasized that between 1960 and 1980 national
defense expenditures had shrunk from nearly 50 percent to less than
25 percent of federal spending and from 9.1 percent to 5.3 percent of
GNP. The new buildup, they argued, would not come close to restoring
even the defense share that existed in the mid-1960s. Therefore, it was
really quite modest. Table 1 gives the data.

Percentages are misleading because they depend on the denominator,

TABLE 1.   The Shrinking Defense Share of the National Economy and
of Federal Activity, 1960–1980

	Defense Outlays as % of GNP	Nondefense as % of GNP	Defense as % of Federal $	Human Resources as % of Federal $
1960	9.1	9.5	49.0	27.7
1965	7.2	10.8	40.1	29.9
1969	9.5	12.0	43.2	34.5
1972	6.8	13.7	33.2	44.8
1975	5.8	16.1	26.4	51.4
1976	5.5	16.8	24.5	53.8
1977	5.2	16.7	24.3	53.3
1978	5.0	16.4	23.5	51.9
1979	5.0	15.8	24.0	52.3
1980	5.3	17.1	23.6	52.1

SOURCE: OMB, Federal Government Finances, 1984 Budget Data, February 1983; Historical tables,
Tables 10 and 13. This is one of a set of background tables that OMB provided to those who asked
but did not publish with the annual budget documents. It has been superseded by a published volume,
Historical Statistics.

the size of the economy. The percentage fell quickly in the early 1960s because the economy grew quickly and the Kennedy administration, despite expansions of both strategic and conventional capability, felt the actual need for defense spending was expanding less quickly than the economy. There is no particular reason an expanding population should require larger armed forces, but domestic spending will inevitably increase absolutely (though not necessarily relatively) with a greater number to be served. Because economic growth was used to finance a large increase in nondefense spending, the defense share of government fell along with its share of the economy.

Argument from proportions was impressive but misleading. Constant-dollar expenditure would have made a better measure of effort. Adjusted for inflation, defense expenditure—the numerator—held fairly steady (in 1960, $72.9 billion in 1972 dollars; and in 1980, $72.7 billion). Expenditures rose during the Vietnam War and fell to a low of $67.1 billion in 1976. But for many reasons—particularly ending the draft and incorporating more advanced technology into weapons—the same amount of dollars bought less defense in 1980 than in 1960. The military budget had been squeezed but not so much as the GNP arguments suggested.

Trying to keep up on weapons, Congress and the military skimped on quick-spending readiness: for example, ammunition for practice, maintenance of existing airplanes, and training of personnel (which, if it involves flying advanced airplanes, can get very expensive). Liberals like Senator Hart and one-time Carter speech-writer James Fallows—not ordinarily supportive of higher military spending—therefore argued that the military neglected readiness in favor of expensive, high-tech weapons. The arguments, possibly true, allowed them to merge Vietnam era distrust of the military with a concern for national security. Yet publicity about readiness problems (soon heightened by a failed mission to rescue the hostages) added to the normal demands for new equipment, increasing the claim for more total spending.

There were further pressures for more pay. Jimmy Carter had held all spending down somewhat by giving federal employees—both civilian and military—smaller raises than those won by comparable workers in the private sector. When these elements were added to a comparatively tight private labor market, the military had problems getting and keeping soldiers.[3]

Senators Nunn and John Warner (R-Va.) sponsored a package of special benefits (in addition to Carter's budget) that garnered heavy support in the Senate. The Joint Chiefs were lobbying hard for a compensation increase. In early March, the commandant of the Marine Corps dramatized this argument by sending all Marines a bulletin advising them of their potential eligibility for food stamps. Neither the military nor its supporters, however, were willing to give up equipment in return for compensation.

The budget resolution had to give a total for defense; in no way could pressures for more equipment, maintenance, and personnel compensation be accommodated within the total the president had proposed. Republicans would demand more. So would southern Democrats, for the South is far more promilitary than other regions of the country. House Budget Committee Chairman Robert Giaimo (D-Conn.) knew he could get beaten on the floor by a coalition of Republicans and southerners if his resolution had too little for the military. Even if he won, he then would have to secure an agreement with the Senate, which, due to both bias created by equal state representation and happenstance, was substantially more prodefense than the House.

The House Divided

The left wing of the Democratic party wanted to cut defense if the budget were to be balanced. Yet such a plan would go nowhere in the full House, never mind in the Senate. Giaimo therefore chose to write off some portion of the liberals, for example, the Black Caucus, and rely, if necessary, on Republican support to pass the first resolution.[4] Republicans had never delivered as many as twenty votes for a resolution; it took quite a leap of faith to imagine that, with the Democrats reeling in a presidential election year, the GOP was going to help them pass a budget.[5] Yet he had no safe alternatives.

Giaimo first worked to get as much agreement as possible among the rest of the Democrats. Two days of private caucusing by HBC Democrats yielded some agreement.[6] On March 20 HBC approved, in principle, a package of $16.4 billion in cuts (as adjusted for new estimates of inflation) from Carter's January spending levels. They were not about to cut big entitlements like social security. The major areas available for cuts were therefore the federal bureaucracy itself—its pay, benefits, and staffing—and aid to state and local governments[7] (which, after all, were running surpluses).

The cutbacks included the state share of General Revenue Sharing, a proposed antirecession package for local governments, half a billion dollars from the CETA program (which unofficially funded local governments), a billion from a 2 percent reduction in agency operation and administrative costs, and another billion from federal civilian and military retirement benefits. Cutting the Postal Service subsidy would save $836 million.

In order to keep some liberal support, Giaimo shaved defense slightly. He positioned himself as resisting spending of any type, a stance that might elicit support from budget balancers. Democratic votes were used to beat attempts to raise defense. Giaimo maneuvered enough votes among Democrats to join with Republicans and beat an amendment, sponsored by David Obey and endorsed by Carter, to raise revenue sharing for local governments by $500 million. Giaimo's plan also allowed a $10 billion business tax cut—on the condition that the budget still be balanced.

Giaimo's tactics worked within the committee. He recognized that "it isn't the kind of budget that liberals and city people can vote for."[8] Ranking HBC Republican Delbert Latta (Ohio), however, proclaimed, "You ended up in the same place where we wanted to end up—and that's with a balanced budget and a tax cut."[9] As a result, in final committee vote on March 26, the budget survived the defection of six committee liberals, passing 18 to 6.[10]

Committee passage did not say much about the House floor. All sorts of factions wanted changes. At the end of March the administration finally released its budget. Carter's plan looked much like Giaimo's, with two conspicuous exceptions: the $500 million in aid to cities and funding for Saturday mail delivery. The differences foreshadowed a liberal challenge. Republicans meanwhile worked on their own substitute. Giaimo's plan might be acceptable, but they would try to do better.

The House leadership wanted to pass a meaningful budget that united Democrats. Reacting to extended brawls in previous years, the majority leadership brought the budget resolution to the floor in early May under a complex rule that allowed eight amendments (and several amendments to those amendments) ranging from a Black Caucus substitute that would raise social spending by $5.3 billion to a Republican plan that would cut spending by another $15 billion, allowing a larger tax cut. The GOP plan, developed by the Republican House leadership, foreshadowed future Reagan/Stockman cuts. It

Tightened eligibility requirements for entitlement programs, especially in the nutrition area, for savings of $7.9 billion.

Consolidated categorical into block grant programs for health, education and social services, accompanied by cuts of $7.1 billion in the program totals.

Repealed antirecession aid to cities and public service jobs programs, while creating new rules for revenue sharing that would effect a further cut in categorical grants. These proposals totaled $8.8 billion.

Cut a variety of government domestic activities, for example, the third class mail subsidies and regional development, totaling $6.5 billion.

Froze federal hiring and cut budgets of federal regulatory agencies, for savings of $5.4 billion.[11]

The differences between Republican and Democratic proposals in 1980 resembled those in 1981. Neither party wished to take on the giant universal entitlements of social security and medicare. Both parties were willing to cut intergovernmental assistance. But Democrats wanted to maintain national control of policy, allowing for later program increases; Republicans wanted to reduce programs and federal control permanently by consolidating categorical grants into block grants, which give recipient states more choice about using the money. Some Democrats were willing to cut poverty programs by reducing program eligibility, on the grounds that the pain of cuts could be limited by better targeting benefits for the needy. Other Democrats, however, worried more about missing somebody who needed benefits, and they were reluctant to go as far as the Republicans along these lines. Both parties viewed the federal employee payroll as a relatively painless place to find cuts. Republicans, however, saw these cuts as an opportunity to reduce the activity of federal regulatory agencies.

Democrats saw budget cutting as something they were forced to do by the needs of economic management; they could clean out a few rather moldy programs. But, for Republicans, the deficit fight was an opportunity to redirect the course of American government. They would use greater social spending cuts to finance greater defense spending, as well as tax cuts; Democrats understandably were unenthusiastic about these objectives.

Giaimo won the first round of the struggle. He beat off a $5.1 billion shift from domestic spending, sponsored by Marjorie Holt (R-Md.) and Phil Gramm (D-Tex.), by telling conservative Democrats that defense was sure to go up after conference with the Senate.[12] He also beat a proposal by David Obey, who was supported by the president and Speaker, for a $1.2 billion increase in social spending. Most Democrats followed Obey, but Giaimo had all but 36 (urban) Republicans, many southern Democrats, and a group of budget-balancing moderates, enough to win by twelve votes. On May 7 Giaimo's plan passed, 225 to 193.[13] Unfortunately for Giaimo, the Senate had a different plan.[14]

The Senate United Means the Congress Divided

Following requests by the Armed Services Committee and Joint Chiefs of Staff, Republicans and conservative Democrats led by Senator Ernest "Fritz" Hollings raised Muskie's defense outlay target by $7.5 billion. To make room for this increase, they had to cut other spending. After a week of tough bargaining, SBC emerged on April 3 with a package significantly higher than HBC's on defense, lower on domestic spending, and equal on revenues. Foreshadowing its choices in 1981, the Senate committee protected veterans, agriculture, and defense programs. It thus showed its natural bias, compared to the House, for the interests of smaller southern and western states and against the industrial North-east and Midwest.[15]

Agreement between House, Senate, and president became less likely when, on April 28, Secretary of State Cyrus Vance resigned in protest of the April 25 aborted attempt to rescue the hostages in Iran. Needing support in Congress, Carter convinced Senator Muskie to replace Vance. Muskie's departure made Hollings, leader of the Democratic hawks, the new chairman of Senate Budget.

The Senate's plan, passed 68 to 28 on May 12, promised a balanced budget.[16] Barely. The next step was the House-Senate conference on the resolution.

Giaimo was willing to come up some on defense, but Hollings would hardly come down at all. Late on May 21, Giaimo agreed to $5.8 billion more in defense outlays and $10.5 billion more in budget authority than the House had allotted. He thereby lost support not only from Obey but also from a group of moderate Democratic budgeters (Representatives Timothy Wirth of Colorado, Leon Panetta and Norm Mineta of California, Richard Gephardt of Missouri, and William Brodhead of Michigan) who had supported him to that point. They joined Carter and O'Neill in urging the party to reject the agreement. Republicans could not resist the urge to torpedo a Democratic resolution. On May 29 the conference agreement was overwhelmingly defeated. Ignoring the arguments of Majority Leader Wright (and the *Washington Post*) that the size of social program cuts had been overstated, most Democrats also voted nay, 146 to 97.

The budget resolution "was defeated last year," said Obey, "and there was no great harm done. The Senate simply learned it had to listen more closely."[17] But this time the message was immediately scrambled. On a motion by Delbert Latta, the House followed its rejection of the agreement by instructing the conferees to accept the resolution's high defense figure. In his thinking, Giaimo had been right that the House wanted more defense, but wrong that a majority would support more defense *and* a budget resolution. Flummoxed, he called the combination of votes "ridiculous." "When you vote down one resolution because it's too high on defense and turn around and instruct the conferees to accept the Senate defense numbers, it's questionable," he understated. "Now I've got two mandates."[18] It was May 29, and the first resolution had been due May 15.

Back to work went the conferees. If it had been a normal year, they could have added some more social spending, increased the deficit slightly, and made a deal. That was what they had done in 1979, changing the social/defense balance at the expense of the deficit. In 1980, however, the conferees could not "budget by addition" because they were supposed to be "budgeting by subtraction" in order to balance the budget. The fact, obvious to all by early June, that they were not going to balance the budget anyway, did not make things better.

The participants had begun to discover they cared for other things besides the deficit. Yet they could not—partly believing in balance, partly believing in the value of public belief in balance—give up that idea. Instead, they added deficit and balance together, arguing that following their policy preferences would balance the budget. How could two "rights" make a "wrong"?

A Procedural Revolution

Though the House and Senate could not agree on the contents of the budget, they had agreed on a potentially much more significant matter: a procedure to enforce the first resolution's targets. The procedure was reconciling the first resolution; in 1981 it would provide the means by which Ronald Reagan would win his spending cuts.

The leadership of both houses concurred that the spending cuts and tax hikes in the resolution had to be enforced. Even Speaker O'Neill, no fan of budget cuts, was convinced to accept new procedures so as to make the budget resolution stick. Now, if you can't agree on what you want to do, making agreements binding does seem premature. But, as they argued endlessly over defense spending, legislators might find some cuts on which they could agree. Majorities certainly favored reducing the deficit while making budget resolutions that would bear some relation to government's fiscal policy.

Under the Budget Act, reconciliation—a strange name for a very conflictual process—was supposed to occur on the second, binding, resolution. If the law existing at the time of the Second Resolution did not jibe with that resolution's targets, Congress could instruct committees to report out legislation to reconcile spending and revenue law to the targets. Although the committees would decide on the details of their savings, reconciliation clearly infringed on their formal authority (a committee's choice of whether to act at all is the heart of its power) and informal relationships (if the budget process could force changes in agriculture policy, then interest groups had to cultivate the budgeters). The committees had a legitimate complaint; ten days was far too short a time for drafting legislation.

During debate on the FY80 Second Resolution in 1979, the Senate could see that supplemental appropriations to cover the annual federal pay raise and costs of "appropriated entitlements," such as food stamps and the Commodity Credit Corporation, would force spending over the totals. Therefore, the SBC draft resolution instructed seven different committees to cut projected spending by more than $4 billion. The two biggest targets, Appropriations and Finance committees, resisted. In a caucus, Senate Democrats negotiated a compromise, scaled-down reconciliation plan, but House Democrats, in their own caucus, rejected reconciliation.

In conference on the second resolution, HBC Chairman Giaimo led the fight against reconciliation, arguing that he couldn't "take on seven committees in the House" over it. In a separate vote on the conference agreement, reconciliation was beaten 205 to 190. Giaimo had argued that it was too late to make reconciliation work. Committees should be given a chance to comply voluntarily, but they did not.

Preparing for the FY81 budget battles, some Senate staffers had a brainstorm: Why not try reconciliation during the First Resolution? That would solve the scheduling problem, a big advantage for the budget committees, whose staffers, of course, wanted their own process to control subsequent action. By reconciling on the First Resolution, the budget committee might get at entitlements directly. In fact, as Allen Schick notes, that would shift the focus from legislation enacted during the current session (mostly appropriations) to that taken in previous years— thus plugging a big hole in the Budget Act.[19]

Reconciling to the First Resolution implicitly meant turning the resolution's figures from provisional targets into binding totals, thus changing the whole nature of the budget process. Although reconciling wasn't part of the Budget Act, the omission was resolved by referring to the act's "elastic clause," allowing a resolution to add to the act's enforcement mechanisms "any other procedure which is considered appropriate to carry out the purposes of this Act."[20] Were members of Congress so eager to show that they could cope with the deficit, the real issue, that they would willingly abandon old ways of doing business?

In general, leaders of authorizing, subject matter committees had the most to lose. And Republicans (who usually lost in authorizing committees anyway) had most to gain because reconciliation would force Republican spending-reduction proposals onto the committee agendas. Thus, in 1979 House Minority Leader John Rhodes (R-Ariz.) said that he considered "reconciliation so important" that he "would be willing to vote for this budget, even though the spending figures are way out of line."[21]

Most important, however, was the attitude of the Democratic leadership in the House. Normally attentive to committee chairmen, Speaker O'Neill had to worry also about his party's image. When Giaimo and other budget balancers like Jim Jones demanded that he support reconciliation, O'Neill agreed. A powerful group of sixteen committee and subcommittee chairmen, led by Morris Udall (D-Ariz.) of Interior, protested reconciliation in a "dear colleague" letter. Significantly missing from the list were Chairman of Ways and Means Al Ullman (D-Oreg.), Chairman Richard Bolling (D-Mo.) of Rules, and Thomas Foley (D-Wash.) of Agriculture. Bolling, a close confidante of Speaker O'Neill, might have been able to swing him against reconciliation. Yet Bolling was a reformer who believed, as did the Speaker, that budgets should be party documents. He thought it was a close call, making the legislative process messier than ever, but decided it would be an observable instance of majority choice. With Bolling and Ullman, House Budget's first chairman, supporting reconciliation, Speaker O'Neill gave the complaining chairmen no help, and they prepared for a floor fight.

Both House and Senate budget committees included in their draft resolutions reconciliation instructions to authorizing committees requiring about $9 billion in spending cuts. There was little debate in the Senate about this new reform. Debate in the House on the budget resolution included a watershed vote on the Udall amendment to remove reconciliation instructions. Chairman Udall lost badly, 127 to 289. The institutional significance of the vote and the attitudes revealed in debate justify more discussion than the lopsided margin suggests. Many events in the Reagan years were foreshadowed by arguments made there.

Conservative Republican Delbert Latta provided the basic rationale for reconciliation:

> When we are presenting a budget to the American people supposedly in balance, and there is about $9 billion worth of revisions which must be made in present law in order to obtain that balanced budget, can we truthfully say that we have passed a budget resolution which is in balance, without providing the mechanism, namely reconciliation, to bring about those $9 billion in savings? You know the answer as well as I do. You cannot do it with a straight face.[22]

Representatives Udall and Neal Smith (D-Iowa) provided the most fundamental objection: in making reconciliation instructions, the Budget Committee was in the business of deciding which programs could best be cut, without possessing the substantive knowledge of the authorizing and appropriations committees.

Liberal John Seiberling (D-Ohio) stated one dilemma: "If we do not have reconciliation in the first budget resolution . . . we have gone through a charade. . . . On the other hand, . . . the committee on the budget cannot possibly develop the knowledge and expertise to substitute for the authorizing committees and the appropriations subcommittees."[23]

Chairman Giaimo continually emphasized that "you, the Members of this great House of Representatives"—not the Budget Committee—

would be the ones to impose any instructions on the committees.[24] In other words, Budget was not grabbing power. He was right in that members could vote for different instructions if they wished. If Budget drafted instructions, however, it inevitably decided on substance; otherwise, how could it decide to which committees the cuts should be assigned?

The choice was really what kind of error to make: bad decisions on programs or an unacceptable total. Jim Jones called reconciliation "the litmus test" of how much the House cared about budget balance.[25] The budget totals, Richard Ottinger (D-N.Y.) argued, were nonsense.

> The entire assumptions on which this budget was formed have evaporated. . . . [Yet] the Budget Committee says . . . the only important thing before the Congress . . . is to see to it that those ceilings are maintained. . . . Why bother? People who cannot afford an adequate diet should not have adequate diets. But we have got to keep that budget ceiling.[26]

The strongest statement of the traditional liberal's distrust of spending constraints was made by Representative James C. Corman (D-Calif.), chairman of the Subcommittee on Public Assistance and Unemployment Compensation of the Committee on Ways and Means. He raised a basic question: How would budget constraint change the conduct of politics?

The draft reconciliation instructions assumed that Ways and Means would find $4.2 billion in revenues or spending savings, mainly by extending income tax withholding to interest income. Administrations and the Treasury had wanted that change for years; Corman had no quarrel with the idea. But, he argued, everybody knew that, politically, withholding was a nonstarter. Ways and Means would never do it. (He was right and wrong simultaneously, as we shall see!) Ways and Means certainly would not cut social security, Corman continued. Because the committee had to get the money somewhere, it would come from the weakest group, the constituents of Corman's subcommittee: "It will come from a very narrow base of people, the poorest of us, and they will be seriously affected. That is my problem."[27]

Having served in the House for twenty years, Jim Corman knew how hard it was to win liberal victories. He saw a politics of interests against interests; if times were tough, then the weakest would be shouldered aside in the scramble for what was left. How, indeed, could it be otherwise? His younger Democratic colleagues, however, were far more confident. In reply to Corman, they argued in terms that will look familiar when we meet a man who was otherwise their nemesis: David Stockman.

Richard Gephardt, a member of the Ways and Means Committee, argued that if withholding were impossible there were other choices:

cuts previously staved off by powerful special interests would, when the issue was clear, suddenly become possible:

> Do we want to cut off orphan children, do we want to hurt people who really have need or do we want to pass higher user fees on people who have private aircraft? . . . I would like to have that debate go on in the House. . . . We can bring these things out of our committee and pass them on the floor if people see that as the stark choice they have to make.[28]

Echoing Gephardt, Tim Wirth mentioned aviation and tobacco tax breaks. In short, if an open argument about justice, not clandestine politics, was at issue, then the good guys would win.

These mostly younger members saw reconciliation as a matter of procedural honesty; they believed it would favor their side because they were right. George Miller of California, a very liberal member of the Watergate class of legislators, declared that he would support reconciliation because for years Republicans had voted for more defense spending, then castigated Democrats as spenders, while themselves voting against budget resolutions. With reconciliation making the budget meaningful,

> Nobody again will be able to run off with the entire store. . . . Those people who are interested in the defense of this country and interested in it in the sense of any contract that will go to their district must be good, will no longer be able to create a deficit at my expense, and no longer will many of us have to pay for their sins.

He described reconciliation as a way to prevent a "deficit that is there for no other purpose than to protect the special interests in this country, many of whom tell you at the end of the letter, 'By the way, I believe in a balanced budget.' "[29]

Seiberling added, "We are never going to reassert priorities, we are never going to get tax reform, we are never going to get that kind of liberal democratic program that I think this Congress is, to some extent, deserting" *without* reconciliation! Only a process that forced the hard choice would force the right choice.[30]

Thus, a faction of liberals—frustrated by years of being blamed for deficits, convinced enough of Keynesian theory to believe deficits had something (if not a lot) to do with inflation, and dedicated to government as a way to redress economic injustices—saw a tough budget process as a means toward better policy. Gephardt, Wirth, Miller, and Seiberling were arguing that, as David Stockman would put it later, in a budget crunch "weak claims," not "weak clients," would lose.

Probably most supporters of reconciliation saw it mainly as a way to reduce the deficit. Certainly that was most Republicans' stated reason. Liberal support for reconciliation nevertheless was crucial: it kept the

Udall vote from being close, and it divided Democrats. Consequently, the principle of reconciliation was established in a nonpartisan manner, making it a stronger precedent in 1981.

The liberal political theory for reconciliation turned out to have some holes. Corman was at least as right as Miller, for the notion that the right side can be determined by clearly posing choices is questionable. Even some conservative calculations may have been a bit off: reconciliation would become the vehicle for a series of tax hikes after 1981. Some authorizing committees would find that reconciliation had advantages; a lot can be tucked away in a large package. Whatever its consequences, reconciliation was established when the Udall amendment lost on May 7, 1980.

More Economic Pressures

A major procedural change, reconciliation would not have seemed necessary without the drive to balance the budget. Nor would the politics of budget priorities have been so serious. Thus, Majority Leader Jim Wright and Giaimo both argued that Congress had to reconcile to show its seriousness about inflation.[31]

Events in the economy during spring 1980 made budget balance less likely, yet they increased both the sense of panic and the desire to calm the markets, feelings that fed the pressure to balance the budget. The March 15 economic package had failed to reduce interest rates—far from it. By early April the prime rate had risen almost five points, to a record 20 percent. *Newsweek* reported:

> There had never been anything like it in modern American history, and even veteran moneymen stood in awe. "It's just unbelievable that this is happening to us," exclaimed a governor of the Federal Reserve Board last week, after he heard that the nation's commercial banks had raised the prime lending rate to their best corporate customers to an astronomical 20 percent. "We are in a South American inflationary environment now, and I'm surprised the banks haven't started quoting their interest on a monthly basis as they do there."[32]

Bankers and moneymen devoutly prayed for a recession but still believed that Carter did not. *Time,* in late March, quoted "one Zurich banker last week in a rueful sentiment that was almost universally shared among business leaders and economists everywhere: 'I'm afraid that at the first sign of a sharp recession, there will be a change in course.' "[33] They were wrong. The recession was well under way, and the administration was staying on course.

Interest rates headed up because the Fed's moves were pushing them higher. Housing starts had already slowed drastically, even before the March 15 credit control actions. Secretary of the Treasury William Miller told a delegation of housing lobbyists that they could expect no help. Two hundred thousand autoworkers were already on layoff, yet the administration took no action to help that gasping industry whose union is one of the most powerful forces of American liberalism.[34] In April unemployment jumped to 7 percent.[35]

Economic activity dropped more sharply than at any time since the depression. In May, the recession began to have some of its intended effects; interest rates fell, and bond prices rose. Yet short-term rates were extremely volatile, falling too quickly for comfort, while rates on long-term bonds fell by only a couple of percentage points, suggesting investors were skeptical that inflation would disappear. As OMB's chief economist said, "We have been forecasting a recession's development since last July, and it's rather nice to be finally getting it. A mild recession is unavoidable if we're to do anything with inflation."[36] But it was not clear that this was the "nice," "mild" recession they had been looking for.[37]

From the left, Senator Kennedy called for wage-price controls, combined with jobs spending. From the right, Republicans increased their calls for tax cuts. Carter's image as a waverer caused his aides to favor steadfastness for its own sake. Noting the high interest rates on long-term bonds, administration economists feared granting the markets further excuses to believe that inflation would accelerate. Its judgments of both politics and policy led the administration to stick to belt-tightening.

Due to lower tax revenues and higher entitlement benefits caused by the recession, the budget could not be balanced. As early as May 5, congressional budget experts knew there would be a deficit.[38] Yet, like the Holy Grail, the mythical balance was still pursued. Comments from politicians and media suggested the point was in the quest itself. The *Washington Post* editorialized that a balanced budget as such was less important than the government display of restraint it symbolized.[39] Senator Byrd acknowledged on May 3 that economic changes might make balance impossible, cautioning that "the worst thing we can do is jump ship too soon."[40] "As long as inflation remains so high," the *Wall Street Journal* quoted a treasury official on May 2, "the financial markets will be watching our moves very carefully. Right now there is very little anyone can do to break out of the balanced budget mode."[41] Promise had become more important than performance.

Economic policy attempted to manipulate the financial markets through symbolic action that everyone could see through, but it didn't work any better with the voters than with the markets. By late March the political advantages Carter had gained from the Iranian hostage crisis were wearing off. The public became impatient with the president's failure to bring the hostages home. In the polls Carter's lead over Reagan dropped sharply. More voters expected the economic package to increase rather than to decrease inflation, and by large margins they expected the package to increase unemployment.[42] Carter's show of resolve was losing the Democratic party's advantage on the unemployment issue, without winning compensating gains on inflation.

Ted Kennedy's weaknesses allowed Carter to move toward clinching renomination, but the blue-collar base of the Democratic party was considering defecting to Reagan. According to Gallup, members of labor union families were more skeptical than their fellow citizens about Carter's economic policies. In six major primary states, nearly half the voters in hourly paid jobs had voted for Reagan in Republican primaries. In Wisconsin, for the first time since Eisenhower had been a candidate, the Republican primary drew far more voters than did the Democratic contest. In West Allis, Wisconsin, a housewife and long-time Democrat expressed the sentiments that haunted Democratic officeholders in their fitful sleep: "Inflation is eating us up, welfare is a mess, we don't have any power in this country—why shouldn't we switch? Kennedy has a moral problem and Carter can't decide anything. Reagan would return us to this country's true meaning."[43]

June 1980 brought even worse economic news. In April the Commerce Department's leading indicators had fallen 4.8 percent—the largest drop in the thirty-two years that the index had been calculated. The Labor Department in May announced that unemployment had soared to 7.8 percent.[44] *Time* summarized the consequences neatly: "Business tumbles, the political fallout hits, and tax cut talk begins."[45] Because desire for a balanced budget did not fade, budgeting became even more difficult.[46]

After all the publicity about balancing the budget to fight inflation, politicians feared both the public and "the markets" might panic if they admitted defeat. "The problem," Leon Panetta (D-Calif.) explained in mid-June, "is that we're in a kind of transition where we're still hurting from inflation while we're beginning to hurt from a recession. We can't afford to bounce either way until we see what's going to happen."[47]

However we characterize their psychology, many Democrats were more scared to change course again than to stick to the present path. Republicans, not (yet) responsible for blazing the trail, gleefully criticized the guides.

But merely watching while people lost their jobs made them all uncomfortable. Congressional Democrats and Republicans therefore joined to inter Carter's barely breathing oil-import fee. Then a president's veto was overturned by a Congress of his own party for the first time since Harry Truman held office.[48] In an era of rampant inflation, Congress was reluctant to add another price increase. At a time of increasing unemployment, Democrats refused to increase the burdens of poorer people while, as they saw it, oil company profits swelled. Neither budget balance nor energy concerns could convince Congress to impose immediate pain in a way that would affect almost everybody.

Traditional liberals, represented by Senator Kennedy, thought the recession justified turning from deficit worries to antirecessionary public jobs spending. The limits of their appeal were shown by a victory: at the Democratic National Convention in August, delegates endorsed Kennedy's $12-billion package of "job-creating" spending. Kennedy won because Democratic convention delegates are more liberal than members of Congress[49] and because only Democrats go to their convention. Rosalynn Carter identified the problem: "I don't know how [Congress] will vote $12 billion, when we tried so hard to get $2 billion for new employment, and both houses of Congress went home without doing it."[50]

Activists, oriented toward winning benefits for their deserving groups, did not have to deal with the conflicting pressures that caused many Democratic politicians to doubt the value of further spending. They were less influenced by the growing literature of policy criticism created by social scientists and more influenced by their responsibility for managing the economy; Democratic reaction caused politicians like Budget Committee Chairman Muskie to question their faith.[51]

Liberals were at a huge disadvantage because in the late 1970s the undesirability of direct government spending to create jobs had become conventional wisdom, stated as fact, not opinion. Like other major media, *Time* reported:

> It would be costly and dangerous for the Government to become an uncle with a job for everyone. Says one Administration economist: "We calculate that to employ a single person in a public-works job, such as building a school, a road, or a bridge, costs about $69,320 per year in taxpayer money."
>
> Moreover, such programs are almost always started too late to have any immediate impact on unemployment. . . . The major impact of the federal spending is to feed inflation later.[52]

Kennedy may have spoken for the heart and soul of the party; but his view of that heart and soul seemed outdated.

Within Congress, tax cuts were far more fashionable than jobs spending. Republicans liked virtually any kind of tax cut while Democrats were attracted to "productivity-enhancing" plans such as the Bentsen and Jones-Conable schemes. Even the left had conceded the need for greater productivity, believing that the social goals of the welfare state could not be financed without it. Liberal Democrats did not reject capitalism, but they did not entirely trust capitalists. Instead, they endorsed government intervention, as a *New Republic* article emphasized, to "save capitalism from its friends." Liberal intellectuals, such as economist Lester Thurow and the *New Republic*'s editors, had their own menus of tax changes, designed to encourage business to invest in ways that increased jobs.

In spite of all the tax-cutting arguments, however, the Democrats remained hesitant, for the two parties also disagreed on the kind of tax cuts desired. Factions in both parties wanted incentives for business investment: liberals wanted cuts at the low end of the income tax so the scheduled 1981 social security tax increase would not make the overall tax system more regressive, but Ronald Reagan and the supply-siders favored sweeping personal tax cuts that would give more back to those who already paid most.

President Carter's aides knew that the Midyear Budget Review, due in July, would show the economy in a parlous state. They began drafting a tax-cut plan.

Back in budget land, nobody was willing to be the first to admit that the FY81 budget would not balance. Urgent 1980 supplementals awaited passage of the FY80 third resolution, which was attached to the FY81 first.

From Bad to Worse

Delay in passing the FY81 First Resolution meant that a third resolution, revising targets for FY80 because the economic projections had been far off, was also delayed. That in turn delayed $16.9 billion in urgent supplemental appropriations for programs such as food stamps and medicaid. As the Senate and House negotiators battled over defense and domestic budget authority figures (outlays had been set by Latta's motion to instruct), each side was holding the supplemental appropriations hostage. Neither would give in. Finally on June 11, a day after a smashing victory in his primary campaign, Hollings agreed to transfer $800 million from defense to domestic budget authority. He also accepted a $300-million increase in transportation and low-income energy assistance at the expense of the mythical budget surplus.

Giaimo's vision of a bipartisan budget disappeared as the budget became clearly partisan. The House leadership backed the compromise in the strongest terms. O'Neill, Wright, and Brademas (D-Ind.) wrote to their colleagues:

Today you will be asked to decide the future of the Congressional budget process and at the same time to resolve a fiscal crisis of dramatic proportions. . . . At stake is the ability of the Democratic party to govern the House. The danger crosses philosophical lines. Failure to adopt the first resolution would demonstrate clearly that the Democratic Congress cannot deal with the budget. It would discredit the party and the Congress. . . . This may be the most important vote you will cast both as a member of the 96th Congress and as a Democrat.[53]

On June 12 the House finally passed the first resolution (Democrats 195 to 55, Republicans 10 to 140); the Senate followed.

Because few analysts believed the resolution's economic projections, both legislators and commentators widely remarked that it was a dead letter. But that was true only if one cared for nothing beyond budget balance. The budget resolution indicated a change in government's priorities, from domestic to defense spending. In that sense, June 12, 1980, foretold the Reagan revolution.

On Wednesday, June 25, Senate Republicans tried for another installment. They announced agreement with Ronald Reagan to support a 10 percent across-the-board tax cut and faster depreciation write-offs, effective January 1, 1981. They would offer the package as an amendment to all pending finance legislation, beginning with the next day's debate on raising the debt ceiling. The 10 percent individual cut could be viewed as either the first year of the Kemp-Roth plan (for three consecutive such reductions) or as reasonable compensation for recent bracket creep. It therefore united supply-siders with the more neoclassically oriented Republicans. "All agreed to take the first year of the Kemp-Roth bill," Senator Robert Dole (R-Kan.) explained, "but we carefully didn't call it that because we were looking for broad support."[54]

Reagan's maneuver was designed by business lobbyist extraordinaire Charls Walker, who had helped design the Jones-Conable and the 1978 Jones-Steiger depreciation changes. Because the Republicans were united, Majority Leader Robert Byrd feared the proposal might pass. In an about-face that shocked both Carter and the House leadership, Byrd called a caucus meeting for June 26, at which Senate Democrats formally asked the Finance Committee to draft tax-cut legislation by September 3. Senator Bentsen was made head of a twenty-one-member task force to hammer out recommendations.[55]

Byrd's maneuver allowed Democrats to justify voting against the Republican plan. They could say that they wanted a better tax cut rather than no reduction. Reagan reacted with mockery:

Yesterday I urged the Congress to enact an immediate tax cut . . . to come to grips with the country's desperate economic decline. Today the Democrats in the Senate answered. Their pitiful response: "We need a study, a task force." What are they waiting for? And where have they been all these months? What do the Democratic leaders expect to learn . . . that millions of American families don't already know?[56]

Explaining the Senate's quick move, Richard Bolling said it proved "how desperately upset the Democrats are. This looks like one of those elections when the Democrats are terrified and the Republicans sense the kill."[57]

As the recession grew, major Democratic economists joined the tax cut chorus. Otto Eckstein said that "it would be the extreme of irresponsibility and the worst economic policy since the 1930s Depression to let taxes increase at the rate planned."[58] Walter Heller argued for a $30-billion cut, proclaiming that "that $30 billion isn't going to begin to be inflationary."[59] These Keynesians had begun to regain their bearings. Yet other opinion leaders went on opposing tax cuts. The *Washington Post* called them "a subject for next year. . . . Most people would welcome lower taxes, but for a great many Americans this summer a drop in interest rates is far more urgent."[60] Bankers, including New York Federal Reserve President Anthony Solomon, agreed. "Good politics," *Time* commented of Reagan's plan, "does not necessarily make good economics."[61]

At a June 28 meeting of his economic team, Carter reaffirmed his hard line against tax cuts. He reports in his diary that "lenders of the key financial institutions on Wall Street . . . had liked the budget and had not recommended any income tax reductions for 1980. They had expressed a preference for a moderate tax cut in 1981 of $20 or $30 billion at most—provided our anti-inflation program continued to work."[62] He wanted to maintain "public confidence in our commitment to maintain discipline and fiscal restraint."[63] When their Midyear Economic Review came out, it predicted 9 percent unemployment by the end of 1980. Yet Carter rejected his own economists' proposals for a $25-billion tax cut in 1980.[64]

Speaker Tip O'Neill heard no "hue and cry for a tax cut" in the House. He and Giaimo opposed any action before the election; Congress would Christmas-tree the bill (cover it with a variety of benefits), and members probably could not resolve disagreements among House, Senate, and administration in the short time remaining before recess anyway. In spite of their skepticism, Senate Finance Committee Chairman Russell Long (D-La.) (who had his own doubts) accepted his caucus's instruction to report out a cut. The Democrats were not only terrified but divided.[65]

Through a combination of bad luck and bad timing, the president and his colleagues were heading for an election with disaster looming on all economic fronts: unemployment, inflation, and the budget deficit. "That's not a very inviting picture they paint for us," commented Representative Jones. He felt his constituents would willingly forego a tax cut in order to balance the budget. Now they would have neither. "This," he said, "is the worst of all worlds."[66]

Voters generally agreed with Jones. Carter's approval rating in the polls had turned mildly negative by early March, then drifted lower, and in mid-July bottomed out at 21 percent—even lower than Richard Nixon's in the darkest days of Watergate. The following list shows the demise of Carter in opinion polls.

	Approval	Disapproval
February 1–4	55	36
March 7–10	43	45
March 28–31	39	51
May 2–5	43	47
May 30–June 2	38	52
June 27–30	31	58
July 14–25	21	63

By early August, 52 percent of Democrats wanted the party to select somebody other than Carter at its convention. "Never before," said Gallup, "in the almost fifty years of Gallup polls has an incumbent president entered a convention with less grassroots support from his own party."[67] Democratic officeholders, unhappy about campaigning with Carter around their necks, began an "Anybody but Carter" movement. Out of sixty marginal House districts, Carter, who had carried twenty-two of them in 1976, was leading the polls in only four in 1980. The difficulty, said David Obey, was that "we'd be in as bad shape or worse shape" with Kennedy at the head of the ticket.[68] In Gallup's polls Kennedy was even less popular than Carter, and Reagan had big leads over Muskie and Mondale. There was nobody but Carter, and Carter looked like a loser.

The Election, the Economy, and a Fragmented Budget

The Democrats still controlled the government, so they still had to govern. Budget deadlines required that they unite to pass the reconciliation and appropriations bills. Having disposed of the First Resolution, they still had to deal with the Second Resolution. Because the second set required binding targets, they would have to admit they would fail to balance the budget, cut spending further, ignore the resolution, lie, or all of the above. In the meantime, the economy would continue to gyrate so wildly as to confuse everyone about what good policy might be.

Carter had to find an economic plank on which to campaign. Because he did not wish to change his policy, he repackaged it as an emphasis on the "future"—including future tax cuts. One aide described Carter's strategy as "the past is behind us—may it rest in peace."[69] His tax plan emphasized business tax cuts (55 percent), and personal cuts took the form of a social security tax offset. Some observers remarked on the irony of Republicans emphasizing personal and Democrats emphasizing business tax cuts, but the *Wall Street Journal* correctly argued that the "basic concept" for Democrats remained "that the government must play the central role in managing economic change."[70]

Carter tried to exploit fears of the Republican platform's "Kemp-Roth" tax cut, which called for 10 percent cuts in income tax rates over three successive years. Kemp-Roth seemed to many a dangerous experiment that risked inflationary budget deficits. The Reagan campaign tried to blunt fears of such deficits by issuing projections that showed budget balance largely by assuming that inflation continued.[71] (If that sounds strange, you're right. It was strange but important; see Chapter 4). Skepticism remained.

Senate Democrats were torn between the commonsense notion that voters were hurting and would like a tax cut and the contrasting considerations: it would help nobody to get into a fight with their own president; the public was worried about deficits; House leaders would side with Carter; and the Senate's budget-balancers, led by Hollings, still opposed a tax cut. At a meeting of the party caucus, Byrd reversed course again, siding with Hollings and the president rather than fighting Carter just before the election. The party decided to have no votes on either tax cuts or a second budget resolution until after the election. The House had already decided not to admit the unbalanced budget until then.

Senator Moynihan swore that his party had just blown five or six Senate seats; and Senator Long never forgave Byrd for preventing the vote for a tax cut.[72] Yet the opponents of tax cuts could argue that they were being responsible, for the economy seemed to have zigged again.[73] The leading indicators began to rise sharply in June, as did retail sales.[74] Arguments could be made (and were) for any economic prediction.[75]

But economists, as Alfred Malabre of the *Wall Street Journal* reported on October 1, could not even say if the recession was over. "Some say yes. Some say no. And some, a cheerful few indeed, say there hasn't been a recession at all this year." And the politicians were supposed to know what the economy would do next.

Having contracted at an annual rate of 10 percent in the second quarter of 1980, the economy, we can see now, turned around and expanded at a rate of 2.4 percent in the third quarter. Although no one can say for sure what happened, the most plausible story centers on the Federal Reserve's monetary policy.

The economy collapsed so suddenly at the end of March that all but the most hardened inflation-fighters at the Fed were concerned. They had been trying to slow the growth of the money supply in order to (a) seem to be following monetarist prescriptions to control inflation, thereby making monetarists in the markets happy; and (b) raise interest rates enough to provoke recession. Interest rates had gone through the roof, then the money supply had begun to shrink. It shrank by 4 percent in six weeks. Maybe people were paying off debts or maybe they were putting their money in long-term accounts. But whatever they were doing, money was disappearing from the checking accounts where it serves as the medium of exchange.

"The Federal Reserve," William Greider writes, "had not intended anything like this."[76] The question was, was it a blip or real? If the Fed ignored the monetary numbers, saying they were a blip, it would (a) lose the support of monetarists; (b) lose the political cover Volcker gained by claiming to be monetarist, which had allowed him to drive up interest rates while disclaiming that as his goal; and (c) risk what Board Governor Charles Partee called "the Big Mistake."[77] If the numbers were real, ignoring them could mean a depression.

Unwilling to take all those risks, Volcker convinced his divided colleagues to step on the monetary accelerator. The aggregates responded sluggishly. Within ten weeks after the Fed put the pedal to the floor, the short-term price of money was cut roughly in half. For good measure the Fed, with Carter's approval, dismantled its consumer credit controls, which no longer seemed necessary to bring on a recession. Suddenly the economy leaped back on its feet; the inflation and money-supply numbers soon followed. The Fed, it seemed, had lost control.[78]

There was a lesson and a consequence. The lesson was that nobody knew what was going on. An October survey of business executives showed they had no better vision than the economists.[79] Even the governors of the Federal Reserve were confused. The consequence was that the Fed's governors determined not to repeat their "mistake." They decided to squeeze hard, damning both the election or any puzzling numbers.[80] Interest rates returned to 13 to 14 percent by late September, confounding analysts.[81] They would go much higher.

In Congress, members had to decide on specific policies. Budget resolutions don't spend money; appropriations do. Budget resolutions don't cut programs; reconciliation might. Congressional action on spending and taking while rushing toward a preelection recess revealed three patterns that would recur continually in later years.

The First Resolution didn't determine the balance of defense and domestic spending. Warren Magnuson (D-Wash.), chairman of Senate Appropriations, tried to move $4 billion from defense to social within his committee. He failed only because he didn't have the votes. The prodefense mood controlled action while House Appropriations and then Senate Appropriations raised previous bids on the military. "The only debate on the committee's overall funding recommendation," the *Congressional Quarterly* reported about the House vote on September 16, "was on whether the increase was large enough."[82]

By then Congress was running short on time; the fiscal year would begin on October 1, Congress would recess on October 4. Only two of thirteen appropriations had passed, so Congress needed a massive continuing resolution (CR). Traditionally, continuing resolutions bridged the gap between expiration of one year's appropriation and enactment of a new one by allowing agencies to continue activities at the previous fiscal year's levels. On September 16, however, Norman Dicks (D-Wash.) proposed breaking with the tradition. Because both policy and inflation meant the FY81 defense figures would be much higher than FY80 figures, the Senate would not act before recess, and the election would delay action for another two months. Therefore, Dicks proposed including the House's FY81 defense numbers in the CR. Thus, the resolution was not at all a stopgap but a new grant of authority. House leadership demanded equal treatment for domestic programs, but the Senate disagreed. The CR, once a housekeeping device, became a battleground over policy and priorities.[83]

The confrontation was made more serious because, earlier in the year, the attorney general had ruled that most agencies would be unable to operate if their appropriations authority lapsed. If the CR did not pass, agencies would have to shut down.[84] The prospect of a government shutdown could encourage either settlement or hostage taking. Bogged down over a rider restricting federal funding of abortions, conferees did not settle until late on October 1. Only defense was funded at FY81 levels,[85] revealing again Congress's tilt toward military, against social, spending.

The battle over policy on the formula for the CR prefigured developments under Reagan. The CR would become one of two vehicles for omnibus action on the budget; the other was reconciliation.

Senate committees quickly complied with their reconciliation instructions. On July 23 a package of spending cuts passed, hitting the targets though cheating a few: some cuts were temporary; others involved changing the dates of payments; Senate Finance and assorted House committees added some sweeteners to the package of revenue increases.

Reconciliation meant cutting people, which was politically difficult. Members hoped that by packaging lots of cuts no group could claim to be singled out; thus, the total would make enough of a dent in the deficit that members could say they had to support the bill. House leaders wanted a closed rule on the package, forbidding amendments, so that cuts would not be subjected to individual votes. The closed rule, by allowing the sweeteners Republicans wanted a chance to cut, also gave Democrats on the committees some stake in an unpleasant process.

The rule therefore was crucial. Unfortunately the leadership—all Republicans united with three Democrats—nearly lost control of the Rules Committee, which by 8 to 7 allowed a separate vote on one of the biggest cuts, a reduction in civil service pensions.[86] The leaders held the rule to that one amendment, however, and then made the floor vote on the rule a party matter. They won, with only fourteen Democrats defecting. They then lost on civil service pensions (seemingly proving the point that members were more likely to vote for cuts if they were not singled out) before the whole package passed easily. All representatives wanted to appear thrifty.

The bill then had to go to conference, where its unprecedented breadth required more than a hundred conferees. Disputes had to be settled over (to name only the most important) civil service pension COLAs, medicare and medicaid provisions, child nutrition, mortgage subsidy bonds, and the windfall profits tax.

October was spent campaigning. The public hesitated, torn between the devil whose performance it knew and disliked and the devil whose words were vaguely disquieting. Exploiting the uncertainty about Reagan's foreign policy and tax cuts, Carter drew close in the polls. But in the climax of the campaign—the debate just before the election—Reagan managed to quell many doubts. An expected close election turned into a landslide. Most dramatically, Republicans captured the Senate, as a covey of liberals in fairly conservative states fell to defeat. Democratic senators had had good reason to be jittery.

Lame Ducks

The Democrats returned to Washington licking their wounds and joking about being an endangered species. The prospect of a Republican president and a Republican Senate changed everybody's judgment about the value of delay: suddenly Republicans saw no reason to hurry, and Democrats saw delay as irresponsible.[87] Yet, because everybody was looking forward to January, both sides indulged in political maneuvers to inconvenience the other in the coming battles. The second resolution, which had the least direct effect on policy, was occasion for the greatest level of posturing.

House Democrats produced a resolution that admitted a deficit of $25 billion, but they managed that low figure only by reducing estimated spending by 2 percent across the board. Chairman Giaimo explained that the incoming president had claimed he could find so much in cuts from "waste, fraud, and abuse"; the Democrats were just taking him at his word.[88] In a very rushed conference, Senate negotiators accepted the House revenue figure and agreed on spending numbers even though their figures differed.[89]

The *Post* called the second resolution a fake. Senator Henry Bellmon (R-Okla.) noted that appropriations already in the pipeline were likely to exceed the "binding" resolution's totals by about $10 billion.[90] Senator William Armstrong (R-Colo.), in the spirit of the holiday season, called it a "turkey." Hollings claimed that the budget would have been balanced save for vitally necessary increases in defense spending. "Now that he has landed as Pilgrim Armstrong on the shores of leadership, and he gets this turkey," Hollings added, "I want to see how he carves it."[91]

Reconciliation conferees projected a deficit reduction of $8.2 billion. They also added reauthorizations of two child nutrition programs to the package. "I am deeply disturbed," Barber Conable commented, "that [reconciliation] seems to have become a new mechanism for holding the government hostage, agglomerating a lot of very important substantive issues . . . and being accepted only because we are under great fiscal pressure at this point in our budget process."[92] He and the Republicans, of course, would not think of doing such a thing—unless they could control it. Whatever their objections, members of both parties agreed with Delbert Latta that a vote against the reconciliation report was a "vote for $8.2 billion more deficit for fiscal 1981."[93] The conference agreement passed overwhelmingly on December 3.

Without the 1980 reconciliation as precedent, committing Democrats to the procedure, that of 1981 might not have occurred. The experience of 1980 also foreshadowed the rules battles, scorekeeping problems, and rider vulnerability that would make reconciliation a mixed blessing for budgeters.

Only the appropriations—most of the government—remained. Defense was settled fairly easily. Liberals knew they would do even worse in the next Congress, so they did not fight too hard. Conservatives wanted to get the money out to the military as soon as possible, returning for more in supplemental appropriations.[94] On December 5 Congress passed a $159.7 billion Department of Defense (DOD) appropriation, the major part of a 9 percent real increase in budget authority for the military,[95] the biggest peacetime increase in history to that point.

Congress faced two obstacles to passing the other appropriations: conflict over various riders, especially busing, and the Second Resolution's binding spending limits, which included a 2 percent cut Reagan was supposed to find. Congress was not about to redo all bargaining and decisions that had led to the appropriations bills passed and pending. Either the last one or two bills considered would be out of order, or Congress would have to waive the resolution that it had just passed.

Congress avoided all these choices by wrapping the last few bills in a continuing resolution that expired on June 5. Lopping off the last four months of the year meant that total authority was under the budget limits, but that everybody could spend at the desired rate until June 5, at which point they would think of something. Clever as this solution was, it had a problem. The CR became an immensely tempting target for nonbudgetary riders. Once again, the government nearly ground to a halt as the House and Senate battled over the CR's provisions.

On December 1, House Appropriations reported out a simple bill by voice vote. Chairman Jamie Whitten (D-Miss.) managed to keep all but a few amendments off the draft, which provided for funding levels at the rates mandated in the most recent congressional action, expiring June 5. This bill, H.J.Res. 637, passed the House on December 3. Senate Appropriations then tacked on dozens of amendments. On the floor, the Senate removed two of the Christmas tree's ornaments: senators excluded the offending busing rider (that forbade using Justice Department resources for lawsuits that might lead to court-ordered school busing for desegregation[96]) because conservatives, led by Senator Jesse Helms (D-N.C.), were convinced that in January the new president would be on their side;[97] the second exclusion was the senators' own pay raise.

Congressmen, comparing themselves to other high-powered lawyers and assuming extraordinary expenses (like two homes), feel underpaid. Voters, almost all of whom make much less, disagree. Therefore, members who want more compensation go through exceedingly complex maneuvers to get it, while other members, wishing to curry favor with voters, keep challenging such maneuvers. The issue affects the entire top level of the civil service because members keep bureaucrats' salaries at a level ("cap") below their own. As lower levels receive raises, they bump into the cap; thus civil servants holding different positions in the hierarchy end up with the same salaries.

Senate Appropriations took the opportunity of CR debate to raise the cap on a voice vote, allowing a $10,000 raise for members of Congress and raises for more than 30,000 federal executives. Given the public's intense distaste for congressional pay increases, on the Senate floor, in a recorded vote, senators reimposed the pay cap, 69 to 21.[98] Having pleased the public (they hoped) by attacking themselves, the senators turned around and hung many more baubles on the holiday tree (beetle eradication, a Baltimore Harbor, hurricane disaster relief, etc.). Thus decorated, the CR was passed on December 11 and sent to conference.[99]

The pay raise returned in the conference agreement, which slipped through the House on a voice vote. But the Senate removed the raise, sending the CR back to conference. The House in turn passed a new CR (H.J.Res. 644) that included neither the pay raise nor the dozens of Senate amendments to the original CR (H.J.Res. 637). Chairman Whitten told the senators to take their pick: a bountiful Christmas tree including the pay raise or a scrawny, sparsely-decorated one.[100] The Senate amended H.J.Res. 644, removing the House's limited decorations and giving the House a choice between the Senate's bountiful tree, without a pay raise, or a totally bare tree.

Now there were two CRs in conference along with many irritated legislators. "There ain't gonna be no pay raise," said Senate Minority (soon to be Majority) Leader Howard Baker (R-Tenn.).[101] At the last moment, in the early morning of December 16, conferees agreed to a CR with only a very few, noncontroversial amendments. That was roughly where Chairman Whitten had begun on December 1. The final battle was a fitting conclusion to 1980: neither side felt the result was worth the struggle to get it.

There They Go Again

Congress had more or less completed its work. Democrats prepared to abandon power.[102] President Carter devised a budget that, like its predecessor, tried to lower deficits with higher taxes. This plan was ignored, however, rather than scorned, as Democrats and Republicans awaited the new administration's budget revisions.

Reagan's administration was slowly taking shape, choosing its members and debating political strategy.[103] Believing in crisis and/or seeing crisis as opportunity, the incoming government began planning a quick effort to cut taxes and domestic spending. Speed was required to exploit the new president's normally short honeymoon period with Congress. The financial markets had to be reassured. "The main thing is to start and to start drastically and dramatically," explained Caspar Weinberger, who headed the transition team on the budget. "I think it's absolutely essential to send a signal, not only to the U.S. but to the world, that the new U.S. government is firmly committed to fighting inflation and to restoring the strength of the American economy."[104]

Preparing signals of resolve and of public faith in order to meet the nation's (and now the world's) expectations, Reagan's group, like Carter's, set itself up for judgment by a standard, market behavior, only dubiously related to anything it did. Unlike the outgoing administration, Reagan could hope for emotional support from business interests. "Reagan is a businessman's populist," commented Democratic banker Felix Rohatyn. "Under the Carter Administration they considered themselves the whipping boys, over regulated and over-Naderized. Now they all see a better climate coming." Business reacted to the election with a burst of optimism that sent stocks up forty-nine points in eight trading days while setting a record for volume.[105] The question was, would such happiness counter the effects of real variables, especially interest rates, which the Federal Reserve was driving to new heights in its war against inflation? At the end of 1980, the prime rate hit 21.5 percent. A better climate might be coming, but only rain, wind, and lightning were to be seen.

As Ronald Reagan's presidency came to an end in 1988, common rhetoric about the budget sounded like the story that began with Reagan's election: Reagan's military buildup created a struggle over priorities; Reagan's tax cuts produced deficits that gave financial markets the jitters; David Stockman dreamed up a new procedure, reconciliation, to package cuts in domestic spending. Reagan certainly would take the military buildup and deficits to extremes. Although some tax cut was inevitable, the massive cut in 1981 would not have happened without him. Yet the whole story of Reagan's presidency makes no sense if we forget what came before.

It matters that the military buildup and reconciliation preceded Reagan because otherwise one could not explain why, in 1981, the Speaker allowed reconciliation to happen with so little fight over defense. Attitudes within Congress, shaped by events (like Afghanistan) and beliefs (liberals' idea of how government should run) that were entirely separate from Reagan's beliefs and strategies, allowed his victories. Events were already moving his way.

The 1980 panic over deficits puts much of our story into perspective. It should make us realize that no one knew what the economy was doing; uncertainty would dampen skepticism about Reagan's implausible sounding theories. It helps explain why Democrats basically went along with the goal, though not the programmatic details, of spending reduction in 1981. It should tell us that, while Democrats were trapped partly by their own opportunism into a position of attacking deficits after Reagan's ballooned, they had already been pushed in that direction by a large segment of their party, including the economists who once had rationalized a prospending bias.

Most important, the near-unanimity among organs of respectable opinion that the budget had to be balanced to stop inflation should give us pause. This was the first of many wrong arguments about expectations; the new administration had its own fantasies. Being wrong is not so bad. Being wrong and scornful of those who don't conform to a false standard is. Being wrong and ashamed of yourself for not living up to the false standard is even worse. The Democrats' failures to "control" the budget began the cycle of politicians losing self-confidence because of the deficit. They began one unique aspect of budget politics in the 1980s: the political center, the voices of "responsibility," would be most upset with the status quo.

This crisis of confidence was an opportunity for the new president, a man whose vision of political economy was very different from respectable opinion.

FOUR

Preparing for the Reagan Revolution

In a landslide the might of the electorate in a democratic order appears in a most spectacular fashion. The people may not be able to govern themselves but they can, through an electoral uprising, throw the old crowd out and demand a new order, without necessarily being capable of specifying exactly what it shall be. An election of this type may amount, if not to revolution, to its functional equivalent.

V. O. KEY, *POLITICS, PARTIES, AND PRESSURE GROUPS*

V. O. Key described a landslide election as one in which the incumbent party is rejected by a heavy plurality, losing votes among virtually all segments of the populace.[1] Reagan's victory, like those of Eisenhower in 1952 and of Roosevelt in 1932, was a classic illustration of the type. Carter lost support in every demographic category, except blacks, and in every region of the nation. As Key suggests, however, a landslide that seems to demand a new order does not necessarily convey its own explanation of what the new order should be.

Politicians cared about what the vote meant for two reasons: First, if the public actually wanted something in particular and the politicians opposed it, defiance could lead to disaster in the next election. Second, the ethos of American politics proclaims that the popular will (so long as it does not contradict the Constitution) is to be enacted into law. Accordingly, presidents always claim that election gives them a "mandate" to do something or other, a moral authority derived from their selection by the whole people, after a grueling and nearly endless campaign. What is the point of all that hoopla and agony if the people, in choosing a president, do not choose what their government is to do?

Although fully aware of the reasons why an election generally cannot be viewed as a referendum on specific issues—voters can oppose a candidate's preferences on most issues and still prefer him for other reasons[2]—politicians are loath to oppose a president immediately after his election, unless his proposals are clearly off the popular map. Even if they think his policies unpopular, they are inclined to let him prove it. As Tip O'Neill put it soon after the election, "We're going to cooperate with the President. It's America first and party second. . . . We're going to give 'em enough rope. They can use it either to herd cattle or to make a mistake."[3]

Accordingly, while opponents hesitate, the president's allies work to identify all sorts of detailed proposals with the popular will. Soon after the election, for example, the Heritage Foundation, a conservative think tank, published a comprehensive set of proposals, *Mandate for Leadership,* discussing mostly issues about which the average citizen would have no opinion.[4] Somehow, political actors had to decide in what sense the public had been demanding the kinds of changes proposed by the Foundation. Politicians, like academics, therefore pored over the entrails of Jimmy Carter's sacrifice, searching for signs. For guidance they also looked to candidate Reagan's speeches, polling data, and results in the congressional election. Let us do the same.

Not a Mandate But an Opportunity

As in virtually any election, poor people, blue-collar workers, union members, the less educated, and racial minorities were more likely to vote Democratic than were white, middle- and upper-middle-class citizens. In a less typical result that caused much speculation, women were less pro-Reagan than were men. Almost all demographic groups preferred Reagan, voting Republican far more than in 1976.[5] Although these results suggested that the new administration would be less supportive of affirmative action, antipoverty proposals, and job programs than had its predecessor, they did not suggest that voters expected Reagan to attack unions, the poor, and the variously disadvantaged. Otherwise, all these groups (always excepting blacks, who were to have rather serious problems with the new president) would not have moved toward the Reagan camp.

Because election returns themselves cannot convey their own meaning, we must look to polls to see what voters expected when they voted Republican. More than anything else, the election demanded some action about the economy. Everybody wants less inflation and less unemployment; in fact, Table 2 reveals those as the two most common reasons for the vote—followed by budget balance. Foreign policy issues trailed badly. The heralded "social issues" emphasized by the "Moral Majority"—at least as symbolized by the Equal Rights Amendment and abortion—were mentioned by only 7 percent of respondents. Perhaps more telling, the "Needs of Big Cities," items that would tap the concerns for poverty and distributional equity (and self-interest) fueling "Great Society" liberalism, were hardly mentioned at all. Those concerns were not even on the agenda.

Carter did well among voters most worried by unemployment. But that was more because unemployment's victims are traditionally Democratic than because they had faith in Carter. In fact, Gallup in September

TABLE 2.   Issues and the 1980 Vote

	1980 Percentage of Electorate	*Percentage of 1980 Vote*			*Swing to Republicans 1976–1980[a] (percentage points)*
		Carter	Reagan	Anderson	
All voters	100	41	50	7	11.5
"Which issues were most important in deciding how you voted today?" (up to two answers)					
Inflation and economy	33	28	61	9	16.5
Jobs and unemployment	24	48	42	7	13
Balancing the federal budget	21	27	65	6	15
U.S. prestige around the world	16	31	61	7	16
Crisis in Iran	14	63	31	4	4
Reducing federal income taxes	10	29	64	4	14.5
ERA/abortion	7	50	38	10	14
Needs of big cities	2	77	13	7	1
Don't know/none	20	45	46	7	8
"We should be more forceful in our dealings with the Soviet Union even if it increases the risk of war."					
Agree	54	28	64	6	16
Disagree	31	56	32	10	8
"Cutting taxes is more important than balancing the federal budget."					
Agree	30	42	50	6	15
Disagree	53	37	53	9	11

TABLE 2 *(continued)*

	1980 Percentage of Electorate	Percentage of 1980 Vote			Swing to Republicans 1976–1980[a] (percentage points)
		Carter	Reagan	Anderson	
"Unemployment is a more important prob- lem today than inflation"					
Agree	39	51	40	7	11.5
Disagree	45	30	60	9	14
"I support the Equal Rights Amendment —ERA—the constitu- tional amendment concerning women."					
Agree	45	49	38	11	11.5
Disagree	35	26	68	4	14

SOURCE: CBS News/*New York Times* National Election Day Survey, at polling places nationwide on November 4, 1980. From William Schneider, "The November 4 Vote for President: What Did It Mean," in *The American Elections of 1980*, ed. Austin Ranney (Washington, D.C.: American Enterprise Institute, 1981), pp. 212–63; table on pp. 237–38.
NOTE: $N = 12,782$
[a]Swing is defined as the average of the Republican gain and the Democratic loss, 1976 to 1980, in each group. The 1976 vote is measured by voter recall, which overstates Carter's support somewhat (57 percent Carter, 43 percent Ford for the sample as a whole).

and the *Los Angeles Times* in October found that the historic advantage of the Democrats as the party best able to prevent unemployment had dissipated. Both polls showed Reagan as better than Carter on unemployment by around four to three. Voters who cared most about inflation, budget balancing, or cutting taxes—traditional Republican themes—favored Reagan by large margins.

A more interesting question, in view of Reagan's endorsement of the Kemp-Roth tax cut, was the relative weight of tax balance and inflation concerns, because most informed observers saw a tax cut as preventing budget balance and potentially allowing inflation. Carter had campaigned against the Kemp-Roth proposal (for three annual 10 percent tax cuts) on just those grounds. By a 53 percent to 30 percent margin (see Table 3) the public disagreed with the claim that "cutting taxes is more important than balancing the federal budget." We therefore might have expected the Kemp-Roth proposal to hurt Reagan. The voters clearly did not favor cutting taxes *if* that would produce an unbalanced budget.

The story is in the "if." Reagan's supporters, unlike Carter's, tended to believe that the tax cut and budget balance could be combined.[6] Much of Reagan's campaign attempted to show that they could be.

Some supply-siders argued that growth resulting from their tax cut would balance the budget, and perhaps Reagan believed it. That was not, however, the crucial argument. More important was Reagan's (and the public's) belief that domestic spending could be cut by eliminating "waste, fraud, and abuse." In the campaign's showdown debate, President Carter challenged Reagan about his plan to cut taxes, increase defense, and balance the budget. Reagan replied,

> Well, most people when they think about cutting government spending, they think in terms of eliminating necessary programs or wiping out something, some service that government is supposed to perform. I believe that there is enough extravagance and fat in government. As a matter of fact, one of the secretaries of H.E.W. under Mr. Carter testified that he thought there was $7 billion worth of waste and fraud in welfare, and in the medical programs associated with it. We've had the General Accounting Office estimate that there are probably tens of billions of dollars lost in fraud alone, and they have added that waste adds even more to that.[7]

The challenger's answer in the debate was what he had been saying on the campaign trail for months; it was a prominent part of his formal statement on economic policy given in Chicago on September 9, 1980; it was his own deep belief; and it was what his advisers told him.

When Reagan promised to cut 7 percent of the budget in this manner, "experienced Washington budget specialists" (as *The Economist* put it) were "divided as to whether that initial pledge was naive or disingenuous."[8] As one put it, "it would be the budgetary coup of the century if cuts of such magnitude could be made by eliminating 'waste and fraud' without dropping programs of substance."[9] We have seen, however, that the public thought waste was massive. The message that Reagan wanted to cut domestic spending got through: a September CBS News poll found that 49 percent believed Reagan wanted to cut domestic spending, and only 14 percent thought he favored raising it.[10] Given the usual low level of public awareness—people care more about personal matters than politics[11]—this seven to two ratio, even with the nonresponses, reveals an unambiguous image. But people, or at least Reagan's supporters, did not expect his cuts to hurt them.

In light of what we know about general public attitudes on spending, specific attitudes on the tax cut, and the appeals made during the campaign itself, clearly the election was no mandate to cut taxes at the expense of a balanced budget. But when Reagan maintained that choice was unnecessary, he represented his supporters.

IDEOLOGY AND REAGANISM

An election is more plausibly viewed as a referendum on such generalities as "less government" or "more fairness" than as a vote on complicated policies. The claim of a mandate by Reagan's supporters was really a claim to general endorsement; the Heritage Foundation report was a statement of policies that could be deduced (or so they claimed) from the ideology that (they assumed) the public had embraced in the person of Ronald Reagan.

"Reaganism" and "Reaganomics," Laurence Barrett observed, are terms that suggest particular biases and ways of thinking, if not specific policies.[12] Unlike Carter or Ford or Nixon, Reagan's ideas were clear enough that his name could be used as shorthand for them. Proud (maybe bellicose) patriotism, enthusiastic capitalism, exaltation of the individual, and condemnation of big government—these themes gave Reaganism its appeal. From the other side, that same combination animated a passionate resistance to his leadership.

Reaganism's potential appeal is best understood if we call it by the name his supporters might prefer: "Americanism." Americanism in this sense had always combined individualistic capitalism and distrust of government with fervent nationalism. Americans were defined not by their origins but by adherence to a life-style; moreover, life's superiority was confirmed by the hordes of immigrants who flocked to U.S. shores from all over the world for a chance to live it. Reagan thus had a very powerful imagery at his command; when invoked, it sounded familiar and inspiring and true to many Americans. Those who opposed him might have trouble explaining why, being reduced perhaps to a lot of "yes, buts." Yet, for all its power, Americanism was a contested creed.

Even after fifty years, the greatest obstacle to Reagan's vision of the nation was the Great Depression. The crash and its aftermath of unemployment had dampened Americans' enthusiasm for unfettered capitalism. "Leave it to business," the motto of Republicans throughout their history, was rejected during the New Deal by a very American experimentalism: people were suffering, and the government helped them. New Deal policies followed no coherent economic theory, but there was a coherent political theory: government is the agent of the people.

The New Deal liberals and their heirs did not reject capitalism and individualism. Instead they argued that the actions of government in a democracy were needed to keep the promise of American individualism: anyone, of no matter what birth, could rise and prosper according to one's merits. To liberals the great tension of American politics was between democracy and capitalism because capitalism too often meant entrenched private power. When Reagan invoked the "American way," liberals saw a history of efforts to preserve injustices and protect established power within society by impugning the patriotism of reformers; they remembered the "Red Scare" of 1919–1920, McCarthyism in the 1950s, the constant attack on labor unions as "socialistic," and resistance to the civil rights movement of the 1960s. Reagan invoked the federal system and states rights, citing Jefferson and other founders of the nation; his opponents heard "states rights" and saw racist consequences. As far as liberals were concerned, Americanism had been invoked on the wrong side far too often.

Reagan would continually stumble on one issue, symbolizing the public attachment to government action: social security. The free market was still the ideal of most Americans, but they wanted some protection.

Surveys revealed the public's attitude toward the two main strains of American ideology. In 1980, as in previous years, Americans preferred to call themselves "conservative" rather than "liberal" by margins ranging from four to three to about two to one. Yet as many Americans rated themselves as "moderate" as would admit to conservatism and liberalism combined. Ordinary Americans, suspicious of both sides, were more centrist than politicians.

Voters normally support the more moderate candidate who is safer and closer to their preferences. In 1980 that was clearly Jimmy Carter. Ronald Reagan was viewed as substantially more conservative than the norm, while Carter moved during the campaign from almost exactly normal to somewhat more liberal. In September a Gallup poll reported that 82 percent of respondents agreed that Carter took "moderate, middle-of-the-road positions." A *Los Angeles Times* poll reported that 41 percent described Reagan as "too extreme," but only 13 percent said the same of Carter.[13] In short, Reagan's world view worried a lot of people.

They did not, however, see Reagan as so extreme that they should reelect a president who had failed.[14] Ultimately, dismay with Carter overwhelmed fear of Reagan. The most common reasons for a Reagan vote were "it is time for a change" and "he is a strong leader." Reagan's victory was not ideological.

The general public did have broad preferences on public policy that fit both Reagan's appeal and the course of events in 1980. Considerable majorities believed that defense needed more dollars and that social welfare needed less, but the desired changes were modest.[15] Reagan's election thus showed a public willing to risk a dash of conservatism, considering the available alternatives.

Even if the public had not become more conservative, the 1980 election guaranteed a conservative Congress. A massive purge of the liberal establishment took place: four House committee chairs (the first losses by Democratic leaders since 1966), House Majority Whip John Brademas, and a raft of famous liberal senators were ousted. The Republicans' twelve-seat gain in the Senate contained elements of luck; a number of Democrats lost by paper-thin margins. Yet the losers' liberalism clearly had not helped them, and the victorious challengers were a rather conservative group.[16]

In the House, the Republican thirty-three-seat gain was no fluke. If anything, the Democrats were protected by the well-known advantages of incumbency. The freshmen Republicans looked like a solidly conservative group, just as freshmen Democrats seemed fairly liberal, but there were many more Republicans. "On important issues freighted with ideological implications," political scientist Charles Jacob reported, "the possibility of a working conservative majority in the House is at hand."[17] If holdover members voted as they had in the recent past—by no means a certainty—and if the new members were loyal to their parties—another big "if"—Republicans could win budget battles by about twenty votes. The potential margin was slim but extant.

Democrats in House and Senate had to hope that Reagan, given enough rope, would tie himself in knots. Gary Hart expressed the sentiment: "I give the Reagan administration about eighteen to twenty-four months to prove it doesn't have any answers either."[18]

The President and His Advisers

The incoming administration's strategy depended on how it resolved the tensions in its agenda: build up the military, reduce social spending, "ease the burden" of government regulation of industry, cut taxes, and balance the budget. Both the tax cut and military buildup could make it hard to balance the budget. To say that social spending should be cut was insufficient; specific programs had to be targeted, which meant that specific constituencies had to be angered. Whatever policy mix was adopted would have to convince those jittery financial markets that better times were coming. Reagan's program had to portray both credible economic theory and something Congress would accept—a combination Carter had not achieved.

ROUND ONE, THE CAMPAIGN

Reagan had strong biases; he wanted both to limit government's role in the economy and to drastically reduce tax rates. Given his lack of interest in or knowledge about many details, however, often the judgments of his subordinates were necessary to translate those biases into action. The president knew where he wanted to go; their job was to help him get there.

Ronald Reagan did not like the domestic federal government. Although he had toned down his rhetoric during his campaigns, he had long objected to not only the Great Society welfare programs but also the New Deal employment programs and the progressive income tax. As far back as the 1950s, while lecturing General Electric employees, Reagan had castigated

> the myth that our graduated income tax has any resemblance to proportionate taxation. The entire structure was created by Karl Marx. It simply is a penalty on the individual who can improve his own lot; it takes his earnings from him and redistributes them to people who are incapable of earning as much as he can.[19]

He viewed taxes and the welfare state as impositions upon a suffering public by Washington bureaucrats. His attitude is shown in how he explained the decline of the Republican party:

> One reason came out of the Great Depression. There was a loss of confidence in the system itself. Democrats came in on the great surge of 1932 and they embarked on the great social reforms and so forth. If you look back in hindsight, you find that these social reforms really didn't work. They didn't cure unemployment, they didn't solve the social problems. But what came from that was a group of people . . . entrenched in government in the permanent structure, who wanted social reforms just for the sake of the social reforms. They didn't see them as temporary medicine as most people saw them, to cure the ills of the Depression. They saw them as a permanent way of life. . . . Now peacetime came and there was no question about the Democratic party having solidified its hold on the people.[20]

In this view, much of the welfare state was essentially a scam. Unfortunately many people had been duped, yet Reagan knew better than to base a campaign on assaulting the progressive tax or the New Deal. He would attack taxes as too high rather than as too redistributive, and he would condemn government as wasteful and arrogant rather than denounce social security as bad in itself. However, the ability to temporize, to compromise for the moment, or to adjust one's rhetoric to the audience should not be confused with moderating goals.

It is difficult even now to judge what Reagan understood about the economy he wished to revitalize. His understanding of such institutional aspects as the role of the Federal Reserve Board was limited. Reagan once wondered to his aides why the Board didn't just lower the prime rate, which in fact it does not set.[21] What he knew, he was certain about: government spending and taxes weakened the personal initiative that made capitalism a great engine of prosperity. When his own marginal income tax rate as a movie star reached 90 percent, Reagan had seen no point in working more; from that extreme case, he concluded that people would work harder at lower levels of taxation. Disputes over timing of policies, effects on markets, and plausibility of forecasts would not shake Reagan's preferences; his decisions would be guided far more by the implications of each option for his overall agenda than by the disputed details.

The great contradiction in his own agenda involved the balanced budget. Reagan had preached against deficits for years, asserting flatly that they were the cause of inflation. How, then, was he to rationalize a Kemp-Roth style tax cut? His advisers helped confirm his belief that the problem could be managed.

In his major Chicago campaign speech on the economy, Reagan urged his audience not to "just take my word for it. I have discussed this with any number of distinguished economists and businessmen, including such men as George Shultz, William Simon, Alan Greenspan, Charls Walker, and James Lynn." All these men, former high officials in Republican administrations, made careers of influencing the policy of whichever Republican was in office. One of them, who had supported another candidate before 1980, recalled that Reagan's "fiscal policy left a lot to be desired—cut taxes and stand back, watch the Laffer Curve work. I let it be known that I was willing to help." Soon he was among the candidate's economic policy advisers. These establishment Republicans, whom we have dubbed neoclassicist, were just as convinced as Reagan that Democratic policies were in error, and in all the same ways: taxes, spending, and deficits were all too high; regulation was too intrusive; money was too loose. In spite of all the publicity for "supply-side" and "Kemp-Roth," Reaganomics, as one participant put it, "came out of the heart of the Republican establishment."[22]

The most thorough rationale for Reaganomics was provided by economist and policy analyst Martin C. Anderson, who was Reagan's chief adviser on domestic policy. Anderson's job was to turn Reagan's ideas into defensible proposals.[23] His "Policy Memorandum No. 1," dated August 1979, outlined the Reaganomics they were to follow throughout the campaign and Reagan's presidency.

The memorandum denied that "any attempt to increase employment would lead to more inflation, and that any attempt to reduce inflation would result in more unemployment." Doubts about the "iron law" relating the two, wrote Anderson, had recently "blossomed into rampant skepticism and full disbelief, even among economists." He cited a 1978 Federal Reserve Bank of Minneapolis study in saying it was "possible to reduce inflation and stimulate economic growth without having an economic bellyache, recession, or depression."

The memo blamed inflation, the economy's greatest problem, on the "massive, continuing budget deficit of the federal government." But the deficit was a function of revenue and expenditures, so the most effective way to reduce the deficit was "to reduce the rate of growth of federal expenditures and to simultaneously stimulate the economy so as to increase revenues in such a way that the private share grows proportionately more than the government share." Economic growth could be stimulated by reducing taxes, which were "stifling the incentive for individuals to earn, save, and invest." Growth could also be stimulated by an income tax cut of the Kemp-Roth type, with lower top marginal rates and lower capital gains and corporate income taxes. Then the tax code should be indexed to prevent the "insidious" effects of bracket creep. The last part of this supply-side stimulus package would be extensive deregulation. Anderson cited Washington University economist Murray Weidenbaum's estimate that federal regulations cost business over $75 billion in 1977—and that those costs were passed on to the consumer in higher prices.

As the economy was stimulated without increasing inflation, given a supply-side rather than a demand-side analysis, federal spending would be controlled. "It is not necessary to cut federal spending from its current levels," Anderson told his candidate, "but it is necessary to reduce the rate of increase in federal spending." That rate would be reduced first by attacking the "legendary" amount of "fraud, waste, and extravagance in federal programs." Anderson's own best-known work on urban renewal enabled him to believe that some programs were wasteful and extravagant in the sense that they did not provide sufficient benefits for the money. Citing an OMB estimate that annual waste might be as high as $50 billion, he suggested citizen task forces, as Reagan had used in California, to search out waste in all programs. Anderson also recommended a transfer of programs back to the states, eliminating one layer of administrative costs, and concluded that the recommended steps could bring the budget to balance. Then balance should be locked in with a constitutional amendment that might also include other procedural proposals, such as a line-item veto and super-majorities (three-fifths or two-thirds) for new spending, in an economic bill of rights.

Anderson's memo became an internal working document. We can see much later policy—choices, justifications, even what others considered diversionary tactics like the item veto—in that paper. It shows that Reaganomics was not something Jack Kemp and David Stockman sold the president. Absent were numbers: an argument that the whole thing could add up over a period of years.

The campaign's economic and political advisers recognized that media attacks on the program's plausibility had to be blunted. Alan Greenspan, for example, predicted in a letter to Anderson on June 10, 1980, that Reagan would face "a degree of scrutiny to the details not accorded other presidential candidates of recent years" and suggested that the campaign should develop budget plans with detail comparable to budget resolutions. Credibility might have been pursued by changing some premises. Reagan, however, would not budge on defense increases or tax cuts. Defense was more important than the budget; "nothing was so vital, in Reagan's thinking, as the strengthening of United States defense capabilities."[24] Reagan was adamant about tax cuts. When told by some advisers that the tax cut would be easier in five years, the candidate reportedly replied, "I don't care." Because they were not allowed to change the premises (and not all of them wanted to), the advisers had to find another way to make the program add up. They solved their problem (sort of) with help from Democrats.

After estimates using CBO's economic forecast showed that the package would not balance the budget before 1985—and that assumed a smaller defense buildup and smaller corporate tax cut than eventually occurred, together with a 6 percent cut from "waste, fraud, and abuse"— the Senate Budget Committee, fortuitously, came out with its more optimistic economic estimates. Reagan advisers adopted these numbers that the Democrats could hardly attack. The Senate numbers on defense were nearly what Anderson had projected anyway; by accepting them and assuming slightly higher "waste" savings, Reagan's advisers fixed it so that the basic plan would yield a surplus by FY83.

Reagan's Chicago statement added one element to Anderson's year-old memo: a sound, stable, and predictable monetary policy. No one said much about the possibility that monetary restraint could knock the economy for a loop: supply-siders believed the tax cut would overcome the monetary squeeze; neoclassicists were more worried about inflation; and Democrats thought Carter's chairman of the Federal Reserve supposedly was pursuing the same policy as the neoclassicists. In drafting the speech, the various constitutional proposals of Anderson's economic bill of rights were removed; the point of the speech was to defuse, not provoke, controversy. Proposals unlikely to pass would not convince a skeptical public that the Republicans had a practical plan.

The September 9 plan promised "waste" savings of 7 percent (2 percent in FY81, 2 percent in FY82, and 1 percent each following year) by the end of FY85. Beyond the promise, the plan announced an even more optimistic "goal" of 10 percent savings. "If these goals are reached the efforts will be redoubled, because certainly more than 10 percent of the money the federal government spends every year is misspent."[25] How would this waste be found? By appointing administrators who shared Reagan's philosophy of spending control; freezing federal employment (which actually had not grown in years); creating citizen task forces; and having a special transition team, directed by former OMB Director Caspar Weinberger, find "specific ways to search out and eliminate waste and extravagance." There was no word about the exact programs.

Who believed this? Clearly Anderson believed some of it, but the new goal went beyond his original caution. The candidate believed it. When we asked if anyone believed in the waste-fraud-and-abuse, a mainstream adviser replied, "They believed it's there, they didn't believe there was much money in it. The president still believes it. It was a political thing in the September speech, the only way to get balance in the plan." The speech in fact took most of the budget off the table:

> This strategy for growth does not require altering or taking back necessary entitlements already granted to the American people. The integrity of the Social Security system will be defended. . . . This strategy does require restraining the congressional desire to "add on" to every old program and to create new programs funded by deficits.[26]

Unless inflation adjustments were defined as "adding on" to old programs, any plausible interpretation of "entitlements already granted," added to defense, meant that Reagan's 10 percent cut from waste was more like taking 30 percent from what was left.

The September 9 package nevertheless did dampen some skepticism. Although the numbers really did not look plausible, they were not impossible; the press at least did not mock the spending projections. The trouble was that to make all of Reaganomics work part of Reaganomics had to fail. Its first point was to stop inflation, but the economic projections assumed inflation would drive revenues up enough to compensate for the tax cut. Herbert Stein put the case well:

> There was one major flaw in this picture. The economic assumptions used . . . implied 8.7 percent per year annual inflation from 1980 to 1985. This was inconsistent with the Reagan promises for conquering inflation, but it was a major source of revenue. Basically, their forecasts abstained from the supply-siders' unrealistic estimates of the revenue-raising effects of a tax cut and relied instead on the revenue-raising effects of an all-too-realistic, but undesired, inflation. The argument was as unrealistic as the supply-side argument, but it was unrealistic in a more conventional way.[27]

In other words, a policy that promised to balance the budget in order to reduce inflation was going to attain budget balance by assuming the very inflation that balance was supposed to eliminate!

The funny numbers on September 9, 1980, put into perspective David Stockman's later mea culpas about unrealistic forecasts. Not only Reaganomics but also the willingness to fudge in order to attain the good things in the package, worrying later how it would add up, "came from the heart of the Republican establishment"—the advisers who cleared that speech. The best that can be said in their defense is that the Federal Reserve got the price level to drop a lot faster than anyone thought. A substantial part of the Reagan deficit came from the lack of revenues premised upon the effects of bracket creep no one, in or out of the Reagan camp, expected to drop so suddenly.

MAKING POLICY

Ronald Reagan's election changed the decision-making process within his coalition because the decisions now meant something different: instead of campaign stances, they would be the "president's program." His defense advisers, no longer letting election worries restrain their arguments for a massive buildup, emphasized their vision of military needs. In response to their briefings, one close aide reports, Reagan "continually upped in his mind the need for spending more."

Economic advisers were organized into a series of task forces to define the program more precisely.[28] The tax policy task force "tried to put together a program which expressed what the President wanted, a marriage of the capital formation and the populist people." With Charls Walker as chairman, capital formation, represented by the "10–5–3" depreciation plan wed individual tax-cutting populism, the Kemp-Roth plan at a meeting of Reagan's Economic Policy Coordinating Committee on November 15. "You would have liked it," a participant told us academics, "the notes were taken by a Nobel prize-winning economist, Milton Friedman." Both the higher defense spending and bigger tax cuts meant that balancing the budget, still a key and publicized part of the economic package, would be more difficult.

Reagan and most of his advisers did not really ask *whether* the conflict *could* be resolved; instead they asked *how* it *might* be resolved. They developed a laundry list of reasons; if any were true, the tax cut would work. The reasons contradicted each other; political argument, however, is not validated by logical consistency. Coalitions for any policy, such as the 1974 Budget Act, usually involve groups with different purposes and ideas about how it will work out. A member of a coalition need not care why others are his allies, so long as he believes his own reason for supporting the bill.

By one argument, Kemp-Roth was nowhere near as big as it looked. Because inflation would drive up peoples' taxes during the years to come, most of Kemp-Roth would merely keep taxes from reflecting the rise. The issue then was not how to balance the budget but what to do with the huge, expected tax increases—fund more government spending, or give money back to the people. This argument would prove misleading given flaws in the economic projections, but at the time no one could have known that. The real difficulty was that if Kemp-Roth were not much of a tax cut, it would do little to relieve the economic disaster that Reagan and much of the public perceived. But it also would do little harm.

Supply-siders claimed that their tax cut would produce so much economic growth that revenues on the increment of growth would exceed the loss from lower tax rates. Based on intuition and his own experience, Reagan agreed. He would tell visitors, for example, that every other modern tax cut had resulted in the government ending up with more revenues that it started out with, and "we're just convinced" that it would happen again. Aides said Reagan really did believe it, but many advisers did not.[29] The campaign's projections always assumed an overall revenue loss. Still Reagan spoke of dramatic economic change, which required a real policy change, and therefore contradicted the first argument.

The third argument, the "children's allowance theory," received less attention than it deserved in 1981. Reagan expressed it best himself in his February 5, 1981, address to the nation on the state of the economy:

> Over the past decades we've talked of curtailing Government so that we can then lower the tax burden. Sometimes we've even taken a run at doing that. But there were always those who told us that taxes couldn't be cut until spending was reduced. Well, you know we can lecture our children about extravagance until we run out of voice and breath. Or we can cure their extravagance simply by reducing their allowance.[30]

Taxes would be cut first. Only by using deficits as pressure to reduce spending could spending be reduced enough to reduce deficits.[31]

The Republicans' natural good-thing-for-people, lower taxes, was foreclosed by the need to cut spending first lest the deficit rise. Cutting taxes first would reverse the political dynamic that had frustrated Republicans for years. The Democrats, until Carter, had something to offer people—spending programs. Now the Republicans could offer tax cuts.

Reagan's characterization of politicians as children or as irresponsible "spenders" neatly fit his distrust of domestic government and therefore was easily accepted by many of his allies. The argument did, however, contradict the supply-side: if tax cuts raised revenue, they did not reduce the allowance.

All three arguments—it was not really much of a tax cut; it was a dramatic change that would create enough economic growth to pay for itself; it would create deficits, but deficits themselves would restrain spending and thus eventually deficits—were blithely employed by the administration, often by the same people and even at the same time. The best way to justify the tax cut, for the many people who believe in budget balance, however, was to translate rhetoric about waste, fraud, abuse, and extravagance into spending cuts. Enter David Stockman.

STOCKMAN

Stockman, who became Reagan's director of the Office of Management and Budget, was the point man in enacting Reaganomics. He also became the president's harshest critic. In spite of these disagreements, he stayed longer than any budget director since the Second World War.

Stockman impressed a series of influential elders who helped him in his career. They included Daniel Patrick Moynihan, then a counselor to President Nixon and later Democratic senator from New York; David Broder, dean of the nation's political columnists; and Representative John Anderson (R-Ill.), chairman of the House Republican caucus. When Stockman was twenty-five, Anderson made him executive director of the Republican Conference, the House Republicans' organ for developing new party positions. There Stockman became a true-blue believer in the gospel of the free market.

After serving Anderson for four years, Stockman decided to run for Congress in his rural Michigan home district against incumbent Republican Ed Hutchinson. A staffer challenging an incumbent is, as Stockman notes, "the ultimate sin in Congress. . . . There would be absolute havoc with it; congressmen would be looking over their shoulders every minute."[32] Although smart enough to see the institutional stakes, Stockman ignored them—believing he was far more able than Hutchinson—for his ambition was overwhelming. Hutchinson bowed out rather than face a tough primary, so Stockman triumphed easily in that bedrock Republican district. In Congress, Stockman quickly became a conservative leader on economic policy. The *Almanac of American Politics* noted that he had "provided congressional conservatives with some of their freshest thinking and strongest advocacy in some time."[33] He dramatized his allegiance to free-market principles as the only representative from Michigan to vote against the 1979 federal bail-out of the Chrysler Corporation. He also became a member of the small group of supply-side theorists clustered around Jack Kemp. And, working with Phil Gramm (D-Tex.), he became a leader of budget cutters in the House.

By 1980, when just thirty-four, Stockman was a congressional veteran who, at least technically, understood how the House worked, knew the budget far better than most, commanded respect for his talent and energy, and dedicated himself to all aspects of Reaganomics—cutting taxes, building the military, deregulating, cutting domestic spending, establishing stable money, and balancing budgets. Yet he was no Reaganite. Here is Stockman's account of his reaction when told by Jack Kemp that

Kemp had negotiated a role for the supply-side clique in the Reagan campaign:

> After I hung up the phone, I didn't know whether to giggle or kick the side of my desk.
> Ronald Reagan?
> The man was more ancient ideologically than he was in years. I considered him a cranky obscurantist whose political base was barnacled with every kook and fringe group that inhabited the nasty deep of American politics.
> So there I was, thinking, "How is this antediluvian going to help us? He's exactly what the establishment needs to discredit our ideas."[34]

Stockman was a newcomer to the Reaganites and therefore not a member of the inner circle. He did not understand that he and Caspar Weinberger, or Ed Meese, or Martin Anderson, or even James Baker were not on equal terms before the president. They had proved themselves before he came on the scene. Nor did he see the president's deep commitment to tax cuts and the ways that eminent advisers such as Greenspan and Shultz reinforced Reagan's preferences.

Traditional Republicans preferred markets to government on principle and distrusted government power as a threat to private enterprise (or power, depending on your own ideology). Stockman's real objection to government programs was moral: they embodied no principle of justice, whether equity or people meriting what they earned. He saw the federal government as distributing its benefits according to power and greed rather than need. Traditional Republicans found the government alien; Stockman thought it corrupt. Because his position was based on ideas rather than a sense of "us" and "them," his loyalties were less solid than, for instance, those of the corps of economists who had served Republican administrations for a generation.

Stockman's critique of politics resembled, as he notes, one of the most influential polemics in the academic literature, Theodore Lowi's *The End of Liberalism*. Lowi argued that the "public philosophy" of the post–New Deal state was something called "interest group liberalism," which combined nineteenth-century fear of governmental power and twentieth-century practical need for government action, by having government cooperate with interest groups. Because groups existed to represent their members, their involvement in legislation, particularly administration, could be called democratic, and government would not be seen as coercing anybody. The problem, Lowi wrote, was that the acceptance of groups in a process of normless, endless bargaining left the political process adrift; without standards, authority could never be legitimate, for it would be arbitrary. "In such departments as Agriculture, Labor, and Commerce, delegation of power has become alienation of public domain—the gift of sovereignty to private satrapies."[35] There are no clear rules or processes, just endless bargaining, the results of which are determined by group power.[36]

We shall return to his themes. Here, we care about what Stockman did with Lowi. His critique of the process looks a lot like that of liberal George Miller in defending reconciliation, an accusation that interest-group games overwhelmed politics of principle: "Might had become Right."[37]

In early 1975 Stockman had published a well-received article, "The Social Pork Barrel," in which he argued that

> The vast increase in social welfare outlays . . . has created in its wake a political maintenance system based in no small part on the cooptation and incorporation of Congress itself. If members were ever legislators and statesmen, they have more and more taken on the characteristics of constituency ombudsmen and grant brokers.

Once a program was started, the "money sluice" would never be closed. Even Republicans were locked into programs as their constituents began to receive benefits and the programs were diverted from their original radical purposes, as with the Community Action Program. In the end, liberal programs were not serving liberal ends, but government grew, draining society nonetheless.[38]

Stockman's particular dislike of social programs had three related consequences. First, Stockman was far more willing to cut business subsidies and other advantages for the middle-class and wealthy than were most of Reagan's advisers except Anderson. Second, Stockman thought he could explain and justify his position to some liberals—most consequentially, William Greider of the *Washington Post* in interviews that would cause a great stir at the end of 1981.

Stockman's version of the Reagan revolution was far more radical than Reagan's: Stockman wanted to change the very way that government functioned, replacing politics with justice. To change the processes, however, Stockman had to work through them; in order to push Reagan's proposals, Stockman had to play the game of assembling coalitions. Stockman had to sin in order to win the kingdom of virtue; therefore, the third consequence, he was trapped by a contradiction far more implacable than those of Reaganomics. Reagan could function without inner conflict, for the means fit his ends. Stockman would feel his ideology was more pure; yet, since he was down in the ditch making compromises, Stockman knew he too was covered in mud. That led to the agony, anger, and cynicism revealed in the book he wrote after his resignation.

Stockman believed that for supply-side policy to work it had to be logically valid in a way demonstrable to the establishment. To Stockman that meant explaining the chain of events that led to the desired end. Because he posited a means-end chain, his theory could be falsified; because it could be falsified, he could imagine—indeed he would have—a moral duty to change his mind. Most Republican economists would settle for the right kind of policy operated by their guys; they did not insist on coherent argument about how the economy would get from the inflation and stagnation of 1980 to the growth and stable prices Reagan promised. Stockman misjudged the establishment and, like all of us, understood less than he believed about macroeconomics. But he stuck to his model, so that, when a part of it was falsified, Stockman lost faith in the whole structure.

Stockman elaborated his economic vision in an extraordinary memo, "Avoiding an Economic Dunkirk," that he and Jack Kemp sent to the president-elect in November 1980. The memo was written in order to convince Reagan to appoint Stockman OMB director.[39] The "President," the memo began, "will inherit thoroughly disordered credit and capital markets, punishingly high interest rates, and hair-trigger market psychology poised to respond strongly to early economic policy signals in either favorable or unfavorable ways." The key to favorable expectations was "decisive, credible" cuts in outlays, removing the specter of deficits.

But, covering some of the same ground covered by Anderson over a year before, Stockman wrote:

> Achieving fiscal controls over outlays and Treasury borrowing *cannot be conducted as an accounting exercise or exclusively through legislated spending cuts in the orthodox sense.* Only a comprehensive economic package that spurs output and employment growth and lowers *inflation expectations* and interest rates has any hope of stopping the present hemorrhage.[40]

Any dilution of the Kemp-Roth tax cut for short-term outlay gains would be, in the long run, counterproductive. Or so Stockman then thought.

At the same time, markets had to be convinced that the tax cut did not mean long-term inflation. In order to show that the money supply would not accommodate inflation, thereby reducing expectations, Stockman recommended that Volcker and Reagan should meet, with Reagan stoutly endorsing a tight money policy. If the budget could be shown to be on a path that would within a reasonable time remove both the deficit and money growth as causes of inflation, investors would adjust their long-term expectations accordingly.

As a start toward credible long-term spending control, Stockman suggested at least $25 billion in FY82 spending cuts, essentially along the lines of the defeated House Republican alternatives in 1980. Stockman's sense of urgency was shared by the rest of Reagan's team, though they saw no need to be so dramatic.

His outline, however, had a few revealing holes. One was defense spending, which he did not consider. Another was excluding some real big programs, like social security and the Veterans' Administration. But the real difficulty was Stockman's reliance on changing long-term expectations before any change in performance. Herbert Stein has nicely summarized the extent to which the policy adopted, basically following Stockman's line, was like the house that Jack built:

> Thus the parts of the programs were tied together not only in the sense that all the parts had to be put into place but also in the sense that they all had to work. The announcement of the program had to have the desired effect on expectations. Otherwise, the monetary restraint would cause an economic contraction, which would, among other things, keep the budget from coming into balance, and that would impair the growth of production and productivity, further affecting the revenue and deficit and so on in a general unraveling. Similarly the tax rate cuts had to have the promised effects on the supply of output on the desired scale and time schedule. If they didn't the budget would not come into balance, investment would be held back, productivity growth would be sluggish, the monetary restraint would cause unemployment and the whole scenario would unravel from a different direction.[41]

Stockman understood all this. When the markets did not behave as he had hoped, he began to doubt his theory. Other advisers' rationales for supporting the president were less elaborate, less easily falsified, and thus more solid.

Appointments besides Stockman's would shape budget politics. For our purposes, the key appointees were Cap Weinberger at the Defense Department and Donald Regan at the Treasury Department.

Ironically, Weinberger's appointment drew cries of dismay from the Pentagon and its supporters. Tough talk in previous stints at OMB and HEW had brought him the nickname, "Cap the knife," though those who worked with him at OMB knew better. Accordingly, many took his appointment as a sign that the Pentagon buildup would receive skeptical review in the office of the secretary of Defense. Yet Weinberger discussed the budget in terms of defense "need," not deficits, and saw defense as a far more fundamental reponsibility of the federal government than social spending.[42] No one knew, however, what Weinberger thought the needs might be. An enemy of a strong defense, Weinberger certainly was not.

Donald Regan at the Treasury would be the point man for tax-cutting efforts; as such, his role was as crucial as Stockman's at OMB. Regan was viewed as a man experienced in the financial markets but relatively in-experienced in Washington. Yet, Regan was no political novice. As president of Merrill Lynch, the nation's largest brokerage house, he had been a leader of the very political revolution, during the 1970s, in the financial services industry.[43] A businessman rather than an economist, Regan had spoken out little about economic theory. Supply-siders were uneasy about him, so Kemp and his allies arranged to surround Regan with assistants—strict monetarist Beryl Sprinkel (under secretary for monetary policy), Norman Ture (under secretary for tax policy), and the *Wall Street Journal*'s Paul Craig Roberts (assistant secretary for economic policy)—who would, they hoped, guide their boss in the right direction. And Regan certainly was sympathetic to individual rate cuts. Echoing the attitude held by the president-elect, Regan believed that "the only argument against reducing the top marginal tax rate is that it would remove a penalty for being successful."[44]

Along with Regan and Stockman, the third member of the economic troika was Murray Weidenbaum as chairman of the Council of Economic Advisers. As the first microeconomist (his specialty was regulation) chosen to head the CEA, his appointment showed the new government's interest in making economic arguments to reduce government interference in the market. It also showed Reagan's disrespect for the economic fine-tuning under which traditional macroeconomists had been trying to manage the economy.

Nevertheless, Weidenbaum would have to sign off on the economic forecast, which meant making macroeconomic judgments. In that he was essentially a neoclassicist.[45] Bearing no direct policy responsibility, Weidenbaum would be less influential than Regan or Stockman. Even for a microeconomist, representing the economics profession within the Reagan administration would not be one of the world's more rewarding jobs.

The most important advisers are those closest to the president: leaders of the White House staff. Their job, as they saw it, was to help Ronald Reagan be a successful president. "It was not our role," an official later commented, "to go in there and try to reshape the President's policies."[46] But they would watch for danger signals in the economy, which could have dangerous political consequences. Because they were selected more for political than policy skills, the chief staffers were not all totally committed to Reagan's vision, though all, as Republicans, leaned that way. Ironically, in dealings with the media and Congress, the more centrist views of some of Reagan's aides may have given an impression that if things went wrong the administration was more flexible than the president in fact proved to be.

The three top White House aides were Presidential Counselor Edwin

Meese, Chief of Staff James Baker, and Deputy Chief of Staff Michael Deaver. Although Meese had cabinet rank, there was no clear hierarchy.

Formerly Reagan's chief of staff in Sacramento, Meese was close to the new president in ideology and many personal attitudes. He commanded the White House policy staffs, prepared the agenda for cabinet meetings, and coordinated cabinet councils. He was supposed to reconcile differences in the cabinet, that is, to get disputes into a shape that would either allow presidential decision or, better yet, make it unnecessary. Though his authority reached into all areas of policy, Meese was more a guardian of Reagan's general ideology than an architect of new initiatives.

Mike Deaver was personally close to both Ronald and Nancy Reagan. He went to work for them in 1966; over the years he became the man, more than any other, who took care of Ronald Reagan's image. To do this he had to submerge whatever policy preferences he had; otherwise he would have been suspected of having hidden agendas. Because most Americans, indeed most of the world, were to the left of Reagan, keeping him popular meant going where the voters and opinions were.[47] Deaver knew his man well enough to judge what situations were trouble and what were opportunity. In the White House, his office adjoined the Oval Office.

Chief of Staff James Baker was an anomaly: unlike Meese or Deaver, he had no past background with Reagan. He had been Ford's campaign manager (against Reagan) in 1976 and George Bush's campaign manager in 1980. Born to the law in Houston, a successful attorney who moved easily in all the right Texas circles, from the boardroom to fishing in the salt marshes, Jim Baker was chosen chief of staff because of the skill he had displayed in various campaigns. Baker was an extremely good administrator, bargainer, and tactician. He was responsible for the political, as distinguished from policy, side of the White House—negotiations with Congress and other political actors. He would prove a master at appraising the political climate and using this understanding to promote the president's program.

A number of other aides had independent responsibility as well as close association with this threesome. Although Vice President George Bush had once labeled the Reagan program "voodoo economics," he worked diligently for the Reagan program and proved an effective lobbyist. Bush was a man of generally conservative values with a long record of service and total loyalty in important jobs, from head of the Republican National Committee to director of the CIA. Max L. Friedersdorf and his deputy, Kenneth Duberstein, were experienced congressional liaisons (the lack thereof had been a real weakness in the Carter administration).

Richard Wirthlin, the president's pollster, had no official position, but his soundings of the public pulse helped shape the presentation of policy. Staff director David Gergen, another aide in charge of making the president look good, had been a speechwriter for Nixon, directed Ford's office of communications, and was well-connected throughout both the Republican and wider Washington intellectual and media establishments (he became editor of *U.S. News and World Report* after leaving the White House).

Richard Darman, Baker's assistant, had the seemingly uninteresting job of ensuring that policy papers destined for the president were fully and fairly staffed. Yet, with Baker's backing, he would become a most influential presidential aide. The thirty-seven-year-old Darman was not only not a Reaganaut but a living, breathing liberal Republican, a protégé of Elliot Richardson, with experience in four departments. "His dirty little secret," writes Barrett, "was that he believed in government, including the federal government."[48] Like Baker, Darman was an incorrigible centrist whose self-assumed task was to make government work. Darman's main interest was problem solving for its own sake. Darman suggested creating the Legislative Strategy Group, cochaired by Meese and Baker, which coordinated the efforts of White House, OMB, and Treasury lobbyists and over the long months to follow directed the negotiations that led to Reagan's victories. That group enhanced Darman's influence, and he—the closest to Stockman in age and brilliance, if not in temperament—would become the budget director's closest ally in the coming internal administration battles over the shape of the economic plan.

As assistant to the president for policy development, Martin Anderson reprised his campaign role with greater resources. His forty-one-member staff included the executive secretaries of each of the five cabinet councils. Although off the lobbying track, Anderson could intervene in internal White House decision making where he saw a need.[49]

On the whole, Reagan had assembled a generally conservative and politically sophisticated staff.

Tactical Considerations

Once assembled, the new team had to devise a strategy that exploited their opportunity. Speed, focus, and maintaining momentum with a series of wins were obvious tactics.[50] Former OMB Director Caspar Weinberger, formerly Reagan's budget director in California, and secretary of HEW for Nixon, led a transition team that was also busily drawing

up lists of cuts. The minority (soon to be majority) staff of the Senate
Budget Committee as well as numerous lesser party officials were also
making lists and checking them twice. Weinberger, following the campaign line that the House Democrats challenged with their Second Budget Resolution, wanted cuts in FY81.[51] Stephen E. Bell, staff director for
SBC, was more interested in quick action on FY82. "You can kiss it
goodbye," he commented, "if you let it go past three or four months. If
you get down the road and Senators are getting a ration of grief from
people whose benefits would be cut, then you've lost it. Suicide is just as
unpleasant for Republicans as for Democrats."[52] Everybody agreed on
the need for speed.

Stockman suggested that spending cuts be attached to the debt-ceiling
raise that would have to be passed in February, thus bypassing the Demo-
cratic-controlled committees in the House. But Howard Baker, the new
Senate majority leader, warned him that riders work only on bills that
people want to pass, saying "you'll pick up all the enemies of the debt
ceiling without gaining any new friends."[53] Stockman dropped that idea,
though it returned many times, garbed finally as Gramm-Rudman. The
Senate Budget Committee, particularly Chairman Domenici and Staff
Director Bell, convinced Senate leadership and then the administration
to use reconciliation on the first resolution, as the Democrats had in
1980, to package cuts and move them quickly.

The administration took a series of steps to ensure its own bureaucracy
did not resist cuts. The administration's personnel operation made sure
that appointees below cabinet level were committed to Reagan's political
philosophy. Carter-era employees were booted out even when no replacement was available. "We felt an empty office was better than to have
a holdover," explained Ed Meese.[54] Frequent cabinet meetings were held,
in Elizabeth Drew's words, to "make sure that the Secretaries were
'aboard' on the President's proposals to cut spending, and to make it
clear at whose pleasure they served."[55] Advised by conservative task
forces before they went into their department, secretaries participated
in economic briefings with Reagan before becoming involved with their
own particular business. Then, while the package of reductions was being
devised, cabinet members had to support their positions—not just to
Stockman but also to panels of critics, such as Martin Anderson and
Murray Weidenbaum. Some more experienced cabinet members, like
Richard Schweicker at Health and Human Services and Alexander Haig
at the State Department, were able to win a few battles in that setting,
but more often they lost.[56]

Reagan personally lobbied the people he had to win over. Having run
against the government, Carter had tried to govern like an outsider.

Reagan realized that he could treat members of Congress as fellow insiders yet, when he spoke to the public, adopt an antigovernment rhetoric. Precisely because the Washington world was not the same as the one outside, the public would not notice or care much if Reagan went to the Hill, greeted as fellows the same legislators whom he was blasting, and invited them to Camp David. Members were used to similar behavior, so they saw no hypocrisy. Reagan and his staff strove to build a reservoir of personal goodwill that might help win the undecided. Before he took office, he went to the Capitol to greet legislators and to Washington parties to meet such movers and shakers as Katherine Graham of the *Washington Post* and *Newsweek*. Reagan later used those social contacts to ask for help.

In putting together its program, the administration faced two substantive problems with tactical implications. First was "fairness": how to cut spending and programs without seeming to pick only on the vulnerable. Everyone knew that most money was in giant programs—old-age, medicare, and social security—that were vital to a large group of voters and popular with everyone. If those programs were not attacked, most of the burden would have to fall on either the means-tested programs or business subsidies. To choose the former would mean taking from the most vulnerable; choosing the latter would anger the administration's political base. Because poor people paid little in taxes, save for social security, Kemp-Roth was likely to do them less good than the spending cuts did harm. The logic of the situation resulted in a package that focused on people near the poverty line. The administration, of course, would argue vehemently that a revitalized economy would help everybody. Perhaps, but those results lay in the future while programs would be cut in the present.[57] Given this inevitable disparity, the administration had to minimize, rationalize, or limit its political importance by making other factors more salient to debate.

For Carter, budget reductions had been a sad necessity. For Reagan, they were a principle. Therefore, Reagan wanted to cut in ways that would permanently decrease pressure to spend, such as either abolishing programs and their bureaucracies or eliminating federal support for interest groups, such as poverty lawyers, that might fight for further spending. Naturally, permanent cuts are more difficult than temporary cuts, preferred by moderates who disliked deficits but liked programs. In fact, the permanence of cuts was the hidden stake in many subsequent spending battles.

Above all, Reagan's most vital priority, the big tax cut, made his own party uncomfortable. He had to calm worries about deficits and promote considerations like party loyalty that would keep Republicans together.

Then he needed some Democratic votes; the administration would be helped by their opponents' troubles.

Senate Democrats were in the minority; they could only hope that the Senate's traditional bipartisanship in budgeting would leave them with some influence. That tradition, however, had been built upon the co-operation of Ed Muskie and Henry Bellmon, neither of whom was now in the Senate, and on a Democratic majority large enough so that it could be expected to prevail in a pinch but fractious enough that Republicans felt they were in a position to deal at the margins. In 1980, even a Democratic Senate kept pushing for defense hikes, social spending re-ductions, and tax relief. The replacement of twelve largely liberal Demo-crats with twelve largely conservative Republicans shifted the Senate's balance further to the right. In such a situation, only strong leadership and near unanimity could give Democrats much bargaining power, but those were the last things anyone could expect.

The center of Democratic resistance would have to be in the House of Representatives. Tip O'Neill had been a fairly successful partisan leader. In 1981, however, he would not only have fewer troops but also limited choices of weapons. The Speaker often exploited his control of procedure, either through the Rules Committee, or scheduling, or his relations with committee heads. Given the election and the economy, he could not use his full power. A fair, or even a slightly rigged, fight would be okay, but some such standard obstructing tactics as delaying votes or refusing to report legislation would make the party look like it was de-fying democracy while playing games with the fate of the economy. Throughout the coming struggle, Democrats in the House would have to ensure that the press did not, in the Speaker's words, "quibble about dragging our feet."[58]

That left the Speaker to lead by persuasion and a bit of procedure. Because Republicans had never voted for Democratic budgets before, O'Neill could expect few if any Republican supporters. If the GOP united, defection by twenty-six of his own troops would mean defeat.

Unfortunately for the liberal O'Neill, his troops included about forty boll weevils, a group of distinctly conservative, cotton-state Democrats. These weevils were in a position of excruciating delicacy, fraught with danger and opportunity. Because power in the House was normally associated with committee positions and because committee positions were determined by the Speaker and the Democratic caucus, a member who defied his colleagues too often was unlikely to win many plums.

The leadership emphasized party loyalty in appointments to the most powerful committees—Rules, Ways and Means, and Budget.

Suddenly in 1981 the Speaker needed the boll weevils as much as they needed him. Representative Charles Stenholm of Texas organized his colleagues in a "Conservative Democratic Forum" to lobby for their preferences, bargaining with both O'Neill and the White House. In December, Guy Vanderjagt (R-Mich.), a Republican leader, was exploring a coalition of Republicans and conservative Democrats to organize the House. Although that was highly unlikely, the prospect did increase the leverage of Stenholm and his colleagues. In search of better treatment, they met with O'Neill and Majority Leader Jim Wright (D-Tex.).

O'Neill and Wright tried to win over the weevils by meeting many of their demands. When O'Neill expanded the Steering and Policy Committee (the main party organization) from twenty-four to thirty-one members, he appointed three Conservative Democratic Forum members to the new slots. Conservatives got some other plum appointments. Stockman's friend, Phil Gramm, won a place on Budget after leading Jim Wright to believe that, while advocating his own views, he would support the committee product.[59]

Stenholm praised the Speaker's "good job in accommodating the interests of our party and being fair to everyone."[60] But that did not ensure the boll weevils' loyalty on budget matters. With his Republican majority in the Senate, the president was in a far better position than House leaders to deal on policy because Reagan could deliver if he won in the House. Many southern Democrats also felt conservative political pressures in their districts.[61] Because many boll weevils' districts still held residual Democratic loyalties and had weak (if any) Republican organizations, party switching was risky. And if the conservatives backed Reagan yet kept their Democratic identification, they risked being in the position, as Ralph Hall of Texas worried, "whereby if the GOP holds the House in 1983 they won't need us. If the Democrats hold the House, they won't want us."[62] Perhaps the best possible outcome for the boll weevils would be for them to win concessions from both sides, followed by a 1982 election that maintained the status quo and thus their own pivotal position.

The House Democratic leadership could only try to put itself in a good position for bargaining; O'Neill's bows to the boll weevils were one step in that direction. The second step, selecting chairs for Ways and Means and Budget, would be central in the coming dispute. Al Ulmann's defeat put Dan Rostenkowski of Chicago next in line to chair Ways and Means, but "Rosty," a close ally of the Speaker, was also in line for John Brademas's spot as majority whip. His choice of the Ways and Means post served both his and the Speaker's interests. Rostenkowski got a position of great formal power and independence. O'Neill could hope that the pragmatic Rostenkowski would be able to find allies, among boll weevils and more moderate Republicans, for a Democratic, alternative tax proposal.

The Budget chair was more problematic; each of the two major candidates had disadvantages. David Obey, as chair of the Democratic Study Group, was a leading liberal and the Speaker's ally in the 1980 battles. He was also abrasive, with many enemies (including Rostenkowksi), and could not be expected to win over the party's right wing. His rival, James Jones of Oklahoma, chaired the Democratic Research Organization, a group of moderate to conservative Democrats. As a former chief of staff to Lyndon Johnson and successful Democratic campaigner in an extremely Republican district, Jones obviously was an adroit politician, although, like Obey, he lacked the backslapping touch of, say, the Speaker. Unlike Obey, Jones had real problems with liberals like the Speaker and Rules Chairman Bolling. He won his seat on the Budget Committee in 1979 against their wishes. They distrusted Jones because of his policies: he wanted bigger tax breaks for business, endorsed a statutory limit on federal spending, and clearly favored spending cuts. Jones had sponsored the big business tax cuts in 1978, beating the party leaders. He worked closely with business lobbyists, who helped him survive in his ultraconservative Tulsa district because, as one told us, "he was our leader on the tax side." Rostenkowski preferred Jones to Obey at Budget, not because of any love for Jones, but to stop Obey and keep Jones preoccupied, away from the tax fights. The battle then was between two extremely able but flawed members, each with strong supporters. A third candidate, liberal Paul Simon of Illinois, was eliminated on the first ballot within the caucus; on the second, they deadlocked at 118 votes each. On the third, Jones won, 121 to 116.[63] This left Democrats with a budget chairman whose relations with the Speaker were rather dicey but who had some chance to keep the boll weevils on board.

The ascensions of Jones and Rostenkowski made a policy of damage control more likely than confrontation. Both would work hard to cut a deal with the Republicans that would protect Democratic preferences. The choice of Jones in particular shaped the terms of the spending debate. With a fiscal conservative leading the Democrats, Reagan was bound to get, at least in dollars, much of what he wanted.

Many liberals expected to lose. Toby Moffett of Connecticut believed that the Republicans and conservative Democrats would have a "majority coalition" on many issues.[64] Another liberal commented that "we shouldn't spend time nickel-nursing around the edges. We don't have the votes."[65] Jones naturally was more optimistic, predicting "a broad coalition of moderates from both parties who want to get us on the road to economic recovery."[66] If Jones were right, he and Rostenkowski would blunt the president's attack, limit the tax cut, and bring spending policy closer to Democratic ideals of equity. Domestic spending cuts would be smaller but so would defense increases and tax reductions. If Jones were wrong, the Democratic party would sit still for cuts in their programs, but they would get no credit for reducing the deficit as tax decreases and a rise in defense overwhelmed their sacrifice. The Reagan revolution might cure some ills, if successful, but the deficit was not likely to be among them.

FIVE

The President's Program

On inauguration day, the prime interest rate stood at 20 percent. The dominant economic issue remained inflation, not unemployment; thus, both media and politicians still emphasized reducing spending to balance the budget. The air of panic remained from 1980. "When Ronald Reagan steps into the White House next week," *Newsweek* wrote, "he will inherit the most dangerous economic crisis since Franklin D. Roosevelt took office 48 years ago."[1] Lack of support for social spending was revealed, in another way, by President Carter's valedictory budget; it was as tight as his FY81 plan and closed with a call for further reductions in entitlements.

Reagan's Attack Takes Shape

The new president had to nurture this mood to "do something." Reagan thought that he could lead the public against the politicians; when he was governor, as he said, "on the major things I took the case to the people. . . . Sometimes it is necessary to make the legislature see the light, you make them feel the heat."[2] His strategists agreed that only massive public pressure would overcome resistance in Congress. "To win this fight," declared Stockman with a bit of hyperbole, "the president is going to have to generate a million cards and letters a month to Congress."[3]

While the administration was still working out the details of the plan, Reagan took to the airwaves on February 5 to gather public support. He began with a litany of economic woes, dramatizing inflation by displaying first a dollar bill and then a quarter, dime, and penny to show the how the dollar had shrunk to 36 cents since 1960. Then, in a gentle, unaccusing tone, he described how it had happened; the rhetoric is worth repeating:

> We forgot or just overlooked the fact that Government—any Government—has a built-in tendency to grow. Now we all had a hand in looking to Government for benefits as if Government had some source of revenue other than our earnings. . . . Some Government programs seemed so worthwhile that borrowing to fund them didn't bother us. . . . We know now that inflation results from all that deficit spending.[4]

The president sought to create the impression that his plan was nonpartisan—but opposing it would be partisan. He was setting up the presidency as the pubic interest and his opponents as the special interests.

To an aide surprised at the speech's tone, Reagan explained, "Listen, if I were making this speech from the outside, I'd kick their balls off."[5] In a tactic from Greek drama that was to be repeated, the bringing of bad news was left to Stockman, the messenger.

Who's on First? Taxing or Spending?

The February 5 speech earned rave reviews; the Democrats saw that the president was putting his position in appealing terms that would be difficult to oppose at the same level of generality. But once matters got down to specifics, the president faced trouble within his own coalition. One issue was: Which came first, tax cuts or spending cuts? Traditional wisdom had it that spending cuts, if any, had to precede tax reductions—pain before pleasure—because only the prospect of pleasure would persuade congressmen to accept the pain. Senate Republicans agreed and pushed spending to the forefront in both counsels and procedures. Donald Regan responded that business needed to plan for the future, so the tax cuts should be pushed without regard to the spending schedule.[6]

In the Senate Budget Committee, the new leadership—Senator Pete Domenici (R-N.M.) and his chief aide, Steve Bell—was, to say the least, skeptical of Kemp-Roth. Stockman refers to Bell as "an avowed opponent of supply-side economics."[7] Bell could be scathing against what he considered the inflated claims of some supply-siders. When told at one dinner that the Reagan revolution would increase savings to 12 percent of income, Bell replied that "savings have never varied from a 4 to 8 percent range. After 100 years, if you're a slow learner, you can figure out that there is something in the system that keeps savings from going to 12 percent." He did not think it was 1980's tax rates. Bell believed that cutting taxes had always been easier than cutting spending, and there was no reason to see that pattern as any more mutable than the savings rate. Stockman scorned such reasoning, but Bell's concern was shared by GOP senators such as Domenici, Dole, and Majority Leader Howard Baker. Although resolved to keep his party together and govern the Senate in support of the new Republican president, Baker wanted independent advice and hired his own economist, Dan Crippen, to provide it. Though quieter and more academic in style than Bell, Crippen was not much more of a supply-sider. Senate leaders and their staffs wanted to follow the president, but they were not about to be sold on the tax-cut-first strategy.

In fact, Senate leaders favored an extreme version of a spending-cut-first strategy. They adopted procedures to make cuts happen fast and be final: reconciliation was slated not only before the tax cut but even before the budget resolution. Senate Republican leaders chose also to extend the reach of reconciliation past entitlements to authorizations for annually appropriated programs. If those authorizations were cut below prevailing appropriation levels, the appropriations committees would have to follow along, for they are not allowed to appropriate more than is authorized. Such cuts would stick in future years (over the term of the authorizations), rather than just in the one year of an appropriation; but the key advantage of reconciling authorizations was speed. If appropriations reductions were delayed until their bills were passed in (at best) September, the drive for spending reduction might have dissipated.

Domenici, Baker, and their staffs had to convince Senate Parliamentarian Robert Dove that such a sequence was allowed under the rules. Convincing Dove was made easier by the actions in 1980 of Senator Lawton Chiles (D-Fla.), a leader of Democratic budget balancers. Chiles shared Republican Domenici's budgetary preferences and his desire to increase the Budget Committee's power, so the 1980 resolution was drafted to establish precedents that gave the committee a lot of running room. It was not the last time Chiles and Domenici would find themselves on the same side. While Stockman got credit for using reconciliation, it was hardly his idea.

As the resistance to tax cuts became obvious, the children's allowance theory took on some unspoken amendments. Spending cuts would be made to ease the worries of skeptics about the deficit picture in the immediate future. Such cuts would be a down payment, in the sense of a token of intent and ability to pay. If tax cuts did threaten deficits, the fact that Congress had cut spending once would soothe worriers, who might believe it would happen again.

Who was to be convinced? Both Republican and conservative Democratic politicians and, as usual, the financial markets. Politicians were easier to convince than markets. Soon after being sworn in, Reagan showed that business had a friend in the White House. He abolished the Council on Wage and Price Stability, decontrolled domestic oil prices, and placed a sixty-day freeze on pending regulations. But confidence in the White House did not translate into optimism about the economy. A mid-February *Forbes* article was subtitled, "Reagan's team won't engineer a crisis to cure inflation—but there may be one anyway." Bond market guru Albert Wojnilower was quoted: "Today, only extraordinary and unacceptable increases in interest rates are able to slow credit expansion—usually by precipitating bankruptcy crises."[8] With respected conservative voices doomsaying, the markets were going to be a tough sell.

The Rosy Scenario

In this context of market skepticism advisers battled over the assumptions that would accompany the economic plan. They could not use the September 9 inflation assumptions, but any forecast within the bounds of experience would make it difficult to project a balanced budget with the big tax cut. Neither the Senate leaders nor, naturally, House budgeters thought the two fit together. House opposition could be dismissed as partisan, but, if the forecast were denounced by Senate leaders as well, the administration's game would be up. Luckily for Stockman and Reagan, Senate leaders wanted to support their new president and at least the basic outlines of the new policy: real domestic spending cuts and some tax relief. Stockman therefore needed an economic forecast that was optimistic but not totally off the wall, one that could be criticized but not simply dismissed out of hand. He got what he needed, not from calculation but from last-minute compromise.

The original drafting team for the economic forecast—Stockman with his chief economist at OMB, Lawrence Kudlow, and Beryl Sprinkel, Norman Ture, and Paul Craig Roberts from Treasury—were a mix of supply-siders and monetarists. They wanted economic growth of 5 percent to 6 percent, twice the historical norm. "Otherwise," Stockman writes, "what was the point of the whole miracle cure we were peddling?"[9] But they also wanted low growth of money supply. There were two ways to get there; the most obvious was to assume a quick collapse of inflation, falling to 2 percent by 1984. Accordingly, in late January, Stockman's draft forecast was predicting a quick rebound in the second half of 1981, followed by GNP growth of 4.5 percent for each following year, all with low inflation. Conceding that conventional economic models predicted nothing of the sort, the budget director declared those models "can't even predict the next quarter, let alone the next year."[10] That was too true, but wishful thinking was not necessarily a better guide.

Stockman could not sell the forecast to any but his supply-side colleagues. Alan Greenspan was particularly critical (internally), and he was hardly alone. CBO estimated that under realistic assumptions the Reagan package as roughly outlined would lead to $70 to $80 billion deficits.[11] More important, Senate Republicans balked at the developing forecast; Domenici told Stockman that he could not accept it.

Into this mess strode Murray Weidenbaum, the new CEA chairman. He knew that no one would believe the combination of fast growth and 2 percent inflation. His protests were interpreted as a threat to resign, which would be very damaging. There they were in early February with no economic forecast, and, as part of the overall strategy of moving quickly, the administration had already announced that it would reveal the full package in a speech to Congress on February 18. Estimates in the budget documents depend on the economic forecast, so the matter had to be settled fast. "You're going to be sending the President of the United States up that Hill with a blank piece of paper," Dale McComber, chief career official at OMB, warned his new director. "The prospect," Stockman notes, "lacked charm."[12]

Stockman, Weidenbaum, and the rest, therefore, bargained out a forecast. Weidenbaum won agreement to predicting slower long-term growth (4.2 percent annually after 1983) and acknowledging the need for a very small ration of recessionary pain in 1981. The final forecast assumed slightly higher (7.7 percent) unemployment in the fourth quarter of 1981 than had prevailed in the first quarter (7.4 percent). It also assumed a much more gradual fall-off in inflation (to 6.0 percent on the CPI in 1983; 5.1 percent in 1984).[13] The CEA chairman described the result:

> A forced marriage. Supply-side people insisted on the possibility of rapid growth in real terms, and monetarists demanded rapid progress in bringing down inflation. Each of them would go along with a set of numbers as long as their own concern was satisfied. The monetarists weren't that concerned about growth and supply-siders weren't that worked up about inflation.[14]

The result, Herbert Stein wrote, "strained credulity."[15] Weidenbaum later claimed that the final result was "extremely optimistic," but not "off the wall. . . . Was it technically feasible? I think so. But everything had to work well."[16]

The numbers about which there was such controversy appear in Table 3, with comparisons to figures in Carter's budget. The forecast's optimism was not so unusual as presidential forecasts go, though it would prove far less justified than normal. The problem was in the internal logic: this was all supposed to happen with slow monetary growth. The monetary squeeze could wipe out the forecast by creating a recession—the usual concomitant of slowing the flow of financial blood to the economic system. But even without recession there was a mathematical inconsistency.

The revenues to balance the budget, at the lower rates from the tax cut, called for a large growth in the nominal (current dollar) economy and therefore in both real and inflationary growth. Growth in the nominal size of the economy means that more money is changing hands. Either there is more money (i.e., the money supply increases), or current

TABLE 3. Economic Forecasts for 1981–1983
(in percentages)

	1981		1982		1983	
	Carter	Reagan	Carter	Reagan	Carter	Reagan
CPI increase	12.5	11.1	10.3	8.3	8.7	6.2
Interest, 91-day T-Bills	13.5	11.1	11.0	8.9	9.4	7.8
GNP change	0.9	1.4	3.5	5.2	3.5	4.9

SOURCES: *CQ Almanac*, 1981, pp. 272, 279; *National Journal*, Feb. 21, 1981, p. 307.

money is moving faster (i.e., "velocity" increases). If the money supply were squeezed, then money for the projected growth in nominal terms would have to come from unprecedented increases in velocity. People would have to turn over their money much faster than ever before. Unless velocity increased then, as Paul Craig Roberts later wrote, by "jacking up the inflation assumption" above what the supply-siders wanted—so as both to seem reasonable to those who believed that inflation could only fall slowly and to give an appearance of budget balance that might reduce inflation expectations in the long term—"Stockman showed higher nominal GNP than was consistent with the assumption of monetary restraint."[17] To wring more money from lower taxes demanded a higher nominal GNP; that in turn required high growth and inflation. But, because the money supply was not supposed to grow nearly enough for this, something had to give.

Inconsistency at this level of analysis was not something that economists could explain very well to themselves, let alone to the American public or to politicians. But it suggested that the administration package would be less than convincing to those skeptical bond markets; when they did not react with glee, Stockman, rather guiltily, concluded "they don't think it adds up."[18]

Economically it didn't add; politically it did—barely. No one knew either if the Federal Reserve would hit its monetary targets or what target was really consistent with what rate of inflation. The uncertainty of 1980, plus the difficulty of appearing partisan, inhibited CBO from taking a strong stance against the estimates.[19] Republican economists—Greenspan, for instance—who wanted the administration to look as good as possible withheld public criticism.

The rosy scenario fooled neither budget experts nor leaders of House Democrats and Senate Republicans. But because the administration had avoided totally implausible economic or budget deficit forecasts and was only technically inconsistent, Senate Republican budgeters would have trouble explaining a break with the president. They would seem to be siding with the Democrats, and that the Republicans could not do. The issue could still be posed as "us" versus "them"; anyone who questioned the figures was opposing the president. Democrats, of course, could say anything they wanted about the Reagan plan, and it would be dismissed as partisan.

Contemplating Cuts

Even under the optimistic economic assumptions, to detail domestic spending cuts that would balance the budget yet pass the Congress was a daunting task. From his previous work with Phil Gramm on a FY81 budget alternative, the Dunkirk memo, the transition (Weinberger/Taft) team work, Senate Budget Committee lists, and so on, the new budget director had collected a large bag of cuts before he walked in the door of OMB. Some were big and obviously politically difficult (the "A" list); others were small and more technical (the "B" list). Once inside that door, Stockman suddenly had a large, highly professional organization to price out all his suggested changes, draft justifications, suggest further cuts (many from hoary OMB lists passed from director to director), and warn him of hidden difficulties (why cuts had continually been passed on). The OMB staff generated additional big and small proposals (the "C" and "D" lists). Among all his new resources, one, however, was scarce: time—Stockman's and particularly the president's and that of his colleagues.

Stockman needed his colleagues' time to make OMB's position the administration's policy. Stockman, for example, wanted to slash non-military foreign aid. New Secretary of State General Alexander Haig thought that budgetary restraint did not justify OMB's changing foreign policy over his head, so he resisted with all the power that a personally forceful bureaucratic veteran could muster.[20] Few other cabinet members had either the facts or the savvy to protest as effectively, but all at least had to sign off on cuts before they were sent to the Hill.

After trying to consider cuts in cabinet meetings, which wasted the time of anyone not immediately on the chopping block, Stockman resorted to a tried-and-true measure of budget cutters worldwide, a separate review board stacked with high officials whose bent was toward cutting. To review contested OMB proposals, his Budget Working Group included Bill Brock, Don Regan, his deputy Tim McNamar, Martin Anderson, and Murray Weidenbaum. Jim Baker and Ed Meese were members but rarely had time to attend. Anderson excelled at doing Stockman's work for him, overawing cabinet secretaries and their bureaucrats with his expertise. Because it was so early in the administration, not many department heads knew much; because few new lower-level appointments had yet been made, department heads were forced to rely on the word of suspect (by definition) career bureaucrats against a group of their administration colleagues. Not a good position for the cabinet members.

Stockman thereby won acquiescence, if not support, to cuts that were then presented to the president for final approval as the product of a group of his cabinet officers. Stockman believes the process made cuts seem more consensual than they were.

> If the President learned any lessons from [the process] . . . they were undoubtedly the wrong ones. When he later found himself being challenged by congressmen and senators, I would hear him say again and again, "The fellas in the cabinet round-tabled all this and are in one hundred percent agreement that these cuts should be made."
>
> In fact, they hadn't and they weren't. We had brow-beaten the cabinet, one by one, into accepting the cuts. It was divide-and-conquer, not round-tabling. In my haste to expedite the revolution, I had inadvertently convinced the chief executive that budget cutting was an antiseptic process, a matter of compiling innocuous-sounding "half-pagers" and putting them in a neatly tabbed black book.[21]

It is fairer to say that Reagan, who on his own upped the estimate of "waste, fraud, and abuse" to 10 percent of all spending, was not educated to the contrary by the process.

There was no point in bashing cabinet officers over the head to back something that congressional Republicans were going to nix. Opposition had to be gauged and then overcome. And so as "black books" of proposals flew around the executive branch, a similar blizzard of paper was carried to the Hill. An OMB source explained that "to get the most politically saleable, $40 billion lowest common denominator, you need to start with $70–$80 billion . . . [but] it's not a smooth glide path from 70 to 40; more like 70 to 30 and then back up to 40." Many cuts failed to pass political muster. Because Stockman had to win support one by one for individual cuts, which were controversial enough, there was no way to assess the totals.

"Fairness"

This process of politically setting cuts, within both administration and Congress, raised the issue that Representative Corman and Democratic budgeters had debated in 1980: Would budget cutting go where the money was or where the power was not? Stockman wanted to defuse liberal criticism by cutting business and middle-class subsidies as well as programs concentrated on poor people. As he told William Greider, "We are interested in curtailing weak claims rather than weak clients. . . . We have to show that we are willing to attack powerful clients with weak claims. I think that's critical to our success—political and economic."[22]

Over in the Senate, Budget Committee Chairman Domenici agreed: "You never heard Pete Domenici make the argument that you could balance the budget, have significant defense increases and multiyear tax cuts simply by eliminating waste and fraud." He told David Broder, "You have to restructure the entitlement programs, either by adjusting the inflation indexes or redrawing the eligibility rules."[23] To Domenici that meant not just rule changes for the means-tested programs such as Aid to Families with Dependent Children (AFDC) and medicaid—weak clients—but reductions in the COLAs for the big middle-class programs, particularly social security.

The social security COLA in 1980 had far exceeded comparable wage increases, thus transferring money from current workers to the retired; that is, when prices rise faster than wages, as during 1979's inflation, and benefits are indexed to prices, beneficiaries do better than people who pay taxes. If cutting the COLA were ever to seem fair, now would be the time; and, because the inflation adjustment would be large, there was a lot of money in it. SBC leaders estimated that a one-year COLA freeze in 1981 would save $88 billion over five years.[24]

In the House, one Ways and Means aide recalled, "I and other staff had assumed, because there were huge increases then, that there would be some deal on the COLAs. Jones was looking at it, and I and the other staffers in the back room expected it." In the Senate, a source recalls, the sense was that "we had to get the social security COLA now. Our first notion was a crude suppression of the COLA. Hollings was on board. We knew that here we've got the old man, elected by a big electoral margin, the SOB could sell ice cubes in Alaska, it was time to do it." In short, the budgeters of the center wanted to go after social security.

As his later actions and his own report make clear, Stockman was quite interested in reducing federal commitments on the middle-class entitlements. If anything, he wanted not just to restrain the COLA but to reform the "capricious hybrid of out-and-out welfare benefits and earned pension annuities"[25] that social security had become. Inside OMB, Stockman and his staff considered a very big cut: eliminating "early retirement" at age sixty-two and forcing people to wait for (supposedly normal) retirement at age sixty-five. People who retired early did receive reduced benefits, but the reduction fell far short of the system's cost of paying benefits for an extra three years. The early-retirement provision was a classic example of Stockman's plaint: a provision unjustified in both actuarial terms and the welfare notion of need. Anybody who qualified and wanted could take the benefit.

But retirement at age sixty-two is the clearest case of budgets as commitments. People plan, save, and make life-choices assuming they can retire and receive social security at age sixty-two. To suddenly break that promise to millions of people would be extremely controversial—too big a thing to try to slip through as part of some other package. "We didn't want to take it on in that context," an OMB source recalls. "There would be too much disruption of the system." So early-retirement changes went back on the shelf, never making it into the black books for Congress to see.

That left COLAs. There existed a technical problem for the Social Security Administration, a political problem for Reagan, and a strategic problem for Stockman. A change to the July 1 COLA had to be adopted very quickly so social security computers could be programmed, certainly by late April. For that technical reason alone, OMB publicly urged SBC to forego any change; it could not be passed on time. Because technical expedients can always be found, the political problem was more important; under campaign pressure, Reagan had promised not to touch social security. Both the perceived and real lack of commitment to that program was his, and perhaps his party's, biggest weakness. Neither James Baker nor Howard Baker wanted anything to do with reopening the social security issue. Finally, from Stockman's point of view, going after the COLAs had all the risks of fundamental reform without all the benefit. Knowing he would face massive protest, he wanted to get more than the COLAs for his trouble. An OMB aide explained:

> Stockman thought that if we did the COLAs we wouldn't be able to come back to it again. . . . If you look at social security as a fiscal problem, the COLAs five years out are maybe 8 percent of programs costs. It's a small part of social security. . . . If you want to make progress, you have to take some checks out of the mail.

The budget director convinced himself that he could get what he needed for 1981 from small tag-alongs to social security, like the student and minimum benefits ($1.7 billion worth), without rousing the core constituency.[26] No one in the administration was likely to urge the budget director to go any further.

With social security off the table, Stockman's cut lists emphasized the means-tested entitlements, intergovernmental assistance, economic development or subsidy programs, and a few special targets (particularly the regulatory agencies, where reductions, by making it harder for them to operate, would kill two birds with one stone).[27] One cut with large symbolic value for equity (accordingly, prominently leaked[28]) was a reduction in the lending authority of the Export-Import Bank, which subsidizes exports for large companies. Stockman proudly reported to Greider how he had beaten back its defenders within the administration with "a demagogic tirade about how in the world can I cut food stamps and social services and CETA jobs and EDA jobs and you're going to tell me you can't give up one penny for Boeing?"[29] It was not so easy. Secretary of Commerce Malcolm Baldrige lost the first round of intra-administration sparring but, in his first meeting with some top business lobbyists, had warned that Export-Import was on the block and had begun rallying them to save it. In the end, Stockman would do less well than he hoped on Export-Import. But he did manage to clear the way for substantial cuts in economic and technological development programs favored by some Republicans.

One cannot estimate precisely who benefits from many federal programs. Does the Urban Mass Transit program benefit needy riders or middle-class bus drivers? Who gets what part of the subsidy for school lunches? No one knows. We can say that between one-third and one-half of the OMB package took from people who already were not doing very well. Some people on the border of poverty did very badly.[30] Our estimate fits common reactions at the time. When the final package was announced, its reverse redistribution drew extensive criticism.[31]

The brunt of the burden fell on the "working poor," those employed Americans who earn little and therefore live near the poverty line. Benefits for that group had risen during the 1970s for two reasons. First, the poverty line was set at a rather low standard of living, and people who were not below it could still use help. Second, making that line a cutoff would drastically reduce the incentive to work, especially for low paying jobs that might nonetheless provide training useful for a later career. Benefits for the working poor were thus expected to make it easier for them to escape from poverty.

The Reagan administration was eliminating or trimming a wide variety of programs focused at those margins of eligibility. Small individual cuts added to large effects.[32] *The Economist*, hardly a left-wing rag, concluded that the benefit cuts "will reduce to virtually nil any incentive for these poor mothers to keep on working." The distributional tilt was well-publicized: in an April CBS/*New York Times* poll 82 percent felt that some groups, particularly the poor, would be hurt more than others.[33]

Part of the package's distributional tilt was a residue of other decisions. If you leave out the military, social security, and interest, the amount of cuts to programs that helped the poor was not quite so out of line as a proportion of the remainder. Yet Stockman also intentionally zeroed in on low-income programs. He wanted to change the "welfare state premise" in favor of the state helping people who might otherwise help themselves. His changes were at the high end of eligibility because that was where the recipients who were not lame or blind or otherwise disabled, who conceivably could make their own way, were to be found. Those cuts also met less internal administration resistance. An OMB civil servant explained, "I've never met a Republican at a community health center."

The administration included no advocates for the poor, but many members feared that, if the program seemed to beat too much on the poor and give to the rich, the media and centrist politicians would condemn it as unfair.[34] When the cabinet met on February 10, a number of members "complained that the administration was getting a 'black eye' because of the proposed social cuts."[35] In order to defuse such criticism, the administration announced that it would not propose cuts in a "social safety net" of programs: social security, medicare, veterans' benefits, Head Start, and Supplemental Security Income (SSI) were the main ones.[36]

At an Urban Institute conference in 1984, Martin Anderson objected to the idea that the safety net was a serious policy commitment. He told the conference that

> Providing a safety net for those who cannot or are not expected to work was not really a social policy objective. The term *safety net* was used in the 1980 Republican platform and then adopted by the Office of Management and Budget to describe a set of social welfare programs that would not be closely examined in the first round of budget changes because of the fierce political pressures that made it impossible to even discuss these programs without invoking a torrent of passionate, often irrational, criticism. . . . The term safety net was political shorthand that only made sense for a limited period of time.[37]

Perhaps, but the safety net was emphasized in strong language in the documents announcing Reagan's budget package.[38] Most participants, and certainly the president, would agree with Anderson. But what they wanted is not as important as what they felt forced to do. The language of safety net expressed what most Americans accept about government social policy: People's lives should not be damaged through no fault of their own, due to hard luck or hard times. In fact, many key programs for the needy, like AFDC, were not in the net. Rather, it included those whose recipients were hardest to stigmatize—the elderly, the elderly sick, veterans, the handicapped—or had most political power. The safety net device did not increase the program's "fairness." Yet it was a major concession. One member of the administration saw the safety net as "a very important concept to have a hyper-conservative government commit to. Bear in mind that Reagan and his supporters feel that social security should be voluntary and medicare should not exist."

The overall package was biased against the working poor also because Stockman was blocked from attacking tax expenditures. Many things government does for the better-off people form exceptions to the tax code. The mortgage interest deduction, for example, is only useful to people who buy houses, and its value increases with the recipient's tax bracket. A number of other government programs provide services that only better-off citizens can use, for example, improvements of airports and traffic control serve people who own their own airplanes. In theory, government could charge a "user fee" for some of those services. Eliminating such tax preferences and increasing user fees were difficult because they involved Republican constituencies. Late in the game, however, Stockman made a run at them. Pressure from Martin Anderson, Pete Domenici, and others to increase the prospect of budget balance gave him his chance.[39] Stockman believed that, if accepted, the "Chapter Two" proposals would have "dramatized the underlying fairness and justice" of his program.[40]

Stockman boasted about Chapter Two to Greider, claiming budget pressure was allowing him to be more fair, to "force acquiescence in the last minute into a lot of things you would never see a Republican Administration propose." It was the same political theory the Democratic reconcilers had propounded in 1980. Greider was skeptical. Stockman reminded him that he had pledged secrecy. "If you tell your guys about this shit, I'll have 160 people calling the White House." The *Washington Post* reporter replied, "You will anyway."[41]

Phone calls were not necessary. On February 11 Stockman brought up the Chapter Two tax preference proposals for approval, beginning with reducing the oil depletion allowance. To Stockman, as for most liberals, there is hardly a better example in the federal government of a program justified only by the naked power of black gold. He was shocked and demoralized, therefore, by what transpired:

> All of a sudden, the President became animated. Our proposal unleashed a pent-up catechism on the virtues of the oil depletion allowance, followed by a lecture on how the whole idea of "tax expenditures" was a liberal myth.
> "The idea implies that the government owns all your income and has the right to decide what you can keep," said the President. "Well, we're not going to have any of that kind of thinking round here."[42]

Stockman retreated.

The tax side was at the heart of the fairness issue. For business interests and the better-off people, the benefits from tax reduction far outweighed any losses from spending cuts. The poor, who pay little or no taxes, got little from all the tax changes, even as they lost the benefits of government spending. Later analyses of the effect of Reagan's program continually showed both the poor losing and benefits increasing with income; an across-the-board rate reduction in a progressive tax system had to give the most to people with the highest incomes. And the tax cut was bigger than the spending cut. Ultimately, the "unfairness" of the Reagan program emerged, above all, from the original policy choice to reduce tax rates across-the-board.

The Defense Buildup

Another choice, essentially the president's preference, was his commitment to a huge defense buildup, no matter what the budgetary consequences. OMB never had much influence on defense matters in Republican administrations; all had relied on the office of the secretary to provide most review of the services' requests. Having so much else to worry about, Stockman told himself that Cap Weinberger, once established in office, would take his famous budget-cutting knife to the DOD: "I think Cap's going to be a pretty good mark over there," Stockman told Greider. "He's not a tool of the military-industrial complex."[43] Stockman misjudged both Weinberger and the president.

An exchange with Elizabeth Drew reveals Reagan's attitude in early 1980:

> *Drew:* I ask Reagan if he thinks we can regain military superiority over the Soviet Union. "Yes," *Reagan replies.* "I think the Soviet Union is probably at the very limit of its military output. It has already had to keep its people from having so many consumer goods. Instead, they're devoting it all to this military buildup. I think it's the greatest military buildup the world has ever seen. I think it tops what Hitler did. And therefore, when people talk about an arms race, this doesn't mean that the Soviet Union escalate to twice what they're doing now. We're the ones who have actually played along with the treaties and, if anything, actually reduced our weapons." He continues, "Now, what I think Russians would fear more than anything else is a United States that all of a sudden would hitch up our belt and say, 'OK, Buster, we've tried this other way. We are now going to build what is necessary to surpass you.' And this is the last thing they want from us, an arms race, because they are already running as fast as they can and we haven't started running."
>
> *Drew:* "Where are you going to get the money to pay for this military buildup?" *Ronald Reagan:* "Out of the economy."[44]

Unlike Carter, Reagan refused to subordinate the defense budget to fiscal policy.

Jimmy Carter's FY82 budget called for 5 percent real growth per year for five years. He also proposed a $6.3 billion supplemental for new (mainly inflation-related and pay) expenses for FY81. Many observers felt that Carter's request would be hard for Reagan to top. They were wrong. Reagan felt obliged to do significantly more. If Jimmy Carter wanted 5 percent, then that must not be enough.

Unfortunately "need" cannot be defined concretely. The formal DOD Planning, Programming and Budgeting System (PPBS) only encouraged the services to estimate need as broadly as possible in the planning and programming steps, leaving hard choices to the budget process. "No one knew in the Carter years what the real number would be," one DOD budgeter recalled, "but the general assumption was that the [planning figures] were never-never land."

Carter's final budget, even with 5 percent real growth, therefore proposed far less spending than his own administration's 1980 estimates of "need." The navy would get 121 new planes instead of 217; 80 ships over five years instead of 97. Some of these differences came from the military's special talent for inflation. An extreme example was the Phoenix missile: Carter's 1982 budget estimated that 72 could be purchased at almost the same cost projected for 210 a year before.[45] Moreover, there are large economies of scale in defense purchases.[46] Reagan's men argued that a much bigger buildup was more efficient and met a "need" already defined by the professional military.[47]

Weinberger relied on the services to define need, downgrading his central DOD staff. He entered office with a "fix-up" package designed during the transition largely by a cadre of people working for Senator John Tower, new chairman of Armed Services, including appointees Richard Allen (national security adviser), Fred Ikle (undersecretary of policy in the DOD), Edward Rowney (chief arms control negotiator), John Lehman (secretary of the Navy), and a few others. "When Weinberger took over," a participant recalled, "the report was complete, the services had it, and their submissions reflected those priorities." Stockman accepted not only the package but also, as his associate director for national defense, Dr. Bill Schneider, a former aide to Jack Kemp who was "totally plugged into" the Tower group. The package was mainly procurement increases on existing weapons, with a 3 percent supplemental increase for FY81; on that new base, it represented not a 5 but a 15 percent real increase in budget authority for FY82.

Instead of Jimmy Carter's $200.4 billion, DOD wanted $226.8 billion. And it was almost all in procurement, raised from $49.1 billion to $68.8 billion.[48] *Newsweek* described the result as "a gusher of cash that stunned even conservatives in Congress and quickly erased Secretary of Defense Weinberger's reputation as a ruthless enemy of fiscal excess." "Marveling at the display of largesse," a Pentagon official "joked that 'Cap the Knife' should be known henceforth as 'Cap the Shovel.' "[49]

The "get well" package was nice, but for its planning the Pentagon needed some sense of what to expect in later years. Stockman also needed long-term defense numbers because he needed to project budget balance in the future. On January 30, he, his defense deputy Bill Schneider, Weinberger, and Undersecretary Frank Carlucci met to work out some ballpark figures. The discussion assumed the get well package for FY82. Because the economic forecast was not ready, they bargained in terms of real growth; they would translate that into concrete dollar amounts when the forecast was done. Frank Carlucci said 8 or 9 percent was the minimum necessary. Stockman, who knew enough to want more than Carter's 5 percent and expected Martin Anderson, "a flinty anti-spender on everything," to "go off the deep end" if they took Carlucci's number, suggested they split the difference—7 percent. Weinberger shed a few crocodile tears. "In light of the disgraceful mess we're inheriting," he replied, "seven percent will be a pretty lean ration." Then he agreed, swallowing Stockman whole in the process.[50]

By his own account, Stockman missed the fact that 7 percent for the years after FY82, compounded upon the FY81 and FY82 increases, resulted in a 10 percent real growth rate per year from 1980 to 1986. Essentially, Stockman forgot to figure the first year into his calculations. The budget director not only didn't know he had been skinned, but he didn't realize that he and Weinberger were on opposite sides. Stockman thought he had agreed on "plug" numbers, but he anticipated that "Cap the Knife," once entrenched in the Pentagon, would find all sorts of fat to cut so those totals would never be met. Weinberger, however, saw a commitment to dollar figures that he could use ever after to justify requests. Not that he was opposed to finding "fat," but, if they found any, he and Carlucci figured they should be rewarded, allowing the savings to turn into more muscle.

Stockman Proposes and Reagan Disposes: The President's Program

With all the compromises, defense, and the forecast, Stockman knew and could tell his colleagues by February 7 that the package was coming up "short" by at least $30 or $40 billion. The budget director told himself that the shortfall was not so great a problem. Some more "cats and dogs" cuts could be found after February 18 (planned for release March 10). Beyond that point—well, the children's allowance theory might work: "I knew that the remaining $44 billion gap was huge. I remembered it was probably going to end up even larger, due to our cockeyed economic forecast. But I saw in this only the potential leverage it provided to . . . force Congress to shrink the welfare state."[51] For the moment he needed some way to downplay the gap. Stockman resorted to what Howard Baker was to call "the magic asterisk"[52]—"additional savings to be proposed later" of $29.8 billion in FY83 and about $44 billion in each following year.[53]

Anderson raised a red flag; he argued that, if the future-savings numbers were too big, they could "undermine the whole credibility of the program from day one."[54] His objections were not enough to cause much internal hesitation. The president expected his cabinet to find more "waste, fraud, and abuse." Stockman writes that no one asked the "essential political feasibility question: How many congressional horses do you need to cut $40 billion more—on top of the black book full of cuts already proposed? How many horses do we actually have?"[55] Feasibility, however, is not a radical's question. Reagan considered the status quo a full-fledged disaster. Not to try to enact his full package was, to Reagan, the same as abandoning the country to a terrible fate. If he didn't get it all, he would try again later. The less radical advisers suspected they would not get the whole tax cut anyway, so they did not believe the deficits would come true. Both the revolutionaries and the pragmatists therefore were willing to push the president's program as far as possible, seeing where they would came out.

Reagan announced his Economic Recovery Program on February 18. The administration was ready to announce savings of $34.8 billion. A further $6.7 billion was promised.[56] Foreign policy and defense were barely mentioned; the point was to rally support for solving the nation's economic problems.

Reagan tried to minimize the pain. Referring to "exaggerated and inaccurate stories" that social security was threatened, he declared:

> Those who through no fault of their own must depend on the rest of us, the poverty-stricken, the disabled, the elderly, all those with true need, can rest assured that the social safety net of programs they depend on are exempt from any cuts.
>
> The full retirement benefits of the more than 31 million social security recipients will be continued along with an annual cost of living increase. . . . All in all, nearly $216 billion worth of programs providing help for tens of millions of Americans will be fully funded.

Here was the commitment to social security that would come back to haunt the administration. "But Government," Reagan went on, "will not continue to subsidize individuals or particular business interests where real need cannot be demonstrated."

He proceeded to announce what would be cut. His list, from food stamps to NASA to the post office, must have impressed listeners with its scope. The documents released at the time of his speech listed eighty-three "major" program reductions. Some programs would be consolidated into block grants, with reduced funding; the added flexibility and reduced administrative costs to state and local governments would supposedly make up for the funding losses. Subsidies to business, justified as aids to development, would be reduced because business would develop better if it followed market incentives. Synfuels would be axed $3.2 billion, the Economic Development Administration would be shut down, and subsidized lending would be slimmed down in many agencies from the Export-Import Bank to the Farmers' Home Administration. Reagan highlighted the cuts to "profitable corporations" funded by the Export-Import Bank. Nutrition programs would be better targeted, he said, removing from eligibility "those who are not in real need or are abusing the program." Medicaid federal contributions would be "capped," and states encouraged to save costs in the program's management and provisions.

Having described his spending proposals, the president moved on to his tax program. He called for Kemp-Roth, with an effective starting date ("I had hoped we could be retroactive on this") of July 1. While it would "leave the taxpayers with $500 billion more in their pockets over the next five years," it was "actually only a reduction in the tax increases already built into the system." These increases included social security, bracket creep from inflation, and "windfall" taxes on oil.

The other part of the tax-cutting program would directly stimulate productivity through increasing depreciation allowances. Many other desirable and needed tax changes—indexing, the marriage penalty, tuition tax credits, estate taxes—would be requested at "the earliest date possible" after enacting the Kemp-Roth "10-10-10" of 10 percent individual cuts and the Jones-Conable "10-5-3" accelerated depreciation plan. That Reagan later matched Rostenkowski bid for bid should not have been a surprise.

In the balance of the speech, Reagan announced regulatory policy initiatives and the administration's full support for the Federal Reserve policy of monetary restraint. He concluded by invoking once more the urgency of the situation and the bankruptcy of the opposition: "Have they an alternative which offers a greater chance of balancing the budget, reducing and eliminating inflation, stimulating the creation of jobs and reducing the tax burden? And if they haven't, are they suggesting that we can continue on the present course without coming to a day of reckoning?" If the Democrats had such a plan, they would have a hard time articulating it without the "bully pulpit" of the presidency. In fact, they had no plan as yet; they had been waiting to see what the president would propose.

SIX

Gramm-Latta 1

The February 18 message impressed but did not please the Democrats. "They've put a giant-sized package together in 30 days," said Tip O'Neill. "Are there inequities? You can bet there are inequities." Democratic interest groups, particularly labor, minced no words: "It is a soak the poor and give it to the rich proposition," said Steelworkers' President Lloyd McBride; Albert Shanker of the American Federation of Teachers called the plan "Robin Hood in reverse."[1] Labor Department programs had been cut drastically, from $34.5 billion in the Carter budget to $26.7 billion. Nearly all the remaining activities of the department, in addition, would be directed by friends of business.[2]

Some Democratic intellectuals, however, approved many of the cuts. Stockman had harpooned many beasts, such as Impact Aid and dairy price supports, that budget analysts had been attacking for years. In an article that blasted many cuts as inequitable, the *New Republic* nevertheless agreed "that the present federal budget is full of fluff and waste and needless subsidy. . . . Those who hope for a greatly expanded government role, as well as those who want a greatly reduced one, should be happy to see the Republican administration clean up the Augean stable." Reagan's argument for better targeting a number of programs seemed right to many observers; Carter himself had tried to reduce the school lunch "middle-class subsidy." Many programs attacked—for example, CETA, EDA, and rent subsidies—were, in the *New Republic*'s words, "badly conceived, or redundant, or top-heavy with administration, or otherwise not cost-effective." For liberals the problems with those reductions was that "all of Reagan's proposed cuts, taken together, don't rationalize government largesse—they simply reduce it."[3] These reformers would have liked to replace those programs with something better.

The Democrats also sensed the public mood to cut spending; Senator

Pryor reported that his Arkansas constituents were even willing to see farm mortgage programs reduced.[4] Massachusetts liberal James Shannon found that his constituents largely believed that federal programs had benefited the undeserving poor at the expense of hard-working middle-class citizens.[5] Therefore, on February 20 when they replied to the president's speech on a television show, Democrats avoided a frontal attack on spending cuts. Jim Wright declared that Congress would support "refurbishing the nation's defenses, encouraging private investment to modernize America's industrial machinery, lifting the burden of unnecessary government regulation, cutting expenses, and restoring more local control over the schools"—in other words, "us too!"[6] Instead they attacked the tax cuts. Senator Gary Hart suggested a one-year trial for the plan; and Chiles declared that it would be no favor to send the taxpayers "a tax refund written in red ink."[7]

Early in March Senate Minority Whip Alan Cranston summarized the Democrats' options:

> 1) give [Reagan] everything he wants, on the theory it will prove disastrous and the Democrats then would benefit politically from Reagan's failure; 2) propose a complex substitute for the Reagan package; 3) give Reagan most of what he wants, but fight tenaciously against the worst of his cuts. Cranston dismisses the first as "irresponsible," the second as impractical and "not politically bright," which leaves him with the third.[8]

Throughout this period there were rumors that the Democrats would take the first approach—roll over, play dead, and hope for the best. But that made little sense. If they wanted Reagan to get the blame for failure, Democrats would have to oppose him. There was no way to vote secretly.

The first test of Democratic strategy came in March, when the Senate Budget Committee reported out reconciliation instructions before a budget resolution, as a way of locking in support for spending cuts. Democrats submitted a blizzard of amendments; they all failed. Baker and Domenici attained virtually unanimous Republican support on every key vote. In the face of this unprecedented GOP unity, Democrats had little hope of winning. Yet they were handicapped further by their own divisions.

A GOP aide recalled that "there were individual [Republican] defections. But there was a hell of a lot of reliance on conservative Democrats to make up for them. . . . You knew you would lose Hatfield on defense, but you got Stennis and Nunn." The package was designed to appeal to the southerners; as another put it: "Sure, we wouldn't screw with TVA, Impact Aid, farm programs; we wouldn't cut a lot out of dams—Bennett (Johnston) was ranking minority on Energy and Water. Tennessee-Tombigbee, Clinch River—we had our eyes open, we knew what we had to do." All the Senate Democratic Policy Committee could do was keep a list of embarrassing votes for campaign use.[9]

Back in the House, Jones kept trying to assemble a plan that could unite the party. Stockman, who watched Jones through the eyes of new Budget Committee member Gramm, was impressed by Jones's performance.[10] The new Budget chairman, however, had trouble with his own party. Much of the leadership still distrusted him. Jones's personal style did not help; one experienced staffer commented that Jones "was pretty good at communicating with people but not good at making people *feel* they'd been communicated with." This perception was shown in another aide's comment that "the problem with Jones was, he held things tight to his vest. You never knew what he was going to do."

Yet Jones was heading in the same direction as two groups of his colleagues who were drafting their own proposals. These two groups— the 1980 Mineta, Panetta, Wirth, and Gephardt "Gang of Four," and liberals Steven Solarz and Thomas Downey of New York, Paul Simon of Illinois, and Les Aspin of Wisconsin—merged, worked out a detailed scheme, and then arranged to meet with Jones. At that meeting on April 2, the participants discovered their proposals were quite similar. A centrist Democratic consensus was forming.[11]

A Pause for Public Opinion

As they looked at policy to see what they could bear to concede, the Democrats watched public opinion to see what they would have to concede. The polls showed some support for the Democrats' skepticism about the tax cut. A CBS/*New York Times* poll taken in late January pictured the public more interested in budget balance than a tax cut by an overwhelming 70 percent to 23 percent margin. Respondents (52 percent) preferred a smaller tax cut to either a larger one (24 percent) or none at all (16 percent). As many as 61 percent of respondents wanted to spend more on defense, but a *Time* poll taken a little earlier showed respondents doubtful that tax cuts and defense hikes could be combined with a balanced budget; when forced to choose, respondents preferred budget balance. Both polls evinced little enthusiasm for any spending cuts save welfare.[12]

Legislators had other barometers of opinion; Reagan's speeches generated a flood of mail to Congress that, combined with their own soundings back home, made them leery of opposing him. The Speaker reported that his mail and his constituents showed strong support for Reagan. But, as time passed, the margin of support in letters and from constituents diminished.

Opinion soundings told a mixed story about Reagan's own popularity, which is what mattered if the issue were posed as for or against the president. He was quite popular, but not by the standards of new presidents. A Gallup poll showed Reagan's disapproval rating of 24 percent to be far higher than for any other president at a similar period; his 59 percent approval, moreover, was lower than that for any previous new administration.[13] Reagan's pollster, Richard Wirthlin, concluded that people were polarizing, with a strong majority favorable to the plan.

Through most of the winter Speaker O'Neill was relatively quiet. He didn't want his party to seem to be obstructing the new administration, but he did encourage hearings on the budget proposals to focus attention on their consequences. Majority leader Wright took a more public stance against the Economic Recovery Program, but he also wanted to have it both ways: accepting budget restraint but criticizing specific cuts. Some liberal Democrats saw in the Speaker's quiet and in Wright's and Jones's compromise positions "a timid leadership and a runaway Budget Committee chairman determined to sell us out in the false hope of gaining conservative votes."[14] They would criticize the leaders throughout the battles of 1981 for not allowing the chips to fall where they may. Tip O'Neill cared too much about programs not to try to save some, but knew he couldn't save them all. And so he temporized, partly due to the lingering shock of the election and partly out of a political veteran's sense that, in politics, timing is everything. Anti-Reagan trends had to be nursed, not assumed. Why not see what Jones could do?

On March 12 Jim Wright, citing poll data, wrote to his Democratic colleagues: Reagan did not really have a mandate for the policies he was proposing; the Reagan plan imposed "a grossly unfair burden on those least able to carry that burden, those Mr. Reagan describes as the 'truly needy' "; and "the people want Congress to be cooperative. They do not want it to be supine."[15] By the end of March, Democrats were rallying around the idea of a comprehensive budget alternative that would reduce the deficit by reducing the tax cut, cut spending but protect some social programs. On April 6 Jones unveiled his plan, which was supported by the double quartet of members who had been working separately on their own plans. The rationale for the alternative came two days later in a Statement on Economic Matters adopted by the House Democratic Caucus.

"For half a century," the caucus statement declared, "the Democratic Party has been an engine of equity and progress in America. . . . The Democratic Party has seen our American government not as an enemy, not as 'the problem,' as President Reagan said it was in his Inaugural Address, but as a necessary instrument for achieving vital public goals." Although inflation had many causes, Democrats argued that reducing spending would help and would also bring down interest rates. They accepted the need for lowering taxes raised by inflation bracket creep, but they would not "join in any program of fiscal control that puts the main burden of fighting inflation on the backs of middle- and low-income workers [through spending cuts] while providing unprecedented benefits for the privileged few [through tax cuts]." The tax program, they argued, "is inflationary because it will stimulate demand before supply, creating enormous deficits in the process." They wanted to stimulate investment but did not trust the holders of capital; they therefore wanted business tax cuts to be more strictly targeted than in the 10–5–3 plan. They justified individual program cuts as helping curtail inflation, not as freeing market forces. The caucus statement made clear that the ultimate stake of the battle, the point where conservative Democrats like Jones and moderates like Gephardt most differed from Reagan, was the role of government. Throughout American history, "private enterprise has been strengthened, rather that hindered, by government-aided research and development, development of basic transportation facilities, and aid to small business, urban areas, and farmers."[16]

The missing piece was willingness to attack Ronald Reagan head-on. As events turned slightly in their favor in March, Democratic leaders gained confidence. The Speaker, deciding it was time to take the gloves off, scheduled a major attack in a speech before the AFL-CIO Building and Construction Trades Council, which met the week of March 30. But it didn't happen.[17]

The president spoke to the Council on March 30. As Reagan left the Washington Hilton that afternoon, a young man named John W. Hinckley, Jr., emerged from the crowd, pulled a pistol, and began firing. Once again, violence slashed into our political body, as with John and Robert Kennedy, Martin Luther King, Jr., and George Wallace. But this time the victim lived; and, unlike George Wallace, Reagan emerged from his ordeal, not hobbled, but larger than life. The nation held its breath, and Speaker O'Neill cancelled his speech.

A mad gunman, as the courts concluded, came within an inch of ending the Reagan revolution. Hinckley's story and his motives need not concern us here. The assassination attempt alone serves to remind us of the tenuousness of history. The scene was confusion; the president himself did not know that he had been shot, though he was in "paralyzing pain." Three unintended victims were seriously wounded—Secret Service Agent Tim McCarthy, patrolman Thomas Delahanty, and White House Press Secretary James Brady. Both the operation to remove the bullet from the president's lung and the subsequent recovery period were far more dangerous than the White House let on.[18] The president and his staff worked to paint a picture of stability and strength; hints of confusion and weakness, it was feared, would encourage challenge overseas. They did not want to lose the initiative in their fight to change American government.

To demonstrate that the president and his administration were still in charge, Baker, Meese, and Deaver (on April 1, the morning after the shooting and the three-hour operation) brought Reagan the dairy price-support freeze legislation. "Hi, fellas," greeted the president, "I knew it would be too much to hope that we could skip a staff meeting."[19] He shakily signed the legislation.

Reagan used humor to reassure himself and those around him; his staff, and doctors, relayed his jokes to the general public for the same reason. "Please tell me you're Republicans," he quipped to the surgeons as he was being wheeled to the operating room; when told by Lyn Nofziger that the government was running normally, he responded, "What makes you think I'd be happy about that?"[20]

The shooting, and his brave reaction to it, garnered Reagan an extra dose of not just sympathy but also respect and awe. At a time when the polls showed his popularity beginning to slide, he received a new wave of personal support. This was not just a movie-star president but a heroic president. His pollster concluded that the event made a permanent impression on the public, creating a reservoir of good will that would go on protecting him even when his policies were controversial.[21]

As Reagan convalesced, his administration's lobbying effort had to slow, for its most effective lobbyist had to take it easy. His opponents were equally disarrayed because it would be bad form to attack a recuperating president. A muted tone would not help the Democrats rally their supporters.

The Republicans: Some Victories, Some Doubts

In some ways it is easier to understand the Democrats in 1981 than the Republicans. The Democrats fought in the open, as is their wont. Most Republican maneuvering went on behind the scenes.

Howard Baker called the whole program a "riverboat gamble." At a luncheon meeting at the *Post* on January 7, Senate Finance Chairman Robert Dole presented not Kemp-Roth but instead the much more limited previous year's Finance Committee bill. Dole said it was his job to guide the Reagan program through the Senate, but he doubted that it would survive undiluted. Around the same time Barber Conable, ranking Republican on Ways and Means, was saying "I don't think for a minute that if the president proposes a flat-rate cut, Congress will agree. Congressmen have other measures, the cost of which will be a trade-off against the tax cuts."[22] He was right about "other measures," wrong about the tradeoff.[23]

The lobbyists were not about to wait for a second bill. As one of them put it, "the judgment around here is that there won't be a second bill or that it won't move in Congress. We're going to have to make every effort to get onto that first bill."[24]

The president was very sure of his position. A presidential adviser recalled:

> You look at all the stories being published about backing and filling and they give the impression that Reagan was changing back and forth. That's wrong. The people around him were changing, or some of us were. We were having doubts, and the news coverage reflected that. Reagan hardly moved at all. At one meeting [in January] Reagan got a little impatient with us. He said, "Listen, you guys are talking to each other and no one is asking me what I think. I'm sticking with it [the 10-10-10 approach]."[25]

Republican economists were divided over the merits of the emerging package, but former Federal Reserve Chairman Arthur Burns was unusual in saying that "if I were an economic czar there would be no personal income tax cuts at all this year. We need to be very cautious about adding to the swollen budget deficits that are already in prospect."[26] No one really knew how the markets would react to the tax cuts; most preferred not to attack their own side.[27]

Republican politicians, even more than economists, hesitated to criticize the new administration.[28] This was their chance to govern; criticism was aid to the other side. Members of the administration like Darman and Baker, with backgrounds in other wings of the Republican party, had to show their loyalty to conservative ideals. Dole and Baker were in a similar spot, having both lost the nomination to Reagan; if they were critical, they could be suspected of trying to make the president look bad.[29]

The remarkable unity of Senate Republicans throughout 1981 resulted both from this desire to govern and careful efforts by the administration and Howard Baker to nurture the notion that they were all working together. In December Baker gathered Stockman, Regan, Jim Baker, Anderson, Dole, Hatfield (chairman of Appropriations), Domenici, and Jake Garn (chairman of Banking) to begin working out the program and strategy. Baker met with Reagan two or three times a week, and the White House lobbying staff was instructed to defer to his wishes. Every Tuesday Baker met with the Senate's committee heads, coaxing them toward unity. Although some Republicans had doubts, Senate Majority Whip Ted Stevens reported, they agreed to maintain public silence "because we realize that if one Senator tries to break down an agreement, then the others will do so."[30] Consultation and unity were enhanced by the fact that Reagan was loyal to his troops as well. When Baker announced on March 26 that the executive committee of the Senate Republican Policy Committee had agreed to postpone considering "social issues" to 1982, he was blasted by the New Right. Reagan immediately told the *Post* that he agreed with the decision.[31]

Unity was easier on spending cuts than on tax cuts because, to a certain point, spending cuts fit both the Republicans' preferences and all politicians' perception of the public mood. Thus, *Newsweek* reported "private agonizing" by the nation's governors at their national conference but, by 36 to 2, they announced they were "prepared to accept budget cuts."[32]

An even better example of the mood came when Congress in March froze the price support for dairy products, preventing a scheduled increase worth $147 million in FY81 and $1.1 billion for FY82. There is a lot of money in milk, and it flows both ways, from Congress and to Congress. When Agriculture Committee Democrats in the Senate caucused about the issue, they began by talking about how to kill the proposed cuts but were soon discussing how bad it would look to be on the wrong side. "I would have found it very difficult," said David Pryor of Arkansas, "to vote for that particular program and then go home over the weekend and give speeches about the need to cut spending."

The Senate Budget Committee's maneuver in reconciling first, before a budget resolution, was designed to maximize both unity and spending cuts. It also seemed to accommodate the need to demonstrate spending reductions so that the tax cut would look more plausible. In SBC and floor action through March and into early April, the strategy seemed to succeed brilliantly. Republican unity on the Senate floor was overwhelming. Yet not all was as it seemed.

The most dramatic event went unreported until much later. Both protagonists have written about it. David Stockman writes,

> A warm fire was crackling in Howard Baker's office, when we arrived at 9:30 a.m. on March 17. The Senate Republican leadership and Budget Committee members were already assembled. . . . Reagan led off with an Irish joke, and the meeting got down to business: their proposal to attack nearly one quarter of a trillion dollars in indexed pensions, affecting roughly 36 million Americans.[33]

In defiance of Stockman's plan, Domenici and his GOP allies had decided to attack the COLAs. As honest budgeters, interested not in policy revolution but in restraining spending per se, Domenici, his staff, and Democrats like Hollings and Chiles believed that spending control had to include a diet COLA. Domenici told of the incident in an op-ed piece for the *Washington Post* on January 21, 1986. Its title, "Ghosts of Deficit Forever," conjures up Dickens's *Christmas Carol*. The scene in Howard Baker's chamber is the last revealed to the guilty politicians by the Ghost of Budgets Past. The end, revealed by the Ghost of Budgets Future, is collapse under Gramm-Rudman-Hollings. That should give the flavor of how Domenici felt about the scene he described:

> The president leans across the table and tells the 12 Republican members of the Senate Budget Committee that he will not support a bipartisan attempt in that committee to freeze cost-of-living adjustments for Social Security recipients as part of a deficit-reduction plan. He asks them to join his opposing effort. In front of the senators is a sheet showing savings from a one-year freeze on the COLAs—$88 billion over five years, and more than $24 billion in the year 1986 alone.
>
> The senators relent. They go back to committee and vote against the move to freeze the COLAs. Social security, although larger than all domestic non-entitlement spending programs put together, is protected in future budget battles; it comprises almost 25 percent of the non-interest spending in the federal budget.

Jim Baker did not think Republicans could ever touch social security; Howard Baker had helped arrange this meeting as a way of slowing down Domenici and his troops. The president told the group, "I promised I wouldn't touch Social Security. We just can't get suckered into it. The other side's waiting to pounce."[34] Stockman writes that the senators wanted to cut the COLA so they could put money back into other programs. That ascribes to the senators a quite remarkable lack of political acumen.[35] Rather, the meeting on March 17 became part of the long-term price of 1981, grounds for resentment and recriminations when the deficit blew up.

Republicans Shot Down

Besides social security, Senate Budget Republicans attempted and made only a few changes in the administration's domestic cuts. On the Senate floor, the major test of unity occurred on March 31.

Five veteran Republican senators were a liberal remnant within their party. Those senators were Charles Mathias of Maryland, John Chafee of Rhode Island, Lowell Weicker of Connecticut, Robert Stafford of Vermont, and Mark Hatfield of Oregon, who as the new chairman of Appropriations was really on the hot seat. At Mathias's instigation, the group began meeting regularly soon after the election. All were longtime party loyalists, but all had ideological and constituency problems with the administration. They hoped to use their pivotal position, given their party's slim Senate margin, to moderate policies. None had any relations with Reagan, but all five were close to Howard Baker and wanted to help him control the Senate.

Torn between party and belief, Hatfield and company faced the blizzard of Democratic amendments. An aide recalls that it was

> this Draconian thing. There was a Metzenbaum amendment on child vaccines, all sorts of terrible votes. They were all "people" sort of votes, like AFDC, and the Republicans all in lockstep were voting them down. Chafee, Stafford and Weicker were all up in 82 and they got very nervous. Their advisors were saying, "These are your constituents, they elected you in the past, you're taking this Republican stuff too far!"

Chafee decided to offer an amendment restoring funds for programs of particular interest to northerners and urbanites, such as home heating assistance, Urban Mass Transit, Urban Development Action Grants, and education funding. Because the increase in the deficit would be limited to just that package, the administration would be protected; moderates could use the Chafee amendment as evidence that they were representing their constituents and to excuse voting against all the Democratic changes.

Greider reports that "Stockman had no objection. The amendment wouldn't cost much overall, and it would 'take care of those people who have been good soldiers.' "[36] But if Stockman did not really mind, other Republicans did. At the least, the administration's opposition was muted, and Domenici seemed willing to go along. Then Domenici decided to try to beat the amendment. Putting a little back into the basic package "made it easier" for fence-sitting moderate Republicans. As a symbol of the vote's importance, Vice President Bush was in the Senate chair if necessary to break a tie.

Chafee lost 40 to 59. Majority Whip Ted Stevens of Alaska admitted he was voting against Chafee reluctantly, adding that "many of us have been saying no not only to programs we supported in the past, but sometimes to programs we initiated."[37] Eleven Republicans still stood up for Chafee. Hatfield, as a member of the leadership, could not join his "Gang of Five" colleagues; but John Heinz and Arlen Specter (Pa.), William Cohen (Maine), David Durenberger (Minn.), Mark Andrews (N.D.), John Danforth (Mo.), and Charles Percy (Ill.) joined Stafford, Weicker, Mathias, and Chafee. Those Republicans, however, were more than balanced by the seventeen mostly southern Democrats who opposed the amendment.

The Chafee failure showed there would be no coalition of moderate Democrats and liberal Republicans. "Chafee was the one shot we had at making inroads," said Chris Dodd (D-Conn.). "When that failed, any hope of making additional inroads went out the window."[38] The vote also dramatized the situation of the northern "gypsy moth" Republicans of the House and Senate.

Moths, Weevils, and the Unexpected

Any plan that slashes domestic and increases defense spending is necessarily biased against the Northeast and the Midwest. The military and its contractors flock to the sun; but old, decaying industry lives near the great water sources of the North, especially the Great Lakes states. Also, northern Republicans come from a different ideological tradition than did Reaganites: a Protestant activism that Daniel Elazar has called a moralistic or "commonwealth" view of society.[39]

The commonwealth ideology gave rise to movements of conservation and government reform that reflect a hierarchical view of noblesse oblige and proper procedure. Leaders in society have special obligations to give back—to sacrifice for the whole.[40] Ronald Reagan's radical individualism was not congenial to those who believed in a nurturing role for government. Nevertheless, these gypsy moths fundamentally were defenders of authority, uncomfortable with the Democrats' egalitarianism. Trapped between their policy preferences and their identity as Republicans, they were particularly susceptible to appeals for preserving the party's ability to govern.

The Chafee vote showed that, in the Senate, where representation by state favors the South and the West, gypsy moths could not find enough Democratic allies to triumph on the floor. In the House, however, they could tip the balance. There were about half as many Republican gypsy moths as Democratic boll weevils (the other set of potential defectors)—just enough, between the groups, to balance almost perfectly the two sides. In general, the gypsy moths ran well ahead of Reagan in their districts. If they were to be pulled toward the administration, therefore, the attraction would be less electoral incentives, although they might worry about their financial backers and party organizations, but more desire either to be part of a governing team or to avoid being one of a few Republicans who had handcuffed a new president of their own party.

In the early months of maneuvering, the moths, like the rest of their Republican colleagues in the House, had little to do. They had to wait to see the Reagan package, but then they also had to wait to see what alternative Representative Jones would devise. The stage was set for the battle over the first budget resolution.

NUMBERS AND PRIORITIES

The Democratic package included many of Stockman's major cuts but revised some others. On the average, Jones cut social programs by only 10 to 12 percent, instead of the administration's 25 percent plan. EDA and Legal Services were saved. Food stamps would decline by $950 million instead of $1.6 billion. Child nutrition programs would lose $1 billion instead of $2 billion. Medicaid payments would not be "capped" (i.e., limiting federal spending that meant kicking the problem back to the states); they were estimated at $1.15 billion higher than in the Reagan plan.

Jones had tried to win administration support for his package. He had negotiated with Stockman throughout February and March, and, just before announcing their package, Jones and Leon Panetta met with the budget director one more time. Jones thought he was giving Stockman about 85 percent of what he had asked for. But Stockman objected particularly to their efforts to protect low-income programs like medicaid; he saw reducing those welfare-state programs as a matter of principle. Democrats felt the same about maintaining them, and Jones knew even his party's budget balancers could not accept Stockman's cuts.

Jones produced lower deficits with smaller social cuts by shaving the defense buildup and allowing a smaller tax cut. Some of his other moves were more questionable. He "saved" $1.5 billion by assuming that the government would borrow funds to fill the Strategic Petroleum Reserve (off-budget)—not absurd because the oil would be an asset but not really a spending reduction either. Across-the-board administrative savings would yield $4.8 billion, a device by which Jones essentially spread out costs that Stockman had targeted on specific programs, without explaining what was really supposed to change. Another $1.3 billion would be recovered from oil companies, supposedly in actions against them for various price infractions. Again this was not absurd, but, given delays in the court system, it was doubtful.[41] After a few revisions in committee, the reduced FY82 tax cut and other new savings left Jones with a deficit of $25.6 billion, compared to the administration's $45 billion.

Many observers agreed with Jones that the HBC resolution gave Reagan most of what he wanted; it was adopted by a 17 to 13 vote on April 16, as boll weevil Gramm voted with the Republicans. "A bemused Republican staffer in the House probably put it best: 'We are being dragged kicking and screaming to victory.'"[42] The administration disagreed. Stockman objected not only to where Jones made cuts and their amount but to how. Democrats were allowing only $18 billion in savings through the reconciliation process; the rest would be done in appropriations. The Senate had assumed $36.9 billion in reconciliation savings. Undoing cuts from reconciliation would require new authorizations, which the president could fairly easily veto. By contrast, reductions through appropriations would occur through thirteen separate bills over a period of many months, and those appropriations could change the following year when support for cuts might diminish.[43]

Although many Democrats, especially authorizing chairmen, still disliked reconciliation, Jones, backed by his committee, had the Speaker's support for using the process again.[44] Jones was not willing to reconcile authorizations (i.e., reduce them to fit within a resolution) when savings in appropriations were technically plausible; reconciliation, in his view, was to be used for entitlements.[45] The Republican insistence on reconciling discretionary program authorizations, therefore, also raised an issue of congressional procedure that left much bad feeling in 1981, recurring in later years.

HBC reported out its budget shortly before Congress adjourned for Easter recess. Jones wanted to push his budget to the House floor immediately, exploiting its lower deficit to appeal to the boll weevil Democrats. The weevils would have been less influenced by the pro-Reagan campaigns whipped up in their districts over the recess. The still shaky Democratic leadership, however, had too little confidence in either Jones or their own control of the House to push events forward. The Republicans, therefore, had the rest of April to lobby while revising their own package.

As Stockman and Gramm worked on the House boll weevils, the administration suddenly ran into trouble in the Senate. On April 9, Republicans William Armstrong of Colorado, Charles Grassley of Iowa, and Steven Symms of Idaho defected from their party and joined the Democrats in voting down Domenici's proposed budget resolution. Apparently, Senator Hollings had been right back in 1980; arrived on the shores of leadership, "pilgrim Armstrong" was not so happy with the way his party was carving the turkey.

Domenici refused to put Stockman's magic asterisk of unspecified savings in his draft resolution and also adopted more realistic interest rate assumptions than the administration had employed. These blows for a more honest budget caused the Reagan plan's FY84 balance to disappear, replaced in Domenici's estimate by deficits of $40 to $50 billion per year from FY82 to FY84.[46] All three conservatives had campaigned for office pledging to balance the budget, and Domenici was saying it wasn't true. Armstrong could not accept that—"I'm so committed to a balanced budget," he declared, "that I am prepared to vote against the defense budget, which I've never done before, and against water projects, something no Senator from Colorado has done in 80 years." Domenici called the vote "ridiculous," "more pathetic than serious."[47]

Although it looked like the disagreement was between the three defectors and their chairman, the real conflict was between Domenici, representing the doubts of Senate Republicans, and the administration. Domenici was focusing attention on the fact that the administration's program did not add up. He rejected "unspecified" savings on the ground that, without knowing where savings would come from, the committee could not project totals for each budget function (e.g., national defense) in FY83 and FY84.

Domenici, however, was in an impossible position. He wanted to use other Republican senators to force the administration to see the light. But if the administration persisted in making its entire plan a test of party loyalty, then the contest became Pete Domenici, a rogue (if correct) Budget chairman, against his president for the support of other senators. Presidents have more weapons in such a fight than do budget chairmen. Domenici's vote alone, of course, might beat the president's plan in the narrowly split (12 to 10) Budget Committee. Yet that would make Domenici the Republican who busted Ronald Reagan's presidency before it had gotten going, and Domenici could not do that. He really needed the administration to flinch, but neither Reagan nor Stockman would. Instead Stockman urged the *Wall Street Journal,* in a scathing editorial, to place all the blame on the Budget chairman,[48] and the administration's heavy guns began targeting Domenici and the defectors.

Howard Baker had already decided weeks before, in a meeting of Senate and White House leaders, that the only reasonable solution to the "future savings" conflict was to punt—and hope the ball never came down.[49]

When the administration refused to blink, Domenici was forced to retreat, devising a set of changes that looked like progress compared to the package that had been voted down (so Armstrong and company could save face) while not really changing anything. He reestimated the outlays created by the assumed budget authority; projected a one percent saving from the ever-popular waste, fraud, and abuse; and with a few other maneuvers, ended up with a smaller magic asterisk of about $15.3 billion in FY83 and $27.7 billion in FY84. Whether because they were satisfied by this rather questionable adjustment or because they had nowhere else to go, Armstrong, Grassley, and Symms returned to the fold on April 18, joined by Democrats Chiles, Johnston, and Sasser.[50]

Domenici did win one victory, though of dubious meaning. Hollings's proposal to include a COLA freeze in reconciliation had been defeated by the committee Republicans after their fateful meeting with the president, but now he moved that the budget resolution assume that COLAs, including social security, would be delayed from July to October and set at the lesser of the increase in wages or prices. Domenici and six Republicans joined Hollings, and the proposal passed 9 to 8. Because the reconciliation had already been passed, the COLA change had little chance of being implemented unless the House adopted it; this may explain the lack of outcry from lobbies for the elderly.

After these glitches, the administration's package emerged safely from

Senate Budget. Lockstep Republican votes for reconciliation left little doubt that the resolution would pass the Senate. The situation on the House floor was much more unpredictable.

Stockman and his friend Phil Gramm reduced their deficit by adopting some of Jones's tricks, such as moving the Strategic Petroleum Reserve off-budget, making general "waste" reductions, and collecting penalty money from those overcharging oil companies. They also added back some money for programs favored by southerners. Extra funds for V. A. hospitals, for example, were the price for the support of Veterans Affairs chairman G. V. "Sonny" Montgomery of Mississippi, a boll weevil leader of greater stature and respectability than either Gramm or Conservative Democratic Forum (CDF) organizer Charles Stenholm (D-Tex.).[51] It is easier to defect when one's elders are doing so. The new package, cosponsored by Gramm and GOP Budget Committee leader Delbert Latta (thus "Gramm-Latta") shaved $6.7 billion more from the deficit.

Stockman and Gramm's new adjustment made their package more attractive to the boll weevils but did little to help the gypsy moths. The moths organized, as one of their leaders, S. William Green (R-N.Y.) put it, "to work for our regional interests within the context of our overall desire to restrain the growth in federal spending."[52] The Northeast/Midwest coalition, a bipartisan caucus whose vice chairman was Carl Pursell (R-Mich.), led in criticizing regional consequences of the economic plan. "We always seem to be selling out Northeast interests and Midwest interests to pick up southern Democratic votes," Bill Green declared. Stockman worked to reassure the gypsy moths as cheaply as possible.[53]

While his members went home to meet the voters during Easter recess, Tip O'Neill went to Australia and New Zealand. A number of Democrats thought that in doing so he made "a very serious mistake of political judgment," as James Oberstar put it. Another midwesterner maintained that "we had the momentum going for our budget when we went into recess. Then Tip goes off on a junket for two weeks. Meanwhile the White House is at work, they put on a real campaign, and we had only a half-baked effort."[54] It was not clear, however, exactly what the House leadership was supposed to do while most members were back home. They had already played their best cards, committee assignments, and they would be of no help with the gypsy moths. The leadership's main tools were appealing to party loyalty and shifting provisions in the package, but neither was possible while everybody was out of town.

When the Democrats returned from their recess, Foley told the Speaker they were fifty to sixty votes short. O'Neill groaned that "only the Lord himself could save this one," and another Democrat declared,

"We're going to get the crap kicked out of us." To O'Neill, the difficulty was not *his* trip but rather the other members' trips back home. "The President had overwhelming support," he said, "and that's what the members found out."[55]

The evidence suggests that O'Neill was right. One summary found that the messages in the districts were conflicting, but these were the liberal districts. When a Massachusetts representative has heavy district pressure for a conservative program, that program is likely to be pretty popular overall.[56] The polls in late April revealed strong support for the president's policy. Reagan's popularity had surged after the assassination attempt; now CBS/*New York Times* showed his spending proposal favored by 35 percent to 14 percent and his tax proposal approved by 37 percent to 11 percent. (More had no opinion, which should give us pause.) Even more than half of the 38 percent of the responders who expected to be hurt personally approved of Reagan's performance as president.[57] An Associated Press/NBC survey found respondents disagreeing (54 percent to 36 percent) with the proposition that the spending cuts were too drastic. In a separate question, 20 percent thought they did not go far enough.[58] In short, a substantial minority of the population disliked Reagan's proposals, which helps explain his relatively high disapproval in polls cited above, but a substantial majority liked the program.

By mobilizing constituents directly (including lobbyists contacting campaign contributors to ask them to pressure waverers) and by appealing to the public in a speech to a joint session of Congress on April 28, the president's strategy kept the pressure on at home. The president also continued a soft-sell approach to both weevils and moths, meeting with small groups and, without giving away anything, trying to put them at ease with his program.

Carroll Hubbard (D-Ky.), a representative since 1975, was one object of this attention. He was invited to a state dinner for the prime minister of Japan, scheduled a day after the budget resolution vote, making it embarrassing to vote against his host. Jimmy Carter had never done that sort of thing. Hubbard was "wooed with phone calls from the President, box seats at the Kennedy Center for the Performing Arts, and a steady parade of White House lobbyists bringing one clear message: The President is too popular in your district for you to vote against him."[59] "I sincerely believe," Hubbard told the *Times,* "that if the President's program is adopted there will be much unhappiness across the nation in a few months." But even with these beliefs and a district that supported Jimmy Carter in 1980, Hubbard hesitated. His constituents, he reckoned, "have serious doubts about the Democratic Party in 1981. They think the Republicans are more serious about fiscal restraint and balancing the federal budget. . . . I have solid citizens calling me up and saying, 'We've tried everything else, let's try something new, vote with the President.' "⁶⁰

Hubbard ultimately stuck with the Jones resolution, but most of his southern colleagues did not. Secretary of the Treasury Donald Regan assured waverers that a vote for the new "Gramm-Latta" package's large spending reductions did not commit them to its three-year across-the-board tax cuts. Budget resolutions set a floor for revenues, not a ceiling. The administration was telling southerners they could have their cake and eat it too: support a popular president, yet preserve your option on the tax cut. "If we get them to the first plateau," Regan said, "we'll just let them sit there. Then we'll try to go to the next plateau."⁶¹

The administration also tried to make defection easier for boll weevils by presenting the Reagan plan as bipartisan. Gramm was the first sponsor of "Gramm-Latta," which reflected his actual role. With a Democratic first sponsor, the administration could claim that *its* plan was bipartisan while Jones's plan, without Republican sponsorship, was a party document—a disadvantage because most Americans, unlike political scientists, consider partisanship a synonym for divisiveness and other bad things. Delbert Latta, in his twelfth term in the House, found deference to second-term member Gramm difficult. After lengthy negotiations, George Bush called Latta and told him the president was relying on his cooperation.⁶² Some southern Republicans wanted the issue joined in a more partisan manner to force the weevils either explicitly to endorse the Republican plan or to defy the president. Ed Bethune of Arkansas felt that drawing the line would increase his party's chances of carrying the South in 1982. Stockman, however, was gambling for policy control; building up the southern GOP was not his concern.

That left the gypsy moths. Lobbying these Republicans, the Administration used the same kind of arguments as it had with the boll weevils: Yes, you may not like everything here, but it's just the first step. It can be fixed later, but if the president's beaten now and you're the ones who beat him, you get the blame, and no change from the status quo will be possible. The gypsy moths, however, objected to different parts of the package, especially the defense buildup. Representative Bill Green reports that, whenever he told Stockman the defense numbers were too high, the budget director replied that they certainly were but he viewed them as a reserve. They could be pared later to pay for a natural disaster like Mount St. Helens or an unnatural disaster such as continued high interest rates.⁶³ Stockman reports that "between thirty and fifty 'soft' Republicans" badgered Bob Michel to restore various cuts. Finally Michel exploded: "Geeminie Christmas! When are you guys going to recognize that this is only a budget resolution? It doesn't cut anything! It's all assumptions! If you've got problems, write 'em down and send 'em to me. We'll take care of them later!"[64]

In 1981 the budget resolution, furthest from policy substance, was the vote most easily presented as, Are you for or against the president? Therefore, the most important and dramatic act of the budget resolution campaign was the president's speech on April 28. Although a third speech on the same subject in three months was a bit much, House leaders could not refuse this platform to the wounded president.

In his first formal appearance since the assassination attempt, Reagan spoke to a joint session of Congress. A "senior White House aide" commented:

> Normally you have the idea that a new President has an open window for just so long and it shuts very quickly in terms of public interest and support. But the shooting incident and the way the President handled it, the character he showed, has reopened the window and given him a second opportunity. Tonight the country was watching again to see how he looked, what his voice sounded like, how he handled himself and what he had to say.[65]

Ronald Reagan looked ruddy and vigorous, sounded slightly hoarse, and received, in Robert Michel's words, "the kind of reception that makes a few of the waverers feel, Gosh, how can I buck that?"[66] He received two standing ovations before he even began to speak. When he spoke, he surrounded some of the same material contained in his first two speeches—statistics about the nation's economic plight, assertions that the election was a message that government was too big and spent too much—with passages that tugged at the emotions of his audience. In those passages the president spoke about America and identified himself and his plans with what Americans hope their country can be. America, he said, was not failing but, listening to doomsayers, had merely lost some of its faith. He evoked powerful symbols—the sacrifice of those wounded in the assassination attempt and the flight, two weeks earlier, of the first space shuttle—to argue that America was good and America was strong.

His budget (or rather, Gramm-Latta) should be adopted over the alternative Jones plan, Reagan said, as an affirmation of what makes America great: "dedicated police officers like Tom Delahanty, or able and devoted public servants like Jim Brady." Within the body of the speech, Reagan spoke also of the tax program's problem with the balanced budget and his three possible arguments—supply-side, children's allowance, and the tax reductions that were not so large after all. He emphasized the last, which had greatest appeal to moderates:

Now I know that over the recess in some informal polling, some of your constituents have been asked which they'd rather have: a balanced budget or a tax cut. And with the common sense that characterizes the people of this country the answer, of course, has been: a balanced budget. But may I suggest, with no inference that there was wrong intent on the part of those who asked the question, the question was inappropriate for the situation. Our choice is not between a balanced budget and a tax cut. Properly asked, the question is: Do you want a great big raise in your taxes this coming year or, at the worse, a very little increase with the prospect of tax reduction and a balanced budget down the road a ways. . . . A gigantic tax increase has been built into the system. We propose nothing more than a reduction of that increase.

Although Reagan was arguing his plan was not so radical, the depth of the spending cuts alone was enough to convince Congress that the plan was not business as usual. He proclaimed that "the old and comfortable way is to shave a little here and add a little there. Well, that's not acceptable any more. I think this great and historic Congress knows that way is no longer acceptable." The Republicans gave that statement a standing ovation, with as many as seventy Democrats joining them. Max Friedersdorf turned to an aide and asked, "Can we count this as our vote and pack up and go home?" Tip O'Neill turned to George Bush and said, "Here's your forty votes."[67]

After the speech, the Speaker declared that "we'll either win it by five or six votes, or lose it by sixty, because if you start to lose it, the swing will come." O'Neill expected votes to switch because members would want to be on the winning side, especially because Gramm-Latta seemed more popular. Nevertheless, Democrats desperately looked to adjust Jones's package, giving it a better chance to pass. Deputy whip Bill Alexander (D-Ark.) suggested scotching the first year of the tax cut to balance the budget in FY82; the idea was an appeal to the boll weevils. After polling members on April 29, it turned out that, in Alexander's own assessment, it "didn't buy us enough votes." In another appeal to the weevils, the Democrats added back into their plan the $6.5 billion difference in budget authority for the military. Worries that this might upset liberals were erased by the knowledge that losing would upset them even more.[68]

The final blow came on May 2, when Senate minority leader Robert Byrd announced that, although he did not like the president's budget, he would support it because the public wanted "to give the president the benefits of the doubt." Byrd's concession merely ratified the situation in the Senate, where the Senate resolution would pass overwhelmingly on May 12, but his words put the last House gypsy moth holdouts in an impossible position. "We can't be hanging out there," one complained, "if your people are throwing in the towel."[69]

On May 6 the two liberal alternatives were handily beaten. The debate on May 7 symbolized the defensive position of the Democrats. "Let history show," said House minority leader Robert Michel, "that we provided the margin of difference that changed the course of American government."[70] Speaker O'Neill replied, "Sure, in the 1970s my party made mistakes. We overregulated. There was too much red tape and probably too much legislation. And we paid for it at the ballot box last year. . . . [But] do you want to meat-ax the programs that made America great? Or do you want to go slow in correcting the errors of the past?"[71] One could hardly find a better phrase—the *programs* that made America great—to capture the difference between the liberal Democrats' vision of the role of government and that of the president. The Speaker could have claimed, in fact, that the actors who starred in Reagan's speech a week before—the policeman, secret service man, the astronauts, and indeed all of NASA itself—were part of government programs. Then the president could reply that America was great long before big government and the New Deal. On this occasion the president won. Gramm-Latta passed, 253 to 176.

The president won sixty-three Democrats; no Republicans deserted him. Some Democratic defectors would have voted with their party if the vote had been close; eleven of them would not defect in any later major budget votes. The Democrats had lost badly, but they had lost a public struggle in which, despite the fury, no final decisions were made. When actual program legislation was changed, the results might differ. Tip O'Neill was already looking ahead to the reconciliation legislation. "You don't think I'm going to do this in one package, do you?" the Speaker asked. "I'm going to have some selected votes and I'm going to pick some beautiful ones."[72]

Social Security

Victory on the budget resolution did not win over the moneymen whose judgments were so crucial to the administration's economic goals. The president might appeal to the public with his call for daring, but bankers, looking at the numbers, were unconvinced. Stockman conceded in his private conversations with William Greider,

> that his own original conception—the dramatic political action would somehow alter the marketplace expectations of continuing inflation—had been wrong. . . . They don't think that it adds up. . . . I take the performance of the bond market deadly seriously. I think it's the best measure there is. The bond markets represent worldwide psychology, worldwide perception and evaluation of what, on balance, relevant people think about what we're

doing. . . . It means we're going to have to make changes. . . . I wouldn't say we are losing. We're still not winning. We're not winning.[73]

The early bond market rally that Stockman had predicted in his Dunkirk memo had not arrived. Interest rates on bonds, after edging slightly downward in January, were slowly climbing.

There was some good news: the economy seemed to head off on a boom in the first quarter, leaping forward at least at a 5 percent annual rate of growth. Perversely, that growth, if anything, raised inflation fears, so the administration had to downplay the good news to maintain the sense of urgency needed to justify that "something new" in economic policy was required. In spite of the growth, employment was stagnant; interest rates were edging back up from a March low of 17.5 percent for the prime rate. On the day that the House passed Gramm-Latta, a *Wall Street Journal* headline read, "Wall Street Is Greeting President's Program With Jitters, Turmoil."

> "We're in the midst of a very strange financial crisis," says Peter Solomon, managing director of Lehman Brothers Kuhn Loeb Inc. "You'd think Wall Street would be happy. The President is doing just what you'd like him to. Congress is about to give him his budget cuts. Oil prices are falling." But the financial markets are nervous.[74]

Donald Regan argued that it was a case of different horizons—the administration looking toward fiscal 1982, the markets looking at the "disaster" of existing financial conditions. That meant Stockman's theory of expectations wasn't working.

Alan Greenspan declared that the administration had to prove it would curb inflation by cutting the deficit further. That meant taking on social security. Institutionally and ideologically disposed toward budget cutting, Stockman agreed. Independently, that program's difficulties were bringing it stage front within the administration.

The new secretary of Health and Human Services (HHS), Richard Schweiker, was determined to use his position to help solve the impending crisis in social security financing. High payments and low collections in recent years, due to the greater growth of prices than in wages, had left the trust fund in danger of running dry in 1982 or 1983. (The nature and causes of social security's difficulties will be discussed in a separate chapter.) In the meantime, J. J. (Jake) Pickle (D-Tex.) was holding hearings in his Ways and Means subcommittee, developing a bill, and asking the administration for reactions. He made some tentative proposals the administration would not accept, and he pressed them to make their own suggestions.

Democratic leaders' fondest dream was that the administration would only be so dumb. "I was praying and working to see if I could get them first committed to gutting Social Security in some fashion," one Democrat recalls. They could never have dreamed, however, that they would succeed as quickly as they did.

April 9, the day Gramm-Latta was unveiled, was also the day Pickle announced his modest reform plan. Even as Stockman pushed to pass Gramm-Latta or something like it, he felt that continued skepticism in the markets required bigger savings, quickly. Pickle's plan could help, but it made up for only a "tiny fraction" of the budget gap Stockman thought was freaking out the markets. "I did desperately need a reform plan that saved a lot more than Pickle's paltry proposal."[75] Stockman hoped that "the impending insolvency of the retirement fund would be a handy cattle prod" to force politicians to cut the most sacred of cows.

In an April 10 meeting, Stockman and Martin Anderson insisted that Schweiker develop proposals to close the gap by reducing benefits rather than increasing coverage. (The standard way of handling fund crises had been to include a new category of worker, in this case government employees, who begin paying immediately but do not collect for a couple of decades.) Anderson and Stockman saw many benefits as unearned and unjustified. Stockman's goal was the proposal he had brought with him to OMB and then held out of his original package: raising the penalty for retirement at age sixty-two to a point where there was no actuarial difference between retiring at sixty-two or sixty-five. Schweiker's staff warned that the changes Stockman wanted would never fly on Capitol Hill. In particular, the rules could not be changed suddenly on retirees; rule changes could not be used for significant, short-term savings. Stockman dismissed that as the bureaucracy's standard inertia. Like many political administrators, the budget director refused to believe that civil servants could help him by telling him things he did not want to hear.[76]

On May 11 the issue was brought to the president who, following his own inclinations, vetoed the coverage expansion as a tax increase and accepted the early retirement changes on the grounds that the existing provisions were one reason why "I've been warning since 1964 that Social Security was heading for bankruptcy." Martin Anderson praised Reagan's courage in choosing to "honestly and permanently fix Social Security." An enthusiastic Reagan signed off, then and there, on a package whose major component was an immediate, major retrenchment of the government's biggest program, changing the rules in midstream on millions. The Legislative Strategy Group was left to work out the plan's presentation and sale.[77]

The political aides, particularly Baker, Deaver, and Darman, were horrified. One recalls,

I heard about the Stockman and Schweiker proposal only on the Friday or Saturday before the decision. I asked how the Social Security package could be bipartisan just because you had one subcommittee chairman saying something should be done, but the train was a long way down the track by then. . . .

[We] spoke to [the President] for a long time but I guess we decided that it had gone a long way—maybe we could surface it?

In retrospect I wish we had been more forceful. We got killed on it. We Republicans can't lead the charge because anything we do or say is interpreted as a reduction in benefits.

Right, particularly if it *is* a reduction in benefits. While the basic retirement age was sixty-five, people had been able to retire at age sixty-two with around 80 percent of their benefit. The Reagan plan would reduce that rate to roughly 50 percent and then gradually raise the proportion to 80 percent at sixty-three years, eight months. People would have to either delay retirement or retire on much less. If retirement at age sixty-five was the basic promise of the system, then the proposal violated no promise. Chiefly it caused the expected total payout to any recipient to remain virtually unchanged whatever the age of retirement, a sound principle of insurance practice. But for anyone who had planned to retire at age sixty-two, the proposal meant a major change. Along with other changes, it also promised to save between $82 billion and $110 billion over the next five budget years.[78]

The political aides, unable to protect the president from himself and Stockman in the morning, were determined to limit the damage when the Legislative Strategy Group met that afternoon. Baker and Darman insisted that the package was a Health and Human Services initiative. Schweiker, hearing the limb being sawed out from under him, tried to show that the political alignments were not so threatening. "This is a bipartisan initiative, *bipartisan*," he insisted. "Damn it, I spent twenty years in Congress. I should know how things work."[79] Jim Baker had spent no years in Congress, but he had a pretty good idea. He ignored Schweiker's argument that, "if there's *any* doubt as to where the President stands, this'll be dead on arrival when it gets to the Hill."[80] Both Baker and Darman figured it would be dead, no matter what. Stockman argued the package was integral to Reagan's economic plan; Baker and Darman said it was deadly to Reagan's plan, and his popularity. So Baker, as chief of staff, ruled that the announcement would come from HHS in Schweiker's name.[81] Darman wanted the announcement to come from Social Security Administration headquarters in Baltimore (i.e., as far away as possible). The next day Schweiker had his press conference. Then the roof caved in.[82]

People anywhere near age sixty-two were furious. The reaction was immediate—a deluge of cards and calls to Congress followed by a Republican retreat. Just to make the point clear to their leader, Senate Republicans on May 20 brought to the floor a resolution pledging to protect social security; it passed, 96 to 0. Bob Dole exclaimed, "They threw a life rope to Tip O'Neill."[83] Senator Moynihan imagined what Republicans were thinking: "My God, the Democrats have an issue here that will confirm every doubt anybody has ever had about us for the last fifty years—that we are going to tear up that social security card."[84]

How could Stockman, Schweiker, Reagan and company—sophisticated politicians all—have thought they could get away with this? Well, politics is the science of the inexact. The target was tempting (think of all one's problems solved with a single cut) and the uncertainties sufficiently stimulating (think of how Stockman learned bit by bit that the unfeasible was becoming feasible) to tempt even grown men. Presumably, if no one dared, nothing new ever would be done. Of course, one should remember also that one who dares too much may never get to do anything ever again.

Believers in budget balance could not afford to be amused. The feeling that "they ought to have known better" gives only a temporary feeling of superiority, a feeling that fades fast when the appropriate counterquestion is raised: How can the budget be balanced if its largest programs can never be cut?

SEVEN

Party Responsibility
Comes to Congress

The administration had fought for and won passage of its Gramm-Latta budget resolution in order to obtain two things: a revenue target that left room for its tax cut plans and reconciliation instructions to various House and Senate committees that ordered bigger spending cuts in different places than Democrats wished. But the resolution itself cut neither taxes nor spending; that required legislation. Now Reagan and his team moved to the next stage: passing the tax cut in the Economic Recovery Tax Act of 1981 (ERTA) and the spending cuts in the Omnibus Budget Reconciliation Act of 1981 (OBRA).

The Omnibus Budget Reconciliation Act of 1981
(OBRA, aka Gramm-Latta 2)

OBRA was the most sweeping legislation in modern American history. The budget resolution instructed thirteen Senate and fifteen House legislative, authorizing committees to report back to the budget committees with changes in programs ranging from Amtrak subsidies to Women's, Infants' and Children's nutrition, from AFDC to the Veterans Administration. More than its substance, the 1981 reconciliation was seen at the time as a revolution in process. For nearly two centuries Congress has been organized around its committees; in these sublegislatures members used their greater expertise, knowledge of substance plus connections with the affected interests, and power not to report legislation, to dominate policy making in their domains. Now the committees deliberated, but they did so, "meeting with a gun pointed at our heads," as Carl Perkins, chairman of Education and Labor, described their plight. They could not stall, or hold much in the way of hearings, or even represent their members. They were under orders to report out cuts, like it or not. Democratic budgeters insisted that the committees respond, and the leadership backed the budgeters because it felt the party could not be seen as opposing deficit reduction. Suddenly, the American Congress, the most nonpartisan of national legislatures, saw an immense package of policies treated as a matter of party loyalty. The Republicans did not like the committees' work; they produced a substitute bill, once again cosponsored by Gramm and Latta and therefore called Gramm-Latta 2. The final showdown between the Democratic version of OBRA and the Gramm-Latta 2 substitute was a partisan battle unprecedented in its scope. Party responsibility and, most amazing, its enforcement had at long last come to Congress.

The budget resolution provided each committee spending reduction targets that had been justified by detailed assumptions about cutting methods. Only the targets, however, not the detailed assumptions, were binding. Committee members could meet the targets however they chose. They did so very differently than the administration and its allies had intended. The latter, therefore, consulting with GOP leaders and some conservative southern Democratic boll weevils, prepared a substitute for the work of seven committees. In the haste and last-minute bargaining, no one saw the alternative in final form until the day of the debate. Stuart Eizenstat, head of domestic policy in the Carter White House, described the implication of having a vote on such a package:

> Passage of a Stockman-sponsored substitute on the House floor would create something akin to a parliamentary system, in which the prime minister's legislative package is voted on with little committee action and limited capacity for modification. . . . Congress would be forced to make the most sweeping changes in a generation in the substances of federal programs without going through the historic deliberative process to assure sound results or paying heed to the work of its own committees.[1]

Having deliberated under the pressure of time limitations that made it impossible to have hearings allowing a voice to those affected by changes, the committees themselves were in danger of having no say. If Reagan was proposing a revolution in spending priorities, reconciliation was a revolution in our form of governance.

"Congressional Government," wrote Woodrow Wilson long ago, is "Committee Government." Hence congressional power is committee power; the Reconciliation Act, by overruling committees, was widely viewed as imposing on the rights of Congress itself. "Reconciliation," proclaimed Richard Bolling, "is the most brutal and blunt instrument used by a president in an attempt to control the congressional process since Nixon used impoundment." From another point of view, congressional power is the ability to confront problems and apply to them the judgment of the people, as filtered through a representational process. From this very different perspective, Leon Panetta, chairman of the House Budget Committee reconciliation task force, declared that "no one . . . can question that this document represents the ability of this institution to do its job, and to that extent I think our democracy has been well served."[2]

The sheer sweep of OBRA made its substance seem more revolutionary than it really was. It was very important, but other acts of Congress had had greater effects on our nation. In 1964 alone, at least two— the Civil Rights Act and the Gulf of Tonkin Resolution—were more important: the first committed the federal government to battle for racial (and later other categorical) equality in our society; and the second facilitated escalating the Vietnam War. In 1981 ERTA, to which we will return, was more important because it reduced taxes far more steeply than reconciliation cut spending, thereby shaping the politics of a decade.

The importance of reconciliation, however, could not be judged solely by policy outcomes in 1981. A better question is whether reconciliation represented a new pattern of decision making through which actions outside the committee—interest group relationship—whether ideological forces, or party, or the independent frustrations of politicians themselves—would become dominant.

Conciliatory Name, Hostile Process

After reconciliation became a matter of public debate, it was generally viewed as a brilliant maneuver by the Republicans, often ascribed to the wizardry of Budget Director Stockman. Even later it was possible to find offhand references to reconciliation as a 1981 innovation.[3] In fact, as our readers know, the crucial decisions to employ reconciliation emerged not from the Reaganites' need to pass their program but from the Democrats' desire to make the budget process meaningful. "For a chairman or anyone else to say he won't cooperate [in 1981] is not an option," declared James Jones. "The Speaker agrees with that. The budget process will prevail."[4]

House support for reconciliation came from a group of moderate Democrats, like Leon Panetta, who believed that process was necessary for responsible budgeting. Other leaders, such as Rules Chairman Bolling, who agreed with Jones on little else, did not want the party to appear to be using procedural tricks to thwart the president. Therefore, in spite of resistance by many who fought reconciliation in 1980, there was never any doubt that the House would reconcile in 1981. The 1981 reconciliation procedure differed from 1980's in two ways: the instructions required savings over a three-year period, and the process was extended from entitlements and taxes to authorizations for nonentitlement programs.

Much of the 1980 reconciliation had solved the FY81 problem by spreading reductions over future fiscal years. Robert Reischauer, former assistant director of CBO, explains:

> Both OMB Director Stockman and the Budget Committees had learned a lesson from Congress' initial experiment with reconciliation in FY 1981. In this experiment the tax-writing committees had circumvented the spirit of the one-year reconciliation instructions and had obtained some of their required savings by pushing year-end Medicare payments into the next fiscal year; other committees had reported legislation that provided only temporary savings.[5]

The major tax change in 1980 had involved a one-time revenue increase by changing the payment date for corporate estimated taxes.[6] Because the budget now included three-year spending and revenue projections, three-year reconciliation made sense. Democratic budgeters approved the shift.

Multiyear reconciliation could be quite significant, for budgeting was now no longer annual; decisions taken in 1981 would change events in FY84. The ideas were extending control and preventing some budgetary games; however, there were some drawbacks. Multiyear budgeting must rely on multiyear economic forecasts, whereas forecasters are even less able to project three years ahead than to predict the next year. As for preventing games, where committees pushed next year's spending into the following year, we will see that the move to a three-year budget focus, as the British treasury discovered when it tried something similar,[7] just meant that smart actors would push the same kind of action into the fourth year.

In 1981 there was little debate over the switch to multiyear reconciliation. House Democrats never did agree to reconciling discretionary program authorizations as well as entitlements; on that they had to be beaten on the floor. Reconciling authorizations may be necessary if you want to cut before appropriations are passed, making cuts that will last for more than one year. It so vastly increases the reach of the budget process that authorizing committee members of both parties disapproved. It also makes it hard to tell what, exactly, is being cut.

Because appropriations rarely call for amounts as high as those in authorizations, it is hard to project accurately the reductions involved in an authorization cut. The Senate solved this problem by comparing its new authorization levels to the CBO "current policy" projection—existing spending plus an estimate for inflation—of the likely appropriation. In the political circumstances of 1981, however, the assumption that appropriations committees would give all programs an inflation adjustment was dubious. Stockman, for one, did not believe it. After the bill was passed, he remarked to Greider that "there was less there than met the eye. Nobody has figured it out yet. Let's say that you and I walked outside and I waved a wand and said, I've just lowered the temperature from 110 to 78. Would you believe me? . . . The government never would have been up at those levels in the CBO base."[8] Reconciliation of authorizations for discretionary programs was both more and less than it seemed: more permanence, less reductions.

Aside from objecting to reconciling discretionary program authorizations, the Democrats, of course, objected to the budget resolution assumptions about where cuts would be made. Unlike in 1980, therefore, Speaker O'Neill was willing to allow amendments during final floor consideration. This time he encouraged liberals to fight for their programs. "If it breaks the budget," O'Neill declared, "then that's the will of Congress. We are not going to roll over and play dead." Disagreeing, Budget Committee Chairman Jones argued that the Democrats' credibility required conforming to the instructions. "Tip wants to protect programs," Leon Panetta summed up the dispute, "and Jones wants to protect the process."[9] Until the committees met the June 12 deadline for reporting their proposals, however, decisions about possible amendments could wait.

When the House committees met, a number reached a consensus among their Democrat and Republican members. Bipartisanship in committee did not, however, guarantee a result the administration would like. The Interior Committee, for example, following its Senate counterpart, rejected the administration's plan to cut funding for purchase of new park land, cutting instead from other Interior Department programs; Public Works and Transportation cut aid to highways more than requested, met the targets for Economic Development Administration outlays but far exceeded them on budget authority, and refused to stop work on three major water projects. If the administration did not like the results, it would have to force Republican members of those committees to reject their own handiwork—not a good way to win their votes.

In devising the Gramm-Latta budget resolution, Stockman had proposed specific cuts to fit the resolution totals. "To remain consistent with the architecture of the Reagan Revolution fiscal plan," in Stockman's idiosyncratic view, the committees had to cut exactly the items on the "included" list. Those cuts alone were "legitimate"; Stockman blasts the "hirelings" at CBO for allowing the committees to count "unreconciled" cuts toward the reconciliation targets.[10] Ways and Means, for instance, planned $27 billion in cuts over three years instead of the expected $30 billion, but Stockman's real problem was where the cuts were made: "The bill had achieved only $16 billion, or half of the instruction savings."[11] In short, they were *instructed,* in Stockman's mind, to make *specific* changes in the law; other changes were cheating.

Actually, reconciliation "instructions" consisted only of totals.[12] Reconciliation instructions in the budget resolution contained not a word about AFDC or unemployment benefits or any specific cuts. Instead, each committee had two categories of targets: (a) savings from entitlements and (b) savings by reduced authorizations on annually appropriated programs. What Stockman calls "instructions" were the assumptions or suggestions made, not in the resolution, but in the conference report that accompanied it. Members treated them as they had always treated the assumptions used to justify budget totals. Members fought over them because having something in a report is better (or worse) than having nothing at all. But nobody believed report language was final; thus, Bob Michel could tell his members that problems could be fixed later, and the Speaker could plan a challenge in later rounds.

Stockman's interpretation of the process was far more revolutionary than desired by any semblance of a majority of the House. When he began to talk about assembling a substitute bill, his colleagues, particularly those whose committees had reached bipartisan agreement, reasonably started muttering about his dictatorial manner.

Seven committees, however, controlling most of the spending, could not agree. In Energy and Commerce, a committee that tilted toward the boll weevils, three Democrats—Gramm, Richard C. Shelby of Alabama, and James D. Santini of Nevada—sided with the Republicans against Chairman John Dingell's proposal, leaving the committee deadlocked at 21 to 21. Therefore, Chairman Dingell and ranking member James Broyhill (R-N.C.) each submitted plans to the budget committee, a quirk that may have been decisive in the outcome. In six other committees, majority Democrats made choices that Republicans could either not accept or at least try to avoid. Some were phantom cuts; some were real but immensely unpopular; some were just different.

The Agriculture Committee cut food stamps by the full $1.458 billion demanded by putting a cap on appropriations for the program. Because this altered neither benefit nor eligibility rules, the change was no more real than any of the many previous caps on food stamps, all of which had led to supplemental appropriations that exceeded the caps. That committee also reported $167 million in reduced Agriculture Department salaries and expenses through a 15 percent personnel reduction. Of course, it is always easier to attack the bureaucrats, but here even OMB warned that this slash would hamper department services.

The stakes in the Banking Committee were complicated by the fact that most programs spent their appropriations over a long period. Budget authority—for the Export-Import Bank, community development, or housing rent subsidies—would pay for the interest subsidies on long-term loans, fund projects that would take ten years to build, or subsidize rents over the next thirty years in the units authorized this year. Differences in FY82 outlays, therefore, were far less important than differences in budget authority. A $40 million difference between the House and Senate in housing outlays was actually a $2.7 billion difference in budget authority, reflecting the Senate's decision to subsidize 150,000 new units compared to the House's decision to subsidize 176,000. In order to pay for the extra costs over the period covered by the reconciliation, only a small portion of the thirty years over which rent subsidies would be required, the House committee cut the Export-Import Bank by $1.1 billion more than the Senate had. OMB's attack on the Democratic plan declared that it "would have the effect of shutting down all new lending operations . . . with severe consequences for U.S. foreign trade." Had Stockman changed his mind about Ex-Im? No, but he was more interested in cutting housing. "In short-order advocacy," one colleague explains, "one uses the arguments that the audience will find convincing."

The Science and Technology Committee took the opportunity of their small expected changes in energy research to forward legislation that would close down the Clinch River breeder nuclear reactor project. This was another project that Stockman considered an absolute boondoggle (though it goes without saying that he, like many others, may have been mistaken), but it was in Tennessee and very important to Howard Baker; now Stockman objected when the Democrats did something he had previously proposed.

Stockman objected to the Ways and Means Committee's package because the House Democrats suggested (of all things) giving only half the 1982 social security COLA in July and the rest in October; they used the $1.9 billion savings to preserve some benefits in AFDC, ignoring the administration's proposed consolidation and reduction of social-services grants. Hardly anybody believed the administration's claim that added flexibility from its proposals would make up for a 25 percent reduction in funding for those grants. Cutting social security was a serious policy choice, but it could also be a version of the "Washington Monument" game: a cut rousing such protest had to be rejected now or repealed later.[13]

The members of the House Post Office and Civil Service Committee (HPO&CS) were specialists in creative compliance. Rather than switching from semiannual to annual COLA for Civil Service Retirement—that issue again—the House committee proposed ending another aspect of retirement law that frequently came under fire: "double dipping," in which military retirees collected their military retirement while still working on the civilian side of government. Civil Service pay would be reduced by the full amount of the military retirement pension. Besides the possible inequity of changing the rules on those veterans in midstream, the catch was that the estimated $870 million in savings would disappear if affected employees then quit the federal service and took jobs in the private sector. Most might not, but nobody knew. As with social security COLAs, the cut itself was not a scam; budget analysts had been protesting the double dip for years. But the administration had reason to doubt the savings would really materialize.

In the Post Office area of its jurisdiction, HPO&CS was expected to find $956 million in savings. Postmaster General William F. Bolger thought this much could be saved by allowing a nine-digit zip code. Neither authorizing committee liked that idea; instead, the House committee suggested closing 10,000 small post offices. This cut had long been suggested by observers, even by the Postal Service itself. The difficulty was not in its merits; it had not and would not come to pass because it was extremely unpopular. People like to have nearby post offices. To minimize the resulting pain, the House committee provided that the Postal Service would submit a plan for the office closings, which either house could veto within sixty days of its submission. It was widely suspected that such a veto was inevitable; thus, in the end, there would be no cut.

The most complicated maneuvering went on in the Education and Labor Committee where the leadership had to pressure the dominant liberals into complying with reconciliation. Chairman Carl Perkins of Kentucky reported that the committee voted for cuts because he was assured that floor amendments would be allowed; Perkins did not want a plan drafted by those whose "hard-hearted actions . . . brought us to this situation in the first place." Once it agreed to cut, the committee decided to slash those programs that Republicans or boll weevils most favored, on the theory that it would be nearly impossible for such cuts to survive on the floor. Impact Aid, most useful in areas with military installations (i.e., the South), was closed down; student loans were banned for families with incomes over $25,000 a year; 25 percent of the elderly who received nutrition support would lose it; and 68,000 children would be removed from the Head Start program. In short, the Education and Labor Committee went after the more middle-class programs, those serving categories whose legitimacy (unlike people on "welfare" or in public service jobs) was difficult to challenge. The chairman, representing a coal-mining area, was the main sponsor of the black-lung disability pension program; he used reconciliation as a chance to deal with the financial problems of that fund, which was projected to have a $2 billion deficit by the end of FY82. Rather than follow budget instructions to save $60 million through eligibility tightening, he added a new fee on coal sales that would raise $553 million; he now had an extra half a billion dollars to give back to other programs.[14]

When you do not want to go there, wherever it is, many paths will take you to some other place. The committee Democrats were meeting the targets but not ending up where Stockman wanted them. The proper analogy for the reconciliation battle of 1981, however, is not that of a traveler but rather a series of military maneuvers: you try to get somewhere, but have to face an opposing army with other ideas; where you end up depends on relative resources and who maneuvers best. Perkins and, originally, the Speaker felt that they could best protect liberal programs by first playing the Washington Monument game on a grand scale and then allowing amendments to restore funds. Jones, who wanted to meet the budget's targets because he thought the Democrats should not be seen to obstruct a stronger budget process, disagreed; he wanted a closed rule, allowing no amendments: Take it or leave it. O'Neill's strategy was also questioned by both liberals and moderates at a May 20 Democratic caucus meeting. Some liberals felt O'Neill's approach might let Republicans off the hook by giving them a chance to vote to fund the more popular programs; or that the middle-class programs with greater Republican support would be restored and poor people's programs would not. Some budget balancers wanted to allow "zero-sum" amendments, restoring social cuts but compensating with reductions in other programs. While the Education and Labor Committee drafted its plan, assuming it would, as the Speaker promised, be alterable on the floor by amendments, support for such tactics steadily eroded within the caucus.

Thus in early June, seeing that most committees would not cut the budget as they had desired when drafting the Gramm-Latta Budget Resolution, Stockman and Gramm decided to produce what they called a "Son of Gramm-Latta" reconciliation bill, which others would call Gramm-Latta 2. OMB staff began the drafting secretly. On June 2, when he met with the president and GOP leaders, Stockman harshly criticized the emerging committee bills; he won approval from Minority Leader Michel for a round of meetings with committee Republicans to present the administration's case. Echoing other Republicans, Michel declared that "a committee has to have some latitude to do its thing" but added that, "if the committee system does not work, we should be backed up with a substitute to conform to the budget resolution."[15] In private, he insisted that Stockman downplay threats of an alternative.[16] Stockman then held another meeting with leaders of the GOP/boll weevil coalition in which his "pitch for this comprehensive substitute to the committee reconciliation bills elicited a torrent of criticism." Michel concluded that OMB should keep on with its drafting but also keep quiet. Committee sensibilities had to be protected. As Stockman reports,

> "We can't have the appearance that this is being written downtown," [Michel] said. He told his aide, Billy Pitts, to mobilize the minority staff on each committee to begin drafting a substitute bill to cover each of their jurisdictions.
> "Make sure OMB has complete input," he admonished Pitts, "but it's got to be written on our typewriters."
> It was a start, but his orders were ambiguous. The committee staff could—indeed, would—deduce that it was a mandate to draw up the bill their way, as long as they let OMB put in its two bits.[17]

On June 12 Michel, Gramm, and Latta announced their agreement on a framework for a substitute. By late Saturday, June 13, Stockman had a draft of a plan almost identical to the budget resolution "instructions"/assumptions.[18] By that time it seemed that the Education and Labor plan was heating up objections to the overall package, for other Democrats did not want a substitute to destroy their committees' work just because Education and Labor had gone too far. Jones claimed on June 15 to have the backing of thirteen committee heads for a closed rule forbidding a substitute. Such committees as Agriculture and Post Office, for example, could afford to let their bills be passed because the kinks in their packages, as designed, could be dealt with later. Education and Labor, however, did not want a closed rule because the committee did not want to cut Head Start and had not included ways to get the cuts to self-destruct.[19]

Responding to these other committees, the leadership pressed Perkins to "persuade his Education and Labor Committee Democrats to revise their reconciliation report so that no floor amendments would be necessary."[20] Education and Labor restored impact aid and Head Start money, allowed student loans regardless of income (the Senate had put on a "needs" test), and restored some money for the elderly. Instead, committee Democrats slashed another $1 billion from public service jobs and about $400 million in miscellaneous programs. The adjustments moved the package toward the administration but not near enough.

At Stockman's instigation, President Reagan, at his June 16 press conference, the first since his wounding, called the House package "unconscionable." "This is a fine time to start picking and choosing between who's being hurt by a $37 billion cut," retorted Leon Panetta.[21] Speaker O'Neill denounced as "dictatorial" the president's attempt to impose his own details. Democrats stressed that 85 percent of the cuts in the package were either recommended by the administration or approved previously by the House.[22]

Even if some committees had pretty much ignored Republican preferences, the idea of a substitute drafted by OMB, bypassing the committee system altogether, did not sit well even with GOP legislators. In spite of their earlier win on the budget resolution, the administration's strategists knew they could lose. Richard Darman assessed the stakes in a memo to the president on June 17: winning would provide momentum and an increased perception of Reagan's leadership and commitment; losing would have the opposite effect. "The votes for Gramm-Latta II are not there now," Darman wrote, "and it will take a major effort to get them." The president chose to take the risk.[23] There were also risks in doing nothing. Success with the tax bill, linchpin of his whole package, was still in doubt; a win on reconciliation could create momentum for that fight. Final passage of the tax bill, by agreement with Senate leaders, depended on making the spending cuts. But that in turn required conference agreement on reconciliation, which could be very difficult if the two houses passed very different bills—a point emphasized by Senator Domenici.[24]

The issues were so complex that Reagan's aides did not believe this was a good place to employ Reagan's television skills.[25] Although sixty-three Democrats had sided with the Republicans on Gramm-Latta 1, only about forty showed up when a breakfast was organized for those defectors.[26] Meanwhile, at least fourteen gypsy moths were unhappy with a number of administration proposals and bargained for changes.[27] In a meeting of the Conservative Democratic Forum, Ed Jenkins of Georgia pounced on Phil Gramm for repeating the Reagan and Stockman claims that the Democratic cuts were fraudulent. "We're still Democrats," he fumed. "And if you can't live with that, you ought to go work with Stockman and become a bureaucrat."[28] Both boll weevil and mainline Democrats said that Reagan could count on about twenty boll weevil votes.[29] But twenty was not the needed twenty-seven. Besides, provisions designed to lure the conservative boll weevils, now that the votes were about real cuts, might only alienate the more liberal gypsy moths. Michel led rounds of negotiations with Republicans on each committee, with the gypsy moths, and with the administration to develop a package from which no Republicans would defect.

One's view of those negotiations depends on who you are. To Stockman, Republican gypsy moths were demanding an unconscionable list of concessions. He saw Bill Green of New York as "the chief trouble-maker of the lot."[30] Green reported that he and his colleagues had simply "fought for the programs most important to our region and met with considerable success."[31] Medicaid, mass transit operating assistance, guaranteed student loans, energy conservation, and the Legal Services Corporation were among the programs on which Stockman had to compromise. Stockman reports as well that Republican committee staffs were a "smoldering hotbed" of revolt. No doubt they felt they were doing their job, drafting legislation that reflected their members' preferences.

"Fluid" hardly describes the situation; turbulent comes closer. Republicans were having a hard time finding enough votes. After a series of meetings on June 17 and 18, however, Michel won a crucial change: the administration would challenge only the seven committees on which Republicans had not helped to produce the HBC plan. Hence Republicans on the other committees would not face a direct challenge from their own party and president. Instead, Republicans, cut out of committee deliberations, were now getting a voice in the administration substitute.[32]

Republican amendments, announced on June 19, largely involved entitlements: of the more than $18 billion in added cuts in entitlements over three years, over $12 billion would come from programs that served mainly lower- and lower-middle income groups.[33] Republicans restored funding in a number of areas to attract boll weevils—for example, the Clinch River reactor and Impact Aid.

The Budget Committee had no formal authority to modify the other committees' plans. Nevertheless, its Democratic majority removed the provision for a later vote on shutting down the 10,000 post offices. The Budget Committee also added the Dingell package of Energy and Commerce Committee cuts. Because Energy and Commerce had divided evenly, Budget suggested that the Rules Committee allow the alternative package, sponsored by Joel Broyhill (R-N.C.), to be voted on as an amendment. Otherwise, Budget requested a closed rule.[34]

While a majority of Democrats strongly supported preventing amendments, enough objected to the closed rule that a whip poll suggested it might not pass.[35] Besides, additional cuts proposed by the Republicans did not seem popular. Why not allow amendments, but only for those further cuts? The Speaker could have some "beautiful" votes, not on Democratic proposals to remove cuts from a package (the original idea), but on Republican efforts to increase them. There could be votes on extra Republican slashing of the poor, the students, the hungry, and less sympathetic (but perhaps more powerful) groups like federal employees. The prospect was too tempting; the leadership changed its mind and had the Rules Committee produce a new rule.

The rule was announced on June 24, and it was a beauty. Not one but six Republican amendments would be in order. Each would include some less popular changes; none would include the "sweeteners"—

which, after all, would increase spending—that the Republicans had inserted to win votes, such as targeting impact aid and increasing funding for the Export-Import Bank. The president's supporters would have to separately approve cutting food stamps, "capping" medicaid, housing cuts, federal employee COLA changes, deeper cuts in child nutrition and student loans, cuts in AFDC and social security. Furious, knowing that if the vote occurred as the rule intended they would lose, Republicans and boll weevils would have to fight to change the rule, the Speaker's strongest ground. If the GOP indeed could count on only twenty boll weevils to begin with, it would be a very close fight.

Stockman feels the new rule actually did him a favor. Republicans were so angry, he writes, that "it got their partisan dander up, and for the first time in weeks they felt that the enemy was the Democrats, not me."[36] Steven Smith reminds us that if a few Republicans had defected, and if that had been enough to beat their president, they would have been left with an awesome responsibility. The vote was bound to be partisan.

The White House lobbyists' count on the evening of June 24 showed the Republicans several votes short.[37] The president, when he heard of the Democrats' plan, inserted an attack on them into his speech at the National Junior Chamber of Commerce convention in San Antonio. "Without these added reductions," he proclaimed, "we will have nearly $22 billion of red ink, an unbalanced budget and a more inflationary pressure in the next few years. . . . It's a sad commentary on the state of the opposition, when they have to resort to a parliamentary gimmick to thwart the will of the people."

Jim Wright declared that what was at stake was "the right to make a choice," that Congress owed the president cooperation but "not . . . obeisance, obedience, and submissiveness."[38] The president was invoking popular sovereignty; the Democratic leaders were invoking separation of powers. Both sides waved the banner of the public good; Democrats called on party loyalty, while the president asked waverers what he could do to help them with their particular problems.

The question was, What have you done for me lately? And Ronald Reagan would not be found wanting. He found six Texas Democrats at dinner with home-state utility executives in the University Club. He didn't talk to Martin Frost, a party loyalist, but spoke to each of the other five. "At least three of them—Ralph Hall, Charles Wilson and Jack Hightower—were on the fence until they heard from the president, even though they voted with him on the budget resolution in May," according to Frost.[39] Reagan called at least nineteen congressmen in the final day of lobbying. On some, as they reported, he used soft sell:

Rep. Charles Wilson conceded he was going to stick with his party on the procedural vote Thursday, but a telephone call from the president helped persuade him otherwise. Wilson said the president told him, "You've gone this far with me, it would be a shame after we took all this heat to lose it now."

But Wilson said Reagan also asked him, "Is there anything you're really interested in that you'd like to talk about?" Yes, replied Wilson, synfuels. The administration's sharp cuts in federal subsidies for these projects troubled him. The congressman said the gist of Reagan's reaction was, "My door's open. Come on over and talk when this is over."[40]

It is nice to be president; just being friendly and showing interest can make a member of Congress feel like progress is being made. John Breaux of Louisiana was more demanding. "I went with the best deal," he declared after he extracted from the president a rather vague promise not to oppose sugar price supports in the House's later consideration. This was not exactly the same as support for the sugar subsidy, but it was a distinct change of administration position, made the morning of the crucial vote on the rule, potentially costing consumers $2.2 billion annually (but costing nothing if liberals in the House managed to kill the program on their own).[41] Breaux and Billy Tauzin (D-La.) claimed that the sugar switch determined their vote. When asked if that meant he could be bought, Breaux replied, "No, but I can be rented."[42]

By including in the revised package extra money for medicaid ($350 million), $400 million more in low-income fuel assistance, $260 million more for mass transit and some extra for Conrail, the administration also bid for the support of the gypsy moths.[43] Because it was a party matter, and they did not much like the Democrats' tactics, the gypsy moths were likely to back the administration on the rule fight. They also were won over by a sense that they could not be nailed as hard-hearted budget slashers because the Democrats themselves had gone so far in that direction.[44]

As time for the vote approached, the president expected to lose. His speech, written for that evening in Los Angeles, included a lot of "we shall fight on the beaches" rhetoric designed to show determination in the face of defeat.[45] In a battle fraught with drama and bitterness, Bolling's motion for the previous question, preventing amendment to the Democratic rule, was voted down, 217 to 210. The Republican substitute rule, allowing separate votes on the Gramm-Latta package and on the Energy and Commerce (Broyhill) section, was adopted, 214 to 208. The president had won his gamble; he changed his speech.

Gramm-Latta 2, made available only the next morning, was a hastily stapled, scribbled-on mass that included the phone number of a CBO staffer and a raft of provisions whose meaning was at best unclear. But its basic drift was clear enough for members to make their choices. *Newsweek* estimated that "the projected Reagan savings melted from nearly $22 billion to $12 billion as sweeteners were offered, some handwritten, into his draft bill."[46] Dennis Farney of the *Wall Street Journal* got the story right:

> The highest stakes in the battle aren't dollars, as unprecedented as the deep cuts are. The highest stakes involve legislative policy and the opportunity Mr. Reagan has to rewrite in a single bill scores of programs affecting millions of citizens. Because of yesterday's victory, Mr. Reagan now has the opportunity to achieve much of his domestic legislative program before the House recesses for the Fourth of July—and without ever submitting the package to the scrutiny of House committees.[47]

House Democrats had given in to fiscal restraint, but they had tried to cushion and direct the blow; they had come within inches of victory, only to lose because of twenty-nine defectors, some of whom they had expected to hold. Their bitterness ran deep: "Traitor," "Judas," "You sold out to the fat cats." "Don't ever speak to me again." "It's amazing what a call from the president does to people who otherwise have character."[48] William Brodhead convened a meeting of the executive committee of the Democratic Study Group to make recommendations for enforcing party discipline, possibly including revoking committee memberships, such as Representative Gramm's on Budget.

The final vote was yet to come. Stockman had been dealing on the details of Gramm-Latta 2 up to the last moment before the vote on the rule. "We ain't gonna make it," Bill Thomas, Republican of California, told him, "unless you open the soup kitchen." Unable to tell if the waverers Thomas spoke of would really defect or were just holding him up for more goodies, Stockman held his nose and went for a final half-dozen deals.[49]

Assembled in such a last minute rush, the Republican substitute so grossly violated congressional standards of draftsmanship that Democrats hoped to evoke legislative pride, especially among senior southerners, to switch a few votes.[50] In the confusion, liberal leader Phil Burton (D-Calif.) was reported to have surreptitiously obtained the draft so his side could have a first chance to figure out what was in it. A Democratic leader (no friend of the late Burton) later claimed that "if Phil Burton hadn't been screwing things up, we might have won. . . . Somehow he got a hand on it, and we lost our virtue, the claim that we were better than they were." Perhaps that blunted Democrats' claim that Republicans were not playing by the rules with their ludicrous-looking draft; perhaps not. The vote was so close that anything might have altered it.

The Gramm-Latta 2 amendment passed 217 to 211, almost the same as the crucial rule vote (217 to 210). The similar numbers, however, hid some flux. Five Democrats who had voted with the Republicans on the rule then opposed Latta's amendment, while five other Democrats supported Latta on June 26 after supporting their party on June 25. If the Democrats had held nine of those ten waverers on either vote, they would have won. The closeness of Reagan's margin was shown again when, in a complicated maneuver, Jones tried to get the bill recommitted to require changes in social security, student loans, and block grants; he failed by only 215 to 212.

Then came the separate vote on the Energy and Commerce provisions. The Republicans had spent all day dickering for support for the Broyhill provisions. Four Democrats who voted for the president on the rule, however, had cut a separate deal with Dingell involving natural gas issues. They did not want to back out of the deal with their chairman, one of the tougher characters on the Hill. A number of gypsy moths preferred Dingell's version because it did not cut medicaid so severely. Ultimately it seemed as if Dingell had the votes. The Republicans chose not to offer the Broyhill plan. "It was one of those decisions," Stockman recalled, "made in about four minutes as a result of sheer chemistry— the time of the day, the sequence of events, how tired the players are. Basically it was the right decision because if we had lost it, we also might have lost the whole reconciliation bill on final passage."[51] Preserving the appearance of control of the floor was vital for preserving actual control.

The tactics worked; when the reconciliation bill was voted on as amended, it passed 232 to 193. The wider margin occurred because a number of Democratic committee leaders, sure that the bill would pass, wanted to guarantee themselves a role in what would be a highly complicated conference with the Senate. These votes also ensured that Phil Gramm did not get to that conference. James Jones explained, "We had to go pretty much on seniority, and we couldn't name Stockman."[52]

All but a very few members voted ideology and party. But the balance on those lines was so close that a few defections either way could determine the result.[53] Legislators exploited the closeness of the vote to win concessions from the side they were likely to support anyway. Boll weevil leader Charles Stenholm, for instance, got a solar energy plant in his district. Ultimately, the victory had less to do with what Reagan himself did than with the idiosyncrasies of a small group of House members.

The administration was so nervous about its slender margin that it feared bringing the bill back from conference for another vote. Two of Howard Baker's staffers later wrote that "many planners, particularly David Stockman, did not believe these coalitions would endure or could be rebuilt for the vote on the conference report. Consequently, the administration undertook a major campaign to persuade the Senate to accept the House bill."[54] Ronald Reagan asked Baker on July 17 to accept the House version. But when the Senate leader met with his chairmen the next day, he found them distinctly unenthusiastic about the idea. First, they had worked hard for many things in the Senate bill and did not wish to give them up. Second, the hastily prepared Gramm-Latta 2 needed considerable technical cleaning up; the Senate's leaders had reports that many of the bill's supporters had voted for it assuming the conference would fix the glitches. They unanimously rejected Reagan's plea and went to conference.[55]

We have already seen why there might be doubts about Gramm-Latta's drafting. The other side of the Senate's resistance to Reagan requires a short description of the Senate bill.

There was never any doubt that the Senate's package would closely resemble Reagan's. The major exception was in some block grant proposals. Congress just does not like to give up its voice in programs. Consequently, in the Senate Labor and Human Resources Committee, two liberal Republicans, Lowell Weicker and Robert Stafford, sided with the Democrats to water down the block grant plans. Noting a general lack of enthusiasm for the whole idea, the administration decided not to challenge the committee's decision. Beyond the block grant issue, there was little Senate conflict about the spending-cuts package.

For precisely that reason, however, the bill became the perfect vehicle to carry various riders. "People saw the train pulling out of the station," as Howard Baker put it, "and they just all got on."[56] Or, as Robert Reischauer describes it, "the committees ran amok, stuffing their reconciliation legislation with authorizations, reauthorizations, new regulations, and all sorts of 'extraneous' legislation."[57] Senate Democrats, particularly Byrd and Hollings, objected to this process just as Barber Conable had complained when House Democrats did the same a year before. After negotiations, the leaders agreed that Baker would offer an amendment stripping the bill of a wide variety of provisions; individual amendments would then be offered on the floor to restore a number of those to the bill. "If we are going to go down this road of including extraneous matter," Byrd explained, "I want it to be done here, on this floor—come in the front door and let every senator, with his eyes open, have a chance to vote on it as we now have in connection with adding legislation to an appropriation bill."[58] Only some deleted passages could be offered as amendments.[59] These latter provisions, in the jurisdictions of Banking and Commerce committees, were in fact restored on the floor.

The conference itself lasted until July 28. It was of extraordinary size—184 House members and 72 senators meeting in 58 subconferences. Yet it was remarkably calm and uncontentious. The only real controversy involved the social security minimum benefit. Both houses had endorsed repeal of this $122 per month payment, which OMB claimed largely benefited state and federal retirees who were covered by other plans but had also worked for a short time under social security. With the social security forces finally mobilized and pressuring legislators, Richard Bolling tried to get the conference to reopen the issue but was not supported by other House leaders. Instead, the House voted on a separate resolution to restore the benefit; it passed 404 to 20. The Senate then refused (57 to 30) to consider the motion. Perhaps they knew that they could gather no more votes than they had on June 26; perhaps process-oriented Democrats like James Jones were not willing to sabotage the reconciliation process at that late date; perhaps their defeat on the tax cut on July 29 left the Democrats with no desire to fight. That was the extent of Democratic maneuvering; House leaders didn't even bother calling for a recorded vote when, on July 31, Congress passed the conference report on the Omnibus Reconciliation Act of 1981.

How large were the reductions in the act? Truthfully, nobody knew. The most careful analysis of Reagan's policy, the Urban Institute's Changing Domestic Priorities Project, analyzed the changes for the entire year, rather than those in the reconciliation act alone. But many caveats included in the project report should be noted.

> Congress made certain accounting shifts and mandated technical assumptions that led CBO's reported numbers to substantially exaggerate the impact on nondefense reductions. Largest among these was the shift of the strategic petroleum reserve to off-budget status. . . . However, the most egregious example of specious savings was the shift of $685 million in Medicare payments from the first month of FY 1982 to the last month of FY 1981, so that it would show up as 1982 budget savings. Congress had done just the reverse the year before when it wanted to show cuts in the 1981 budget. So credit was taken twice for a nonexistent reduction.[60]

Furthermore, as Stockman had noted, the CBO baseline assumed increases, to keep up with inflation, which probably would not have been made even without reconciliation. Not only was that adjustment to the baseline questionable, but inflation, as it turned out, was lower than predicted; the baseline, therefore, was too high to begin with. For all these reasons, the estimated FY82 reductions of $35.2 billion that emerged from the conference were certainly too high.

Nevertheless, no matter what the course of the economy, substantial changes in government policy would have both immediate effects on millions of Americans and long-term fiscal consequences: altering food stamp, AFDC, and unemployment compensation eligibility; encouraging states to reduce medicaid costs; limiting hospital reimbursements for medicare; eliminating more than three years of impact aid except where children lived on federal property; terminating public service jobs; nearly terminating Trade Adjustment Assistance; substantially changing the school lunch program; arranging annual instead of biannual COLAs for Civil Service pensions; allowing higher tenant payments, stricter eligibility, and fewer units of subsidized housing; and terminating student and minimum social security benefits.

Whose bill was it, anyway? The common interpretation—that, as one Republican budget leader put it, "it was an administration package engineered with the boll weevils"—is a bit too convenient. It lets Republicans blame the pain they inflicted on the administration and allows Democrats to stigmatize the OBRA package as not merely bad policy but poor procedure. Ultimately Gramm-Latta 2 was drafted on the typewriters of Republican staffs of the affected committees. One of Stockman's colleagues expressed the OMB perspective in a way that fits the situation. When we asked if Gramm-Latta 2 were "assembled by OMB," he replied,

> Would that that were true. We sent down a draft reconciliation bill. The minority staff directors were told to review the thing, and they stuffed in their own proposals. . . . A lot of those things had been on the Republican committee members' agendas for years. The Gramm-Latta section on education was the 1979 and 80 Asbrook [John, R-Ohio] higher education amendments. Everybody cleaned out their closet. In the first stage we cleaned out our closet, and in the second stage, the real stage, they cleaned out theirs.

The actual drafting of legislation, not its proposal, is, in fact, the "real" stage. There were no hearings, but most provisions of Gramm-Latta 2 had been floating around for years. Few understood many of the provisions, but then legislators rarely know what is in a bill. They count on colleagues and staff, committees or party, to alert them to problems, and, for the Republicans at least, the process was not really so different in 1981. The provisions for each committee were approved by that committee's Republicans. Thus, the decision to challenge only the sections committee Republicans had not approved was crucial. It was Reagan's victory, but it was Congress's bill. That is the bottom line: Congress did what *it* wanted. Gramm-Latta 2, the Omnibus Budget Reconciliation Act of 1981, defined the boundaries of what Congress was willing to cut from domestic government.

Cosmos, it is said, is a special case of chaos. The reconciliation of 1981 looks like chaos, but there was direction. Between the district concerns of the boll weevils (who were glad to cut spending so long as agriculture and water projects and impact aid and the military were protected) and the similar concerns of gypsy moths (who would support their party but not if it meant cutting transportation or fuel or education assistance in a way that looked as if they were really hurting their districts), the river of budget cuts was more channeled than its speed and turbulence suggested. Some committee heads were carried along kicking and screaming. Others grabbed logs, holding on to maintain the full panoply of benefits to which they were pledged, preserving a bit here, losing bits there. Amidst the pulling and hauling, trickery was joined to ideology; illusion became an instrument of policy. As if in a house of mirrors, expenditure cuts changed shape when looked at in different ways.

Stockman and perhaps others wish all the churning and illusion could have been circumvented by a few clean decisions. But that is neither American democracy nor Congress at work. Consent had to be built through a series of compromises, and those bargains (or agreements; the word used affects how the process sounds) defined the limits of consent in a democracy in which neither Ronald Reagan nor David Stockman was elected to provide a specific package of spending reductions.

The fuzzy areas would surely need settling. Stockman had his agenda of future cuts. Even what was seemingly agreed would be fought again, as the Democrats attempted to overturn the verdict of 1981. The losers did not consent to the result, and were almost as numerous as the winners. Getting it back would be difficult because they would have to beat a veto but, when conditions improved, the Speaker would try again. OBRA was only the first of many battles, but it was the biggest and the most decisive. The question for the future was: Would conflict be contained or expanded to a point where it threatened to break the budget process that, in its messy way, had produced Gramm-Latta 2?

Actually, there was another question for the future. All these domestic spending cuts had been justified in the name of a balanced budget. Yet Republicans had also rationalized that spending cuts would make room for tax reductions. If they cut taxes much, they might lose budget balance. Could they find some happy medium of lower taxes and a balanced budget?

The answer to both questions, whether they could find a happy medium and limit future conflict, depended on what would happen to the tax bill.

EIGHT

Starving the Public Sector:
The Economic Recovery Tax Act
of 1981

How could the nation have gone from hope to gloom in less than two years? It is a critical question as the 1982 election approaches. Yet there is another, possibly more significant question to be asked: How could Mr. Reagan's economic plan have been enacted in the first place? For it was a program that lacked any sort of traditional constituency in Congress or in the Government, a program whose premises were challenged by conservative and liberal economists alike and that was widely characterized as a risky gamble with the nation's future.

STEVEN WEISMAN, NEW YORK TIMES

The business and finance community, popularly considered to be great worriers about the budget, suppressed its anxiety on this occasion—being so eager to have their taxes cut. When the tax bill was passed, in August, that was celebrated as a great victory for the President. Yet there was never any doubt that a tax bill very much like the President's would pass. It is, after all, one of the hoary axioms of political life that a Congressman should and will vote for every tax cut. When the tax cut provides some relief for all taxpayers, and when it is certified as essential by the most conservative President in fifty years, its adoption is assured.

HERBERT STEIN, FORMER CHAIRMAN, COUNCIL OF ECONOMIC ADVISERS

From one view the passage of the Conable-Hance, née Kemp-Roth, Economic Recovery Tax Act of 1981 is inexplicable, and from another inevitable. Weisman argues that few members of Congress actually believed in the supply-side theories that justified the reductions; Stein suggests that legislators like to give out benefits and, when encouraged by the president, have little reason not to do so. The journalist cites beliefs about the economy; the economist cites political truisms.

From President Reagan's perspective, politics always overwhelmed economics. Perhaps it is better to say that they both sprang from the same principles, which had little to do with economics as conceived by economists. Perhaps the tax cut would free productive energies previously chained by confiscatory tax rates. Certainly the obtrusive public sector could not grow any fatter if it were starved for funds. Whatever the short-term (or even permanent) fiscal effects, the tax cut could only favor the individual over the government. That, in Ronald Reagan's mind, was what his revolution was all about, and so he fought for his tax cut with a certainty and persistence that overcame the doubts of his own staff and congressional allies. Large spending cuts might have passed without Ronald Reagan. The form of the final tax bill reflected the many contours of the American political process and the special circumstances of 1981. But the fact of the big individual rate reduction may be credited to the president.

"I had to subordinate my own feelings," recalled one senator. "I figured, Ronald Reagan was elected the Republican President. That was always in the back of my mind. I'm not here to pick a fight with a brand new President."[1] When Robert Dole suggested that some compromise might be necessary, he was reprimanded in a note from the hospitalized Reagan.

Reagan's reaction—rejection of any compromise—was loud and immediate. When White House aides wanted Reagan to know he might have to compromise, they had Barber Conable, Republican leader on Ways and Means, brief their boss on the political outlook. Conable reported that the president told him, "if he started compromising now, what was left over wouldn't look like his original program."[2] Conable couldn't argue with Reagan's tactical judgment. In all these cases, the president, by refusing to show any give, forced his somewhat reluctant allies to stand with him or against him; they stood with him.

Most Democrats believed that some tax relief was mandatory, not only to help the economy but also to lower taxes that had risen considerably in the previous three years. Between social security changes and bracket creep, a family of four with a 1977 income of $10,000 had seen its federal taxes rise from 10.2 percent to 13.8 percent of its income. In 1981 a 13.3 percent rise in inflation would cause a family of four earning $15,000 to lose $120 in real after-tax income.[3] The tax increase was highest for low- and middle-income workers.[4] As in 1980, most Democrats preferred smaller tax cuts distributed more to the lower end of the scale, but both policy and obvious political pressure meant they would produce *some* tax bill. As on spending, House Democrats could not simply stonewall.

Given uncertain control of the House and a Republican Senate and president, Ways and Means Chairman Rostenkowski's ideal had to be an agreement with Conable and Republicans on his committee. But Rostenkowski and other Ways and Means leaders, moderates used to bargaining across party lines, could not get a deal.

As a first cut, Rostenkowski adopted proposals justifiable on policy grounds and particularly attractive to Republicans. He proposed to reduce the "marriage penalty," in which, due to the progressive rate structure, some couples who filed jointly paid more than if they lived together unmarried and filed separately. Rostenkowski also adopted estate tax reductions that some liberals disliked but were favored by a number of tax analysts. Most tellingly, the chairman and his staff decided to lower the top rate on capital income from 70 percent to 50 percent—a proposal that Reagan, on Meese's urging, had excluded from his program because it could be attacked as helping only the rich. The policy experts felt that, as one recalls, "to the extent that you wanted to stimulate investment, and there was not much money there anyway—nobody pays 70 percent—why don't we just go ahead and do it? We had studies showing that it would cost very little." "I guess it would be pretty hard for the Republicans to vote against that, wouldn't it?" asked Rostenkowski. "If Danny goes with that," Ways and Means Republican Bill Gradison commented, "he'll just steal the ball and make a basket."[5] So Rosty hoped to make his slamdunk as a few liberals watched with despair from the sidelines.

With Republicans quietly nervous and conservative Democrats loudly skeptical about the deficit effects of the Reagan package, Rostenkowski's strategy—targeted policy changes for a smaller total tax loss than Reagan planned—made sense. It fit conservative policy preferences; even better, polls repeatedly showed that the public, too, believed a balanced budget more important than a tax cut.

Yet Conable would not deal. He blamed the Democrats for having stacked Ways and Means—twenty-three Democrats to twelve Republicans—at the beginning of the year. Given the stakes—if the committee endorsed Kemp-Roth, the game was over—the leadership wanted some extra margin of safety. "I told Danny," Conable reported in March, "that he robbed me of my independence. So I've got to go with the administration to have any impact."[6] Ways and Means Republicans also hesitated to negotiate because nearly half the Republicans in the House had campaigned in support of Kemp-Roth. Rostenkowski and Conable, by many reports, were not the most congenial pair—the former a Chicago pol, the latter a more reserved self-conscious intellectual.

Conable had always preferred targeted savings incentives to across-the-board cuts because he believed, all other things being equal, people would spend rather than save. Conable never bought the argument that Kemp-Roth would increase savings. But he could see tax policy reasons to prefer rate cuts: preferences have to be paid for with higher rates, which in turn encourage tax avoidance and resentment.[7] A wider tax base means more compliance, less administrative problems, and generally less frustration involved with raising revenue; this policy, which Conable and everyone else abandoned in July, would shape the 1986 tax reform. But beyond the policy argument the Ways and Means Republicans had one overwhelming reason to sit tight: Reagan had far more political weapons than Rostenkowski.

If the Democrats had the votes to beat Kemp-Roth, it was better for Republicans to keep quiet rather than to risk a fight with their new Republican president. Although Kemp-Roth was less than popular, there was certainly no outcry against it. On taxes as well as on spending, Ronald Reagan, with his veto and control of the Senate, was in a far better position to deliver on or to thwart any bargain than were House Ways and Means Democrats.

Republicans gained much momentum for the tax fight when they won on the first budget resolution (Gramm-Latta 1). "If the White House decides to go to bat on Kemp-Roth the way they did on the budget," Leon Panetta predicted, "they're going to get it."[8] At that time, however, the administration did not have the votes to pass its tax package in the House. Within the White House, the same deficit fears that fueled the ill-fated social-security initiative also fed worries about fiscal hemorrhage from the tax cut.

Don Regan and the Treasury had primary responsibility for negotiating with Congress. Regan, the salesman from Merrill Lynch, wanted to sell the president's program.

Senate Republican leaders Baker, Dole, and Domenici, worried about the deficit, also wanted to support the president. Their leanings fit their positions: Baker most interested in keeping his majority together; Domenici increasingly nervous about the deficit; Dole eager to pass a tax bill that satisfied his Finance Committee. Dole sent messages that 10-10-10 wouldn't fly; the final bill had to include other provisions of interest to his members.[9]

Senate Democrats were still out of the game. Senator Byrd appointed Bill Bradley (D-N. J.) to head a task force to write a Democratic plan; it went nowhere. Russell Long kept blaming Byrd for having prevented a tax cut back in 1980 when he thought it might have saved the Senate majority. Every man for himself. House Republicans had taken themselves out of play. The White House essentially took them for granted, concentrating on cutting a deal with either Rostenkowski or the House boll weevils. The Administration's difficulty was that Rosty had to satisfy House Democrats to maintain his chair, while the weevils were worried about deficits and leery of defecting from the Democratic party on taxes as well as spending.

President Reagan and his advisers met on May 12 to discuss strategy. The advisers thought Rostenkowski might accept a two-year bill. The president accepted both adoption of the 70/50 reduction for the top rate in unearned income, which the Democrats had kindly endorsed (thereby temporarily solving Reagan's equity problem) and proposals to reduce the marriage penalty. These provisions as well as short-term deficit worries could be accommodated by reducing the first year's cut to 5 percent, making it a 5-10-10 package. But that was as far as the president would go, and he did not want to go that far if he could help it.

Reagan authorized Regan to continue separate negotiations with Rostenkowski and the boll weevils in pursuit of the new, unrevealed bottom line. The Treasury secretary would report to the Legislative Strategy Group (LSG). An LSG member explained, "We needed either to deal with Rosty, where he had to worry about his Democrats (to his left) or do what we eventually did, creating a coalition with the boll weevils on the floor. The approach we hit upon was to use the threat of a boll weevil floor fight as leverage for a deal with Rosty." Negotiations proliferated both between the administration and congressional factions and among House and Senate leaders. Meeting with four boll weevils, Regan concluded the weevils would "go for 5-10-10 and a couple of other little things."[10] Publicly the four southerners were noncommittal; they told Regan that they wanted to support a compromise from within their party, if possible, and that the membership of the Conservative Democratic Forum was split on the merits of Kemp-Roth. Rostenkowski, meanwhile, had been fattening his plan with more tax breaks, hoping thereby to attract wavering conservative Democrats and mainline Republicans. Among these temptations were reductions in the estate tax (justified as a particular burden on family farmers) and increases in the amount of money that could be placed in tax-free retirement plans (an investment incentive). Regan countered by offering Rostenkowski—and Dole, and boll weevil Kent Hance, a second-term Texan and member of Ways and Means who had assumed the role of mediator between southerners and the White House—a menu of items from the second planned tax bill in order to bring Rosty along on the three-year cut.

The bargaining had now taken a particularly bizarre turn; Rostenkowski was offering provisions to the House Republicans and boll weevils to avoid Kemp-Roth while Regan was offering them back to Rostenkowski to win support for the three-year cut. Rostenkowski, although he told reporters on May 27 that he might go for more than a one-year cut, was not willing to go for three. He met with Regan and Dole, who offered 5-10-10. Rostenkowski came back, "What about a two-year program instead of three?" And the Treasury secretary countered, "If I went to the President with that offer, I'd be fired."[11]

Rostenkowski went back to his committee and reported to a caucus of twenty-three Democrats on the state of the negotiations. All but one rejected compromise on the available terms; "If that's the bottom line," Richard Gephardt declared, "then there are no further negotiations."[12] Only two members favored even a two-year cut.

Rostenkowski relished the fact that business lobbyists had to learn to pronounce his long Polish name; he wanted to be a powerful chairman of Ways and Means, which meant, as he told his caucus on June 4, winning on the tax bill. He wasn't interested in being a principled loser: "Look, I want a tax bill that can win." Rostenkowski contrasted himself to his good friend, the Speaker, in an interview with Martin Schram of the *Post:* "Tip stands solid like an oak because he's got a basically liberal chemistry and he's got great pride in protecting what has been built in the last thirty years by the Democratic Party. I'm still at liberty to be the palm. I can sway."[13]

Unlike James Jones, who had been out in front on budget and tax issues (in a conservative direction) long before he became Budget chairman, Dan Rostenkowski had no obvious, set views on most issues that came before his committee. But his interest in winning above all led him, like Jones, to search continually for grounds of compromise with either Republicans or conservative Democrats on his committee.[14] Rostenkowski's career also revealed no objections to dealing with interest groups, whether hospitals or commodity traders or the savings and loan industry; searching for support, therefore, his willingness to use provisions that favored business groups was not out of character. Were concessions to other groups required for victory, he would have made those, too.

President Reagan told Democratic leaders on June 1, "Three years is a matter of principle with me. I'm already backed in a corner and I can't back up any more." Speaker O'Neill challenged Reagan's recitation of the supply-side premises, "Mr. President, you don't really believe that!" And he concluded, "If you roll us, you roll us."[15] The Speaker told reporters that there was no hope of compromise, though Rostenkowski still claimed it was possible. Seeing a picture in the paper of the glum Rostenkowski, Reagan sent him a note: "Honest, Danny," wrote the president, "things aren't that bad. . . . Come on back—we'll try again. Warm regards, Ron."[16] It was classic Reagan—friendly, personable, but behind that, unyielding.

Democratic leaders were split, with O'Neill adamant for a one-year cut, Wright arguing for a 5-5-5, and Rostenkowski leaning again toward two years. Both Ways and Means Democrats and the Conservative Democratic Forum caucused on June 2. The first group reached a loose consensus for a 5-10 plan; the second agreed to Reagan's idea of proportionately equal cuts but were split between supporters of two and three years. The next day the Ways and Means Democrats settled on a 5 percent cut on October 1, 1981, and 10 percent on July 1, 1982. The *National Journal* reported, "Many opposed a three-year cut out of fear that it would severely limit funds for social spending programs."[17] Southerners Ed Jenkins and Ken Holland endorsed the plan.[18] Only one Ways and Means Democrat did not: Kent Hance, the second-term conservative from a very conservative Texas district who, like Gramm, had reaped a plum committee assignment as part of Jim Wright's effort to win over the boll weevils. "Hance was fidgeting in the corner, still on the fence," a participant recalls, "and we knew he had a meeting that afternoon at the White House." If he went, Hance knew his relationships with other members of the committee might never be the same; that afternoon he finalized his agreement with the administration.

The Die Is Cast: June 3–9, 1981

The day after telling Rostenkowski to "come on back," the president took the boll weevil option. The new package, announced on June 4, was cosponsored by Hance and Conable—a forced marriage if ever there was one, since Conable saw Hance as a pork-barreling oilman. At a breakfast that morning, Reagan told the southerners that though he could not prevent Republican opposition in their districts, if they supported the new bill, he would not campaign against them. That was one enticement; another was that Conable-Hance managed a smaller deficit than the original plan, while still adding some of Rostenkowski's appetizers.

Hance had suggested postponing the effective date of the individual cut as well as reducing the first year to 5 percent. He accepted a three-month delay, matching the Democrats' schedule, in return for a $700 million tax break for oil producers.[19] The deficit projections were reduced, however, by deleting some parts of the original business tax package—precisely what Conable, and many other traditional Republicans, cared about most. Stockman was encouraged: the new steps "were consistent with good tax policy and also reduced the revenue loss by tens of billions of dollars in the out-years."[20] But it was not to last.

Policy on depreciation involves formulas for estimating the useful lives of categories of capital plant. The rule for any item thus becomes part of the price the business pays for it. The inflation of the 1970s fueled demands for more generous depreciation rules, both because companies' assets were being overvalued and because more generous depreciation would lower the after-tax price of new investment. A lower price in theory would mean more investment and, eventually, more productivity. A crucial segment of Democrats—Jim Jones, Lloyd Bentsen, and Representative Sam Gibbons (the number-two man on Ways and Means)— wanted to liberalize depreciation rules on these grounds. Traditional Republicans like Barber Conable agreed.

The 10-5-3 accelerated depreciation plan reduced the many categories and useful lives of equipment developed by the Treasury and Congress over the years to three categories: ten-year, five-year, and three-year writeoffs. Businesses loved the idea because most items could be depreciated much faster under 10-5-3 than under existing law. A series of other provisions, particularly tax credits, in the package made it even more attractive.[21] The Treasury Tax Policy staff, and their political leaders, were less enamored. In the words of one participant, "It was considered too simplistic, too meat-ax. Machinery and equipment do have different useful lives. And it was too generous, it created *negative* tax rates." In essence, the government would give companies money to invest.

The argument blaming declining productivity growth on too little investment was dubious to begin with. The Commerce Department reported: in 1980 total investment (apart from housing) accounted for 11.3 percent of gross national product; in 1970 it had been 10.5 percent, 9.6 percent in 1960, 9.5 percent in 1950. For some reason, old levels of investment did not create the same productivity growth as before, but in that case more investment might not be the answer. Neither was more generous tax treatment clearly the key to greater investment. A survey of business reaction to the investment tax credit showed that "while business welcomes the tax reduction" firms "buy little or no additional equipment as a consequence of the tax credit."[22] Yet the basic argument for business tax cuts seems to have been widely accepted.[23]

Whatever its economic merits, the administration's original "Accelerated Cost Recovery System" (ACRS) was fervently supported by business interests and traditional Republicans. The new Conable-Hance package reduced the estimated tax cut by $15 billion over three years (and more later).[24] This angered Ways and Means Republicans who didn't much like not having been consulted about it either.[25] While they grumbled, the administration faced two threats that could provoke a defection.

The first difficulty involved the administration's economic projections. Senator Domenici had numbers from his staff and enough contacts with other sources to believe that the deficit picture was far worse than OMB had revealed. Because he was losing sleep over the prospects, the Senate Budget chairman finally told Chief of Staff Baker that he might have to lead a revolt against the tax bill. Baker, Darman, Stockman, all tried to get Domenici to back off. "I couldn't convince him," one senior aide recalls. "None of us could." They assured him they would seek more cuts, including those in defense, later in the year if necessary. Finally, "he went up to the residence with the president and practically got down on his knees to say he couldn't vote for the tax bill, and the president said, 'Pete, trust me, it will work.' And against all the advice of his staff, of Bell, he voted for it." Domenici would huff and puff but simply could not defy his president. One of his aides reported in late 1982 that the New Mexico senator was still tortured about the decision; it would "haunt him for the next ten years."[26]

The administration itself was divided over its projections. Regan, Baker, Darman, Stockman, and mainstream Republican economists all subordinated worries about long-term deficits to a concern with winning now as much as possible of the good things in the president's agenda. "As a group," Murray Weidenbaum would tell the president two months later, "your advisers decided that the midyear review should not be changed. It would have confused the tax picture."[27]

A second and more powerful challenge to the revised tax package emerged from the business establishment. Most of Washington's top business lobbyists met regularly in a breakfast group at the Carlton Hotel. At White House urging this informal gathering had expanded into a more formal Budget Control Working Group that lobbied Capitol Hill for President Reagan's package. They "were not enamored of 10-10-10. . . . But [they] wanted the Accelerated Depreciation" and weren't sure that the tax cut would create horrible deficit problems. According to a group leader: "We did have some economists who said it would work, that the boost in the economy would be so great that we'd get it back in three years." One faction in particular, led by Chamber of Commerce President Richard Lesher and its chief economist Richard Rahn, included some fervent supply-siders. Groups like the National Association of Manufacturers (NAM) were more skeptical, but all had rallied to the president's side with uncharacteristic fervor. They were thrilled to be rid of Carter, wanted help from the new administration on environmental and other regulatory issues, trusted Reagan's old-hand advisers, and so had subordinated doubts about the tax cut.

On Thursday, June 4, at a routine morning meeting at the White House, the business community suddenly learned the administration couldn't confirm the business part of the package. Richard Rahn of the Chamber (whose black eyepatch and boots made him a fitting symbol of that group's individualism) erupted, declaring the new plan "a breach of faith." News of the business reaction spread quickly. Rahn and his colleagues were shocked by this new twist, but White House advisers with liaisons to business were equally stunned by Rahn's response. And "for some reason . . . they in the White House thought we *would* bolt."

Who could be sure? Looking back, it seems unlikely, but White House strategists were working on such a longshot game that even a lessening of enthusiasm might be dangerous. It was not as if they had enough boll weevils to give a cushion. Charles Stenholm estimated only fifteen to twenty members of the conservative Democratic Forum were with the president on taxes.[28] If business really wanted its own cuts, maybe some more traditional House Republicans would ally with Rostenkowski to help business, thereby torpedoing the individual reductions, which, after all, is what they wanted to do anyway. Another source reports:

> The next morning all of us, about fifteen, met with Regan, Baker, and Ture. Regan said, "I hear you're unhappy; we want to do something about it." He looked at Rahn and said, "Let's not just complain." I asked Regan, are your feet in concrete on this? Regan said yes. I told him, "All I have to say is, the Roundtable [chief executives of the nation's largest corporations] meets Monday, and they've never really liked 10-10-10. The two guys who sold them were Wriston and Shultz, who are out of the country right now." Silence. Baker said, "Can this be fixed?" I said, "Three days ago it might have been fixed. Now you're set in concrete."

This participant reports that at the June 5 meeting someone suggested "that they just restore the last part but move it out past the third year of the budget horizon." In other words, they would postpone but not eliminate the deficit effects, moving them far enough into the future for the boll weevils not to have to look at them. There are conflicting reports about who came up with the idea and when, but it held the most promise of solving the political problem of holding both business and the boll weevils.

Secretary of the Treasury Regan was no fan of most of the excised provisions, but Baker was pressuring him to solve the political problem any way he could. The secretary then thought the most important part of his own job was to serve the president, which meant above all maintaining a coalition to support the individual tax reduction.[29] Over the weekend, the Treasury redrafted Conable-Hance along the lines suggested by the business representatives. The revised package, actually introduced in the House on Tuesday, June 9, produced the same revenue loss for the budget period, FY82–84, as had the June 4 plan. But for FY81–86 it cost $163 billion, $10 billion less than the February plan but $40 billion more than on June 4.[30] If business was bluffing, the bluff had worked.

The administration now had 5-10-10 on the individual side, a delayed version of the original business plan, and many provisions designed to win marginal, particularly Republican, votes.

The Democrats Respond

The Democrats' strategy had been, in essence, to beat the individual rate cuts by using special provisions to win marginal votes. Now the Republicans had matched those bids. Tip O'Neill mused that "when they had the pure Kemp-Roth and the 10-5-3 we had them licked and they knew we had them licked. But where we made our mistake was . . . in allowing them to get the information of what was in our bill . . . the sweeteners. . . . They took the goodies that were under our table."[31]

The bidding for marginal votes could only continue; any bid, however obnoxious in itself, would seem the lesser evil compared to losing on the individual rate cut. Of the proposals circulating in Ways and Means Ken Holland (D-S.C.) remarked, "It used to be that these kinds of things were only being advocated by rednecks and Republicans."[32] Anticipating the dynamic that would follow, the *New Republic* commented that "liberal citizens can only hope that the Democrats will come to terms before Reagan threatens to compromise further."[33]

The bidding war that followed should not, however, obscure the real disagreement on policy. In mid-June, Ways and Means Democrats endorsed a 5 percent rate cut on October 1, 1981, and 10 percent on July 1, 1982, substantially tilted toward middle- and lower-incomes. In order to argue that their bill would be as generous as Reagan's, if the deficit allowed—a pretty good reading of opinion polls—Ways and Means designed "a gimmicky trigger that we knew could never be pulled," allowing a third-year, 10 percent cut if the economy did some miraculous things.

On the business side, Sam Gibbons, chairman of the task force responsible for drafting a Democratic plan, set the size of the Republican package as a rough standard. There seems to have been little controversy over that decision. The question was how to match the Republican offer. In mid-June Ways and Means Democrats pulled a whopper out of their hat; they endorsed "expensing," the provision under which a corporation could write off all the cost of an investment in the first year.

Although it essentially eliminated taxation on investment, expensing would not subsidize anything in particular—unlike the administration plan, which was estimated to cost $1.07 for every $1.00 of new investment. Economists, who dislike government trying to influence market actions, had to prefer expensing to the messy details of Reagan's Accelerated Cost Recovery System and to the investment tax credit. Former Senate Finance Chairman Russell Long commented that business had always wanted expensing; "they only didn't ask for it because they thought they couldn't get it."[34]

In addition to expensing, the Democrats proposed reducing the corporate income tax, with top rates falling from 46 to 34 percent between 1984 and 1987. People with short memories, especially those who seek to judge responsibility for the deficit, should remember not only what Republicans got but also what Democrats were prepared to give.

Expensing was a bold stroke, attractive to businessmen and economists, a real reform that would simplify the tax code (eventually) yet, supposedly, cost less than the GOP plan.[35] Naturally the Democrats could not keep it all this simple; they added an investment tax credit for the smokestack industries (cars, steel—think of Chrysler) in trouble, particular beneficiaries of the GOP plan. The tax credits could be received as refunds even if these ailing companies had no profits to be taxed. "You guys have come a long way toward being Republicans on taxes," W. Henson Moore (R-La.) commented, "but this goes too . . . far."[36] In the end Republicans matched the bid by allowing unprofitable companies to sell unused tax credits to companies that could use them, a variant that in a rather twisted way preserved a market role in this process— without reducing the government's loss and while strengthening the already strong. Sales of tax credits became a prime target for repeal in the 1982 tax act.

The Democrats' bold maneuver might have worked if politics was only about competing for support on the basis of the best offer. But that is the politics of amateurs, people in the game for only one round. To the professionals, long-term alliances are more important than short-term offers. The professional's question—here we include not only party politicians but also partisan policy experts and leaders of interest groups— is not, Whose proposal sounds better? but Who are my friends? Business lobbyists ignored the attractive Democratic proposal, rationalizing their disinterest with doubts the Democrats would actually follow through.[37] A business lobbyist explains, "We didn't take expensing because it was just not invented here, that's all." Another says, "It was very late in the game, and in politics you don't change sides so easily." A Ways and Means source summarized what happened: "They were just on the president's side. We're big kids, we talked to these guys, and the message was coming from the CEOs. I don't care what we did, they were going to back Ronald Reagan." The fact that the Democrats' plan was slightly less generous surely did not help, but it would have required a much more generous plan to get business to defect from a Republican president. Sentiment as well as hard-sell motivates the managers of corporate capitalism.

Senate Finance Moves

As Ways and Means Democrats worked on their package, public conflict shifted to the Senate, where Chairman Dole was working to report his bill before the July 4th recess. Dole wanted to keep the pressure on Ways and Means. He circumvented the constitutional requirement that revenue measures originate in the House by attaching the bill to a House-passed increase in the debt ceiling. His real difficulty was how to accommodate the intense pressure within his committee for "goodies" while keeping the deficit down.

In a markup that began June 18 and ended June 25, Finance adopted 5-10-10, the rerevised ACRS, and a raftload of additional provisions, ranging from a tax credit for oil royalty owners to one for rehabilitating old buildings included in the Conable-Hance package.

Finance then added, among other things, a reduction in the windfall (oil) profits tax and deductions to help truckers cover the costs of deregulation. The biggest addition was something called the All-Savers plan, under which savers could deduct from their income the first $1,000 of interest ($2,000 for couples) on special one-year CDs, paying 70 percent of the current T-bill rate.

As originally proposed by the savings and loan industry, the point of All-Savers was to generate deposits for thrift institutions, which had severe problems because inflation had made many of their old mortgages money-losers. The thrifts claimed that the tax break would encourage savings. Because that was such a good idea, senators extended it to banks and credit unions. Most observers assumed that All-Savers would just cause a shift of money from one kind of account to another. CEA member William Niskanen called it "one of the worst ideas I've seen in public life for a long time. I see no reason why it would increase savings."[38] Dole called it an "all-subsidy" plan.[39] Treasury and tax committee specialists were horrified, but pressure from senators, particularly Democrats, was too great to resist.[40]

To compensate for some of these valuables, Dole included a few reforms. One would eliminate the "commodity tax straddle." When Finance approved its package, 19 to 1, on June 25, it seemed that Dole had fought off enough other tax breaks to have worked a miracle.[41] He had hit the FY84 revenue-loss target of $150 billion almost exactly but included enough attractive items to get a nearly unanimous vote from his committee.

Only by the standards of the Senate was Dole's a victory for fiscal responsibility. He met the original target by first adopting the administration's compromise to 5-10-10 and then postponing the third-year business tax cuts beyond the budget horizon. Finance had not exactly reduced costs. On one major issue, the indexing of tax rates, Dole had arranged to increase the tax cut substantially, but Stockman didn't know that.

Indexing means raising the brackets each year by the amount of inflation, thereby not pushing people into a higher bracket by a wage increase that gives them no increase in real income. Like repairing the marriage penalty and reducing the estate tax, indexing was Reagan administration policy but not part of the first tax bill package.

Along with Finance member Bill Armstrong (R-Colo.), Dole had sponsored indexing proposals in 1979 and 1980.[42] Because of inflation, Dole said, some families' taxes were "nearly 50 percent higher than in 1965." Indexing, he said, "is more honest"; raising taxes was a decision "Congress should take responsibility for, rather than ceding that duty to the Consumer Price Index."[45]

Although the administration supported indexing in principle, Regan, Baker, Stockman, and even the president insisted that indexing not be added to the bill. In reply, "Dole assured us in plain English," a member of the Legislative Strategy Group recalls, "that indexing would not be in the package at the time it was considered in Senate Finance." Whatever he said to the administration, Dole had his staff working on ways to add indexing from the time the Reagan package was added in February. About a week earlier they had adopted a neat tactic: indexing, beginning in 1985, would be reported as a separate, committee-supported amendment. The date and separate reporting meant indexing would not count in the FY82–84 tax cut totals. The amendment (sponsored by Armstrong) was reported by a vote of 9 to 5. "There were a lot of absentees," one aide reports, "out of deference to the chairman."

By Stockman's account, the administration still thought Dole was on their side.[44] Perhaps that is why, when Dole and Armstrong spoke for the amendment on the Senate floor on July 1, he and Senator Long had the following exchange:

> *Mr. Dole:* The Senator from Kansas would like to speak in favor of the amendment prior to the vote.
> *Mr. Long:* If the Senator wants to speak, go right on ahead.
> *Mr. Dole:* If there are other speakers, I would sort of like to blend in with the group.[45]

Understandably! According to estimates when the tax bill was passed, in FY86 indexing accounted for as much extra revenue loss as all other additions to the original package combined.[46] The reasons for indexing were compelling, nonetheless, for an establishment politician like Dole, who worried about the perceived legitimacy of the tax code.

With only one Democrat, Bill Bradley, voting against Dole's plan in the committee, the game was essentially over in the Senate. The only question was how many riders would get on the tax-cut train. In late June, Russell Long had told the president, "You have the votes in the Senate to pass your tax bill," and the former Finance chairman was not one to misjudge such matters. Yet Long urged that the third year be subject to a trigger in the event of high deficits. Reagan refused. "Government," he replied, "spends all the taxes it gets. If we reduce taxes, we'll reduce spending."[47] This restatement of his children's allowance theory was the essence of Reaganomics. There would be no further compromise.[48]

Ways and Means Democrats were uniting behind a package that would have provided 80 percent of individual cuts to persons earning less than $50,000, compared to 65 percent in the Senate Finance bill.[49] They would change depreciation to better fit their remaining principles. Ironically, the very fact that the Democrats had lost twice in a row encouraged unity. How many times could the boll weevils reject their party on crucial votes and still be able to live with their colleagues? A number of boll weevils wanted to make amends to the House leadership; they had done enough for Reagan. Charles Wilson, a defector on reconciliation, was working with the leadership to hold his Texas colleagues. When Congress returned from its July 4 recess, most estimates held that the Democrats might well win in the House.

The Bidding War

Which side are you on? Most members knew, but some were on the fence. Neither side could abide the prospect of losing, so they began an all-out bidding war for the swing votes. That war provided the year's most lurid political dramas, which almost obscured the battle's serious policy stakes.

Senate Republicans had saved money by attacking tax straddles. On July 10, House Democrats, on the instigation of Marty Russo (D-Ill.), reduced the savings from $1.3 billion to $900 million by allowing commodity traders to continue using tax straddles. This proposal was drafted by Joint Tax Committee staff after meeting with Russo, the chairman of the Chicago Board of Trade, and the special counsel to the Board of Governors of the Chicago Mercantile Exchange. Nothing could look more like "special-interest" politics. Each organization had given hefty campaign contributions to Russo and Rostenkowski. On July 14 President Reagan, in a speech in Chicago, proclaimed that the Democrats "have gone out of their way to offer 2,500 commodity speculators a tax break of over $400 million."[50] Before the fight was over the president would abandon such rhetoric and raise Russo's bid.[51] The real high-stakes auction, however, involved oil.

What could be more old style politics than oil? Long before OPEC, long before energy shortages and worries about the national security implications of war in the Persian Gulf, oil was at the center of politics. For years a precondition of appointment to Ways and Means was supporting a tax break for oil—the depletion allowance. Texas, Oklahoma, and Louisiana oil money—originally Democratic for reasons of either state politics or opposition to giant eastern oil companies (whose pipelines and market power continually threatened smaller but still rich operators)—became a major financial prop of the Democratic party.

As the Democratic party became more liberal, its conservative southern wing became less influential. The "small" operators of Texas and its neighbors came to realize that they were rich men, sharing some interest in national politics with the "Seven Sisters" of the international oil business. On the whole, Democratic biases, favoring price controls and other measures to ease customers' pain from the dramatic oil price run-ups during the 1970s, did not sit well with oil men. Republican biases toward letting the market decide were much more congenial to people who, for the moment, supplied a commodity for which there was great demand. Democrats had lost their grip on the oil money; it was missed.

The oil industry was not merely of interest to a few fat cats. Many thousands of people received royalties from oil wells; hundreds of thousands more depended on the health of the industry. In Oklahoma there are oil wells on the grounds of the State Capitol; in Baton Rouge, capital of Louisiana, the giant Exxon refinery is a symbol of petroleum's importance. Oil is important in its region in the same way the auto industry is in Michigan or the federal government is in Washington and its suburbs. James Jones said that as many as twenty votes on the tax bill would depend on the treatment of oil. Secure in upstate New York, Barber Conable could call Kent Hance a "knee-jerk oil man";[52] Hance had little choice in the matter if he was to serve his district.

Oil politics focused on redistributive issues: who would pay and receive more or less depending on governmental policy. When OPEC drove up prices during the Carter administration, the oil states raked in money from the rest of the country. In order to assure supply, Jimmy Carter worked for a phased decontrol of prices (which oil interests liked); to prevent further regional redistribution, however, he fought for the windfall profits tax. In this battle over energy policy, the oil-producing states had ideological allies in the Republican party; but it was essentially a regional battle of oil interests against everybody else's, and oil was outnumbered. In 1981 fortunes dramatically reversed. Instead of a losing protagonist in a policy battle, oil representatives found themselves—because of their ideology and the balance of power within the House—a crucial swing group, courted by both sides.

Democrats appointed Richard Gephardt—budget reformer, flat taxer, and deal maker from Missouri—as their negotiator with the oil Democrats. Senate Finance's proposal to increase the tax credit against the windfall-profits tax from $1,000 to $2,500 for royalty owners (generally, landowners who have sold rights to drill on their property) would be justified as an aid to the "little guy," the farmer who just happens to have an oil well on the back forty. The Ways and Means Democrats were looking for something more.

They came up with a plan for a tax credit of $4,300 for royalty owners, that is, a windfall-tax exemption rising to three and a half barrels a day by 1986. This latter provision could be worth far more than the credit. With other exemptions for newly discovered oil, their bid was estimated to cost $7.1 billion through 1986.[53]

Over in the Senate, during debate on the Finance Committee bill, Lloyd Bentsen proposed to more than double the House offer. Although Dole got Bentsen's amendment tabled, 61 to 38, the Finance chairman concluded that some compromise was necessary. He therefore proposed a further reduction, beyond the Ways and Means plan, in the windfall profits tax on "new" oil. Administration lobbyists were unhappy with the cost of this proposal (raising the ante to $11 billion) but could not say much because Reagan was known not to like the windfall profits tax.[54] Northern Democrats, however, now began a filibuster—enough was enough. Dole found that he did not have the votes for cloture to limit debate, a development that may not have disappointed him very much; so on July 22 he dropped his amendment. As of that day, therefore, the Ways and Means bill was superior to either the Senate's or Hance-Conable as an oil subsidy. Charles Wilson was confident about the final outcome: "I will state categorically that we have the Republicans beat on this bill."[55]

Christmas in July

That would not do. On July 23, the *Post* reported, "The Reagan administration, preparing for a confrontation in the House . . . abandoned all pretense of seeking a 'clean' tax bill and substantially altered its tax package to include special interest amendments for the oil industry, savings and loan firms and a collection of other groups."[56] Stockman provides a vivid explanation of what had happened: "Everyone was accusing everyone else of greed, and cynically auctioning off the tax code. . . . At a White House strategy meeting, Minority Whip Trent Lott summed up the mood: 'Everybody else is getting theirs, it's time we got ours.' "[57] Republican House leaders, over the resistance of Stockman and, more important, Treasury Secretary Don Regan and Assistant Secretary for Tax Policy John "Buck" Chapoton, won a series of concessions. Opposition to All-Savers was abandoned, and the commodity tax break, which Reagan had blasted on July 14, became part of the package on July 23. Regan explained that these revenue reducing "giveaways" were necessary for the "greater good" of passing the administration tax bill.[58] Among other provisions added were a reduced holding period for capital gains from one year to six months, the generous Democratic treatment of estate taxes, and indexing.

In a separate meeting with the boll weevils, the administration upped the ante on oil, adopting not only Dole's proposed Senate treatment of new oil, but a series of other adjustments that raised the revenue loss to an estimated $13 to $16 billion. The White House had doubled the Democrats' bid.[59]

The oil provisions were the most publicized aspects of the tax battle, but there were many, many more. The Senate adopted 80 of 118 proposed amendments to the Finance Committee bill, creating a beautiful Christmas tree. These ranged from lowering the minimum corporation tax rate to a one-time $1,500 credit for adoption of certain disadvantaged children to a $10 credit for each pecan tree planted in South Alabama to replace each one blown down by Hurricane Frederick in 1979.[60] In short, the Senate adopted many amendments serving many ends.

The administration's July 23 agreements, about which Conable now had more of a say (some wags suggested calling it "Hance-Conable 2"), included special provisions ranging from sops for gypsy moths (tax credits for rehabilitating old buildings and for woodburning stoves) to a credit for investing in television shows, which Dole dubbed the "Gong Show amendment." By this time all parties to the great tax debate were embarrassed. "It's awfully easy to focus on the add-ons," declared Conable defensively. "If I were writing the bill, I would write it differently. Everybody would write it differently."[61] Liberals in the House finally began crafting an alternative. "It would probably be cheaper," David Obey suggested, "if we gave everybody in the country three wishes."[62] "It's terrible that we should be involved in a bidding war," Rostenkowski admitted. "But it all depends on whether you want to lose courageously or to win. I like to win."[63]

Stockman and Darman were beginning to wonder. As the budget director watched Ways and Means Republicans extract concessions from the Treasury on July 23, he passed a note to his colleague. " 'I hope they're enjoying this,' it said. 'They've just put themselves out of business for the rest of the decade.' "[64]

The oil deal distressed Stockman further. He and Darman had assumed all along that they would have to compromise with Rosty: "[We] expected to have to give in on some spending, but it wouldn't matter because we wouldn't get all the tax cut." Instead the tax package kept getting bigger.

On the afternoon of July 23, the two most independent-minded members of the administration considered heresy: "Maybe," Darman suggested, "we should take a dive on this." If only they managed not to cut a few extra deals—they could see that more deals were needed—the tax cuts might not pass. "But in the end," Stockman reports, "we chickened out." Always the tactician and institutionalist, Darman told himself he was preserving the president's ability to govern. Stockman, more the moralist, recalls that "calculated sabotage of the President's most cherished initiative was beyond the pale."[65] At least for awhile.

With all the ornaments attached, however, the biggest bucks were in the most defensible addition: indexing. Its cost was estimated, by Joint Tax Committee staff, at $12.6 billion in FY85, and $37.4 billion in FY86. When the administration added indexing to its House bill, the proposal was now in the Republican packages on each side. The editors of the *Washington Post* objected:

> Congress has shown itself fully capable over the last decades of legislating tax cuts sufficient to offset "bracket creep." . . . Legislating a massive three-year tax cut in an economy as uncertain as the present one is folly enough. Sharply limiting the freedom of future Congresses to deal with whatever failures of current policy or unforeseen shifts may emerge is mid-summer madness.[66]

A realist had to assume that fiscal policy would work better if choices were phrased as how much to cut taxes rather than how much to raise them. Democracies, in this view, need institutions that can help representatives do the unpopular and the necessary—in this case, match taxes and revenues. President Reagan, of course, would say the issue is too much spending, not too little collecting.

Whether sound or not, the argument against indexing based on grounds of fiscal flexibility is hard to sell. If the reader disbelieves us, try arguing that tax increases should be surreptitious, done in the dark of night, which is how bracket creep takes place. Indexing had already passed the Senate on July 16, 57 to 40 (Republicans, 43 to 8; Democrats, 14 to 32).

In the House, by July 17, Willis Gradison (R-Ohio) had 223 cosponsors on a separate indexing bill. Rostenkowski acknowledged that Gradison's bill would sweep through the House if a vote were taken but vowed to keep it off the House floor. Thus, Treasury Secretary Regan was under intense pressure when he capitulated on July 23.[67]

"It's like the arms race between the United States and the Soviet Union," said Representative William Brodhead (D-Mich.). "For every move, there's a countermove; for every weapon, a counterweapon."[68] There was one big difference: in the tax battle all the weapons were used.

The parties organized home district lobbying of possible swing votes. Democrats set up a "boiler room" in the Capitol with telephone banks for calls to newspaper editors in key districts. Party Chairman Charles Manatt asked contributors to contact wavering legislators. Democrats also tried to pressure the gypsy moths, particularly through labor unions, since many of the more liberal Republicans represented districts with strong union organizations.[69] The gypsy moths were uncomfortable at being placed under such continuous pressure by the administration's unwillingness to compromise. "They don't have to put us to the wall every week," declared Carl Pursell (R-Mich.).[70] But it was hard to see how union pressure could be any stronger on taxes than on reconciliation. Ed Madigan (R-Ill.) concluded, therefore, that the "tax vote should not be too tough for them, but," he added presciently, "if Stockman tries for another $20 billion in cuts next year, it will be very hard."[71]

Republicans had bigger guns. As on reconciliation, they were helped by the fact that they controlled the Senate and the presidency. They had the money ($500,000) for a series of radio ads in swing districts. Most of all they had the president. He used the soft sell, inviting fourteen waverers to a barbecue at Camp David on Sunday, July 26. The waverers generally reported no change of mind; Charles Bennett declared that he felt that any tax cut was a bad idea and had told Reagan so three times. In the end, a sense of being personally courted could not have hurt as eleven of them did back the president. With some members Reagan made specific deals. Then on Monday, July 27, he went on television to sell his program.

Mobilizing the Public

Reagan's audience that night was basically favorably inclined toward him but not convinced about his policies. His job approval rating, which was 68 to 21 percent favorable in early May after his dramatic recovery from the wounding, dropped to 59 to 28 percent in early June, where it remained through the summer. The most likely cause of this decline was Reagan's social security package, which the Republicans' own polling showed to be very unpopular.[72]

Reagan's approval rating, as Table 4 shows, was based more on attitudes toward his leadership than on his budget policies; the latter were as likely to produce opposition as support.[73]

A *Time* poll a little later in the month, however, showed 32 percent of the public supporting the three-year tax cut, while 36 percent supported a one-year cut, and 22 percent no cut at all.[74] These figures could give the Democrats some hope.

Yet the public did not share the Democrats' intense opposition to Kemp-Roth. In a July poll only 16 percent expected the big tax cut to increase inflation; far more people expected the cut to help them through increased employment.[75] The public's seeming preference for a smaller tax cut had more to do with preferring moderation on principle than with objecting to the cut itself.

When Reagan gave his speech on July 27, he therefore had a chance to define the issue in his favor. He wanted to use the speech to make

TABLE 4. Reagan Approval Is Not Based on Policies—
But Disapproval Is
(in percentages)

Approval (58%)	
Deserves credit for trying (general)	26
Approve economic plan and budget cuts	19
Leadership qualities; like him	16
Needed a change of leadership	11
Reducing government size and waste	6
Disapproval (28%)	
Dislike economic plan and budget cuts	44
Reducing social security benefits	24
Helps business and rich people	22
Has not done anything positive	8
Outspoken military posture	7

SOURCE: George A. Gallup, *The Gallup Poll: Public Opinion 1981* (Wilmington, Dela.: Scholarly Resources, 1982), pp. 118–19.

NOTE: Also asked of those who expressed an opinion on approval or disapproval of the way Reagan was handling his job as president (87 percent of the sample): Why do you feel this way?

the case for both his tax and social security cuts. That coupling might well have been a mistake.

Howard Baker and Robert Michel were so worried by that prospect that they sent Reagan a written request that he confine his speech to taxes. "I think it would be a terrible mistake to drag the Social Security issue into the tax and budget fight," added William Armstrong, one of Reagan's strongest supporters on that issue. Republican pollsters advised that the issue had almost caused Republican Michael Oxley to lose a special election in a very Republican congressional district in Ohio.[76] The president backed down, saying in his speech only that he had been unfairly attacked on the social security issue and that his administration certainly wouldn't take away anyone's benefits—correct, though not for lack of desire.

His speech about taxes was a stunning success—"by common consent of ally and adversary," Laurence Barrett reports, "his best television performance up to that time."[77] Reagan called his plan "the first real tax cut for everyone in almost twenty years." In simple and powerful language he attacked the main Democratic objections (that is, his plan's distribution of benefits and riskiness) and suggested what the real reasons for Democratic objections might be:

> The majority leadership claims their [bill] gives a greater break to the worker than ours and it does—that is, if you're only planning to live two

more years. The plain truth is, our choice is not between two plans to reduce taxes, it is between a tax cut or a tax increase. There is built into our present system, including payroll Social Security taxes and the bracket creep I've mentioned, a 22 percent tax increase over the next three years. . . . If the tax cut goes to you, the American people, in the third year, that money . . . won't be available for Congress to spend, and that, in my view, is what this whole controversy comes down to. Are you entitled to the fruits of your own labor or does government have some presumptive right to spend and spend and spend?[78]

Reagan asked his audience to phone their congressmen to urge support. The response was overwhelming:

Until the President's Monday night speech on television, House Democrats honestly believed they had a margin of 10 or more votes. But after the speech, Mr. Rostenkowski related . . . he sat in his office until 11:30 p.m., listening to the phone ringing in response to Mr. Reagan. It was then that Mr. Rostenkowski began to worry. His apprehension deepened Tuesday morning, when most Democrats in the Georgia delegation informed the House leadership that they were going with the President.[79]

What the Speaker called "a telephone blitz like this nation has never seen" set switchboards ablaze on Capitol Hill.[80] Offices were flooded with calls, according to one estimate, favoring Reagan by about six to one. On Gramm-Latta 1, Carroll Hubbard had resisted the blandishments of a state dinner and the president's appeal, but on the tax bill his office received 500 calls, 480 of them siding with the White House. "It is obvious that the president's tax cut has overwhelming support in western Kentucky," said this previously loyal moderate who then voted for Hance-Conable.[81] Beverly Byron had not been convinced by the Camp David barbecue, but 1,000 phone calls won her over to the president's side. Bo Ginn of Georgia received a call from Jimmy Carter urging him to hold fast, but, though Carter was Ginn's 405th caller, he was only the fifth to back the Democrats.[82] Ginn also defected. "The constituents broke our doors down," he explained. "It wasn't very subtle."[83]

Some lobbying was orchestrated by interest groups. The Chamber of Commerce, for instance, organized a telegram blitz of forty-three Democrats whom the White House suggested might be winnable, and twenty-nine of them did defect. Most congressmen, however, concluded that many of their calls were from "real people."[84]

The lobbying after the speech was intense. Dan Glickman (D-Kan.) reported calls from the secretaries of Agriculture, Energy, and the Treasury, and two from the president. Bob Traxler (D-Mich.) reported that at 10:00 a.m. on Tuesday he was called by the president and turned him down. He was called again at 1:30 p.m. by a White House aide. Beginning twenty minutes later, he received calls from top executives of General Motors and Dow Chemical, a Ford vice president, and then a Chrysler lobbyist. Traxler continued to resist, but Glickman, loyal to his party on spending votes, gave in. So did Dan McCurdy of Oklahoma, who explained that after Reagan called him on July 28 (McCurdy also had been at the barbecue), he finally decided to support the president for the sake of "accessibility. You like to know you have access and I feel I have it more so now. The president said he would remember. . . . I have three military bases in my district. I just want to know that if we come to a crunch over that, they're going to remember me."[85]

Other Democrats received more tangible considerations. Reagan gave Glenn English a handwritten note promising to veto "with pleasure" any windfall tax on natural gas. That was no concession for Reagan who already opposed such taxes. The note, however, did enable English to look especially good in his district; it sealed his vote. Some members took kind words as promises; Mario Biaggi of New York announced that Reagan had promised to back legislation to reverse the Gramm-Latta 2 repeal of the social security minimum benefit. That was a big change, if true, as the minimum benefits issue was simultaneously part of the controversy over the conference on Gramm-Latta 2.[86] In every way available to a president, Ronald Reagan sought votes for his tax plan, the centerpiece of his program to change the course of American government.

We cannot judge whether members were convinced by the indicators of Reagan's popularity or found it instead a convenient excuse for a vote shaped by other considerations. Georgia Representative Bo Ginn, for example, explained his vote by constituency pressure; yet both Stockman and one key Democratic strategist had a different explanation: peanuts. As Stockman explains, "The Georgia delegation notified Ken Duberstein [the administration's House lobbyist] it was 'for rent.' . . . I gagged at the prospect. They wanted us to stop our attempts to abolish the peanut subsidy program." Peanuts symbolized, for Stockman, the "corruption of state power." It was "a government-subsidized producer's cartel."[87] Still he agreed; the prize was too big. As his Democratic rival put it, "We had votes we could muscle; they had some; but when you lose eight at once. . . ." Most likely it was peanuts *and* popularity. One member of the Georgia delegation told us he gave a series of speeches against the tax cut in his district, but people wouldn't hear it.

Emphasizing the attack on programs, on the federal government's social mission, inherent in the tax plan, Democratic leaders pleaded for support. "Let us cut spending, yes. Let us cut taxes, yes," Jim Wright proclaimed, "but let us leave the round table intact at Camelot. Let's not burn it for firewood to warm the wealthy."[88] Reminiscent of the New Deal language of class differences ("malefactors of great wealth"),

Speaker O'Neill declared that passage of Hance-Conable would, when added to the Prince Charles wedding in London that day, make it "a big day for the aristocracies of the world."[89] Republican leader Robert Michel defined the stakes a little differently, telling the House, "Let us face it, the Speaker wants to hold onto as much federal revenue as he can."[90] The Speaker lost, 238 to 195. Forty-eight Democrats voted for Hance-Conable; one Republican opposed it. That same day, after approving eighty amendments in twelve days of debate, the Senate passed the Finance Committee's bill, 89 to 11.

Meanings

What were the political lessons of the tax battle?[91] Ultimately Reagan won all but two of those who had voted with him on the reconciliation rule. His lobbying and the public outcry picked up a few moderates, like Glickman and Biaggi. He showed that a president can successfully appeal to the people or to some of them. The tax cut was popular when it passed; in mid-August a Gallup sample approved it by a two to one margin.[92] Reagan was helped, in a way, by the Democrats, who created a package they had trouble defending because they did not much believe in it. "All the Democrats achieved by compromising was to undercut their own arguments against our position," commented a Reagan adviser.[93] But the president also sold the package by continually downplaying its radicalness.

It was hardly a tax cut at all, he argued, much as the spending cuts had not really been spending cuts. There seemed, to be sure, some truth in these arguments. The Kemp-Roth tax cuts would serve in some sense to offset previously established tax increases from social security and bracket creep. Yet while Reagan invoked brilliantly the residual American suspicion of "the guvmint"—always speaking of government as if it were some strange creature with a mind of its own, separate from the people who voted, lobbied, demanded and complained, paid taxes, pocketed the benefits, and staffed the bureaucracy—he did not make his case against the welfare state on its merits. He had some desire to try, as with social security, but was talked out of the attempt.

In short, Reagan's great victories were not truly revolutionary. He did not change the minds of the American people. But he did rouse existing beliefs to a point where many people petitioned their senators and representatives. Reagan used all the powers at his command to obtain, in only seven months, a major redirection of the priorities of the American government. Yet he had not won the public over to "Reaganism."

Congress passed the conference report on the tax bill on August 4. Conferees compromised on various benefits attached to the package during the bidding war. Some miscellaneous special-interest provisions—pecan trees, "the gong show amendment," the freeze of the oil depletion allowance, tax credit for wood-burning stoves—were removed. The mild cleanup of the tax bill was just as traditional as the previous Christmas-treeing of the package.

The bidding war was the most dramatic aspect of the 1981 tax battle. Yet the fact that Reagan won all but three of the votes on taxes that he had won through reconciliation should remind us that the basis of his victory was a coalition created by the 1980 election: Republicans held together by party unity and a minority of conservative Democrats from conservative districts. There was uncertainty, so members of Congress exploited the situation to demand benefits for their districts. Yet the auction proved not that the president had to dominate Congress but that even he had to lobby it. As surely as he raised a political windstorm, just as surely he knew there were limits to how hard he could push. When Charles Wilson was committed to his party on the tax bill, the president ceased his personal lobbying.[94] When Claudine Schneider opposed him on the final Gramm-Latta 2 vote, he called her the next day to pledge his support against unhappy Republicans in her district.[95]

Stockman drew another conclusion; Greider quotes him:

"I now understand," he said, "that you probably can't put together a majority coalition unless you are willing to deal with those marginal interests that will give you the votes needed to win. That's where it is fought—on the margins—and unless you deal with those marginal votes, you can't win."[96]

He added something that meant more then he perhaps realized: "Power," said the disappointed budget director, "is contingent."[97] The oil auction was a wonderful example. Oil interests, relatively weak in the late 1970s, took full advantage of the new contingencies. If power is contingent, however, so is weakness. The oil interests exploited the bidding war, but that was possible only because the bidders chose to play. The game could change very quickly and with it the seeming distribution of power.

Some legislators exploited the need for their votes in late July for personal ends. But to party leaders, and (we hope by now) to our readers, the "situation" meant more than the tax battle of July. That battle was set in a larger context—economic crisis, Democratic party disarray, elite confusion, a dramatic election, Republicans enjoying the prospect of governing, a new president at the height of his power. Those were the circumstances Reagan used, not only for short-term ends but also to shape the long-term results.

The attention paid to the special-interest battle also should not be allowed to obscure the fact that if that battle had not occurred and the president had won his original cleaner bill, deficits would still have been huge.[98]

The fiscal crisis that followed had far more to do with the original plan than with the add-ons. Estimates at the time projected that big differences would not show up for five years (in FY86, $46 billion). There was plenty of time to fix up those differences, if they were significant. The original $221.7 billion revenue loss for FY86 was far more intractable.

From the beginning of the battle, both sides knew that the real stake was constraining government in the future. The Speaker and his allies fought to prevent constraints; they did not believe in the supply-side boom. The president believed in both the boom and in spending cuts. Taxes were the worst part of government, so cutting taxes would cut government, reversing what Reagan believed to be the pernicious momentum of the federal machine. The tax and authorization changes were now part of the law. Attempts to change these would have to overcome not the president's popularity but his veto. He held the key to later action. In that sense, he had set the agenda for coming years.

But the agenda would depend as much on the economy as on Reagan's victories. The crucial consideration was raised by veteran Pennsylvania Republican Representative Joe McDade shortly after he voted for the Hance-Conable bill: "Pray God it works. If this economic plan doesn't jell, where are we going to get the money for anything?"[99]

NINE

Return of the Deficit

Can anyone here say that if we can't do it, someone down the road can do it? And if no one does it, what happens to the country? All of us here know the economy would face an eventual collapse. I know it's a hell of a challenge, but ask yourselves: If not us, who? If not now, when?

The speaker was Ronald Reagan; the audience was his cabinet, the time, September 1981, his subject, reducing budget deficits.[1] As soon as the reconciliation and tax-cut battles ended, the deficit panic began again— indeed, even before Reagan signed those two bills on August 13 and left on a California vacation. The alarm was sounded by David Stockman, privately to the president on August 3 during a lunch meeting of the administration's top economic policy makers, not so privately in a series of leaks to the media. Some critics have argued that Stockman's fear that the deficits would spook the markets was self-fulfilling. But the "markets," with their own supply of gloomy gurus, did not need Stockman to spook them.

The Markets Say No

When the tax cut passed, the coming deep recession was not obvious, though the economy had begun to slow and private economists were nowhere near as optimistic as the administration.[2] The recession was coming in large part because the Federal Reserve had finally taken a choke hold on the economy. An upward blip in the money supply in April supposedly spooked the markets, so the Fed decided to make sure it did not happen again. In early May the central bank raised the discount rate one point to 14 percent with a four point penalty for frequent, large borrowers, allowed the federal funds rate to rise above 20 percent, and began an unprecedented monetary squeeze. M1-B shrank in May and June, not regaining its April level until November.[3] It took a while for what the Fed was doing to be noticed or believed. By the end of June, however, Jerry Jordan of the CEA, commented that the Board was being very strict; Edward Yardeni of E. F. Hutton said that the Fed might push the economy over a cliff; Lacy Hunt of Fidelity Bank predicted that unemployment would rise above 8 percent.[4]

Inflation was still slowing, but so far that seemed mainly a result of good luck on commodity prices. Governors of the Federal Reserve Board were worried that inflation might accelerate again, and so were bond-holders. "I assume markets are so skeptical now," Mellon Bank's Norman Robertson suggested, "that no amount of talk will change people's anticipations. The markets will have to see actual results."[5] By mid-July CEA member William Niskanen was declaring that "I think we should acknowledge that we are puzzled. . . . People don't change their expectations of long-term inflation very fast."[6] Trying to soothe European worries about American interest rates, Treasury Secretary Donald Regan was explaining that "you cannot get inflation under control without having high interest rates. . . . It's a result of supply and demand for money."[7] Interest rates were not coming down, and the arguments they would were daily growing less credible.

Federal Reserve officials expected interest rates to ease "only if we get real softness in the economy." They believed as well that inflation could be controlled only if the economy were weak enough to hold down wages in basic industries like steel, trucking, and automobiles.[8] In July, although money supply growth was running below target and the economy was at a virtual standstill, the Fed lowered the announced targets for 1981. On July 21 members of the House Banking Committee blasted Volcker. Representative Henry Gonzales (D-Tex.) accused the Board of "legalized usury." "Can the country," Norman Shumway (R-Calif.) asked, "stand the cure for this [inflation] problem?" The chairman of the Federal Reserve replied that "turning back the inflationary tide, as we can see, is not a simple, painless process, free from risks and strains of its own. All I would claim is that the risks of not carrying through on the effort to restore price stability would be much greater."[9] The politicians were being judged on many criteria, including employment; Volcker was being judged only on one—inflation.

Instead of a boom, passage of Reagan's economic package preceded the worst economic slump since the Great Depression. From Stockman's Dunkirk memo to Reagan's comments upon the passage of the tax bill, the administration had dreamt that expectations, raised by enacting its program, would cause an investment boom, while tight money would assure price stability. By mid-July that position was becoming very difficult to maintain. Perhaps they hadn't meant that tight. Investors had not been inspired to optimism by the Reagan package, or, if they had, they had not been inspired to pay or charge less for their money. In the June 5 meeting, Reagan's advisers decided not to acknowledge in the midyear review that a rosy scenario was losing credibility. Yet they had to forecast the deficit for their own use, not just to sell their tax program; by late July only the supply-side coterie at Treasury was willing to defend the old forecast.

Stockman, Weidenbaum, OMB chief economist Larry Kudlow, and monetarist Jerry Jordan of the CEA believed that the unlikely assumptions about money velocity should be corrected. The tax and spending packages also produced larger tax cuts and smaller spending cuts, particularly for FY85 on, than had been planned. The administration's Senate allies were expressing strong doubts about the old forecast. Finally, as one policy maker puts it, "The closer you get to the actual, the more realistic you have to be. . . . You move the optimism into the out-years." In late July the economic troika put together a new, more realistic forecast. Even assuming 5 percent real growth of GNP from late 1981 on— a very fine economy indeed—the new forecast, as worked up into budget projections by OMB, implied a deficit of $83 billion in FY83, heading over $100 billion in later years.[10]

On August 3, Weidenbaum briefed his colleagues and the president on the new economic forecast; Stockman followed with a long briefing on the budget bad news. "The president," a participant recalled, "looked stunned." Donald Regan, who had accepted the new economic projections, raised some doubts about the deficit numbers but confirmed the main point: the deficit was likely to be worse than previous projections admitted.

No formal decision came out of the meeting, yet there seems to have been a general, undiscussed conclusion that the administration should respond. Reagan commented that the news would make Tip O'Neill look like he had been right all along; when Stockman suggested (rhetorically) that they abandon the target of a balanced budget in FY84, the president responded, "No, we can't give up on the balanced budget. Deficit spending is how we got into this mess." He added that precise balance in FY84 wasn't necessary, but they should come close and show they had made the effort.[11]

What response was possible? Stockman broached the subject of scaling down the defense buildup; Reagan would have none of it. He emphasized that in the campaign he had said national security was more important than the deficit; he believed it, and the people cheered. Stockman brought up the avenue of tax increases; Don Regan, happy to fight the deficit but with spending cuts, opposed the budget director. Stockman discussed "draconian" cuts in social programs; the president suggested savings from "waste" from federal personnel. He said the federal bureaucracy was "layered in fat."

No doubt Reagan believed it. He had said it before, believing 10 percent of the budget could be cut by eliminating waste, and he would say it again. At the end of 1981 he told Senate Republican leaders as much as $40 billion could be saved from general government overhead.[12] Unfortunately for Stockman and other budgeters, no matter how much waste there may be in the government, people could not agree on what it was. Certainly $40 billion couldn't be taken out of overhead; total payroll for all the civilian agencies wasn't much more than that. Reagan wanted deficit reduction that hurt only "free-loading" bureaucrats, but Stockman had to take checks and benefits away from citizens.

Stockman's difficulty, as he left the inconclusive meeting on August 3, was that, as *Newsweek* reported, "The easy cuts have all been made." By definition, everything the boll weevils or gypsy moths had forced out of his earlier package was difficult, never mind the cuts that never made it to public view.

Stockman versus Weinberger

But one thing hadn't been tried before—the military. Although the magic asterisk in the Economic Recovery Plan referred to domestic spending savings, Stockman and other presidential advisers had long assumed defense could take a hit if necessary. They had assured Domenici, Bill Green, and other doubters that defense could be cut if the deficit headed out of control. When the Legislative Strategy Group met on August 4, Stockman convinced his colleagues that the administration should launch a "September offensive" to fix the deficit. They agreed that, while the president was in California, a series of meetings would be held to work out a new deficit-reduction package.

Baker and Meese agreed that Stockman should prepare a new package, including defense scale-backs, to present to the president in Los Angeles on August 17 and 18. The Senate was asked to delay action on appropriations until late September so the administration could devise this new package. As Reagan prepared to head west, he held a thank-you ceremony for his tax-cut allies. "The fight to control the Federal budget," Reagan told them, "is just beginning."[13]

Before the long budget battle in Congress, Stockman and his deputy, Bill Schneider, were agreeing with Weinberger and Frank Carlucci on 7 percent real growth for the Department of Defense from FY83 on, after 15 percent in FY82 and 12 percent in FY81. Weinberger treated that as a commitment, and the Pentagon began working out a five-year plan to spend its $1.46 trillion.[14] He was following a logical strategy for an agency in a competitive environment where support could fluctuate quickly: get it while you can, a big commitment, and as much up front as possible. His job was to fight for his department; plenty of other people could worry about the deficit.

Pursuing his responsibility to control spending, the OMB director disagreed with the secretary of Defense. Stockman saw no hope of support for much more in domestic cuts unless the military also chipped in; he believed there were plenty of items that the military desired but, for good budgetary reasons (they didn't work, something else would do the same job, the contractor was having trouble producing), could be dismissed. OMB produced a $130 billion reduction (7 percent) out of Weinberger's $1.46 trillion, five-year plan. Their cuts included the usual suspects in such exercises: aircraft carrier groups, the Bradley armored fighting vehicle, the DIVAD antiaircraft gun.[15] The first two were still on the list during the 1988 campaign for president; DIVAD had been cancelled.

The big showdown was set for August 18 at the Century Plaza Hotel in Los Angeles. Trying to build a sense of public urgency in support of their position, OMB staff did a lot of "public handwringing" over the extent of the deficit.[16] The national media picked up the message that defense must be reconsidered.

While Stockman built pressure on the outside, resistance had developed inside the administration. Prepped by supply-side advisers who were not so worried about the deficit and having a salesman's sensitivity to his client's moods, Donald Regan came to oppose arguments that hinted at any retreat on the tax cut. When Stockman began his case by predicting a $75 billion deficit in FY84, Regan objected that, because the administration's program would not take effect until October 1, projections were premature.

Regan's objection stretched the boundaries of reasonable inference. The economic forecast was quite optimistic; fiscal policy beginning in October would not be much of a change from before October;[17] if expectations were to rescue the economy, they should have already begun to work. However, President Reagan didn't believe in macroeconomics anyway; thus, he did not attend to such details. He always wanted a more optimistic forecast. His secretary of the Treasury's objections would help the president conclude that he did not have to accept prescriptions he preferred to avoid.

The secretary of Defense was even less helpful to Stockman. Objecting even to the form of Stockman's numbers (constant 1984 dollars instead of 1982), Weinberger argued that *any* reduction in the defense buildup would be dangerous. He stonewalled by refusing to discuss where cuts might be made. Secretary of State Alexander Haig added that to flinch would send the wrong message to the Soviets. Weinberger echoed that argument, which appealed strongly to his chief's sense of what the buildup was all about. Reagan would make the argument himself continually whenever his aides or congressional allies pressed him for defense scale-backs. Reagan also emphasized that defense had represented a much larger share of the federal budget under President Kennedy, which was true; but, if entitlements had grown, and you could not get rid of them, did that mean defense had to grow to match? Amidst all this resistance, Stockman did have some support from the more legislatively oriented Baker and Meese, who argued that it would be political folly to make new proposals for soaking the needy while sparing the Pentagon. Said one participant, "It can't be done. We'd never win that fight." The president told Weinberger and Stockman to work out a compromise, but that was most unlikely.[18]

On August 26 Reagan's top advisers, led by Meese, met once more to discuss the defense budget. Cap Weinberger again adamantly opposed reductions. Meese asked Weinberger and his deputy, Frank Carlucci, to produce an analysis of defense-budget options. On September 3 they complied, providing charts that showed tanks and airplanes sawed in half and consequences such as deactivation of the division to which Meese's son was assigned. Reagan took the charts for study. He understood the political arguments of his advisers, but he also believed that "if it comes down to balancing the budget or defense, the balanced budget will have to give way."[19]

Having announced they would be remaking the budget, the administration, as in January and February, was continually consulting with its supporters in Congress. A big segment of the latter wouldn't touch further domestic cuts without a defense cut to show fairness and, with defense heading from one-quarter to over one-third of the budget, to give the fiscal program a chance of adding up. Throughout the internal deliberations, interest rates stayed high, stock prices fell, and members of Congress visiting their districts were met not by praise for passing tax cuts but by screams of pain over high interest rates amidst the first signs of recession.

The politicians instinctively and correctly blamed the Federal Reserve's tight money. Back in Kansas, Bob Dole called Paul Volcker and then handed the phone to an agitated constituent so that the Federal Reserve chairman could share the heat. "We can't live with a 20 percent prime," worried Robert Michel, back from his district in Peoria, Illinois. "Something has got to give in the next ninety days." Howard Baker summarized the mood: "I have not witnessed the sort of anger and indignation I'm seeing today in a long time. On the floor, people are talking about credit controls, reorganizing the Federal Reserve, a 'windfall profits' tax on interest income, and wage and price controls. Some of this is coming from Republicans."[20]

Reagan himself joined in bemoaning the Fed as if he wasn't a part of it. At a GOP fundraiser in Santa Barbara, he declared, "The Fed is independent, and they're hurting us in what we're trying to do as much as they're hurting anyone else."[21] This, however, was Reagan the politician trying to soothe the supply-siders, who saw their doctrine being unfairly discredited, by telling them he was sharing their pain. Reagan the policy maker was a hard-line anti-inflationist, a believer in the monetarist doctrine that inflation should be reined in by a tight hand on the money supply. For most of the spring, the monetarists in the administration, particularly Under Secretary of the Treasury Beryl Sprinkel, had been taking shots at Volcker for being too loose. These critics in the administration, along with extreme nervousness in the bond markets (based on remarkably dubious judgments about monetary policy and thus, apparently, equally wrong fears of coming inflation), had helped push the Fed into its tightening in May. Now the bulk of the administration's economic policy makers—Weidenbaum, Stockman, Jordan, Kudlow, Sprinkel—opposed pressure for looser money. Neither did the establishment press approve the politicians' laments. After all, so the common wisdom went, if the Fed loosened, inflation might accelerate.

Most members of the Reserve Board itself, including the chairman, were so concerned about inflation and worried about establishing their credibility as inflation-fighters that the Board was determined, if it erred at all, to err by being too tight. Furthermore, the logic of expectations said that high long-term interest rates, despite quickly falling inflation, must mean the markets were expecting further inflation. Volcker and his colleagues, in turn, blamed that on the deficit projections. If fiscal policy didn't credibly offer relief for bondholders, the Fed had to work even harder to show its dedication to reducing inflation by crunching the economy. From the beginning of 1981, Volcker had maintained and would continue to insist that future deficits forced him to tighten money immediately. Never again would he allow other people's pain to deflect him from his duty or (recall 1979–1980) lead to the Fed being discredited.

William Greider's history of monetary policy during this period tells this unhappy tale well and in great detail.[22] He places a bit too much emphasis on the secrecy and undemocratic aspects of the Fed as cause of a policy that, as he sees it, sacrificed the economic fates of millions to the irrational fears of bondholders. He is right that the policy favored bondholders in the first instance, but his own story makes it obvious that the responsibility for policy extended far beyond the Fed. Panic about inflation, willingness to err toward severity rather than ease, and insistence on leaving the Fed alone came not from the Fed itself but from the establishment (particularly non-Keynesian) economists, the press, and the administration. Reagan believed in hard money; he was willing to use new worries about deficits to demand a new round of spending

cuts. Those Republican and moderate Democratic budgeters, who, unlike Reagan, were willing to raise taxes or restrain defense to reduce
deficits, still believed that inflation and high interest rates were due to
fiscal irresponsibility. Howard Baker would privately urge Volcker to
loosen up, but Stockman, Weidenbaum, Jim Baker, Domenici, Dole,
Hollings, and Chiles all directed most of their attention to the deficit.

Congress essentially had no answer when Volcker demanded that it
put its own house in order. The economic logic may or may not have
made sense; the political logic was overwhelming. As in 1980, if the
government could not control its budget, how could the politicians criticize anyone else?

Thus, the administration was committed to "doing something" about
the deficit, and its mainline Republican allies were demanding as much
when its leaders gathered on September 9 for one more round of Stockman versus Weinberger. The president's speech about his new package
had already been postponed from September 14 to September 24; his
staff still had to figure out what he would say.

Weinberger again made the general case for the defense buildup. He
talked about Soviet advantages in tanks and bombers, even though OMB
had accepted DOD numbers on those items. DOD graphics dramatized
the Russian threat but said little about real differences between plans.
The best of these graphics was a cartoon showing three characters: one,
a pygmy with no rifle, was Carter's budget; a second, "a four-eyed wimp
who looked like Woody Allen, carrying a tiny rifle," was OMB's budget;
DOD's plan was "G.I. Joe himself, 190 pounds of fighting man."[23] Stockman did not know what to say against this hour-long blast of what he
considered irrelevance. There was too much to say and too little time;
he couldn't be sure of agreement on anything, from the numerical bases
to the need for any deficit package at all. As in a number of previous
instances—most strikingly the meeting on "Chapter 2" business subsidies
back in February—Stockman was too discouraged to take the issue right
to his adversary, but he "could tell the President wasn't listening."[24]

Ronald Reagan did not enjoy working with details, and this disagreement, though Weinberger kept trying to obscure the issue, was essentially one of facts and particulars. He organized his presidency by
setting clear policy directives and finding people who would run that
way. He did not want to confront, never mind resolve, conflicts created
when people working out parts of his agenda collided. He preferred
they work it out among themselves so he could say his troops all agreed
on a policy. Put differently, the president had given general policy direction; whether it leaned a bit this way or that need not, he felt, concern
him, nor would he decide better had he considered it. Once more, there-

fore, the president told his secretary of Defense and budget director to work out a compromise.

Because Cap didn't want to compromise and Stockman was furious at Weinberger's "intellectually disreputable . . . demeaning" presentation, that was none too likely. Meese and Baker, therefore, ganged up on the president to force him to make the choice—any choice. He did, but the three nonexperts in the room confused budget authority with outlays; what they thought was "splitting the difference" turned out to be the whole loaf for Weinberger. On Friday, September 11, Reagan had to go over it all again with Stockman and Weinberger. The president was fed up; the staff stayed away. Cap still refused to budge. Finally, Stockman, exhausted and discouraged, agreed to a $13 billion outlay reduction: $2 billion in FY82, $5 billion in FY83, and $6 billion in FY84.[25] Even then they disagreed about the base from which cuts would be made, but Reagan finally imposed a truce with a signed presidential directive.

"If I had to pinpoint the moment when I ceased to believe that the Reagan Revolution was possible," Stockman recalls, "Sept. 11, 1981, the day Cap Weinberger sat Sphinx-like in the Oval Office, would be it."[26] How could this be when even Stockman had no real desire to restrain defense? The answer lies in power over process. Until the defense dust-up, Stockman believed that he always had some arrows left in his quiver. Some solution or maneuver would be found. The events of September 1981 showed that the budget director was not making policy. They showed as well that Stockman's vision of policy making—clear debate on the merits—would not be attained. Stockman had been rolled by a Defense secretary who, in Stockman's mind, had not played fair. Whether the Reagan revolution ended on September 11 is open to doubt. By some calculations it still continues; by others, it ended on August 13 when Reagan signed the tax bill. But Stockman's revolution, his confidence, and his power did end on September 11, 1981, though his responsibility for budget numbers remained.

Reagan Loses Control

The defense decision was announced on September 12. As Stockman expected, it infuriated the gypsy moths and those who considered themselves responsible budgeters. On September 15 Howard Baker and Domenici urged Reagan to reconsider, but he refused. Senate Budget staff drafted an alternate proposal for much greater defense savings, though it still would have left a 7 percent increase. They also wanted to limit medicaid costs and change the formula for entitlement COLAs. But they would be stymied by House Republicans, never mind Democrats, and the president.

In a leadership meeting, one by one Republican leaders vetoed alternatives. Silvio Conte (R-Mass.), Republican leader on House Appropriations, declared that "we've got those domestic appropriations bills so tight they squeak." Bob Dole protected the means-tested entitlements: "Somebody else is going to have to start taking a hit besides welfare recipients." Bob Michel exclaimed, "Judas Priest! There's got to be more than $2 billion of fat [in defense]. We've got to have some more give on defense, or we might not get anything at all up there in the House." John Tower replied that defense cuts would redound "to no one's benefit except the Kremlin."[27] As for social security, the Democratic Congressional Campaign Committee was all geared up to blast any Republican move, and the Republicans knew it. An aide to Howard Baker recalls that staff and Domenici had convinced his Senate majority leader that shaving entitlements "was necessary and appropriate," but House Republicans, especially Kemp, wouldn't touch it; Baker saw no point in a losing battle. This aide neatly paraphrased Kemp's position: "I'm the heir to Reaganism, but that's nothing if the entitlements get cut." Stockman quotes House Minority Whip Trent Lott on the same subject: "There ain't a corporal's guard," Lott said, for touching social security.[28]

Hemmed in on all sides, Stockman and Darman finally decided to try to delay the second- and third-year tax cuts. They agreed on September 18 to try to convince first Baker, then Meese, then Regan, and finally the president. On Sunday, September 20, Meese agreed that Reagan should at least see the option. On Monday Regan objected, and his opposition only buttressed the president's. Reagan asked the obvious political question: "What would the people think?" He added, "We shouldn't even be discussing that idea. If our critics ever heard about it, they'd jump for joy."[29] A salesman who condemns his own product doesn't make many more sales. A leader cannot suddenly go back on his major promise to followers. But what, then, was the fast disappearing September offensive to include?

Meese immediately backed down, while providing the formula that would be used to justify tax hikes in future years: "If we do anything in the revenue category, it should be strictly under the heading of loopholes."[30] Loophole closings could be justified as matters of fairness, without going back on the general promise of lower rates. With only three days to go before the president's September 24 speech, however, Meese's suggestion was little help to Stockman.

At Monday afternoon's leadership meeting, House Minority Leader Michel told his president that support for a new package "just ain't there." The defense number was too small; he couldn't get the votes for cutting other things and leaving the military virtually unscathed. Reagan insisted the whole administration agreed on defense need; anyone who read the papers knew better.

The next day the president slammed the door on tax cuts, saying "damn it, Dave, we came here to attack deficit spending, not put more taxes on the people."[31]

On September 24 Reagan went on television to announce the new, improved deficit-reduction plan, which was supposed to win the confidence of the markets. He proposed to reduce the deficit by $35.8 billion in FY84. Donald Regan at the last minute had offered $22 billion over three years in what were euphemistically called "revenue enhancements." Examples included eliminating some energy tax credits and restricting the use of tax-exempt industrial development bonds. Federal civilian employment would be cut by 75,000 people by 1984 (reducing "waste," of course), though no one knew where or how reductions might be made. Defense would be pared by $13 billion over three years; entitlements, except for social security, would be cut by $2.6 billion in FY82 and a total of $25 billion in the following two years. Here, as with revenue enhancements, Reagan did not have the details, promising only to provide them within a few weeks.

The president did speak about social security, but not to argue for reduced benefits. His allies had convinced him not to fight a battle he could not win and in which they might get killed. Reagan bowed to public pressure and announced support for restoring the minimum benefit. He also proposed a fifteen-member commission—with Reagan, Tip O'Neill, and Howard Baker each appointing five members—to prepare a proposal (in early 1983, safely after the midterm election) to solve the system's financing crisis. Until then, the pension trust fund could borrow from the medicare trust fund, which still had a surplus.[32]

There was, in short, no proposal, another magic asterisk, as Stockman says, save for a 12 percent across-the-board cut in domestic appropriations. Even there OMB was forced to announce exceptions, such as the Immigration and Naturalization Service and VA hospitals. Across-the-board cuts always sound good until someone points out what is actually getting cut. One also always has to ask, cut from what base? Here the administration disturbed a hornet's nest. They decided to cut from neither assumptions in Congress's budget resolution nor the reconciliation act but from proposals in the March budget revisions. The cuts therefore would undo all the bargains and adjustments of priorities that had been made over the previous six months. Table 5, prepared by the rather irritated Northeast-Midwest Congressional Coalition, provides some striking examples of the result.

Given February and March revisions, May and June deals, and Sep-

TABLE 5.   Spending Cuts Inflict Deeper Pain

	Reagan proposal—March 10 (in $)	*12% cut (in $)*	*Reconciliation level (in $)*	*Percentage of cut*
Low-income weatherization plan	0	0	175	100
Economic Development Administration	32	28	265	89
Conrail	50	44	262	83
Amtrak	447	394	735	46
Low-income energy aid	1,400	1,232	1,875	34
Handicapped education	890	783	1,150	32
Public housing operating aid	1,205	1,060	1,500	29
Vocation education	616	542	738	27
Impact aid for schools	401	353	475	26
Comprehensive Employment and Training Act, Titles IIA-C, IV	3,567	3,139	3,895	19
Highway aid	8,000	7,040	8,200	14
Community development	4,166	3,666	4,166	12
Northeast corridor rail aid	200	176	200	12
Mass transit aid	3,880	3,414	3,670	7

SOURCE: *National Journal*, Oct. 3, 1981, p. 1779.

NOTE: The Northeast-Midwest Congressional Coalition has found that the 12 percent across-the-board budget authority cut proposed by President Reagan would actually mean substantially deeper cuts for many of the programs of interest to its members. The table shows the administration's March 10 spending proposals (in millions of dollars) for fourteen programs, the effect of a 12 percent cut on those proposals, the spending level authorized by the reconciliation bill enacted summer 1981, and the percentage cut below the authorized level that is represented by a 12 percent cut from the March 10 administration proposals.

tember changes, the media and politicians greeted Reagan's third and maybe fourth annual budget of 1981 with derision. The administration, *Newsweek* headlined, was "Running to Stay in Place."[33] The *National Journal*'s summary was "Reagan's budget plans generate tepid support, plenty of confusion."[34] *Time* commented that the president was "backpedaling furiously" on social security.[35] The attitudes of politicians and chief aides in Congress were no more encouraging. On the Republican side of House Appropriations, "They didn't really take it very seriously. That was their private perception. Publicly there was some outrage." Over in Senate Budget, a source reports, "We thought they had been smoking dope. There was no way you could cut those things again."

The Economist summed up the reaction of the financial community while pointing out what was puzzling about the whole business:

> At present the Reagan administration is surprising informed people mainly by its implausibility. The president's latest spending minicuts did not persuade investors that interest rates will come down, except investors who trust to Murphy's law that everything which can conceivably go right will from this moment be deemed to do so. Every private analyst who is not called Murphy is now forecasting a bigger American budget deficit in 1982 through 1985 than the White House does, especially as the fastest increasing spending program, which is defence, is the one most prone to overruns on costs. The difference of opinion is whether it is logical or rather nuts to suppose that a budget deficit of around 2 percent of gnp could send American inflation and interest rates soaring.[36]

Whether or not it was "rather nuts" to be so worried about the deficit, the worry, as *The Economist* noted, could be a "self-fulfilling expectation." In spite of his great victories, in September 1981 Ronald Reagan had placed himself in a situation similar to Jimmy Carter's in January 1980. Reagan's budget proposals were being mocked as too little to help and too big to be believed. Had he brazened it out, claiming that the deficit was part of putting the country on a new course, the president would only have had to deal with its size, not with his own credibility on insubstantial reductions. But then he would have needed a staff, especially a budget director, who shared his priorities. Like Carter before him, Reagan was now in the grip of a budget deficit panic that seemed more a matter of faith and group-think than a coherent model of the economy.

Bye, Bye, Balanced Budget

Senate Republicans outlined an alternative package of budget savings that would cut social spending less while raising taxes and slicing defense slightly more than the president had suggested. The gypsy moths were supporting larger defense reductions (which, we should always remember, still meant large increases in real defense expenditures).[37] Their willingness to defect was demonstrated by two votes on appropriations bills. In spite of opposition from the GOP leadership, the conference report on the HUD-Independent Agencies bill got enough Republican votes to pass on the House floor. Then thirty-nine Republicans, led by Silvio Conte, opposed a motion to recommit the Labor/HHS/Education bill so as to implement the 12 percent cuts. The motion failed, 168 to

249. Meantime the administration had not developed the promised package. Neither entitlement cuts nor revenue enhancements were revealed, as promised, on October 20. Not unreasonably, with his own men stymied, Reagan gave Howard Baker private approval to see what kind of deals the senators could work out for their proposed package.[38]

Democrats were emboldened by a September 23 rally in Washington, organized by a coalition of labor and civil rights groups, that drew 250,000 protesters of Reaganomics. As the recession deepened, the Democrats became assertive. "It is a shame," the Speaker declared, "that it takes the human tragedy of unemployment to show the Reagan economic nonsense for what it is." As their programmatic cuts were implemented, the result most embarrassing to the administration was the issuance of new regulations for school lunches, including one and a half ounce hamburgers with catsup defined as a vegetable. After Democratic senators munched a sample lunch at a press conference, the new regulations were withdrawn for redrafting.

The leading economic indicators had slumped 2.7 percent in September; the recession was looking longer and deeper all the time. On November 2 his economic advisers met with President Reagan for another round of crisis talk. Stockman and Senate leaders worked up an outline for changes that would eliminate the $100 billion deficit that senators (publicly) and Stockman (privately) expected in FY84. Senate Budget Committee Republicans envisioned, over three years, $80 billion in tax increases and $30 billion in defense spending decreases, compared to the March budget.[39] Now Stockman, aided by Baker, Meese, Weidenbaum, and Martin Anderson, sought the president's support. Donald Regan led the opposition.

Backed into a corner, the president declared, "I did not come here to balance the budget—not at the expense of my tax-cutting program and my defense program. If we can't do it in 1984, we'll have to do it later."[40] Or much later, for Reagan would not budge. When Stockman reminded Reagan that he as president was publicly committed to balancing the budget by 1984, Donald Regan disagreed, saying that this was only a target; the press had pushed Reagan into viewing it as a promise. Regan won on Monday; Stockman tried again on Tuesday, with commerce secretary Malcolm Baldrige's support, but to no avail; on Wednesday (November 4) the Treasury secretary told Senate leaders that there would be no tax hikes. Because the senators were unconvinced, on Thursday the president made a strong statement to a meeting of private money managers opposing tax increases. Reagan agreed with his advisers that it was not possible to balance the budget. "That's very obvious," he told them, "but a larger deficit is the least of our problems. What we have to do is get inflation down and business activity and em-

ployment up. If there's a bigger deficit then, the man in the street will
say, 'That's okay, things are better.' "[41]

House Republicans supported the president in rejecting the OMB/
Senate "Fall Offensive." "You don't raise taxes during a recession," declared Jack Kemp. Barber Conable called fine-tuning the deficit in order
to achieve a major reduction in interest rates "an exercise in moon-
beams." "Changing your policy every Thursday afternoon isn't an economic program," he snorted.[42] Given enough mainstream conservative
support, Reagan saw no political reason to budge. One can ask how all
these people could be so foolish, as Stockman does, or why the president
of the United States kept advisers who wanted him to be something other
than he repeatedly insisted he was. The inconsistency was not within the
president himself but within the advisory apparatus he created.

As for policy, Reagan did not accept the same analytical framework
as either his frustrated budget director or most of his other aides. As he
told Pete Domenici, in the final meeting of 1981's efforts to design a
package, the issue was not the deficit; rather, "when government starts
taking more than 25 percent of the economy, that's when the trouble
starts. Well, we zoomed above that a long time ago. That's how we got
this economic mess. We can't solve it with more of tax and spend."[43]
That the rest of the industrialized world and, indeed, the United States
had enjoyed the greatest prosperity in human experience with total government expenditures above the danger line did not enter Reagan's
calculations: as we have seen, he saw that as "false" prosperity. Stockman,
Domenici, and others kept trying to point out that even under very
optimistic assumptions (5 percent real growth), the nation faced massive
deficits. But Reagan accepted no such thing as a historically validated,
reasonable limit to growth. As he felt later with his Star Wars initiative,
the president was not convinced that just because something had not
been done was no reason it could not be tried.

On November 6, 1981, Ronald Reagan publicly admitted that he could
not expect to balance the budget in 1984; he adopted Regan's line that
it had always been a goal, not a promise. On November 10, bowing to
the lack of agreement within his congressional party and staff, the president announced that he would put off decisions on the promised tax
and entitlement measures until the FY83 budget was issued in January.
Retreat on two fronts made the administration all the more eager to
show its toughness on the third. Reagan took a hard line on discretionary
appropriations: "I stand ready to veto any bill," he told reporters at his
press conference, "that abuses the limited resources of the taxpayers."

On that same day, *Atlantic* magazine hit the newsstands with William
Greider's long article, "The Education of David Stockman." There was
little in that piece that Stockman had not said in one form or another

to other reporters. Yet the blunt language—"supply-side was trickle-down theory"; "the hogs were really feeding" on the tax bill; "there are no true conservatives in Congress"—and the powerful effect of seeing it all in one place created a sensation.[44] Democrats pounced on Stockman's admissions; the OMB wizard had been revealed as a blue-smoke-and-mirrors artist who admitted not only that all the numbers were bad but also that nobody understood them. Senator Hollings declared for the Democrats that "after the Stockman performance, I don't see how we could undercut the President."[45] White House and congressional figures were widely quoted, though not for attribution, claiming that the budget director had betrayed the president.

Anyone shocked by Stockman's revelations had not been following Washington politics very closely. The surprise was not Stockman's beliefs but his secret arrangement with Greider, assistant managing editor of the unfriendly *Washington Post*. It was not even a matter of feeding a reporter; experienced hands could usually identify the unnamed source of a reporter's story. The unusual part was Stockman's revelation of his own doubts. Washingtonians expect officials to use reporters to plant their private versions of reality into the public debate. The puzzle was how to explain the Stockman/Greider relationship in these terms. Either the budget director all along had been preparing an escape hatch—a defense so he would not be blamed if the policy blew up—or he was obtuse. Such were the conventional reactions, and there was surely some self-promotion and foolishness in the arrangement. There is something wistful yet wrong about wanting it both ways, as if only good intentions mattered. There was something more as well.

After one reads both Greider's and Stockman's books, it seems evident that their relationship was peculiarly equal. Rather than looking for information to publish, Greider was challenging Stockman's view of the world. And Stockman accepted it; as an ideologue who nevertheless believed in exchanging ideas, he was refreshed by a chance to question right and wrong, how the world works. Stockman's penchant for changing his mind seems almost immoral in the political world where commitment is everything; but for an academic, the continual willingness to criticize his own ideas and to take other critics seriously may be admirable. This is to endorse neither Stockman's policy judgment nor even the Greider arrangement. Rather, the fact, not merely the content, of conversations with Greider show how much Stockman remained the policy-oriented theorist who dreamed of a politics of justice resting on free-market economics.[46] Cynical in his manipulations, Stockman still could be shocked by Weinberger's failure to provide a good, clean, analytical debate on defense. He wanted to believe that a liberal like Greider could be won over by argument.

None of this garnered points for Stockman in November 1981. Instead he had to dramatically display loyalty to the administration, showing above all that he served at the pleasure of Ronald Reagan. Jim Baker provided the script: "You're going to have lunch with the President. The menu is humble pie. You're going to eat every last mother-f'ing spoonful of it. You're going to be the most contrite sonofabitch this world has ever seen." In a lengthy press conference after lunch, Stockman proclaimed his loyalty and described the lunch as "a visit to the woodshed after supper." An Oliphant cartoon showed Reagan and the paddled miscreant; a little creature in the corner of the drawing commented, "You should have used the other side of the axe!"[47] The public drama of a chastisement helped soften the scandal of Stockman's supposed apostasy.

In their meeting, Stockman reports, the story was quite different. Apologizing, he told the story of his long ideological journey—how he had worked to make Reaganism work only to be thwarted by the ways of politicians. The president, after all, had traveled the same path from small town values through a rejected liberalism and back to the right wing. Reagan, too, resented the politicians' obstruction; he was more than willing to believe that the press was the real enemy. He had read the article and judged, as we do, that the whole story was more about a frustrated zealot than an apostate. He had never liked to fire people; besides, Stockman knew the budget details that Reagan did not want to know, and the president also knew his budget director's biases. Reagan told Stockman to stay on.[48]

Although he stayed, the *Atlantic* article, as Laurence Barrett explains, deprived the budget director his "shield of purity. Now he could be attacked for his character as well as his policies."[49] Still, many felt better about an administration with Stockman than without him. Thirty-two Republican senators signed a letter to the president declaring that "we need him as part of the team."[50]

The *Atlantic* article, combined with Reagan's retreat from the balanced budget, raised questions about the administration's resolve on fiscal policy. With things sliding out of control, both budget director and president looked for a chance to reassert their authority.

Into the Heart of Budget Darkness

After the Senate had delayed all the appropriations in anticipation of the September 24 package, Congress passed a continuing resolution, expiring November 20, to buy time to figure out what to do with the new proposals.[51] As that deadline approached, congressmen wanted to go home before Thanksgiving. Both House and Senate leaders decided to wrap up all appropriations in one big continuing resolution and extend it through September 30, 1982, so they could go home. On November 12, the House appropriations committee reported H.J.Res. 357, funding twelve remaining appropriations by a total of six different formulas.[52] From the administration's standpoint, there were two main difficulties: H.J.Res. 357 ignored much of the president's September reductions and allotted too little for foreign aid. All presidents, whatever their ideology, wind up fighting Congress for a bigger foreign aid budget; it is as inevitable as the Red Sox always breaking their fans' hearts in the end. The administration promised to veto the House CR.

"It's creepy," Silvio Conte declared. "There could be a real showdown. . . . Those guys up there [in the White House] are really adamant."[53] Congressmen showed little interest in the 12 percent cut. Both sides would have to compromise, bringing them to the *really* creepy part: no one knew how to keep score.

How could anyone tell if the CR met targets for deficit reduction? The CR provided budget authority, but outlays created deficits. If two (or three) sides were to negotiate on outlays, they would need to go through the bills account by account because in each account translating BA into outlays occurred at a different rate. There was no time for such detailed work. Instead there were across-the-board formulas, applied to such a variety of bases (conference reports, probably closer to the president's wishes; House committee reports, possibly further; and so on), that no one could fathom their relation to the president's proposals. As House minority whip Trent Lott described it, "We were working with different base lines and three different sets of figures, and the computers weren't talking to each other."[54] Worse still, much of annually appropriated domestic spending—food stamps, agricultural price supports, unemployment compensation—is really entitlement. In budget parlance, these are mandatory appropriations. An across-the-board cut, without changing underlying entitlement law, makes no sense. For that matter, House Appropriations leaders believed, one should only judge appropriations bills by whether they met targets for the discretionary balance of spending. If the economy went sour and mandatory estimates rose, Appropriations should not be blamed. House Budget agreed. OMB did not. By House scoring, therefore, the CR was only $1.9 billion over the September request for domestic spending and $6.3 billion below for defense. OMB instead claimed the CR was $10.3 billion over on domestic accounts.

Robert Michel proposed that the bill be recommitted with instructions to reduce funds by 5 percent for most nonentitlements, estimating a $4 billion savings. His motion lost, 189 to 201, as eighteen Republicans joined the majority. On November 16, the House CR, of indeterminate cost, was passed and sent to the Senate, where, on November 19, the Senate stayed up all night to take twenty-three roll call votes and tie itself into knots.

Senate Democrats, meanwhile, unlike their House colleagues, would not support the September 30 expiration date. They wanted a number of items in the defense appropriation bill debated, particularly the MX missile and B-1 bomber. After a filibuster threat by Carl Levin (D-Mich.), supported by Hollings and Nunn, GOP leaders changed the CR's expiration date to March 30. After considering a raft of options, GOP leaders also decided to support Howard Baker's plan to reduce domestic discretionary spending in the CR by 4 percent. A comment from *Congressional Quarterly* illustrates the complexity of the proposals that senators were being asked to understand:

> As proposed, the amendment excluded defense, military construction, foreign aid and food stamp programs from the cuts. James A. McClure, R-Idaho, outlined on the floor a complex procedure for applying the amendment that narrowed its scope substantially. He said a program would not be affected by the cut if it was in a bill that overall was at or below the president's budget, or in a section of a bill that was at or below the budget, or even in an account listing within a section that was not over budget. Programs that were still eligible for cuts would be reduced 4 percent but not below the level of the budget.[55]

Got that? Good. Nobody else did.[56]

This new Republican proposal, which gave the president maybe about half of what he wanted, passed the Senate. On the evening of November 20, twenty-eight senators and twenty-one representatives met to resolve their differences in conference. It was a Friday night, so even though the previous CR would expire at midnight they had some time for negotiations. The major differences were over defense, which the House had reduced and the Senate had not, maybe $2 billion in domestic discretionary spending, and a similar amount of foreign aid. As the conferees wrangled, they finally decided that to represent the administration and make sense of the numbers they needed some help from Stockman. The budget director was glad to be wanted after two weeks of abuse stemming from the *Atlantic* article; he settled down with his pocket calculator and began pricing options.

By Saturday evening, the conferees were willing to accept the House proposal, more or less. When most participants went home around 1:30 Sunday morning, they thought they were near a deal, but they most certainly were not.

Stockman went back to OMB, fed that bargain into his computer, and decided that the new bill's changes in budget authority would not yield the outlay reductions—roughly those in the Senate's bill—that he had defined as an acceptable compromise. Therefore, a Senate Appropriations source recalled,

> Stockman recommended a veto on grounds of outlay. On Sunday morning there was a meeting in Howard Baker's office with Baker, Laxalt, Hatfield, McClure, Garn, Schmidt, Stevens, Jim Baker, Freidersdorf, and Stockman, and to a man the senators said, tell the president to sign it! Jim Baker said thank you very much, went downtown, and an hour later called back and said, "we're gonna veto it."

Conferees were upset. Referring to comments about "balancing the budget with mirrors," Senator Mark Andrews proclaimed that "we all thought we had done the job. But Stockman found he was using the wrong mirror, so he got himself another mirror."[57]

Congress had good reason to distrust Stockman's numbers, aside from his own statements in the *Atlantic*. At that point, House Appropriations, which had been building its computer system since 1974, was far ahead of either OMB or CBO on the technical side of scorekeeping. House Appropriations had a simple position on outlays: they should be ignored. Its staff and leaders said then, and say to this day, that outlays are a swamp; everybody should stick to things (i.e., budget authority) that are actually in the bills. Ultimately even OMB had to admit that House Appropriations had a point: One top official recalls that "we wanted to do the technically impossible"; another said that he "found out after that November veto that our numbers were as screwed up as on the Hill."

Nevertheless, House Republican leaders showed their loyalty to the president by opposing the conference agreement. Angry House Democrats chose to pass the bill so Reagan could veto it; then he would be blamed for shutting down the government on Monday morning for lack of funds. Reagan, however, expected to get credit for a veto against spending. This made the loyalist vote a bit difficult for senators to determine, as the *Congressional Quarterly* describes:

> Majority Leader Baker gave conflicting signals on how he wanted party members to vote. At first, he announced his support for a vote to approve the conference report in order to get it to the president. But, in a debate that was repeatedly interrupted by laughter, Democrats relentlessly needled Baker about the contradictions of his position. "Do you vote for or against this conference report if you are trying to be a friend and supporter of the president?" asked J. Bennett Johnston, D-La. Finally Baker threw up his hands and urged members to vote however they felt. "All I want to do is make sure we get rid of this thing once and for all. As far as I am concerned, we could have a vote and you can vote it up or you can vote it down, but just vote it and get it over with."[58]

They voted it up; H.J.Res. 357, passed on nearly straight party-line votes by House Democrats and Senate Republicans, was sent off to the White House. Reagan, who privately had been arguing that economic and deficit problems were separate, then vetoed the bill, shutting down much of the government on November 23 and going on television to declare that spending $2 billion more (maybe) than he had been willing to accept risked "higher interest rates and inflation, and the continued loss of investment, jobs and economic growth."[59]

Under guidelines prepared after the 1980 near-misses, many functions did continue; but nonessential employees of many agencies were told to secure their files and go home. The White House made a point of phoning lawmakers to tell them that White House tours for their constituents had been canceled on account of the budget impasse. Everybody having made their points, House Democrats then extended the old CR. They wanted it to expire on February 3, but, when the Republicans insisted on December 15, the Speaker only mildly resisted Conte's motion to change the date. The new CR passed both houses with ease.

The political implications of the CR fiasco far exceeded what small effect it may have had on policy. It foreshadowed years of byzantine battles over scorekeeping, posturing by all sides to make the other look bad, and conflict over priorities masquerading as a contest over fiscal policy. It fed Senate Republicans' distrust, later converted into a sense of betrayal by the administration. And it made the stakes not only policy but also tests of will among the factions controlling parts of the government. Most of all, the erosion of the September offensive, from a serious assault on the deficit to a conflict over about 2 percent of domestic discretionary spending, showed how much the tide had changed in four months. No longer the initiator and leader, the administration was now just one player, better at blocking action than controlling it.

Everybody went home for Thanksgiving, where Robert Michel hoped that they might "have a little bit of wine and turkey, and all the rest . . . back with the home-folks, and come back here with a fresher view."[60] When everybody returned from Thanksgiving, everyone was fresher, but nothing was easier.

TEN

A Government Divided

What members found at home was no cause for thanksgiving. Unemployment climbed to 8.8 percent in December. As people stopped buying their products, businesses stopped investing to produce more. The public's reaction to the slump eliminated the sense that Congress had to follow the president, without providing a clear alternative message.

The Initiative Shifts toward Senate Republicans

In December only 36 percent of voters said they were better off than a year before; 59 percent felt they were not.[1] In January a Gallup poll reported that 53 percent wanted Democrats to win their congressional district, compared to 41 percent for Republicans. The public still approved Reagan's performance but by the lowest marginal percentage ever after one year of a presidency (52 to 38). On any particular issue—the tax cut, greater emphasis on inflation than on jobs, effectiveness on inflation—narrow margins continued to endorse Reagan. But that seemed, as Gallup's president put it, "hope—not conviction."[2]

The voters distrusted the Democrats even more than Reagan; one-quarter had "a lot of confidence" in his ability to solve the nation's economic problems, while only one-tenth had confidence in the Democrats. In the abstract, people favored "greater cuts in government spending." They also opposed higher income or gas taxes. Unfortunately for Reagan, there was little support for cutting specific programs. A plurality wanted to reduce defense.[3]

The economy continued to slide. Unemployment rose to 9.8 percent by July and 10.8 percent in November. Gross private domestic investment fell by more than 20 percent between the third quarters of 1981 and 1982. By December 1982, industrial production fell to the level of

1977. Supply-siders had argued Americans would work harder because of lower marginal tax rates. However, there were many implicit qualifications; for example, a sufficient supply of money should manifest this incentive, and the cuts should be not merely anticipated but actually effected. But no one was hiring.[4]

As the recession deepened, so did public skepticism about Reagan's leadership, the military buildup, and scheduled tax cuts.[5] Strong majorities opposed further cuts in aid to the poor. In March the most popular option for reducing the deficit, by a 5 to 3 margin, was eliminating the July 1982 tax cut.[6] There would be far less support for raising taxes once people had the cut in their pocket.

Unlike other presidents, however, Reagan's support would not go into a free-fall. By July the decline had halted, even though the economic slump intensified further. His hard core of supporters, present since early in his administration, held firm at around 40 percent of the electorate. Thus, he would not feel as pressured as Carter; yet he also could not rally public support behind him.

Public opinion encouraged stalemate. So did economic logic: massive deficits fueled calls for budget restraint, but the recession provided a strong argument against spending cuts or tax increases. Both concerns, deficit reduction and the recession, lessened the confidence of Reagan's original supporters. "We really believed—and still do—that what we did was right," said boll weevil Billy Lee Evans of Georgia. "All of us would just like to see some indication that these things are working."[7] Donald Regan argued the program had not gone far enough; if the tax cut had been 10 percent in July, none of this bad news would be happening. This classical argument to do more—equally applicable to bombing North Vietnam or spending money on poverty programs—was drowned in a sea of economists condemning the deficit. Of course, as the early December meeting of *Time*'s Board of Economists revealed, the economists differed widely about both the relevant evils and their solutions.[8]

Elite opinion was revealed most clearly when CEA member William Niskanen, on December 8, told a seminar at the American Enterprise Institute that, according to his research, "there is no direct or indirect connection between deficits and inflation."[9] Niskanen had resigned from the Ford Motor Company because he refused to offer arguments contrary to his personal beliefs in regard to the undesirability of restricting foreign competition. On this occasion, Niskanen had correlated size of deficit with all manner of bad things and had found no relationship. So, as usual, he told the world what he thought. Niskanen was immediately blasted by all the organs of "responsibility," such as *Time* and *Newsweek*. "It was a 'How I Learned to Stop Worrying and Love the Deficit' performance that stunned me nearly speechless," said Republican and former OMB chief economist Rudolph Penner (who in 1983 would replace Alice Rivlin as CBO director).[10] The spiraling deficit numbers made it easy to accuse the administration of trying to slough off responsibility.

"Responsible opinion," with its horror of deficits, was deeply entrenched in the White House itself. It just didn't include the president, who identified deficits only with deficit spending. He wanted to cut spending, but, if he could not, Reagan would live with the contradiction between his present results and his past efforts as the scourge of budget deficits. *The Economist* expressed the divisions within the administration very nicely at the end of 1981:

> "We stick with our tax programme," Mr. Reagan told his news conference on December 17th. "We go forward with the reduction in tax rates. I have no plans for increasing taxes in any way." Both in the White House and at the treasury his advisers are divided about the extent to which the president means what he says. Those who doubt the magical revenue-yielding properties of supply-side economics think he is going to have to ask for some new taxes sooner or later, and so they explain that when he says "taxes" he only means income tax, he is not ruling out the customs or the excise. Their only ground for this contention is that, if it is not so, the budget prospect becomes too horrible to contemplate. Mr. Reagan has given no sign at all that he shares their alarm. Unlike the Democratic economists, he does not see a remission of tax as an expenditure; to him it is a beneficent shrinkage of government interference in the life of man.[11]

Both sides were correct: the president did not accept his aides' logic, but he was going to be forced to raise taxes anyway. He was determined, but the pressure was intense—and his credibility was reduced as the economy went to hell in a handbasket.[12] Like Carter in 1980, Reagan would be pressed to "do something."

Reagan did want to balance the budget, but he didn't want to give up the rest of his program to do it. Far better, in his view, he strove to make deficit reduction compatible with his preference for smaller domestic government. Reagan so disliked domestic government programs that he could give a little on taxes and defense to get some social-spending reduction. The difficulty was that Reagan's idea of compromise—given his rather extreme position relative to other politicians on most of these issues—might not look like much of a deal to others. Still, the bounds of negotiation could be revealed only by experience. If some package could win the president's approval, he might, in turn, be able to help it pass in Congress.

From that day to this, the search has been on for a formula to compel Congress and the president to do right, that is, to balance the budget quickly and sensibly. Senate Republicans played the central role in the search for this formula-to-end-all-formulas because they cared the most about balance. Liberal House Democrats and conservative Republicans in the administration cared about deficits as well. We will see why the Democrats became even more interested in balance than they had been in Carter's time. Yet the two wings stood for other things as well. The right was against domestic government and taxes and for a strong defense. The left was for domestic government and its efforts to provide social security in the widest sense. The center, however, stood for balance above all; balance as proof that the system was working, that they as politicians and the nation as a community were responsible, that they could govern. At times, Senate Republicans had help from these moderate Democrats. Hollings, and later Lawton Chiles (D-Fla.), led Democratic budget balancers. The great organs of opinion—*New York Times, Washington Post,* and the newsweeklies—also led demands for action against the deficit. Mainstream economists found certainty again and joined the chorus. Still, the protagonists of that period from August 1981 through December 1982 would be Senate Republicans, continually searching for a position on which they could unite and to which they could win over the president.

Senate leaders (Howard Baker, Robert Dole, Pete Domenici, and Appropriations Chairman Mark Hatfield) had made clear all along they were worried about deficits but thought that a new Republican president should be given a chance. When the economy began to deteriorate, they could argue for modifications in the program, suggesting alternatives, without seeming to abandon either principle or the constituents who elected them.

Selling a deficit package to all the other factions in the government would not be easy, for Ronald Reagan's victories obscured many divisions within Congress.

Lots of Attitudes Mean Little Latitude

We have argued that the bargaining over Ronald Reagan's taxing and spending package was shaped by the difficulty of uniting southern Democratic boll weevils and northern Republican gypsy moths. The circumstances of early 1981 were ideal for overcoming such divisions. A new president was on his honeymoon; the failures of his predecessor fed a demand to "do something"; the president had no failures of his own to defend; the public was willing to give him a chance; members of his party, elated by control of one branch of Congress for the first time in a generation, united to show they could govern. Senate Republican unity on budget votes was unprecedented.[13] House GOP unity, though limited to far fewer votes, was nearly as impressive. Thus, Reagan was able to hold his party and win over enough House boll weevils to build a majority. All the favorable circumstances vanished by the end of 1981; they are summarized in the fact that the president was no longer leading. After the September offensive fizzled, budget votes were no longer matters of support for "the president's program." As program content became more important, therefore, so did the divisions of preference among congressmen.

These divisions, shaping decisions in both chambers, were both more visible and more effective in the House. Senate Republicans, under the skillful leadership of Howard Baker, trying to make the most of their rare opportunity to govern, knowing that if they could settle differences among themselves that would be enough, remained remarkably unified. The House had no such governing party; Republicans needed help from the boll weevils, who in turn were very different from most Democrats.

Party, region, and ideology are the major cleavages among American politicians and voters. They overlap in large measure, but nowhere near perfectly.

Broadly defined, a party is an alliance of politicians united to help each other win elections, control Congress and the presidency, and thereby enjoy the fruits of government. Members of Congress vote with their party because this stable, if rather weak, system helps them know who their friends are. But party also has a strong, often forgotten, ideological component. The budget battles highlighted deep differences within parties in attitudes toward the government and the market. In the United States, what makes party divisions rather messy is a disjunction between party as alliance and party as ideology. That disjunction is mainly a consequence of regional divisions.

The heritage of slavery exacerbated regional economic differences. Until the 1960s, Civil War memories and the search for allies to defend the remnants of its "peculiar system" left the Democratic party as the only party in the South. Republicans, who waged the Civil War, were not welcome. The Great Depression gave Democrats something like parity in the Northeast and Midwest, making them, because of their southern monopoly, the normal party of government. Yet the powerful unions and ethnic groups in the North fit very badly with the WASP conservatism of the South. In the 1960s, when Democrats in the North finally turned on their southern compatriots over civil rights, Republicans began to court the South. At the same time many more liberal Republicans in the North moved toward the Democrats.

From 1964 to 1980 the disjunction between ideological and regional bases of the parties diminished. Yet many Democrats in the South held ideologies that did not much resemble northern liberalism. Especially on issues of race, religion, and social values, Republicans in the Northeast, upper Midwest, and Pacific Coast states were far from comfortable with their party's courtship of the South. They were descendants of the Yankees who, though quite capitalist, had a "commonwealth" ethic of noblesse oblige and community governance that fit poorly with both Reaganite individualism and New Right moralism. As we saw, their districts' material interests also made these gypsy moths more supportive of social programs than were most Republicans.

For most legislators, the 1981 battles on the budget resolution, reconciliation, and tax cut saw party, ideology, and regional interest support each other. The boll weevils, however, followed ideology and interest over party, while the gypsy moths favored party. All that was possible because attention was focused on general characterizations of policy rather than on program content. When the issue became content, as on the tax auction, less grand definitions of interest became more relevant.

Groupings

Every bill will tap partisan and regional interests. Both a bill's debate and its provisions shape attitudes. We know, for example, that members of Congress are more willing to cut programs if they can focus attention on the money saved, not the programs cut. That was one point of reconciliation; it is also seen in the popularity of across-the-board cuts, rather than targeted ones, like those at the end of 1981.[14] Because each bill poses issues differently, we need to look at many bills in order to understand the cleavages within Congress about budget policy. When we look at such a variety of bills, we see less stable coalitions than our previous story suggested. Yet amidst the cacophony of roll calls is a modicum of order, enough to suggest why Congress would have trouble solving the budgetary dilemma.

House members in the 97th Congress may be divided into six groups, more or less from right to left: domestic opposers, responsible conservatives, Sunbelt conservatives, Frostbelt moderates, Democratic loyalists, and diehard liberals.

Approximately forty opposers were fervent supporters of Ronald Reagan, and almost all were Republicans. They were distinguished from other Reaganites by their unwillingness to compromise even as much as their leader. They opposed the domestic government at every opportunity. They voted against individual appropriations that almost all other members supported. They voted against continuing resolutions. They voted against a tax hike even when endorsed by the president. They voted for spending cuts everywhere but in defense; for example, they supported cuts in farm programs and water projects.

About fifty responsible conservatives included most of the Republican leadership and a few Democrats. They were stronger for budget balance, as opposed to simply opposing spending. Thus, they would support the 1982 tax increase, casting far fewer symbolic votes against routine appropriations, while supporting Reagan's basic priorities.

Unlike the first two groups, the ninety or so Sunbelt conservatives were united more by region than by party. About two-thirds were from the South, and Republicans constituted a slight majority. These members were quite conservative, but regional interest came first. They backed Reagan in hiking defense and cutting urban programs but, unlike the previous two groups, strongly supported rural "pork": water projects and farm subsidies. They also voted against the 1982 tax hike.

The sixty Frostbelt moderates were the regional mirror of the Sunbelt conservatives. Almost all from the North, they were willing to cut farm subsidies and water projects. While they supported Reagan on most big votes, they were uncomfortable with the military buildup, particularly when forced to choose between it and medicare. This largely Republican group was the broadest definition of the gypsy moths.

Around seventy members were Democratic loyalists, mostly southern and western Democrats who shared regional concerns with Sunbelt conservatives but who were much more comfortable with the Democratic party. Some were liberal; some were senior; all were pretty loyal. Their regional interests showed up in strong support for agriculture and water projects. They were more prodefense than were Frostbelt moderates. They opposed Reagan on major votes and strongly supported the appropriations bills, compromises no one loved, which kept the government running.

The last and largest, though outnumbered, group was around 110 diehard liberals who were northern Democrats. They opposed Reagan at almost every turn. They particularly opposed the defense buildup. They agreed with Stockman and Reagan, however, in one area: they didn't like rural subsidies, crop supports, and water projects. Some of this opposition was regional interest; some was the attitude toward business subsidies represented in support for reconciliation by Representatives Seiberling and Miller, the liberal side of Stockman's argument about justice and corruption.

The administration's maximum coalition consisted of the first four groups, between 240 and 250 members. But it would not be so easy to get because the Frostbelt moderates and Sunbelt conservatives did not agree on much of substance. Furthermore, a moderate-conservative budgeting compromise, if it lost the opposers, would need backing from members of one of the two Democratic groups. House Democrats, meanwhile, would have their own problems assembling a majority. They could rely on only two groups, about 180 to 190 members. If they allied with the Frostbelt moderates, the loyalist Democrats would worry about defense and rural programs; alliance with Sunbelt conservatives was even less likely because they and the diehard liberals disagreed on virtually everything.

These groupings only reflected tendencies; on any particular issue, local concerns and the merits of the individual case would affect many members. If a vote was on one issue, rather than on a package, members could be targeted and lobbied, as on civil service retirement in the 1980 reconciliation. The clearest case of pressure occurred in May 1981, on the Export-Import Bank.

Congress had to pass a very large supplemental appropriation, H.R. 3512, before the FY81 CR expired on June 5. Reagan used the opportunity (so kindly granted by the Democrats' maneuvers) to request $15 billion in rescissions and an extra $12 billion in military spending. He had the whip hand because spending was expiring; the rescissions were mainly in slow-spending programs like housing; and, after reducing the rescission slightly, Congress passed the package easily. In the course of House consideration, however, Appropriations split the difference between the Export-Import Bank's $5.9 billion existing FY81 loan authority and Stockman's request of $5.1 billion. Diehard liberal David Obey submitted an amendment to cut to Stockman's level.

Export-Import's biggest beneficiaries are very large corporations (like Boeing) and big, very liberal unions (for example, the machinists, who work for Boeing). Good Republicans and good Democrats. Obey won, 234 to 169, on a ballot that split the parties (Republican 113 to 70, Democrat 121 to 99) and our six groups. Only the opposers, who disliked all subsidies (by 36 to 4) and the Sunbelt conservatives (who represented little industry that benefited from the Bank, by 62 to 21) came down strongly on one side of the issue. That night the affected groups got to work, and the next day the House reversed itself. The biggest switches were among the subsidy-oriented Sunbelt conservatives and the Democratic loyalists. The former went from 62 to 21 in favor of cutting to 42 to 40 opposed. The moderate loyalists went from 35 to 30 in favor of cutting to 52 to 14 opposed. Only the opposers and the responsible conservatives of the diehard liberals hardly moved at all after the lobbying blitz. Obey lost, 162 to 237. A program supported by business and labor groups was still hard to reduce. Lobbying pressure was most effective on an isolated issue, especially when applied to those members with least ideological or partisan commitment to reductions per se.[15] They, however, were a majority.

Diverse preferences were highlighted most clearly in a series of votes on the reauthorization of the Legal Services Corporation (LSC). Reagan had wanted to kill Legal Services ever since, when he was governor of

California, California Rural Legal Assistance, funded by Legal Services, had blocked some of his policy initiatives in the courts. Local legal services agencies had a disconcerting and well-publicized habit of suing local and state authorities who, the poverty lawyers believed, were administering programs in ways contrary to the law. The LSC lawyers also won frequently. Many conservatives did not approve of the federal government paying liberal attorneys to sue the locals; even some moderates were uneasy with the idea. Liberals admired it: because everybody else had access to the courts for such purposes, so should the poor or, at least, their self-appointed legal advocates.

An amendment to ban political action by legal services agencies passed 275 to 146, with diehard liberals heavily opposed and moderate loyalists split evenly. It should be noted that, because few Republicans worked at the typical legal services agency, political action generated massive Republican opposition. A ban on lawsuits against governments also passed. The most revealing vote came on a motion to recommit (that is, kill) the legislation. It was phrased as allowing a hearing on the president's proposals (i.e., to eliminate the LSC), thereby making the vote more a matter of loyalty to the president than it would otherwise have been. Yet recommittal lost 176 to 233, as forty-two Republicans voted against it. Opposers and Sunbelt conservatives strongly supported the motion. Diehard liberals and moderate loyalists strongly opposed it. Responsible conservatives mainly supported their president, but the Frostbelt moderates voted almost two to one against recommittal. Even in June 1981 they would go only so far in support of the president.

Farmers

The Export-Import Bank showed how group pressures could limit spending cuts. Legal Services showed the ideological limits on Reagan's revolution. The farm bill, later in 1981, showed why both budgeting and politics are very difficult. Sometimes you just can't tell who will ally with whom or what a proposal will do if it passes.

Agriculture is the nation's largest industry and, going back to clipper ship days, a major export industry. Modern agriculture is very capital-intensive; for most crops, tractors, land, and feed cost far more than the labor employed. Farmers often carry considerable debt, so they are at risk in bad years. Bad years come fairly frequently because prices fluctuate greatly. Prices depend on supply, which depends on weather, not only in the United States, but in the rest of the world. The only thing as bad for a wheat farmer as bad weather at home is really good weather in Argentina.

Farmers, therefore, always want assurances of what they consider reasonable prices. Since the Depression, the government has tried to help. Economists have argued all along that these attempts to help farmers could only make them inefficient. They have been wrong and right: American agriculture gets steadily more productive and efficient, meaning the number of farmers continues to decline. No generation has been quite willing to take the economists' advice. The result has been a complex system whose terms change as market conditions change or costs get too high or some crop's supporters come up with a new idea.

The variety of programs and crops makes farm subsidy politics a fragmented arena. There are, however, some natural alliances by region: cotton, sugar, tobacco, and peanuts from the South; wheat, corn, and soybeans from the North. Certain crops, particularly the grains, are more vulnerable than others to the vagaries of weather and international markets. The combination of regional histories and crop peculiarities has divided the farm bloc into a liberal/radical side (the National Farmers Union and, somewhat, the Grange) and a wealthier conservative side (the Farm Bureau).

Farm Bureau types were more likely to look to export markets for higher profits; the Reagan administration hoped to reduce costs while helping their constituents by promoting exports. Many farmers, however, saw no need to take risks; if the government wanted to help exports, that was great. But if prices went down, those farmers wanted to preserve the existing system, built from a series of logrolls. They stuck together, recognizing their individual weakness: tobacco helped corn, cotton helped soybeans, and milk helped peanuts.

One more giant logroll lay at the heart of farm policy. Nonfarmers had at best a mixed interest in high prices for farmers because, after all, nonfarmers had to pay for the farmers' food. Also, farmers, in spite of their risks, were frequently quite well-off and distinctly Republican. Even the more liberal farmers tended to come from areas, like the Dakotas, of traditional Republican loyalty. So the big city liberals and the farm representatives made a deal; the former would support farm programs if the latter would support food stamps. Food stamps and farm programs were authorized every four years or so in the farm bill. It was an unstable marriage because, although the partners did not much like each other, they needed each other.

The farm bill came up again in 1981. Its consideration was shaped by events during the battle over reconciliation. When a number of farmstate legislators made food stamp cuts real by voting for Gramm-Latta 2, they broke the alliance with urban liberals. The liberals would remember.

The farm bill was already in trouble when it hit the House floor in October. It originated in the Senate, where Agriculture Chairman Jesse

Helms was not likely to ask for, or get, much help from his more liberal colleagues and Republican leaders were leery of the deficit. "We've never had such a hard time, believe me," said one peanut lobbyist. "Agriculture needs to stand together, but we seem to be getting nothing but splinters."[16] First, the Senate cut the milk price support level from 80 to 70 percent of "parity." (Parity is quickly defined as the price when times were very, very good.) That was what the Reagan administration wanted. Then, even though the administration sat on the sidelines, as it had promised Georgia House members in the reconciliation fight, Richard Lugar (R-Ind.) led an attack on the peanut allotment system. Despite Howard Baker's support, a motion to table Lugar's proposal was beaten 56 to 42. A senator commented that the vote reflected antagonism against Helms. Only a hastily drafted compromise preserved a weakened peanut support system. The farm coalition barely protected sugar and tobacco. Robert Dole led a move to trim back increases that the Agriculture committee had mandated for wheat, rice, corn, and cotton. "I'll be criticized by some in my wheat-growing state for this," Dole explained, "but the farmers want us to stop spending, and they are willing to make some sacrifices."[17] Senate events made farm block House members justifiably nervous.

The House then passed a bill that was more generous than the Senate's. The key consideration was that the administration, in cutting deals with the southern Democrats on sugar, peanuts, and tobacco, so as to pass the tax cut and reconciliation, lost its ability to ask midwestern Republicans to sacrifice their programs on the altar of deficit reduction. Therefore, they allied with northern Democrats to (a) protect the North and (b) take revenge on those southern crops whose programs were protected in the earlier deals.[18] Diehard liberals, Frostbelt moderates, and responsible conservatives led the charge to repeal the peanut allotment system and sugar price supports. Diehard liberals had no reason to support fellow Democrats, like the Georgians and Louisianians, who had deserted them on food stamps. Only on tobacco, where the North Carolina delegation had supported the Speaker on the big budget votes, did the diehard liberals have no reason to take revenge. And enough of them supported the program for it to go unscathed.

The bill went off to conference. Tobacco, peanuts, and sugar survived, but, by the standards of previous years, the compromise seemed favorable for the Reagan administration.

Democratic leaders did object to giving Reagan another shot at the farm bill in 1983. So after a series of mostly nonpartisan votes, as Frostbelt moderates and diehard liberals cooperated to cut subsidies, the proposal to cancel FY84–85 reauthorizations resulted in nearly party-line division. Democrats won 201 to 188, picking up 9 Republicans and losing only 22 Democrats. The farm bill then passed 205 to 173, with mostly Democratic votes. The administration was unhappy with its totals; some liberals thought it was too generous; some moderates felt things had worked out just right; and some Sunbelt conservatives decided they had better take what they could get.[19]

The greatest irony in the farm story was yet to come. The administration, which had not quite understood how farm programs worked, made some mistakes. As the year went on, it became clear that the farm economy was in a serious depression. Prices slumped; farmers defaulted on their loans; and the federal government spent three times more than planned on aid to farmers.[20] All the permutations of ideology and interest, ambition and revenge, had far less effect on spending than did the inexorable workings of the economy.

With a series of uneasy compromises 1981 drew to an end. In late November, the House passed a DOD appropriation. Support for the military was still high as the House gave the administration almost all it wanted. Proposals to delete funds for the MX missile and B-1 bomber received only 143 and 148 votes, respectively. Yet a 2 percent cut in procurement and R&D lost by only 204 to 209, with northern Republicans, such as Bill Frenzel, using the opportunity "to warn the Defense Department that, unless it demonstrates a real commitment to reduce wasteful, unnecessary spending, it will lose the strong coalition that now supports the strengthening of our defense."[21]

Congress also faced the embarrassing task of passing a second budget resolution. Senate Budget reported out a second resolution that, as the *Congressional Quarterly* reports, "merely reaffirmed the first. . . . The report accompanying the resolution was a long disclaimer for the committee's action. 'Approval of the resolution, without recommendation, is a stopgap solution to a problem that the committee found intractable at this time.' "[22] The resolution passed 49 to 48. Democratic and Republican budget leaders cooperated in getting the Senate's resolution passed on the House floor, 206 to 200. The leaders all admitted they were just trying to get rid of the darn thing. "There should be no confusion that this will get us through the year," said James Jones. "But this is the only thing upon which we can reach agreement."[23] When the only thing people can agree on is pure fantasy—budget balance without budget action—they are in trouble.

As Congress passed this pro forma budget on December 11, it also finished work on a third continuing resolution. H.J.Res. 370, as passed, followed negotiations among administration and congressional Republican leaders, particularly Mark Hatfield and Silvio Conte, moderate leaders of Republicans on the two appropriations committees. The resolution cut discretionary spending by 4 percent from the levels in Senate or

House pending bills, whatever that meant; the provisions as to which bill applied were as complicated as those in the aborted second CR. The package also increased spending for education block grants, railroad retirement pensions, and low-income energy assistance—sweeteners for gypsy moths like Hatfield and Conte. All in all, H.J.Res. 370 was estimated to reduce domestic outlays by $3.7 billion from previous estimates of the totals for the bills included.

Work continued on regular appropriations. The HUD bill totaled $1.7 billion more in budgetary authority than the president's September request for $58.7 billion, but it also allowed Reagan to cut by 5 percent any budget account that exceeded the September request. It therefore was essentially a victory for the president.

The most complicated battle at the year's end involved foreign aid. The foreign aid bill had not passed in either 1979 or 1980, in part because Congress thought it was in the domestic aid business and in part because of bitter partisan divisions over the proper balance between military and economic assistance. The tortuous bargaining process within both the House and the conference committee ended in a compromise that not only preserved the usual balance between economic and military assistance but actually produced a bill. If there was a hero in the process, it was Jack Kemp, who designed and fought for the crucial compromise on International Development Association funding.

Thus, the year ended with three bills still financed by a CR (Labor-HHS-Education, State-Justice-Commerce-Judiciary, Treasury-Postal-General Government), while Ronald Reagan, Jack Kemp, and Tip O'Neill worked together for a foreign aid spending increase!

The CR and foreign aid compromises might encourage the moderates who hoped all good men could agree on a responsible deficit-reduction package. The budget resolution sham could only discourage them. In retrospect, the signs were discouraging, but that is more obvious now than it was then.

The gypsy moth–boll weevil coalition had already been pushed as far as it could go. Without that coalition, there was no governing majority in the House. The politicians, however, could not know as much. Take the Democrats. They could see that the gypsy moths' ideology and district interest should keep them from supporting further social spending cuts, but the trouble was that the moths, by that logic, should not have supported Reagan to begin with. When you have been clobbered three times in a row, it is hard to believe that won't happen again.

Reagan's victories, even though they had ended five months before, were so dramatic, so different from results in previous years, that no one could be sure of their calculations. Stockman had lost a lot, but he had won some, too. The Republican budgeters in the Senate had been thwarted in the fall. But they controlled their chamber; they had won smashing victories on spending earlier; Reagan had not been around long enough for the senators, or even his staff, to appreciate the depth of his preference for tax cuts and a defense buildup over budget balance. The shifting coalitions we have detailed in the House could mean many things; on peanuts, for example, the House floor had gone beyond the Reagan administration's efforts to cut programs.

The forces of responsibility could also be encouraged by 1981's budget processes. The first resolution was enforced as fully as could be reasonably expected; as CBO later reported, deficits stemmed from the economy, not from congressional failure to keep budget promises.[24] Reconciliation obviously provided a means to package major deficit reductions. If agreement could be forged, it could be enacted.

Carter's January 1980 deficit projection had been $15 billion; Reagan's December 1981 projection, based on the evident recession, was ten times as much. The problem kept getting larger; agreement, so fervently desired, was growing correspondingly more difficult. And the Republicans were divided. Howard Baker pressed for reductions in the defense budget: "I cannot believe that out of a budget as large as the Pentagon budget . . . we can't find $5 billion or maybe $10 billion that we can save."[25] He was skeptical about further cuts to discretionary programs: "We may have overdone it already with some of them."[26]

Taking in the deficit prospect and the cleavages in his own party and the rest of Congress, Silvio Conte concluded, "What we really need is a magic wand. There's going to be a hell of a crunch here."[27]

The Party of Responsibility

As 1981 ended, the governing Republicans in the administration and Congress were deep into maneuvers over a budget plan for FY83. A year earlier the president had clearly set the tone and direction. Now the issue was not how or even how far to pursue his radical agenda; rather than a basic position altered at the margins to win crucial votes, with most votes taken for granted, the very nature of the entire package now had to be negotiated.

Over the course of many months, Senate Republicans would craft a package and convince the rest of the political system to support it. With the economy at its worst in more than forty years and with an election imminent, GOP senators managed a tax increase, called the Tax Equity and Fiscal Responsibility Act (TEFRA, or the 1982 act, to be distinguished from the 1981 Economic Recovery Tax Act, ERTA; the names say much). Passage of a tax increase under such circumstances was surprising enough; perhaps equally interesting were the bill's provisions.

Straw-bossed by a mainstream Republican senator, Finance Chairman Dole, aided by quiet advice from Treasury, Senate Finance produced a package including many tax reforms long coveted by the Senate's dying breed of liberals. In other legislation, social spending was reduced, but not so much as the president might have hoped at the time he agreed to the deal. All in all, the 1982 budget battles were bravura performances by Senate Republicans, particularly Howard Baker and Robert Dole.

Baker was the consummate insider, a self-described "congressional brat," son of a House member, son-in-law of longtime Senate Minority Leader Everett Dirksen (R-Ill.), himself minority leader from 1976 to 1980. Baker was best known to the public for his performance on the Senate Watergate committee. He appeared earnest and diligent, continually asking, "What did the president know, and when did he know it?" (He could not then have imagined trying to protect another president against similar questions.) It is probably a sign of Baker's talent that Nixon's men thought he was aiding them, while as informed an analyst as Michael Barone of *The Almanac of American Politics* was convinced that Baker was trying to discover the truth. With his colleagues, Baker's greatest skill seemed to be the ability to make them feel good about going along with him. His personal skills, along with a fine sense of timing and maneuver, made him, by general acclamation, the most effective majority leader since (the very different) Lyndon Johnson.

Baker combined basically conservative policy preferences with an emphasis on doing the work of government. He deviated from conservative positions on matters that could be construed as questions of responsibility; for example, he supported the Panama Canal treaty and rejected ideological crusades on emotional issues like abortion.[28] Balance was Baker's policy, compromise his forte.

Robert Dole, who became chairman of Finance in 1981, was known mainly for his acerbic wit and partisanship. As chairman of the Republican National Committee in 1971 and 1972 and vice presidential nominee in 1976, Dole had seemed more a hatchet man than a creative politician. But Bob Dole was complicated. Badly wounded in World War II—after months of recovery, left without the use of his right hand—he was both an advocate for the handicapped and an architect of the food-stamp program.

In the United States it is especially important to know where a person comes from because the meaning of left and right, liberal and conservative, varies from one place to another. In *The Almanac of American Politics*, Michael Barone described Dole as a man

whose values and beliefs remain very deeply rooted in Kansas, but who is also a Washington insider, a politician who knows the Senate, the lobbyists, the media—and has been around long enough to see the individual senators, lobbyists and reporters come and go.

To understand Dole's politics, you have to understand that he . . . comes from a state where Republicanism is the natural affiliation of the majority and where the Republican Party's base is broad. . . . Kansas Republicanism believes in free enterprise, but it also understands that the untrammeled operation of the free market is going to hurt a lot of people. Kansas' populist past, and its frequent farm revolts, reinforce that lesson: Republicans as well as Democrats here believe in some sort of safety net. And, living in small towns where everyone knows, or knows something about, everyone else, they see the problems of the poor, not as theoretical, but as practical and personal.[29]

Unlike David Stockman, Robert Dole could not cut social programs merely on the basis of a theory about the causes of poverty. Like Stockman, Dole abhorred deficits and high interest rates, as do most Kansas Republicans and all farmers. It was easy for him to believe that irresponsible government borrowing could ruin decent productive farmers who needed loans for their businesses. That attitude had been common outside the financial centers since the days of Jefferson and Hamilton. Dole therefore was willing to cut social programs so as to reduce the deficit, but he also wanted bondholders and the military to bear some burden.

In part because no one else wanted it, an interesting trio seized the budget initiative: Howard Baker continually fostered a spirit of unity among Senate Republicans; Robert Dole carefully crafted TEFRA and then defended it skillfully; and Pete Domenici stubbornly insisted that the deficit problem be faced, by draconian measures if necessary. Reagan had no desire to attack his own tax cuts, little more in looking as if he wanted to cut social security benefits. Liberal Democrats were quite willing to oppose the defense buildup or the third-year tax cut, but they wanted Republicans to take the blame for any assault on universal entitlements, such as medicare and social security. House Republicans were looking for someone to follow who would not lead the country further into the depression or push the party off a cliff in November.

When Baker, Dole, Domenici, Hatfield, and Laxalt met with the president on December 18, after Congress had wrapped up the budget for FY82, their confrontation revealed real differences in substance. Dole said that he would not help cut food stamps unless something were done about defense. Laxalt held that unless the FY83 budget pointed credibly toward balance in 1984, Congress would see little reason to endure the pain of further spending cuts. Domenici argued that increased economic activity could in no way make up the revenue lost from the tax cut.[30] The president still wanted to slash social spending, not raise taxes. Senators and their allies in the administration wanted a big package, including a tax increase.

Thus, senators and their allies turned their efforts toward making the tax increase medicine as palatable as possible for their recalcitrant president. First, they had to demonstrate that the patient was sick. If the FY83 economic forecast showed fast growth, there would be no need to close the deficit. But preliminary projections by monetarists—led by Jerry Jordan, CEA member with primary forecasting responsibility, and leaked on December 7—showed a considerable slowdown in real economic growth. The forecast was resisted by supply-siders. After the leak, Donald Regan insisted that "we don't have an economic forecast we've agreed on yet. I'm the one who isn't agreeing. I'm a little more bullish than my conferees."[31] CEA Chairman Weidenbaum, however, won that battle. Responding to his critics, he called the forecast "very optimistic, though not quite as optimistic as the supply-siders would like. If our forecast is dismal, the prevailing private-sector forecasts are the end of the world."[32]

The administration's projections were not too terribly out of line with historical experience.[33] Other forecasts were less optimistic because the Fed's monetary restraint would provide a level of downward pressure on the economy that had not existed in previous recoveries from a recession.[34] Supply-siders, such as Paul Craig Roberts and Norman Ture at the Treasury, argued that if any economic mistake had been made it was not the large deficits but rather the tax cut postponement. When the president asked Weidenbaum what would have happened if the original plan's 10 percent cut in July had been implemented, the CEA chairman replied that it would have boosted output in the third quarter, though with only small, "measurable but not significant," effects overall. Roberts then denounced Weidenbaum for a conclusion "inconsistent with the reasoning upon which Reaganomics is constructed"—a fair enough claim, but relevant only if Reaganomics did not include the monetary freeze. Roberts, who viewed himself as keeper of the flame, soon resigned in frustration.[35] Supply-side influence was steadily diminishing. Donald Regan lessened his own objections to new taxes, so long as they were fairly small and on consumption.

The next step for Reagan's aides was to find nice wrapping paper for the tax package. They found it in "federalism." Reagan had long advocated devolution of federal responsibilities to the states, so that decisions would be made by people at the grassroots. Analysts with very different ideologies than the administration's might be attracted by a plan that made some activities wholly federal and others entirely state activities. The difficulties were in determining which programs might be shifted and financing the resulting transfers. White House policy development staff had already been working on these issues when the political staff began to search for something positive that the president could say in his State of the Union message—preferably something to divert attention from the deficit.

The transfer of programs—called, say, a "New Federalism" or "New Partnership"—looked as if it might work. "We've got numbers showing the idea favored by margins of 8 or 9 to 1," *Newsweek* quoted "a Reagan strategist."[36] The senior staff decided to make federalism the centerpiece of the State of the Union address, so Stockman became involved in turning that policy into something that could be put into the budget. There was the opportunity for the deficit cutters.

The package being developed in late December began with a swap in which the states would take full responsibility for Aid for Dependent Children and food stamps, while the federal government would take over medicaid. In addition, more than forty other programs (sixty-one in the final package) would be transferred to the states. In order to finance these programs, a trust fund would be set up to receive revenues from various federal excise taxes. The trust fund would expire (in the final package, begin to phase out) in four years, by which time the states, presumably, would have decided which transferred obligations they wished to maintain and at what cost.

The whole package was definitely in tune with the president's predilections. He proposed such a transfer in his 1976 campaign, only to get in trouble when President Ford's campaign told New Hampshire voters their state would need an income tax to pay for it. In March 1981 Reagan declared that "I have a dream of my own. I think block grants are only the intermediate step. I dream of the day when the federal government can substitute for those the turning back to local and state governments of the tax sources we ourselves have preempted."[37]

On the budget front, the federalism plan provided two opportunities Stockman could hardly resist. If programs were being transferred to states, then, just as with block grants, Stockman could claim administrative savings that would justify expenditure cuts.

Better yet, the trust fund had to include revenues from taxes that the states could themselves impose, if they wished. Income tax revenues would not do because some states, as Reagan had learned to his chagrin in 1976, do not want an income tax. The fund instead would have to be built from various excises. But the available excises in no way added up to the cost of programs being transferred. Therefore, new excises—temporary, of course—would be needed to finance the fund. The fund and the spending would go off budget because they were "really" state activity. What remained in the budget would be reduced on the revenue side by the lost (smaller) old excises and on the spending side by the (larger amount of) transferred programs. Then the budget would be both smaller and closer to balance. It was all remarkably neat: a tax increase needed to accomplish the Reagan dream of smaller federal government.[38]

On December 22 and 23 Reagan met with his top aides to discuss the budget and the State of the Union. At the first meeting, he commented, "Well—I understand you're here to talk me into a tax increase." After hearing some details, he remarked, "Well, they're right, you *are* trying to talk me into a tax increase."[39] Don Regan made the main presentation of the proposal. Normally the leader of antitax forces, Regan disliked taxes on consumption (excises) far less than taxes on income or capital. The president gave a tentative go-ahead to the plan but wanted to see more details. He told reporters, "I don't think that consumption taxes are in direct opposition to the tax program we have instituted."[40]

Most excise taxes involved, such as those on beer, liquor, and cigarettes, had gone many years without change. Increases could be justified, though House Republicans, including Bob Michel, worried about taxing Joe Sixpack to give Daddy Warbucks defense contracts.[41] Senate leaders, however, joined to urge Reagan to support about $45 billion in tax increases over two years.[42]

At a meeting on January 20, Reagan rejected a number of tax increases listed in a decision memo drafted by Richard Darman, but said others were acceptable. Aides leaked the decision to the *New York Times,* no doubt to commit their troubled leader to his decision. As Washington and Wall Street were learning of the president's support for a package yielding $30 billion in FY84 and half that or less in FY83, however, an uneasy Reagan was meeting with Chamber of Commerce leaders. The Chamber lobbied hard for defense restraint rather than tax increases. In fact, they said, they would sit out the budget fight in Congress if Reagan proposed new taxes. Reagan heard the tax argument more clearly than the defense part. The Chamber's reaction made all of Reagan's own doubts seem politically more reasonable; he had begun to feel isolated as all of his aides ganged up on him. "I just want you to know that I've taken everything you've said into my heart, *deep* into my heart," he is reported to have replied. Then he told his aides that he had reconsidered. Even with federalism sweeteners, Ronald Reagan simply could not swallow the tax pill. "I haven't been able to sleep because of this. I just can't do it," Reagan told Michael Deaver the next (Friday) morning. "He stood up and was bouncing again," Deaver reported. "He felt better down to his toes. He was comfortable again. You shouldn't try to change him on basic things and it was a mistake for us to try."[43] (Here, as we say in California, was a man in touch with his feelings.)

Thus ended the cleverest of all Stockman's maneuvers. Reagan kept the federalism initiative in his State of the Union where it got much publicity. The *New York Times*'s headline read, "Reagan Vows to Keep Tax Cuts; Proposes $47 Billion Transfer of Social Programs to States." The revenue hole was plugged by using the windfall-profit tax to earmark revenues for the trust fund for transferred programs. Because only the oil states would be able to replace the windfall tax, the device was of no help to most states or their senators and representatives.

Although it remained a major news story for a number of weeks, the federalism proposal had no obvious constituency. State and local officials, buffeted by recession and unhappy with 1981's block-grant legislation, quickly endorsed the idea of the transfer but remained skeptical about its costs. Rich Williamson of the president's staff, Governor Snelling of Vermont, and others negotiated extensively in attempts to create a plan that the locals could support, but their efforts were doomed to fail. More power and responsibility with less money was a lousy deal, and local politicians rejected it.

National politicians might have liked to dump their fiscal problems on the locals, but, because each of them came from somewhere, they would catch the grief, too. New Federalism seemed irrelevant. "My enthusiasm has to be muted a bit because it doesn't create one new job now," observed minority leader Robert Michel. "The President didn't discuss 1982 or 1983 at all," said Vermont's Senator Stafford. "We've got to live through them first." Senator Hollings, as usual, was the most biting commentator; Reagan, said that senator, had "just shifted around the deck chairs on the Titanic."[44]

If state and federal responsibilities were to be realigned, the process was going to be much slower and less direct. As the federal government was hamstrung by the deficit and while states that raised taxes to balance their budgets in 1982 got extra revenues during the subsequent recovery, states picked up a portion of the programs the feds were unwilling to finance. Indirectly, perhaps inadvertently, Reagan got a small part of what he wanted.[45]

In his State of the Union address, the president reiterated his faith:

> Higher taxes would not mean lower deficits. If they did, how would we explain that tax revenues more than doubled just since 1976, yet in that same six-year period we ran the largest series of deficits in our history? . . .
>
> Raising taxes won't balance the budget. It will encourage more Government spending and less private investment. Raising taxes will slow economic growth, reduce production and destroy future jobs, making it more difficult for those without jobs to find them and more likely that those who now have jobs could lose them.
>
> So I will not ask you to try to balance the budget on the backs of the American taxpayers. . . . I will stand by my word. Tonight I'm urging the

American people: seize these new opportunities to produce, to save, to invest, and together we'll make this economy a mighty engine of freedom, hope and prosperity again.

Whatever was happening conveniently could be made to justify the president's preferred policies. That this was pure rationalization, albeit heartfelt, is evident. We should be less sure that it is an unusual way to govern. Among other things, to govern means to lead, and to lead means to get others to follow. A leader works to (retrospectively) rationalize what is happening in terms that can support present and future policies. In this way the leader tries to give followers a coherent picture of the world so they will not only feel better but also understand their part in the scheme of things. Coherent, however, does not mean true by definition. Ultimately there must be contact with the world of events, which may prove the president wrong.[46]

Reagan's leadership style made more sense in dealing with the public than with the Congress with whom he shared authority in the divided U.S. political system. Reagan's rationalizations came from a world that Congress did not recognize; thus, he could not lead it. His definition of "uncontrollable" spending illustrated the problem. As he explained it in the State of the Union, "uncontrollability" was not, as understood by the budget community, a prior obligation through contract or law to spend. To Reagan "uncontrollable" meant wasteful.

Contrary to some of the wild charges you may have heard, this Administration has not and will not turn its back on America's elderly or America's poor. Under the new budget, funding for social insurance programs will be more than double the amount spent only six years ago. . . .

But it would be foolish to pretend that these or any programs cannot be made more efficient and economical. . . . There's only one way to see to it that these programs really help those whom they were designed to help, and that is to bring their spiralling costs under control. . . . [People are] cheating the system. . . . Not only the taxpayers are defrauded—the people with real dependency on these programs are deprived of what they need because available resources are going not to the needy but to the greedy. The time has come to control the uncontrollable.

The president used statistics in ways that would sound better to the public than to the pros. Few budget experts in Congress would pay heed to his comparison in current dollars to those of six inflation-prone years before. Other comparisons Reagan made—such as a 16,000 percent growth in food stamps, from the time when it was a small pilot program— were equally flawed. Congress could as well have said that the increase was infinite because once there had been no program at all. Congressional leaders continually fumed about Reagan's reliance on anecdotes about food-stamp recipients who used the stamps to buy vodka, and similar stories, when he argued for his program in private meetings. Anecdotes serve more to reinforce a believer than to convince a skeptic.

The mutual misunderstanding was inevitable. Only our congressional opposers could understand because they agreed with the president. Reagan saw government as a child to be disciplined—remember the children's allowance theory; uncontrollability was sort of like not being toilet trained. Most members of Congress, by contrast, saw government as themselves. They saw uncontrollable spending not as waste but as their obligations, and they disliked the thought of going back on past promises.

Reagan's plan to gain control by limiting waste had nothing to do with the problem of being locked in by past commitments—save the possibility that, if a majority could agree that some provision of law was undesirable, Congress might remove any legal entitlement under that law. Barring such easily identifiable policy error, Reagan and many of his listeners were talking about very different things even if they used the same words.[47]

Reagan and Senate leaders perceived a budget crisis, but, where Reagan saw the problem as insufficient control *of* the government, the senators saw insufficient agreement *within* it. Reagan tried to use the deficit as evidence of the evil of social programs. To those who did not share his premises, however, there was another, more compelling, interpretation of the crisis: spending could be out of control because Reaganomics was not working.

The case against Reaganomics was made just hours before the president gave his State of the Union address, when Federal Reserve Chairman Paul Volcker, testifying before the Joint Economic Committee, gave his own version:

> I am very concerned about the deficit in the out years because we do obviously want to look forward to recovery and growth in those years. . . . If the Government is going to stand out there and pre-empt a very large share of the savings flow, you call into question what financial market conditions will look like out there in 1983 and 1984. Anticipation of that situation tends to block the markets today.[48]

The president urged the American people to seize opportunities; Volcker warned against wishful optimism.

Pushed to the wall by events, President Reagan preferred to downplay the deficit. He was reported to have asked why the pessimistic projections had to be calculated at all. Told that the law required these forecasts, the president appealed to Stockman, who confirmed that it was so.[49]

Among the many tensions in Reagan's program, receiving most attention was the one between tight money and promised economic recovery. Politically, however, the most important tension was between the promise of economic recovery—necessary to maintain political support—and the desire for a general sense of urgency required to make people willing to cut social programs that were, individually at least, popular. Reagan seemingly wanted the politicians to believe both him and Volcker.

The goals of these two powerful officials differed: Where the president wanted to legitimate a reduction in the size of domestic spending, the chairman wanted price stability, at whatever level of spending existed. The center in Congress—Senate Republican leaders such as Dole and Baker and moderate Democrats and Republicans like Leon Panetta and Silvio Conte in the House—believed Volcker's version of the state of the union. But Ronald Reagan, as he reminded Senator Baker, was still president.[50]

ELEVEN

Fake Budgets and a Real Tax Hike

By the time the president gave his State of the Union address, his own forecasters were projecting a fiscal year 1982 deficit of $101 billion, rising, if policies were not changed, to $168 billion in FY85. CBO predicted larger deficits, rising more quickly. Ronald Reagan, Paul Volcker, by far the largest part of the political establishment, and, indeed, the public agreed that such deficits were unacceptable. If Carter's $60 billion deficits were bad, much larger deficits must be worse. Yet in trying to get the numbers down for the president's FY83 budget proposal, Stockman had to accept the defense buildup. The president rejected his tax initiatives. Nobody considered touching interest payments. Social security, certainly, was not for Stockman and the president to put on the cutting board. That left Stockman looking for deficit reductions out of the remaining 40 percent of the budget. By CBO's figures, the deficit was half as big as the programs available to cut.[1] Stockman, if 1981's conclusion was any guide, hadn't a prayer of getting much of what he needed out of what was left. The administration's somewhat more optimistic-than-the-norm forecast helped only a little.

Trapped, the budget director reports,

> I finally did what the *Atlantic* story seemed to accuse me of. I out-and-out cooked the books, inventing $15 billion per year of utterly phony cuts in order to get Ronald Reagan's first full budget below the $100 billion deficit level. As on prior occasions, I rationalized this as a holding action. When the President finally came around, we would substitute new revenues for the smoke and mirrors.[2]

Ironically, the smoke and mirrors did not do the job they were supposed to do, but they did a job they were not expected to do. Even with phony cuts, the new budget's deficit of $91.5 billion was too high to be accepted

227

in Congress. Even with the phony cuts, the real cuts needed to lower the deficit to a level that was still too high were too severe to be accepted during a recession. The FY83 budget, therefore, became the first in a long series to be termed "dead on arrival." The phony numbers were not replaced by a tax increase; instead, even bigger phony numbers were used to sell a tax increase to the president.

A Stillborn Budget

Reagan's FY83 budget was met with a torrent of criticism, tempered mainly by the desire of the president's allies to leave some room for an orderly retreat.[3]

OMB claimed that "current policy with adequate defense" would produce deficits of $147.3 billion in FY83 and $167 billion in FY84. "Adequate defense" was the Weinberger/Stockman deal that Stockman had failed to repeal: real growth of 12.7 percent in 1982, another 13.2 percent increase in 1983 and, over the entire 1981–1987 rebuilding period, an 8.3 percent annual rate of increase. Defense would rise from 24.3 percent of federal outlays in 1981 to 37.2 percent by 1987.[4]

Entitlement savings would "restore the focus of social welfare programs on the people who need them most and . . . prevent overcompensation of benefits." *User fees* would be increased for activities that "provide direct services above and beyond those that accrue to the general public." *Discretionary and other programs* ranged from housing to Amtrak to job training. *Tax revisions* were supposed to "eliminate unintended tax benefits and remove obsolete incentives." Finally, *management initiatives* constituted a potpourri of savings, from will-o-the-wisp reductions in "waste, fraud, and abuse" to changes in tax collection and federal pay.[5] The savings projected from all these means are summarized in Table 6.

The administration was proposing social program cuts of more than $58 billion by FY84. AFDC and food stamps would be cut by nearly 20 percent; the employment programs remaining under Comprehensive Employment and Training Act (CETA) would be cut in half. Amtrak, Mass Transit, and Elementary and Secondary Education assistance were all to be reduced by 17 to 20 percent. Not all reductions were targeted on the poor; Amtrak was a middle-class program (poor people ride buses); federal retirees are middle-class; and medicare savings were expected to come from hospitals and doctors as well as patients. But the overall effect of these changes did mean considerably reduced benefits for low-income groups.

Stockman's book-cooking occurred in the category called management initiatives, for example, the restraint of federal pay raises to 5 percent—

TABLE 6. The Administration's Fiscal Year 1983 Budget Deficit
Reduction Proposals (in billions of dollars)

	FY83	FY84	FY85	Total	Percentage
Entitlement savings[a]	11.7	17.1	22.8	55.6	21.5
Medical	5.1	8.3	12.5	25.9	
Cash assistance and nutrition	4.6	5.2	5.9	15.6	
Federal retirement	0.9	1.8	2.3	5.1	
Other	1.1	1.8	2.1	5.0	
Discretionary and other programs	14.2	26.1	35.3	75.6	31.6
Management initiatives[a]	20.3	24.0	23.9	68.2	28.5
Improved tax collection and enforcement	5.5	5.5	4.7	15.7	
Tax revisions	7.2	13.5	13.5	34.1	14.3
User fees	2.5	3.5	3.8	9.8	4.1
Total	55.9	84.1	99.3	239.3	100.0

SOURCES: *President's Budget for Fiscal Year 1983*, pp. 3–8; Congressional Budget Office, *An Analysis of the President's Budgetary Proposals for Fiscal Year 1983*, February 1982, p. 8.
[a]Includes revenue increases, such as medicare premiums.

a level that few if any policy makers had expected to be exceeded, even if the formal comparability process projected larger increases. Estimates of revenues from accelerated leasing of offshore oil sites were even more dubious. Between them, pay and oil lease "savings" totaled $31 billion over three years. Increased enforcement by the IRS was supposed to yield nearly $7 billion.[6]

The package was not, however, purely spending cuts and mirrors. More than 20 percent, including the highly controversial management initiative of withholding (just like on wages) a portion of dividend and interest income, consisted of revenue increases. These proposals—including a new minimum tax on corporations and changes in some accounting procedures—were, the CBO concluded, "heavily weighted toward increases in corporation income taxes, which account for about three-quarters of the net tax increases proposed for the 1983–85 period."[7]

Professionals in the Treasury Office of Tax Policy had begun an effort to repair some of what they considered mistakes—simply bad policy—in ERTA. They were less concerned about deficits than about anomalies such as negative taxation of corporations; on that basis the secretary of the Treasury, otherwise an opponent of tax hikes, agreed with them.

One would hardly have guessed it from the balance in the president's budget alone, but the fact that the Reagan administration, of all things, was attacking business represented a change in the political balance. Business suddenly was on the defensive; consequently its components began trying to stick each other with the burden instead of uniting to fight all change. How does business fight a supposedly probusiness administration?

The reactions of Republican leaders made it evident that the new plan would last no longer than Jimmy Carter's January 1980 draft. House Minority Leader Michel commented, "Most of the members feel that they went along with a precipitous increase in defense spending last year, and that you can't have that two years in a row. With the kind of deficits we're looking at here, and the need to cut expenditures, you just can't leave defense out of there." Iowa's Republican Senator Charles Grassley declared, "I have spent two weeks touring twenty-seven counties in western Iowa, speaking in twenty-seven courthouses, and there wasn't a meeting where concern with the rapid escalation of defense spending didn't come up."[8] "I don't think anybody likes the budget," said Wyoming Senator Malcolm Wallop.[9]

Economists who previously had gone along with Reagan joined the chorus of critics. Former CEA chairman Paul McCracken declared that "there is a hard-core part of the deficit that's going to have to be covered by some additional revenue."[10] And Martin Feldstein, soon to be Reagan's own CEA chairman, thought that "the Administration has put itself in an impossible position. . . . We may just have a long, flat bottom with very little growth."[11] That he would turn out to be incorrect did not mean he would be uncertain about being correct.

Trying to rally grassroots support for his budget, the president declared that he had a plan but his opponents did not. "To the paid political complainers," he proclaimed in Indianapolis, "let me say as politely as I can, 'Put up or shut up.' "[12] So they did. Most significantly, Senator Hollings proposed to eliminate the July 1982 tax cut, reduce taxes by only 5 percent in 1983, freeze all domestic (including social security) spending at FY82 levels, and increase defense by only 3 percent in real dollars annually. Howard Baker immediately praised Hollings's plan. Republicans such as Slade Gorton of Washington, Rudy Boschwitz of Minnesota, and Domenici began drafting possible compromises; Hollings could be used as a lever to move Reagan.[13]

Iowa's Representative Jim Leach, a leading gypsy moth, explained:

> The President's budget was dead in its tracks the day it was delivered. Conservatives rejected it on the ground that the deficit was too large, and the liberals on the ground that its priorities were askew.

As a moderate, I agree with both. The feeling here is one of lost confidence. No one elected Ronald Reagan to preside over a recession.[14]

The President Retreats

If the president's budget was not good, Congress would have to make its own. But if it wanted to avoid Stockman's social spending cuts and management initiative fudging, Congress would have to cut defense and raise taxes just to attain President Reagan's figures—never mind reducing his deficit. A top Senate Democratic aide explained the box in which the legislators found themselves and the confinement's likely result:

> If you start with wanting to have a balanced budget, anything you do that's real . . . it's gonna cost you. If you have honest numbers it raises the deficit. You have to cut spending more and raise taxes higher. The politicians' tendency, the whole system pushes them, to do what Stockman did, to jimmy the numbers.
>
> Everything you have to do on the deficit is bad. It's a no-win situation for members of Congress. The president can go on TV and make speeches, but they have to vote. In the deficit era the whole budget process is just an albatross for members.

The incentive to fake it was greatest for those with most responsibility, not those with least.

> The House would adopt some of that phony stuff because *they* had to govern. There was always this tension between the House and Senate [Democrats]. The House felt they had to govern. [Senate Democrats] said, hey, we're the minority, to hell with governing, they drove us out of office by saying they could balance the budget with tax cuts for Christ's sake!

Minorities are going to get beat on a partisan issue like the budget anyway. In neither house could they control either procedure or the votes necessary to make anything happen. No solution could occur without the majorities' support. But if the majority—House Democrats or Senate Republicans—knew what they wanted to do, it almost surely would involve pain for someone, so the minorities might as well let those who made the decision take the blame. Trying to reduce the strains within their own coalitions, the majorities, like Stockman, would be sorely tempted to jimmy either the numbers or the procedure. Because everybody was keeping score by total deficit, once one side cheated the others felt they had to as well just to keep up. Both sides would claim that had happened in 1981.

Musical Chairs

In spite of the incentives to fudge, Congress still had to find some serious deficit reductions—just to match those of Stockman. The centrist budgeters wanted to zap everybody—an equitable "three-legged stool" (social spending, defense, taxes) of deficit reduction. A general deficit-cutting mood may allow politicians to assemble a vast number of small changes that otherwise no one would trouble to put together. Recipients might accept small cuts on the grounds they could be recovered later. In 1982, however, the deficits looked so big and cuts in 1980–1981 had been large enough that any useful cuts on the deficit were sure to be resisted. Thus, everyone would oppose a broad package that hurt everyone.

Budgeters who hoped the public interest in deficit reduction would overcome interests in specific government activities, or in the private activities lost to a tax increase, faced two fundamental difficulties. First, people value what they have more than what they might have. They will object far more strenuously to giving up their benefits than the value of those benefits might suggest.[15] Second, the pain of deficit reductions would be obvious and immediate; the supposed benefits were indirect, slower, and dubious. For both reasons, any group that contributed its fair share to deficit reduction would feel it was contributing too much and resist.

Synoptic rationality—one mind imposing order on a system—might yield a pattern of shared sacrifice. Political rationality, a process of groups bargaining and struggling, was more likely to resemble a game of musical chairs, in which the slowest (weakest) player was left standing. That was what Representative Corman had predicted in 1980, what largely occurred in 1981, and what the Democrats feared would continue: the poor, particularly the working poor, would be least able to save their place in the budget.

But politics is not just every man for himself. No one imposes order, but players do watch, help, and hinder each other. A group's success depends not only on its own resources but also on how others see it, in short, on its enemies. Therefore, Stockman's distinction between weak claims and weak clients is inadequate. If a claim is seen as questionable, opposition to the claim can render its supporters relatively weak (as befell dairymen in 1981). The elderly were strong not only because of their own resources but because they had few enemies; almost nobody opposed their social security claim.

Now, if any claim were really opposed by majorities, it probably would not be there. A program of interest only to a minority is not opposed by everybody else; the majority generally just does not care. Farmers want farm programs; city dwellers do not object so long as they are getting something they want, say, housing or mass transit subsidies. People object not to other people getting benefits but to somebody getting too much. The normal practice of incremental budgeting, a kind of rolling agreement on resource allocations, marginally altered each year, creates notions of "fair shares." Participants are most concerned with their own shares; they will care about others' shares only if they seem to be getting out of line.

The Reaganauts justified their policies to other players by arguing that defense had fallen below its historic share and most domestic programs had risen above it. Many 1981 cuts were in programs—housing, nutrition, CETA—that had grown recently. Their share had not been ratified as normal through the passage of time. The very process of rearranging in 1981 (and 1980) created a new history. Domestic spending that survived was more obviously accepted. At the same time a new set of beneficiaries—corporations and the military—had done extraordinarily well. Nobody is entirely neutral; everybody has something to which he is committed. Politicians of the center looked for ways to reduce the deficit; meanwhile, the norms of fair shares, which inhibited taking from last year's victims, favored taking from those who had just done well. Moderate Republicans like Dole and Baker felt the working poor had paid enough; even Robert Michel was telling the administration to slow its defense increase.

These Republican budgeters' notions of fair shares, liberal Democrats' ideology, and the tax experts' disgust with the 1981 auction combined to place corporate taxes high on the deficit reduction menu. Defense also could not do as well as the president wished, but there was still broad support for a substantial increase.

Despite the recession, the rejection of social spending stimulus and fear of budget deficits that we saw under Jimmy Carter had been intensified by huge deficit projections. Even the AFL-CIO executive board, at its annual meeting in February, called only for maintaining social programs at existing levels. Labor had long supported defense spending; but the Reagan budgets forced unions to ask if they were willing to build up defense at the expense of social spending. The answer was "no."[16]

Business interests, as an alternative target, asked how much it was worth to build up defense at the expense of a higher deficit. A wide variety of business representatives, including the National Association of Manufacturers, the Chamber of Commerce, and the Business Roundtable, felt that the military buildup was too rapid in two ways: too expensive and too fast for the defense industry to be capable of supplying new weapons at the rate demanded. Paul Thayer of LTV Corporation,

David Packard of Hewlett-Packard, and Reginald Jones of General Electric were among the leaders of major defense contractors who believed the defense increase could be slowed.[17]

Even if the president's budget were not acceptable, assembling a majority in Congress would still be difficult. At one end were those who wanted to reduce the deficit solely through defense and tax changes, maybe even adding some social spending for sectors of the economy in bad shape (for example, housing). At the other end were those who wanted to reduce the deficit through smaller tax and defense changes and larger social cuts, particularly in universal entitlements. Speaker O'Neill led the defenders of social spending; Senator Domenici led supporters of larger deficit reduction.

The Gang of 17

On February 23, 1982, Domenici announced his own budget proposal: hold defense to a 5 percent real increase for each of the next three years; freeze discretionary spending at FY82 levels for three years, thus allowing erosion through inflation; deny federal pay raises for FY83; and freeze COLAs for benefit programs. In addition, $122 billion in new revenues would be raised, preferably by reducing tax preferences but if necessary by delaying the third-year tax cut. The administration criticized the defense and tax provisions. But the Senate Budget chairman emphasized that "the 1983 budget, like the 1982 budget, fails to respond to the perception that it is inequitable. Congress must redress that perception."[18] Democratic budget leaders Hollings and Jones expressed interest in Domenici's proposal.

The president's staff, particularly Stockman, Darman, and James Baker, tried to get him to cut a deal with Domenici, sending a steady stream of visitors urging compromise toward the Oval Office. But Reagan had a selective ear. Just as in January he had heard the Chamber of Commerce's warnings against tax hikes but not those against defense increases, when Reagan met with economists from his advisory committee he concluded they supported him.[19] The president also insisted that the political situation did not require retreat. "I still think the issues will be ours this year," he told Senate leaders. "What are the Democrats going to run on? Raising taxes? Bargain basement defense when our planes won't fly? Where the hell have they been for the past forty years? They've been in charge and look at the mess they've created. That's why I say, 'Draw sabers and charge.' "[20] But not only liberals might be run through. The Democrats were going to run on the state of the economy, and that was steadily declining. For the first time in forty years, *Time* reported, "highly respected business analysts" were "saying out loud the dread word, depression."[21]

As the skies darkened, the administration's economic advisers fell into what *Newsweek* columnist Jane Bryant Quinn called "profound and angry disagreements [which] are not the sort of thing that engenders confidence."[22] Martin Anderson, believing that much of what the administration could hope to accomplish it already had, departed.[23] Paul Craig Roberts left Treasury, soon to be followed by other supply-siders. As they departed, Reagan's advisers became more united in pursuit of tax increases. Commerce Secretary Malcolm Baldrige was brought in to tell the president that the long-expected surge in capital investment was not on the horizon. The economic advisory board met again, but this time with Donald Regan, who summarized the board's advice in a March 19 memo designed to ensure that the president got the message:

> The group as a whole were more gloomy than I have ever seen them.
>
> There was agreement that the greatest barrier to a healthy and sustained recovery was high interest rates. . . . Most felt that large prospective budget deficits (1983 and beyond) are the primary cause for the high levels of current interest rates, and that the financial markets are convinced that deficits and prospective deficits matter, regardless of the academic debate on the subject.[24]

If all the bad economic news were not enough, Darman prepared a memo indicating that the budget was going nowhere in Congress, and pollster Richard Wirthlin reported a large drop in public support for Reaganomics.

With all this bad news in hand, Reagan met on March 19 with Meese, James Baker, and Mike Deaver. He agreed that it was time to open discussions with the Democrats in search of a budget compromise. By a willingness to talk, the administration would blunt criticism of its intransigence. They knew the Democrats would go along; James Jones had been secretly pressing James Baker to negotiate. Reagan decided that Baker could give up $10 billion in defense and accept up to $15 billion in new taxes beyond what was then in the budget, so long as the Democrats went along with proposed domestic-spending reductions. COLA changes could be accepted as long as the Democrats were induced to share the political blame. Even other members of the administration (save Darman) were not told that Baker had been given a bottom line.[25] Thus, David Gergen, the president's spokesman, was able to insist to reporters that Baker "had only the authority to listen."[26]

On March 22 James Baker requested permission from Tip O'Neill to begin talks with Jones and Rostenkowski. For public relations reasons, the Speaker could not refuse, but he wanted Richard Bolling (whom he trusted as a fellow liberal) rather than Jones to take the lead. Senate Republicans shot their way into the game on March 30. Howard Baker told Domenici to go ahead with marking up a budget resolution (that wasn't likely to be the president's) and the committee voted 16 to 1 to abandon OMB's economic assumptions and use CBO's instead. That forced Reagan and O'Neill to include the senators and established the principle of using CBO numbers for the economy. Using CBO's more pessimistic assumptions made deficit reduction more difficult, but market confidence would not be won with an OMB forecast that almost no one believed.

The negotiators became known as the "Gang of Seventeen." James Baker, Donald Regan, David Stockman, Richard Darman, and congressional liaison Kenneth M. Duberstein represented the president. Senate Republicans were Dole, Domenici, and Laxalt, with Hollings and Long for the Democrats. From the House came Robert Michel, Delbert Latta, Barber Conable, and Minority Whip Trent Lott for the Republicans, and Jones, Rostenkowski, and Bolling for the Democrats.

Designing a budget compromise proceeded on two tracks. At one level was the big picture—the balance among various types of spending cuts and revenue increases. Only the seventeen negotiators could bargain on the big picture, and, of them, only Jim Baker, representing the president, and Dick Bolling, representing the Speaker, could set a deal. Forming the second track were the concrete proposals that would add up to broad categories of deficit reduction. Here policy and political consequences had to be estimated by staff, serving their principals. Judging the consequences of various deficit-reduction measures required considering other values; therefore, the values of staff and the principals most directly concerned came into play.

On the second track, a number of players saw a chance to fix social security under the cover of the Gang's secret deliberations. Knowing he eventually was going to get stuck with the hot potato, Rostenkowski would gladly have gotten rid of it in early 1982. Jones, as a budget balancer and Ways and Means member, had double incentive to find measures that, by solving social security's imminent funding shortfall, would also reduce the deficit. Stockman wanted savings wherever he could get them; Jim Baker wanted the political problem to go away. Staff, therefore, very quietly drew up proposals to deal with the giant entitlement. The tax players also largely agreed on the need for new revenues, so the Senate Finance and Treasury tax staffs developed a series of revenue proposals. These tended to reflect their own judgments that ERTA had gone too far with business giveaways and the political attractiveness of "compliance" measures as opposed to rate increases.[27]

After floating a series of proposals, on April 6 the administration put together a package dubbed the "Baker plan," which claimed $450 billion in deficit reductions over three years. Revenues would be raised by $115 billion; defense increases pared by $66 billion. Domestic spending would be cut by $145 billion, including limiting and delaying COLAs.[28] The balance, 30 percent of the total, consisted of management initiatives and savings on debt service projected to result from all the other savings. The ratio of revenues to other deficit reductions was roughly $1 to $3.

The Baker plan exempted SSI, aid to the disabled poor, from COLA cuts. The administration's negotiators emphasized they were allowing $22 billion more for discretionary programs and $16 billion more for medical, nutritional, and public assistance than in their original budget. Many of these compromises involved leaving a popular program at the FY82 budget level. Because inflation and recession meant the needs had increased, Bolling was not so thrilled by such compromise. Because the proposals helped answer Senate Republicans' notions of fairness, however, Bolling worried that Jones too might be tempted by the offer.

"Frankly," Domenici suggested on April 8, "I believe that those of us who have been negotiating could reach an agreement tomorrow."[29] He may have spoken accurately of the majority of "Gang-sters," a fairly conservative group who valued deficit reduction above all. Domenici, Dole, Baker, Stockman, Jones, and Hollings might have been able to agree. Representing the Speaker and the Speaker's supporters, Bolling could not. The Baker plan still involved both big social cuts and a big defense buildup during a recession. "I knew we couldn't concede the things that they wanted us to concede for one vital reason," Bolling later explained. "We couldn't deliver them." Domenici also did not speak for many House Republicans. "How many people in the House of Representatives," asked Trent Lott, "would vote to cut Social Security in an election year? Maybe seventeen, and most of those retiring."[30] Domenici was in a sense wishing away deep conflicts of ideology and political interest. But he was also putting pressure on Reagan and O'Neill, trying to create the impression that a deal was there for them to make, if only they would be reasonable.

The president and the Speaker used the same tactics on each other, each asserting that he could not be moved but playing up hints (emerging from the negotiations) that the other might begin to give in. Reagan trumpeted a hard line on the tax cut; O'Neill a hard one on social security.[31]

Behind the public maneuvering was a residue of private distrust. Bolling and O'Neill felt they were being asked to clean up Reagan's deficit mess, which they had fought to prevent. Now Bolling was dealing with Stockman, who had lied before and, as far as Bolling knew, could lie again.

Despite this distrust, neither side wanted the blame for failure. There was also some movement. The menus of revenue initiatives produced by the Joint Committee on Taxation (April 6) and by Dole (April 7) included such good things for Democrats as a minimum corporate tax, modification of tax leasing, a cap on depreciation tax breaks in the out-years, and a 4 percent income tax surcharge. By April 13 some negotiators, but not Bolling, were reported to be converging on a package that would have put a 4 percent surcharge on taxable incomes over $35,000, added a tax on crude oil, repealed income tax deductions for most consumer interest, capped COLAs at 4 percent in 1983, and accepted a number of further social cuts. Hoping to lock Reagan into a deal, Howard Baker all but endorsed the surtax, warning that without quick agreement the Senate would go off on its own.[32]

The Speaker of the House was not enthusiastic. Saving discretionary programs by cutting social security was not Tip O'Neill's idea of a compromise. Both his staff and Rostenkowski's, however, did like the idea of doing something about social security—perhaps a revenue solution? Reagan, meanwhile, kept up his public campaign for accepting the original presidential budget priorities. On April 16 he told a group of newspaper editors and broadcasters,

> The one sure way to reduce projected deficits, bring down interest rates and still encourage growth is to reduce government's share of the gross national product [that is, cut spending]. . . . We hear so many judgments about compassion—who has it and who hasn't. . . . Where was the compassion in those bankrupt spending policies that brought the pain of high inflation and interest rates to so many people? Where is the compassion now in raising tax rates again on our people, making it even harder for them to work and compete?[33]

These are not the words of a leader about to retreat very far; they are the words of a leader trying to give his followers acceptable arguments against the "fairness" issue.

The negotiators were unable to overcome the differences. Bolling said he would have to consult with the House Democratic Steering and Policy Committee before going any further. The president's men began to look for ways to turn any breakdown of negotiations to their political advantage. Reagan told a news conference that he would "go the extra mile" to win an agreement, to which the Speaker scoffed that "President Reagan proved he was willing to walk a mile—for a camera."[34] These, too, were not the words of a leader planning a retreat.

The president announced that he would be willing to go to the Capitol to meet with the Speaker on Wednesday, April 28. The Democrats could hardly refuse but insisted that the talks essentially were stalemated.[35]

When the Speaker and the president met, the essential differences between the two proposals involved the three fiscal years from 1983–1985:

1. Bolling proposed $145 billion in new revenues over FY83–85: the administration proposed $105 billion.
2. House Democrats were scaling back military outlays by $42 billion; the administration by $28 billion. The budget authority differences projected to a larger outlay difference later.
3. House Democrats proposed $23 billion in domestic discretionary cuts; the administration wanted $35 billion.
4. House Democrats would cut the targeted entitlements (e.g., food stamps, medicaid) by $12 billion; the administration wanted $25 billion.
5. Bolling would accept limiting the COLAs to 5 percent in both 1983 and 1984, an estimated $16 billion savings. The administration, no longer proposing a delay, wanted a 4 percent limit from 1982 through 1984, saving $26 billion.
6. House Democrats wanted to fix social security by raising $19 billion in new revenues, with the COLA savings, and by dedicating $24 billion in old revenue from taxes on alcohol and tobacco to the social security trust fund. Their most likely source for new revenue, according to our interviews, was a tax on some portion of social security benefits received by higher-income elderly. The Speaker and Robert Ball, former commissioner of the Social Security Administration and the Democrats' expert on the issue, long had favored such taxes. The administration would have matched the Democrats' $60 billion package with its COLA caps, a smaller amount of new revenue, benefit cuts to be suggested by the Greenspan commission, and delaying the COLA date by three months beginning in 1982 (about $17 billion).

The two sides roughly agreed on some big, but dubious, numbers: $54 billion from management initiatives, including pay restraint, and $105 billion from lower interest payments. Of the latter, $64 billion would result from borrowing less because of the other deficit reductions. Less credibly, the markets were supposed to be so happy about deficit reduction that expectations would change and rates would come down enough to reduce debt service by $41 billion.[36]

In the terms that would later become matters of great recrimination, counting the more concrete social security proposals and the dubious numbers as spending reductions, the Democratic package was about three to two in spending cuts to revenue increases; the administration's plan was closer to five to two. If we exclude management initiatives and interest, however, and group defense cuts with tax hikes as changes the administration did not want, while it wanted to cut social spending, the difference in priorities is even more clear. The Democratic package was about 80 percent tax increases and defense cuts; the administration's proposal was about 60 percent, and the differences would grow in the out-years.

What hope there had been quickly evaporated in a fiery confrontation of strongly opposed principals. The president and the Speaker clashed bitterly over the fairness of the Reagan program. "Your budget was unfair. It had no equity," O'Neill accused. "I've heard all that crap," snapped the president. "You had a depression when I took over."[37] "Each saw the other as the archetypal representative of the opposing ideology," a participant recalled.

Howard Baker proposed a compromise in which the 1983 tax cut and 1983 COLAs would each be delayed by three months, but that foundered on social security politics. According to the *New York Times*,

> The President wanted the group to know that he had never approved of cuts in the cost-of-living adjustment for Social Security benefits. "He said he had nothing to do with the COLAs," the Speaker said. "You fellows are going to offer the COLA to me. I said, 'I offer you nothing.' " "I told the President in no uncertain terms that they were trying to set us up," Mr. O'Neill said. When Republicans insisted that reductions in the cost-of-living adjustment had not come from them, Mr. O'Neill said, "They're not coming from us—I'll take them off the table."[38]

O'Neill didn't want the blame for a proposal he didn't even approve. Reagan felt he had already given a lot from his original budget; at the least, the president and his party did not need the blame for the package's most unpopular part. Bolling and the Speaker, meanwhile, did not want to cut more from domestic spending than they had offered. Liberals felt those programs had taken too big a hit in 1981; they wanted program increases in response to the recession. The fireworks between the principals merely widened an already unbridgeable gap.

So the blame shedding began. OMB's summary of the differences, reported in the *New York Times*, excluded all but the COLA limit aspects of the social security dispute—an obfuscation to which neither side objected!

Trying to show that the Democrats were being unreasonable, in a televised address on April 29 the president reported on the spending side: "Our original cuts total $101 billion . . . but they were rejected, believe me. Our own representatives from the Congress proposed compromising at $60 billion. Their counterparts from the Democratic side of the aisle proposed $35 [billion]." He, too, didn't mention social security COLAs. He added that "I swallowed hard and volunteered to split the difference between our $60 and their $35, and settle for $48. And that was rejected. The meeting was over."[39] Implicitly, although criticizing Democratic unreasonableness, Reagan also acknowledged that his own party had torpedoed his original budget plan. The president's rueful "they were rejected, believe me" reveals that the opposition to his original cuts was overwhelming.

Bolling summed up the Democrats' case succinctly:

> He believes his program is working. And he believes that he hasn't hurt anybody. But the fact of the matter is that that is not what's been happening. . . . His program didn't work and his new budget was not acceptable, not only to many Democrats but also to many Republicans. The revolt against the President was in the Republican Senate.[40]

Why, then, one might ask, should the Democrats dig Reagan out by sacrificing social programs to the deficit?

Passing a Budget: The Senate

The Reagan budget was dead; the bipartisan budget was stillborn; now it was Domenici's turn. The day after the Reagan-O'Neill meeting, SBC met and began drafting. Senator Moynihan proposed a vote on the president's budget so as to embarrass Reagan before his television address that evening. Domenici prevented that vote, but not until he insisted that "we don't have to be subtle. The President's budget will not pass."[41]

Although Reagan used his speech to appeal for support, the response, as in September, was minimal. Kent Hance reported that he had received only fifteen calls compared to one thousand after one of Reagan's 1981 appeals. "People want to support the President," said Louisiana's John Breaux, "but the enthusiasm has worn off, except for the hard core."[42] There was little reason for representatives to fear presidential wrath for interring his budget.

The SBC chairman went to the White House on Monday, May 3, to discuss his plans. Then, while admitting that congressional leaders and President Reagan showed "much concern and consternation" about his plan, Domenici announced his proposal to the press: a three-year tax increase of $125 billion, a one-year social security benefit freeze, and many other spending reductions. The SBC chairman emphasized that "this is not a Republican plan, this is not a White House plan, this is my plan." Domenici was going to force everyone else to react to him; he had taken the position that Reagan had always claimed to (but no longer did) occupy: the man with a plan, challenging others to articulate alternatives. Slade Gorton of Washington and Steven

Symms of Idaho voiced their support, and William Armstrong, leader of SBC's conservatives, announced that the plan's "sense of rough justice" won his support.[43]

SBC met to begin its drafting on Tuesday, May 4; Hollings moved for a vote on the Reagan budget. Domenici agreed and, sending a message to the president, began the voting with his "no." The senators laughed and cheered the 20 to 0 wipeout.[44] So much for any Reagan hope that the Gang's breakdown would resurrect the original White House budget.

Hollings then proposed his own alternative, including a one-year social security COLA freeze followed by two years of COLAs limited to 3 percent less than actual inflation. In his draft, Hollings (like Domenici) allowed increases in food stamps, veterans' benefits, and supplemental security income. Unlike Domenici, SBC's ranking Democrat would not have frozen domestic discretionary spending; and Hollings's $36 billion three-year defense slowdown was larger than that in Domenici's plan. Hollings also proposed a $198 billion, three-year tax hike, including a halving of the 1983 tax cut.

By going out front on social security, against the advice of his party leaders, Democrat Hollings let Republicans hope that they might not have to take full blame for pension changes. Furthermore, Hollings's proposal provided an alternative that, from Reagan's perspective, looked far worse than the Domenici plan. Robert Kasten (R-Wis.) proposed only a $73 billion three-year revenue increase, guaranteeing the third-year tax cut, but that proposal was rejected 17 to 4. The Kasten vote made it obvious that the committee meant business on taxes. Domenici's plan began to seem both more necessary and more attractive to the president than it had been a few days earlier.[45]

That morning Reagan had met with James Baker and Stockman to devise new budget numbers. When SBC recessed late that afternoon, Stockman and Baker met with Domenici. They agreed that the tax hike would be reduced to $95 billion in return for presidential leadership on social security. The freeze was abandoned. Instead, the budget would require social security savings, to be produced by the Greenspan commission, of $6 billion in FY83 and $17 billion in both FY84 and FY85. Republicans hoped to present the cuts, not as balancing the budget on the backs of the elderly, but as securing the pensions by instigating needed reforms. Domenici took the package to a caucus of SBC Republicans and won their support. The president pledged his support in a phone call; and the compromise passed the committee on an 11 to 9, party-line vote.

Reagan strongly endorsed the Senate Budget Committee plan the next day. The tax hike was less than he had been prepared to accept in the Gang-of-17 negotiations; defense spending would be more; social spending cuts would be substantial. When asked about social security, he suggested that the savings might come from "an entire restructuring of the program," a line that revealed the president's old distrust of the program and, fortunately for him, received little publicity. Unfortunately for Reagan, the proposal's raw numbers were trouble enough. Democrats began blasting the social security provisions even before they emerged from committee on the night of May 5. "This is a time bomb designed to raid and loot the Social Security system," declared Michigan's Senator Riegle, "but they want to wait until after the election."[46] "The President proposes to mortgage the future of the elderly to keep alive the folly of his Kemp-Roth tax cut," declared Minority Leader Byrd.[47]

Vulnerable Republicans, including Senators Lowell Weicker, John Chafee, David Durenberger, and John Heinz, all up for reelection in 1982, ran for cover. Out at the grassroots, Republicans already were in a near-panic about the political impact of the recession. Governors Robert Ray of Iowa, William Milliken of Michigan, and Albert Quie of Minnesota had declared that they would not run for reelection in what promised to be a very bad year for their party. Now, the *New York Times* reported, Republican pollster Robert M. Teeter "said he had been getting calls from worried Republican candidates all day. He said he had been told that Democrats were so overjoyed at the political opportunity they had been handed that 'they can't believe what they're hearing.' He commented sourly, 'Me neither.' "[48]

Republican House leaders declared against the compromise on May 11. Robert Michel insisted that members who had to run for reelection could not be saddled with the social security cuts; the matter would have to wait for the report of the Greenspan commission. Trent Lott added, "Social Security is out, Period. No plug, no honorable mention."[49] Back in the Senate that same day, Daniel Moynihan proposed an amendment to the defense authorization bill that would repudiate the social security cuts. Howard Baker won the votes to defeat Moynihan only by promising an amendment that would put the Senate on record as opposing any but "corrective" actions "to save the system."[50] So died the social security part of the SBC budget. *Newsweek* (in "The Third Rail of Politics—touch it and you're dead") quoted a White House aide, "All Republicans should be required to get a lobotomy before they can say the words 'social' or 'security' again."[51]

Senate Republicans dumped the social security provisions on May 18. They also added back $3 billion in domestic spending so as to aid the reelection prospects of nervous Frostbelt Republicans. As adjusted, the package was fairly similar to that of the Gang of 17. Despite some grumblings, these changes were enough to unite the party. The united Republicans took the resolution to the floor, beat back numerous Democratic amendments, and passed it, 49 to 43, on May 21.[52]

Passing a Budget: The House

After one nasty screwup, the dominant party in the Senate had passed a budget resolution. The House had no dominant party; its action was therefore almost a parody of everything bad that has ever been said about Congress. Disorganization? Posturing? Legislation by exhaustion? The House provided these—and more. About all that can be said of the House's activities is that they were very (small "d") democratic. Everybody had a say; although agreement may have been achieved only through fatigue and creative accounting (that fooled no one), the result did represent opinion on the House floor.

"There are three ways you can pass a budget," said Representative Timothy E. Wirth of Colorado. "One is to get all the Democrats. A second is to get all the Republicans and the weevils. And a third is to find a compromise right in the middle."[53] Or maybe there was no way. No one expected to unite all the Democrats. The 1981 Republican/weevil coalition was in shambles because of gypsy moth dismay about priorities and boll weevil distaste for deficits; and the ranks of centrist Republicans and Democrats—Frostbelt moderates, some Sunbelt conservatives and moderate loyalists, maybe a few of the responsible conservatives—were unlikely to yield a majority. Nonetheless, Wirth and his "Gang of Five" partners (Panetta, Mineta, Gephardt, Aspin) went to work with gypsy moths to design a centrist budget. James Jones and Delbert Latta, meanwhile, worked the partisan sides of the budget track.

On Thursday, May 6, ten gypsy moths told James Baker that it would be "politically stupid" and "indefensible" for them to vote for the Senate budget plan. They released their own alternative, which included greater reductions in the defense buildup, higher social spending, and no foolishness on social security. On Friday, Republicans Jim Jeffords (Vt.), Jim Leach (Iowa), and Tom Tauke (Iowa), along with the centrist Democrat Gang of Five, signed a bipartisan budget plan. "I would like to work with my own party," proclaimed Claudine Schneider (R-R.I.). "But we have been pushing and pushing and we haven't got any response. I think we need to work with the Democrats."[54] This moderate proposal, known as the Aspin budget after its Wisconsin Democrat coauthor, would test the proposition that there was a hidden moderate majority.

On May 13 the House Budget Committee, in a party-line vote (Phil Gramm abstained), adopted a plan that claimed to meet the Senate's deficit reduction targets but relied on substantially higher tax ($147 billion versus $102.3 billion in the final Senate version) and defense savings ($47 billion versus $22 billion) to achieve that deficit target. This was the Jones budget. Essentially, it matched the Democratic Gang-of-17 proposal but left out social security and cut defense more.[55]

Robert Michel established a nineteen-member group (including five boll weevils and four gypsy moths) to try to recreate the Republicans' 1981 coalition. "It was like being in a snake pit," reported Silvio Conte, both a party leader and a gypsy moth. "The boll weevils gave some. We gave some."[56] On May 19 Conte and others joined GOP leaders in announcing support for what would be called the Latta budget, with totals similar to the Senate's plan. But, by further cutting domestic discretionary programs ($41.3 billion versus $27 billion) and through matching the other House plans for larger "management initiative" savings, as "iffy" as could be imagined, Latta projected a lower deficit.

David Obey and the Black Caucus each proposed more liberal budgets; Republicans John Rousselot and William Dannemeyer of California proposed a plan that had massive social spending cuts so as to achieve balance. California Democrat George Miller produced a "pay-as-you-go" plan: spending would be frozen, and then all increases, including those in defense, would be funded by new taxes. This was a neat variation on Miller's theme that the military "spenders" created deficits (see his comments on the 1980 reconciliation).

Having tried to limit choices in 1981, House leaders now maximized them. One Democratic leader recalls, "There was . . . a good deal of frustration in the House; everybody thought *they* could come up with something politically and economically acceptable. I figured, let them see how easy it was." In addition to looking at seven comprehensive budgets, they proposed a rule that would allow extensive amendments to the three main proposals. First, the House would vote on the Miller, Obey, Black Caucus, and Rousselot plans, in that order. Then amendments could be offered, applicable to any of the three main alternatives (Aspin, Jones, and Latta). All three would be debated simultaneously. Then Latta, Aspin, and Jones would be voted on in sequence. The last one to get a majority would win. It was, Richard Bolling admitted, a "very complicated" and "unique" rule. But the Republicans found it fair, and there was no rule fight.[57]

"Does Anyone Have a Budget?" *Time* asked, and then described how it appeared to outsiders:

> Seven competing budgets. Flocks of nuisance amendments proposed for the sole reason of forcing opponents to cast embarrassing "no" votes. . . .
> The scene in the House, which begins voting on the budget this week,

was fairly close to legislative anarchy. . . .House Republican leaders produced a budget that looks very much like the Senate document but, somehow, projects $15 billion less spending. How did they accomplish this feat? An aide to Senate Republican chiefs had a simple answer: "They lie." Retorted an aide to the House GOP leaders, "Our numbers are no phonier than anyone else's."[58]

On May 24 the Miller, Obey, and Black Caucus plans were defeated; each received almost no Republican support. The next day the Rousselot plan lost by 242 to 182, receiving 47 Democratic votes but losing by 53 Republican defections, almost all Frostbelt moderates. The Rousselot vote may be the best measure of the ideological thrust within the House to balance the budget by drastically cutting spending: the cutters were outnumbered.

During the votes on the three major resolutions, Mary Rose Oakar (D-Ohio) offered a crucial amendment. She proposed to increase medicare and decrease defense spending in all three budget plans. When her amendment was offered to the Latta plan, about 60 conservative Republicans chose it as an opportunity to express unhappiness with that plan and to remind Robert Michel that he could not take them for granted. Accordingly, they voted "present." Their moderate colleagues, however, seeing that Oakar had a chance to win, voted for her amendment and were joined by diehard liberals and moderate loyalists. This victory by the Democratic/Frostbelt coalition left the Latta plan with lower defense numbers (by $4.5 billion in FY83) than conservatives could accept yet with larger social cuts than moderates could stomach. It was widely argued to have ensured defeat of the Latta plan, which lost 235 to 192 as 20 Republicans defected.[59]

In spite of pleas by Democratic and Republican leaders that the House pass something—anything—all three plans were defeated. The Aspin, supposedly centrist, budget turned out to have no real base, losing 109 to 129 among Democrats and gaining only 29 Republicans. Jones's plan also was beaten decisively, 253 to 171.[60] Republicans were unanimous against Jones because the rule gave moderates a chance both to oppose Latta and to vote for the Aspin alternative; so the gypsy moths' discontent did not help the Democrats.[61]

The leaders had one trick left. Following seven budget defeats, the original HBC plan (without the amendments added during floor debate) came up for a vote. "We come to the moment of decision," declared the Speaker. "The hour is late. Most Americans have retired for the evening. Tomorrow morning, when they wake up, I want them to know that Congress did its job and passed a budget."[62] The members weren't interested in what anybody thought at breakfast, at least not on the Budget

Committee's terms, and voted down the eighth plan 265 to 159. Surveying the wreckage, Les Aspin commented, "Right now, you haven't got the votes out there to pass the Lord's Prayer."[63]

President Reagan denounced the budget process as "the most irresponsible, Mickey Mouse arrangement that any governmental body ever practiced."[64] For some reason he had not felt that way when he prevailed under the same rules in 1981; ridicule, moreover, would not produce a budget.

Politicians were beginning to wonder why they should go through so much pain to get down to a $100 billion dollar deficit. But people don't necessarily get to choose their problems. Or, if they have chosen them, it becomes hard to avoid them when there is an audience. The audience remained, not so much the voters as the markets. Something had to be done about interest rates; and so, in the logic of the time, something had to be done about the deficit.[65] The next event reflected the seemingly contradictory notions that unless something were done about the budget, disaster portended;[66] because budget resolutions didn't mean much anyway, however, any resolution would do. Basically, the Democratic leadership chose to force adopting a budget even if the Republicans were to win.

"I think the Speaker felt," one leader recalls, "that this was a Republican game, don't muddy it up, and we would straighten it out through the election." To clarify the choice, both parties moved away from the center. "At least we'll go with the true philosophy of our party," said Tip O'Neill. "To pass something," said Delbert Latta for the other party, "we have to go farther to the right."[67] Democratic leaders estimated that a more liberal proposal might attract only about 180 votes, but they still added a few billion dollars in social spending to the Jones budget.[68] Bowing to the lesson of the Oakar amendment, Republicans cut medicare by less, but they financed the change by reducing medicaid and nutrition programs.

"Will we do what the medieval bleeders did," Jim Wright responded, "and, if the patient doesn't respond to the first bleeding, bleed him some more?"[69] Yet while the Republicans were leaning on their members to vote for the Latta proposal, Wright told reporters, "Last week the official party line vote was to vote against Latta. This week, the official party line vote was to vote for Jones. After the Jones vote, we told everyone to vote his conscience."[70] First the Jones and then the Latta budgets would be considered as amendments to the original Reagan budget. If both failed, Congress would have to vote on the original Reagan budget, a prospect few Republicans wished to contemplate. When Jones failed, therefore, Republicans had an extra incentive to vote for Latta.

Jones lost 202 to 225; 39 Democratic defectors made the difference. Then Latta passed, 221 to 208, supported by 46 Democrats and opposed by 15 Republicans. On the final vote to pass the budget as amended by the Latta substitute, Republicans again won 221 to 207, as symbolic votes against the deficit by "opposers" were offset by new defections among moderate-to-conservative Democrats.[71]

Happy to end the long fight, the representatives cheered the Latta budget's passage on the House floor. Hawaii Democrat Cecil Heftel explained that the budget passed "not because it was a good budget or fair budget or an accurate budget. But because it was the only budget."[72]

Off went the plan to a conference dominated by three days of private meetings among Republicans. At the end of these meetings, conferees had pretty much accepted the House plans on revenue (slightly smaller increases) and defense (slightly larger reduction from Reagan's plan). The most objectionable of the Latta plan's entitlement cuts, for example, medicaid and food stamps, were sharply reduced, back to the numbers in the Senate plan. Discretionary spending choices tended toward the House position.

Conferees also moved to reduce the appearance of deficits, changing economic assumptions and accepting all the House's management initiatives. By conjuring up these reduced deficits, it became possible to predict lower interest payments. The Democrats scoffed at the result. Hollings declared, "We know it's out of whole cloth." And Domenici came back, "It has about as much realism as any budget we've produced." Fatigue leads to cynicism.[73]

Table 7 summarizes the conference report that squeaked through the two houses; now Congress had to make it come true. The congressional task was not as big as the totals suggested. Congress could not legislate the management and interest savings. Federal pay, as in 1981, was only being restrained relative to an unrealistic baseline. The defense and nondefense discretionary savings would begin in the FY83 appropriations, but they also depended on action for FY84 and FY85. With virtually no disagreement, the 1981 experiment in controlling appropriations through cutting discretionary program authorizations had been abandoned in early 1982. Republican leaders made clear they would not again do that to the authorizing committees.[74] Reconciliation instructions, therefore, covered only the entitlement and revenue changes, a third of the total savings.

A $100 billion tax hike would be difficult enough. Bob Dole and his allies, however, had spent most of the year putting a package together. The budget resolution would provide the argument that brought the president into their camp.

TABLE 7.   The "Three-for-One" Package: Fiscal Year 1983 Budget
Resolution for Three-Year (FY83–85) Deficit Reductions
as Estimated by the Senate Budget Committee

	Billions of $	*As percentage of total*
Revenues (including user fees)	98.3	26.0
Defense (except pay and pensions)	26.4	7.0
Nondefense discretionary	34.8 ⎫	
Entitlements (including COLAs)	30.8 ⎬	19.4
Other program reductions (includes some user fee spending offsets)	7.8 ⎭	
Federal pay raises	26.1	6.9
Management savings	46.6 ⎫	40.8
Net interest	107.7 ⎭	
(lower rates)	(54.9)	
(lower borrowing)	(52.8)	
Net non-revenue	280.2	74.0
Total	378.5	100.0

SOURCE: Senate Budget Committee estimates, June 23, 1982 (typescript).

The Tax Equity and Fiscal Responsibility Act of 1982 (TEFRA)

The 1982 tax hike was devised and pushed through by politicians and
staff who believed it was good policy and who, in the case of Republican
leaders, singled out their own constituents to be the victims.[75] Until the
1986 tax reform, we could hardly ask for a better demonstration of the
limits of interest group power. Business lobbyists had collected a string
of victories in the late 1970s, and in 1981 Democrats, led by Jones, had
joined Republicans to encourage investment through favorable tax provisions. Suddenly, in 1982, the momentum reversed. The palaces of K
Street, where lobbyists and lawyers dwell, glistened no less and the coffers
of corporate PACs bulged as tightly; but their influence had waned.
Convinced of the need to do something about the deficit, politicians
believed that "something" should include new revenues. Businesses
themselves were screaming about the deficit and interest rates, so they
could not deny the problem. But when revenues were needed, in the
words of one tax lobbyist, "The main individual [tax] preferences are
health, homes, and retirement. And on the business side there is the
investment tax credit and accelerated depreciation. . . . Where do *you* go

for the money?" Politicians, particularly Republicans, may not have wanted to raise business taxes, but it would certainly be better than either abandoning the third year of 5-10-10 or going after homeowners. The question changed from How do we encourage productivity? to Whose taxes shall we raise? Then business lobbyists went from occupying the high ground to being up to their necks in alligators.

Corporate tax breaks, as loopholes for undeserving fat cats, always had been subject to criticism; publicity about the auction of 1981, along with some provisions of the 1981 act—its negative rates for some profitable corporations, especially "Safe Harbor Leasing"—only intensified that image. Under "Safe Harbor" provisions, businesses that could not use deductions for investments because of low income or no income against which to offset the expense essentially were selling their tax breaks to profitable corporations. Whatever the argument for subsidizing the nonprofitable corporation, it was hard to explain why the purchasing corporation should be able to rake off a portion of the tax advantage in the process. A business lobbyist described safe harbor leasing as "a PR fiasco." Some Republicans, particularly Barber Conable, thought leasing worked. But on February 19 Senator Dole went so far as to unilaterally announce its demise: "However desirable many tax theorists find the current . . . leasing rules in the abstract, they are indefensible in a year in which the federal deficit will reach nearly $200 billion. . . . Corporations entering into leasing deals after today do so at their own risk."[76] He was partly grandstanding, but the Finance chairman knew the fans were on that side.

The January budget had proposed a minimum tax on corporations and, far more potentially controversial, a tax withholding on interest and dividends. While Reagan disbelieved in the corporate tax, his Treasury did not, and the politics clearly favored the tax. Interest and dividend withholding was far more risky. A Carter withholding proposal had been riddled with grapeshot in 1980. Treasury staff saw it as a compliance issue: if everybody who should pay taxes did, rates would not have to be so high. Regan and Reagan agreed.

With tax increases looming, business groups had to choose between two strategies: oppose all change, or try to shift costs to somebody else. Charls Walker, business lobbyist and past chairman of Reagan's tax policy transition team, remarked that "there is the potential for goring all sorts of oxen. . . . People are scared to death."[77] He took the second tack, testifying to Ways and Means that the third year of the individual tax cut might be postponed or that tax breaks for oil and natural gas could be reduced.[78] The Business Roundtable suggested higher excises and user fees. Others, particularly the Chamber of Commerce, opposed all tax increases, reflecting in part its devout supply-sider leaders. Yet the

Chamber's split from the Roundtable also reflected their different constituencies; the Chamber's small(er) business members had different concerns than the Roundtable's CEOs of major corporations.

Every threatened tax break had defenders. Airlines and aircraft makers claimed they depended on Safe Harbor Leasing.[79] The administration's minimum tax proposal was said to fall most heavily on banking and oil industries. Normally, groups are able to protect themselves by claiming unfairness: "Why me? Why am I worse than anyone else?" In 1982, however, there was an answer: "We have to get somebody, and you've done well lately. It's your turn." The chief counsel and staff director of Senate Finance, Robert Lighthizer, expressed that basic principle: "How can you do anything about a $150 billion deficit if you can't assure that major corporations pay a 15 per cent tax?" He asked, "What can you do if you can't do that? Go out and nail some more students, or make some more cuts in food stamps?"[80] Staff—on both tax committees and in the Treasury—felt policy was out of control, and they were determined to correct it. "We didn't know what was coming until it was in the report," a business lobbyist ruefully reported.

By filling in the blanks of something like $100 billion of revenue increases over three years, Treasury and Finance staffs were serving their leaders, particularly Bob Dole. If business interests were left off, everything would be contested, and Dole could not allow that.[81] An administration member of the Gang of 17 recalls that "there was not much difference of opinion. [The troika,] Stockman, and Treasury all were on board because we had come up with $750 billion in revenues [lost in ERTA] when the original target had been more like $600 billion."

The Tax Policy office was very active. "We were providing him [Dole] all sorts of help," a participant said. "It was an ideal situation to us, we could make very good changes in the tax law and he would take the heat."

Determined to proceed with business tax increases, Dole let the administration know that, if it backed down, it might get something it wanted far less. "We're willing to raise revenues, and we believe we can protect the third year" of the individual tax cut, the senator reported telling Reagan. "But if people in the Administration are dealing off different tax provisions that affect business and others, they will put more pressure on the third year."[82]

In late May Dole presented a list of thirty-four proposals to Finance Committee Republicans and asked which each found unsupportable. Each senator's staff aide then began meeting with Chief Counsel Lighthizer. The aides agreed on about $68.5 billion in tax increases that, at least to them, were noncontroversial. Other provisions, such as the minimum tax, an energy tax, and tax leasing (the latter being as strongly defended by Minnesota's David Durenberger as it was disliked by Chairman Dole) were considered contentious. As of mid-June, Senate Republicans were still divided over the last $30 billion.[83]

On June 30, the last day before the start of the second phase of Reagan's three-year tax cut, Senate Finance Republicans tentatively approved a package that met their budget target.[84] During markup, however, four of them jumped ship on interest withholding. Dole hinted that total repeal of tax leasing might be needed to make up the resulting $12 billion revenue loss. After more bargaining, the defectors backed down, and withholding was adopted on a party-line vote. In order to appease banks and other interest or dividend-paying institutions, some smaller tax breaks were added to the package.

Within Senate Finance, Russell Long proposed to defer the third year of the tax cut on higher incomes (raising $37 billion over three years); he lost 7 to 12. On a party-line vote on July 2, the committee adopted a plan that would raise $98.5 billion over three years; $17.5 billion would come from measures to increase taxpayer compliance, such as collecting taxes from restaurant owners on waiters' tip income. Withholding 10 percent of interest and dividend payments was expected to yield $11.6 billion. The twenty-five provisions ranged in comprehensibility from repeal of the modified coinsurance tax loophole (your guess as to what that was is as good as ours; but, anyway, its estimated worth was $5.2 billion) to doubling the excise tax on cigarettes ($4.8 billion).[85]

The Finance package was brought to the floor as an amendment to a minor House-passed revenue measure (H.R. 4961), so as to circumvent the constitutional requirement that revenue bills originate in the House. It then was considered as Finance's reconciliation bill, including $17 billion in spending savings. Senator Bradley proposed a Democratic alternative that would limit the third-year tax cut for persons earning above $46,400 per year and repeal it (ostensibly, delay it until the budget was balanced) for persons with incomes greater than $78,700. "It's the last stand on the third year," Dole predicted; and indeed, on a nearly party-line vote, Bradley was defeated.

Dole beat off, or compromised on, a series of smaller challenges. Kasten and Hollings tried to delete the withholding provision, but Dole won (48 to 49) after exempting lower incomes, with help from liberals Ted Kennedy, Alan Cranston, and Chris Dodd. A Democratic proposal to limit medicare cuts was headed off by a smaller adjustment, proposed by David Durenberger. After several attempts by tobacco state senators to defeat or reduce the cigarette tax increase, the Senate agreed to make the increase expire after three years. Once again games were based on the three-year budget horizon! At 4:30 a.m., July 23, the Finance Committee reconciliation tax bill, H. R. 4961, passed 50 to 47 on a nearly party-line vote.

Back in the House, Rostenkowski came out of the Gang of 17 with a rough sense of revenue-raising targets. Ways and Means staff worked with Rostenkowski and Conable to put together a package, which Rosty then brought to a caucus of committee Democrats. But the discussion did not go well:

> At our meeting some members said, "Why are we taking the lead, Danny?" And some disagreed on the details, going after oil particularly. So the meeting broke up and only three members, Rosty, Shannon and Brodhead, were really for it. Brodhead thought it was the best reform package in years. Eighteen were against. . . . The meeting broke up with a consensus there would be no bill. And a few of us sat down . . . and agreed to get *some* bill about *anything* to the Senate, to let them do it and then we'll do our part in conference.

Seeing that the Senate would be able to piggyback on H. R. 4961, Ways and Means' staff consulted with Dole's people during his markup. Then, on July 28, the committee voted to go straight to conference on the Senate's amendments to the originally rather innocuous H. R. 4961. Agreeing that it was the only way to get a bill and hoping (wrongly) they would have some influence in the conference, Conable and three other Republicans joined the committee majority. That afternoon on the House floor, Rostenkowski admitted "deep personal misgivings" about going to conference without House consideration of the issues. Nevertheless, he argued that "any attempt to craft a tax-increase bill in the House would lead to political chaos, severely reducing the chances of its passage." Conservative John Rousselot challenged the Ways and Means maneuver; but his motion to table lost 229 to 169. With the support of forty-five Republicans, mostly "responsible conservatives," the House agreed to send H. R. 4961 to conference.

Rousselot predicted that the president would be lucky to get one hundred Republicans to support the tax increase when it reached the House floor. The Democrats liked the idea of making the president fight for a tax increase, especially since they did not trust his support. They were glad to see Reagan pushed out front by his own troops. "I want there to be presidential leadership, and sheer pain, as there was sheer pleasure last year," said Richard Gephardt.[86]

Reagan's allies were badly divided; even his long-time aides, Lyn Nofziger and Martin Anderson, publicly opposed the tax increase and had to be reined in by White House staff. After Senate action, however, Reagan heartily supported the TEFRA tax increase. He did so in part because many components were described to him as mere matters of ensuring tax code compliance or correcting mistakes in the tax code.[87] More important, however, Reagan thought he had gotten a very good deal. As he continually declared in appealing for Republican support for the tax hike, for every dollar in new revenues, the budget plan provided three dollars in outlay savings.

Table 9 shows where Reagan got that idea: revenues were, in fact, only 26 percent of the total package. Stockman pointed that out to Reagan as part of the argument for TEFRA. It also shows what was wrong with Reagan's idea: the 1982 *reconciliation* would be three to one *revenues*; even counting all the spending savings, Congress could itself deliver, including defense, a balance more like 1 to 1. Most outlay savings were items Congress could not, and had not promised to, deliver: for example, lower interest payments.

In essence, the funny numbers, meant to impress voters and maybe markets, fooled the president. They also fooled Donald Regan and Ed Meese.[88] When eventually someone (Stockman blames Kemp) told Reagan that Congress did not give him any three-for-one, the president felt betrayed. Believing the administration had been "snookered," "screwed," "hornswoggled" on TEFRA, Reagan, Regan, and Meese became very suspicious of other compromises.

To Stockman, Baker, Darman, and congressional leaders, this sense of betrayal was ludicrous; no one ever said Congress would pass three-for-one. The resolution was clear enough about that. But when Stockman perceived, during the fight to pass TEFRA, that Reagan might have missed the point, there wasn't much the budget director could do. If he tried to clear up the confusion, Reagan might have changed his mind on TEFRA itself. Instead, Stockman let it slide and hoped for the best. He could not have anticipated the endless recriminations that would follow, outlasting him in the administration. In a letter to Reagan on January 16, 1984, for example, Senator Dole had to write:

> The most frequently voiced objections to packaging new spending cuts and revenue increases together is that Congress would enact the new taxes but renege on the spending cuts. These critics cite as evidence the alleged failure of Congress in 1982 to deliver any of the promised three dollars in spending cuts for each dollar of tax increase. I respectfully submit, Mr. President, that you were not "taken in" by this budget plan.

Nevertheless the president decided he had been taken in, a perception that would explain the later Gramm-Rudman Act. Actually Reagan was not all wrong: while the deal never was three-for-one, he did not get all the social cuts he might reasonably have expected. On the other hand, Reagan and Weinberger tried to renege on the defense cuts!

In August 1982, however, Reagan still believed. In Billings, Montana, on August 11, the president opened his campaign for the new package of tax hikes. "The bottom line is this," he told his audience, "would you rather reduce deficits and interest rates by raising revenue from those who are not now paying their fair share? Or would you rather accept larger budget deficits, higher interest rates, and higher unemployment?" The president had convinced himself that the Senate plan was reform of unfair "loopholes." "In order to get $280 billion in reduced outlays over the next three years," he declared, "we had to agree to the added revenues of $99 billion. The ratio of reduced revenues to outlays is three to one."[89]

The Republican National Committee taped two spots with the president asking voters to urge their representatives to support the plan. The spots carefully avoided describing the package as a tax increase, but the message to wavering Republicans—that the president wholeheartedly favored the package—had to be clear. On Monday night, August 15, Reagan would urge support for the plan on national television.

As Reagan campaigned for TEFRA, there was one minor complication: the bill did not exist. Conferees still had to settle many issues, and the administration lost on virtually all of them.

It was a very strange conference, beginning with an about-face by the administration on the tax side. "We went up to a meeting with Dole, Darman, Regan, Baker, Chapoton and so on," a House source recalled. "We thought it would be a pep-talk meeting, and found they wanted changes in the out-year (depreciation) and other business-type things." A coalition of business groups had finally managed, as a lobbyist put it, "to draft an alternative that was revenue neutral. . . . Dole wouldn't introduce our plan, and Jim Baker didn't approve it until a few days before the conference." At the last moment, Treasury supported these "more satisfactory schedules for business," as the lobbyists put it.

It was too late; TEFRA's business cuts were loosened only slightly. It was great stuff for Democrats: political jujitsu in which the Republicans became victims of their own momentum. "We kept receding to the Senate positions," a Democrat said, "which they kept denouncing in the Senate." The bargaining situation—Reagan out front, the only formal proposal from the Senate, the administration needing Democratic votes—gave Rostenkowski the advantage.

If the administration did badly on taxes, it did worse on spending. Ways and Means had taken a vote on spending provisions on July 15 but had bypassed the floor with its approval to go straight to conference. The conferees protected AFDC and restored some medicaid cuts in 1981. On AFDC, a key staffer estimated, "We were up $400 million; they were down $1.8 billion." After they "hung on to the nth degree," Ways and

Means held the cuts to "maybe $100 million." They cut a similarly good deal on unemployment compensation. Savings were produced by coupling an extension of benefits to a small increase in the employer portion of the tax.

Conferees cut medicare even more than, but not in the same way as, the administration desired. The administration wanted to cut medicare costs by reducing benefits and raising patient costs, which, by market logic, would reduce "unnecessary consumption" of medical services. Congress agreed that medicare costs were soaring out of control, largely because under the third-party payment system neither providers nor consumers had to worry about costs. The committees also wanted to do something about the problem before the medicare trust fund went broke, expected around 1990. Reconciliation made for a great cover. Ways and Means and Finance, however, hit the providers, not the patients; instead of allowing prices to hurt customers, the conferees moved to regulate prices.

The conference agreement set temporary limits on physicians' fees and hospital prices. Then it ordered HHS to develop a procedure for "prospective" payments to hospitals and nursing homes by which costs for patients would be anticipated (based, in the end, on the diagnosis) and payments would be held down to a set amount for each diagnosis.[90] TEFRA's cost restraints hit medical providers so hard that, when HHS completed its study, the new prospective payment system, though quite complex and regulatory, looked better to the hospitals than the alternative. Therefore, when the new system was enacted as part of the 1983 social security rescue package, hospitals did not resist strongly. Ironically, Ronald Reagan, who opposed medicare from its inception, was dragged into endorsing greater government regulation of the medical profession in the course of his own campaign against the welfare state.

On almost all categories of spending, results were closer to the House than the Senate numbers for an important reason. Republicans could hold only half their own troops in the House for a tax hike and knew it; therefore, there was no hope of a GOP/boll weevil coalition. Only the Speaker could deliver the necessary votes. If spending had not been packaged with revenue increases, Senate leaders might have fought harder (we cannot know; Dole certainly lacked enthusiasm for AFDC cuts). As it stood, however, they couldn't even protest much. "If I had screamed too hard on the [spending] compromises," a TEFRA advocate explained, "that would have given Gingrich and Kemp and the other guys the smoking gun to get rid of TEFRA. They could tell Reagan he was [getting shafted]." TEFRA was big, bigger than it seemed; it made no sense to complain about "$5 to $7 billion out of three years" when the tax might be "$300 billion over six." Executive branch aides and the senators kept quiet so as to keep Reagan on board, while conceding to the Democrats to keep them on board. This time, packaging favored the Democrats.

Fearful of deficits and browbeaten by a heavy dose of jawboning from the White House, even most business groups went along. Although their proposals were rejected at the end, the Roundtable helped rally business interests behind Reagan who was, after all, "their" president. Donald Regan declared that business had to understand that new revenues must come from corporations and the wealthy: "Because of last year's tax and budget cuts, a mistaken impression is abroad that this administration favors only the rich. Business must understand we have to correct this mistaken impression."[91]

Liberals did not quite believe their good fortune. "Liberals should be behind this bill one-hundredfold," proclaimed the national director of the Americans for Democratic Action. "The bill includes in it reforms we have sought for years." "From a tax standpoint, we closed a lot more loopholes than we opened," said Ways and Means Democrat Fortney (Pete) Stark of California.[92] The Democrats, too, felt the bill was redistributive, away from the rich and toward the middle class.

On Monday Reagan went on television to explain his support for the tax increase. Once again he presented himself as surrounded by rumors, out to set things straight. The tax increase was not "the largest tax increase in history" as some would claim; but it might be the largest tax *reform* in history. The tax package had to be passed to "end the bickering here in the capital" and allow the Reagan program and economic recovery to proceed.[93] Now, he could hope, his third year of tax cuts was safe.

This speech, like the others since September 1981, provoked no upwelling of support. Yet, reading it closely, we suspect the speech served another purpose: its rhetoric continually sought to reassure people that Ronald Reagan hadn't changed, that a few great principles informed his policy, and that the public should pay no attention to confusing reports from Washington that suggested otherwise. Reagan's speeches succeeded in maintaining his bond with supporters in the face of criticism and bad news that had undermined his predecessors.

In response, Democrats declared they had not supported Reagan's extreme tax cuts in 1982 but would now support him in rectifying some of his own worst excesses. Their language was restrained, emphasizing bipartisanship. The most important result of the speeches was not the weak public response; the speeches helped to cement the temporary alliance between House leadership and the president.

H.R. 4961 finally emerged from conference on Tuesday, August 17, after a series of last-minute deals.[94] In the two days before the vote, both the president and House leadership worked their troops furiously. In spite of the leaders' efforts, both parties were badly split. It was a big tax increase close to an election. In the five districts where, due to reapportionment, incumbent Democrats were running against incumbent Republicans, all ten candidates opposed the bill. The GOP could not even use its regular whip structure because the whips were split. Kemp, Rousselot, and other strongly antitax Republicans led the opposition. The Chamber of Commerce,[95] National Federation of Independent Businesses, and Farm Bureau fought against TEFRA; aside from labor, there was no real countervailing force back in the districts.

The key vote came on an attempt to revise the closed rule for considering the conference report. As Trent Lott put it, "If we try opening this package of tax and spending cuts at this point, and then succeed in knocking just one provision out on a point of order or a vote, then we risk losing the whole package for good."[96] The rule held, 220 to 210, with mainstream and diehard liberal Democrats joining responsible conservatives in a rather unusual alliance. Republican leaders held only 75 of their troops on the rule vote, but, on the final vote on the conference report, 103 Republicans supported the president. As Democratic support for the plan declined between the two votes, the result was a narrow 226 to 207 victory for TEFRA, the Tax Equity and Fiscal Responsibility Act of 1982. After the House vote, Senate action was anticlimactic, although the margin was narrow. With crucial support from nine Democrats led by Ted Kennedy, Robert Dole and Ronald Reagan triumphed, 52 to 47.[97]

The deficit mattered. Without that threat, such substantial action was unlikely. Morality mattered. How the deficit was reduced was determined by shared notions of equity. Politics mattered; it looked awful, but it worked well.

As the tax-hike debate reached its peak, Wall Street took off on a rousing rally.

TWELVE

Economics as Moral Theory:
Volckernomics, Reaganomics,
and the Balanced Budget Amendment

Long awaited, yet unexpected, the market boom finally came as Ronald Reagan was fighting for a tax increase. Business seemingly celebrated as its taxes were raised. What did it all mean?

Throughout the battle of the budget the participants responded to or invoked notions of how their actions would affect the economy. We have emphasized that a budget is many things, and fiscal policy is but one. Yet even those most skeptical of government intervention in the economy, including Ronald Reagan, judge economic performance to be the key criterion of political performance. Are you better off today than you were four years ago? was not merely Reagan's tactic for attacking Jimmy Carter; according to most students of politics, it is the most important question in any election. Encouraging the nation's productive forces—whether by directing them or by leaving them alone—is a primary responsibility of our elected officials.

Consensus on that responsibility gives economists their power, yet consensus on the economy per se is more rare. Throughout this narrative we have traced disjunctions among aspects of economic policy making. Not only did schools of economic thought proceed from different premises and advocate different solutions, but also, as times changed, individuals (and groups) made radically inconsistent arguments. The administration's arguments for a tax increase were but one example of such inconsistency; the turn in 1980 of such eminent figures as Paul Volcker to the "logic" of expectations was another.

Much about the economy was simply unknown or unknowable. To this day we cannot say what caused the decline of productivity; if anything, the puzzle has increased with time.[1] Action often reflected no one's intent. The battles of 1981 produced a policy that was neither supply-side (too little stimulus, early) nor Keynesian (too much stimulus, late). As we saw in 1980, our governors had a hard enough time figuring out what the economy was doing at the time when they were looking at—never mind knowing—either what would happen next or what to do about it.

Trying to govern by one set of theories, politicians were forced to compromise with others who held different theories; the result was policy that fit no theory. Hardly anyone anticipated what actually happened to the economy, but everyone at the time interpreted it with overconfident vigor.

Because the stakes were so high and arguments about economic effect so pervasive, we must try to explain what was happening in the economy. We cannot settle these issues. Even if we were right, we could not prove it, and, right or not, many might disagree. The absence of correct answers is part of our point; we must look for meaning outside the terms used in much economic debate. Rather we will ask about the ways of life that participants believed in and hoped to preserve; about the groups that they identified with and wanted to favor; and about the primary terms of economic thought (labor, capital) that are part of not only economic analysis but the economy as power relationships. We must appreciate how much—for economists, business interests, and politicians—economic philosophy is another form of political philosophy. The October House debate on budget balance is the most obvious case of melding political and economic philosophy.

First we ask, What was driving the economy? It is time to focus on not budget politics but Volckernomics. What was the difference, we ask, between Volckernomics and Reaganomics? We move, then, from observed events in the stock market to their possible causes: a banking crisis, the actions of the Federal Reserve, and the beliefs and acts of Ronald Reagan and his supporters. Finally, we look at the debate over budget balance in which the principles of constitutional design mix with group interest.

The Stock Market

By August 12, 1982, the Dow Jones average of 30 industrial stocks had slid from 822 to 777. On the 13th it climbed to 788, on the 16th to 792. On Tuesday, August 17, the market suddenly leaped upward by a then-all-time record of 38.81 points (with a near-record 93 million shares traded). The next morning, the rally continued with 37 million shares traded in one hour as the Dow soared by another 18 points.

Wednesday and Thursday were roller-coaster days: a sharp rally followed by profit taking and an all-time record 133 million shares traded on Wednesday; a rally, fall (over rumors about banks and Mexican debt), and finally a nine-point gain on Thursday. On Friday, after the tax bill passed, the Dow leaped ahead by nearly thirty-one points.[2]

The stock market frenzy continued during the following week, with 550 million shares—a daily average of 17 million more than the previous record—traded. The rally continued until it finally leveled off in April 1983, with the Dow hovering around 1200.[3]

What did it all mean, and who deserved the credit? With the November election approaching, would the stock market rally support what *Time* called a "strong new hope that Reaganomics might work to pull the American economy out of stagnation"?[4] As a matter of logic, both questions depended on whether whatever caused the stock market upswing was part of Reaganomics. As a matter of electoral politics, Reaganomics might be seen as whatever happened during the Reagan administration, whether Reagan was responsible or not. However, logic and politics were not the same.

Secretary of the Treasury Donald Regan declared, "The market forces are beginning to believe our resolve in redirecting the economy. Perhaps it took something like the tax bill to convince people that we're serious about fiscal responsibility." By his account, there was no difference between the tax bill and Reaganomics, which was finally paying its expected dividends. Others thought that the administration was a late convert to "fiscal responsibility."[5] If Reaganomics represented supply-side economics, then the tax bill reversed policy, as Jack Kemp claimed, and the market rally could not be credited to the original policy's wisdom. A third possibility was that the rally had less to do with the tax bill, whether Reaganomics or not, than with monetary policy and hence "Volckernomics."

We lean toward the third position, but we can never know what the markets are thinking because markets do not think. The overall trend of a market results from uncoordinated individual hunches and guesses. Individuals consider not only the economy but also many other things: How will companies perform financially, and thus what will be the dividend or capital appreciation on investment? What else could people do with their money, comparing the return on equities to, say, Treasury bills? And, hardest of all, what will other actors do? Consequently, political interpretations of stock market behavior are more important for their effects than for their validity.

Conceivably, the stock market rallied at this time because the economy was such a disaster. Why were investors suddenly willing to pay more for stocks (and therefore, in percentage terms, receive smaller dividends) than they had before? The most obvious explanation in August 1982 was an expected decline in return on other investments due to a drop in interest rates. Lower interest rates might mean greater corporate profitability. Stocks and old bonds would become more attractive as alternatives to new bonds and savings of various sorts.

Let us go back to Wall Street the week the rally began and reconsider the reporting of *Time*'s enthusiastic correspondents.

> The first hint that something extraordinary was about to unfold came on Monday morning. The First Boston investment firm announced that Albert Wojnilower, its chief economist, had revised his economic forecast. After warning for months that the huge federal budget deficit could send interest rates shooting back up again, Wojnilower now admitted that the cost of money would probably continue to decline over the next year. On Tuesday morning, rumors whirled through Wall Street that Henry Kaufman, chief economist of the Salomon Bros. investment house, had also changed his mind on interest rates. Word that these two gurus, known on the Street as Dr. Doom and Dr. Gloom, had reversed themselves electrified the stock exchange. . . . Because few portfolio managers were willing to risk missing a major market rally, a buying panic quickly built up.[6]

Newsweek told a similar story. Lower interest rates could mean that recovery and higher profits were on the way. But Kaufman forecast lower rates because the economy was so sluggish that demand for credit would be weak. Kaufman was right. Capital investment, the engine of recovery according to supply-side doctrine, did not begin to increase until summer 1983. Businesses were hunkered down to wait out the recession. Throughout the first half of 1982, as businesses had scaled back on capital investment, analysts had looked to the second installment of the income tax cut to spur consumer demand and economic recovery.[7] As the magic date approached, however, no surges occurred in either demand or supply.[8] The demand side of high interest rates was diminishing. The governors of the Federal Reserve joined Dr. Doom and Dr. Gloom in observing that trend. They, however, saw a particular kind of gloom and doom in the trends—a debt problem far worse than the federal deficit. As the demand for money slowed, the Fed decided to increase the supply.

The Federal Reserve and the Banks

Chairman Volcker and his colleagues faced an extremely delicate choice. Over two years, beginning in October 1979, the Board had reduced inflation through an unprecedented squeeze on the money supply. On the few occasions, when the monetary aggregate figures had suggested some loosening of the grip, commentators had raised the alarm of runaway inflation. The rest of the time, the Federal Reserve had to listen to screams of pain from the interest-sensitive sectors of the economy. Throughout this period, the Fed's governors felt their only choice was to squeeze hard because any loosening might drive up interest rates as panicky investors predicted worse inflation. By July 1982, M-1, the basic measure of the money supply, had risen barely 4 percent in fifteen months; unemployment and bankruptcies were climbing steadily toward heights last reached in the Great Depression. Yet neither investors and business interests nor the public at large seemed to believe, in spite of the real reduction in inflation, that prices would stay under control. In June, for example, a *Business Week* poll of 600 top corporate executives found that 53 percent expected inflation to take flight again within a year.[9] If the Fed loosened its grip on the money supply, inflation fears might keep interest rates high, no recovery would follow, and the hard-won progress against inflation would be lost. But if the Fed did not loosen, interest rates certainly would remain high. Talk about Representative McDade's no money for anything.

Not only was the American economy choking, but the recession was equally bad in Europe, with prospects there even bleaker. High American interest rates and worldwide political worries strengthened the dollar dramatically against foreign currencies. To prevent an even greater outflow of their capital to the safe, high-interest United States, European finance ministers raised their own interest rates, and in turn those rates crippled European economies. As unemployment rose in Europe and America, consumer demand accordingly stagnated or fell. The world economy entered a classic downward spiral.

If Europe and America were in trouble, the struggling nations of the second (communist) and third worlds were, literally, on the verge of bankruptcy. The strong dollar meant that these nations had to exchange more of their products for fewer dollars, reducing both American inflation and Mexican, Polish, and Brazilian incomes. Dollars could barely be earned and only dearly borrowed. Yet dollars were needed, for the nations of the world owed hundreds of billions of dollars to American and European banks.

We have been talking throughout this book about the Federal Reserve as an institution for economic management. Fundamentally, however, the Fed is a bank—a rather big and unusual one (serving only other banks, not individuals or businesses) but a bank nonetheless. Its bedrock responsibility is not economic growth but the banking system's health—on the well-grounded assumption that a sick banking system will infect the whole economy. By a banking system, we do not mean simply a place for people to put money and have it safe. Rather, we mean a system for creating money and credit, for ensuring the flow of that very peculiar commodity that is the means of payment for all other commodities.

In June 1982, the Board's governors saw the economy doing rather worse than was tolerable. The Board also saw many foreign loans on the banks' balance sheets. Perhaps some of those nations would default. If they did, the debtors might take the banking system with them into bankruptcy.

The massive international debt crisis that reached public attention in late summer 1982 had been building since 1971, the year when OPEC discovered its strength in negotiations with the big oil companies. In October 1973, OPEC raised oil prices unilaterally, and the price held. A few months later, the price more than doubled again. The greatest transfer of wealth in the history of the world had begun. The world's rich nations suddenly were paying tribute to less-developed ones. Those envious of the West might have been happy for a moment; economic writer George Goodman (aka "Adam Smith"), with nice irony, described

> a feeling of jubilation in all those countries of Asia and Africa. What an upset! Ragheads, 66; Giants, 0! . . . So much for the imperialist exploiters who wanted us to be a nation of busboys!
>
> And then somebody—maybe the financial people . . . would say, "But now we have to pay four times as much for the oil, and we have no oil. Where do we get the money?"[10]

More or less fortunately, there was yet another problem: What on earth would OPEC countries, particularly the sparsely populated Arab states, do with the money? They put it in banks, and the banks lent it all over the world. Many loans were less than wise, but this recycling of the OPEC surplus through the banking system prevented the oil price hike from generating a massive worldwide slump. The cycle repeated after 1979.

In late 1981, Mexico owed various banks $56.9 billion, of which half was due in 1982. Brazil owed $52.7 billion, a third due that year. Venezuela, Argentina, South Korea, and Poland all owed more than $15 billion.[11] To make matters worse, throughout this period, the banks—competing with each other for the international loan business—had expanded their loan/reserve ratios. Thus, the banks were at great risk if defaults occurred.

In all the strife about the budget and the economy little had been heard about third world loans. But to bankers and policy makers of the international financial system the problem loomed ever larger and more menacing. A big default might start a process in which the flow of money and credit that is the lifeblood of the world's economy collapsed like a row of dominoes. Warning signs abounded: a large government securities trading company went under in May and a medium-sized bank in

July; the entire savings and loan industry was in trouble. As August approached, Mexico neared default.[12]

A number of lines of defense against a chain of defaults spread from some weak link across the banking system. First, debtors and creditors negotiated to reschedule the debt; that defense was crumbling as creditors demanded higher interest rates for greater risks. Next came the International Monetary Fund (IMF); third parties could guarantee loans, or offer them, in return for policy changes that would make repayment by the debtor nation more credible. But IMF conditions for loans might be too tough for recipient governments to accept and still survive politically while IMF reserves themselves were limited.

Within each country the national central banks themselves would be "lenders of last resort" to their respective private banks. If a major American bank was about to collapse, the Federal Reserve might provide loans to tide the bank over the crisis or allow some other, profitable bank to assume the liabilities (and assets) of the collapsing institution, thereby protecting its creditors. The Bundesbank in Germany, the Bank of England, and other central banks would try to do the same in their own financial systems.

What if none of that were enough? What if the doomsday scenario occurred, and the dollars could not be found to stem the chain reaction of collapse? Well, only one organization in the world could invent the necessary dollars. The dollar is the world's currency; the system of money and credit for the world, not just the United States, ultimately is the responsibility of America's central bank. The Federal Reserve is the lender of last resort for the world.

In 1981, at the height of concern with hyperinflation, George Goodman reported a conversation with his understandably anonymous "banker mentor." "Where will the Federal Reserve get the money?" Goodman asked. "It will print it," the banker replied. But that, said Goodman, is superinflation, too many dollars chasing goods. Perhaps, his banker replied, but there was no choice:

> The System must survive. A burst of liquidity at the right time can save the System and buy time to solve the problems. Otherwise we will have a massive depression, and the Western nations will battle one another for the scraps, as they did in the Depression. . . . We hope that a burst of liquidity, properly handled, would restore confidence, not destroy it. . . . Remember, there is nowhere else to go.[13]

This is melodrama but melodrama with a point. In July of 1982, the crisis was uncomfortably close; the Fed's governors knew it. They knew one more thing: an ounce of prevention is worth a pound of cure. The time for a "burst of liquidity" was *before* panic set in.

Yet the Fed's governors worried that if they loosened, those with money to lend, attending to monetarist theory rather than deep recession reality, might fear future inflation and keep interest rates high. The Fed, therefore, had to loosen while maintaining its reputation for tightness. As Volcker told the story,[14] the Board merely decided to let monetary growth move from the low end to the high end of the year's target range. In fact, M-1 overshot its 1982 target by three points as the Fed jammed the monetary accelerator through the first half of 1983. The money shortage was met by a large infusion of cash. Simultaneously the Board embarked on a publicity campaign, reiterating both its determination to prevent inflation and its contention that inflation was finally under control. Board governors gave rare public interviews. Volcker stoutly resisted congressional pressure to "loosen up" while doing exactly that. Expectations were confronted with rhetoric.

"In just one week," Chase Manhattan Bank economist Richard Benson asserted, "they [the Federal Reserve] did a coupon pass [bought Treasury notes on the open market], a bill pass [bought T-bills] and a system repo [borrowed securities from a bank or broker for cash] five days running."[15] In August, both before and during the stock market rally, the Fed cut the discount rate three more times, down to 10 percent. Short-term interest rates fell, the stock market boomed, but long-term rates remained sticky; the economy did not recover. The Mexican crisis was postponed but not resolved.

Monetarist logic about the relation between the money supply and prices was being invalidated, as Volcker argued, by an unprecedented, since the depression, reduction in the velocity of money. Instead of spending and circulating it, people and businesses were holding on to cash, anticipating even harder times. Keynes had a name for this: he called it a "liquidity trap," in which nervous people clung to liquid assets; that unwillingness to spend or invest made their fears for the economy self-fulfilling. It was the exact opposite of the burst in velocity needed to make the Rosy Scenario come true. Volcker's version was understated: because standard relationships "over time between the monetary and credit aggregates and the variables we really care about—output, employment and prices . . . did not hold in 1982," M-1 targets had to be overshot because "that policy, in practical effect, would otherwise have been appreciably more restrictive than intended in setting the targets."[16]

On October 5, 1982, the Federal Open Market Committee met again. In spite of the market rally, economic conditions remained parlous. Describing conditions in the most gloomy of terms, the chairman led his colleagues in deciding to loosen further, formally abandoning monetarist money-targeting procedures adopted in October 1979. In an unusual step meant to reassure market participants that the Fed wanted interest rates down, Volcker publicly announced the change on October 9.[17]

Would beliefs about the catastrophic effects of deficits overcome the real effects of greater supply and slack demand for money? No; nominal interest rates did come down. The prime interest rate, having slid three points in July and August, declined three more points, to 10.5 percent in February. Other short-term interest rates dropped accordingly. Long-term rates, more influenced by expectations and less by the immediate money supply, fell more slowly. But they, too, dropped three points by November. As money expanded and interest rates fell, prices were steady. The Consumer Price Index (CPI) rose only 2 percent from July 1982 through June 1983. Real interest rates thus were extremely high and in some ways crippling. Yet for investors who had to put their money *somewhere*, lower nominal rates made stocks more attractive.

We can say now that in August 1982 the Fed, for the time being, had won its battle against inflation; a 13 percent increase in M-1 over the next year did not reignite the fire. Volcker's gamble worked. For quite a while the economy remained in miserable shape; unemployment rose into double digits in September and stayed there until June 1983. In spring 1983, however, a robust recovery began.[18]

We have come a long way from the stock market, but we can now draw a few conclusions. The decline of interest rates, the need of large institutions to invest somewhere, and the dynamics of a buying surge among a small group of actors[19]—rather than optimism about the economy or confidence in Reaganomics—fueled the market rally. Even if investors expected further inflation, declining short-term interest rates justified moving funds into stocks. Businessmen were not confident, as long-term rates showed, that the battle against inflation had been won. Business investment did not lead the nation out of the recession. But the economy had passed a watershed; whether or not anyone believed it, the recession had killed inflation.

Volckernomics

Businesses were too scared to raise prices; labor was too scared to demand higher wages. Slumps in demand and increases in production depressed the prices of crucial commodities, especially agricultural and petroleum products. High mortgage costs terminated the boom in housing prices. Across the economy, people did not demand higher payments because they were afraid of losing the sale or their job.

That, at its heart, was Volckernomics. In spite of the fanfare that accompanied the Fed's alleged conversion to monetarism on October 6,

1979—when the Board announced it would focus on monetary targets and ignore the interest rate results—that decision had been mostly public relations. But the Board had a majority that believed inflation had become so debilitating that it had to be wrung out of the economy even at a very high price. Monetarism provided a convenient rationale for letting interest rates rise, thereby decreasing demand and investment.

The money supply, however, was never the real target of Fed action.[20] A target is what you try to hit; you score your effort by some measure on the target. In that sense there were a number of targets. Perhaps the most important was the rate of increase in prices, but the rate of increase in wages ran a close second. Volcker and company in essence agreed with Carter's economists who had sought to reduce core inflation by restraining wages. Consider these excerpts from the Federal Reserve's report to Congress on monetary policy at the beginning of 1983:

> In many ways the slowing of inflation this past year has reflected the pervasive influence of the recession on product and labor markets. . . . The wage-price interactions that served to perpetuate inflation through the 1970s appear to have lost much of their momentum. Workers generally are agreeing to smaller pay increase[s] than in earlier years, and in some sectors in which long-term wage agreements are prevalent, the settlements concluded in 1982 will help ensure diminished labor cost pressures in coming years. Lower labor costs are relieving pressures on prices, and, in turn, an improved price performance is reducing expectations of inflation and thus leading to a further slowing of labor costs.[21]

Lower wages were good news. This is not to say Board members were "capitalists" out to crush "workers." Smaller wage hikes did not necessarily hurt the interests of workers—*if* prices rose more slowly. In fact, wages went up faster than prices in 1982 for the first time since 1978—*if* you were working.

Yet the recession fundamentally changed business and labor behavior, to labor's disadvantage. Previous recessions had been viewed by most participants as normal, if unpleasant, swings of the business cycle. When the recession was over, things would return to an acceptable level; companies interested in the long term would try to maintain a stable labor force, minimizing the dislocations caused by large layoffs. Output would fall more quickly than employment, so productivity statistics would decline.

For two reasons, 1982 was different. First, the high interest rates meant that the debt portion of companies' fixed costs had grown; thus, worries about financing the debt made companies more willing to cut other costs. Second, fear of diminishing competitiveness of American industries left companies less confident about regaining their markets when the recession ended. In steel, autos, and many other industries, managers felt that costs had to be reduced sometime to meet foreign competition. The recession, when there were few customers anyway, was the right time to shed unnecessary labor. That is what companies did; employment declined more, relative to production, than in previous slumps. High unemployment meant that workers in manufacturing industries had nowhere to go. If they struck, companies that were losing money anyway might close down. As the balance of power between business and labor shifted, the wage-price spiral flattened.

Although Volcker regretted the pain of recession, he believed he had no choice. The war against inflation came first. The chairman put the Fed's case in his March 8, 1983, testimony to the House Budget Committee, replying to Representative Bill Hefner (D-N.C.):

> *Mr. Hefner*: . . . you can't have it both ways. If monetary policy is responsible for inflation coming down, monetary policy has to be responsible for some of the interest rates being high and unemployment setting records. . . .
>
> *Mr. Volcker*: . . . We have had a recession; there is no question that that has helped importantly in precipitating lower inflation. . . . I don't think we had an either/or choice, that we could do something about it or not; I think economic performance would have been unsatisfactory—ultimately more unsatisfactory—if we hadn't through monetary policy very largely, coped with the inflation problem.[22]

Mr. Volcker's remarks may be simply summarized: Yes, we beat down inflation with unemployment, and we did it on purpose. There was no alternative.

The taming of inflation became the great achievement claimed for Reaganomics. Reagan's real contribution was that by proclaiming hope in the face of the grim task of Volckernomics, he allowed the Fed to do its nasty job. How did Reaganomics allow Reagan not to flinch—and his political supporters to stay with him?

Reaganomics as a Moral Economy

Reaganomics was a political, not an economic, philosophy. The solution to the deficit problem, for example, was always seen as a matter not of calculation but of conviction: If everybody practiced capitalism, there would be a recovery, and then—shazam!—their wish would come true. Stockman's position in the Dunkirk memo—that the very change in policy would alter expectations so dramatically that a surge in investment could revitalize the economy—was merely the most detailed statement of the administration's reliance on self-fulfilling prophecy. What unified

Reaganomics, and its fractious proponents, was not what was included but *who* was included and *what* was excluded. Reaganomics excluded demand, that is, ensuring a market, as an object of policy. Supply-siders and monetarists ignored demand because their basic models emphasized different factors. In 1980–1981, due to spiraling inflation, the last thing neoclassicists were worried about was ensuring demand.

Each part of Reaganomics had particular attractions for business. Deregulation, personal tax cuts, and business tax reductions provided direct benefits. These policies also reduced the size and influence of an organization, the federal government, which many businesses viewed with suspicion as a rival to their power and a threat to their independence.[23] Spending cuts, particularly in the Gramm-Latta package, barely touched business. A balanced budget, if attained, would mean less government borrowing and, other things being equal, lower interest rates. It would also symbolize restraint on the alien power of the politicians. Most important, given what actually occurred, businesses were willing to accept the monetary squeeze. They accepted it in part because the uncertainty associated with inflation was so disorienting. They accepted it also because, like Chairman Volcker and the neoclassical economists, businesses believed that the squeeze could help them regain control of wages so as to adjust their operations for international competition.

Policy to restrain wages was more extensive than we have shown because what did not happen was significant. There was neither a rise in the minimum wage nor the usual long-term extension of unemployment benefits during the recession. It also is impossible to estimate the impact of the administration's hard line in the face of an air traffic controllers' strike; breaking their union in 1981 symbolized the new pattern of labor relations.

Because they liked specific provisions of Reaganomics and could accept the recession, business stayed loyal to the president even when the economy turned down. Thus, while the general public was far more negative, businesses endorsed Reaganomics by large margins in spring and summer 1982. Yet these same business interests were very pessimistic about the economy. In early spring only 23 percent of *Business Week*'s executive sample said that the Reagan package encouraged them to expand capital spending, and half expected no economic upturn before winter; meanwhile the administration and some economists predicted recovery in the summer.[24] After a long period of economic bad news, practical people demand premiums against risk. Most likely, they assume, the future will look like the past; that is the normal logic of expectations. "We're betting on the downside," said the chairman of Boeing Aircraft Corporation. "If we bet on a fast recovery and it didn't happen, we could be in real trouble."[25] *Business Week* reported that, as the Federal Reserve also noted, three-quarters of its sample was planning to "utilize labor more efficiently" because of the recession.[26] Here was the paradox of encouraging business with policies: it won political support, but businesses' economic behavior still responded to their judgment of economic conditions.

Reaganomics as a probusiness worldview helps explain why the pain of Volckernomics did not turn business against Reagan. What about other people? Why would they support something very like Republican "old-time religion" with a charming new preacher? Was it just, as Greider got Stockman to say, "trickle-down" disguised as a new "supply-side" theory?

Actually, much of Reaganomics was rejected. The political system delayed and reduced the first year of tax reduction. Although some deregulation occurred, administration efforts frequently bogged down as the courts and Congress demanded that the laws be enforced more strictly. Initiatives, such as the subminimum wage for teenagers and further taxation of unemployment benefits, were blocked. Yet polls kept showing support for Reagan's policies in general.

The Republican campaign for the 1982 congressional elections called for the country to "Stay the Course." The imagery was obvious: the ship battered by storms, the skipper standing tall by the wheel, steering against the gale, sure of his direction. The sense of purpose and command that Reagan worked so hard to project was a bulwark of his political popularity. So also was the public belief that the previous skipper and his mates had led the nation into the storm. Reagan did his best to encourage that memory, referring over and over, inaccurately, to the "depression" conditions prevailing when he took over.

Reagan's view of economics was not a set of theories about the effect on outputs of a particular structure and process of inputs. He could sound like a monetarist, a neoclassicist, or a supply-sider, depending on the subject and his political needs. When he made policy, however, he chose not by inference about how some balance of policies would affect economic outputs but by reference to core principles, mediated by political philosophy. Those principles—reduce government, encourage profit, support individualism—included, but were not limited to, the interest in production and therefore producers ("suppliers," if you will) that united those economic schools allied with the administration.

Stockman's book is filled with examples of what he sees as decisions to fund business at the expense of individualistic principle. Thus, Reagan defended the oil-depletion allowance, subsidies for the nuclear industry, synfuels, and auto import quotas.[27] For each action, however, the president found an individualistic reason: taxes were too high anyway, or nuclear and auto industries were crippled by regulation, or "we can't cause an honest business to lose money." Even if the president were just rationalizing the politically necessary, the form of rationalization reveals the ideology. Others might have admitted the political pressure for import quotas or said that national security required energy subsidies; Reagan found ways to blame government.

Reagan's individualism was moral and personalistic. He opposed high taxes because of his own wartime experience; he identified with the browbeaten business interest. The exceptions, when he opposed business, proved the rule that his attitudes essentially involved beliefs about individual reward for behavior: he supported tax-compliance measures, such as interest withholding, because they were posed as issues of obeying the law.

When Reagan's ideas broadened to the system level, he blamed government for removing the moral basis of a healthy economy. He believed the New Deal to have been a scam; the postwar economy was not an unprecedented boom but an escalator ride to perdition. On July 28, 1982, Reagan told a press conference that all the previous recessions

> have been ended by a quick fix, a flooding of money into the market, temporary spending, artificially stimulating the economy which resulted in high inflation but did give you a kind of quick fever that seemed like prosperity. And the next recession came usually about two years later. We're trying to restore the economy. To get back to a growth economy that will be based on solid principles.

The language used—"solid principles," "artificially stimulating," a "quick fever" of unreal prosperity—expressed his moral view as a proponent of private, not public, enterprise.[28]

From an economic standpoint, federal spending and deficits are different problems; both might be bad, but spending matched by taxes creates one set of problems and deficit spending creates another. For Reagan, the two problems were one; even when it seemed in his interest to disentangle them, his heart seems not to have been in it because "deficit" and "spending" fit together in his own head so neatly. The deficit was the token of irresponsibility, excess, and corruption caused by spending (remember, he assumed that there was great waste). Deficits opposed self-reliance, the moral uprightness that Reagan saw threatened in modern America by Big Government. When people relied on government, instead of on themselves, bad things would happen: recessions, inflation, a loss of precious freedom.

This attitude toward deficits lived deep within American society as well as Ronald Reagan. It shared with supply-side promotionalism the emphasis on individual responsibility and initiative. But true-blue supply-siders did not care much about deficits; to them, deficits were something to outgrow. Free individual energies, proclaimed the supply-siders, offer a big price for winning; then the growth generated by peoples' striving will overcome all other problems. Ultimately, this was part of a tradition—of a "Don't tread on me!" frontier individualism that resisted regulation of all sorts. Ronald Reagan had some of this frontier individualism in his style, his imagery, indeed his life. But he appealed as well to another strain in the American character, the disposition that Max Weber called the Protestant Ethic, which joins moral constraint to economic liberty. The tradeoff is explicit, its logic strong: If you behave properly, strive hard, work, and save, you will be rewarded with success. In this view, good things come as a consequence of right action; therefore, the community has a right to enforce values by restraining social behavior. That activity does not contradict but rather reinforces the laissez-faire economic policy. Social restraints reinforce economic competition. Too frequently people point to the supposed contradiction between social regulation and economic deregulation in Reaganism without realizing these two ideas have been linked, for good reason, throughout American history.[29]

Reagan's Reaganomics may be called a "moral economy." At its heart, it was a set of beliefs about how people should live together. Like other visions of the good life, it could be invalidated by nothing short of a cataclysm. Short-term results were something to be explained away or manipulated in behalf of the larger goal of preserving or extending the way of life. Those who suffer in such a system are searched for defects; the system, if humane, will allow compensation for accidents or bad luck (the "truly needy") but will never accept the blame for peoples' pain. The "system," the American way, is good for you. From this springs the Reaganite attitude toward welfare, the continual separation of the helpless unfortunate from those who could help themselves.

The president's denial that his package could possibly hurt anyone has the same root: right action cannot hurt any but the immoral. Thus, unlike many Republicans in the Senate and some of his own staff, the president worried little about fairness. To Reagan, fairness meant people getting what they deserved. He replied to criticism with stories about cheating: the welfare queen in Chicago or the food stamps used to purchase vodka. He worried mainly about finding a moral ground because moral principles are not so easily turned aside as statements about matters of fact.

Now the moral leader in an immoral world knows that he must meet the unconverted halfway; but he also believes that continual witnessing of the Word will eventually win the day. Strong in a faith that is bigger than the leader, the leader then communicates that belief to the citizenry. This certitude need not appear as the deadly cold fanaticism of a Robespierre. Nor need it be the strictness of a Cotton Mather or a John Calvin. A moral leader can forgive the sinners, like a Stockman after the *Atlantic* article or Jack Kemp after the 1982 tax-hike battle, by recognizing that the world is a difficult place in which to live. The Lord himself forgave Nineveh (much to Jonah's disgust). The Lord even forgave Jonah. Reagan acted as a moral leader first, a policy maker second. Recall that when Ronald Reagan at the last minute in early 1982 rejected his advisers' tax plans—it *felt* so wrong—he reacted physically to the idea.

The believers in the vision, like their president, would not abandon it because of a few bad months. What Reaganomics offered was a chance to believe, a chance to have their country, for a while, pursue their vision.

Herbert Stein has written that, with the breakdown of the Keynesian consensus, Americans have no theory for fiscal policy. What we wish to add is that Ronald Reagan wanted no fiscal theory; he was quite satisfied with the moral economy (some call it capitalism) he already knew. Nor could economists guarantee that their theories would work better than his.

The Reagan administration would feel pressures to reduce the deficit and thereby interest rates, or even to pump up the economy with further tax cuts. But this administration, far more than most, because of its leader, would accept the painful present. Ronald Reagan would campaign to stay the course because he was strong in his own beliefs. Virtue, his version, surely would be rewarded in the end.

Should Spending Be Limited by Constitutional Amendment?

As the midterm elections approached, the overriding concern was whether a public attracted to Reagan's moral economy, but bowled over by the economic gale, would maintain the Republican de facto majorities in Congress. If not, then Republicans had to find some other appeal to help GOP legislators stay in office. What do you do about Reaganomics if your constituents need help now? One response was focusing attention on their strong moral grounds rather than the short-term economic disaster. Hence the Republicans pushed for a constitutional amendment to require a balanced budget. The proposed balanced budget, spending limit amendment was criticized as irrelevant to the existing deficit, but that, we believe, was neither the moral nor the political point.

An amendment to the Constitution that called for balancing the budget and limiting government spending had gathered support slowly since the mid-1970s. Two issue groups, the National Taxpayers Union and the National Tax Limitation Committee, provided most of the lobbying effort. Although balancing the budget was the more politically popular theme, these groups were more interested in limiting government spending; balance at high levels of taxing and spending would be a defeat. Eventually a coalition of legislators and other interested parties formed to push a version of the amendment that would make unbalancing the budget difficult; spending cuts would become the most likely means to achieve budget balance.

Amendment proponents began with little hope of winning the two-thirds of each house necessary to submit an amendment to the states for ratification. Democratic legislators thought it was a bad idea, and their control of procedure, especially in the House, enabled them to keep the issue off the agenda. Amendment proponents, therefore, worked to build pressure on Congress by proceeding on the never-used second route to a constitutional amendment. If two-thirds (thirty-four) of the states so requested, Congress would have to call a new constitutional convention to propose amendments that would, in turn, be submitted to the states for ratification.

No one knew exactly how such a convention would work: who would participate in it, whether its actions could really be limited to balanced budget matters—and so on through a litany of uncertainty. Some argued that a convention might "run away" and radically alter the Constitution. Not likely: getting people to alter a body of law that we have all learned is nearly sacred, and then getting three-quarters of state legislatures to agree, seems wildly improbable.[30] The prospect, however, served as a double-edged scare tactic. Although the specter of a "runaway" convention gave them fits because it was hard to prove a negative—a stick-to-the-budget convention—the amendment's advocates felt that these uncertainties added to the appeal of their strategy. They hoped that fear of a convention would cause Congress to act preemptively, that is, to submit an amendment to the states rather than open that Pandora's box.

Balanced budgets are very popular, in the abstract, with the American public. Spending limits are not necessarily so popular, but, because the amendment was presented as a budget-balancing effort and because the polls asked questions accordingly, its advocates could demonstrate over-whelming support for the idea. The amendment was far more popular, just like the balanced budget, than was any particular action to achieve its goal.

On January 31, 1982, Alaska became the thirty-first state to endorse the call. The mushrooming federal deficit strongly encouraged the amendment, for the cries of woe from all sides, liberals included, about interest rates and other supposedly deficit-related evils made action to restrain deficits seem more important, while the failures of first Carter and then Reagan to balance the budget encouraged the belief that only powerful medicine would cure the deficit disease. In American political thinking, a constitutional amendment is the most powerful medicine of all. With the tally of states nearing the magic thirty-four, and with deficits mushrooming, the amendment movement in Congress grew stronger.

A constitutional amendment to enforce any particular budgeting result takes to an extreme, but hardly unprecedented, point a common political tactic: shaping decisions by changing the rules for deciding. The budget acts of 1921, 1974, and 1985 (Gramm-Rudman-Hollings) were, at least in part, efforts by factions to change budget results by changing procedures. State constitutions include many provisions—such as balanced budget requirements, item vetoes, and limits on how a legislature can alter a governor's budget—designed to ensure balance.[31] The U.S. Constitution is amended far less frequently than are state charters; both the presumption against elevating policy to fundamental law and the difficulty of amendments are greater at the national level. Yet the Constitution itself had emerged from particular concerns, not just abstract principles of governance; the evils of the Articles of Confederation, after all, were more evident to creditors than debtors. The *Federalist Papers* remains the classic text on how rules may shape results.

Martin Anderson's "Policy Memorandum No. 1" (August 1979) proposed a menu of constitutional changes that include "a constitutional limitation on the percentage of the people's earnings that can be taken and spent by the federal government," a line-item veto, and a balanced budget amendment. These proposals were downplayed in Reagan's campaign because they did not respond to the immediate budget problem; therefore, they could easily be attacked as grandstanding.

Early in the administration, efforts were focused on more direct attacks on the deficit and domestic spending. CEA Chairman Weidenbaum was able to declare:

> The President's economic program would accomplish all of the objectives that are sought in the many proposals to balance the budget via Constitutional change. But it would do so without the many drawbacks, such as encumbering the Constitution with matters that more appropriately belong in the policy arena or attempting to rule on matters of technical fiscal administration.[32]

By early March 1982, attacks for grandstanding were still more plausible, but the administration had less to lose by pursuing the constitutional agenda. Getting tough on spending was wearing them down. "We have a lot of Republicans, not to mention Democrats, who absolutely are not going to vote for the size deficits that we face if they can't see a balanced budget at the end of the tunnel," *Newsweek* quoted a "senior Administration official." "What's more reassuring than an honest-to-God constitutional amendment?"[33] Weidenbaum and Regan issued statements of qualified support. The cabinet met to consider a formal endorsement.

Senate Republicans moved a version of the amendment out of their Judiciary Committee on July 10, 1981. As 1982 began, this version, S.J.Res. 58, had not been brought to the floor. A House companion, H.J.Res. 350, was buried in House Judiciary. The House committee had held hearings but had taken no action.

If it were passed and worked, the amendment would help to entrench the Reagan agenda of a smaller role for government in American society. By backing the amendment, the president also could testify to his support for the balanced budget. More important, he could embarrass the Democrats who had been beating him over the head with his own balanced budget rhetoric and big deficits. Some of them, like James Jones, might be as committed to a balanced budget as Reagan himself, but even those believers would resist the amendment as it was structured. Let them try to explain either that they objected to the text because it was antispending as well as probalance or that a balanced budget was fine but not appropriate for enshrining in the Constitution. When Reagan endorsed the amendment at his March 31, 1982, press conference, he could be accused of hypocrisy for supporting it while simultaneously proposing wildly unbalanced budgets. "It was almost as if the nation's leading distiller," *Time* commented acidly, "had suddenly come out in favor of Prohibition."[34] But the White House was facing those attacks anyway and would, with at least equal logic, scorn its opponents who denounced both unbalanced budgets and the amendment. Insofar as the amendment was basically about spending and revenue limits, moreover, the president agreed entirely with it.

On April 29, as part of his television address about the breakdown of negotiations in the Gang of 17, he declared:

> Once we've created a balanced budget—and we will—I want to insure that we keep it for many long years after I've left office. And there's only one way to do that. . . . Only a constitutional amendment will do the job. We've tried the carrot [arguing that budget balance is good for the economy so that sacrifices will be repaid] and it failed. With the stick of a balanced budget amendment, we can stop the Government's squandering ways and save our economy.[35]

The amendment would institutionalize the changes that Reagan wanted so they would live on after him.

In the House the amendment's chief sponsor, Barber Conable (with Ed Jenkins, D-G.), filed a discharge petition with the House clerk. If 218 members signed the petition, then the amendment could be forced out of House Judiciary over that body's opposition. Although the House version, H.J.Res. 350, had 221 sponsors, it remained to be seen whether they would all choose to override the committee or whether some of them rather liked cosponsoring a bill that was safely buried.[36]

On July 12 Howard Baker called up S.J.Res. 58 for Senate consideration. The Senate text provided:

1. "Prior to each fiscal year, the Congress shall adopt a statement of receipts and outlays for that year in which total outlays are no greater than total receipts." Congress could provide for a deficit only by a vote of three-fifths of the whole number of each house (261 representatives or 60 senators; an abstention therefore was identical to a "No"). "The Congress and the President shall ensure that actual outlays do not exceed the outlays set forth in such statement."

2. Total receipts for a fiscal year could not increase faster than national income had increased in the previous calendar year. That is, FY83 receipts could not grow faster than the 1981 economy. Receipts could only grow beyond that level if a majority of the whole number of each house endorsed a bill (thus again, abstention was a "No") which the president signed into law. This was constitutional indexing of the tax system taken a step further: higher *real* incomes would no longer raise taxes through the progressive rate structure.

3. Congress could waive these provisions if a declaration of war were in effect.

4. "The Congress may not require that the states engage in additional activities without compensation equal to additional costs." That is, Congress could not fob programs off on the states to save money. . . .

5. Borrowing did not count as receipts, and repayment of debt principal would not count as outlays. The latter was at best an academic concern for the foreseeable future.

6. "This article shall take effect for the second fiscal year beginning after its ratification"—no earlier, that is, than FY85, and that was highly improbable.

On July 19 Reagan led a GOP rally on the steps of the Capitol in which he asked the familiar question about why the government could not be run like a family: "How can families and family values flourish, when big Government, with its power to tax, inflate and regulate, has absorbed their wealth, usurped their rights and too often crushed their spirit?" James Jones emphasized respect for institutions: "There can only be two results if the amendment is adopted. The most likely is that it will mirror Prohibition—a sham. A second possible result is that it will be enforced, and thus fundamentally change the checks and balances of the three branches of the Federal Government."[37] Policy, power, and political philosophy were all at stake.

The Senate debated the bill for two weeks and accepted two amendments. One, by Domenici, attempted to calm fears about impoundment; the other, an attempt by William Armstrong to ensure the amendment did its job, took all the slack out of the constitutional change. Armstrong proposed that an increase in the debt ceiling should also require a three-fifths vote. Therefore, if the president and Congress tried to ignore the amendment in the event of, say, increases in recession-related outlays, the debt limit would force action. Most Republicans thought it was trouble and opposed it 20 to 31. In a classic case of sabotage, Democrats, convinced Armstrong's modification would make the whole business less palatable, supported him 31 to 14. Nevertheless, the amendment passed the Senate by 69 to 31 (2 votes more than the 67 needed) as a number of senators, after voicing grave doubts, supported the amendment. The vote was as much regional as partisan. Republicans, who had to go on record, voted 47 to 7 for the amendment, southern Democrats 13 to 2 in favor, and northern Democrats 9 to 22 against.

The battle now shifted to the House, where no doubt some senators hoped the bill would be buried. Many Washington leaders doubted that the amendment, even if passed by Congress, would actually be ratified; signs at the state level suggested they might be right.[38] But also they might be wrong, and House leaders were not about to take that chance. Their resistance meant proponents had to blow the amendment out of committee with a discharge petition. On September 29, after a last-minute drive led by Vice President Bush, Stockman, and House GOP leaders, proponents got the 218th signature.

Rather than let the issue sit for a couple of weeks at the height of election season—as standard procedure and Republican hopes prescribed—House leaders responded by bringing the amendment to the floor immediately. Their rule also allowed a substitute by Representative Bill Alexander (D-Ark.), heavily watered down. Alexander's proposal would provide political cover so that some members could vote against Conable-Jenkins yet still say they had voted for a balanced budget amendment.[39]

At 10:00 a.m. on October 1, 1982, the House convened to debate and to vote on enshrining in the Constitution the balanced budget and spending limits. Congressmen pleaded with each other and played to the gallery, rising to impressive levels of rhetoric or descending to equally impressive depths of sophistry. We cannot capture all the arguments, but we can provide the flavor of the debate, a picture of the House at work during one of the rare times when the work really was done on the floor and the differences in political philosophy came to the fore.

Richard Bolling led the debate, professing a nonpartisan worry for the fate of the political process. He expressed sorrow that "the gentleman from New York (Mr. Conable) . . . has truly given up on the essential democratic process. He puts certain things in his resolution . . . which would require super majorities to decide that there will be an unbalanced budget."[40] Conable replied:

> We have already done irreparable damage to the Republic in seventeen of the eighteen years I have served here. . . . Congress should be a place of judgment. When judgment is not wisely exercised it is appropriate that we put some limitations on that exercise of judgment and that is what the Constitution does in many cases.[41]

Delbert Latta scored the big spenders who wanted to grab tax money, spreading benefits now that would have to be paid for by their grandchildren. Where Latta saw spenders, David Obey saw cowards and hypocrites:

> Mr. Speaker . . . this administration is giving hypocrisy a bad name. This administration pretends that it is fighting for a balanced budget. If it is losing that battle, it is losing that battle to itself. . . .
> I have talked to at least twenty members on that side of the aisle, and more members on this side of the aisle. I have asked them how they could sign this discharge petition and how they can vote for this today, including members of the Judiciary Committee. They have hung their heads, and they have said, "Well, I know, I hate to do it, but I just cannot go home and explain it to my people."
> I would suggest that it goes with the territory. . . . If members are not willing to go home to their own districts and tell them what their honest beliefs are about something as crucial as this, then you do not belong here.[42]

After the rule was passed, debate was controlled by the two leaders of the Judiciary Committee: Peter Rodino (D-N.J.) and Robert McClory (R-Ill.). McClory spoke to charges that the amendment would be ineffective.

> I do not accept the notion that Congress will ignore the mandate of the Constitution if House Joint Resolution 350 is proposed and ratified. Congress has made good faith efforts to obey the Constitution throughout its history. While it may have been mistaken about the constitutionality of its legislation, I cannot accept that its errors were willful. . . . In fact, it is my observation that Members would prefer to be so constrained than to be free to be unduly pressured by special interests.[43]

"Forced to be free" was a theme of the debate among those who responded to widespread concern about inability to govern effectively.

In what would be the main opposition speech, Peter Rodino went step by step through the alleged uncertainties in the text—the inability to predict deficits, the antimajoritarian cast, the delegation of powers to the president or the courts. "What do the courts do then?" he asked, "Write the budget? Appropriate the money? Order arrests?" He concluded:

> The proposal would demean the Constitution. The Constitution is a document that guarantees fundamental rights and freedoms and provides for the orderly operation of Government. This amendment is a constitutional guarantee of nothing. It provides a balanced budget—except sometimes: When three-fifths of Congress says otherwise; when revenues fall below estimates; in times of declared war; when Congress cannot agree on cutting spending; when Congress cannot agree on raising taxes. It could be an invitation to fiscal gimmickry or a prescription for paralysis of Government, for confrontation among the branches, for economic chaos.[44]

The proposed amendment led the party of change to a more ardent defense of an unchanging Constitution than had been its custom.

Phil Gramm replied by describing the bias toward spending the amendment sought to correct:

> In the last Congress, the average bill we worked on with amendments cost about $50 million. There are 100 million taxpayers. That is 50 cents a head. The average beneficiary got $500. You do not have to have studied economics at Texas A&M [where he had taught] to know that somebody is willing to do more to get $500 than somebody is willing to do to prevent spending 50 cents. . . . This is a perfect example of where a constitutional constraint on elected officials is required.[45]

A leader of southern Republicans, Ed Bethune, made one of the most interesting arguments against the amendment. Conservatives, he declared, should be leading the opposition to such attempts to hamstring the play of political forces. The amendment would fail because it depended on the "fallacious assumption that budgeteers can accurately calculate one indispensable, exalted number—the deficit—which will tell us whether we are winning or losing the battle for a rational fiscal policy. Nothing could be further from the truth." Not only were estimates wildly unreliable, Bethune continued, but the spending figures did not "begin to reflect the many ways in which the Government can and does impact our nation's economy." The amendment would not deal with what he considered the real problem. The Senate Judiciary Committee, Bethune proclaimed,

> published a wordy finding that Congress is plagued with an institutional "spending bias." They concluded that politicians will not cast "politically

disadvantageous votes" to restrain spending and that a constitutional amendment is the only way to overcome such a disease. . . . That may be so under the circumstances we can see today, but there is nothing new in the Senate findings. These same problems have plagued democratic governments since the origin of man. The strained analysis, however, basically comes down to a contention that the people at large are too stupid and indifferent to know how to correct the problem.

That attitude, Bethune argued, was wrong. The people had perceived and were correcting overspending. Conservatives were being elected to Congress, attitudes had changed, and "the politically disadvantageous vote in today's climate, contrary to the Senate's findings, is a vote for new spending or a vote which does nothing to restrain the growth of spending." New forces were forming; old actors were adjusting to new realities; old institutions, like Senate staffs, were transformed; and "the political parties are competing intensely on the basis that one is better equipped than the other to bring a balanced budget." Perhaps all that would come to nothing. But if the forces were not strong enough, a constitutional amendment would also fail. Although the people had little faith in men and parties, they did have faith in the Constitution. That trust should not be hazarded lightly.[46]

California Republican Jerry Lewis returned to the mythology that surrounds and buttresses our political system: What, after all, would the hallowed Founders have said about this proposal? Where Rodino and Bethune had argued that their work should be left untouched, Lewis proclaimed:

> The Founding Fathers were most reserved about the prospect of expanding central Government. They recognized that Government growth would require taxes and that to tax was to take people's property. Never in their wildest dreams would they have imagined that the Congress would come to the point where they were taking not only high percentages of the productive value of today's citizens—but placing in debt the property and productive potential of their children and grandchildren as well. Mr. Chairman, I suggest it is absolutely reasonable to let the people decide whether or not in the future there shall be required by the Constitution an extra majority of the Congress before it can budget beyond our means.[47]

Lewis's side was invoking the majority's right to adopt an antimajoritarian provision (the people should decide whether to adopt the amendment) while his opponents ultimately were relying on an antimajoritarian procedure (the two-thirds requirement on amendments) in their fight against the antimajoritarian proposal. Ironic, yes, but nothing new. While we eschew the Spockian "mindlock" (recall "Star Trek") with the framers others so easily achieve, the Founding Fathers so fervently invoked remain practical politicians, leaders who lived on the fine line between principle and expedience. Thus, Hamilton would inveigh against the debt if it helped him get the Constitution ratified, and Jefferson, the great apostle of limits on both executives and government itself, was actually the most dominant of presidents, purchasing Louisiana with absolutely no authority. Perhaps there were no Jeffersons or Hamiltons in the House on October 1, 1982, but the task and burden of the politician remained the same.

The Alexander substitute went down 77 to 346, but it provided cover for many southern Democrats who opposed the amendment but wanted to go on record in favor of balancing the budget. Then the balanced budget amendment fell short of the required two-thirds vote, with 236 yeas and 187 nays. Led by the former minority leader, Arizona's John Rhodes, Silvio Conte, Ed Bethune, and Jack Kemp, twenty Republicans opposed the president and their party.

"One way or another we're going to get this," Barber Conable declared. But the amendment did not take hold as an election issue, and 1982 was a bad year for Republicans. The proamendment forces, surveying the postelection wreckage, could see little hope in the states and none in the House.[48] At this writing (summer 1988), it seems that the campaign for a constitutional amendment, after cresting on October 1, 1982, has receded; two states have reversed their support. But the effort to change the politics by changing the rules continues.

In this elevated conversation two truths compete: Efforts to thwart majority rule are likely to fail when people learn how to avoid, use, or circumvent any provision (our book has enough examples of gamesmanship to suit anyone). However, the rules of the game, including institutional biases, help determine the outcomes; this is the truth on which our constitutional structure, including the separation of powers, is based. Like the great constitutional debates of the past, the issues are illuminated but remain unresolved. An occasional conservative may argue in favor of allowing the balance that comes in shifts of public opinion to diminish the tendency to spend more and tax less. A liberal may accept the desirability of erecting institutional impediments to being overly generous, as Congress did when it erected obstacles in the path of new entitlements. On the whole, however, positions about rules followed from opinions about desirable outcomes—moderated by perceptions of constituency pressure. There had to be a moderate majority out there somewhere, or so the budget balancers hoped. TEFRA showed it. If only they could adjust the rules, so the moderates could govern again, then they might find the pony under all the dirty budget work.

Although the term moderate-extremist may appear to be an oxy-moron, the passion of those committed to budget balance would grow in proportion as its realization declined. Then we would be treated to an unusual spectacle indeed: moderate defenders of responsible government violating its procedures in the name of a higher value—the ever-elusive balance.

THIRTEEN

Guerrilla Warfare:
Spending Politics, 1982

Amid battles of ideology and procedure, the nation's elected representatives and chief executive still had to run a government. Of the three 1982 battles already described—the constitutional amendment, budget resolution, and TEFRA—only TEFRA directly affected the goods and services government provided to citizens. Budget resolutions spend no money. The amendment was steps further removed from government activity. When members of Congress turned to legislation and appropriations, vague numbers—a percentage of GNP on the amendment, a functional total on the resolution—became far less attractive line-item reductions in specific programs. Just like the voters, legislators preferred abstract budget balancing to concrete spending cuts. When voting on the latter, it was more difficult to ignore both policy and political consequences: dams were not built; hot lunches were not served; transit fares were raised; and citizens were unhappy. As consequences became more direct, support for budget cutting declined, from a substantial (though not two-thirds) House majority for the amendment, to a bare majority on the budget resolution, to minorities on the appropriations bills.

Reagan and Stockman wanted to use the growing deficit to pressure domestic spending downward. By cutting or eliminating new appropriations, they could slash programs while bypassing the chairmen who would bottle up legislative proposals to eliminate them. Yet neither House nor Senate appropriations leaders, of either party, much approved of Reagan's agenda. In September, Republican leaders on Appropriations finally revolted. First Silvio Conte in the House and then Mark Hatfield in the Senate led their chambers in overriding the president's veto of a FY82 supplemental appropriations bill.

The conditioning event in all of 1982's spending battles was the reces-

285

sion. The ideological shift against public works spending, which we saw in 1980, the giant budget deficits, and Reagan's veto all assured there would be no big new programs. Yet constituencies, including Republican constituencies, were suffering. Slashing the poor's benefits while their ranks grew was difficult to defend. As unemployment rose to the highest level since the Great Depression, even the taboo against jobs spending weakened. By December, Reagan, who in September said only a "palace coup" could win his support for such a plan, was backing a big increase in transportation funding, financed by doubling the gasoline tax.

In terms of the mathematics of deficit reduction, the appropriations battles were not so important. Congress appropriated $7 billion more than the president requested. Although an unprecedented increase, this was a very small proportion of the deficit. Yet it hid a much larger increase in domestic programs, which was balanced by scaling down the defense buildup. To update Senator Dirksen, a billion here and a billion there may not be real money in the macropicture of budgeting, but it is plenty of real policy. The policy stakes in appropriations were big enough that they were transmuted into power stakes, as the administration and its opponents each tried to win battles to establish momentum for the next.

We may push the military analogy further. Spending conflict in 1981 resembled a set-piece battle; the entire forces of each side collided in the House on reconciliation where huge amounts of budgetary territory were at stake. The struggles of 1982 were more like guerrilla warfare, a series of skirmishes over small pieces of territory, at the end of which control remained dubious. The drift of events, however, was clear: the administration, aggressive early in the year, was on the defensive in late 1982.

As 1982 began, the administration proposed not only substantial appropriations cuts in its FY83 budget but also substantial rescissions of funds appropriated in FY82. These proposals reflected a change in policy as well as a change in the role of the president's office, particularly OMB, in budget making. When David Stockman took over at OMB, he accelerated alterations in its relationships with Congress that had begun during the Carter administration. As a top OMB official wrote, the details of cuts were less important than

> the way in which this revision took place. Traditionally the American budget is developed by the executive and presented to the Congress and the public without formal discussions or negotiations. . . . In contrast, the [fiscal] 1981 budget revisions were literally negotiated between executive branch representatives (primarily the Office of Management and Budget and the White House) and the leadership in both houses of the Congress.[1]

Stockman institutionalized the ad hoc developments of 1980 and took them a giant step further. Executive budgeting became far more "top-down." He shifted OMB's focus from examining and assembling agency requests to lobbying the administration's budget through Congress. Staff was dedicated to tracking budget action through the multiple stages of the congressional process, not to examining agency requests. To facilitate this tracking, Stockman ordered the development of a computer system that aggregated budget items by both budget function categories and committee jurisdictions, allowing him to trace the spending implications of action at all levels. Stockman could use his resources this way because he really needed to know nothing about the agencies. For at least a few years he could get by with previous analysis by OMB, the extensive literature produced by GAO, CBO, and the think tanks, and his own prejudices about what government should and should not do. The new OMB approach, Hale Champion commented, "almost excluded cabinet departments and agencies from the formulation of the budget."[2]

Because Stockman (and President Reagan) were interested in achieving their preferred set of cuts, not in using the budget to finance agencies, OMB also moved away from the norm of annual budgeting. The annual budget served many needs, but its primary purpose was to regularize the financing and therefore functioning of government agencies. Funded for a year in advance, an agency would be able to plan its activities. Stockman discarded the norm of the annual budget in 1981 and 1982, proposing large rescissions of spending that meant reneging on commitments; in effect, the budget was being remade several times a year. This would not exactly reduce budgetary conflict. With the budget under continuous negotiation, even a place in the formal budget did not guarantee funding at the formerly agreed level. As part of its budget cutting, OMB also interfered directly in agency administration; for example, OMB issued orders to the Park Service, forbidding hiring up to the levels allowed in the appropriations legislation.

Both House and Senate Appropriations Committees, as part of their job of overseeing program administration, found themselves defending agencies against OMB's attacks. Committee members objected to the repeated cuts on both programmatic and legislative grounds; in rescissions the president challenged the power of Congress through its appropriations committees.

Supplemental Appropriations

The year 1982 began quietly enough. Much of the government was still running on the December 1981 Continuing Resolution (for FY82), which would expire by the end of March. The administration chose not to hold the CR hostage for further spending cuts because the Gang-of-17 negotiations had begun and such a conflict would not encourage deal making. Therefore, after bizarre maneuvers regarding legislators' taxes—which we will ignore for the moment but will confront later—the previous CR was extended with bipartisan support but without attention to the budget targets from the previous year.

Instead, the administration chose to use a supplemental appropriation for a number of other programs, such as Guaranteed Student Loans and sewage treatment grants, as a vehicle for spending reductions. OMB proposed rescissions of more than $9.4 billion, mostly in subsidized housing but also in education programs. It proposed new rules for student loans to shave $400 million from the $1.3 billion extra cost.

Congressional opinion about the education rescissions in particular, and rescissions in general, was best indicated by the remarks of Senator Ted Stevens (R-Alaska), the majority whip, in an Appropriations hearing. He told Ms. Harrison of the Department of Education that to rescind the funds would mean grantees had been misled. She replied that Reagan's administration and previous administrations had opposed the program involved. "But successive Congresses have disagreed," Stevens reminded her, and "the president signed that bill last year." "That's why we are proposing a rescission," Ms. Harrison explained. "I think the Department is just buying itself a fight," the senator responded. "There is a de facto breaking of a commitment as far as the Government is concerned. . . . You people are not reading Congress correctly if you think you are going to get away with this."[3]

With the rescissions, and the pay raises still unfunded, the administration created an "urgent supplemental appropriation" proposal that would reduce budget authority by about $5 billion (subtraction under the guise of addition, a rather neat trick). House Appropriations, unimpressed, rejected almost all the rescissions, although it agreed to defer $3.8 billion. It then added some social spending, reporting a bill that would increase budget authority by about $5 billion.

This large but straightforward difference of opinion was then complicated by the demands of the housing industry for relief from the effects of recession and high interest rates. Republican representatives Tom Corcoran of Illinois and Thomas B. Evans, Jr., of Delaware wanted to take $1 billion from the synfuels program and use it for a new mortgage subsidy program. Majority Leader Jim Wright, an ardent defender of synfuels, objected. With the housing industry in desperate shape, however, the Corcoran and Evans proposal might well have passed with heavy Democratic support. Democratic leadership did not want Republicans to get credit for helping housing. Instead, after a delay, the Democrats produced both a housing proposal that did not take the money from synfuels and a rule that allowed a vote on that amendment, legislation on an appropriations bill, but not on the Corcoran and Evans plan. Seeing little chance of Democratic defections on the rule, Republicans let it ride, and then, although Stockman promised a veto, most Republicans voted for the housing money.

Senate Appropriations acceded to most of the housing rescissions that the lower chamber had rejected. The Senate committee then tacked on a $1 billion appropriation and a five-year $5 billion authorization for a different mortgage subsidy plan, this one designed by Richard Lugar. Making the bill still more controversial, Appropriations Committee members also added provisions regarding senators' tax deductions that could increase their incomes.

Senator Lugar insisted his housing plan was a way to fight unemployment; William Armstrong (R-Colo.) argued that Lugar's plan would only pave the way for bailouts of other troubled industries; the administration fervently opposed Lugar as well. On this issue, the organs of "responsibility," opposed as they were to spending programs, backed the administration. "Getting down the deficit," *Time* quoted a real estate economist, "is the only solution."[4] *Newsweek* reported, with similar skepticism, that "it happens every recession: mindful of plunging economic indicators and—more to the point—upcoming elections, Congress scrambles to bail out the industries feeling the most pain."[5] Reagan risked little media opprobrium for threatening a veto. Because the public at large and the interests involved might be less convinced that aid to housing or for jobs was bad, legislators still wanted to appear to be helping.

In conference the two houses split the difference on mortgage assistance and allowed most housing rescissions. The bill that emerged was still more than $4 billion over the administration's request, so Reagan vetoed it on June 24. A move to override failed when House Republicans supported the president, 131 to 53. Democrats thereby got those Republicans on record against housing aid.

Appropriations and Democratic leaders now turned to devising a supplemental that might get signed. They created, and the House passed, a "fat" and a "skinny" supplemental. The fat bill, H. R. 6682, did not contain the new mortgage subsidies and a number of other items that could wait until the next round; however, it provided lower rescissions and more spending than Reagan had requested. After the Senate passed the fat version on June 25, Reagan immediately vetoed it. Two days, two bills, two vetoes. For good measure, Stockman told Hatfield that the skinny bill, H. R. 6685, also would be vetoed. After those two bargained for a bit, Senate Appropriations reported an amended H. R. 6685 that rescinded more subsidized housing funds.[6] On the floor, a Democratic effort to restore the $3 billion conference version of the mortgage subsidy program was tabled, 48 to 44. Now Republican senators were on record against housing aid.

Democrats' strategy was to get spending increases if they could, but, if not, they at least wanted to get the Republicans on record against them. David Mayhew's classic analysis of position taking applies here:

> A congressman can hardly be blamed if there are not enough right-think-ing members around to allow him to carry his motions. He's fighting the good fight. . . . We do not ordinarily think of losses as being politically harmful. We can all point to a good many instances in which congressmen seem to have gotten into trouble by being on the *wrong* side of a roll call vote, but who can think of one where a member got into trouble by being on the *losing* side?[7]

The president also might believe there was political mileage in using his veto against big spenders. He, however, had more stake in the results. People understand if their representative is outvoted; they may be less sympathetic if their president loses. The president's inside-the-beltway reputation for effectiveness is particularly important, for it shapes how seriously other political actors take those preferences.[8] Reagan therefore had to care more about winning.

With a few minor changes, the skinny bill passed the Senate, and everyone went home to celebrate Independence Day. When the House returned, it tried but failed to override the veto of the fat bill and then went to conference on the skinny bill. More money was taken out of subsidized housing and spread around on more popular programs. (For various reasons, including being a fairly ineffective use of money, sub-sidized housing construction, the primary target, was less popular than almost anything else.) Stockman accepted the resulting package; Howard Baker commented that in any case a veto would have been hard to sustain.[9] The skinny bill was a draw. It provided $390 million more new spending than the administration requested, accepting most housing but no other rescissions.

The appropriations committees' rejection of most domestic spending cuts would be ascribed by Stockman to the politicians' appetite for con-stituency pork. Yet there were at least two other sources. First, the ad-ministration itself tried to deny that its cuts would do harm, while Congress found those arguments incredible. "The impression you give us," Senator Andrews (R-N.D.) told an administration witness, "is that somehow or another you have found a magic way of doing exactly the same thing that has been done years ago for two-thirds of the cost." Andrews did not believe in magic.[10] When told by agency officials that local governments would make up cuts in federal aid to libraries, Senator

Hatfield replied that they were wrong and they knew it.[11] Appropriations members built a record against the cuts. Second, Appropriations elders did not see major policy changes as part of either their jurisdiction or budgeting. "Tell me," Sidney Yates (D-Ill.) of the House Appropriations Interior subcommittee asked the director of the National Park Service, "about the historic preservation fund. Has Congress repealed the basic legislation for which you are eliminating all funds?" "No, sir," replied Mr. Dickerson. "Why are you eliminating the funds then?" asked the chairman. As a senior Republican on House Appropriations commented to us about eliminating programs, "You can do that, but you have to do it in the authorizing committees."[12]

In July OMB requested a new FY82 supplemental, including the annual pay raise, $2.4 billion in new defense authority, and $5 billion more for the Commodity Credit Corporation (CCC). As the agricultural sector's problems mounted, the CCC was turning into an unstoppable money pump. Defense, CCC, salaries, and foreign aid increases accounted for $14.2 billion of a $16.3 billion administration request.

House Appropriations accepted mandatory increases like pay raises and CCC, but otherwise it gave the president none of what he wanted. The supplemental provided only one-sixth of the requested defense funds. House Appropriations also reduced extra medicaid funding, saying that it could wait until FY83 action. These reductions enabled the committee to add about $1 billion to such programs as community service employment for the elderly, education for the disadvantaged, college student aid, and interstate highways—that is, many programs the administration had been working all year to reduce. Yet the defense reductions kept the House committee bill well under the president's proposed spending. It passed easily on the floor. Senate action basically followed the House.

Because their version called for $1.8 billion less than the president's request, members of Congress could argue that the bill was fiscally responsible, differing only marginally from the president's request. Actually, members had rejected his policy preferences and imposed their own on almost every plausibly discretionary item. OMB therefore urged a veto of the bill, supported by political advisers who felt that a veto would mollify conservatives upset about the tax increase. On August 19 Senator Stevens warned that "I don't think anything is to be gained by vetoing this one. A veto would be overridden in the Senate."[13] Mark Hatfield warned he would fight all future defense increases if the president vetoed. Reagan vetoed the bill anyway, denouncing it as a billion dollar budget buster.

Democratic leaders did not expect to override Reagan in the House. But with Silvio Conte leading the effort, the override succeeded, 301 to

117. Members had been infuriated by the president's claim that they had busted the budget; Reagan seemed to be saying that fiscal responsibility meant not just his totals but his priorities. Of course, within Reagan's moral economy, that was exactly what fiscal responsibility did mean; but Congress did not agree. To everyone's surprise, Senate leaders now had to take sides on the veto. Hatfield flew back to Washington on a red-eye flight to lead the override forces.

Nobody can say exactly what shaped that vote. An administration leader said, simply, "They'd [the Republicans] been up the mountain too many times." A House Republican staffer who was deeply involved said, "It was just a tactical error by OMB. What overrode the veto was just the older Americans' money. I never regarded that as other than a tactical success by the elderly lobby. . . . It proved nothing but don't screw around with the elderly."

Certainly part of Reagan's problem was money for jobs for the elderly. The program, that no one except Stockman wanted to close down, was out of funds. Even Reagan, after vetoing, backed off and explained he had not known about the older Americans money. Mark Hatfield used money for the elderly as an example of why Congress should set priorities:

> I have swallowed hard many times. I have literally held my nose on occasion in order to be a part of the majority party . . . to demonstrate the capability of the majority to govern. . . .
>
> There comes a time in a person's life when conscience and principle transcend all the affections and loyalties of the party and to one's president. . . .
>
> The President may later claim an oversight, but we cannot. . . . The question is simple and straightforward. Will the Congress, which passed this measure by substantial majorities, kowtow to David Stockman in his singleminded desire to eliminate programs of great value and importance to the people of this Nation, or will Congress assert its own priorities and prerogatives and responsibilities?[14]

Even Senator Domenici supported the override. The stakes had been exaggerated on both sides, he argued; clearly the bill was no budget buster so there was no point to a confrontation that would shut down the civil service. Howard Baker supported the president but without urgency. "They did their regular whip checks," one aide recalled, "but did not make it a big issue." When the vote was taken, the Senate overrode the veto, 60 to 30.

In politics, why something happened may be less important than why people think it did. Robert Michel's interpretation was telling: "The principle reason we lost was that you cannot make a good argument that

Congress was busting the budget. You couldn't make a good argument on the numbers. Maybe, for the long haul, the administration could learn something from this."[15] Indeed. One lesson was that Conte and Hatfield could beat the White House. Another was that legislators were much less susceptible to pressure when they could not accurately be accused of swelling the deficit. Unlike events in 1981, Congress, not Stockman, was keeping score; if a bill fit Congress's scorekeeping, a veto might yield only an embarrassing defeat.

The supplemental veto override of September 10, 1982, therefore, was a watershed in the battle over priorities. The override also revealed the strength of pressure to restrain deficits. It succeeded where others failed because total spending fell below the amount requested. Congress would not explicitly increase deficits.

Appropriators, meanwhile, had been working on FY83 appropriations. The House committee had always taken pride in appropriating (by hook or by crook) less than the president requested. But Reagan went too far; the second session of the 97th Congress ended up appropriating $7 billion more, including later revisions, than the administration's estimates over the course of 1982. Congress kept the increase that low by chopping $18 billion on the defense side; in fact, it appropriated about 10 percent more for domestic discretionary programs than the president had requested. The committees treated the president's proposals not as a neutral upper bound but as a partisan position, worth consideration only to the extent that Reagan and his partisans in Congress could force its consideration.

Without the president's budget as a guide, appropriators resorted to two other standards. One was the previous year's policy, expressed as the CBO baseline. The huge deficits made spending above that level taboo, but, because of the recession, cuts below it were also questionable. The other standard was the spending allocated to the appropriations committees under the first budget resolution. They acknowledged that the resolution's totals constrained them but refused to accept budget committee assumptions about the line items.[16] They ignored the resolution's priorities, being quite blunt about their opposition to domestic cuts.

Appropriators established the priorities within their allotted spending through the budget act 302(b) allocation process. Under 302(b), each committee had to report a division of the resolution's totals among its subcommittees. In 1982 hardly anyone outside the appropriations committees knew what a 302(b) was. Yet the 302(b) within Appropriations would soon become almost a second budget process, potentially as contentious as that of setting priorities in budget resolutions. Conflict was limited because entitlements and revenues were excluded. Yet, in terms of results—particularly defense versus domestic—the 302(b)s were very important because appropriations spend money; budget resolutions do not.

In both House and Senate, full committee staffers would go to each subcommittee and ask the clerks how much they "needed." Clerks would consult with their chairs, who usually checked in with the ranking minority and other subcommittee members. Some subcommittees would accept Budget Committee assumptions as guidelines; most would not. Subcommittee chairs had to trust the "big" chairman's judgment of what kind of distribution would be both supported by other leaders and helpful to passage on the floor. A House subcommittee chairman commented that "it's a very subtle process. It really works out to be the staff acting as buffers with all the subcommittee chairmen." Members defer to the staff and Chairman Whitten because "it's easier. It avoids the recriminating and hostility."

House subcommittees reported bills that purported to spend less than the 302(b) allocations. Rather than let underestimations of entitlements force reductions in discretionary spending, subcommittees wanted to force Stockman to raise his estimates. Although the bills more or less conformed to the budget resolution, amounts were well over the president's budget in many categories. Appropriators and Democratic leaders, therefore, had to devise a way around the president's veto.

We do not know if anyone plotted the subsequent strategy explicitly; perhaps no one needed to. Our sources claim it happened naturally. House Appropriations held the DOD bill hostage pending satisfactory settlement on other contentious measures. The DOD subcommittee waited until early December before reporting out its measure, but everything else was reported out by September 29. In the end, the most contentious domestic-spending bills would be wrapped into a continuing resolution package with defense; if Reagan vetoed, therefore, he would be vetoing something he badly wanted as well as activities he proposed. This use of the continuing resolution would informally but significantly modify the budget process.

As Congress passed TEFRA and the supplemental FY82 appropriations and as FY83 appropriations worked their way through the process, Congress also had to pass the second reconciliation bill. A *second* reconciliation? one might ask. Wasn't the whole idea of reconciliation to put everything into one big package? Well, yes, that is what everybody said. In 1981 all the commentators remarked on the brilliant strategy of one big vote, but it required the House leadership's cooperation, which was no longer (in fact, far from) forthcoming. Democratic leaders decided that there was no reason to make life easy for their opponents by creating a package. Instead, they brought up separate reconciliation bills for separate votes.

Nothing interesting happened in the separate votes on Veterans and Banking, but the agriculture committees became creative. The budget resolution assumed that food stamps and other nutrition programs would be reduced. The Senate committee mostly complied, although its food stamp savings were less than convincing. With the Commodity Credit Corporation hemorrhaging and farmers in real trouble, Senate Agriculture also felt it could do something more constructive. The Senate side endorsed changes in farm programs of the "pay now to save later" variety. Encouragement of farm exports and controls on production would cost money up front but would also raise prices and reduce yields, thereby increasing farm incomes and (hopefully) reducing federal obligations under the commodity loan and price-support programs. The House committee cut food stamps less and projected billions in savings from new efforts to reduce yields of milk, wheat, and corn.[17] In the short run, the wheat and corn plans would have put cash directly in the hands of farmers.

OMB claimed that the House committee and CBO savings estimates were off by about $3 billion. In fact no one knew. The administration's credibility on the subject was limited; after all, OMB had projected spending cuts in 1981 and now in the course of 1982 was to request nearly $17 billion in extra funding for the CCC (the $10 billion in FY82 supplementals and another $6.7 billion in December). Meanwhile, something had to be done about both costs and the farmers, so the House ignored OMB's criticisms. The Agriculture Committee proposals passed easily. The only strong challenge was on food stamps, where Delbert Latta's larger reductions were defeated when enough gypsy moths voted with the Democrats to balance boll weevil defections.

The Post Office and Civil Service Committee, which was expected to cap Civil Service Retirement (CSR) COLAs at 4 percent, not only refused to do so but proposed minimal other savings in place of that cap. It thus became the first committee to defy reconciliation. The committee's bill was brought to the floor under a rule that kindly allowed Republicans to undo the damage with an amendment placing the 4 percent cap on the pensions of two million politically active federal retirees (and, by extension, another two million military retirees). "We are not considering reconciliation in the context of fiscal responsibility," complained Minority Leader Michel. "We are being forced to consider individual bills tailored to embarrass and frustrate those in the House who supported the budget resolution in June." It was convenient to forget that Republicans had forced a similar situation in 1980. Leon Panetta replied that "members cannot come here and support a budget resolution that calls for certain cuts and then hide from the ability to vote up or down on those cuts."[18] "I challenge you to offer the amendment" to reduce CSR COLAs, chided Post Office and Civil Service Committee Chairman William Ford (D-Mich.).[19] Republicans were not about to take that dare. They challenged the rule but lost 240 to 170; the Post Office Committee package then passed with equal ease.

The conference agreement followed congressional inclinations to restrict agriculture production, interfering with the market. It met civil service pension targets through some extremely creative drafting. CBO had to score the package as meeting the targets, but in the end it wasn't close.[20] The final bill claimed savings of $13.6 billion over three years, substantially more than the committees had been ordered to achieve. Nobody could tell if the claim were true. The bill was generally reported as a victory for Reagan and the budget process, but it is a strange set of cuts that hurts few constituents. As on TEFRA, the administration had negotiated unsuccessfully on programs.

Getting Through the Election

After reconciliation and the September veto override, Congress had to finish up FY83 appropriations so it could recess for the election. Both Speaker O'Neill and Senate Majority Leader Baker were tempted to wrap up everything for the year in the continuing resolution, but the administration refused. On the day House Appropriations reported out its CR, the president called for a lame-duck session. Reagan explained his demand in procedural terms, deploring the attempt "to run the Federal Government without a proper budget." Tip O'Neill scoffed, "You know what happened, the defense figures are so much lower, and they don't want them."[21]

No one likes lame-duck sessions. Howard Baker apparently figured that whatever deal could be cut with the House could be done as easily before the election as after. Barring Republican gains in November—which, with unemployment headed over 10 percent, seemed unlikely—there was no reason to wait. But the president's procedural argument, supported by such unlikely allies as the *New York Times,* was hard to counter. Baker and O'Neill grudgingly agreed to the postelection session.

The House, therefore, with support from some GOP leaders, passed a short-term continuing resolution 242 to 161. In the Senate, Appropriations Committee members set defense spending at their own desired level, tacked a few authorizations on to the bill, and reported it out. In a thirteen-hour session on September 23, senators rejected all major Democratic spending amendments but added a miscellany of authorizing measures. Proponents were grabbing seats on the CR train. Disgusted, Jamie Whitten asserted that the result "attacked the whole idea of being a continuing resolution—it's a catchall legislative bill."[22] Not for the last time.

House conferees realized they could not get away with keeping defense at FY82 levels. The prodefense mood had been eroded but not ended. They settled for allowing DOD to spend at a rate of about $229 billion for the year, albeit with restrictions on some new procurement. The Pentagon was thus assured a 14 percent nominal spending increase, quite substantial because inflation would be under 5 percent. Nevertheless, DOD was unhappy because the spending level and restrictions on procurement represented substantial changes from its request. In our opinion the giant FY83 request had made the final increase seem less huge. For domestic spending, in contrast, the status quo, hemmed in by recession and deficit, was the implicit standard.

Legislators' attention turned to—though it had never really left—the campaign.

The Election of 1982

In 1981 Republicans had thought that 1982 might be the year when they finally captured the House. The president's party normally lost seats in a midterm election, but, if a political realignment were in progress, 1982 could be, like 1934, the exception to the rule. After the 1980 census, redistricting would shift congressional seats from the declining Democratic Frostbelt to the booming Republican Sunbelt.

The Republicans had a further advantage in the Senate, where only 12 of their seats but 21 Democratic seats were at stake. Republicans had also developed a superior campaign apparatus: The GOP could raise more money than the Democrats. That did not ensure that Republican candidates would have more money than their opponents, for Democratic incumbents could generate substantial contributions. But it did mean that Republican challengers would be better funded than Democratic challengers. The Republican National Committee not only provided campaign assistance in each district, but it also helped to recruit attractive candidates, guaranteeing them money enough to make the race, and even training them in electioneering. The Democratic National Committee could not begin to match such efforts. All those Republican advantages only limited damage at the polls, exacerbated by an unemployment rate that hit 10.8 percent in November.

Republicans would complain that Democrats blunted the effect of population shifts to the sunbelt by the hoary political tactic of the gerrymander (named, not quite fairly, for Elbridge Gerry, governor of Massachusetts in 1811). In states where they controlled both houses of the legislature and the governorship, Democrats drew new district lines that helped them stay in charge by concentrating Republican voters in as few districts as feasible. Republicans did the same where they could, but they controlled fewer (or smaller) states. Thus the GOP gerrymander in Indiana hardly compensated for the Democrats' plan in California.[23] Nevertheless, Republican advantages in campaign resources and plain good luck enabled them to win more seats in the House and Senate than their smashing defeat in the popular vote would normally have allowed.

In 1982, as in 1980, most close Senate races—those decided by 2 percent or less—went to the GOP. The GOP held on to its 54 to 46 edge, although roughly 43,000 votes in five states (Virginia, Rhode Island, Missouri, Nevada, and Vermont) would have given the Senate to the Democrats. In the House, the public voted Democratic 57 to 40 percent, a margin that would normally create a landslide in the districts. Republicans escaped with a loss of "only" twenty-six seats—low given the poor economy, but double the norm and enough to restore Tip O'Neill's reliable majority. In the states, Democrats gained seven governorships for a 34 to 16 edge and gained full control of six more legislatures for a total of thirty-four.

The election gave Tip O'Neill control of the House; without shifting, the balance in the Senate was less secure. Columnist Mark Shields pointed out that the problem for Republicans was not their losers but their winners: winning senators such as Danforth, Durenberger, Chaffee, Stafford, and Weicker had run away from the president to save their skins. "In politics," Shields wrote, "which is the art of the imitative as well as of the possible, that lesson will not be lost on any of the 19 Republican Senators facing reelection campaigns in 1984."[24]

Using his nautical storm theme yet again, Reagan and his party had tried to stave off disaster by urging voters to "stay the course." Sure, the ship of state had drifted into a gale, but that was the fault of the previous skipper and crew. If the ship were steered straight ahead, it would emerge into bright sunlight. On October 13 Ronald Reagan went on television to defend his record. He argued that the cure of economic problems caused by government spending required time. The administration's policies were working on everything except unemployment ("always a lagging indicator in times of recession"). The next recovery would be "built to last." Congress, of course, would have to help by such measures as honoring its "pledge" to save three dollars in outlays for every dollar in new taxes.

> But it isn't an easy job, this challenge to rebuild America and renew the American dream. . . . It can be tempting, listening to some who would go

back to the old ways and the quick fix. But consider the choice. A return to the big spending and big taxing that left us with 21½ percent interest rates is no real alternative. A return to double-digit inflation is no alternative. A return to taxing and taxing the American people—that's no alternative. That's what destroyed millions of American jobs. Together we've chosen a new road for America.

In the Democrats' televised response, Senator Donald Riegle of Michigan declared:

> The President says, "Stay the course." But Democrats feel that it's time to change the course. . . . Every month since the President and the Republicans got their program adopted a year and a half ago, unemployment has skyrocketed. Why would the Administration want to stay this course? Maybe because so many of the top officials in the Administration are millionaires who have no understanding of what life is like for most Americans.
>
> Maybe it's because they have their eyes so fixed on the ticker tape on Wall Street that they don't see the growing pile of pink slips and foreclosure notices shutting down Main Street.
>
> The truth is that this Administration has created two courses: one of them a very fast economic track for the few, the other filled with potholes and roadblocks for the rest of us.
>
> That's why staying the course makes sense to them: because they're not paying the price. You are.[25]

Riegle appealed to the traditional Democratic voter. In politics votes, not dollars, counted; for the Democrats the government rather than the economy had been the place of fairness. The party's long-term problem was that Democrats had grown suspicious of that government as well. In 1982, however, the Democrats reclaimed most of their old constituency. Reaganomics might be okay in the abstract, but unemployment in the concrete was terrible.

NBC's election day sample reported that 39 percent of 12,000 respondents believed that Reaganomics has "helped the country," and 40 percent said it had hurt. The president's job performance showed 52 percent disapproval and 48 percent approval. Reagan and Reaganomics did even this well because, another poll showed, 46 percent blamed the recession on "the situation Reagan inherited," while only 33 percent blamed "Reagan and his policies." In the NBC/AP poll, only 6 percent called Reagan's policies a success, but 50 percent declared that they "needed more time."[26]

At the level of theory, voters were not so sure the president was wrong. They liked him personally. With unemployment over 10 percent, however, those closest to joblessness remembered that Democrats were their historic allies. Democrats once again were heavily favored over Republicans as the party to reduce unemployment. Democrats gained most among Catholics, union members, and those with no college education, all of whom had deserted Jimmy Carter when he engineered a recession.[27] They were mobilized by leaders of unions and civil rights movements; turnout increased for the first time in years as these voters protested the new turn in policy.

Although the depression (so, Louis Harris reported, most voters considered the state of the economy) brought voters back to Democrats, it did not create a groundswell for big new social programs. There was no mandate for an alternative Democratic program. Californian Democratic Senator Alan Cranston, his party's whip, concluded that "this election was a call for moderation and modification, not for a return to old-style liberalism."[28]

Republicans agreed in their own way, seeing the message as not rejecting the premises of Reaganomics but showing their concern about unemployment. Minority Leader Bob Michel narrowly survived the election. "We've listened and learned, and we will take what we've learned back to Washington," Michel told his constituents. "There will have to be some adjustments, some modifications in the things we are doing. No question about it."[29]

Politicians are a creative lot; and any situation, however bleak, is an opportunity for someone. The election of 1982 seemed mainly to guarantee stalemate, but Drew Lewis and James Howard had an answer for legislators who wanted to do something about jobs without rejecting Reaganomics.

A Lame Duck Takes Wing, Sputtering

Drew Lewis was secretary of Transportation; James Howard (D-N.J.) was chairman of the House Committee on Public Works and Transportation. Lewis and Howard wanted to spend money on roads, bridges, and mass transit, key components of the nation's "infrastructure"—the capital plant used to move our goods, treat our waste, or store our water. The projects involved are the traditional subject of "pork-barrel" politics, the "internal improvements" beloved by Henry Clay, that dated back to the building of canals and roads at the beginning of our history.

House Public Works has long been the prototypical pork-barrel committee. Contrary to an overwhelming deluge of political rhetoric, spending on such projects had not grown but—as a proportion of national product—had been halved during the 1960s and 1970s.[30] Governments instead shifted resources from public works to transfer payments for the elderly, to health, to education (due to the baby boom and Sputnik), and to antipoverty programs. These new responsibilities crowded out the old ones as government at all levels met resistance to raising taxes.

Spending that could be postponed, therefore, was; that meant less for highways, bridges, sewers, and the like. It was easy neither for Democrats to explain why, when money was more plentiful, these essential services had been neglected nor for Republicans to explain why, when they were in control, they allowed these building blocks of society to decay.

Secretary of Transportation Drew Lewis cared more about highways than sewers. Highway spending had shrunk, in real terms, mainly because the gasoline tax, which financed the Highway Trust Fund, had not been raised since 1959. Lewis felt that after twenty-two years an increase of four or five cents a gallon, from the existing four cents, could be justified. It would be a "user fee"; the people who use the highways pay the gas tax. James Howard and many urban Democrats agreed with the need for higher spending on transportation, but they were less interested in highways. To urban Democrats, cars and highways were middle-class commodities while subways and buses were working-class. Democrats also were uneasy with the gas tax, which was not at all progressive. For years, city representatives had argued that mass transit took pressure off the highway system, that types of transit were fungible, and that cities should be able to choose. Cities had little place to put interstate highways. Many city people bought gasoline, and, perhaps more important, there were lots of urban senators and representatives. By allowing some new gas tax money to go to mass transit, Lewis won liberals' support.

Lewis, Howard, and others worked to bring infrastructure needs to public attention. In 1981 the National Governors Association published a report, "America in Ruins," which claimed that up to two-thirds of the nation's towns and cities lacked the facilities to accommodate new economic growth.[31] Then Republican and Democratic legislators injected the need for new capital spending into the budget debate. Transportation Department officials, in the unusual position (for this administration) of having a program advocate as secretary, lobbied for new spending. The media also joined the campaign. *Newsweek* titled its August 2, 1982, issue, "The Decaying of America," beginning its story with a vision of the chaos that would be caused if a main water tunnel were to crack beneath New York City.[32] The publicity campaign succeeded.

Now, recognizing a problem did not mean (especially if you were Ronald Reagan or David Stockman) that the federal government should pay to solve it. It might be left to the states and localities, or it might wait for economic recovery. Even if federal action were demanded, spending and tax increases could be avoided by shifting funds from lesser priorities. Therefore, on May 18, a day after Howard had reported the bill out of his committee, the president turned down Lewis's proposal. Lewis worked to reverse Reagan's decision, but on September 28, in response to a question at a press conference, the president declared that "unless there's a palace coup and I'm overtaken or overthrown, no, I don't see any necessity" for a gas tax increase.[33]

The election accomplished what the *National Journal* called "Political Alchemy: 26 fewer Republican seats in the House plus 10.4 percent unemployment transforms an unacceptable gasoline tax into an acceptable user fee."[34] In another bit of alchemy, the infrastructure bill became a jobs bill. Legislators in both houses and both parties saw Lewis's proposal as a job provider that could not be criticized as "make-work." Dan Rostenkowski endorsed the idea; the Speaker promised to send something over to the Senate during the lame-duck session where, "if they don't do anything, the onus is on them."[35] On November 18 Howard Baker announced he and Tip O'Neill would work out a bipartisan jobs bill; on November 22 they endorsed the basic outlines of the Lewis and Howard proposal.

The president wanted private, rather than governmental, spending to lead the way out of the slump. He suggested that the July 1983 tax cut be moved up to January. Howard Baker and Bob Michel immediately told Reagan they did not have the votes.[36] On November 23 the president finally jumped on the infrastructure bandwagon: "There's no question but obviously there will be some employment with it," he declared, "but it is not a jobs bill as such. It is a necessity. It's a problem that we have to meet, and we'd be doing this if there were no recession at all."[37] (The president did not explain why the infrastructure bill was a necessity in November and heresy in September.) Robert Dole, skeptical of spending but recognizing the politics, was more straightforward: the transportation package was, he commented, "the best possible jobs bill that could be devised."[38]

In politics, agreement on a proposal may substitute for agreement on purposes. If the objectives of the winning coalition are too diverse, however, they may undermine the initial agreement. With all the major party leaders behind it, the bill seemed likely to pass.[39] Yet conflict about purposes and shortness of time almost enabled opponents to scuttle it.

By early December, Democrats had developed a $5.4 billion plan for "light" public works. The administration then had to explain why one jobs bill was good and required Republican loyalty, while another, which would create jobs more quickly, was bad and required Republican opposition.

On the transportation bill itself, the administration strongly opposed subsidies for mass transit operations; if the users could not pay at least operating (as distinguished from capital or investment) expenses, then the systems probably should not exist. Mass transit proponents argued that users could not pay and that the consequences of letting big city transit systems go under were too terrible to contemplate. For their part, some Democrats wanted to replace the gas tax increase by repealing part of the third-year tax cut. If either operating subsidies were removed or the income tax cut scaled down, however, the coalition might fall apart. In addition, the bill had myriad consequences disliked by the trucking industry and, therefore, the Teamsters—two powerful lobbies. And it was almost universally condemned by the economics fraternity. New CEA Chairman Martin Feldstein told the president and everyone else who would listen that the gas tax bill would just siphon jobs from the private sector. Democrats Walter Heller, Charles Schultze, and Otto Eckstein joined the chorus of skeptics.[40] These objections helped justify the resistance of a small band of conservatives who felt that nearly all domestic government spending was bad and that new taxes were worse. When he jumped on the infrastructure bandwagon, they believed Ronald Reagan had abandoned his principles.

The growing continuing resolution became the second major controversy of the lame-duck session. Disagreements over defense and federal/congressional pay threatened to torpedo it.

The defense disputes involved not just money but policy. House liberal leaders wanted to kill at least one of two nuclear aircraft carriers—the B-1 bomber and, most of all, the MX missile. If they could not do so, defense savings would have to come out of combat readiness, like spare parts, and there was little support for that.

All these weapons could be attacked on strategic grounds: the carriers were too vulnerable to attack by missiles; the B-1 as adding little to the B-52s, and outmoded as soon as the "Stealth" bomber came on line; the MX as a potential first-strike weapon, vulnerable to Soviet attack, and therefore destabilizing. They could also be defended: the carriers were the core of the Navy's strategy for projecting power around the world; the B-1 was better than the aging B-52s and more likely to be produced than the Stealth; the MX was a counterforce weapon and, within the bizarre world of "arms control" reasoning, necessary so it could be bargained away.

Liberals lost badly in Appropriations on the carriers and B-1, but $988 million for five production-line MX missiles survived only because three MX opponents were unable to attend the vote. The MX was vulnerable: production funds could be reduced without eliminating research, development, and test money; it was possible to send a cautionary message to the president with that vote; but most important, no one knew where to put the missiles once they began producing them.

MX had gone from the "racetrack"—100 missiles shuttled among 1,000 silos in Nevada and Utah, so the Russians wouldn't know where to shoot—to "dense pack"—all the missiles would be placed in silos fairly close together so the explosion from knocking out one missile would blow up incoming missiles, thereby protecting the ones that remained in the ground. Members of Congress were skeptical. Charlie Wilson's comment that the pro-MX arguments "sound like PAC-Man" struck a responsive chord. Even three of the five members of the Joint Chiefs of Staff opposed what some congressmen called "Dunce Pack."[41]

When Don H. Clausen (R-Calif.) invoked the memory of Pearl Harbor in a traditional argument for preparedness, Carroll Hubbard, Jr., added that "right or wrong, the words 'Here come the Russians' nowadays do not scare Kentuckians half as much as 'Here come the creditors.' "[42] The House accepted Addabbo's amendment to delete funds for MX production, 245 to 176. Both Addabbo and occasional MX critic Les Aspin conceded that, if the basing issue were resolved, the administration would get the missile.[43] For the first time since World War II, however, a house of Congress had even temporarily denied the president a major weapon.

The major controversy over the Transportation Act was about its tax provisions. Trucking interests objected to the truck charges; conservatives objected to any taxes at all; liberals, led by Richard L. Ottinger (D-N.Y.) and Henry Reuss (D-Wis.), wanted to replace the gas tax increase with a cap on the third-year tax cut, in effect repealing that cut in the upper brackets. House leaders concluded that the tax section of the bill was too vulnerable, that any change in it might unravel the whole package, and that the tax section therefore should be offered without allowing amendments. Thus, floor conflict centered on the rule, which was upheld by a close (197 to 194) margin. The bill passed by a 262 to 143 margin that belied the pitfalls it had avoided.

House Democratic leaders still wanted to attach extra jobs spending to the continuing resolution. On December 10 House Appropriations reported out a new CR with a $5.4 billion jobs bill attached, including $1 billion in new programs. In debate on the floor, Silvio Conte reported that Reagan had promised to veto the CR if it included jobs spending. Democratic leaders again saw no reason to back down early. They managed to defeat Conte's motion to delete the jobs sections, 215 to 191. The CR passed by an even narrower 204 to 200 that included 13 votes from an assortment of not overwhelmingly liberal Republicans who may have wanted to go home.

In spite of the jobs battle and a narrow deletion of funds for the controversial Clinch River breeder reactor, the CR's greatest controversy was congressional pay. Here we have to go back a bit because we have been skirting the subject.

Because legislators are normally scared to raise their own pay, they sometimes look for less visible ways to increase their compensation; these in turn are attacked by members looking for a safe issue with which to get some publicity. In 1981 the Senate managed to sneak through a large tax break for congressional living expenses, replacing the old, insufficient provision with a new, more generous one. Senators also eliminated the existing limit on honoraria from speeches and the like, and House members doubled their own limit on honoraria from $9,100 to $18,200.

It could not last; with members of Congress leading the way, the tax break became the subject of maneuvers on the final FY82 CR that continued throughout the battle on the "urgent" supplemental that finally passed in July. Senators pushed to return to the old tax provision as irritated House members tried to blackmail the senators out of that by reimposing the limit on honoraria. In the final version of the July supplemental, the tax deduction limit won out.

In August Senator Stevens, who headed the Senate subcommittee with responsibility for federal pay issues, tried to tack a byzantine pay raise maneuver onto the reconciliation. He wanted raises for not only his colleagues but also the higher civil servants whose pay was held down by members' inability to raise their own salaries. It failed after a revolt in the House. "Obviously we are in an election period, and it is not a good time to talk about these things," commented Vic Fazio (D-Calif.). The "cap" on salaries, however, was due to expire at the end of FY82. Fazio, chairman of the legislative branch subcommittee of appropriations, made sure that battles were postponed by extending the cap to December 17 in the first CR. He then began a quiet campaign to raise the cap during the lame-duck session. The GAO reported that, if the cap lapsed, under the existing comparability system members would be entitled to a 27.2 percent pay increase.

When the second CR came to the floor, Fazio had left out the pay cap. Two amendments—one by Fazio limiting the pay raise to 15 percent and one by Bob Traxler (D-Mich.) reimposing the cap—were in order. The Fazio amendment passed without comment. Then Traxler's amendment was defeated on a tie vote, but it wasn't easy. The vote was allowed to run well beyond the normal fifteen-minute period. Even the Speaker voted against Traxler. The *Congressional Quarterly Almanac* reported:

> Finally, with the amendment ahead 208–207, lame duck Robert K. Dornan, R-Calif., voted no, and the amendment failed on a 208–208 tie. It was the vote of Dornan and the other 70 lame ducks who voted on the Traxler amendment that sealed its fate. Lame ducks opposed the amendment by 2–1, 24–47. While Republicans overall supported Traxler, 121–65, the 48 Republican lame ducks who were voting opposed his amendment, 21–27.[44]

Lame ducks, of course, did not have to worry about public opprobrium, therefore giving a parting gift to their more "responsive" colleagues.

Any issue that can unite Tip O'Neill and "B-1 Bob" Dornan is bound to have unusual permutations; more were to come. In order to make the raise more palatable—and to create a bargaining chip with the Senate—the House took the precaution of limiting honoraria to 50 percent of pay. Senators had more prestige than representatives and could make more money from speeches. Naturally, when the CR reached Senate appropriations both the pay and honoraria provisions were deleted. Final action would wait for the conference. But there would be no conference until the CR passed the Senate, which, strangely enough, brings us back to the transportation act. Anybody want to be a congressman? The job is so simple! And rewarding!

Back to the Senate

When the Senate began to debate the transportation act on December 10, Senators Helms, Nickles, and Humphrey filibustered against Howard Baker's motion to consider the bill. On December 13 the Senate invoked cloture 75 to 13, ending debate on the motion to consider while allowing consideration to begin. Aided by the need to consider a raft of amendments, some germane and some not, opponents then began a not-quite-filibuster. Ronald Reagan requested they halt the delaying tactics.[45] The senators refused. Howard Baker hesitated to move for cloture again because foreclosing amendments might anger potential supporters.

After a series of amendments, up and down, Carl Levin (D-Mich.) moved to extend the period of unemployment benefits. Not exactly a germane subject, but this was the Senate. A motion to table lost, 47 to 50. Opposed to the cost of the benefit extension, GOP leaders decided that maybe cloture was not such a bad idea after all. Democrats then voted against cloture, even though they wanted to pass the transportation act to force a vote on unemployment benefits. Back at square one, Robert Dole had to compromise with Levin. Under Senate rules another two days had to pass before another cloture vote could be taken; Helms and his allies therefore filibustered.[46]

Because he was afraid that everybody would go home after the CR was passed, Howard Baker wanted the gas tax bill passed before action was taken on the CR. "We're going to pass [the gas tax bill] even if that means that those who are filibustering will shut down the government," he declared.[47] That probably was fine with Helms and his allies. So on December 16, Baker, blinking first, pulled the transportation act off the Senate floor so as to work on the new CR. The old one would expire the next day, but, because it was a Friday, Baker and friends figured they had through Sunday (December 19) to pass the new CR.

Everything was going smoothly, if slowly, until the Senate neared a final vote on Saturday night, December 18. Then John East (R-N.C.), responding to an announcement that the Senate would return to the gas tax after disposing of the CR, began a filibuster on the CR. Cloture could not be invoked for two days, so Baker took two steps. First, the Senate appointed conferees to begin negotiations with the House the next morning, even though the Senate had yet to pass its version. Second, Baker sent the senators home to sleep, staying alone in the chamber to listen to Senator East. In the early morning hours, East made a procedural error, and Baker regained control of the floor. On Sunday evening, as the conferees were actually meeting, the Senate approved its version of the CR 63 to 31.[48]

The president promised to veto the bill if it included a jobs plan; House Democrats were adamant about the MX. Perhaps Reagan could have been talked into accepting jobs in return for getting MX. The new bias against spending won out; the conferees chose no spending and no MX until the dispute over the mode of basing was settled and there was some place to put it. Total defense spending was set at $231.6 billion— $4 billion below the budget resolution and $18 billion below the president's request—a 9 percent real increase.

House members got a raise, and senators did not; but House members' outside incomes were restricted, and senators' were not. Conferees agreed that the CR would expire on September 30, 1982 (end of the fiscal year), meaning that no more action would be required. Senator Hatfield reported that total outlays in the bill might be around $2 billion above the budget resolution. Everyone knew that no one knew for sure. Stockman was quiet about it.[49]

The only question left was whether the pay deal and MX would scuttle the conference report. In the House not enough members requested a roll call, so the CR sailed through on a voice vote. The filibusterers were quiet in the Senate. National Security Adviser William Clark lobbied for a veto because of the MX. But the White House Legislative Strategy Group recommended that the bill be signed because Republican leaders predicted that a veto would be overridden.[50] Jack Edwards (R-Ala.) told reporters that he had called the White House and "told them that if they wanted to see the roof come off the Capitol they could veto this bill."[51] Silvio Conte, who had led the House fight against the jobs bill (and had no use for the MX) warned, "If he vetoes, he'll get a jobs bill like he never saw before . . . and he won't get what he wants on the MX missile . . . and I'd lead the fight."[52]

The president signed the CR on Tuesday, December 21, coyly congratulating Congress for having "completed action on a budget for the full fiscal year before final adjournment." If wrapping most discretionary spending into a CR, while operating under a budget resolution with economic projections (and thus deficit totals) that were wildly out of whack, qualifies as "completing action," then Reagan may have been correct. Congress would gladly have done the same the year before if he had let them; the president, not they, had changed. "On balance," the president said, "the resolution is a significant achievement in our efforts to control discretionary spending."[53] What you want depends on what you can get![54]

As the CR awaited the president's decision, the Senate returned to work on the Transportation Assistance Act. It required five days and two more cloture votes, but the Senate finally passed both the bill and the conference report. At the battle's end, Reagan personally offered senators rides home on air force planes if they would stay in town long enough to invoke cloture and pass the bill. Five took him up on it; "that's what airplanes are for," commented Russell Long.[55]

The 97th Congress

At long last, the 97th Congress came to an end. The lame-duck session had passed a major piece of legislation, but few were happy with the experience. An exhausted Howard Baker agreed with defeated Jesse Helms that the session should never have been held.[56]

Members of Congress had traveled a long way from the dramatic Reagan victories of early 1981; the president's budget had been virtually disregarded; Congress had tied itself in knots. Arguments could be made that each had been successful in 1982. Reagan had won a big military buildup; in the midst of a recession domestic spending had been increased far less than one might expect; and, though forced to raise taxes, he got others to take most of the blame. Democrats at least had stopped the Reagan Revolution; budget balancers had won a major deficit reduction package. Yet no faction was satisfied.

Pragmatic though he could be, Reagan still had to view rejection of his spending cuts as a defeat. From his standpoint TEFRA was a betrayal; his side had been snookered. Preventing new programs was not so great a victory. Even in 1975 facing huge Democratic majorities, Gerald Ford had successfully vetoed a jobs bill in the midst of a recession. Reagan did lock in the military buildup; his high-ball strategy certainly helped. But the final figures had more to do with senatorial than with White House preferences.

Congress had failed to resolve the disjunctions within its own preferences on taxes, spending, and the deficit. The leaders of the Republican Senate had succeeded in pursuing their own version of responsibility: a tax hike, large but scaled-down defense increases, the status quo on poor people's programs. They had failed only on the great universal entitlements. Still, senatorial preferences, like everyone else's, did not add up to anywhere near a balanced budget.

Outside analysts might call the events of 1982 a reasonable package of compromises, crediting Senate Republicans with the lead role. By their own standards, however, all participants had done poorly. And now the grizzly bear of political animals, social security, was bound to awaken after its election-year hibernation. Soon the government would have to act to ensure the solvency of the giant pension system. Policy would have to be made with a Congress at least as ideologically divided as the 97th had been. Moreover, the deficit would not go away.

Republican Senator Slade Gorton of Washington summarized the situation nicely: "1981 was the Year of the President. 1982 was the Year of the Senate Republicans. 1983," he concluded, referring to a well-publicized film, "is the Year of Living Dangerously."

FOURTEEN

A Triumph of Governance:
Social Security

The social security program was going broke. That means revenues from payroll taxes (the FICA deductions from paychecks) dedicated to Old Age and Survivors Insurance (OASI) were smaller than the amount being paid to the elderly. Originally, the system had a cushion of budget authority, to be called upon when revenues exceeded benefits; by 1982, however, that was nearly gone. Unlike the budget-deficit "crisis," social security's difficulties were concrete and calculable: by a specific date, some 31.6 million checks would be held up. The federal government was in danger of defaulting on what is, save for the national defense, its biggest commitment.

Two years of social security politics did not create hope for a settlement. Democrats felt that Republicans exaggerated the problem, wanting to cut social security, not out of concern for the elderly, but as part of their ideological attack on "big government." Republicans felt that Democrats were engaging in unmerciful demagoguery, beating up on the GOP while failing to acknowledge real problems. Each view had a measure of truth. Let us now quickly review the dimensions of the problem to set the stage for the last-minute rescue.

After the May 1981 debacle, and after the president was convinced not to include social security in his "September offensive," Congress, with Reagan's support, passed a bill to restore the minimum benefit, which had been eliminated in the 1981 reconciliation. OASI pensions are just part, though the largest part, of the insurance system funded by payroll taxes under the Federal Insurance Contributions Act. FICA also includes unemployment insurance and the disability and health (medicare) trust funds.[1] Because disability and health funds were still in the black, the Senate, in its version of the minimum benefit bill, provided authority for OASI to borrow from its companion funds for the next ten years.

But Barber Conable, Republican leader on Ways and Means, insisted that this borrowing authority must expire at the end of 1982. He hoped that such an imminent date would encourage other action in the lame-duck session after the 1982 election, when at least some portion of Congress no longer would have to worry about voter retribution.[2] Ideally, the National Commission, on which Conable sat, would report in November, and, in the face of imminent default, Congress would have to act.

The National Commission first met in February 1982. Chairman Alan Greenspan, former CEA chair and future Federal Reserve chair, joked that the fifteen members might produce fifteen minority reports.[3] President Reagan's appointees included three Republican business types—Greenspan, Robert Beck, and Mary Foley Fuller—along with conservative Democrats Alexander Trowbridge (head of the National Association of Manufacturers) and former congressman Joe Waggoner of Louisiana. Howard Baker appointed Finance Chairman Bob Dole, social security subcommittee chairman William Armstrong (R-Colo.), and John Heinz (R-Pa.), chair of the Special Aging Committee. Like Baker, Bob Michel appointed his party's committee leaders—Conable and subcommittee ranking member Representative William Archer. Thus, Reagan had chosen five conservatives, while Senate Republicans had appointed a group of committee leaders divided between those who staunchly opposed revenue increases, Armstrong and Archer, and those who might accept a mix of revenues and benefit cuts. Democrats appointed liberals, passing over almost all committee leaders. Robert Byrd appointed Senator Moynihan, the subcommittee ranking member, and Lane Kirkland, head of the AFL-CIO. Speaker O'Neill appointed Claude Pepper, former Representative Martha Keys, and Robert Ball. Ball, former commissioner of social security and O'Neill's real representative, had helped organize Save Our Security, a coalition of interest groups. He had been in the program since the beginning and was the party's expert. Ball's expertise was matched by that of Robert Myers, the National Commission's staff director; Myers, former chief actuary, at the time was deputy commissioner of the Social Security Administration. Myers was the Republicans' expert on the program.

The Commission thus knew enough and represented virtually everybody. Conservatives could outvote liberals, but that didn't mean much because no agreement rejected by Ball, Kirkland, Pepper, and Moynihan was about to pass the House.

Before the Commission could do much, social security became part of the larger budget fight. Efforts by a few participants to cut a deal under cover of the Gang-of-17 negotiations broke up in animosity. How much to cut COLAs, how much in taxes the president would allow in return, and, especially, who would take the blame were the issues over which the Gang of 17 collapsed during Reagan and O'Neill's acrimonious meeting.

The Gang's collapse put Domenici out front, where, the reader may recall, he talked Reagan into the $40 billion social security "plug" in his First Resolution for FY83. That, too, was blown out of the air quickly. When the National Commission next met, the result was, in *Time*'s words, "a partisan shooting match, with cameras rolling. Senator Moynihan charged that the administration had 'terrorized' older people into thinking that they won't get their Social Security." Republican Senator Armstrong declared that "we have done everything to avoid making this a partisan issue"; then he blamed Democrats for the $40 billion cutback proposal.[4] After that dustup, commission meetings sank into somnolence; congressional Republicans stopped making dangerous proposals; and attention shifted to the election.

It is hard to disentangle the social security issue from the recession and from "fairness" in order to assess its independent effect on elections. Paul Light's analysis makes three important points. First, many Republicans who survived the election did so, particularly in the Senate, only by very slim margins. Therefore, they were nervous about any issue that could anger the public. Second, to defeat them at the polls, social security did not have to work directly, as if the Republicans had done something to harm it; social security had only to symbolize the entire Democratic argument that Reaganomics was unfair. Third, Republicans believed social security had cost them dearly in lost seats.[5] A well-positioned lobbyist summed up the political situation:

> By the time the November election was over, Baker, Darman and that crowd were in charge of the issue. This is an overstatement but from conversations then it was clear that they would take their own grandmothers off social security to get a deal with the Democrats. They were in the trough of a depression, the President's popularity was at bottom, they had lost their House majority, and they wanted it *done*, behind them! The polls showed that if anything went wrong with social security the president would get blamed.

Yes. And clearly something could go wrong by July. Pragmatists in the White House believed that, as one told us, "the only way we Republicans can deal with social security is if the leadership of the Democrats is on board." That gave the Democrats an advantage. But it didn't necessarily mean that the president would go along with a deal.

The administration's best scenario was that a solution—that could be enacted in the lame-duck session—would emerge from the National Commission's meetings on November 11–13. But that would not happen: the session already had enough to handle; the Commission was too divided, and probably too large, to forge an agreement; and the Speaker wanted his twenty-six new Democrats in place before reforms were considered.

The Commission did, however, define the scope of the problem, an action surely necessary to end the extensive disagreement over its seriousness, which depended on the economy's performance. In 1972 the Social Security Administration (SSA) had estimated 15 percent inflation and 12 percent real wage growth from 1973 to 1977. Those assumptions justified indexing benefits to inflation after a 20 percent increase. Unfortunately, inflation turned out to be 41 percent, and real wages rose only by 1 percent. In response, President Carter and Congress put together a rescue package that changed the calculations of some benefits (the formula had been more generous than intended) and scheduled payroll-tax increases at intervals until 1990. Assuming 28 percent inflation and 13 percent real wage growth during 1978–1982, the system would have been quite healthy; but unfortunately inflation was 60 percent and real wages had shrunk by 7 percent. The discrepancy was more than enough to swamp social security again.[6]

As a matter of policy and prudence, this experience might have caused participants to err on the side of pessimism. Yet liberals objected: to define the problem as drastic served the conservative agenda—radical reform as opposed to incremental change. And conservatives were embarrassed because pessimistic forecasts would contradict the administration's economic scenarios. The SSA responded in 1982 by creating a range of scenarios, of which alternative 3 was very pessimistic (shrinking real wages through 1984 and barely any wage growth for the rest of the decade), alternative 2A was the administration's FY83 economic forecast, and alternative 2B represented the actuaries' fairly pessimistic best guess (a weak recovery in 1982, fairly similar to the low-ball forecast on which Martin Feldstein would insist for the FY84 budget).

Alternative 2A predicted an $82 billion shortfall for OASI from 1983 to 1989. At that point, the OASI payroll tax would rise from 9.5 percent to 10.6 percent (half each from employers and employees), and the system would stop losing money. It was not good but not so terrible, certainly no reason to make big cuts. By November 1982, however, alternative 2A was not looking credible; it predicted only 8.9 percent unemployment for 1982. As Senator Moynihan, who had downplayed the crisis, later commented, "There was a point when we thought you might squeeze by, but when unemployment went to 11 percent, there was no point kidding yourself."[7] Greenspan, Staff Director Myers, and most Republican commission members had no stake in the administration's forecast; they were willing to go with something like alternative 2B, which assumed a $184 billion OASI shortage through 1989, larger than the disability surplus.[8]

When the National Commission met, Greenspan suggested they look for savings in a range from $150 to $200 billion, and the members agreed. In these matters, involving huge sums, accuracy plus or minus $25 billion is the most one can hope for. The shortfall was around 14 percent of projected costs of the program for 1983 to 1989. The commission agreed also on the size of the system's long-range problem: 1.8 percent of taxable payroll. To comprehend that estimate requires an understanding of the social security trust fund.

The most important thing to know about the financing mechanism of social security is its pay-as-you-go system. What is paid in during a given fiscal year as contributions goes out that same year as benefits. That is all there is to it. Everything else is misleading—everything.

Social security looks like insurance: individual and employer make equal contributions; the worker collects after retirement. He or she pays into, and benefits are paid out of, a trust fund. The trust fund pays benefits each year out of that year's contributions plus any accumulated balance. If benefits exceed contributions, the balance declines. From 1975 through 1981, the OASDI balance fell from $44 billion to $25 billion.[9] If contributions outpace benefits, as during most of the system's history, the balance rises.

Benefits are shaped by eligibility rules, inflation rates, and demographics. Contributions are shaped by tax rates, taxable income definitions, wage and employment levels, and population. (Only wage income is taxable; in 1982 up to the first $32,400 could be taxed. The rationale for this cap is the insurance principle: higher contributions could be justified only by higher benefits. But as it stands, higher-income participants receive a smaller benefit relative to contributions than do lower income; thus, the system is progressive.) If people live longer, social security costs more. If fewer people are born, there are fewer wage earners to contribute.

Over the long run, population factors have the largest influence on the relation of contributions to benefits. In 1955, when the system was young, there were 8.6 workers per beneficiary. A 4 percent payroll tax was sufficient to cover benefits. By 1982, with 3.2 workers per beneficiary, about 12 percent was needed. The ratio was expected to remain stable as the baby-boom generation began to dominate the work force. After the year 2000, however, this group will start retiring, to be replaced by their children, the "baby-bust" generation. By 2030, under the alternative 2B assumptions, there would be only 2 workers per beneficiary. If benefits were to be maintained at the same level, contributions would have to equal 16.8 percent of the taxable payroll. Because existing law set taxes at 12.4 percent, the system would run massive deficits. If the pessimistic alternative 3, which predicted even lower birthrates, were true, contributions of 23.9 percent of payroll would be needed. Nearly half of all benefits would have to come from the principal of the trust fund.[10] Dollar amounts involved would depend on inflation; over the period, deficits would be in the trillions. And, like all complex calculations, things could turn out a lot better—or worse.

Peter Peterson, former Commerce secretary and organizer of the "Bipartisan Budget Appeal," was among the many conservative critics who used long-term projections to argue for major changes. Peterson wanted a series of reforms that would lower benefits, particularly for people with higher incomes.[11] To his ideological right, the Heritage Foundation reported that "the only way to cure the fiscal dilemma of OASI is through fundamental redesign of the social security system . . . [converting it into] an actuarially sound individual annuity program."[12] Contributions would be invested in a fund tied to the stock market's performance or some other reflection of the private economy. Ronald Reagan wanted to make the program voluntary. The program's defenders felt that the whole notion of such long-term projections was a mite unreasonable. "The feeling that we must make final decisions now for the year 2035," said Henry Aaron of the Brookings Institution, "would be rather as if we had expected Calvin Coolidge to make binding policy for Americans of the '80s."[13]

Polls showed that the proportion of the public who had "only a little" or "no" confidence in the ability of the system to pay benefits when they retired rose from 49 percent in 1979 to 75 percent in 1982.[14] "My children are concerned with whether they ought to contribute," said Dan Rostenkowski. "They're entitled to doubt whether there's going to be solvency when they expect to retire."[15] The critics argued that these fears presaged "generational warfare." In fact, the young supported current benefits at least as strongly as did the recipients.

Though the critics' crocodile tears over lack of support for the program were unjustified, proponents of the program felt that the long-run political consequences of long-term deficit projections might not be so minimal. If they could reduce the size of the long-term "problem" without reducing benefits much, it was worth doing.

"Fixing the problem," according to virtually everybody, meant combining reduced benefits and an enlarged trust fund, so that during bad years the system could live off its "savings." The National Commission defined the target for a long-term solution, not as the shortage in any particular year, such as 2035, but rather as the average shortage over the entire period from 1982 to 2056. According to the alternative 2B projections, this would be 1.82 percent of taxable payroll.[16]

A difficulty with all this went unidentified: *the "trust fund" is a mirage.* To withdraw money from the fund, the government must cash in its assets. The assets, however, are government bonds. To pay off those bonds, the government must either sell more bonds or raise revenue through taxes—which is exactly what it would do if there were no trust fund at all. Merely building up the fund per se makes no difference.

The fund would matter only if it held assets in the private economy: stocks, bank accounts, buildings, whatever. Then cashing in the fund would reduce the need to tax or to borrow. But that possibility poses all sorts of problems: A fund of this sort, large enough to fund social security, would have to own a substantial part of the U.S. economy. Who would control the fund? Or, whom would the fund control? Few politicians have ever seriously suggested that the trust fund hold assets to make it meaningful because this would raise directly the thorny issue of relations between the public and private sectors. What would happen, for instance, if social security were made up of private annuities invested in the stock market and a "Black Monday" caused a great loss in value? Not only would government be damaged, it might well either feel obliged or be compelled to make up the loss. To the cost of employee-employer contributions, therefore, would be added the price of government emergency funding when the market declined. This is not to say that building up the fund has no effect; it just doesn't mean what it is supposed to mean. Each year's surplus, made up of real cash contributions, reduces the unified budget deficit. It thus would reduce federal borrowing, increase the national savings rate, and, by that logic, increase long-run productivity and growth.

But, as far as cumulating resources over time is concerned, the trust fund is empty. Think of it this way: when, in a given year, there is a shortfall (i.e., payments exceed contributions) the government makes up the difference by borrowing, taxing, or printing money. At some future time, some people think that shortfalls would be made up by cumulation of past social security surpluses. Not really true. Treasury bonds or other IOUs from one part of the government to the other might total in the trillions, but these pieces of paper are not claims on private sector assets. Consequently, the government must still make up a shortfall by borrowing, taxing, or printing money.

Social security is funded annually. Consequently, the actual shortfall in, say, 2035 could be ameliorated only by changing the planned benefits and contributions in 2035. Pretending for the moment that those could be forecast (i.e., that alternative 2B projections were accurate), what would a solution involve?

In 2035, according to 2B, OASDI would represent 6.05 percent of GNP. In 1982 it was 5.16 percent of GNP.[17] What, one wonders, was the big deal? If the economy were worse, social security would be just one of many problems. True, the actual burden on workers would increase by more than the change in proportion of GNP. The percent of taxable payroll, an increase from 11.78 percent in 1982 to 17.02 percent in 2035, reflects the fact that when there are fewer workers their wages make up (or are assumed to make up) a smaller portion of GNP.[18] Anyone who wanted to deal with these more worrisome taxable payroll figures thus would have to adjust the ratio of beneficiaries to workers. More children or more immigrants (the latter being far easier to supply) would do the trick, but this was beyond the scope of social security legislation. Instead, as Pickle had suggested in 1981, Congress could raise the retirement age.

The whole argument about the long run was decidedly unreal. The problem was not so big; the solution of building up the trust fund was no solution at all; the most relevant factor, the supply of workers, was not even on the policy map. To complete the unreality, the rhetoric of panic largely ignored one area of really frightening numbers, much worse than for OASDI—medicare. Under alternative 2B, Hospital Insurance (HI) costs were projected to rise from 1.30 percent of GNP in 1982 to 3.97 percent in 2035—more than double the increase in OASDI. The increase was 9.1 percent of taxable payroll.[19] Of course, projections of medical costs were unreliable, involving many more factors than pensions do. And, since the short-term crisis for medicare wasn't expected until, say, 1990, that program was not on the table.

Why, one might ask, did the liberals not simply scoff at the long-term problem? Though we can only speculate, there is a reasonable answer: in order to say that the whole argument (about fund solvency and an average shortfall of 1.8 percent of taxable payroll) made no sense, liberals would have to admit that the insurance notion and the fund itself were mythical. That was too big a risk to take. All in all, some ostensible fix, even if it cut benefits from where they would have been thirty years down the road, was safer. Robert Ball explained that public confidence required "a plan that would result in the Board of Trustees saying officially that the program was in full actuarial balance both in the short- and long-term."[20]

Although both sides agreed on the size of the problem, they were far from agreed on its solution. The fundamental, liberal-conservative, disagreement was the same as that for the rest of the budget: tax hikes versus spending cuts. Conservatives wanted all the latter, liberals all the former, and centrists a mix. On November 11, Senator John Heinz of Missouri, the most centrist of the Republican negotiators, suggested a 50–50 split. Republicans, however, were avoiding specific proposals. Dole figured that proposals to cut benefits were politically dangerous.[21]

On November 12 the Democrats proposed advancing the 1990 tax increase to 1984, which would add $132 billion; tax increases on self-employed workers would mean another $18 billion. (If you don't have an employer, there is no employer contribution. Rather than have no social security for the self-employed, the system would charge them a higher individual contribution—though not as much, even after the fix, as the regular employee and employer contributions combined.) Two other provisions fit the long tradition in social security financing of increasing short-term revenues by including in the program a new group, which would begin paying immediately but begin collecting only decades into the future. These provisions included (1) federal employees within social security (worth $21 billion) and (2) newly hired state and local employees (garnering another $13 billion).[22]

Coverage expansion, convenient as this sounded, was not so easy to achieve. State and local coverage might turn out to be unconstitutional. If made mandatory, social security contributions might be defined as a tax on state and local governments—explicitly forbidden. Federal employee coverage had been urged by social security administrators and resisted by employees since the 1940s. This group already had a pension system with larger contributions that provided larger benefits. If federal employees had to join social security, they would be contributing to both systems, paying more but not receiving more. Employee unions objected strenuously and had been successful for a generation.[23] The AFL-CIO, a strong proponent of social security in all other matters, had backed its federal unions.

"Extending coverage was a given," recalls one lobbyist, "except for the AFL-CIO, which did not want to admit to its federal sectors that it was going to cave." Labor could live with that so long as the rest of the deal was good enough. The liberals wanted Reagan to sign first before they went to O'Neill; then Reagan would look like he was initiating large tax increases. The offer was rejected.

On Saturday, November 13, liberals tried again, suggesting that state and local coverage be replaced by a three-month delay in the date of the COLA. "Delay" may sound temporary, but it was really a permanent cut because, for three months each year, benefits would be at a lower rate (without inflation adjustment) than they would otherwise have been. Over seven years, benefits would be about $23 billion lower.[24]

The Speaker approved this package, which included concessions from both Lane Kirkland (federal employees) and Claude Pepper (COLAs). Yet the conservatives weren't interested in what was still overwhelmingly a revenue solution.[25] Nor was Rostenkowski who, in an open letter to his House colleagues and the commissioners on November 12, asserted his committee's prerogative to draft a solution and expressed skepticism about a payroll-tax increase during a deep recession.[26]

Just as with the Gang of 17, National Commission members' opinions were secondary to whether those who were not there—Reagan, O'Neill, Rostenkowski—could agree. The principals were not talking, and the commissioners did not have the power to bargain out an agreement. The formal sessions of November 11–13 ended without issue. A last meeting on December 10, 1982, was quick and desultory.

What was needed was not formal negotiations but a way for the two sides to feel out, test, and influence each other. Commission member and nominal Democrat Alexander Trowbridge was a Washington veteran who knew all the players. After the November meetings, he began developing packages, talking to other commissioners, asking their positions, moving toward John Heinz's target of the 50–50 split between revenue increases and benefit cuts. Trowbridge had no commitments from anyone, but he created an impression of movement. That gave Stockman something to take to the president. Stockman asked Reagan if Trowbridge's latest plan—$80 billion in taxes; $50 billion in a six-month COLA delay; $32 billion in coverage expansions; and an increase in the retirement age, over the long term, to sixty-seven—would be acceptable.[27] Reagan concurred and authorized Stockman to begin secret negotiations with the commission to get them to report such a package.

Stockman had to negotiate with the liberal leaders; then the White House and the Speaker would try to bring along the rest of the commission. In essence, the president's appointees were replaced by the core White House legislative team—James Baker, Richard Darman, Kenneth Duberstein, and Stockman. The negotiations had to be kept secret: because failure might produce red faces; because interested parties might not keep quiet; and because the Democrats generally distrusted Stockman. The White House team began with personal contact between Stockman and Moynihan, his old mentor, and between Darman and Ball, who knew each other from HEW in the early 1970s. Ball made clear that the Trowbridge plan would not do but did not close the door. The old friends, Stockman and Moynihan, were rebuilding trust. When the Senate reconvened, Moynihan enlisted Dole for "one more try" at negotiating a package on behalf of the commission.

On January 4 Dole, Greenspan, and Moynihan met to arrange the secret talks. By adding Conable, Ball, and the four White House representatives, they had included one member from each of the commission's factions—House and Senate majority and minority and the chairman. Members with strong interest-group or ideological positions—such as Pepper, Kirkland, and Armstrong—were excluded. Meetings began the next day.

Because no staff were allowed, Stockman and Ball were the key players. They knew the most. Everyone understood that President Reagan and Speaker O'Neill held the real votes. Each side used the argument that its own extremists had to be placated, both to force compromise from the other camp and to emphasize that they were all reasonable, in this together.

The meetings could not stay secret if for no other reason than that participants couldn't judge what would play in Peoria without doing some checking beyond the closed doors. The fourteen-million member (according to 1982 records) American Association of Retired Persons (AARP), the AFL-CIO, and such congressional powers as Rostenkowski had to be sounded out. On January 8 Senator Armstrong demanded to be included; Dole had no way to refuse. Armstrong, finding too much support for tax increases, went public and threatened to rally interest groups (including, implausibly, the AFL-CIO) against "a massive tax increase."[28] The other negotiators retaliated by trying to distract Armstrong in the meetings and by keeping him away from Ball and Stockman.

Agreement on cost was crucial, particularly in order to put a price on a COLA delay. Stockman, who wanted as big a package as possible in real dollars (to reduce the deficit), jawboned the Democrats into accepting lower inflation assumptions; this meant that any COLA delay would be estimated to raise less. Democrats, therefore, would have to accept other provisions or a longer delay. The Democrats went along— in part because they were not sure they could win a spitting match over assumptions and in part because, on this one, Stockman seemed right.[29]

After agreeing on economics, the National Commission had to reach its target (still between $150 and $200 billion over seven years) in the most politically acceptable way. That meant allocating as little pain as possible in the present, making no part of the package so big that a major player would feel obligated to defect. Whereas Trowbridge had four major provisions, Stockman and Ball moved toward a much more complex package. The parts were smaller; there were a few side payments, provisions benefiting one faction or another so it would complain less; and many provisions were beyond the ken of most nonexperts. Obscurity might reduce the political heat.

"The principle of equality was very important to the White House," Paul Light quotes one Democrat as explaining, "but if we had gone to a strict 50–50 split we would have needed $80 billion in benefit cuts. That was simply not acceptable to us."[30] A six-month COLA delay and a two-stage acceleration of the previously scheduled tax increases yielded $40 billion each, a 50–50 split. But Democrats did not want to yield more benefits. "The key," Light's source recalled, "was to go outside either pure taxes or benefits, and find some new area of agreement." Democrats found it by taxing benefits.

Social security benefits had never been taxed, partly on the grounds that people were just getting their own money back. People who received social security alone would not be taxed much anyway; their incomes would be too low. Millions of retirees, however, did have other income. The negotiators agreed that

> beginning with 1984, 50% of OASDI benefits should be considered as taxable income for income-tax purposes for persons with Adjusted Gross Income (before including therein any OASDI benefits) of $20,000 if single and $25,000 if married. The proceeds from this taxation, as estimated by the Treasury Department, would be credited to the OASDI trust funds.[31]

Because the tax money was to be fed back into the trust fund, taxing benefits really meant a backdoor cut in benefits for more affluent recipients.

Ball and the Speaker had long been willing to tax benefits. Stockman agreed, for reasons of different principle. The provision was worth $30 billion in the short term and more in the long run. Yet taxing benefits for higher, not lower, incomes threatened the premise that social security was a program for everybody. Instead, social security would become an income-transfer program, creating class divisions that might threaten its political support. In the short run, Republicans could object because the tax was a cut to mostly Republican constituencies. It was also vehemently opposed by AARP, largest of the aging lobbies. AARP is as much a giant buying club as a political group; its power would be diluted by the need not to alienate any portion of its fourteen million members (as of 1982). Yet fourteen million is many voters, voters who were better off and more active than most. In short, taxing benefits involved risks; at the least, neither side wanted to lead the way walking that plank. But the risks were worth taking because the provision provided $30 billion that either side could claim as a victory in the scorekeeping of revenue increases versus benefit cuts.[32]

Coverage expansions, COLA cuts, tax-rate increases, and taxation of benefits would yield $130 billion. Another $18 billion was found through increasing the tax on self-employed persons, who previously had paid 75 percent of the combined employer/employee rate. It seemed fair to have them pay the full rate; after all, they got full benefits. But, because corporations deducted payroll contributions from taxable income, thus reducing the corporate income tax, negotiators chose to allow self-employed individuals to do the same. As a result, the $18 billion in extra trust fund revenues would reduce general revenues by $12 billion, as the self-employed claimed larger deductions. The provision was a veiled transfer of $12 billion from general revenues to the trust fund.

The last large part of the package was another disguised general revenue transfer. Before 1957, soldiers had received social security credit for their service without paying into the fund. Current law required contributions from the general fund each year to cover these "excess" benefits; however, someone came up with the bright idea of crediting all future payments as if they were received together right then and there. The "proper" amount of such payments was, one negotiator recalls, "absolutely arbitrary." It was raised to $18 billion during the last days in response to concerns, particularly from AARP, that the package was not big enough to assure the public that social security was safe.[33] One lobbyist called the "lump sum military wage credit" (the official name) "the tooth fairy." But this money under the pillow was crucial because it was immediate, "a quick one-time infusion to get through 1983–84, to jump-start" the plan. It meant the system was "fixed," in the first year, without cutting or raising taxes. Without it the system would have gone bust in July 1983.

Agreement on the final package was not reached until midday on Saturday, January 15. In addition to the six main proposals, it included a raft of smaller ones.[34] The package, totaling $168 billion for 1983–1989, provided only two-thirds of the long-term target. Although the five core commissioners were agreed, others objected to various parts of the package. In spite of the COLA increase, Claude Pepper went along. His support was essential not only because of his leadership of the elderly but also because, in the new Congress, as chairman of the Rules Committee he would be able to block action. Armstrong and Archer, however, resisted both the tax hikes and the general revenues. They hoped also to get business representatives to object. On the afternoon of January 15, however, President Reagan telephoned Mary Fuller, Robert Beck, and Alexander Trowbridge, strongly urging them to go along. "It was tremendous pressure," a negotiator recalled, and the three complied. After a polite minuet that ended with the Speaker, the president, and the commission simultaneously committed, the commission endorsed the package, 12 to 3. Armstrong, Archer, and ex-representative Waggoner dissented.

For those most interested in reducing the size of government, the package was a defeat. Taxation of benefits did not reduce intrusive government; only the COLA cut was acceptable. It was a victory for those most interested in maintaining benefits. For the needy even the COLA cut was offset by a change in rules for Supplementary Security Income (SSI). In terms of ideology, the Speaker came off better than the president. Yet Reagan was getting the issue off the table; and if benefit taxation were viewed as a benefit cut, then the real cut in benefits ($70 billion) was greater than the increase in taxes ($58 billion). Reagan was less purist, more willing to take the best he could get, than were some of his allies.

From the standpoint of Reagan's aides, the best thing about the deal was its completion. "Once we stopped being revolutionaries and started being system conservers," a Reaganite recalled, "it was a tremendous accomplishment." "We even cut social security," said one proud Democratic politician. "We just didn't say we were doing it. Everyone agreed to say we weren't doing what we were doing." They were showing that they could govern, that reasonable legislators (themselves) could find solutions to difficult problems. But the fact that they felt unable to tell the public what they were doing did not bode well for the future.

All that remained was convincing Congress to go along. First, this meant House Ways and Means. A strong endorsement from the committee would help a lot; a weak or divided endorsement would hurt. As one committee source put it, "the deal was ours to screw up." A fast track was needed to have the agreement in place by July, preferably even before Easter recess. After that came budget time—no time for other problems. Public opinion was confused: mildly negative on the individual provisions, mildly positive on the package.[35] Interest groups, equally confused, were also defensive.

Unlike lobbies for the aging, federal employee groups had little to gain from the package; unlike business, they had few comparable interests that might induce moderation so as to preserve long-term relationships. Indeed, the federal employee lobbies, particularly the powerful postal unions, had few relations with Ways and Means; they would get no satisfaction there. Instead, the coalition of federal retirement lobbies, Fund to Assure an Independent Retirement (FAIR), announced a $3 million lobbying campaign whose goal was to win separate votes on employee coverage on either House or Senate floors. As the 1980 and 1982 reconciliations showed when COLA cuts were defeated, the CSR supporters had a lot of clout.

Rostenkowski at Ways and Means could rely on Pepper at the Rules Committee, backed by the leadership, to protect him from FAIR.[36] Rosty's real problem, one source recalls, was "a fundamental difference between conservatives and liberals on the long-term solution." Pickle wanted to add his own plan to the commission package, raising the retirement age to sixty-seven. Pepper, supported by the AFL-CIO whose industrial and craft workers strenuously objected, wanted a tax increase in the year 2015. "We knew if we went one way Pepper wouldn't allow it on the floor, but Pepper's version wouldn't pass on the floor."

Pickle's subcommittee could not give the package bipartisan backing because its Republicans were led by Archer, who had already dissented from the commission report. The subcommittee reported the bill by a 7 to 4 margin. In full committee, the package was attached to proposals from other subcommittees involving medicare, unemployment insurance, and SSI.

The Ways and Means health subcommittee proposed and full committee accepted a major reform of medicare. The Health Care Financing Administration would establish a schedule of "diagnosis-related groups" (DRGs); each DRG would establish a set fee for treatment for each diagnosis, rather than continuing to pay hospitals for activities (surgeon's fees, tests, number of days in the hospital), as in the traditional "fee-for-service" system. Setting government costs, and thus "prospective" hospital income in advance, would give hospitals incentives to control their costs; thus, the government would have a way—the payment schedule—to regulate its costs. How a few far-away federal administrators would triumph over many close-by doctors in monitoring millions of transactions was not specified.

Clearly, prospective payment was intrusive government regulation. But, in TEFRA, Congress had ordered the Health Care Financing Administration to develop a plan; and the administration decided that this system was its best hope for cost cutting. *Time* described it as "the only element [of administration proposals] that does not automatically send temperatures soaring."[37] Liberals prefer regulating hospitals to cutting benefits. And everybody involved knew that medicare's financing problems, though less immediate than those of social security, were in fact more severe. Therefore, the politicians effectively conspired to short-circuit objections from medical providers by attaching prospective payment to the social security rescue before the providers could mobilize opposition.

Prospective payment sailed through Ways and Means. The full committee gave the GOP a victory by removing a plan by Pickle to allow general revenue subsidies if OASDI got into future trouble. The major issue was what to do about a long-term solution. The full committee faced the same Pickle-and-Pepper dilemma as had the subcommittee. Rostenkowski wanted Pickle's solution, but he had to get past Pepper. Rosty and his allies convinced the Speaker, and Pepper, to leave it up to a floor vote. Let each offer his plan, devoid of sweeteners, with Pepper having the advantage of going last. It was explained to us, by someone we'll call Peter Piper:

> We had to do a massive selling job to convince both Pickle and Pepper to trust us. We knew how it would turn out, that Pickle would win. But both sides thought they could win. The Speaker thought the liberal side would win. . . . Otherwise we would never have gotten a vote. . . . We had 35 members, and the Republicans kept insisting on a vote in the committee. They kept saying, "We have 20 votes." Rosty kept saying, "No, you have more, you have me and some others, but if we adopt it in committee we'll never get a rule."[38]

On March 9, Pickle won a decisive victory. His amendment carried (228 to 202), supported by 152 Republicans and 76 Democrats. Pepper's failed (132 to 296), despite impassioned support from both the Speaker and Pepper whose speech received a standing ovation. The retirement age would increase from sixty-five to sixty-six, in two-month steps, from 2004 to 2009, and to sixty-seven, again in two-month steps, from 2022 to 2027. All Ways and Means Republicans, and a bare majority of Democrats, supported Pickle. Many conservative Republicans, who intended nonetheless to vote against the full package, voted here for what they considered a change for the better.[39] This was not a tax.

After he lost on the long-term provisions, Pepper could no longer endorse the package. The Speaker, even as he supported Pepper's amendment, called on his troops to pass the bill in the end; and it did pass, 282 to 148. The center had held.

Next came the Senate. On the long-term issue, Finance adopted (13 to 4) Heinz's proposal to cut benefits by 5 percent in 2000 and to raise the retirement age, in small steps, to sixty-six by 2015. The Committee rejected (11 to 6) Russell Long's motion to have new federal employees not included in social security until creation of the new, supplementary civil-service pension system. Long was backing employee advocates who had argued that new employees would be paying into both social security and the old civil-service retirement, without being able to benefit from both. Dole maintained that any delay would only help unions in the fight for their real goal—repeal of the coverage extension. Finance adopted an assortment of small changes, enough to satisfy Armstrong, and the committee reported its bill out (18 to 1) on March 11.

The Senate moved quickly to consider the package, only to meet a roadblock thrown up on an extraneous issue: withholding income tax for interest and dividend earnings, a major part of the 1982 TEFRA revenue package. The banks (we will discuss this in a subsequent section) had whipped up a fire storm of demands that such withholding be repealed. John Melcher (D-Mont.) tried to amend the social security rescue to delay withholding by six months. Dole was furious, but Melcher wouldn't budge. At this point, the president, Republican leaders, and the AFL-CIO (particularly concerned about the unemployment benefits attached to the bill) ganged up to break the logjam. On March 22, Vice President Bush, presiding, ruled that Melcher's amendment, by reducing revenues, violated the revenue targets of the FY83 budget resolution and was therefore out of order. Perhaps because the issue had been redefined—but more likely due to pressure from all sides and to a suspicion that withholding could be repealed later—senators rejected Melcher's motion to waive the budget act, 54 to 43.[40]

As is its tradition on tax bills, the Senate passed a series of fairly insignificant amendments. One, however, was important. On March 22, Russell Long offered his amendment to delay coverage of new federal employees until a new supplementary benefit plan was established. A frequent ally of the employees, Ted Stevens, whose subcommittee would have to draft that plan, objected; so did Dole. But the FAIR coalition represented six million angry citizens who did have a point; and some of them, the postal workers, were politically very active in every state. Long's amendment passed on a voice vote. The Senate passed its bill (88 to 9) on March 23.

"Despite the separate victories," Light reports, "there was one 'small' problem: neither bill could pass in the other chamber."[41] That is a bit extreme; both chambers wanted a bill, and, compared to no bill at all, the differences might not look so big. But there was a series of disagreements, ranging from the long-term solution to federal employee coverage, that could be compounded by institutional jealousies. Rostenkowski wanted to "win" the conference, and, had Dole felt the same way, things might have been more difficult.

The conference was also up against time pressure. Congress was due to recess for Easter on March 24, the end of the day the conference began. Bargaining went on for most of that day. The Senate gave in on the long-term retirement fix and, rather willingly, on federal employees. The toughest issue was a "fail-safe" for the short-term solution. The House rejected automatic COLA cuts. The Senate insisted that the House's provision—making the COLA the lower of wages or inflation if reserves fell below 20 percent after 1987—was too little and too late. In the final agreement of the conference, the House provision was set to be effective at the beginning of 1985, and the "trigger" was lowered to 15 percent. The COLA change, therefore, would be announced before the 1984 election—dangerous politics.

With heavy Democratic support, the House passed its conference agreement (243 to 102) late on March 24. The Senate's deliberations ran less smoothly. Some senators sensed an upset when both Armstrong and Long announced their opposition; the House's victories now eliminated the compromises that had won their support. But leaders of both parties rallied, arguing that they could not afford a failure. "I do not like the bill," said Minority Leader Byrd. "I wish the problem would just go away." But defeating the bill would not accomplish that. "This is not a perfect bill," Howard Baker declared, "but we are not a perfect body."[42] Resting on the safety of imperfection, the Senate passed the conference agreement, 58 to 14. At 2:00 a.m. on March 25, the Senate adjourned for Easter. If not altogether resurrected, at least social security had been saved.[43]

The rescue was a triumph of governance. The politicians had shown they could act to avert a crisis, that reasonable people of the center could prevail over polarized, divisive forces that cared more about spending or fending off taxes than about saving the system. The social security issue seemed to have taught a lesson: imminent crisis would force responsibility.

The social security package, on balance, exemplified government. Yet it did not imply that the overall federal deficit problem, as distinguished from social security alone, could be solved. Let us review both the problem and the solution to see why.

Consider the short term. First, the package barely dented the budget deficit; of its $168 billion, over seven years, only about $120 billion, that is, $18 billion a year, reduced a federal deficit that was ten times larger. The balance were transfers from general revenues or account maneuvers: the "tooth fairy" military accounting credit ($18 billion); the partial self-employment tax increases that would come out of income tax receipts (but offset by tax credits); and federal employee coverage (it was not generally understood that new employees who would be contributing to social security would no longer be contributing to the Civil Service Retirement Fund, which actually had a higher—7 percent—contribution requirement). The package amounted to less than half of TEFRA. If we count federal employee coverage as a real step, the total still came to around 10 percent of social security liabilities. The federal deficit was about twice as large a part of federal policy commitments as the social security shortfall was of its overall commitments. *The social security problem (and solution) was much smaller than the deficit problem.*

Yet there was a problem, and they had solved it. We have argued, contrary to much scare talk, that the long-term problem actually was not so big. If the economy, with its demographic multiplier, really went into a tailspin (alternative 3), the system could not be financed; but under those circumstances there would be much trouble in other areas long before social security hit the wall. Given mediocre economic performance (alternative 2B), the problem was manageable—except that the standard notion of how to manage it, building up the fund, was meaningless because the fund's assets, government bonds, were no more than a promise to tax or borrow. Raising the retirement age addressed the real problem—the demographic balance between workers and retirees. Taxation of benefits meant that by 2030, with inflation, most benefits would be taxed—which meant, in fact, they would be reduced. Politicians had addressed the long-term "problem" of underfunding by changing the long-term promise, that is, by reducing future benefits.

We have said that budgeting is about commitments: what kind and how many you make and, in a time of deficits, what kind and how many are broken. The contrast between the short-term and long-term fixes of social security reflects a natural tendency to try to keep commitments on which people have relied for years and a greater willingness to change

commitments when there is a long time—here, a generation—for recipients to adjust to the change. The "tooth fairy" may have been fake;
but it looks more respectable if we recognize it, not as a long-term commitment of general revenue, but as a device to maintain existing commitments that very few Americans wanted to abrogate. If budgeting is
conceived only as a matter of income and outgo—the budgeters' perspective—then the "tooth fairy" is a scam. But it looks more like statesmanship if we see the task of budgeting as choosing commitments so
that members of a society can live together.

The charge of statesmanship on social security we have leveled against
our national politicians is disputed on two quite different grounds. First,
social security now and for years to come contributes its annual surplus
to reducing the deficit. Evidently, this is a worthy act. Why, then, should
the social security program not only be exempt from attacks on the deficit
but also have its surpluses credited against its future shortfalls? A good
reason, which we have previously discussed, is that social security taxes
do have an impact on the deficit because they reduce willingness to pay
other taxes levied on the same individual. Unless the right ear pays
income taxes and the left foot social security, so the person who pays
has no glimmer of the total tax burden, social security is part of the
deficit problem.

Furthermore, proponents of the "social security is not to blame" thesis
talk as if they wanted to eliminate its pay-as-you-go feature in order to
credit early surpluses, when the system starts and people pay in but do
not take out, to later deficits, when more people receive than contribute.
By doing this, however, the conflict between generations that has been
muted by political statesmanship is once again highlighted. The difficulties involved in departing from pay-as-you-go are emphasized by the
other major objection: the quick fix will lead to unacceptably large increases in social security taxes in the first half of the twentieth century.

The debate over social security has been enlivened by contributions
from free-market advocates, especially Peter J. Ferrara, who wish, in
essence, to privatize the system. Their arguments are cogent, even il-
luminating, although we do not find them compelling. It is true that as
social security taxes rise and fewer contributors support a larger number
of beneficiaries, due to the aging of the population and the maturing of
the system, combined with its increasingly redistributive character, a
significant minority of contributors will take out less than they put in.

It is also true that black people, because they do not live as long as
whites, take out considerably less. We would stipulate further that calling
social security a middle-class subsidy is a misnomer; after all, if everyone
were given a chance to opt out, people of middle income might well be

better off financially investing in a private annuity. What neither complaint addresses is whether, given the usual interplay of politics and economics, there is a remedy that is not worse than these maladies; we doubt it.

It is clear to everyone that social security cannot be allowed to default. This means that current and (likely) increased future contributions will continue. Where, then, will the money for private annuities come from? Ferrara has the only idea—income tax credits. While in the past a rescue of social security has often been proposed that would pay beneficiaries out of general revenues, it is now proposed that people be enabled to get out of social security via this subsidy.[44] The deficit, to say the least, would have to decline substantially before this proposal even had a chance to be considered. Should it pass, moreover, a program of phasing in private annuities as a substitute for social security would depend upon the march of the markets. Deep downturns could hardly be tolerated. The temptation to interfere with markets would increase. Making retirement depend on avoiding deep market fluctuations does not seem to us a good way of promoting capitalism, which requires a willingness to face substantial loss.

It is likely that social security taxes will rise in the next century, as they have in this one. In thirty to fifty years, people may not mind so much paying a higher proportion of a much larger income. Or encouraging migration may prove more attractive. For the time being, however, our politicians have maintained the viability of government's most popular program. This is not bad, especially absent evidently superior alternatives.

Sometimes commitments conflict: a commitment to provide certain benefits, for example, counters a commitment to balance budgets. In the social security case, however, commitment to maintain benefits and commitment to fiscal solvency went together: there could be no benefits without solvency. Thus, even the most radical of the program's supporters, Claude Pepper, would, if necessary, give a little on benefits. And solvency had no independent value of its own. Contrast that with the wider budget dispute, that saw "balance" as an independent value, and in which arguments claiming that benefits depended on balance were at best long-run and dubious.

The conflict of commitments was much less severe in social security than in the federal deficit. The short-term social security fix was an effort to maintain existing commitments. Any solution to the overall federal deficit required breaking many such commitments—whether by cutting defense effort, or slashing the poor, or raising taxes substantially, or changing the social security promise. Indeed, it would be nearly impossible to cut social security in later budget-deficit packages because the argument that benefits were being cut to preserve them would no longer make sense. Politicians talked about "waste, fraud, and abuse" because that implied that it was possible to keep the promise to balance the budget without breaking other promises. It wasn't true then, and it isn't true now.

FIFTEEN

Causes and Consequences
of the Deficit

During the reign of France's Louis XVI, Marie Antoinette supposedly once asked the Royal Finance Minister, "What will you do about the deficit, Monsieur le Ministre?" His reply: "Nothing, Madame. It is too serious."[1]

Compared to its predecessor and successor, the 98th Congress was notable more for what it did not do than for what it did. The 98th Congress, from 1983–1984, was not without accomplishment. It passed the package to fix social security; in 1984 it passed the Deficit Reduction Act (DEFRA), a miniature TEFRA. Yet the 98th Congress effected change similar to the tax and spending packages of 1981 in neither federal policy nor fiscal status. The 98th was characterized by the strife and stalemate that set the stage for the dramas of tax reform and Gramm-Rudman-Hollings in the 99th Congress.

Formal budget procedures broke down. The apostles of budget responsibility, of dealing with the deficit, began to turn to procedural irresponsibility, hostage taking, and brinkmanship to get their way. The fact that two years of fighting over the deficit changed deficit projections not a whit—in spite of a better-than-expected economy and real tax increases and spending cuts—left politicians frustrated.

This story, then, is the transition from the action of 1981–1982 to the desperation of 1985. We begin with fundamental questions: Where did the deficit come from? What were its causes, and therefore what were the prospects for a solution? Who or what was to blame? Or was a solution—in one year, five years, ever—really necessary? In the next chapter we provide a real-life evocation of the deficit blues, the 1984 fiscal year (real 1983) budget process, whose discombobulation reveals the profound disagreements over how to reduce the deficit.

The Deficit Dilemma

In February 1983, the Congressional Budget Office published its baseline budget projections for the following five years. The bad news looked like this:

TABLE 8.   The Deficit Trend as Seen by the Congressional Budget Office, February 1983

	Outlays		Revenues		Deficit	
	(in billions of $)	(as % GNP)	(in billions of $)	(as % GNP)	(in billions of $)	(as % GNP)
Actual						
1980	577	22.5	517	20.1	60	2.1
1981	657	22.9	599	20.9	58	2.0
Estimated						
1982	728	24.0	618	20.4	111	3.6
1983	800	25.0	606	19.0	194	6.1
Baseline projection						
1984	850	24.3	653	18.7	197	5.6
1985	929	24.3	715	18.7	214	5.6
1986	999	24.1	768	18.5	231	5.6
1987	1,072	24.0	822	18.4	250	5.6
1988	1,145	23.9	878	18.3	267	5.6

SOURCE: "Reducing the Deficit: Spending and Revenue Options," A Report to the Senate and House Committees on the Budget—Part III, February 1983, p. 1.

CBO was projecting $200 billion deficits as far as the eye could see. "To a great extent," that office explained, the 1983 and 1984

> deficits are attributable to the economic recession, which has reduced federal revenues and increased federal outlays for unemployment compensation and other income maintenance programs. But even as these cyclical crises wither as economic recovery proceeds, the proposed deficits remain at the high level of 5.6 percent of GNP throughout the 1984–88 period. This indicates a long-term mismatch between federal spending and taxing.[2]

CBO projected a deficit in 1988 that would consume 3.6 percent more of GNP than had 1981's deficit, although unemployment in those years would be similar.

This "long-term mismatch" was what President Reagan had called the "structural deficit." This 3.6 percent difference consisted of a rise in outlays of one percent of GNP and a drop in revenues by 2.6 percent. By this standard, then, the major source of the deficit problem was reduced revenue, though there also was a lack of spending restraint. The long-term mismatch could be ascribed, by Democrats, to short-term policy errors—mostly the ERTA tax cut.

Any analysis was flawed, however, if it assumed that 1981's 20.9 percent of GNP was a reasonable base level for federal taxes. The Democrats lost the 1980 election in part because they had let taxes rise to their highest level since 1944. In 1978, revenues had been 19.1 percent of GNP, but bracket creep, payroll tax increases, the windfall-profits tax on oil, and the effects (from 1977 to 1979) of a progressive income tax on rising real incomes had increased the tax burden. Because the corporate tax had been diminished by the 1978 depreciation amendments, most extra money came out of individuals' pockets.

To be defensible, the 1981 tax level had to be argued for, and the public had to be convinced. Neither happened. There is little reason to believe that the American public saw these higher taxes as a necessary price for increasing government services. Rather, this tax increase was an aberration during a twenty-year period in which federal taxes had remained remarkably steady. Not only the overall tax level but, specifically, individual income taxes had increased from around 8.5 percent of GNP (or less) before the Carter administration to 9.9 percent in 1981.[3] Gregory B. Mills and John L. Palmer summarize the trend in federal government tax burdens (as a percentage of GNP), comparing averages over five-year periods to the 1981 level:

FY 1961–1965	19.2%
FY 1966–1970	19.2%
FY 1971–1975	18.6%
FY 1976–1980	19.2%
FY 1981	20.8%

The brunt of these increases fell on lower-income taxpayers. Democratic efforts in 1981 to direct reductions to the lower brackets and to cut somewhat less than the president proposed reflected the fact that the 1981 tax rate was higher than most people or politicians, with the conspicuous exception of Jimmy Carter, desired.[4]

If a normal level of revenues is 19 percent of GNP, not 20.9 percent, then the long-term budget problem was not simply an artifact of the Reagan tax cuts. We must, therefore, turn our attention to the outlay side, where the president kept pointing his finger. Table 9 highlights five crucial relationships.

First, in 1979—a pretty good year for the economy—outlays at 20.83 percent of GNP were 1.2 percent of GNP above actual revenues and 1.8 percent of GNP above the (more or less normal) revenue level. These are the figures from which President Carter, in his FY80 budget, began his drive for spending restraint.

Second, spending growth from 1979 to 1985 can be explained entirely by increases in defense, social security, medicare, and debt interest. The real growth from FY79 to FY83 in income security is entirely a product

TABLE 9. Outlays in Major Spending Categories (as percentage of GNP, by fiscal year)

Function	1977	1978	1979	1980	1981	1982	1983	1984[a]	1985[a]
National defense	5.22	5.00	4.93	5.20	5.47	6.06	6.50	6.68	6.99
Social Security & Medicare	5.61	5.58	5.54	5.85	6.20	6.62	6.91	6.75	6.69
Social Security	(4.4)	(4.4)	(4.3)	(4.5)	(4.7)	(5.0)	(5.2)	(4.9)	(4.8)
Medicare	(1.2)	(0.2)	(1.2)	(1.3)	(1.4)	(1.6)	(1.7)	(1.7)	(1.8)
Income security	3.28	2.94	2.81	3.35	3.44	3.50	3.78	3.16	2.94
Net interest	1.60	1.69	1.81	2.04	2.38	2.78	2.78	3.04	2.98[b]
Total	21.50	21.44	20.83	22.39	22.80	23.82	24.65	23.99	23.79

SOURCES: Congressional Budget Office, *The Economic and Budget Outlook: Fiscal Years 1986–1990, A Report to the Senate and House Committees on the Budget—Part 1*, February 1985, pp. 161–165. Office of Management and Budget, "Federal Government Finances: 1985 Budget Data," typescript, February 1984, pp. 23, 92–93; and authors' calculations.

NOTE: Estimates of future numbers, naturally vary with the source. A more vigorous economic recovery than expected and congressional resistance meant that defense and other spending did not increase as much, proportionate to GNP, as expected in February 1983. But high interest rates caused net interest to increase far more. In 1988, the basic deficit picture faced as of early 1983 had not changed. Pre-1983 figures, being history, are reliable.

[a]Figures reflect estimates.

[b]CBO's end of FY85 interest costs were significantly higher than OMB's at 3.4% of GNP.

of the bad economy; it disguises the significant reductions made in domestic discretionary programs and in means-tested entitlements during this period.[5] This is only one of many instances in which hard political work was, if not exactly undermined, then at least reduced in value by events public officials could not control.

Third, from 1979 to 1983 social security rose from 4.3 percent to 5.2 percent of GNP. This increase stemmed from the recession's effect on GNP and from the Carter-era stagflation. The recession slowed production, but it slowed neither the growth in program recipients nor the delayed effects of their COLAs. Stagflation caused benefits, linked to prices, to grow faster than either the economy or fund contributions, which increased more slowly with wages. These combined effects threw the social security system into crisis. They also caused an increase in the social security share of GNP during a time when economic growth had been expected to exceed demographically driven program increases. Thus, in the mid-1970s stabilization of the social security share had been reversed by unexpected economic bad news. Medicare, meanwhile, grew mainly because of the tremendous cost inflation in the medical business, a trend with which Congress had been wrestling for years.[6] Given underlying demographic trends (more old people), only an optimist could predict even a stabilization of this medicare increase.

Fourth, net interest costs increased drastically because the government had to borrow more as deficits increased; then borrowing and interest began to feed on themselves, generating higher deficits, more borrowing, and, it was argued, higher interest rates. The economy's troubles—inflation and then recession, creating first an insistence by lenders for higher rates and then a great need to borrow—were the major cause of the government's, if no one else's, interest rate problems. Because fiscal policy was rather tight from 1980 until mid-1982, it is fairer to say that the economy caused this part of government spending than that spending caused the economy's troubles.

Fifth, the defense buildup began under the Democrats; indeed, the 1981 outlays are almost entirely a product of 1980 (mostly Senate) action; not until 1983 did the Reagan budgets significantly increase outlays.[7] Some increase certainly would have occurred without Ronald Reagan. Still, a substantial part of the long-term increase in the "structural deficit" was due to administration plans to raise defense spending to 7.7 percent of GNP by 1988.

These trends in the two biggest entitlements—interest costs and defense—suggest that, given the behavior of the economy, any president and any Congress would have faced a serious deficit problem by 1983. They suggest also that only part of the trouble was avoidable. If, like many observers in 1983, we decide that a deficit of 1 to 2 percent of

GNP is actually quite livable—in short, that Carter's original FY81 budget was just fine—we will still have trouble explaining how to get there. Table 1 shows deficits of 5.6 percent of GNP. Where can we get 4 percent of GNP in budget savings? How can we keep taxes at 20.9 percent? That would be a big chunk, but then there might not be a recovery in 1983 or a president in office to support it. Have a slower defense buildup? It's worth a try, but, given first Afghanistan and then the backlog of budget authority from FY81–83 action, it would be very hard to get much below the 1983 figure—only saving half a point of GNP. Reduce interest costs? It's too late.

Cut the other stuff? This was done in 1981 for FY82 and then slightly by attrition (increases slightly below inflation, for example) in subsequent years. Those reductions actually began under Carter. But, as David Stockman explained at the beginning of 1984,

> The Great Society programs . . . peaked out at a cost of $140 billion in 1984 dollars in 1979–80. That cost will be down to $110 billion this year, no matter what Congress does. We have not succeeded in challenging the premise of the Great Society, but the level has been adjusted downward by about 20 percent. . . . Aside from defense, interest, and social security, we have shrunk the government by 15 percent.[8]

Stockman was willing to junk the whole kit and kaboodle of Great Society programs, but he did not have the votes.

One could cut medicare by changing the guarantees of treatment or putting the doctors on salary; cut defense by retrenching America's commitments (why should the United States defend Japanese and German oil supplies in the Persian Gulf or support the defense of rich European nations?); cut interest with legislation limiting rates to, say, 6 percent (the states had long had such usury laws). But we are talking here about drastic changes in national policy, none of which on their own would be enough to solve the deficit problem. Even if you tossed out $110 billion of Great Society programs—food stamps, the Economic Development Administration, medicaid, Amtrak—you would have roughly a $100 billion deficit in 1985. That is experiencing considerable trauma to reach a still enormous deficit.

The mismatch between taxing and spending stemmed, in the main, from much earlier decisions about social security, medicare, and other pension programs, combined with the economy's stagnation after 1973. Table 10 provides data on outlays by major categories of spending. From 1962 to 1979, nondefense spending increased its share of GNP from 9.9 to 15.9 percent, yet total spending rose only from 19.5 to 20.8 percent. Domestic growth was financed not by taxes or deficits but by a lower defense share. Almost all the government's share from economic growth went into domestic programs, so the relative proportions of defense and domestic changed dramatically.

As we argued in previous chapters, and as the administration acknowledged in its FY84 budget, defense need not grow with the economy.[9] Yet in 1979 both the public and elites felt the threat and thus requirements had increased. Therefore, defense was bound to retrieve some of its budget share; the free ride for domestic spending was over.

Most domestic increase came from payments to individuals, such as social security and medicare. These may be divided into direct payments, such as social security, and those administered though the states, such as AFDC and medicaid. Most poverty programs expanded sharply from 1967 to 1972 as the federal government removed restrictions on access and as medicaid took effect. After 1973, however, the government made few new commitments. AFDC shrunk in real terms, but food stamps picked up the slack. Growth of poverty programs, as Table 10 shows, was essentially cyclical.

The growth of "other grants"—the panoply of Great Society efforts to aid and influence local governments: revenue sharing, CETA public service jobs, Urban Mass Transit, Title 1 education fund, and so on— stopped in 1978, under Carter, as the budget crunch began. Poverty programs and these grants were the major victims of the 1981 reconciliation; in early 1983 OMB still planned major cuts. As for other program spending—everything from NASA to the FBI, the census, water projects, and national parks—they had stopped growing as a share of GNP in 1968.

What grew and kept growing were the non-means-tested entitlements funded directly by the federal government: civil service and military pensions and, most of all, OASDHI (that is, social security and medicare). These grew, however, not because of post-1973 decisions but because of pre-1973 commitments. They grew mainly because the eligible population grew: people were living longer, and more and more of them were fully vested in the social security system. In 1962 the Old Age and Disability funds had 16.8 million beneficiaries; in 1972, 25.2 million; in 1982, 31.9 million.[10] In the case of medicare, they grew because virtually nobody anticipated the costs of coverage; Congress began struggling with medical inflation soon after the program began. They grew, finally, because politicians kept benefits in line with rising prosperity but out of line with recipients' contributions; legislators, eager to please a very powerful group of voters, seemed confident that continuing economic growth would enable current workers to pay the bill. The last big increase in 1972 tells both sides of the story: Democrats and Republicans competed to woo the elderly; the resulting increase "was financed largely by a change in actuarial assumptions" that politicians had little reason not

TABLE 10. Outlays as Percentage of GNP, 1962–1988

Year	Total Outlays	Defense Function	Payments to Individuals			Other Grants to State and Local Governments	All Other	Net Interest	Total Nondefense
			Total	Direct	Through States				
1962	19.5	9.5	5.4	4.8	0.6	0.9	3.4	1.3	9.9
1963	19.3	9.2	5.4	4.8	0.6	0.9	3.4	1.3	10.0
1964	19.2	8.9	5.3	4.7	0.6	1.0	3.6	1.3	10.3
1965	18.0	7.7	5.1	4.5	0.6	1.1	3.7	1.3	10.3
1966	19.6	8.0	5.2	4.6	0.6	1.2	3.8	1.3	10.6
1967	20.3	9.2	5.8	5.1	0.6	1.3	3.6	1.3	11.1
1968	21.4	9.9	6.1	5.4	0.8	1.5	3.6	1.3	11.6
1969	20.2	9.1	6.3	5.5	0.8	1.4	2.8	1.4	11.1
1970	20.2	8.4	6.8	5.9	0.9	1.5	2.8	1.5	11.8
1971	20.4	7.6	8.0	6.9	1.1	1.7	2.6	1.4	12.7
1972	20.4	7.0	8.4	7.1	1.3	1.8	2.7	1.4	13.4
1973	19.6	6.1	8.5	7.4	1.1	2.2	2.5	1.4	13.5
1974	19.4	5.8	8.9	7.8	1.1	2.0	2.4	1.6	13.7
1975	21.9	5.8	10.6	9.4	1.2	2.2	2.6	1.6	16.1
1976	22.2	5.5	11.2	9.9	1.3	2.3	2.5	1.6	16.8

	TQ[a]								
TQ[a]	21.8	5.2	10.8	9.6	1.2	2.4	2.7	1.6	16.6
1977	21.5	5.2	10.8	9.5	1.3	2.4	2.3	1.6	16.3
1978	21.4	5.0	10.3	9.1	1.2	2.5	2.7	1.7	16.4
1979	20.8	4.9	10.1	8.9	1.2	2.3	2.4	1.8	15.9
1980	22.4	5.2	11.0	9.7	1.3	2.2	2.7	2.0	17.2
1981	22.8	5.5	11.5	10.1	1.4	1.9	2.6	2.4	17.3
1982	23.8	6.1	11.9	10.6	1.3	1.6	2.4	2.8	17.8
1983	24.7	6.5	12.5	11.1	1.4	1.5	2.5	2.8	18.2
1984[b]	24.0	6.7 (6.4)	11.6	10.3	1.3	1.5	2.1	3.0 (3.1)	17.3
1985[b]	23.8	7.0 (6.5)	11.3	10.1	1.2	1.4	2.1	3.0 (3.4)	16.8
1986[b]	23.4	7.3 (7.0)	11.0	9.8	1.2	1.3	1.9	2.9 (3.5)	16.1
1987[b]	23.3	7.6 (7.2)	10.9	9.7	1.2	1.2	1.8	2.9 (3.6)	15.7
1988[b]	22.8	7.7 (7.4)	10.7	9.6	1.1	1.1	1.6	2.6 (3.9)	15.2

SOURCE: Office of Management and Budget, "Federal Government Finances: 1985 Budget Data," typescript, February 1984, pp. 91–93.

NOTE: Numbers in parentheses refer to alternate CBO estimates. Totals do not add because of rounding and exclusion of "offsetting receipts."

[a] When Congress changed the dates of the fiscal year as part of the budget act, it created an extra quarter—July 1, 1976—September 30, 1976—that was not part of any fiscal year. This was called the transitional quarter and reported separately in federal government budget statistics, thus TQ.

[b] Estimates, assuming changes per Reagan FY85 budget and good luck on interest rates per that same forecast. Defense is too high; interest is too low.

to accept.[11] There were only two difficulties: the economy did not behave as expected, and almost everybody was asking the wrong question.

The economy went into a "quiet depression"[12] in 1973, and social security got into deep trouble. The social security funding question—Would that system's taxes fund that system's expenses?—was politically important. But throughout the program's history, it begged a second question: If social security taxes increased, would those be new taxes or replace old ones? (Tax aficionados speak of "fiscal cannibalism" where one tax eats up another.) One way, the tax burden went up; the other way, either other programs went down or deficits went up. Acting "responsibly" in funding OASDHI, the government had the payroll tax rise from 3.1 percent of GNP in 1962, to 4.7 percent in 1972, to 6.6 percent in 1982.[13] It was already scheduled to go higher; the 1983 compromise would speed up these increases. Whenever the government propelled increasing taxes out into the future—as it did in the original 1935 act and most subsequent modifications—it avoided the choice as to how the increase would affect the rest of federal activity.

Thus, the repetition of what appears a truism—social security is self-financing—by Ronald Reagan, his congressional opponents, and spokesmen for the elderly, though true as far as it goes, leaves the mistaken impression that the biggest program by far would not affect the rest of government. Nonsense. To believe this is to believe that it doesn't matter how high any tax is as long as it supports a given activity. Individuals and businesses feel taxation from all sources, so a big increase here is bound to affect the possibilities of other increases elsewhere.

Here's the catch: maybe the government *should not* have chosen. No one could see the size of any future problems; perhaps they would be small, for economic growth heals many ills. Perhaps it was for people in the future to choose whether they wanted higher taxes or fewer programs, or even (gasp!) higher deficits. If politicians in 1962, say, had decided that other programs would have to be cut by 1.6 percent of GNP (the amount OASDHI would grow) by 1972, how on earth could they have done so? Okay, one might say: If you can't plan, don't make the commitment. Don't have a national retirement plan or any policies with long-term increasing costs. Toss out civil service pensions and medicare while you're at it. But that's not possible or desirable. People in real life make long-term commitments like buying a house, sometimes even with an adjustable-rate mortgage. They have children, plan to send them to college; they will figure out later what to sacrifice to that end. The government, with heavy public support, committed itself to social security. There is little evidence that people, on the whole, dispute either that commitment or its necessity. Some problems come with the territory.

Is there, then, no room for choice? Hardly, one can always exercise prudence. The 1972 increases, for example, could have been smaller. Many provisions, such as early retirement, could be less generous. Here we want to emphasize only that both Carter and Reagan, along with politicians of all parties, got caught in a fiscal tidal wave, beginning in 1979, that had begun long before; much of its force was inevitable. Most of the increase in spending after 1979 constituted old commitments hitting the beach of a new economy. Huge deficits would have occurred even without Ronald Reagan—unless you think taxes were going well above the level that helped defeat Jimmy Carter.

What could the politicians have done, in 1980–1981, about the coming tidal wave? Could they even know it was coming? In the president's FY84 budget, published at the beginning of 1983, Stockman answered those questions. He argued that events from 1970 to 1981 produced a "profound disequilibrium in the inherited 1981 budget." He wanted to get domestic spending down to 1970's share, but that was nearly impossible. The administration's solution was the magic asterisk of unspecified savings in the Economic Recovery Program, to shrink the numerator, and "an immediate, rapid and sustained expansion of GNP" to increase the denominator of the outlays/GNP ratio.[14] This presumed, he reported rather drily, "the transition from rising to falling inflation and from low real growth to rapid output expansion would occur immediately and simultaneously, and without intervening financial and economic disturbance."[15] If everything had worked, spending would have stabilized after 1984 between 19 and 20 percent of GNP.

What went wrong? In 1983 Stockman blamed the economy. Later, in his book, he blames himself and his colleagues for misestimating the economy. Rosy Scenario, he writes, overestimated GNP, and thus the revenue base, by $2 trillion over FY82–86.[16] They thereby hid, from themselves and from others, the deficit consequences of the tax cut. Stockman is partially right: they did rig the forecast; if it didn't fool Domenici, Baker, and other congressional leaders, it did make it harder for them to oppose the package. But Stockman was right in 1983 as well; the economy performed far worse than anyone had expected. For example, the excessive GNP projections in Rosy Scenario were no higher than those made by Carter's CEA in his last (January 1981) budget. Stockman predicted more growth, Carter, more inflation, creating similar nominal GNP.[17] Neither side anticipated the revenue consequences of actually stopping inflation; no one was predicting the slump that occurred or its far greater than normal decrease in revenues.

There is something to be said for erring with the conventional wisdom, as opposed to making up a logically inconsistent theory with which to err. Stockman's mea culpa is not all wrong. But, as we saw, the whole Republican establishment confirmed Rosy Scenario, albeit in some cases grudgingly. The Republicans could do so because, panicked about the state of the economy, no one knew quite what to do.

It is hard to argue that the first two installments of the tax cut, in 1981 and 1982, were excessive either in prospect (when they seemed smaller because people anticipated more inflation, thus increasing revenues) or in effect (for they responded to a much bigger recession than was anticipated). As for business tax cuts, Democratic tax leaders accepted the basic size of the administration's package, for Democratic economists were also pushing "capital formation." The original Hance-Conable compromise, on June 4, 1981, would have cut taxes less than the final bill. But a lot of the add-ons—concessions to business lobbyists on June 9, oil and other breaks in the auction—were reversed, albeit with difficulty, in TEFRA. Given what economists were saying in 1981, as well as the actual course of the economy, it is hard to argue that tax policy as of early 1983 could have been much different, with one glaring exception: the upcoming third year of the tax cut.

The most thorough analysis of the deficit's causes was made by Gregory Mills and John Palmer of the Urban Institute in September 1983; thus, it included the deficit reductions from TEFRA, the social security rescue, and the economic picture as understood by Congress in its FY84 budget resolution. Mills and Palmer also assumed that taxes would not have risen beyond the FY81 level, remaining at 20.8 percent of GNP. Table 11[18] indicates (compare lines 5 and 8) that policy did not significantly affect the deficit until FY84 and after. Even in FY86, only $100 billion of a projected $237 billion deficit would be due to policy choices. Of that $100 billion, similar shares are accounted for by tax cuts and defense buildup (lines 9 and 12, offset by line 13).

In 1983, therefore, the politicians faced $200 billion deficits far out into the future. Over FY84–86, however, $174 billion, $149 billion, and $137 billion (line 2 minus line 8) of those deficits were not, in any plausible way, their fault. After 1980's experience with a $15 billion deficit, we suspect, those deficits alone would have been enough to create political chaos.

Surely something must be wrong with the analysis because "everybody knows" that Ronald Reagan was responsible for the huge size of the deficit. Surely his tax cuts and defense increases are the villains. Aside from encouraging doubters to reread what they have just read, this view is so prevalent and so strongly held that it deserves direct confrontation.

Was Reagan responsible for the deficit? We answer: mostly no, but partially yes. To say that the nation would have stood still for even higher taxes in 1981 and 1982 not only goes against historical experience but also implies that Democrats would not have cut taxes. The evidence is that

TABLE 11.   Sources of Increase in Projected Federal Deficits
(in billions of dollars)

	FY82	*FY83*	*FY84*	*FY85*	*FY86*
Projected total deficit (surplus):					
(1) As of Jan. 1981[a]	62	28	(11)	(50)	(90)
(2) As of Sept. 1983[b]	128	225	213	218	237
(3) Increase in deficit	64	197	224	268	326
Sources of increase in deficit:					
(4) Changes in technical assumptions	−2	29	26	19	11
(5) Changes in economic outlook	71	146	159	180	215
(6) Revenues	49	131	157	179	220
(7) Outlays	22	15	2	1	−5
(8) Changes in policy	−5	22	39	69	100
(9) Revenues	30	50	59	69	83
(10) Outlays (see Addendum)	−35	−28	−20	0	17
Addendum:					
(11) Changes in policy— outlays	−35	−28	−20	0	17
(12) Defense	3	13	30	51	69
(13) Nondefense programs	−38	−41	−53	−58	−65
(14) Net interest	0	0	3	7	13

SOURCES: Table from Gregory B. Mills and John L. Palmer, *The Deficit Dilemma* (Washington, D.C.: Urban Institute Press, 1983), p. 22. Congressional Budget Office, *Baseline Budget Projections for Fiscal Years 1984–1988* (Washington, D.C.: Government Printing Office, 1983), pp. 18, 35, and 57; CBO estimates of legislation enacted in 1983 and net interest outlays as affected by shifts in revenues or program outlay; and authors' calculations.

[a]Estimated under the base line economic forecast published in Congressional Budget Office, *Baseline Budget Projections: Fiscal Years 1982–1986* (Washington, D.C.: Government Printing Office, 1981). Assumes annual real growth in defense outlays of 5 percent in 1982, 4 percent in 1983, and 3 percent in 1984–1986; also assumes no change in corporate tax provisions and nondefense program policies as of January 1981, with full adjustment for inflation in nondefense programs, and tax reductions to offset bracket creep in the individual income tax.

[b]Estimated under the economic forecast adopted by Congress in passing its *First Concurrent Resolution on the Budget for Fiscal Year 1984*. Assumes adoption of the administration's defense request for FY 1984 and subsequent years, plus the continuation of all tax and spending policies enacted through August 1983, including the emergency jobs legislation, social security amendments, and repeal of tax withholding on interest and dividend income.

they would have, albeit not as much. The difference between the two parties is essentially the third year of the tax cut.

Although Reagan did not start the defense buildup, he pushed it farther and faster than a more fiscally prudent president might. That part of the deficit, by no means the largest part but a part nonetheless, is fairly attributable to him. With the benefit of hindsight, we can observe that after 1984 a build-down occurred, thus reducing the impact of defense spending on the long-term deficit. That deficit reduction, of course, was not his fault. Even the famous Professor Hindzeit, less fallible than the rest of us, has not had sufficient time to test whether the rise in defense spending was worthwhile or not large enough.

If not Reagan, who was responsible? A good half or more of the deficit may be attributed to the recession, which, as far as anyone knows, was either inevitable or precipitated by the Federal Reserve Bank under the aegis of Paul Volcker. Having perhaps taken off the monetary brakes too soon in 1980, when inflation surged again, Volcker may have kept them on too long in 1981 and 1982. Possibly another Fed chairman might have brought the economy in with a softer landing. Inflation and employment might have declined more slowly, leading to less individual suffering and considerably more revenue. Maybe. But citizens were so distraught over inflation that "just right"—had anyone been able to figure out then what that would be—might have been considered too little and too late by market and populace. Because Reagan supported Volcker and because both men claimed credit for stopping inflation, credit for the good face of deflation has to go with blame for its bad side in reducing revenues.

Should the ghost of commitments past, as well as present supporters of social security, like Senator Moynihan, Representative Pepper, and Speaker O'Neill, take part of the blame? After all, social security payments (and, therefore, taxes) could well have been lower, thereby leaving more room for other taxes. They, too, or others like them who had the authority in the early 1970s, erred on the side of optimism in expanding the clientele and the awards under social security. No doubt they will accept blame for the most popular program in America.

A reasonable conclusion would be that all who govern now and in the past half century share some blame for the deficit: some more than others, but few are guiltless. Overall, American economic performance since the end of the Second World War has been good. Nevertheless, the 1970s left a lot to be desired. Much of this slowdown may be due to international oil increases or vast numbers of new entrants into the labor market or emergent economic powers on the world scene or too high taxes or insufficient demand or too little saving, some of which government could affect and much of which it could not.[19] Finger pointing does not, in any event, tell us whether (and, if so, how much) we should worry about the deficit—our next subject—or what public officials might do about it (and how), the subject of the rest of the book.

The Economy and the Deficit

Economists' difficulty with predictions was confirmed once again at the beginning of 1983. *Time* reported that people on its Board of Economists were beginning to feel like Vladimir and Estragon in *Waiting for Godot;* they kept thinking the recovery ought to arrive, but it hadn't for so long that they were beginning to wonder if it ever would.[20] Pessimism was mainly based on a belief that high interest rates would "shackle consumer spending and business investment." Surveys of business plans showed no intention to increase investment. *Business Week* commented:

> The sobering experience of the past two years suggests that executives and investors must be prepared for a world quite different from that of the standard forecast—but it also leaves scant guidance about whether the surprise is more apt to be pleasant or unpleasant. Since unemployment and underemployment are so high, there is clear potential for a surge in growth at least as swift as the postwar average. But if the Administration and Congress fail to cut the budget deficits and the Fed returns to stricter adherence to monetary targets, there is also the potential for yet another— and worse—bout with recession.[21]

This conventional wisdom about deficits sounded sensible, but, after the Fed turned to tighter money and the deficit continued, the economy boomed anyway.

Martin Feldstein's first economic forecast for the Reagan administration was fairly pessimistic. He predicted GNP growth of 3.1 percent, inflation of 5 percent, and year-end unemployment of 10.4 percent.[22] The CEA, overcorrecting for 1981's overoptimism, thus ensured that it would not be criticized for trying to make the administration look good. But two wrongs do not make a right. That projection also increased the pressure for action on the deficit. Asked in an interview about the forecast, President Reagan replied, "I just can't help but have an optimistic feeling that the recovery may just be better than we think."[23]

Reagan's suspicions were quickly confirmed. In January unemployment started dropping. Feldstein told the president that GNP growth might be more like 5 percent than 3.1.[24] By mid-February there was little doubt that the recovery had finally arrived.[25]

By late May 1983 the economy was looking ever better, unless you were among those union workers whose wage contracts were calling for actual reductions. Some policy makers, such as Henry Wallich of the

Federal Reserve Board, were beginning to fear that the economy would overheat. Beginning in May, the Federal Reserve moved toward a policy of tighter money. By late June, the Commerce Department was reporting second-quarter growth at an 8 percent rate; business profits were soaring.[26] Walter Heller had been keeping a list of adjectives applied to the recovery. At the year's beginning they included "weak, wobbly, puny, pokey, measly, muted, and miserable." At midyear they had become "rapid, robust, snappy, surging, brisk, bullish, and a barn burner."[27]

Throughout 1983, the economy kept growing beyond expectations. "There's one way we can tell our program is beginning to work," crowed the president. "They don't call it Reaganomics anymore."[28] By October, industrial production had rebounded to an all-time peak.

Unemployment, which had languished near 10 percent, finally fell to 7.2 percent by December.[29] By a number of indicators, mid-1984 was another watershed, with growth slowing markedly to a rate of roughly 2 to 3 percent per year from that time to the end of 1985.

Everyone should have been happy, right? Wrong. Lots of people were miserable. Policy and the overall trends of the economy together seemed to be creating an "unbalanced" recovery; people at the wrong end of the seesaw did not like it one bit. Recovery in 1983 left manufacturing below 1981 levels. Construction was also weak. Industries that had done relatively well during the recession attained new heights during the recovery: wholesale and retail trade, finance, insurance, real estate, and services. The big losers were the heavily unionized blue-collar industries, such as steel and autos, that were vulnerable to foreign competition, or those, like airlines and trucking, that suffered under deregulation.

These differential effects fed a suspicion that, underneath the cyclical movements of interest rates, prices, wages, and unemployment, "something else was going on." That something else might have involved the changing position of America in a global economy, or it might have been the beginning of a new phase of the industrial revolution. The economic age of the automobile, petroleum, and steak might be giving way to that of the personal computer, Electronic Fund Transfer, and croissants. There were signs aplenty of such a broad change—from Sears' metamorphosis into a financial-services supermarket, to the ATM machines that were replacing tellers in banks, to the unemployment remaining in the old middle-American cities of Toledo, Detroit, South Bend, Flint, Gary, and Youngstown.

Many politicians wanted to ride the wave. A new breed of Democrats popped up in Congress, if not among the public. These advocates of high tech were dubbed "Atari Democrats" after the Silicon Valley maker of video games. The computer was all the rage; *Time* even chose that machine as its 1982 "Man of the Year."

Whatever was happening, it was not good for labor. Unemployment did come down, but its slide stopped at a level well above the rate during any previous expansion. Those who were unemployed had been out of work for a long time—an average of 20 weeks in 1983, compared to 15.8 weeks in 1976 (also a first year of recovery from deep recession).[30]

As unemployment stayed fairly high, wages failed to grow. Real wages had fallen from average weekly earnings of $183.41 (1977 dollars) in 1979 to $168.09 in 1982, mostly due to the 1979–1980 inflation. The low inflation recovery that the administration promised, and (after un-expected vicissitudes) delivered, did little to redress the wage loss.[31] In 1984 real, nonfarm business compensation remained below its 1977 level. Where, the obvious question is, did the rest of national product go? Most went to increasing employment and a growing population; the rapid growth in 1983–1984 had to accommodate more workers before wages could increase. The money did not go to the profits of manufacturing industries. Some went into the profits of service industries such as whole-sale and retail trade.[32] Much went to bond holders and other savers due to the higher interest rates. Whether they held government or other debt, people and institutions who had money to lend could benefit most from a recovery that combined high interest rates and low wage growth. In nominal (that is, inflated) dollars, personal interest income doubled from 1979 to 1984, while overall wages rose by less than 50 percent and manufacturing wages by only 30 percent.[33]

This transfer of income from wage earners to rentiers had begun under Carter. The Reagan administration's tax and spending policies directly paralleled these wider economic trends, but we cannot judge how much they contributed to them. Tax policies, such as the failure to adjust personal exemptions in the 1981 tax bill, exacerbated by social security contribution increases, meant that those people who saved less because they earned less also benefited least from the tax cut. Decreased taxes on interest income (such as the 1981 top-rate reduction and capital-gains reduction) also favored interest earners over wage earners, as did the budget deficits (to the extent they increased interest rates).[34]

The trend began with pressure on union wage rates from more basic movements in the political economy. The power relation between labor and management had, by 1982, been dramatically changed. The effect is described by the CEA's 1985 economic report: "Some recent union wage settlements have involved an actual reduction in wages or fringes, a relaxation of work rules, or wage freezes. Concessions have occurred in previous recessions, but the scale of recent concessions is unprece-dented."[35] The unions' problems explain why the AFL-CIO, battered by events under first a Democratic president who barely knew them and then a Republican who opposed them, determined that they would pull out all the stops in 1984 to have a friendly president.

Nominal interest rates came down, but real interest rates stayed high, reaching 7 percent. There are as many possible explanations for interest rate behavior as there are political positions that stand to benefit from explanations. None are entirely persuasive. The administration's favorite explanation was that higher prospective, after-tax return on investment, caused by the 1981 tax changes, made businesses more willing to pay high real interest rates.[36] Changes in financial markets associated with deregulation, formal and informal, may have enabled businesses and individuals to demand a higher price for the money.[37] The most common explanation, however, was that big deficits increased the demand for money, and the Federal Reserve reduced its supply. The causes might not have had the presumed effect, but they did exist. After June 1983 fiscal policy, for the first time in our story, became loose; monetary policy once again became tight.[38]

The Federal Reserve insisted that, in order to prevent inflation, monetary policy was tight *because* fiscal policy was loose, thus blaming deficits for both sides of the pressure on interest rates.[39]

High interest rates favored lenders and borrowers who had profits high enough for the tax advantages of interest deductibility to come into play. High interest rates were very bad for debtors—that is, farmers, young families who wanted to buy houses, and thus the housing industry. They were very bad for Latin American nations. And they were not much help to the federal government, whose debt service costs grew steadily.

To summarize, a consumer-led recovery that began in December 1982 accelerated particularly in mid-1983, maintained rapid growth for an unusually long time into 1984 due to business investment, and then slowed to a pace that was either "moderate" (per Republicans) or "sluggish" (per Democrats) by mid-1984. In the aggregate, the recovery resembled Ronald Reagan's promise of inflation-free expansion. But an unusually large number of people weren't along for the ride.

"Consequences" of the Deficit

In spite of the recovery, therefore, bad things were still going on in the economy. Where there are bad things, there must be blame, and blame means worry about the deficits. In the case of interest rates, blame could have meant worry about the Federal Reserve, the other half of the double whammy that supposedly kept rates high. Yet the consensus of business and political elites in defense of Volcker was so overwhelming that criticism of the Fed was muted.

The power of elite consensus became evident when the administration had to decide whether to reappoint Volcker as the Board's chairman. Although Milton Friedman urged Reagan to replace Volcker, *Time* asked the right question: "Does he really have a choice?" The answer was, probably not.[40] To replace Volcker was extremely risky; it may be hard to win the confidence of "the markets," but it seems fairly easy to lose it. Previous presidents had not dared to take similar risks; thus, both Kennedy and Johnson had reluctantly reappointed Chairman William McChesney Martin.

Feldstein, Stockman, Howard Baker, and Paul Laxalt urged Volcker's retention. As the risks of dumping Volcker grew clear, Treasury Secretary Regan switched to supporting him. No one else had Volcker's credentials for dealing with the other crisis in the Fed's purview, debt in the third world.[41] Ultimately, the chairman was deemed indispensable; on June 18 Reagan announced Volcker's reappointment.[42]

The White House had a schizophrenic position on the evils of the deficit. It was hard to maintain that deficits were both so terrible that spending should be cut drastically but not so bad that taxes should be raised. If asked about tax hikes, Martin Feldstein would say, well, yes, if necessary, while Donald Regan kept claiming that, after all, deficits did not affect much of anything. In one speech Regan declared that "I will offer a prize to anyone who can show me the connection between high rates of interest and high deficits." Yet, *Time* commented, "he seemed to enter his own contest" when the Treasury secretary told another audience that "I do guarantee we will make visible progress in removing the specter which arose from the January budget: record deficits as far as the eye could see."[43]

Regan, while calling spending cuts "the only meaningful solution to the deficit problem," declared also that his staff had found "no empirical evidence that correlates deficits and interest rates." Yet he did add that "deficits constrict capital formation":[44] if not through interest rates, how?[45]

The secretary of the Treasury and the president downplayed the deficit when they thought tax hikes were more likely than spending cuts. CEA Chairman Feldstein continually condemned the deficits: "The president isn't well-served," he declared, "unless he gets honest advice from his advisers."[46] No one could argue with that sentiment; the issue was whether advice should be public or private. As he continued to speak out, relations between Feldstein and Regan and White House staff steadily deteriorated.

Feldstein was not about to divert Reagan from his moral economy. But the chairman's statements added force to the continuing demand by the media and mainstream economists that deficits be reduced. Now the evil consequences were an "unbalanced" recovery, an overvalued dollar, high real interest rates, a massive trade deficit, and, ultimately, excessive risk to the international financial system. A new conventional wisdom said that these consequences, rather than the predicted inflation and stagnation, resulted from the willingness of foreigners to finance American consumption. As one leading Keynesian put it, the deficit hadn't stifled recovery "because we failed to anticipate the ease with which the United States could borrow overseas. That foreign borrowing has played a key role in providing the financing for investment that we have been unwilling to provide for ourselves."[47]

Net foreign investment in the United States increased dramatically as the United States recovered while other major economies stagnated. If we think of the dollar not only as a medium of exchange but also as a repository of value, even as an investment, people around the world, comparing their situation to ours, evidently wanted to hold American currency and to use it in the United States.

As the value of the dollar rose, increasing 79 percent from 1980 to early 1985, so did the relative prices of American goods.[48] Businesses that produced in America but sold abroad found that they could not reduce costs sufficiently to make up for the rapidly rising value of the dollar. American exports suffered, but American imports increased; industries vulnerable to foreign competition in the U.S. market were damaged. This price competition caused by the strong dollar, however, helped keep inflation down, thus encouraging the economy to grow. Bad news for some is good news for others.

The U.S. trade deficit rose from a normal level (1977–1982) of around $30 billion to $60 billion in 1983, doubled again in 1984, and continued to grow. To paint the picture in broad brush strokes, the debt crisis reduced American lending abroad, while weak European recoveries and high American real interest rates attracted capital to the United States from the developed nations. These roughly equal trends caused American net foreign investment—the difference between American investments overseas and foreign investments in the United States—to change from roughly zero to a negative 3 percent of GNP. This was a dramatic reversal of the twentieth-century trend in which the United States had been a creditor rather than a debtor nation. By 1985 the change in investments meant that foreigners, for the first time since World War I, earned more from investments in America than American citizens earned from investments abroad.

The direct distributional stakes in the budget battles were quite clear: to the extent that tax reductions increased interest rates, tax policy had the same effects on corporations as tax and budget policy had on individuals. It reinforced the existing trend of the economy, which benefited those who already had money (to lend or invest) and hurt those who were already in trouble (and had to borrow). Thus, Democrats had fought for a different kind of tax cut and spending priorities. The indirect distributional effects of policy were also sensed by the participants; this would become a major theme of liberal critiques of Reaganism.[49] By their analysis, the consequences of the big deficit strikingly resemble the old Jeffersonian/Jacksonian critique that had been a pillar of the balanced budget norm; federal debt favored those who began with greater resources. We must emphasize, however, that Democratic economists in 1980 and some politicians, including the president and other budgeters, accepted the idea that bad news for bondholders ultimately, through lower investment and productivity, would mean bad news for wage earners. When Senator Byrd protested tight money, he was shot down by other Democrats as well as Republicans. Inflation fighting came first.

As the economy recovered, without inflation, attention would turn to the problem that remained: some industries and jobs were not recovering. Senators and representatives from the industrial heartland could not accept the idea that their industries should die. Too much of the "creative destruction" that, according to Joseph Schumpeter, made capitalism great,[50] was being fed, many feared, not by real efficiency differences but by high interest rates and high exchange value of the dollar. Economists from Alan Greenspan to Otto Eckstein blamed the budget deficit for the trade deficit and thus for the losers in the economy.[51] "If Congress fails to take the necessary steps" to reduce the deficit, Martin Feldstein concluded, "real interest rates will remain high, the dollar will continue to be overvalued and a large segment of American industry will suffer the consequences of declining competitiveness."[52] In 1987 and 1988, of course, as the dollar lost more than half its value, the deficit would also be blamed.

Many suffering industries took it out on their unionized employees. Greyhound Bus drivers lost a bitter strike against management demands for compensation reductions; unionized packinghouse workers faced 25 percent wage cuts; Eastern Airlines employees had to agree to large wage reductions and altered work rules in return for shares of stock. Having won concessions in the most recent bargaining, U.S. Steel demanded more. "We are going to get beat up worse and worse," commented William Wimpisinger, president of the International Association of Machinists.[53] To the extent the deficits could be blamed for the manufacturing industries' and debtors' difficulties, the Democrats' interest-based acceptance of deficits was diluted. Union leaders still preferred to reduce the deficit with tax increases, but Democratic politicians became even less likely than in 1980 to say deficits were not a problem. Furthermore, as the economy recovered, the deficit became the easiest target for Democratic attacks.

Conservative Republicans, who believed in worrying about the future, believed the economists who predicted bad times ahead. High real interest rates linked the antideficit ideology of conservative Republicans to their constituency interests; for example, in the farm belt, heavy farm indebtedness reinforced the antideficit positions of Senators Dole of Kansas and Grassley of Iowa.

In spite of the recovery, therefore, neither Democrats nor mainstream Republicans nor the economic gurus would surrender the idea that deficits were terrible. Ultimately, neither did Ronald Reagan. He still wanted it both ways: deficits were terrible but not so bad that they should be solved by tax hikes or defense cuts. That was his moral economy; therefore, he consistently condemned deficits in general, even as he defended his own. Thus, no one, save a few isolated supply-siders, willingly defended the deficits in economic terms. CBO summed up the situation in its 1984 *Economic Outlook:* "In regard to fiscal policy, it is almost universally agreed that action must be taken to reduce future deficits significantly." "But," they added, "it is not clear how or when the problem will be resolved."[54]

We discuss the shifting and contrary anti-deficit arguments at such length because, while public discourse so often claimed national interest in avoiding the evident evils of deficits, most assertions about how the economy works, including assertions about the deficit, proved inaccurate. It is neither that deficits are inherently good nor that Reaganomics (in its various forms) made them good. The manner in which the evils of the deficit kept being redefined should alert the reader to the consideration that deficit reduction was as much a solution in search of a problem as a response to difficulties.

Is the deficit itself, then, no problem? We would not go that far. There may have been adverse distributional effects. How much of the mid-1980s increase in inequality stemmed from fiscal and monetary policy, how much from other politics (not raising the minimum wage), and how much from the underlying transformation of the world economy, we wouldn't hazard to guess. Furthermore, it is hard to disagree with Herbert Stein that, over the long term, "an economy with a budget deficit equal to, say, 4 percent of GNP will probably have less private investment than with a budget deficit equal to 2 percent of GNP, and, if other things are equal, it will probably have less growth of productivity. . . . Over a long period [this effect] would almost certainly be significant."[55] Almost certainly so.[56] But the relationship between investment and productivity growth is very difficult to judge; the 1970s slump in productivity growth, for instance, was not associated with a drop in investment. Whether the short-term costs of deficit reduction were worth the long-term gains depended on how the economics turned out—unknowable—and how one valued the activities eliminated by deficit reduction—a question the economists never asked.

Large deficits, unless the interest payments are effectively reduced or denied to creditors by the future effects of inflation, do finance current government consumption at the expense of future government spending. That is, future citizens, instead of buying services with their taxes, will be paying a larger and larger proportion just for interest payments. Deficits, therefore, can plausibly be seen as people today engaging services that will be paid for by their children and grandchildren. This fairly consensual analysis of long-term effects explains why conservative Republicans of a more social, that is, hierarchical/paternalistic, bent particularly dislike growing deficits.

Democrats could legitimately fear that interest payments down the line would displace social spending. In 1981 Democrats fought the third-year tax cut precisely because they could see how it would pressure their programs. While Reagan would not have put it in those words—that interest payments would constrain substantive spending—he certainly believed that the tax cut would; he and his opponents thus actually agreed. All sides could agree that increasing interest costs is bad for any organization. So do we. Republicans would avoid burdening grandchildren by cutting spending now; Democrats wanted to protect spending later by financing current spending. Of course, the two parties and their various factions disagreed on which spending was worth preserving.

As a matter of prudence, we believe, any organization should limit its indebtedness. The absolute amount is less important than the burden of its service; thus, we would pay most attention to measures of our ability to pay, interest as a share of GNP; or ability to spend, the interest share of the federal budget. Sometimes going into greater debt makes sense, depending on your return for the money. Reagan would say we bought much greater national security by borrowing for his military buildup. Perhaps, but limiting deficits to a point where the interest share of spending is stable or shrinking is certainly a worthy, even a major, goal. Is balance then *the* major concern of policy making? We cannot see it; certainly it cannot be justified in economic terms.

We have criticized many economic arguments about the deficit. Perhaps the most telling indicator of their difficulty is that no side could say what the deficit should be. The administration had no coherent fiscal policy rationale, for it did not *want* such a rationale in place of its moral vision. As for the Democrats, if they had an argument, they never articulated it. Our colleague, James Savage, has described how Democratic politicians, faced with the difficulty of maintaining Keynesian principles while worrying about deficits, resorted to waffling, trying to have it both ways.[57] Because of the difference between long-term and short-term effects, some waffling was actually appropriate. But the Democrats were never able to marshal an argument about the appropriate level and time of deficit. Their deficit-reduction figures always seemed selected more for comparison to the Republicans' than for any economic rationale. Thus, as Savage argues, Walter Mondale promised to reduce Reagan's deficit as much as two-thirds by 1989. But why two-thirds? Why not a half, or all? If President Reagan came off better, it was because his preferences for a different moral economy needed no economic arguments, only faith and prosperity.

SIXTEEN

The Budget Process Collapses

As 1983 began, Democratic control of the House, deepening unemployment, and the skirmishes of the late 1982 lame-duck session all suggested that the administration would have to change course. If not, it would be outstripped by a Congress that in 1982 had shown it could lead as well as follow. Conservatives such as Irving Kristol, Kevin Phillips, and William Safire joined moderate and liberal columnists in proclaiming that Reaganomics and the administration were in deep trouble.[1] One of the strongest statements came from David Broder, perhaps the most influential of national news columnists:

> What we are witnessing this January is not the midpoint in the Reagan presidency, but its phase-out. "Reaganism," it is becoming increasingly clear, was a one-year phenomenon, lasting from his nomination in the summer of 1980 to the passage of his budget and tax bills in summer 1981. What has been occurring ever since is an accelerating retreat from Reaganism, a process in which he is more spectator than leader.[2]

Reagan's 1982 backpedaling, ending with the gas tax, explains why pundits reached such conclusions; as luck would have it, the economy was about to recover, one reason the conclusions proved false. A different president, however, might have bowed to the pressures, thus failing to benefit politically from the economy's faster-than-expected recovery. Ronald Reagan did not budge.

Reagan Hangs Tough

Reagan adjusted the facts to fit his worldview. At his worst, in a long profile of "How Reagan Decides," *Time* reported, "He has a propensity to seize on one comforting truth and magnify it into the whole truth, blocking out all evidence of continuing or looming trouble."[3] It was not that Reagan learned nothing from events but, rather, what he learned. Events did not make him question his principles; instead, he developed new tactical judgments about how he might better achieve his objectives. "Do you think that any of your preconceptions about problems and policies have been wrong?" *Time's* correspondents asked him. "Well," he responded, "not as to basic philosophy: my belief that government in recent years has been more a part of the problem than part of the solution in many ways. No, I haven't changed my mind in those ways." But yes, he added, you have different information as president than as an outsider. Asked for an example that showed his preconceptions as not matching the information he received as president, Reagan replied,

> I don't think I was prepared for how much of the budget was built in by the original legislation, how many programs were instituted . . . with features in them that made them automatically increase. So you look and say, wait a minute. If there were no recession, the budget would keep increasing at a rate that is higher than the normal increase in revenues, and you find that somehow you have got to find a way to make a structural change that will require the Congress agreeing not just to a cut in the budget but to actually changing the structure of a program.[4]

Note the real, though selective, learning at work. Stockman and other aides had taught the president some budget truths, and he had incorporated them into his tactical understanding (structural changes are hard, so be patient) without altering at all his strategic objectives (abolishing and diminishing domestic programs).

A *Business Week* interview in early February also shows how Reagan adapted arguments to his own purposes. Asked why his economic program did not produce the expected surge of growth, he replied,

> People began talking about whether the program was succeeding or not at a time when only a part of it had been put into effect. We believe that the tax cut will stimulate the economy, savings and investment. But you have to wait until the people get the money. Just signing the bill and saying we've got a tax cut hasn't changed their fortunes yet.[5]

As excuses go, one could hardly do better than this. Yet much of the argument in 1981 claimed that "expectations" created by the new policy would themselves fuel a boom. And Reagan returned to expectations logic when he explained that, although he hoped the taxes would not be necessary, the contingency tax proposal "will psychologically reassure the money markets." Then Reagan rejected repeal of the third year of the tax cut or indexing, explaining "part of the optimism that we are seeing right now is because people and business have been able to look ahead knowing that these things are going to happen."[6] In other words, the tax cuts create optimism so should not be repealed in 1983, but the policy depended on the money actually being in people's pockets to have any effect in 1981.

It makes more sense to view Reagan as a salesman or advocate than as confused or disengaged. In spite of the judgment of pundits, therefore, the president had no intention of changing course. His aides were another matter.

Stockman and Darman in particular strove to get Reagan to sign on to a big deficit-reduction package. They were joined by the new CEA Chairman Martin Feldstein, far more aggressive than his predecessor. Determined to prevent the kind of optimistic error made in 1981 and 1982, Feldstein threatened to resign if he did not get his way when the economic forecast was prepared: prediction of a weak recovery in 1983 and steady GNP growth of 4 percent the following year. His short-term forecast, more pessimistic than many others, added to the pressure on Reagan.

Feldstein would soon become Stockman's most public ally within the administration, predicting horrible consequences from deficits and recommending tax hikes, if spending could not be cut, to reduce those deficits. His disputes with Donald Regan and other members of the administration got so much publicity and raised such acrimony that one might get the impression that Feldstein was a Keynesian mole who had somehow burrowed into the administration in an effort to undermine its policies. Yet that impression would be very wrong; Feldstein, in fact, was the "superstar of the new economists," the most prestigious supporter of "supply-side" emphases (but not doctrines), and an influential critic of the welfare state. He argued that government policies distorted incentives: that unemployment insurance increased unemployment; medicare boosted the cost of health care; social security was "probably the most important cause of our capital scarcity problem."[7] Feldstein's work was sufficiently good and prolific that, at age thirty-eight, he became president of the National Bureau of Economic Research, a prestigious and independent association of economic researchers. He was a strenuous advocate of changes in tax laws that would increase investment. In 1980, while Carter tried to balance the budget, Feldstein attacked those who "made a fetish" out of balancing the budget. Tax cutter and opponent of the most sacred cows among government programs, Feldstein seemed the ideal Reagan economist. The fact that many Keynesians vehemently disagreed with his analyses and conclusions, yet accepted his stature, should have made Feldstein even more attractive. When Murray Weidenbaum resigned, the administration needed a new chairman in tune with its ideology yet so well-respected that his forecasts would receive some credence. Feldstein met the bill; no one could mock his conclusions.[8] The administration's difficulties with Feldstein stemmed from the fact that he shared the president's moral economy but was, for all that, a mainstream economist.

Feldstein and Stockman kept trying to make Reagan face up to the deficit, both by explaining its substance and by creating situations in which Reagan would be under political pressure to endorse a package. Stockman presented the substance to his boss in a lengthy preference quiz in November 1982. The budget director divided the budget into fifty major components with three choices to be made on each, "ranging from a nick to a heavy whack." Policy and political consequences accompanied each option. Reagan spent several days deciding; Stockman then added them up and reported back that, based on the president's choices, the remaining deficit would be $800 billion over five years. The budget director was sure the president would see that the difference had to be made up with revenue; after all, "the $800 billion worth of deficits were the result of spending he didn't want to cut." But Reagan continued to insist that "the problem is deficit spending!"[9]

Stockman and Darman decided (correctly, we think) that Reagan did not believe in the long-term deficit forecasts. "When you sit there going over the deficit projections," Darman said, "the man's eyes glaze over. He tunes out completely because he doesn't fully appreciate that the pony [a reference to a well-known joke about incorrigible optimists] is already built into the numbers."[10] In other words, though the projections assumed a strong recovery, Reagan felt that current deficits were largely due to recession and did not realize that the projections led to deficits even if the economic plan worked quite well.

What Darman did not realize was the president's desire to believe and his experience, as another adviser told us, that over a long career his usually greater optimism than his advisers' had usually been right. Why should this case be different? Why should he give up things he cared about in response to economic forecasts? And, because he was president, nobody would confront him directly; his aides, including Stockman, kept leaving him to draw the conclusion.[11]

A series of "kiss-and-tell" books have documented the president's distaste for conflict among his advisers. That distaste was fed, however, by his aides; even the most opinionated of men may be awed by the office of the president, if not by its inhabitant.[12] Thus, Stockman and Darman would not say "you're wrong"; instead they tried to trick Reagan into a tax hike with a "perfectly disingenuous plan" involving a long-term proposal to create a flat tax.[13] That plan metamorphosed, due in part to suggestions by Treasury Secretary Regan, into a "contingency" tax package, to take effect in FY86 if the deficits were too high and if Congress accepted the FY84 budget's spending cuts. Stockman found no way to argue against those proposals. By passing the tax(es) and the trigger mechanism in 1983, the government might reduce market fears of future deficits.[14]

Reagan's aides trotted in members of Congress to give him their message that the defense buildup had to be scaled back if they were to have any shot at reducing the deficit. Newt Gingrich of the Conservative Opportunity Society urged "pretty much an across-the-board freeze" for two years on defense and domestic outlays. He would sacrifice defense to save the tax cut.[15] Senate leaders also—with conservative Jake Garn (R-Utah) and Paul Laxalt (R-Nev.) leading off so that Reagan would take the message seriously—urged Reagan to back down from his stand on a continued buildup. Weinberger was requesting all the dollars in the 1981 plan, despite both lower inflation and the FY83 budget resolution agreement to scale back increases. Yet congressional Republicans weren't successful. The president's budget cut Weinberger's request but remained higher in real dollars than the original 1981 plan.

Shortly before the State of the Union message on January 25, an honor roll of the "Establishment" issued its own message. Peter G. Peterson, secretary of Commerce from 1972 to 1973 and managing partner of Lehman Bros. investment bankers, along with five former secretaries of the Treasury, organized the "Bi-Partisan Budget Appeal." Its 500 signers ranged from Gardner Ackley, chairman of the CEA under President Johnson, to Admiral Elmo R. Zumwalt, Jr., chief of Naval Operations from 1970 to 1974, from conservative economist Michael Boskin of Stanford to liberal Lester Thurow of MIT, including leaders of some of the nation's most prestigious law, accounting, and investment firms and corporations.[16]

The Bi-Partisan Appeal ad proposed a one-year freeze on universal entitlement benefits and other nondefense subsidies that were not means-tested. Afterward, indexing should be limited (e.g., to 60 percent of the CPI). These steps would (maybe) save $60 billion from the FY85 budget. Another $25 billion could be taken from defense. That would still allow for 7 percent real growth per year between 1981 and 1985. Then revenues would be increased by $60 billion in FY85. Because the Appeal's supporters were particularly concerned about investment, they preferred consumption taxes (such as a national VAT or excises) and user fees. Income tax changes would be approved "*only* in the context of a prior agreement on the kind and magnitude of spending cuts" specified above. In turn, entitlement, defense, and revenue measures to reduce the deficit would lower interest payments by about $30 billion and thus reduce the FY85 deficit by $175 billion.

The Bi-Partisan Appeal went nowhere; given its honor roll of sponsors, this in itself is worth some attention. If there is a "power elite" in American society, Peter Peterson had rounded it up, and it proved powerless.

But the appeal is interesting because, give or take $10 or $20 billion in the estimates, it was actually a serious proposal to reduce the deficits; its logic and failure thereby illuminate the basic difficulty. First, because such a large deficit reduction in FY85 would have to take effect largely in FY84, the Appeal was suggesting a sharp contraction of fiscal policy in the early stages of a weak recovery. The proposed debt reductions would exceed the planned 1983 stimulus expected from the third stage of the tax cut and defense buildup, and thus they would leave fiscal policy tighter than it had been at the time the Bi-Partisan Appeal appeared.[17] As they belatedly realized this, Keynesian sponsors such as Alfred Kahn and Lester Thurow recanted their support for the plan. Second, $60 billion in extra revenues in FY85 was a lot of money. Economists like consumption taxes, but states (because sales taxes are their main revenue source) and Democrats (because they are regressive) do not. Because higher corporate taxes were hardly what the Appeal's sponsors had in mind and because the president would oppose income tax changes, there was no good, that is, harmless or painless, way to find the needed revenues.

Domestic savings of $60 billion might be possible, but it would mean more than a 10 percent reduction (in real dollars) in such benefits. Most Democrats had little interest in that idea; when it came right down to it, neither did many Republicans.

Even in failure, the Bi-Partisan Appeal foreshadowed quick rejection of the president's budget. If such a business-oriented and prosperous group called for scaling back the defense buildup and opposed further cuts in the means-tested programs, citing medicaid and legal services as examples, administration priorities were in trouble. Reagan had lost the center.

Another Dead Budget

The FY84 budget was FY83 with new wrapping: a claimed "freeze" in total outlays, which would be held to a 5 percent increase for inflation. Because the essence of budgeting is the unwrapping and inspection of packages, the decorative rhetoric of a freeze did not help. Defense and interest payments accounted for the entire spending increase, domestic spending would not grow at all, thereby losing by the amount of inflation. The budget included many structural policy changes as well, such as eliminating Legal Services, which had been rejected in 1982. If these were rejected, then the tax package, of course, could not be proposed.

Primed for a fight, House Democrats began 1983 by kicking Phil Gramm off the Budget Committee. Such punishments for opposing the party were extremely rare. But the Speaker now had a secure majority, and Gramm had reported private deliberations to Stockman. As one House leader commented, "In any army he'd have been shot at sunrise."[18] (Gramm replied by resigning his seat; he then won a special election as a Republican and was put back on Budget by his new colleagues. In 1984 he was elected to the Senate, but that gets a bit ahead of our story.)

Still on the offensive for jobs, the Speaker declared that "I can't conceive of a freeze on domestic spending, to be perfectly truthful." Howard Baker was not willing to fight on the president's ground. "There is going to be a real donnybrook . . . a ferocious debate" about defense, he declared, and led a delegation to talk Cap Weinberger into changes before the budget was published.[19] No luck. Robert Dole said food stamp cuts were out and some other programs might have to be increased. Representative Denny Smith (R-Oreg.) expressed the common response to Reagan's proposed freeze when he said that "in order to get a freeze, we have to be fair about it. The President's plan isn't going anywhere."[20] Silvio Conte predicted that as Congress worked on the budget "there will be a hell of a shift from defense to social programs, no doubt about it."[21] A *Newsweek* poll found 49 percent of the public preferring to cut defense spending, 25 percent preferring to cut domestic spending, and 12 percent preferring tax hikes in order to reduce the deficit.[22] *Business Week* found that 85 percent of its sample of corporate executives agreed with the (admittedly rather leading) statement that "Republican senators were right when they told the president he must make substantial cuts in defense spending if the budget deficit is to be attacked."[23]

In spite of presidential calls for bipartisanship, *Time* reported, "the only shred of bipartisan agreement is over Reagan's plan for a stand-by tax increase; almost everyone agrees it will not fly." Barber Conable and Robert Dole announced their opposition even before the State of the Union.[24] With Dole, Conable, and Baker publicly opposed, the contingency tax died. Democrats wanted tax increases sooner and spending cuts much later, if at all. Russell Long joined Tip O'Neill in calling for repeal of both the third year of Kemp-Roth and indexing.

House leaders wanted to use their new majority to establish a strong Democratic position. Budgeters like Jones and Gephardt wanted to reach out to the members, including the leadership, and show how tough the problem was. Both sets of purposes were served by working through the Democratic caucus and by distributing a survey questionnaire titled "An Exercise in Hard Choices" to all Democratic representatives. A senior Budget Committee aide recalled:

The survey was a really good idea. . . . It had two purposes: to educate the members and to get them to internalize the facts of life; and it had more value than expected in detecting consensus. Not on Medicare, which is too complicated. But it was good on defense, where the consensus was heavily at 3 percent.

The Speaker, he added, "got into it. He liked taking it, trying to lower his score, like with golf. He took it a few times." But O'Neill, like Reagan, did not change preferences after the quizzes.

While the survey found areas of agreement, divisions remained. Die-hard liberals, like the AFL-CIO, wanted lots of antirecession spending and a cap on the third year of the tax cut. Ways and Means Chairman Rostenkowski, however, believed that repeal or limitation of the third year would not get through Congress. It was bad politics, he believed, to stand up for an unpopular position without even a chance of winning. His committee told the Budget Committee it could do only $8 billion for FY84. Rosty had his own freeze proposal, suspending all tax law changes scheduled for after December 31, 1983. That would have nixed indexing and raised substantial dollars. His party leaders felt the Ways and Means chairman was undercutting their position on the third year of the tax cut.[25] The disagreement foreshadowed the fact that even if the budget resolution mandated a big tax increase, Ways and Means would not produce it.

The same was true in the Senate, where Dole was not ready for another round. Soon enough, as a perverse fate would have it, Dole was engaged in a bitter battle to keep taxes from being lowered.

An Interlude of Normal Politics

The vehicle chosen for tax reduction was a supplemental appropriations bill to replenish the Unemployment Insurance fund. On February 10, the White House and House Democrats had agreed to add another $4.3 billion to the supplemental jobs bill. Many of its details had been suggested by a House Republican task force on employment opportunities, and the administration had gone along, in part because of heavy pressure from House Minority Leader Michel.[26] The president's staff considered $3.6 billion of that as acceleration of existing projects, to be deducted from later spending. Democrats, following Reagan's rule of taking part of the loaf and coming back for more, reserved the right to add to that spending in later years.[27]

Some jobs proposals required authorization, but, to expedite progress, O'Neill sent the whole package directly to the Appropriations Committee. After some battles on the House floor over the targeting of benefits—to districts with high unemployment and to districts represented by members of Appropriations—the jobs package grew to $4.9 billion. Upon House passage on March 3, the White House began suggesting that this was not quite the original deal.

Senators added supplemental funds for CCC (yes, farmers again) and Small Business Administration (SBA) loans.[28] They also disagreed with the House on the substance and distribution of the jobs bill dollars. Senators provided more for human services and less for construction and more for smaller states (surprise!). The distribution was so controversial that Chairman Hatfield won by only one vote on a compromise to his original plan. The major obstacle to passage of the bill came out of left field, as it were, when Robert Kasten (R-Wis.) on March 10 suddenly proposed an amendment to repeal the withholding of estimated taxes on interest income.

Dole's 1982 victory on interest withholding was probably the year's biggest surprise. As individual banks looked at the new requirements, they became seriously upset. The thrifts and smaller banks were the most concerned. A lobbyist explained that the big money center banks actually liked withholding because "they handle dividends for corporations and they could charge corporations for the service."

By early 1983, the smaller institutions had mobilized. They claimed it would cost $1.5 billion to administer the 10-percent withholding of interest on their accounts.[29] Although that fact explained their concern, it was no way to mobilize voter pressure on Congress; instead, bankers told their customers that the government was going to take their money away. A sample speech declared that withholding would "loot your savings account." One ad led off in large, boldface type: "Warning: 10 percent of the money you earn in interest is going to disappear"—with the word "disappear" fading to white.[30] Although the body of the ad did explain that this was not a new tax and that there were exemptions for the poor and elderly, it raised fears effectively enough. Financial institutions also stuffed annual 1099 interest-report forms with printed post cards for their depositors to send to Congress. Out of maybe 80 million such cards, 4 million or more came to Congress in January and February; that was only the beginning. Dole had thirteen staffers answering nearly 450,000 pieces of mail. Banks and other savings institutions had generated the greatest flood of mail in congressional history.

Legislators will always tell you that handwritten letters, not preprinted cards, get their attention. But at some point, maybe around the millionth card, an organized campaign does begin to be noticed. By the time Kasten chose to add repeal of withholding to the supplemental, various other repeal bills already had 52 cosponsors in the Senate and 320 in the House.

Furious, Dole threatened to fight fire with fire. He announced that twenty of the nation's largest banks had paid taxes of only 2.7 percent on domestic income in 1981. "Now you know," he declared, "why they have so much money to send out mail . . . to intimidate Congress."[31] Immediately he called for a Finance Committee hearing on banking taxes. As committee Democrats dove for cover, saying they would "have nothing to do with such a reprisal" against the bankers, Chairman Dole proclaimed innocently that "there is no relationship" between the hearings and the drive to repeal withholding—"no direct relationship," he amended.[32] In addition to threatening reprisals, Dole held the supplemental hostage by a virtual filibuster. With some states scheduled to run out of money for unemployment benefits during the week of March 13, he hoped to get senators to table Kasten's amendment rather than delay further.

The Finance chairman also enlisted the president. Convinced that withholding was an issue of tax compliance, Reagan accused the banks of "a great distortion of the situation." "I'm deeply disturbed," he added, "that the jobs bill will suddenly become a Christmas tree for special-interest legislation. I think that the banking industry would do a lot better to spend its time thinking about lowering interest rates than lobbying the way they are. I would veto such legislation."[33] Kasten stuck to his guns. It isn't often that a freshman senator gets to be the hero of a huge interest group. Back-bench senators of both parties were caught between their leaders and the massive lobbying blitz. Dole failed to table Kasten's proposal; Kasten failed by one vote to win cloture on Dole.

Here was a true standoff, as both Kasten and Dole now held the unemployed hostage. Finally, they cut a deal in which Dole promised that Kasten could move his amendment onto a trade bill after the Easter recess.[34]

The Senate passed the (by now rather large) supplemental on March 17. Conferees wrangled over distribution and amount of jobs spending; Stockman threatened a presidential veto because $5.2 billion in jobs spending was too high. By March 21, various states began to run out of unemployment money. A conference agreement was passed and signed on March 24, with the extra jobs spending reduced to $4.6 billion, fairly close to the original $4.3 billion agreed between House Democrats and the administration.[35]

This final compromise marked the end of the period, beginning in early 1982, during which Democrats in the House had held the edge in a series of raids against the president's program. It soon became apparent that the recession had ended, but the deficit remained. As the jobs issue faded, Senate Republicans refused to add to the domestic budget.

The appropriations battle settled into roughly a two-year stalemate. The White House lost on spending cut proposals that involved real policy changes, but Democrats did not get anywhere with their selective spending increases. The appropriations committees shaved a little here and there from agency budgets, leaving most agencies with only slightly reduced current spending levels. No one knew it then, but most spending had gone on automatic pilot.

Before we return to the search for yet another package to reduce the deficit, we should finish the tale of Senator Dole and the banks. The proponents of interest withholding hoped that during the Easter recess members of Congress would discover that the millions of cards represented wide but not very deep sentiments, standing only as a passing result of the bankers' massive efforts. They were wrong. "It became an 'issue in which little old ladies in tennis shoes are a problem,' recalled Rep. Leon Panetta."[36] When the Senate returned, members' experience back home was reinforced by the continuing flood of mail—up to 750,000 pieces a day.

Dole won a few provisions to make life unpleasant for the banks, but the Senate repealed withholding 91 to 5. When Rosty stalled, a repeal bill was blasted out of Ways and Means with a discharge petition. By the time it passed, 382 to 41, House members had received 22 million pieces of mail on the issue.[37]

The fights over distributing jobs spending and repealing interest withholding were pure "interest-group politics."[38] This kind of politics has always given Congress a bad name, but at least it was easy to understand. We asked one lobbyist why his side won on withholding but, after 1981, kept losing on depreciation. He replied:

> We tried, but never got the grassroots populism, smaller banks, and citizens that withholding did. On that, Republicans found their donations dropping off. Dole was reduced to holding press conferences with Ralph Nader and Ted Kennedy. You don't manufacture something like that. You could not put cards in the bank lobbies on the Clean Air Act or social security COLAs [to cut them] or the deficit. . . . [Depreciation] affects a narrow portion of the business community, and you can't generate those cards from the employees' lounge.

Exactly. You win if you have the votes; that in turn depends on how many people feel your policy will help or hurt them. By comparison, the battle over the FY84 first resolution involved such confusion and had so little to do with actual spending and taxing that pure interest group politics looks attractively quaint and practical.

The First (and Last) Resolution
or, Wanted: a Budget, Dead or Alive

"The way to reconcile the irreconcilable is to choose the flat-out impossible."[39] Using the results of the questionnaire distributed to all House Democrats, along with the March 15, 1983, committee reports and input from Democratic caucus meetings, House Budget Committee Democrats held a series of closed meetings and drew up a distinctly Democratic plan. They added to the president's budget for FY84 $32 billion in domestic outlays, cut defense outlays by $9 billion, and raised revenues by $30 billion. They cut defense budget authority by even more, $16 billion, allowing a 4 percent real increase rather than either the 10 percent requested by the White House or the 7.5 percent suggested by House Armed Services.

Democrats unveiled their plan on March 17, as the full House Budget Committee met to work on a budget, ramming it through the panel in one day on straight party-line votes and defeating all attempts at amendments. The committee requested a rule that would allow only one comprehensive amendment. Rules agreed, stating that only the Republican leadership would be allowed to offer a substitute. The Republicans wanted to offer a series of amendments, perhaps as many as fifteen, but could not agree on one.

The parties had reversed positions since 1981; at a disadvantage on overall priorities, the GOP now wanted to fight on the specifics. The Democratic plan passed 229 to 196 on March 23. Twenty-six new Democrats made the difference.[40]

The biggest problem for Republicans was the defense number.[41] At the beginning of March, as stories exposing waste in the Pentagon began to hit the front pages, *Time* ran a cover story about a previously obscure Defense Department analyst named Franklin C. Spinney. Chuck Spinney, who worked in the DOD's Office of Program Analysis and Evaluation, was not really saying that the Pentagon needed less money. In fact, one could have concluded from his analysis that the Pentagon actually required more. But his evaluation was such a damning indictment of Pentagon procedures that the natural reaction was to cut the military because they could not be trusted with the money. Clumsy Pentagon efforts to suppress or refute Spinney's analysis only added to the sense of scandal.[42]

From the Pentagon came a series of horror stories. Let the *Post* tell the story:

> Just behind the cockpit in the world's most sophisticated radar plane, on the leg of a folding blue-and-gray stool, sits the world's most expensive plastic cap.
>
> What distinguishes this particular cap from any other lump of white nylon is that the Air Force paid its government supplier $1,118.26 for it, which is roughly the cost of the plastic, plus $1,118.[43]

We will spare the reader further details; suffice it to say that neither Boeing Aircraft nor the military procurement system came out looking very good.

Now, ordinary people can't really argue with the military about the costs of high-tech weapons. But anybody knows that $1,118.26 for a plastic cap is excessive; and most people assume that officials who first suppress criticism and then answer it with false reports probably have something to hide.[44] Even as President Reagan used anecdotes about people buying vodka with food stamps to judge that food stamps could be cut, stories about defense waste convinced the public that, even if a buildup were needed, the Pentagon should finance some of it by getting its own house in order.

In spite of the rash of bad publicity, Reagan campaigned heavily for his buildup. On March 15 he asked Domenici to delay SBC's action on the first resolution while he tried to rally support. The president's rather lonesome campaign climaxed on the night of March 23 (after the House passed its First Resolution) when he made a television address to the nation. Reagan made the usual comparisons of U.S. and Soviet strength and the standard argument about the West's disarmament in the 1930s. But in concluding his speech, the president "launched the debate over U.S. military spending into an entirely different orbit."[45] He proposed a massive new program—the Strategic Defense Initiative (SDI)—in order to create a space-based system of defense against ballistic missiles.

Whatever SDI's merits, they did not include helping win support for the president's defense budget. "I would have preferred that speech during the Easter recess if it was not going to focus on the budget," Robert Michel groused, meaning that SDI had just diverted attention from House Democrats' domestic spending and tax hike plans. For the moment, SDI merely injected an extra level of controversy into the defense spending brouhaha.

On April 5 Reagan met with Senate Budget Republicans. Domenici had put together a tentative plan, including 5 percent real growth for defense. Seeking to avoid a collision, Majority Leader Howard Baker proposed 7.5 percent, with slightly less in the out-years. This was really no different from what had been agreed in 1982, but Weinberger had backed out. Baker warned Reagan that his plan was the best the administration could hope for. Domenici was not exactly enthusiastic anyway. Reagan decided to go along if Weinberger agreed, but then no one could find Weinberger.

> By the time Ronald Reagan put in a call to . . . Domenici, the votes were lined up, the numbers had been written on a big green chalkboard and the clerk was ready to call the roll. But Domenici, his teeth clenched with anger, nevertheless excused himself, stubbing out yet another Merit cigarette as he made his way to the phone booth marked "Senators Only." Domenici listened politely, his face noticeably reddening as Reagan barked into the phone: "I'm the president and I want you to hold off for a while. People in that committee are up for reelection. They're going to be coming to me for help."
>
> Reagan's threat came too late. After Domenici hung up the phone, he joined all but four Republicans on the budget committee in voting for a defense spending increase that came to only half what the president had wanted.[46]

Stockman reports that Weinberger finally had agreed to compromise, but by the time Reagan called Domenici it was already too late. "Why," Senator Grassley asked, "should we dump huge sums of money into the Defense Department when it is rotting with bad management?"[47] His voters were saying, "Turn off the spigot!" As Robert Michel put it, "That consensus . . . you once felt out there to recoup on the military isn't there anymore."[48]

With defense seemingly settled, Senate Budget turned to revenues. That was more difficult. Democrats proposed tax increases of $30.2 billion in FY84 and more in the out-years (figures very like those in the House package), but they lost on a tie vote. Then the president's tax plan was rejected, 8 to 14, with six Republicans against it. They knew what they were against, but what were they for?

On April 18, Stockman bluntly warned the president that "almost none of the huge policy savings" that the administration desired "can be achieved without congressional-administration agreement." Instead, "a runaway anti-administration resolution could emerge through de facto Democratic dominance over [a] split GOP in [the] Senate Budget Committee and through further compromise in budget conference."[49] The budget director was fighting privately (and publicly; the memo was immediately leaked) with Weinberger, who suggested that the president abandon the budget process and go it alone with a veto strategy on appropriations. Simultaneous consideration of defense and deficits, said Weinberger, would work against defense. Vetoes, Stockman argued, excluded any efforts to change entitlement policy.[50] Stockman won approval to negotiate further, but divisions over defense and revenues prevented agreement on April 20, when all twelve Republicans on SBC met with Stockman, Meese, and Jim Baker.

"We must continue to try to get a compromise," Domenici declared, "or the deficits will threaten economic recovery."[51] That refrain could be dropped randomly into any year's debate. But the Republican majority had disappeared. Dole was balking on revenues, and the Gang of Five moderates (Hatfield, Mathias, Weicker, Stafford, and Chafee) were becoming much more independent.

On the Democratic side, Hollings had succeeded to the ranking position on the Commerce Committee; he yielded his ranking spot on Budget to Lawton Chiles. Far more a conciliator and deal maker, Chiles wanted to shape the process, either by offering a Democratic alternative or by dealing with Domenici. A party man, Domenici would do it with Republicans if he could, but he and Chiles were personally close. Around this time, Slade Gorton (R-Wash.) began outlining a package, consulting with both Domenici and Chiles about what might prove acceptable in an emergency. A participant recalls that Domenici "was very sympathetic from the beginning but also thought that he couldn't do it on his own due to his relations with the president, Howard Baker, and the Republican caucus." Domenici would use Gorton as a fallback.

On April 21, a last effort to unite Republicans was stymied by the antitax faction. Domenici then joined Gorton, Mark Andrews, and Nancy Kassebaum in support of Chiles's revenue figures, and SBC passed a resolution that also included the 5 percent defense increase and $11 billion more for domestic spending than the administration had desired. "I couldn't wait any longer," Domenici recalled. "I made a decision there was little chance of getting a solid Republican budget resolution. I think I was right." Domenici would try again on the floor. Dole's response to the Budget Committee's tax figure was "speechless; stronger letter to follow."[52]

On the floor, the Senate rejected, by big margins, four more extreme plans: Hollings's freeze; a conservative Democratic package with large new taxes; a Grassley domestic plus defense freeze; and a more-Reagan-than-Reagan budget, sponsored by Orrin Hatch, taking big chops at social spending. That left three alternatives: the SBC plan; a Domenici-Baker substitute, lukewarmly endorsed by Reagan; and one devised by the Gang-of-Five moderate Republicans. On May 12 the Gang of Five joined Democrats to table the leadership budget, 52 to 48. Then they accepted an amendment by Gorton, whose plan allowed slightly higher defense spending and restructured the tax hikes. Gorton's figures were numbers both Dole and Rostenkowski would accept for FY84–85 and numbers the president's contingency proposed for FY86, but they had the support of neither camp and lost 46 to 53. Then the full Senate rejected the SBC plan because its tax provisions were too high—back to the drawing board.

After this unsuccessful round, Howard Baker wrote an opinion piece in the *Post,* with a promising title, "We Will Pass a Budget Resolution":

> Equating a simple budget resolution with democracy itself may seem a bit dramatic, but the congressional budget process lies at the heart of modern and coherent democracy. What we spend determines how we govern, and nowhere is that fact in sharper focus than when all the problems of government descend on one set of people in one room at one time during budget resolution season.

Baker was joined by CEA Chairman Feldstein and leaders of the National Governors Association in the chorus of calls for responsibility.[53] As usual, exhortation was no substitute for consensus. If only the president would accept more taxes. . . . Instead he had rejected Domenici and Baker's warnings that a compromise on taxes was needed, leaving Domenici, according to one aide, "as angry as I've ever seen him." Then in a radio speech Reagan declared that "governments don't reduce deficits by raising taxes on the people." This was news to state governors, most of whom had been forced to do exactly that, as well as cut spending, to meet their states' balanced budget requirements. Yet neither Howard Baker nor the governors nor much of anybody except liberal Democrats supported specific tax increases. In a letter on April 28, 146 House Republicans—enough to sustain a veto—pledged that they would oppose any change in the July tax cut or indexing.[54] The president was the key not because he was stopping Congress from doing what it wanted to do but because Republicans and moderate Democrats wanted him to take the flak for the increases. Reagan chose not to lead Congress against himself.

Senate Budget tried again on May 18. Domenici supported a modified Gorton-Chiles plan, but it lost 8 to 12. SBC rejected its previous plan by the same margin. Then, reversing its alignment a week before, it passed a new Domenici-Baker plan, 11 to 9. That resolution hit the Senate floor on May 19. By then the Democratic leadership had finally decided to back the Gorton-Chiles plan. Senator Byrd, an aide recalled, "was strongly against passing a Democratic budget" but was convinced by the argument that "Christ, it's only a budget, it doesn't mean anything." A victory would be good for the troop's morale.

The Budget Committee plan went down as all the Democrats and ten Republicans joined to defeat it, 56 to 43. Gorton-Chiles lost, 52 to 48, when thirteen mostly southern Democrats voted against it. As usual with

Senate Democrats, leadership was weak. A revised Domenici plan lost 57 to 43. By then it was near midnight, and Howard Baker in essence conceded. He asked the Senate to reconsider Gorton-Chiles and urged his colleagues to pass *something*.[55] His motion to reconsider carried 55 to 45, as a number of GOP leaders, including Baker, supported the move. Gorton-Chiles then was adopted as an amendment to the SBC plan, 53 to 47, as five Republicans who originally opposed it switched votes.

When the Senate voted on final passage of a budget resolution, now amended as the Gorton-Chiles plan, it got the same twenty Republican votes as before, but four Democrats—Patrick Leahy (Vt.), David Pryor (Ark.), Wendell Ford (Ky.), and minority whip Alan Cranston (Calif.)—now voted against final passage. Because Senator Goldwater had gone home, that left the margin at 50 nay to 49 aye. Democrats had put Domenici on the spot; at the last moment he switched, and the Gorton-Chiles plan passed 50 to 49. Republicans opposed it 32 to 21; Democrats supported it 29 to 17.[56]

The numbers suggest a fairly bipartisan resolution; but the way they occurred shows that there was no real agreement. The Democratic leadership was in no way committed to the substance. A resolution had passed the Senate, but its provisions, particularly for revenue, could not be enacted by that body. There really was no majority for anything. A senior Senate aide recalls worrying that a resolution that could not be enforced would kill the budget process. But so would passing no resolution at all. Domenici had no good choices.

Among a chorus of pessimistic comments, James Jones said that "this could be the shortest Congress to deal with substance." Bob Dole judged that "the odds are even that all bets are off until January of 1985." And a top Senate Republican aide commented that "this Congress is over. Everyone's waiting for 1984."[57] Rather than concede defeat, budget leaders conferred in search of the best possible impossible resolution. On June 20 they settled on a tax increase target close to the Senate number; they split the difference on defense (a 5 percent increase) and accommodated the domestic spending differences by roughly accepting the Senate numbers, while providing a "contingency fund" of $8.5 billion in new spending that would be allowed if authorizing legislation passed. Because authorizing legislation would be vetoed, this was a victory for the Senate. But new authorizations would be vetoed no matter what the budget resolution said, so it wasn't much of a loss for the House. King Solomon could have taken lessons from our legislators on "splitting the difference." More optimistic (and, this time, more realistic) economic assumptions reduced the projected deficits. Reconciliation instructions required $12.3 billion in savings from 1984 to 1985, mostly in civil service pensions, dairy price supports, and medicare.

By most standards, the Senate had "won." Yet because its position had not really been that of Senate Republicans, other Republicans were not satisfied. House Republicans did not even show up for the final meeting of the conference. Senator Domenici called the deal a "miracle"; Representative Latta called it treachery; and Ronald Reagan dressed down the Senate chairman in a meeting with Republican congressional leaders.[58]

All along, the Gorton-Chiles leaders had hoped Dole didn't mean it when he denounced the tax increase plans. "Our assumption about reconciliation," one aide recalls, "was always that it enables authorizing chairmen to say, 'they made me do it.' " "Finance loves getting reconciliation instructions from the budget," one senator recalls. "They don't want to be told how to do it, but love getting a target." They were wrong; Dole attempted to amend the conference report to reduce the revenue figure. "We were speechless," an aide recalls, for that isn't done. "We should have realized," he added, "that if a legislative player like Dole, with all those years of experience, proposes to amend a conference report, he must be serious and you had better listen." Dole was supported by Russell Long, who argued that "to try to pass a tax increase of these kind of numbers without the support of the president of the United States is just ridiculous."[59] Dole's amendment lost 41 to 51. With Howard Baker and seventeen other Republicans supporting Domenici, the conference report passed 51 to 43. Its passage, however, reflected only the senators' desire to finish the battle.

The president, referring to his own budget, not Congress's, promised to "veto their budget-busting bills again and again and again." Dole kept calling the budget a "dead cat" and other unpleasant things. A "budget" had passed, but no agreement had been forged. Being speechless meant being budgetless.

Packages and Formulas

If the budget process had failed to create an acceptable package, the budgeters would try to create a package outside that process. Foremost among them was Senator Dole, who was just as insistent about doing something as about not doing what the budget resolution prescribed. In early July he called for an "economic summit meeting" between Reagan and congressional leaders. The White House refused; David Gergen commented that Congress "would just use [such a summit] to beat the president over the head."[60] When that went nowhere, Dole worked to create a package within Finance.

Why Dole thought he could succeed where Domenici had failed remains a mystery. Perhaps he thought a more "balanced" package could win Reagan's support, and once Reagan was on board his party would have to go along. Reagan publicly opposed Dole's efforts, but the senator persisted. After one particularly strong presidential statement, Dole remarked that "there are a lot of ways to interpret 'no,' " and placed the president in the "undecided category."[61] Most likely Dole felt Reagan would support a more "balanced" package at the last moment, that, as a good politician, the president was driving a hard bargain and was willing to let others do the spadework. There was surely political advantage in publicly leading the forces of "responsible budgeting," a role that won Dole a great deal of favorable media coverage. If he could bridge the gap between Reagan and more traditional budget-balancing Republicans, he would do good (by his own lights) and possibly increase his political support in both camps. The White House political types might win over Reagan. It had happened before. The budget responsibility faction of Democrats—Jones, Panetta, Gephardt et al.—had allies, especially among freshmen and might be able to pressure the Speaker. If the pressure were great enough and if Dole's "solution" looked better than the budget resolution, perhaps the president would seize it. Responsibility would triumph.

Reagan, however, had his own definition of responsibility: keep taxes low and strengthen the nation's defenses. The Speaker's definition differed from Dole's or Reagan's: O'Neill's was to protect the legacy of his party, to use government's power to aid the economy's losers, and to help Democrats win the 1984 election. Because the public and the media believed Dole's (and Domenici's, and Chiles's) version of responsibility, the deficits gave O'Neill and Reagan a fine club with which to bash each other's heads, though neither would get so carried away as to abandon his primary purpose. From mid-1983 to mid-1985, therefore, Speaker O'Neill and President Reagan would continually frustrate the efforts of Dole and his colleagues to enforce budget "responsibility."

This is not to say that Congress wanted to spend wildly. Remembering the chaos of 1982, in 1983 appropriations leaders were willing to cut a few dollars if that would settle the disputes, enable everyone involved to make plans, and give themselves the good feelings that go with having passed a bill. In spite of some messy battles—abortion on the Treasury/Postal bill, for example—action generally was far more orderly than in previous years. Major Reagan policy initiatives such as abandoning Legal Services were, as usual, rejected. But so, after the early supplemental, were efforts of House leadership to increase social spending. The appropriations leaders put together, if barely, bills that everyone could live with, funded agencies and programs, and then let the fight for more spending take place on supplementals and through specific provisions added to short-term continuing resolutions.

House and Senate appropriations leaders buffered the agency funding process from the chaos of the partisan budget wars. They could not have succeeded if Reagan had, as advertised, pursued a tough veto strategy. Stockman mocks his colleagues for proclaiming and then not following that course.[62] Yet, perhaps remembering the 1982 supplemental override and how defense had been held hostage in the CR, a senior White House official recalled that "they presented us with total spending under the limits and moved it around." And "you can't veto the defense bill," he added; "then you get zero . . . .We would have vetoed if we thought we could do anything . . . [but] what would we have accomplished? We would just have gotten it back in a CR. And, as we all knew, most of the excess spending is not in appropriations." Besides, another official recalled, it was not as if the whole administration were united behind that budget: "Even the cabinet members wouldn't support the veto."

Instead, the administration tried to cut deals with Republican leaders on Appropriations. A senior OMB official recalled that by 1983 the administration was working with Appropriations Republicans "with the goal of preventing them from making a deal with the Democrats. We would work with the Senate to get a standard, and then try to get the House senior Republicans to push that standard in the early salvoes with the Democrats." These Republicans opposed Reagan's cuts but were equally suspicious of program increases.[63]

The real conflict on Appropriations involved additions to or riders on continuing resolutions. At one point, when Appropriations members tried to invoke the War Powers Act on the first CR in regard to the American troops in Lebanon, the Speaker took the unprecedented step of referring the CR to the Foreign Affairs Committee for review and burial. As a result, in this first go-around, the Speaker ended up committed to a clean bill as a matter of principle and could not tack on some planned extra spending. The new CR passed the House 261 to 160 on September 28. The Senate, impressed by the House's example or perhaps convinced of plenty of remaining time in an odd-numbered year, also practiced restraint and actually passed the continuing resolution without trouble, and on time, by September 30.

The stalemate on appropriations showed that Congress was not in a spending mood. But the mild squeeze would not help much against deficits that now were greater then the total domestic discretionary budget. Significant spending cuts would have to come from entitlements or not at all. That brings us back to Senator Dole and his allies. "We will have to raise taxes," Dole declared, "but we will have to cut spending first."

During the summer, while Dole called for a process that might yield a package, other legislators looked for a formula around which people might rally. In the Senate, John Danforth (R-Mo.), David Boren (D-Okla.), and Malcolm Wallop (R-Wy.) filed a bill to reduce scheduled adjustments in both COLA benefit payments and the new tax indexing by 3 percent each year from 1985 to 1988. In the House, James Jones and Carroll A. Campbell, Jr. (R-S.C.) joined four Republicans and four Democrats in a similar bill, cutting COLAs and limiting tax bracket indexing by 2 percent each year. The 3 percent solution would bring in $116.7 billion over four years; the 2 percent formula, $77.6 billion. Both left AFDC and other programs for the poor untouched. Richard Cohen explained the attraction of these formulas:

> Each quickly raises a large amount of money by relatively simple legislative actions. Each raises about half its deficit savings from tax increases and half from spending cuts. Each spreads the pain in small doses to most of the population, except for the very poor. And each requires concessions of important political principles by both Republicans and Democrats.[64]

These plans met the prevailing test of equity. But their attacks on the tax cut (Reagan's cherished principle) and social security (the Democrats'), though gradual, still meant more than an 8 percent tax hike and social security cut.

House Democrats already had taken one deficit-reduction measure, passing a $700 cap on the July tax cut, despite skepticism in their own ranks. Leon Panetta feared a "substantial political backlash."[65] A letter sent to O'Neill from seventy-nine Democrats declared that "taking such action without any accompanying cap on spending is flawed policy."[66] In spite of these doubts, the party gave the Speaker a 229 to 191 victory on June 23.

In the Senate, the six moderates who had spearheaded the drive for the eventual budget resolution also called for limiting the July tax cut. But Majority Leader Baker argued that the cap was a futile political gesture, sure to be vetoed, and convinced the moderates to support the cap's party-line defeat, 55 to 45.[67] The liberals therefore had to go back to the drawing board in search of a tax-hike package that would meet the budget resolution's $73 billion target.[68]

When Congress went home for its August recess, it was accompanied by a chorus of criticism. Persistent yet always sardonic, Dole observed that "no one is exactly marching on Washington asking us to raise revenues."[69] "We've met our fiscal enemy and it is us," declared Barber Conable. "We're hypocrites if we pretend anything else."[70] The "us" of Conable's comment should not have been Congress alone; it also was the American people, who, nevertheless, complained to their representatives about the deficit. When the members returned to Washington in September, the stalemate continued at a heightened level of anxiety.

Failure in the House

House Democratic leadership polled its members again about how they preferred to reduce the deficit. This time only half responded, and the results were sufficiently inconclusive or inconvenient that they were filed and kept secret by the staff of the Steering and Policy Committee.[71] The Democratic Study Group (DSG), heart of the liberal faction, pushed for quick action on taxes in spite of the electoral risk; in order to get that far, they would accept some spending restraint. Freshmen Democrats formed another faction that pressed the party to devise deficit-reducing legislation.[72] Between the economic consequences of deficits and the squeeze put on the budget by increasing interest costs, freshman Jim Moody (D-Wis.) argued, the party had "to choose between the early poison of a tax increase and the later poison of not being able to govern."[73] The Speaker put DSG Chairman Matthew McHugh (D-N.Y.) in charge of developing a tax package separately from the work of Ways and Means, along with Moody, the ubiquitous Richard Gephardt, and Donald J. Pease (D-Ohio). Responding to a poll, 106 DSG members supported enough specifics to hit the $74 billion target. But that was no majority. Both Rostenkowski and Democratic Campaign Committee Chairman Tony Coelho (Calif.) were more interested in avoiding Republican attacks on Democratic taxes and blaming Republicans for the deficits than in pushing a tax bill doomed to fail anyway.[74]

A small spending reconciliation bill was considered in late October. As amended by the Budget Committee, it supposedly met its three-year, $10.3 billion target. George Miller (D-Calif.) tried to attach his "pay-as-you-go" plan to this reconciliation, but the Budget Committee convinced Rules not to allow the Miller amendment. This reconciliation passed on October 25 on a voice vote.

Controversy then moved to a small ($8 billion over three years) package of revenue increases, H. R. 4170, reported out by Ways and Means on October 21. Its most controversial provision was a curb on tax-exempt Industrial Development Bonds (IDBs). Issued by state and local governments to help finance and thus attract private business projects, these bonds were immensely popular with local governments. They were less popular with federal officials, who regretted the accompanying revenue loss and questioned the federal government's indirect financing of private investors. H. R. 4170 also extended increased premium payments for medicare part B and therefore was greeted skeptically by Rules Committee Chairman Claude Pepper. Because the major supporter of IDBs, Martin Frost (D-Tex.), was an influential member of Rules, the tax bill got hung up in that committee.[75] Liberals meanwhile eyed it as a potential vehicle for larger tax hikes.

Meanwhile, Chairman Whitten got Appropriations to report another clean CR, through February, by putting thirteen other proposals into a separate supplemental. House leaders, however, got Rules to allow amendments, and on November 8 the House added almost all of Jim Wright's nearly one billion dollars in social spending, plus some fairly bipartisan foreign military aid. All seemed to be going smoothly, until twenty-four freshman Democrats, who had been meeting with the Speaker to urge him to force the Ways and Means bill out of Rules, decided to show they were serious by voting against the CR. It lost by three votes.

The freshmen had no plan of their own, but they wanted the Ways and Means bill reported with amendments allowed, including the Pease/McHugh group's revenue increase package. House leaders began working on Rules; a new CR, with the same amendments, then passed.[76] The Senate knocked off Jim Wright's spending package.

Conferees could not agree in time to prevent a number of departments, including defense, from going without funds. Nevertheless, the president, on a trip to Asia, saw no political gain in shutting the agencies down and didn't. Rules are made to be bent. In the end, the CR passed on Sunday, November 13, with only one-tenth of Wright's package included.

Back in the Rules Committee, Martin Frost had the votes to allow an amendment on IDBs. Rostenkowski objected. On November 15, O'Neill won "a forced, amiable compromise" altering the IDB provision. Pepper got the medicare premium provisions eliminated. A medicaid extension amendment was allowed. Aside from these retreats from deficit reduction, Rules proposed votes on three revenue-raising amendments: a new Rosty freeze (excluding indexing); a cap on the third year; and a Pease/McHugh/Moody/Gephardt $32 billion three-year package "to go after people who don't vote for Democrats anyhow."[77] All these measures combined would meet the budget resolution's revenue target. They were not adopted. The rule itself was defeated, 204 to 214, as all but thirteen Republicans and a total of sixty-five Democrats voted it down. So ended the House's efforts to reduce the deficit in 1983.

"The next time I see Republican crocodile tears about the deficit," Speaker O'Neill declared, "I'm going to ask them where their party was today. Today's vote proves once again that we cannot reduce the deficit with the president sitting on the sidelines."[78] Certainly not over Reagan's opposition. The Senate was discovering the same truth.

No Go in the Senate

While House Democrats worked through ad hoc factions within their caucus and House Republicans retreated to their usual nay-saying position, the barriers of partisanship were not so great in the Senate.[79] Dole and Domenici strove to build bipartisan coalitions outward from their committees. Dole enlisted Volcker to help. At a closed meeting of the Finance Committee on October 26, the Federal Reserve chairman put the antideficit case in strong terms. According to Senator Danforth, Volcker's warning galvanized a majority of each party on the committee to begin drafting an antideficit package.

On Thursday, October 27, Dole unveiled his own "2.5% solution" (as *Newsweek* termed it), modifying the formulas proposed before the summer recess in the House and Senate, good for three years instead of four. Dole's proposal would reduce COLAs on everything except the poverty programs by a small percentage (2.5) each year. Indexing would be changed to allow a 2.5 percent tax increase each year—a major concession by Dole, the sponsor of indexing. Corporate income taxes would face a surcharge of 5 percent for the three years. Spending reductions would be extended to discretionary programs by allowing the president to impound 2.5 percent of appropriated funds each year, with a 15 percent limit on cuts to any single program. But the political costs of cutting social security perhaps would be mitigated by a provision for funneling the savings into the medicare trust fund, which was due for severe trouble by 1991. Senators Boren, Danforth, and Wallop joined Dole in presenting this modification of their earlier proposal.

While Dole worked on a deficit package, he was also in charge of a bill to increase the debt ceiling—the classic innocent victim looking to be taken hostage—by $225.6 billion. Dole hoped that his plan might forestall such maneuvers. Nevertheless, Senator Armstrong won (70 to 15) an amendment reducing the increase to $61 billion, enough only to last until February. Armstrong argued that the February deadline increased the "bargaining power" for deficit reduction. Senators then loaded the debt bill with nongermane amendments on matters ranging from press coverage of the Grenada invasion to Japanese beef imports. Lawton Chiles failed (31 to 53) in a more germane attempt to make the debt limit increase contingent on passage of legislation mandated by the reconciliation provisions of the budget. Opponents of the debt ceiling, such as Russell Long, were arguing that to endorse the increase without taking other actions meant endorsing the deficit. "I'm beginning to get the feeling," Howard Baker remarked, "that the Senate doesn't want to pass the debt limit."[80]

On October 31 Baker moved that the bill be recommitted to the Finance Committee to remove all amendments, including Armstrong's, but he lost 27 to 68. Senators wanted neither to abandon their pet projects nor to pass the debt limit. They then defeated the amended bill, 39 to 56. Most Democrats opposed the debt ceiling because they wanted the Republicans to have to vote for the deficit.

Dole had fought for a clean debt increase. When the debt ceiling was beaten, however, he remarked that its rejection provided "an opportunity to hammer something out."[81]

In a meeting with House and Senate Republican leaders, President Reagan banged on the table and vowed to veto any debt-ceiling bill that included a tax increase. "I've never seen him that mad," reported Silvio Conte.[82] Nevertheless, Dole set his committee to work devising a package that might be attached to a debt bill. Although the senator had not chosen to take the debt ceiling hostage, he could see some advantages in the result. In exploiting someone else's hijacking of the debt ceiling, as in proposing an across-the-board formula and giving the president restricted powers of impoundment, Dole's maneuvers in late 1983 foreshadowed passage of Gramm-Rudman-Hollings in 1985.

After many sessions to consider a number of approaches, including an energy tax and cuts in medicare, defense, and farm subsidies, Finance Committee bargainers put out trial balloons for a $150 billion plan. On November 3, Howard Baker convened a meeting of leaders and ranking members of the Finance, Budget, and Appropriations committees. Domenici, Hatfield, Long, and Chiles agreed that Congress should act before adjournment; but Minority Leader Byrd, who joined the meeting, argued (as also in later public comments) that action should be avoided until the president's consent was secured. Howard Baker responded that, if the Speaker were willing to go along, he would try to win over the president.

That meeting in Baker's office was a high-water mark of the bipartisan effort. That evening, however, President Reagan rejected the whole effort. He told a group of his 1980 campaign workers that "we don't face large deficits because Americans are not taxed enough. We face those deficits because the Congress still spends too much. . . . And I am prepared to veto tax increases if they send them to my desk, no matter how they arrrive."[83]

Dole dismissed this statement as "boilerplate."[84] He quipped that if his committee had to consult Reagan during the president's upcoming trip to Asia, "We'll call him. If we get a bad connection, we'll be all right."[85] Reagan, however, was not Dole's only obstacle. Senator Moynihan commented that "there are things in there we [Democrats] could not accept."[86] For example, the Speaker condemned social security COLA cuts.[87] Finance members went back to drafting a bill that would defuse some opposition, though at the cost of a smaller deficit reduction.

The Senate's reconciliation bill—$14.6 billion in spending savings over three years and $13.4 billion in revenue increases—was reported out of the Budget Committee, without recommendation, on November 4.

Meanwhile, Dole changed his larger proposal in order to defuse the president's opposition and ensure that other committees did their part for deficit reduction; $150 billion would be saved over four years instead of three, much of the tax hike would be delayed, and almost all the provisions would go into effect only if CBO certified on November 15, 1984, that spending reductions had been made. If a large percentage, but not all, had been made, that same proportion of revenue hikes would go into effect. Dole had thus adopted the president's "trigger" idea without specifying that Reagan get his preferred cuts.

At the same time, Dole abandoned the 2.5 percent chops at COLAs and tax indexing, proposing only marginal, "rounding" adjustments. His major revenue provisions now were a 2 percent tax on energy products, a 2 percent extra tax on corporate income, and a surcharge on individuals with large tax bills. Senate Finance's consideration of Dole's new plan on November 16 "quickly descended," the *National Journal* reported, "into a murky discussion of small and obscure reforms." On the Senate floor that day Domenici and Chiles unveiled their own plan, an amendment to bring the reconciliation into compliance with the budget's deficit-reduction totals, essentially by accepting Dole's original 2.5 percent solution but throwing out the COLA reductions, a plan better for Republicans than the budget resolution but worse than Dole's target and very different from Reagan's wishes. Although they denied any such intent, it looked as if they were challenging the jurisdiction of the Finance Committee, and Dole opposed them on those grounds. The budget leaders' plan was easily defeated by an alliance of conservative Republicans with Democrats who believed, in the words of Russell Long, that "it doesn't accomplish much to be one of the dead bodies on the battlefield after the smoke has cleared."[88]

In the early hours of November 17, Howard Baker got the debt ceiling through the Senate, 58 to 40.[89] Conferees agreed on enough debt to get the government through April and threw out the Senate's assorted riders. Congress adjourned.

No reconciliation bill had been passed; the budget resolution's revenue targets had been ignored by everyone but the liberal Democrats. "As we leave Washington," Dan Rostenkowski declared, "word of our impotence will precede us. We have put special interests on notice that we can be pushed around. We have confessed to an already doubting nation that we are ruled by political fear, rather than economic courage." Senator Dole explained, "There are two stumbling blocks. One, Ronald Reagan; the other, Tip O'Neill. Unless we have the two giants in this town on board, we're not going to put together a deficit-reduction package."[90]

If the readers' patience has been taxed, think of the poor legislator. The meal was frustration pie. Everyone had to eat it. Just when they thought this monotonous diet had to end, they ate more than they ever thought possible. What remained was discovering newer and more fiendish ways of exasperating themselves.

SEVENTEEN

Budgeting Without Rules

We could tell three stories about the budget battles of 1984. The first is about shameless electioneering. The second is about the collapse of budget procedures, partly due to the pressure of electioneering. The third is about budgeting as business-as-usual, Congress working just about the way it normally works. All are true.

The Three-Ring Circus

Story number one is a tale of political posturing. The administration split between the deficit reducers, led by OMB Director David Stockman and CEA Chairman Martin Feldstein, and those who would not sacrifice their policies to deficit reduction: Treasury Secretary Donald Regan on taxes and Defense Secretary Caspar Weinberger on spending. President Reagan and the White House political staff sided with Regan and Weinberger, but that left the White House with a political Hobson's choice. The administration could accept large deficits and be pilloried by the media, opposition, and some of its own allies. Or, it could propose big domestic cuts that once more would go nowhere, except to provoke a storm of general abuse about fairness as well as specific complaints from affected groups. Neither seemed a good way to begin an election year, so the administration chose neither; OMB produced a budget with a 13 percent real defense increase and small domestic cuts, then disavowed the deficit totals by calling for bipartisan negotiations. The Democrats, protesting their concern for deficits, could not refuse to negotiate. They seemed trapped between blame if no agreement emerged and losing the deficit issue if they made a deal. They wriggled free by both proclaiming the president's deficit reduction target too small and forcing the defense issue. In the name of budget control, they demanded detailed cuts from a most reluctant Pentagon and, when the Pentagon failed to oblige, blamed the administration for the breakdown of the talks.

Stuck between the Democrats and the president, Senate Republicans could not defy Reagan directly because he was their major party symbol in the coming election. If they kicked him, they would be kicking themselves. GOP senators, therefore, cut a deal with the White House—the March 15 "Rose Garden Agreement." It passed the Senate, but the House would not go for the defense numbers. It didn't have to. If the senators compromised, they would be rejecting their president; if not, there could be no budget resolution. With no way out of that trap, the Senate stalled. Only in September did Howard Baker and Tip O'Neill agree to a defense compromise allowing final passage of the budget resolution on October 1.

A budget resolution not agreed on until October 1 does not guide subsequent action. What subsequent action? The FY85 first budget resolution looked far more like the second resolutions of the late 1970s—a summary of the year's events—than like the first resolutions of 1981 and 1982, which had led to major reconciliation bills.

The fate of that resolution was just the final act in the story of budget process collapse. The first casualty had been the historic role of the president's budget as representing administration preferences. When Reagan in his State of the Union called for negotiations on a deficit "down payment," he as much as proclaimed that his budget, which had not even been released yet, was not his policy; and its structure revealed that the administration was not proud of its handiwork. "Instead of being located at the front of the book, as is customary," *Newsweek* reported, "the budget totals were squirreled away 102 pages into the document. 'It's a perfectly normal budget,' admitted one administration budget official, 'assuming that you're Chinese.' "[1]

The president's budget was quickly forgotten by all concerned. Next to go was the idea that budget resolutions provided reconciliation instructions, which then would be carried out in reconciliation bills. For you could have reconciliation only if you had already agreed on everything else—which, because defense was stalemated, was unlikely. Congress passed DEFRA, the Deficit Reduction Act of 1984 (H.R. 4170) even though there was no budget. DEFRA, in fact, was drafted in each house even before reconciliation instructions were placed in each budget resolution.

The politicians were adapting any available vehicle to the (somewhat inconsistent) twin purposes of reducing the deficit and pursuing other preferences. Republicans believed that an agreement on defense in the budget resolution would not prevent further cuts in authorization or appropriations processes. They therefore preferred to collapse everything into one step. The Rose Garden agreement called for three-year restraint on domestic appropriations—hard to achieve because Congress would only be passing FY85 appropriations but demanded by the White House to ensure that Reagan got the domestic savings. Senate Republicans tried to solve that problem by including in DEFRA three-year "caps" on appropriations, a major change in the budgetary process. The House rejected that proposal and won in the conference.

Senate Republicans were not alone in encouraging the breakdown in budget procedures. The Reagan administration delayed its internal FY86 budget process (actual 1985) so that plans for cuts could not leak before the election. In the House, Budget Chairman Jones announced early in the year that he would hold the debt limit hostage, if necessary, "in order to force the president to put forward, with the bipartisan leaders of Congress, a deficit reduction package."[2] Some Democrats, led by David Obey and Tony Coelho, seriously considered giving Reagan a line-item veto of appropriations for the year. "Ronald Reagan loves to talk about cutting the budget, but when it comes to specifics, he always ducks," explained Coelho. "This way, the president would have a chance to make it known where he wants to cut."[3] But his colleagues really didn't want to find out.

In February House Republican leaders Robert Michel and Trent Lott floated a plan allowing the president to impound funds. Entitlements would be protected, 25 percent of the impoundments would have to come out of defense, and no more than 10 percent could be cut from any one program.[4] The idea sank like a stone. In September a majority of fifty-one senators actually endorsed the line-item veto; the year ended with Senate Democrats sabotaging a debt limit increase so Republicans would have to vote for it. It is easy in hindsight to view all these events as precursors to Gramm-Rudman-Hollings, but surely they are the picture of a budget process in chaos. Legislators were groping for ways either to force action or at least to force someone else to take the blame for inaction.

That is the second story in which the process collapses and budgeting proceeds without rules. We might expect political posturing and abandoning all rules to make budgeting totally unpredictable and to prevent meaningful action; yet the "normal" detailed work of budgeting did proceed apace. Action in 1984 looked a lot like action in 1983, except that after a year the revenue committees had managed to cobble up enough "kittens and puppies"—compared to TEFRA's "cats and dogs"—to produce some extra revenue. The third story then is budgeting as the assembly of preferences about programs within a general understanding about constraints—essentially a freeze on domestic spending and the same defense buildup projected by Congress the year before.

Budgeting in 1984 was a three-ring circus. Action in all rings was continuous, sometimes overlapping. We find ourselves most interested in the center ring where budgeting proceeded without rules because that will best help us understand the show to come, the Gramm-Rudman-Hollings Greatest Show on Earth. But with any ring missing, the circus would not have been the same.

We leave the reader to pursue the analogy further: Where were the trapeze artists, the snarling tigers and lions—and where were the clowns?

A (White) House Divided: Reagan

As the administration prepared its election year budget, Martin Feldstein became the symbol of economic responsibility suppressed by (as most commentators saw it) political expediency. When the president's advisers met on December 1, 1983, to discuss the upcoming budget, Press Secretary Larry Speakes "launched a brutal attack against the Harvard professor turned economic adviser."[5] Feldstein, who had had to assert his right to participate, got the central message; the White House staff was displeased at his electorally embarrassing talk about the deficit. "I completely support the president's program," he told reporters; and then, in a speech that night, he declared that there was no way the government could grow its way out of deficits. With that kind of support, Reagan needed no opposition. Feldstein's goal and loyalties—growth without inflation—were the same as Reagan's, so he decided he was on the same side. It was a disagreement of means, not ends—but policies are means.

Feldstein very loudly, Stockman less so, and Commerce Secretary Malcolm Baldrige quietly continued to work to include some version of the 1983 contingency tax plan in the FY84 budget package.[6] On December 12 an unenthusiastic Donald Regan told the Washington Press Club that the administration would propose such a tax increase, contingent on prior spending cuts.[7] Sometime between then and mid-January 1984, however, Secretary Regan defeated the tax plan. President Reagan had never liked the contingency tax; when it came time for his decision, the president, in Stockman's words, "came down on us like a ton of bricks with a twenty-minute lecture on economic history and theory." In spite of, or perhaps because of, all the publicity about feuds within the administration, the president was making the major budget decisions.

As reported by Stockman, the president's outburst was a stunning collection of misstatements and non sequiturs. It was, however, out of line with neither the president's more careful statements in public forums nor his tendency to make such misstatements when he was not being careful. "There has not been one increase in history that actually raised revenue," Reagan declared. "And every tax cut, from the 1920s to Kennedy's to ours, has produced more."[8] Not so. Most recently, both the 1969 tax surcharge and the 1978 social security tax increases had raised revenues; they did not get social security out of the hole, but that's a different question. Moreover, if tax increases did not usually raise revenues, they would never be adopted.

OMB's FY85 projections showed that the debt would have increased by $587 billion in just the years from 1982 to 1984. By the end of 1985, it would be double what it had been when Reagan took office. By normal logic, that much of the deficit could not be blamed on "them." If you want to retire the debt—Reagan could still "dream of the day when we actually have a surplus, when we can start retiring the national debt"[9]— doubling it seems a strange way to begin. Yet Reagan was right on the politics if not on government finance. He understood, as Stockman and Feldstein did not, that if he adjusted his policies to respond to the deficit he would be admitting he was wrong. He would be denying the whole premise of his presidency—that America could be governed differently.

Reagan responded to the deficit query by telling people either to look elsewhere for the answer (e.g., Congress) or to change the question. Neither response was merely tactical. Congress had rejected his social spending cuts, engaging in "deficit spending"—though so had Reagan on defense. Nor was the deficit the only public concern. *Newsweek* reported:

> Ronald Reagan contentedly boasts that he kept his campaign promises to prune domestic spending, restore America's military might, slash taxes and lift the yoke of needless federal regulation off the back of business. So what if he miscalculated a little on his pledge to provide a balanced budget by 1984? "I've succeeded in four of those five goals," Reagan has said in private meetings. "I'm batting .800 and that's pretty good in any league I know about."

As a politician, Reagan knew that you rarely got everything you want. Therefore, he treated the deficit as only a partial failure. What president enacts his entire platform?

Reagan also expected to take more shots at the spending side. His Grace Commission was nearing release of its report on waste and inefficiency in government, which would confirm the president's belief that private sector experts could find all sorts of savings.[10] Reagan also expected to take on entitlements. He told the *Washington Post* that "it [these programs] just automatically keeps increasing—that is uncontrollable only in the sense that you and Congress and the government are not willing to deal with it and change what you did that was wrong."[11] In short, with courage, entitlements would some day be dealt with. Leon

Panetta and Pete Domenici would say no different. But what changes, and when?

Members of Congress, however, figured that because nothing big enough could possibly turn up, the president would have to give on defense and taxes. That, as an administration official commented to us, was a lousy deal for the president. Reagan already had his tax cut and defense buildup. Now the president was being asked to give them back in hope, but with no guarantee, that doing so would eliminate his deficit error. Not a good bargain for Reagan's batting average.

Reagan's rejection of tax hikes and endorsement of a 13 percent real increase in defense spending make sense for a politician who sees the deficit as only one of a number of major concerns and who is used to postponing problems. Delay made less sense to people who believed, as did Feldstein and Stockman, that the deficit was unspeakably horrible. Delay was anathema also to people—Democrats, moderate Republicans, and budget professionals such as CBO Director Rudolf Penner—concerned with the interest wheel: that bigger deficits meant higher interest payments and thus higher deficits, ad infinitum. Reagan seems never to have believed that delay was making the problem worse. After all, immediate action meant enacting the tax increases he believed would only lead to higher spending and thus larger future deficits.

Reagan's patience matched his political advisers' belief that 1984 was a bad year to propose social spending reductions. The Democrats were geared up to run a campaign on "fairness."[12] The previous two budget rounds had demonstrated that even if the White House proposed cuts, Congress would reject them. Reagan's men preferred discretion to ineffective valor.

A Down Payment

By January 1984, Republican senators were beginning to define their goal not as immediate budget balance but as controlling the debt situation.[13] Stockman testified to the Senate Budget Committee: "I don't think there's anyone here who can think of enough taxes or enough spending cuts to offset [the] explosion of debt service. We are in the same position of many companies on the eve of Chapter 11."[14] The budgetary effects of compound debt interest were indeed impressive. Interest costs for 1984 were projected at $108 billion. Every extra $200 billion of borrowing would increase subsequent interest costs by $15 billion or more per year forever (optimistically assuming 7.5 percent interest)—and that did not account for possibly higher interest rates created by federal borrowing needs. Thus, though Feldstein's economic report assumed deficit reductions that would reduce interest rates, and Stockman used those interest rate assumptions to get his debt service estimates down, deficit reductions were not in the budget. In essence, the economic report assumed some other budget. When Reagan, in his State of the Union on January 25, announced he had arranged negotiations with representatives of Speaker O'Neill and Majority Leader Baker about a $100 billion three-year "down payment" on deficit reduction, he in fact announced that the administration had not been able to make a budget of its own.

In his speech the president reiterated his disinterest in making the down payment with taxes. "Whether government borrows or increases taxes," he declared, "it will be taking the same amount of money from the private sector, and either way it's too much." Besides, he added, in a portent of things to come,

> There is a better way. Let us go forward with a historic reform for fairness, simplicity and incentives for growth. I am asking Secretary Don Regan for a plan for action to simplify the entire tax code, so all taxpayers, big and small, are treated more fairly. . . . I have asked that specific recommendations, consistent with these objectives, be presented to me by December, 1984.[15]

The December (that is, postelection) target for tax reform proposals drew sarcastic laughter[16] because the president appeared to be shifting off some hair-brained scheme until after the election. The last laugh, however (see Chapter 20 on tax reform), would belong to him.

Changing the subject to tax reform did not save a budget that even Reagan did not want to defend. The budget and CBO analyses differed vastly: FY89 interest was estimated at $126 billion by OMB and $207 billion by CBO. Virtually no one, including OMB, believed OMB. The call for negotiations on a "down payment"—finally inserted into the speech the morning it was given[17]—was meant to bridge the gap between economic and budget reports, providing a functional equivalent of the magic asterisk: we'll make it add up later. Feldstein drew the conclusion merited by Reagan's call for negotiations: "This budget is not what we want to see happen," he testified. "My sense is that these negotiations supersede completely the budget that has been sent up."[18]

Tired and testy, Stockman tried to resign before the budget was released. "I can't make a fool of myself any longer, Jim," he told Baker. "This budget is so bad, it's beyond the pale." "You do that and you'll stab the president right in the back," the Chief of Staff replied. "The Democrats will have a field day in the 1984 campaign. Let me remind you of something, my friend. He stuck by you. Now you stick by him." "Because I knew Jim was right," a chastened Stockman reports, he agreed to stay on—even if that meant, as he puts it, giving "dutiful loyalty to nonsense."[19] Stockman was always, however, at least as loyal to his personal version of the truth as to any individual. He therefore strove to get out the truth about the budget situation as he saw it.

Trying to understand what had happened to his dreams, the budget director had initiated a major historical analysis of budget trends. Stockman concluded that his spending history showed broad support for many programs he wished to cut. Surprise! Not Johnson's Great Society but older (social security) and younger (food stamp) programs made up the bulk of the new spending. The budget's analysis was elaborated in the April release of "Major Themes and Additional Budget Details"—an advocacy document that took on a reflective cast. Stockman wanted a wider audience. Therefore, in January he went on record, summarizing his view in an interview for *Fortune:*

> Philosophically I have a large roster of cuts. . . . You could find several tens of billions to throw overboard.
>
> But the point is that we have knocked on all those doors for three years and three budget rounds. And the result is people want to have mass transit subsidies and middle-class subsidies for education. And the agricultural sector wants all those benefits. I can't foresee that anytime in this decade we will have the kind of people in Congress who will abolish those things— even if it is philosophically correct to do so.
>
> We have gone through a great testing process for three years, and that defines the financing requirements of the government. Now we have to figure out how to pay our bills. Some [read Reagan, Meese] still think there are vast pockets of fraud, waste, and abuse out there. In fact, nearly every stone has been turned over.[20]

In background interviews, Stockman's associates continued to press the point: tax increases were essential.[21]

Feldstein's warnings about deficit-by-default sent the same message: a tax hike would be needed. In reply, Donald Regan blasted the CEA chairman. "I have 35 years of experience in the market," he declared. "The CEA has none. . . . Experience in the marketplace is a lot more valuable than time spent in the library."[22] On February 3 ranking Democratic Senator Lawton Chiles told Regan, at a Senate Budget Committee hearing, that the annual CEA report made a strong case for the evils of deficits. The Treasury secretary replied that the president had only written the first eight pages of the report; "as far as I'm concerned," his punch line went, "you can throw the rest away."[23] The White House staff felt that Feldstein's attacks on the deficit were making the president look bad. They forced the CEA chair to cancel a scheduled February 5 television appearance. Rumors flew that Feldstein would resign; but the CEA chairman, who had long planned to resign that summer when his leave from Harvard expired, saw no reason to hurry. George Bush had the hopeless job of denying that the administration was split over the deficit issue.[24]

To the Rose Garden

Before serious work began on creating a FY85 budget, the nominally bipartisan negotiations had to be disposed of. A Democratic aide recalls,

> It was obviously a political way to get through the year. . . . [Senate Minority Leader] Byrd had no choice but to accept, of course . . . [he] was depressed because he was in a false position. He could see that by going along he would lose the issue of the deficit and hurt Mondale—though we might have been better off without that issue, since Mondale's solution was a tax hike!

The Democrats' first problem was who to send to the budget talks. On the Senate side, Long and Chiles were the obvious candidates, but those two, especially Chiles, might make a deal that got Reagan off the hook (any deal would) and would also be too conservative for most Democrats. On the House side, the logical negotiators, Jones and Rostenkowski, presented the same difficulty. What do you do when the president requests a budget conference and you don't trust your budget leaders?

The Democrats declared the negotiations a leadership issue. Senator Byrd decided to send Daniel Inouye (D-Hawaii), a member of the leadership known for his stubbornness and discretion. The Speaker thought that was a great idea, and he delegated Jim Wright.[25] "The speaker," his spokesman declared, "is extremely suspicious" of the president's deficit-reduction proposals.[26] A Democratic aide described the scene:

> Every meeting would begin with [Jim] Baker chairing, and he would say, let's see what is doable here, about $30 billion per year. Wright would say, no way, let's do something that would really help, $200 billion total. Here's what we can do on taxes, what specifics can you do on defense? Inouye would keep saying, if this is so easy and so doable, why do we have to be here? I could be back at Appropriations, doing something real. . . .
>
> I watched Stockman and Domenici, who would talk to each other, and clearly they wanted to make a deal. . . . Stockman would say, we might consider something—and then Regan or Baker would shut him down and say, no way. I'm sure that is where the [Stockman] book came from in a way. It was clear he had become a functionary, not a policymaker.

By early March, Democrats Wright and Inouye had dropped out of the budget negotiations. Talks continued among various Republican factions, searching for some common ground on defense, taxes, and social spending.[27]

On March 1 Ways and Means reported a $49.2 billion package (over three years) attached to the FY84 reconciliation that had been hung up back in December (H.R. 4170). Finance worked through early March assembling a similar package.[28] Though the two plans had many differences, each appropriated some small tax proposals found in Reagan's budget, conspicuously excepting taxation of employee health benefits. Each increased some excise taxes, restricted industrial development bonds, changed tax shelters, and included a few sweeteners for the tax increase pill. As in 1982, the committees received quiet help from Treasury and from professionals at the Joint Committee on Taxation. The real target was Wall Street.

Essentially the tax professionals, under cover of the deficit panic, proposed reforms involving "a lot of reporting, penalties, the time value of money, imputing interest"—highly technical matters "absolutely," as one participant put it, sold to the president as compliance. They were so technical that, as a Ways and Means aide put it, "no one viewed anything in there as particularly egregious, in part because no one understood it." The major interests affected, stockbrokers and other financial institutions, were narrow enough that most legislators could afford to oppose it in pursuit of what they deemed the greater good of deficit reduction.

By assembling detailed tax proposals, Finance and Ways and Means changed the overall budget picture. As the White House and congressional Republicans bargained, tax-hike proponents could point to menus of increases that protected the president's individual tax cut, sounded fair, and, most important, had some chance of passing. On the basis of a three-legged stool of defense restraint, domestic cuts, and tax hikes, the emerging tax proposals allowed a three-year $150 billion overall package.[29] After the Senate Republicans' third meeting with Reagan on March 14, Domenici reported that agreement was coming closer. The holdup was spending; he, and particularly Hatfield, were pushing for defense reductions greater than Senate Armed Services Chairman John Tower and Cap Weinberger would accept.[30]

The issue was how to make a three-year cut in discretionary spending (entitlements were out). No one was willing to repeat the 1981 reconciliation of discretionary-spending authorizations. Congress could try multiyear appropriations, but then what would future appropriations committees do? Rejecting these approaches, the Senate leadership proposed to legislate "caps" on discretionary spending for FY85 and the two subsequent years. Caps would allow discretion on details and an annual review, but they would also constrain total appropriations. A defense cap would allow an average 7 percent real growth over the three years. The nondefense cap would freeze spending in FY85 and then allow inflation adjustments in FY86–87.[31]

Hatfield (never mind House appropriators) objected to both the principle of caps and the particulars. Pete Domenici and Howard Baker, his personal friends, argued that the party had to agree on a program. Under intense pressure, Hatfield gave in on March 15, 1984, but, when the Senate leaders and the president announced their agreement in the Rose Garden that day, the chairman of Senate Appropriations was conspicuously absent. He kept a prior engagement at Harvard University, refusing Howard Baker's offer to get him back from Boston on an Air Force jet.[32]

This Rose Garden agreement included $149.5 billion in savings from the highest possible base—that is, keeping current services on domestic spending and accepting the president's request on defense. From that base, defense and domestic would be reduced by $40 billion and $43 billion, respectively, taxes increased by the $48 billion planned by Senate Finance, and interest costs accordingly reduced by $18 billion. Given these baselines, the figures provided a rough equality of sacrifice. Except for the appropriations freeze, all the other spending savings in the plan were already moving through Congress on their own.

If the Rose Garden's tax and domestic spending changes were on the way, and if so-called defense reductions were being calculated from a base that no one believed, what was the point? Clearly the agreement had far more to do with uniting the Republican party than with reducing the deficit. Yet this plan was better than no plan—what had happened in 1983. As Dole put it, "It's not a $100 billion down payment. When you net it all out it's probably $30 billion. But if you don't do anything, it's zero."[33] Hatfield could console himself that, because Congress cannot bind itself, the caps could be ignored later.

The Rose Garden agreement was fragile. Each faction might back out if the whole package did not stick together. In particular, the president might not accept the tax hike if he felt betrayed on domestic spending and defense, which under normal procedures could not be attached to the tax increase. "Normal procedure" would not do; it would draw attention to the (politically) wrong things. Budget resolutions would highlight the bad deficit result instead of the good, supposed, deficit reduction. Senate Republican leaders, therefore, decided to bypass the budget resolution by packaging the Rose Garden agreement in a separate bill.

A Thicket of Thorns

As Republicans plotted procedural maneuvers to hold their factions together—and reduce the deficit a bit—Democrats searched for ways to unite themselves, embarrass the Republicans, and outbid them on the deficit.

As a minority, Senate Democrats did not control procedure. They could, however, use the Senate's loose structure, including the threat of filibuster, to resist Republican innovations. Lawton Chiles, their leader on Senate Budget, strongly believed in the budget process and balanced budgets. More partisan Democrats, such as Majority Leader Byrd, did not want the Republicans to deflect attention from the deficits themselves to a deficit-reduction package—exaggerated because it was spread over three years and from an overstated defense base. Senate Democrats, therefore, wanted to force votes on a budget resolution.

On March 22 the Senate Democratic conference endorsed a Chiles package that allegedly would save $50 billion more than the Rose Garden package. Chiles held defense to 4 percent real growth per year and raised taxes by about $25 billion more than the Rose Garden total, by deferring the first two years of income tax indexing. The Chiles package showed that conservative Democrats, not just Ted Kennedy and other liberals, wanted to raise taxes and reject the president's defense numbers. Other Senate proposals would show the same pattern of conservative support for less defense spending and higher taxes.[34]

In the House as well conservative southerners were moving toward their liberal Democratic brethren. House Democrats spent most of March in internal debate about (a) what their budget should include and (b) how it should be packaged. They finally settled on George Miller's "pay-as-you-go" plan, which he had been pushing since 1982. He would establish as the base current spending and revenues (as increased in future years by inflation). Then any increment of spending would have to be paid for by new taxes. Because the proposal's major increments were in defense, Miller's plan offered the administration a simple choice: if it wanted the military buildup, then it should pay for that buildup. The plan was particularly attractive to liberals because it rejected the existing baselines that favored defense.[35]

Nonetheless, support for Miller revealed just how much of a bind liberals were in. Focusing attention on paying for defense discomfits conservatives; yet if everybody assumes the vast majority of increases will go to the military, then liberals can hardly be happy. To say that any new spending demands new taxes does not sit well with advocates of government activism. Imagine how few new programs would be started if each also included a tax hike! Such a rule would radically transform the budgetary process.

The House Budget Committee resolution of March 28 created three classes of programs: those increased by 3.5 percent, slightly less than the projected 5.2 percent inflation; those fully adjusted for inflation; and those increased by 3.5 percent above inflation. The latter increases, in defense and mostly means-tested entitlements, were to be paid for by new taxes. The total of increases and new taxes was, not coincidentally, nearly the same as that in the Ways and Means bill.[36]

Democratic leaders were improving at a strategy of substantive and procedural inclusion by which they helped their policy minorities feel like they were well treated. Thus, veterans' benefits were favored, giving the southerners a sign that they were heard. The leadership also allowed many amendments on the floor, so members could see that the whole House, not the leadership alone, prevented any package that reduced the deficit by more than the Budget Committee's plan. Although nobody would propose a higher deficit, nobody could pass a lower one.

Freshman Democrats, led by Representative Buddy MacKay of Florida, who wanted to apply new taxes to deficit reduction, not to new defense and poverty spending, had a chance to see that only 108 members agreed.[37] The Republican leaders' budget plan increased the Rose Garden's deficit reduction by freezing discretionary domestic programs below inflation for three years instead of one and by assuming some management savings suggested by the Grace Commission; that received only 107 votes. Another, more conservative Republican proposal (raising hardly any revenues, but adopting even more Grace Commission spending reductions) was rejected 51 to 354. Purely to embarrass their rivals, the Democrats forced a vote on Reagan's original budget, which won only the lonely vote of Jack Kemp.

The House handily defeated three alternatives sponsored by Democrats. The Black Caucus budget funded new social spending with big defense cuts and tax hikes to produce easily the biggest deficit reduction, $324 billion. It won 76 votes, tapping as always the hard core of liberal sentiment. The Conservative Democratic Forum proposed a $225 billion package that obtained extra savings by shaving 2 percent off indexing of both benefits and revenues. It showed that the boll weevils were putting deficit reduction ahead of both conservative change in government priorities and the safety-first politics of ducking the COLA issue, but it received only 59 votes. The third, and most popular, alternative, from the DSG, would have held most spending, including defense, to inflation adjustments and would have raised income taxes by delaying indexing. DSG's plan also revealed sentiments: liberals now felt they could oppose any defense buildup; it won all of 132 votes.

"Pay-as-you-go" was bitterly denounced by Republicans. Minority Leader Michel called it "pray-as-you-go," given the defense slowdown.[38] Phil Gramm scoffed that "it's kind of crazy to talk about pay-as-you-go when you have a $175 billion deficit."[39] Yet, as the votes on alternatives showed, there was, if anything, more sentiment for lower defense spending than for bigger domestic cuts. Tapping what substantive agreement existed, the House Democratic plan won by the biggest margin ever for a first resolution in the House, 250 to 168.[40]

House Democratic leaders pushed forward. On April 11, the Ways and Means tax bill, H. R. 4170, came to the floor under a closed rule. After only three hours of debate, it passed easily 318 to 97. The next day, Democrats brought up a spending reconciliation (H.R. 5394) mandated by the budget resolution passed only the week before. Under the formal budget process, reconciliation was supposed to follow agreement between the two houses on a budget resolution, but the House was not about to wait around for the Senate. House leaders wanted to claim credit for action on the deficit, and they also wanted to make sure the action occurred. Support for the formal budget process took a back seat.

Spending reconciliation hit a snag when provisions that related to freezing physicians' fees under medicare were beaten by a coalition of Republicans and rural Democrats. Rural members feared that a sole resident doctor, so common in some areas, might refuse care under the rules being proposed; House Republicans (and the American Medical Association) won that fight. The GOP failed, however, to eliminate Henry Waxman's (D-Calif.) spending increases for certain poverty programs. Waxman (like his ally, the late Phil Burton) was a liberal who played hardball. In politics, Waxman was building a machine, funneling campaign money from his Los Angeles base to other Democrats whose needs were greater than his own. In policy, he kept finding "motherhood" ideas for program expansion—proposals that would be hard for Republicans to oppose. The 1984 batch included the Child Health Assurance Program (CHAP), expanding medicaid coverage for maternal and pediatric care. CHAP and a few other ideas were worked into the reconciliation package. The bill, which despite those increases would save $3.9 billion over three years, passed, 261 to 152.

By April 12 the House Democrats had established their control of the lower house, with votes on a budget resolution, spending reduction, and tax increase bills. Armed Services had already acted to reduce the administration's defense authorization to a 5.5 percent real increase—below the Rose Garden, surprisingly low for that committee. The House leadership soon gave Appropriations a green light to begin reporting bills even if no budget resolution was agreed, using the House-passed version for guidance. As Democratic factions warred over the presidential nomination, they united within the House, providing a semblance of coherent party government. Unfortunately for fans of order, a different party controlled (if barely) the Senate. Without the services of a rules committee, Howard Baker had more trouble managing his majority than did Tip O'Neill.

Baker and Domenici had cooperation from some key players. Reagan himself visited the Hill on March 21 to lobby his party for the Rose Garden package. Knowing the Rose Garden was the best deal the military could hope for, John Tower worked hard to push it through. Chairman Dole whipped his tax hikes and spending cuts through Finance. *Business Week* reported that "lobbyists quickly lowered their profiles, and the members snapped into line behind Dole. In a matter of days, in fact, they voted for the whole $73.8 billion deficit-reduction package, including $25.8 billion in spending cuts, by 22–0."[41] Finance voted out the Deficit Reduction Act of 1984 (DEFRA) on March 21, and Senator Baker planned to attach it to the leftover reconciliation from 1983, along with the appropriation caps and various other Rose Garden deals. Even as the president lobbied his party and Finance reported out its bill, however, the Republican strategy in the Senate began to run into trouble.

The right wing wanted domestic cuts guaranteed. From the Republican left (so to speak), Lowell Weicker complained that the agreement "just absolutely would raise havoc with spending in health, education, and science."[42] Other Republicans such as Slade Gorton, Nancy Kassebaum, and Charles Grassley wanted bigger deficit reductions. Mark Hatfield resisted plans to bypass the budget resolution because he wanted a budget debate that might change the balance between defense and domestic. Democrats agreed, feeling they were being denied a place in policy making by Baker and Domenici's planned tactics. Russell Long threatened to filibuster by reading the entire U.S. Code.[43]

Senate Republicans were torn between the desire to do more than the Rose Garden and fear of delay. The Gorton-Kassebaum-Grassley faction favored debate in order to forge consensus on bigger defense reductions; yet they feared delay even more, endangering the Finance Committee bill given their conservative colleagues' suspicions. Moderate Republicans and Democrats wanted quick action as well because the financial markets were getting skittish. Interest rates were climbing; bond and stock prices sliding; as usual, the bad news was blamed on (CBO) projections of mounting deficits. "When the prime rate jumps, so should Congress," declared Bob Dole.[44] The difficulty was that considering alternatives is a powerful norm in the Senate; many members would object to being rushed on a major issue like the budget, and they could use procedure to slow things down.

"Domenici will not show a lot of patience with delay," his top aide, Steve Bell, warned in April.[45] Patience, however, was Domenici's lot. He and Baker allowed the Budget Committee to meet and consider alternative plans. That short delay was enough to abort Baker's plan to attach the Rose Garden agreement to H.R. 4169. That leftover reconciliation involved some COLA delays that had to be programmed into the computers by early April. The Senate, therefore, passed H. R. 4169 (67 to 26) on April 5, while budget committee members maneuvered over a resolution and Howard Baker searched for an alternative vehicle. He found it in an already rather deceptively named House-passed tariff bill. "When it's finished," the majority leader declared, "the Federal Boat Safety Act will carry a cargo of valuable commodities."[46]

Finance's package, DEFRA, reached the Senate floor on April 9. Democrats immediately began delaying tactics in order, as Chiles's top aide Richard N. Brandon declared, "to get the real numbers and deficit figures on the board."[47] Meanwhile, the badly divided Senate Budget Committee struggled to pass a budget resolution.

The most complicated maneuvers involved a budget plan prepared by Republicans Kassebaum and Grassley with Democrat Joseph R. Biden, Jr., of Delaware. These three took the idea of a freeze seriously and proposed freezing *everything*—defense, domestic discretionary, and entitlement spending (entitlements would grow with population, but COLAs would be canceled)—for FY85. Joined by Max Baucus (D-Mont.) at a later point in the debate, the sponsors explained their proposal:

> Unfortunately, the major [other] proposals still are more political than substantive. Although they are supposed to reduce the deficit significantly, most of the proposed reductions come not in 1985 but instead in the elusive "out-years."
>
> This kind of deferred solution won't convince the American people that Congress is serious about reducing the deficit. It won't convince the managers of our financial markets that Congress is serious about reducing the deficit. And it doesn't convince us, either.[48]

They hit all the right notes: a freeze would be "fair," "simple," "right"; it would stop the growing interest bill and protect "our children's future."

If deficit reduction were the overriding criterion, the "K-G-B" freeze (as it was rather ominously dubbed) would have been a nearly ideal plan.[49] The catch was that most Democrats were uncomfortable with important parts of the freeze. Some Democrats conceded that they would not vote to cancel social security COLAs in the real life of legislation.[50] Republicans who suspected as much could feel good about the freeze only if they believed the Democrats were sincere; otherwise, it would ratchet defense down but change little else.

In the Budget Committee on April 11, John Tower declared that the defense freeze would "almost be tantamount to unilateral disarmament." Pete Domenici told members they should oppose the freeze because its social security COLA elimination was unrealistic. Because he had proposed such things before (and would again), that argument sounded strange in his voice; under election-year circumstances, however, Domenici was counseling moderation in deficit reduction. Yet the freeze carried, 10 to 9, with heavy Democratic support. Then Bob Kasten switched his vote, declaring that "I didn't anticipate this vote would take on a political tone." As the margins changed, Democrats who didn't want to be associated with the social security provisions jumped off the wagon, while Republicans who wanted to posture against the deficit but not to torpedo their party climbed back on. The K-G-B plan was a strange kind of trolley: only popular so long as it wasn't going anywhere. In the end, it lost 7 to 13.[51]

Party battle lines having been drawn, the SBC then defeated Chiles's Democratic plan (described above) 11 to 10 and endorsed the Rose Garden package by the same margin. Thus, on April 11 the Rose Garden proposal passed its first hurdle. Barely.

On April 13 around 5:00 a.m. (the leadership wanted to finish before Easter) the DEFRA tax bill passed as an amendment to H.R. 2163 (that handy Boat Safety Act). Amendments made only minor changes. Finance had done its job well by ferreting out a relatively less contentious set of revenue raisers; the Senate passed Finance's package, 76 to 5. The next stage, in which Howard Baker would try to add the more contentious spending caps to the growing Boat Safety bill, would be far more difficult.

Though it was formally a reconciliation fight, the Senate debate that began during the week of April 23 looked a lot like a budget-resolution debate, as senators proposed a variety of comprehensive packages. Because it involved real legislation, it was also more serious. Senators drafted nearly forty amendments. "Believing that the one offered last would have the best chance of prevailing," ten senators asked Baker to give them the last shot.[52]

Senators quickly disposed of conservative plans offered by Senators Helms (27 to 68) and Symms (11 to 84). The fight then moved to two rival freeze plans—a Hollings-Andrews and the Kassebaum-Biden-Grassley-Baucus proposal. Hollings had more taxes and defense, and less deficit, than the K-G-B plan. Each would reduce COLAs. Neither did very well. Hollings was defeated 57 to 38 on May 2. The Kassebaum plan, supported by several normally Republican groups, including the Chamber of Commerce and National Association of Manufacturers, was expected to do better. "It's fair. It exempts nothing. It is a cut now, not in later years," NAM Vice President Paul Howard explained.[53] These business groups could accept the defense cut produced by a nominal freeze; but defense advocates, and most senators, could not. Majority Whip Ted Stevens called the freeze so "drastic that it would require the draw down of our troops committed to the defense of our interests abroad."[54] That freeze was beaten, 65 to 33.

Never let it be said that the deficit has not been reduced because plans for larger reductions were not offered, or because no "fair" plans were put forward, or because the packages were not big enough to be worth the pain. On the Senate and the House floors in 1984, as in other years, there were plenty of large, balanced proposals. They kept losing because more pain means more opponents.

After the freezes were defeated, the situation recalled 1983: a Republican plan, a Democratic plan, and a group of moderate Republicans torn between party loyalty and program preference. On May 8 the Democrats almost won. Chiles's plan lost on a tie vote, 49 to 49, with Hollings and Glenn absent; 6 Republicans had joined the unanimous remaining Democrats. We suspect that in a pinch one Republican could have been switched; nevertheless, Republican leaders had to see that vote as a bad sign. Other Republicans, like Gorton, might switch the other way.

In a way that presumed $37 billion less for defense and $20 billion more in domestic spending than the Rose Garden agreement, Republican moderates Chafee, Weicker, Andrews, and Stafford proposed combining defense and domestic caps, allowing Appropriations to determine priorities later. Howard Baker replied that without the caps the budget package would collapse; that is, Reagan would veto the tax bill. The leadership managed to table Chafee's amendment 48 to 46 only after Charles Percy (R-Ill., facing a difficult reelection fight) switched his vote. Now Baker and Domenici really had to worry. Of the six absent senators, five (Hart, Inouye, Tsongas, Glenn, and Mathias) could be expected to side with Chafee if he tried again.

It looked as if the Rose Garden plan would fail by one or two votes. But if the Rose Garden failed, then maybe no DEFRA act, a veto war over domestic spending, and lots of bad publicity about the split in the Republican party would follow. Howard Baker had no choice but to pay off the moderates as cheaply as possible. After a few days of negotiating he worked out a deal to take unspent budget authority of $2 billion from synfuels and spread it around other domestic programs. Baker told the conservatives the extra money would not increase the deficit because it already had been appropriated for synfuels. The argument was a bit disingenuous—synfuels was highly unlikely to spend the money—but it worked. Democrats blasted the moderate Republicans for settling so cheaply when Chafee's much larger amendment had so nearly won. "You don't have a majority," was Weicker's reply," for any significant decrease in defense spending or for any meaningful increase in education and health programs."[55] And Stafford looked to the conference that, he asserted, "will reduce military expenditures significantly toward the House's figures. That always happens."[56]

On May 17 the amendment, adding spending caps and other savings to the heavily loaded Boat Safety Act, carried 65 to 32. Republicans were unanimous; they were joined by mostly conservative southern Democrats. The entire package, as amended, then passed the Senate 74 to 23, winning more liberal support with its tax provisions. The next day the Senate quickly adopted a budget resolution to conform to its reconciliation (instead of the other way around) and sent everything off to conference.

Who Wants a Budget?

Because any resolution to emerge from conference would be worse for the administration than was the Rose Garden, the White House had no strategic interest in passing a budget resolution. The president cared little about the process. Stockman had been accustomed to use the budget resolution as a benchmark in his bargaining with Hatfield about appropriations bills; but because Hatfield had (however grudgingly) signed on to the Rose Garden, Stockman already had a benchmark.

Many Senate Republicans preferred no budget resolution to one that gave in on defense—that is, any compromise that Reagan and Tower did not accept. Baker and Domenici believed a budget compromise on defense would only lower the baseline for the later fight in appropriations, ensuring spending below the Rose Garden level but not guaranteeing the budget figure.[57] True. "We couldn't pass a conference report on the First Resolution," an aide adds, "until the administration backed down because if we made a defense agreement the White House could accuse us of breaking the Rose Garden agreement."

Democrats wanted a budget resolution for all the reasons Republicans did not. House Democrats had one further motive: the House always produced its debt-ceiling extension as part of the budget conference agreement; lacking that agreement, the House would have to vote directly on a debt ceiling, something it never liked to do. By the time the Senate finally passed its budget, however, the debt deadline had been reached. House leaders grudgingly brought the debt ceiling to the floor on May 22, offering a $30 billion extension that would expire on June 22, so as to keep pressure on the Senate to agree to a budget resolution.

House leaders hoped the short-term, small debt increase would discourage the usual posturing. A majority of Republicans opposed the increase, many Democrats bailed out, and the bill failed 262 to 150. Two days later, when Treasury threatened that social security checks might not go out—and because members wanted to go home for Memorial Day recess—the House passed the same increase 211 to 198. Only 69 Republicans backed it. The Senate next passed the $30 billion increase but removed the expiration date. Senate leaders wanted no extra pressure to force action. For the moment, House leaders conceded.[58]

Passing DEFRA

Congress returned in early June to conferences on the budget resolution and the reconciliation. The reconciliation conference, which began June 6, was the largest since 1981, involving twelve subconferences and sticky issues. Five of its subconferences were particularly important. We list the committees to make a point: in politics, much depends on who has a place at the table when the meal is cooked.

1. Taxes: House Ways and Means, Senate Finance
2. Medicaid, Hill/Burton, CHAP (health programs other than medicare): House Energy and Commerce, Senate Finance
3. Medicare Hospital Insurance (Part A, the trust fund program, which is part of social security): House Ways and Means, Senate Finance
4. Medicare Medical Insurance (Part B): House Energy and Commerce, House Ways and Means, Senate Finance
5. Appropriations Cap, Synfuels Rescission: House Appropriations, House Rules, Senate Appropriations

Not only the committees but the individuals involved mattered. Senate Finance had to cover four subconferences, so those with the least money involved (the second and fourth) got the least attention. Senators Dole, Packwood, and their colleagues put most effort into negotiating with Chairman Rostenkowski and his colleagues on the tax conference. Energy and Commerce Chairmen John Dingell and Henry Waxman could concentrate totally on medicaid and medicare part B; on the latter, liberals Charles Rangel (D-N.Y.) and Harold Ford (D-Tenn.) of Ways and Means played a major role while the more conservative, more senior Democrats—Rostenkowski, Gibbons, and Pickle—negotiated on taxes and hospital insurance. The negotiators on taxes were committed to meeting the targets, and House negotiators on medicare part A were quite willing to go even farther than their colleagues for spending reductions. The House had its toughest advocates of spending programs negotiating the non–trust funded health programs. Needing his own troops on taxes—and perhaps for more Machiavellian reasons (like keeping him busy)—Senator Dole had Russell Long, although a Democrat, represent the Senate on those health programs. Long was a southern conservative, but some of his father's populist blood still ran in him; he would prove rather responsive to Waxman's arguments. Thus, the participants in the subconferences helped guarantee the substantive result:

agreement on taxes and movement toward both the Senate position on medicare part A and the House's expansionary plans for poor peoples' health programs.

The fifth subconference on caps is important for what it did not do. It did not negotiate on appropriations caps. House Appropriations and Rules didn't think there was much to negotiate about. Their answer, simply, was "No!" Of the Senate conferees only Stevens really supported the Senate position. Senate Republican leaders therefore declared the caps a matter for negotiation between the two budget committees. The caps had to be negotiated there, anyway, in order to settle the budget resolution.

By June 14 the entire conference was deadlocked because of conflict over the caps. The Republican position—the entire package could not move without the caps—had a corollary if the caps were not settled. Senator Dole stated it succinctly: "I don't see any need to beat our heads against the wall in a tax conference if nothing else is going to happen."[59] A special meeting on June 14 produced only recriminations. "Why should our conference go out on a limb early," one conferee asked, "if the Budget Committees may not be able to resolve their differences and the process may collapse?"[60]

Domenici insisted more on the cap's principle than substance. His House counterpart, Representative Jones, however, argued that only after they agreed on priorities would it make sense to work on the process. Jim Wright suggested that Domenici was trying to "avoid dealing with the substance."[61] Wright was correct, but two other considerations were also influencing Domenici. First, caps in principle increased the power of both his committee and the budget (as opposed to appropriations) process. Second, the caps were Reagan's guarantee that he would not be bilked on DEFRA as he believed he had been on TEFRA. Unfortunately for Domenici, his approach could mean no tax bill at all because there would be no conference agreement.

With the Fourth of July recess and the presidential nominating conventions coming up, time was scarce. Conferees set midnight, Thursday, June 21, as a deadline for agreement. Much was settled before then; in fact, $40 billion of the tax increase had been agreed by June 8. But contentious issues of politics, privilege, and policy remained—from cigarette excise taxes to commodity traders, capital gains taxation to policy about doctors who refused to take medicare patients on assignment (that is, agreeing to the medicare rate as full payment). Midnight passed with no solution. Finally, on June 22, the crucial compromises were made. Conferees bargained from morning to night and almost to morning again, finishing at 5:17 a.m. on Saturday, June 23.

The administration and Senate Republicans abandoned the spending caps. Instead conferees agreed to "sense-of-the-Senate" language—that the Senate would abide by the separate defense and domestic targets in its appropriations bills. House leaders didn't care what the Senate said it would do, so long as the bill did not claim to bind the House. Meanwhile senators could say that nothing had really changed, which, in a sense, was true. After all, Hatfield had been right all along when he argued that one Congress could not bind another Congress (or itself). What then, we may ask, was the fight about? The House had resisted because Appropriations objected to the caps on principle, and Democrats saw no reason to vote for a defense/domestic distribution to their disadvantage. The Senate waited because, at the very least, its leaders had to show good faith with the president by waiting until the very end.

No common theme unified the final $50 billion in tax increases; it could have been a classic product of tax committees, except that it raised revenues instead of lowering them. There were winners and losers and others who couldn't quite tell. There were benefits for poor people (the earned income tax credit), insurers, some investors, and governments.

Many tax increases involved provisions that seemed abusive, though in some nonideological way. The real estate depreciation period was raised to eighteen years; few believed a building's useful life to be as short as fifteen years or that office buildings and hotels needed help. Conferees tightened the rules on individual income-averaging, making that procedure, originally designed as exceptional, less routine than it had become. Such changes accounted for one-third of the tax increases. The tax writers also limited the pain of the tax increases by changing the law without changing people's circumstances. At least one-third of their revenue raisers were through delays of scheduled tax breaks (e.g., an exclusion for interest income, worth $7 billion alone) and extension of temporary taxes (e.g., for telephones, $3.2 billion). People were not losing anything they already had.

Time suggested that the result be called not a tax hike but "a bill to raise revenues largely by blocking extensive tax changes, and thus to make deficits get worse more slowly, assuming some guesses turn out right."[62] Bismarck observed that those who enjoy sausage and respect the law should never watch either of them being made. The process that created DEFRA whetted no appetites, but nonetheless the government would find the tax hikes quite nutritious.[63]

The spending subconferences produced $13 billion in spending cuts. We cannot quite say the House won. House Democrats wanted less social spending reduction than they got, and Senate Republicans, particularly Dole and some moderates, seem not to have minded those settlements that resembled Democratic victories. The president definitely did poorly. There were fewer reductions in social programs than he wished, some of them were undeniably flaky, and few fit his philosophy. Poor people's programs like AFDC and medicaid were expanded.

Almost all of the $7 to $8 billion cuts in social spending came in medicare. Waxman, speaking for many liberals, explained that "we would have preferred not to cut medicare at all. But we were dealing with the reality of an administration that has as its primary objective cutting medicare by asking the elderly to pay more."[64] Cutting doctors' fees seemed like a way to reduce spending without making the elderly pay for it. The major issue was how to prevent physicians charging patients more than a frozen medicare fee level. Lobbyists for the elderly were quite satisfied with the final terms. No more than 20 percent of the $7 billion medicare savings would be charged to the recipients.

Negotiations on medicaid and AFDC went down to the wire until the conferees settled on a package of changes that increased spending by at least $500 million. Some costs were unclear, which suited the Democrats just fine. "I remember coming out of there," a House aide recalls, "and I called somebody I knew at CBO to find out what [one provision] cost. I had a notion we had made a great deal, and told the CBO guy, don't tell anyone else unless they ask." Conferees rejected the Senate's medicaid cuts and accepted a scaled-down version of Waxman's CHAP program.

The administration, through Stockman, always had a voice in the settlements. However, no major participant, other than Stockman, had a real bias toward cutting welfare programs. Instead the leaders, and especially their aides, focused on welfare policy in its own terms: Who is served? What are the incentives? Are there people whom we want to help but do not reach? Budget worries, instead of provoking a search for cuts—any cuts—had produced a minilegislature, the spending subconferences, whose members took the opportunity to make a series of small changes that increased spending. "Waxman said the Senate conferees—Dole in particular—were 'very helpful, very cooperative.' An aide to Dole said the Senator 'was very pleased' at the outcome of the conference. 'We did the sort of juggling that no one ever thought we could do, and we did good things.' "[65]

DEFRA's spending settlement confirmed, if any doubt remained, that the Reagan revolution against welfare spending was finished. One might conclude that the special interests of the poor and the elderly (represented by politicians like Waxman and Dole) were asserting their power at the expense of the general interest in budget reduction: the spenders were back in the driver's seat. That is only partially true. Waxman and Dole supported welfare increases because they believed in the policy. On medicare the question was not whether some interest group would lose out but which group—the elderly or the providers—would bear the burden. Nobody ever wants to mess with the elderly or the doctors. That they chose to mess with either shows that legislators really felt compelled to do something about the deficit.

Congress approved the conference report on H. R. 4170, the Deficit Reduction Act of 1984, on June 27.[66] Stockman advised the president to sign. He did.

Life Without a Budget

Once DEFRA was passed, one might have expected a budget resolution to follow. After all, raising taxes and cutting medicare should have been the hard part. On June 27 Senate conferees proposed that the resolution set a range for the national defense function, with the House's $285.7 billion as the low point and the Senate's $299 billion in budget authority as the high. Senators could then tell the president that the budget resolution accepted the Rose Garden level of defense expenditure and that the previous year's "reserve fund" provided a precedent for flexible totals. House Democrats rejected the Senate offer. Instead they offered a 5 percent real defense increase, which the Senate refused. Chairman Jones then called on his colleagues to reject a new increase in the debt limit; the House did so on June 28 by a large margin. The senators called Jones's bluff by refusing to meet with House Budget conferees, so Congress passed another short-term extension. Congress departed for most of July, the president signed DEFRA and the debt increase during its absence, and the budget resolution languished. Congress had acted on the deficit, not the budget. Instead of the deficit being a residual of the budget, the budget had become an afterthought to the deficit.

Both houses had already provided for functioning without a budget resolution. DEFRA included "sense-of-the-House" and "sense-of-the-Senate" language that established their respective fiscal plans as targets for appropriations action. When the House adjourned at the end of June, it had passed seven bills; only the perennial headaches—Labor-HHS-Education, defense, and foreign aid—remained to be reported by House Appropriations. The Senate passed four appropriations in June; when Congress recessed, three bills had already been enrolled, gone through conference, and sent to the president for his signature.

The appropriations committees could do quite well without a final budget. Appropriations committees need to know three things: what will pass their own chamber, what the other chamber can live with, and what the president won't veto. Each chamber's budget resolutions and experience tell legislators more about sentiment than they could learn from a conference agreement. Each chamber judges the other by the actions of its conferees and its votes on the appropriations bill itself. Each house judges the president by what he or his OMB director says about each bill. The administration had announced that the Rose Garden's 2 percent nominal increase would be the standard on domestic spending. Appropriations members knew that, if they could live with that restriction, their bills would be signed. Following that guideline, Energy and Water and HUD-Independent Agencies were signed in June.

When Congress returned after the Democratic Convention, however, the waters got choppy, and the sailing became more difficult. Members of Congress wanted to increase some domestic spending—for example, Labor-HHS-Education—by more than 2 percent. The administration had to worry that if it approved 2 percent increases in places where it had proposed major cuts (like Interior and Commerce), Congress would hold back the more popular bills with bigger increases until the end. In other words, an overall 2 percent increase assumes some less and some more; if the most likely "more" is saved until the end and if everything else is judged separately by the 2 percent standard, then all the "less" will hit the mean, and everything else will exceed it.

While the White House grew more critical of individual bills, the defense hang-up spread from the budget resolution to the defense authorization bill to the appropriations. The actions and comments of Senator Stevens on August 3 neatly summarized Senate Republicans' dilemma. With the defense authorization bill deadlocked in conference, Majority Whip Stevens convened his defense appropriations subcommittee to mark up the DOD appropriation. His subcommittee approved a bill that conformed to the Rose Garden targets. Having done that, however, Stevens admitted that "whether we like it or not, we'll get 5 percent. . . . We'll be lucky to get that." As a leader Stevens was supporting his administration, yet neither he nor anyone else expected to win. The White House insisted that it had no interest in compromise. Stevens had told the truth, and everyone knew it; but the majority leader refused to give his president the bad news.[67]

Chiles feared that the Republicans' maneuvering could kill the budget process. When the Agriculture appropriation reached the Senate floor on August 1, the Florida senator, who had allowed five previous appropriations bills to receive a waiver of the requirement that the First Resolution be passed first, objected. "What we are doing," he declared, "is trying to wipe out the mandate of the Budget Act and take us back to the old days when we went ahead, passed appropriations bills, and then just added up the total." Right. Then Chiles launched into a filibuster. On August 8 the Senate invoked cloture on Chiles, 68 to 30, proceeding to pass its version of the agriculture appropriation on August 10. But Chiles announced that he would object to every subsequent appropriations bill until the budget impasse was resolved, thereby presenting the threat of a totally clogged Senate schedule. He suggested that all the defense figures be settled at once in a summit among the party leaders, budget and armed services committee heads, and defense appropriations subcommittee leaders.

A Senate leadership aide commented that by holding up appropriations, Chiles actually helped Howard Baker. The majority leader could tell the White House that if he did not bargain, the Senate would become unmanageable. Nevertheless, negotiations dragged on past the Republican convention and into mid-September.[68] Finally, on September 20, Senator Baker and Speaker O'Neill announced their agreement. They allowed a defense authorization total of $297 billion but limited the appropriation to $292.9 billion—the 5 percent increase that everybody had expected all along.

Reagan and his defense advisers may have calculated that they would lose nothing by delaying compromise so long. Yet Howard Baker was retiring from the Senate, and Pete Domenici was getting tired of fighting battles for the White House, especially since he and Chiles were natural allies on both substantive and institutional grounds. The president and his staff were using up their personal credit with Senate allies. That may have something to do with the fact that there were to be no defense increases in either the next round or the round after that. On September 20, 1984, though no one knew it at the time, the defense budget had reached a plateau. In real dollars, it was about to begin sloping downward.

Such is hindsight. At the time, Congress was rushing to complete its work and go home to campaign. Legislators and the president wanted to show how much they cared about reducing the deficit. They also wanted to do good things for their constituents. Once again, the end of the session produced a chaotic clash over appropriations.

Commerce, Justice, State, and Judiciary went through fairly early. The programs that Stockman and Reagan disliked received about one-third more than requested; law enforcement and foreign policy ("national interest") programs got about 3 percent less than the president asked for. Total action averaged out to small (2 to 6 percent) real increases in the major accounts. Failing to induce Hatfield to enforce its priorities, the administration chose to sign rather than risk a political veto battle.

Other less fortunate bills were bogged down by controversies somewhat tangential to questions of government finance: abortion, on Treasury and Labor-HHS-Education; deterrence strategy (the MX), on the Department of Defense; orange marketing orders, on Agriculture; a turf fight between the Public Works Committee and Appropriations, on Transportation. The most acrimonious policy dispute involved Central

America. The El Salvador issue was settled in August and September. Both the election of Christian Democrat José Napoleon Duarte as president of El Salvador and Duarte's own lobbying convinced skeptical Democrats to support aid. They did not want to sabotage a leader whose professed policies were essentially their own. The Nicaraguan Contras, however, had no Duarte, and they did not get into the House CR.

Congress was also confounded by the now familiar question of which authorizations would be attached to the CR. When the Rules Committee, responding to a veto threat, stripped a series of authorizations from the CR, a coalition of House members of all sorts, demanding a chance to put more baggage on the CR freight, beat the rule, 225 to 168. The next day, Rules reversed itself and allowed eleven amendments, including an $18 billion water projects authorization, start-up water projects funding, and the foreign aid authorization. On September 25 the House added the water projects and foreign aid authorizations. It also inserted an omnibus anticrime bill that had been passed by the Senate; members hoped that by so doing they would make a veto less likely.[69] The administration reiterated its veto threat.

After the House passed its CR, the Senate bogged down in "a spectacular, ever-deepening procedural snarl" over civil rights, school busing, gun controls, and tuition tax credits.[70] The conflict began when the Supreme Court held, in *Grove City College v. Bell*, that federal grants could be withheld as punishment for sex discrimination only if that discrimination had occurred in the activity funded by the grant. Previous policy, upheld by lower courts, was to withhold funds if discrimination occurred anywhere in the institution; athletic departments were the prime example. Liberal and moderate legislators wanted to write the old interpretation into law; conservatives, led by Judiciary Chairman Strom Thurmond, used procedural means to block a vote in the Senate. Civil rights forces, led by Minority Leader Byrd, Senator Packwood (R-Oreg.), and Senator Kennedy, decided to attach the change to the CR. When Howard Baker did not object, Orrin Hatch (R-Utah) began delaying tactics. After a 92 to 4 cloture vote on September 29, Hatch and his allies began offering other amendments, for example, against busing, as both a semifilibuster and an embarrassment to the liberals.

On Monday, October 1, the Senate had to pass a two-day CR; the civil rights fight still blocked a vote on the real thing. On October 2, the liberals gave in: "Shame on this body, shame on this body," Ted Kennedy proclaimed, blasting Reagan for letting his conservative allies block the legislation.[71] That left the Senate and House with a day to settle abortion, the Contras, the MX, and a perennial favorite, aid to Turkey (Greek-Americans object).

Howard Baker proposed another interim CR, but the Speaker refused. On October 4, Reagan, who had seen no need to do so under similar legislative circumstances in 1983, shut down "nonessential" government agencies due to the lack of funding. Reagan blamed House Democrats. "Just once," he declared, "it would be great to have a budget on time." Furious Democrats pointed out that the delay was in the Republican Senate. Reagan, the Speaker charged, "stopped the government today not for purposes of good public policy but for purposes of melodrama."[72] Democrats suspected the president sought a chance for an antispending demonstration before his debate with Walter Mondale on Sunday, October 7.

Congress passed a thirty-six-hour interim CR. All three rings of the budget circus—political posturing, budgeting without rules, and detailed budget making—were filled with activity as the CR battle continued in conference. On Friday, October 5, Congress passed another interim extension, and the conference stalled over the same issues.[73] By Tuesday, October 9, the third interim CR was running out; Congress passed a fourth. "We are essentially in a state of gridlock," Senator Rudman declared. Stockman explicitly threatened a veto over water projects. He had long argued that users should pay more of the costs for such projects. "If we were to permit the approximately $6 billion worth of new projects in the tentative conference agreement to go forward," he wrote, "any future effort at reform would be virtually meaningless." In spite of the partisan politics surrounding veto threats, the water projects fight was a classic struggle over an important budgeting value: Who would pay for the "pork-barrel"? Spending advocates were using the famed "camel's nose" technique: by letting the start-up funding nose of the camel into the spending tent, one hopes the rest of the beast will follow. Stockman was objecting, as budget directors always will. Amid the fury over Nicaragua and Star Wars and after a year of totally convoluted process, the penultimate battle included a standard budgeting dispute that could have occurred twenty or one hundred years earlier.[74] On Wednesday conferees finally settled, by scuttling the water projects and delaying Contra aid at least until February.

The Contra aid battle was to be fought again and again and again. Frustration would lead the administration into unwise maneuvers known as the Iran-Contra affair, but that is outside our story, except in one respect: the divisions over the Contras that so poisoned relationships were integral to larger ideological divisions reflected in funding disputes—defense versus welfare.

House Democrats proceeded with the compromise only after assurances that the White House would go along. Silvio Conte proclaimed that Reagan had no choice: "No way he could veto that thing now," the House Republican leader on Appropriations declared. "There'd be a revolution up here if he did." Declaring "no limitation to their lust" for military (at the expense of domestic) spending, Hatfield blasted administration aides, accusing Democrats as well of "caving in," but in the end he went along. The battle had been reduced to Congress against the president; the CR passed by wide margins.[75]

As in previous years, they settled by cutting spending that each side had desired. The deficit pressure made that the compromise of choice because members in the middle, undecided on policy, preferred not to increase the deficit. But on most issues majorities wanted to spend roughly what they were already spending, so there was little deficit reduction in the appropriations. Reagan got smaller increases in law-and-order programs than he wished. And Congress insisted on small real increases in education, mostly college student aid. The president was not about to take a strong stand against education funding in an election year.[76] Other bills, such as transportation, were held to the Rose Garden standard of a very small real cut.

Congress, as always, liked the idea of cuts more than the actuality. The House had passed amendments for across-the-board cuts of 4 percent on Commerce-Justice-State-Judiciary, 3 percent on Interior, 2 percent on both Foreign Aid and Legislative, and 1 percent on Agriculture and Treasury. A 6 percent cut in the discretionary accounts of Labor-HHS-Education, however, went down 279 to 144, as 74 Republicans, including Conte, objected. David Obey mocked these proposals by offering a 64 percent cut on Agriculture; if you excluded defense and entitlements, he explained, you had to cut 64 percent of everything else to balance the budget. That's what all this posturing is about.

Throughout the year Republicans had tried to give the president authority to cut appropriations. Robert Walker proposed that Reagan be allowed to cut up to 10 percent from any account in the HUD-Independent Agencies bill. In late September, 51 senators proposed a temporary line-item veto; then they backed off. A similar proposal by Mack Mattingly (R-Ga.) had been kept off DEFRA, 56 to 34. Both Phil Gramm and Newt Gingrich proposed impoundment or veto authority on small spending bills early in the session, receiving 131 and 144 votes, respectively.[77] Efforts to discharge the balanced budget amendment from House Judiciary gathered 190 signatures, not enough.[78]

House Democrats proclaimed that balanced budgets were a great idea. "Any time the president wants to send up a balanced budget," Tip O'Neill promised, "I guarantee I will get it on the floor within 48 hours." So there! The House on October 2 adopted James Jones's motion requiring the president to submit a balanced budget to Congress. Republicans blasted the Democrats for gimmickry and then passed the bill 411 to 11. The Senate did not act.

Every year's deficit was adding another $20 billion a year to future interest payments—$20 billion, as someone put it, to the end of time. Although legislators voiced anguish about the deficit, the political forces favoring programs were too strong. As the election approached, even Reagan reversed himself on aid for debt-burdened farmers.[79] He also supported legislation to guarantee social security COLAs if inflation stayed below the 3 percent trigger level. Congress's actions in reconciliation and on the Labor-HHS-Education bill showed that education and poor people's programs, if anything, were on the upswing. Legislation on social security disability or eligibility sent a similar message: Cuts that could make a dent in the deficit were nowhere in sight.

In a last burst of partisanship, the Senate defeated the debt ceiling on October 12, as Democrats forced Republicans to take responsibility for the deficits. Howard Baker even had to send Air Force jets to bring some senators back to Washington to pass the increase, 37 to 30. Members then went home to campaign. Pressured by Walter Mondale during the election campaign, President Reagan ruled out tax hikes and cuts in social security and medicare.

Otherwise, the election changed very little. It produced the same president and roughly the same partisan balance in Congress to deal with the same deficit. The president, who had downplayed the problem in the campaign, renewed his attack on social spending. Stockman released some more pessimistic forecasts that had been delayed until after the election. Congress prepared for more of the same agony. Frustration mounted. Indeed, so far as we can tell, frustration was the participants' most frequently used word describing the budgetary process.

Frustration could bring collapse; that had already happened to the budgetary process. Thus when 1985 began, there was adherence to neither institutional norms nor budget balance. Frustration could breed desperation. That too would soon be evident, as a "shoot-on-sight" budgetary mechanism called Gramm-Rudman-Hollings came into being. If thought would not bring balance, maybe thoughtlessness would. Out of frustration could also come creativity. Its name was tax reform. What it shared with Gramm-Rudman-Hollings was an overriding desire to show that, despite the circus we have just witnessed, the clowns could govern.

EIGHTEEN

The Deficit in Public and Elite Opinion

In the 1984 presidential election, Democratic nominee Walter Mondale made the deficit his major charge against the incumbent. Not only did Reagan win in a landslide, but also voters who cared most about the deficit split their votes nearly evenly between the candidates. Voters with strong feelings about solutions to the deficit favored Reagan; they tended to oppose either taxes or spending. Why, one might ask, did Mondale focus on such a loser of an issue?

Democrats and the Deficit

The short answer is that Mondale focused on the deficit because it not only formed one of Reagan's few glaring weaknesses but also obstructed traditional Democratic proposals to use government to address society's ills. Mondale's campaign thus became part of the larger process by which the Democratic party moved from the Keynesian position that had served the party so well during most of the postwar era to the me-too-ism in which the Democrats would support Gramm-Rudman-Hollings. The Democrats' journey may have been unwilling; it surely abounded in political calculation. Whatever their sincerity, however, Democrats changed their positions, and that is a major part of the story of how the deficit recast American politics.

We have seen that stagflation caused a crisis of confidence in which many Democrats, including President Carter, seized the banner of deficit reduction, in spite of its danger for their constituencies (see Chapters 2 and 3). We have seen that Ronald Reagan's deficits, combined with tight money, could be argued to favor creditors, mainly Republican, over debtors, mainly Democrats (Chapter 15). By 1984 a plausible constituency-based argument supported Democratic concern about deficits. The end of inflation, however, should have eliminated the Democrats' first objection to deficits. The redistributive concern, as we will see, was emphasized by only one faction of the party. Given the pressure that the deficit exerted against good things Democrats wanted to do, including good things for the worst off, Democrats had plenty of reason to downplay the deficit; instead they emphasized it.

No doubt Democrats calculated that if they ignored the deficit and proposed new social-spending programs, they would be pilloried by the media and the public, be defeated in their efforts anyway, and possibly split their party. Any politician who read *Time* or *Newsweek*, or who remembered 1980, knew that Democrats who acted as if they approved of the deficit would suffer withering abuse. By 1984 the mood was such that Richard P. Conlon, executive director of the liberal House Democratic Study Group (DSG), declared that "there's no way you can talk about liberal social programs—there's no way you can talk about anything—until you talk about deficits." DSG Chairman Matthew McHugh hastened to distance the group from "the old spend-spend-spend liberalism."[1]

Although the public liked programs, it condemned deficits in principle. A large faction of Democratic politicians would also object to any effort to show that deficits were a "good thing." These included not only the boll weevils but also more mainstream figures such as Lawton Chiles, James Jones, and Leon Panetta.

If the Democrats could have found a way not to join in the antideficit clamor, to make clear to all concerned the reasons why they disliked Reagan's deficits but not all deficits, subsequent history might have been different. The panic about deficits might have been moderated by discussion of their nature and effects. That certainly would have been in the interest of the Democratic party, if not the nation. Instead, the party actually intensified the antideficit din. Part of that was practical politics: the Mondale campaign seized one of the only weapons available with which to attack Ronald Reagan. Part was visceral reaction against Ronald Reagan; impaling him on his own antideficit rhetoric gave Democrats immediate satisfaction.

Democrats condemned the deficit, but what could they do about it? Reagan could condemn the deficit, say it was caused by domestic spending, and propose slashing programs. Although he could not rally a majority for that position, at least it was consistent and won support from a substantial minority of the public. Democrats blasted the deficit, but most of what they wanted to do cost money. They were reduced to being mealy-mouthed or campaigning for higher taxes.

Both in the House and during the presidential campaign, a group of black Democrats and their left-liberal allies managed to merge deficit reduction with their social agenda. The Black Caucus budget plans (when offered) and Jesse Jackson's campaign combined liberal priorities with an attempt at serious deficit reduction. It was easy: clobber the military and raise taxes. Many black and left-liberal activists thought that America's mission to protect the "free world" from communism too often turned into the domination of "people of color." Why should they worry about protecting the national community from evil outsiders when blacks had been exploited for four hundred years by evil insiders? In their view, America's military might could be seen as extending the police forces of Selma or Los Angeles to El Salvador, or Chile, or Angola. Yes, the Soviets did threaten Europe, but the liberals would add that if Europeans spent more on their own defense we could spend less. When Berkeley's black congressman, Ron Dellums, proposed large defense cuts, he did not have to worry that it would compromise America's world role; Dellums opposed that role anyway.

Black Caucus members and Jesse Jackson and other diehard liberals had less difficulty than most members in proposing tax increases on the upper brackets. Too few of their constituents were in upper-income groups to be worth worrying about. A large proportion were precisely the people, those with incomes under $10,000, who most depended on the federal spending that was threatened by the deficit. Furthermore, many Black Caucus and other urban liberals who most strongly supported large tax hikes had very safe districts. Their political circumstances were reinforced by their policy preferences: to redistribute income from richer to poorer groups. This hard core of diehard liberals, therefore, saw neither defense cuts nor upper-bracket income tax increases as painful costs of deficit reduction.

In his 1984 presidential campaign, Jesse Jackson proposed large, immediate reductions in the deficit and large increases in social spending. He would have cut $80 billion (roughly a third) out of the military budget, added $50 billion in taxes, and then increased domestic spending by $60 billion. The resulting $70 billion immediate deficit reduction, combined with much smaller interest payments and defense growth in later years, would have made a big dent in the out-year deficits. The package reflected Jackson's basically redistributive intent; economic arguments about growth of the whole were less important.[2] Timothy Clark of the *National Journal* summarized both Jackson's policy and its possible appeal:

> Jackson's deficit-reduction program rested on reasoning likely to appeal to his rainbow coalition and perhaps to the majority of Americans. The federal debt, he [Jackson] said, constitutes "a near-permanent engine for the redistribution of income from the general public to leaders. The

chronic and expanding budget deficits, combined with bloated interest rates, are speeding this revenue transference along at a dizzying pace, saddling future generations of Americans with an issue containing highly explosive conflict potential."[3]

Jesse Jackson, opponent of deficits, tight money, and high interest rates, meet Andrew Jackson, early opponent of same: 1980s Democrats had good reason to return to the antideficit position of 1830s Democrats. Yet doing something about it was a much different proposition than it had been 150 years before.

In Andrew Jackson's day, egalitarians criticized government spending as providing special privileges to a favored few. Even massive internal improvements that benefited millions were financed by a transfer from a great mass of taxpayers (tariff payers) to smaller groups of beneficiaries. Andrew Jackson's Democrats saw the market as a force for, and government as a foe of, equality; obviously Democrats of the 1980s could not follow Andrew Jackson's lead. Moreover General Jackson was an assertive nationalist and military man; the hero of New Orleans and the Indian Wars was able to join intense aggressive nationalism with "small government" because the nation's enemies were extremely weak. Modern Democrats either had to play down their nationalistic assertiveness— hardly a popular course—or pay up for a military comparable to the Soviets'. When Andrew Jackson rallied debtors against creditors, he could appeal to a series of ideologically helpful, reinforcing cleavages, such as farmers against the city and non-Yankees against New England's self-righteous puritans. When liberal Democrats in the early 1980s wanted to symbolize their group of the exploited, they talked about "minorities" or "a rainbow," but many Americans saw only blacks. Blacks in 1980 were far fewer and less popular than were agrarians in 1830, and the symbolic politics of redistribution was less promising.

In Search of a Program

Democrats who were not left-liberals, or those with less safe constituencies, could not or did not want to propose huge defense cuts and big tax increases. What, then, could they do about the deficit, other than become Republicans? Democrats understood that the deficit prevented new programs. They understood that their party's basic political principle was government activism. They believed the public was skeptical of spending; they objected to Reagan's market ideology not as fundamentally false, as would a Marxist or old-line labor leader, but as extreme. Needing not only to assert a role for government but also to make a viable budget, mainstream Democrats became defensive.

The difficulties for most Democrats and their responses are evident in two papers prepared by the House Democratic Caucus. The first, "Rebuilding the Road to Opportunity," was produced by a Special Task Force on Long-Term Economic Policy and published in September 1982. Task Force Chairman Timothy E. Wirth (D-Colo.) and member and Caucus Chairman Gillis W. Long (D-La.) described the responses to their widespread process of consultation in a cover letter to the Speaker as "indicating a shared concern to answer the question we are so often asked: What do the Democrats propose?"[4]

After producing this "Yellow Book," the House Democratic Caucus joined with the Democratic National Committee (DNC) to create the National-House Democratic Caucus. The new organization, cochaired by Gillis Long and former DNC chairman Robert Strauss, included House and DNC leaders and a roster of private members that spanned the breadth of the party, from old hands like Clark Clifford to academics like Lester Thurow. In Gillis Long's words, the new organization's blue-covered statement in 1984, the "Blue Book," meant to provide "a public philosophy and an action program on which most Democratic candidates can agree—although they need not embrace every detail—and can be proud to run." These documents of the party center, however, served best to document the party's difficulties.

When the Democrats condemned Reagan's recession in 1982, they declared:

> Once more they [the Republicans] have chosen to pursue the discredited policies of "trickledown" economics. So it is up to our party to rekindle the entrepreneurial spirit in America, to encourage the investment and the risk taking—in private industry and in the public sector—that is essential if we are to maintain leadership in the world economy.[5]

Objection to trickledown was standard, but the key terms—entrepreneurship, risk taking, economic leadership—sounded Republican.

The Democrats' goals, they declared, were growth and fairness. Their distinctive means to these ends included cooperation (among business, labor, government, academics, and other sectors of society; or among nations) and a positive role for government, both of which stood in contrast to the Republican model of growth from competition in the private sector. Reagan blamed government, but Democrats did not blame the market. They declared that "free-market capitalism is the basis of our economy and remains the first and best hope for long-term growth and jobs. But just as it has done through our history . . . government must be a vital partner."[6] This formulation was just one in a series of "yes, buts."

Our Democratic author could only shake his head in sadness as he read the following passage:

> Achieving a balanced budget is very important to our economic future. We do not believe that the federal government should continue to spend an ever-increasing percentage of the nation's wealth. We need to limit spending and to set tax rates in order to generate a balanced budget during periods of sustained economic growth. To achieve the goal of a balanced budget, while limiting taxes, we must strengthen our congressional budget process, and we must constantly review existing government spending and tax programs.[7]

In the middle of this passage we see the Keynesian logic: a balanced budget during sustained growth means full employment. But that is the subordinate assertion; primary is "the importance of a balanced budget to our economic future." Next is a criticism of "ever-increasing" spending—a bow to opponents of "big government." The need to raise taxes is also subordinated with an emphasis on "limiting" them. The hairy hand was the hand of Democrats, but the voice was the voice of Reagan. If Democrats wanted spending and balance, they had to justify higher taxes.

Sensitive to the charge that Democrats were merely redistributive, failing to help create wealth in their urge to do good with other peoples' money, the Blue Book declared that "this volume helps Democrats to re-establish our identity as the party of growth, for growth is the prerequisite of opportunity." The blueprint for the future in *Renewing America's Promise* consisted of eight pillars.

The first was "a concerted, multi-year effort to eliminate the structural imbalance between the government's spending obligations and its revenues"—politicalese for "reduce the deficit." At the end of 1983, this was the primary policy goal of the New Force within the Democratic party. "Before we can target our efforts on growth," the Blue Book declares, "we must target the chief obstacle to it: the Reagan deficits. We must begin a program of economic expansion with a campaign of deficit reduction."[8] Again, Keynesian caveats were subordinated in the text.[9]

What was needed, the Blue Book argued, was "a new understanding between Americans and their government, insuring that the people know and accept the burden they must share, defining for them the common good their sacrifices will advance."[10] They did little, however, to create that understanding. Tax reform, for instance, would have to be "the cornerstone of new revenue measures" because otherwise the average taxpayer wouldn't accept a tax hike. Talk about tax reform, however, was cheap; everybody does it. Action is much more difficult because it attacks a host of interests whose immediate stakes far outweigh the average citizen's. The Democrats could have made tax reform a dramatic issue, distinguishing themselves from the Republicans by pushing the existing Bradley-Gephardt bill through the House in 1984. But because that would have led to protests by those who had to pay more at the height of the campaign, the Democrats hesitated; in the end, they allowed the president to steal the issue. That is material for another chapter.

Reagan's belief that the deficit could be reduced while taxes were unchanged and defense increased was not credible. The Democrats' promise to reduce deficits by negotiation was no more so. Yet incredible promises to reduce the deficit still committed them to the task, even as they did not win over those voters who cared most about deficits. Democrats, once again, were placing themselves in the worst of both worlds.

The Blue Book especially provided the beginnings of a new rhetoric to build a sense of community that might later encourage the individual sacrifices necessary for deficit reduction. This notion of community was expressed in imagery of the family. Thus, Reagan's spending cuts masked "an assault on poor families with pious rhetoric about 'cutting waste in government.' "[11]

By family, Democrats meant those people who have to take you in— the primary community in which differences of age or health or gender serve as reasons for some members to help others. For many, however, the family is the school of conformity and right conduct, the model hierarchy with distinctions of gender and age that order all relations. In the family people learn values and behavior. The Democrats' version of family, a subtheme in the Blue Book, would reach its greatest visibility in New York Governor Mario Cuomo's keynote address to the 1984 Democratic Convention. Whether the compassionate family was a more powerful symbol than the moral family supported by the striving individual remained to be seen.

All Democratic presidential candidates in 1984 campaigned on the themes of deficit reduction, government activism, and cooperation. The three who reached the convention were all liberals; neither Senator Gary Hart nor Reverend Jesse Jackson had substantive reasons to refuse supporting former Vice President Mondale against Reagan.

Because Walter Mondale won, his positions are of greatest interest. Mondale looked at Reagan's Republicans and saw a group of people who exalted the pursuit of wealth. Mondale—who was doing quite well, of course, as a lawyer after leaving the White House—included himself when, on September 15, 1983, he told his business advisory council that he would favor raising taxes on business and the well-to-do because "most of us in this room received more tax cuts than we needed" from President Reagan. Though met by tepid applause, Mondale continued that "I just happen to believe it. I think most wealthy Americans are a little embarrassed by the amount of tax cuts they have received."[12] Mondale looked at unions and saw not an interest group but working men and women.[13] "Since when is it a special interest to be for organized labor? I'm for organized labor. We have to stand up and make our case unashamedly." If Mondale were less redistributive than Jesse Jackson, he nonetheless defined his party's mission in terms of underdogs against topdogs.

If there is such a thing as a liberal establishment, Mondale was a perfect member. He considered himself an insider, emphasized his experience in government, and defined the president's task in terms of knowledge and management—insider considerations. "I've been there," he would declare. "I know where the buttons are." He could not shed his membership in the liberal establishment because he was of them and they were of him. In particular, he was the candidate of labor, the first candidate for the presidential nomination of his party endorsed by the AFL-CIO. The unions, with wages being slashed as companies demanded "givebacks," strikes failing left and right, and their membership declining, needed a president who would make reviving their movement a top priority.[14]

At the beginning of the presidential primary season, Mondale, with his labor base, was the front-runner. Therefore, he took the fewest risks on the deficit, proposing, for example, smaller tax hikes than did his major rivals.[15] He became the prime target in a game of "bash the candidate for not saying how he'll solve the deficit." When the eight Democratic candidates shared a stage in Hanover, New Hampshire, on January 15, Mondale and Senator John Glenn (D-Ohio), then front-runners, generated headlines with a heated exchange. Glenn called Mondale's position "vague gobbledygook," and Mondale denounced Glenn's "baloney figures."[16] In response to attacks, all the candidates had to become more specific about their budget policies.

Many campaign professionals, such as pollsters Peter Hart and Patrick Caddell, believed their party could make the deficit an issue. A few Democrats dissented. Economist Lester Thurow argued that the deficit was too big and taxes too unpopular. Victor Fingerhut, a Democrat consultant with strong union ties, scoffed that "if you walked into a bar and told three guys the Democrats had a super plan to balance the budget, what kind of response do you think you would have? . . . the American people will sit back and roar with laughter."[17] These skeptics may have been right; yet, as the campaign season wore on, the Democratic party became more and more committed to using the deficit as its major economic issue against the president. The deficit helped candidates combine worries about the future, the family, and the caliber of Reagan's management into one symbolic appeal. The trouble was that any Democrat who seriously campaigned against the deficit would have to run a campaign whose most visible policy proposal was a tax hike. Yet Mondale the candidate, as a decided underdog, had to take risks. He also had to respond to charges that he was a candidate of the special interests and a bit of a wimp, a designation meaning soft and fumbly, not a leader. So it happened that on July 19, 1984, a triumphant Walter Mondale stood on the podium at the Democratic National Convention in San Francisco to accept his party's nomination for president, declaring his courage by calling for higher taxes.

Mondale proclaimed a "new realism" based on listening to the message of the 1980 election for a strong defense and faith in the private economy, but he declared that the voters had not chosen to "savage social security and medicare," "poison the environment," create $200 billion deficits, or to create a "government of the rich, by the rich, and for the rich." He emphasized his own decency, small town roots, and sense of fairness, and then he tried to make honesty about the deficit a test of leadership, the issue on which he would show that he was more forthright and upright than the president:

> Here is the truth about the future: We are living on borrowed money and borrowed time. These deficits hike interest rates, clobber exports, stunt investment, kill jobs, undermine growth, cheat our kids, and shrink our future.
>
> Whoever is inaugurated in January, the American people will have to pay Mr. Reagan's bills. The budget will be squeezed. Taxes will go up. And anyone who says they won't is not telling the truth.
>
> I mean business. By the end of my first term, I will cut the deficit by two-thirds.
>
> Let's tell the truth. Mr. Reagan will raise taxes, and so will I. He won't tell you. I just did.
>
> There's another difference. When he raises taxes, it won't be done fairly. He will sock it to average-income families again, and leave his rich friends alone. I won't.
>
> To the corporations and freeloaders who play the loopholes or pay no taxes, my message is: your free ride is over.
>
> To the Congress, my message is: We must cut spending and pay as we go. If you don't hold the line, I will: that's what the veto is for.
>
> Now that's my plan to cut the deficit. Mr. Reagan is keeping his secret until after the election. That's not leadership; that's salesmanship.
>
> I challenge Mr. Reagan to put his plan on the table next to mine—and debate it with me on national television. Americans want the truth about the future—not after the election, but now.[18]

There was some posturing here—whom was Mondale kidding about the veto and domestic spending?—but the main thrust is pretty clear: I am going to raise your taxes. The political calculation was partly that some voters would care more about the deficit than taxes, partly that aggressive pursuit of the issue would put the president on the spot. Perhaps Mondale's challenge would make Reagan waffle, change the terms of political debate, and alter the public's perception of the two candidates as leaders.

Over a century ago, Walter Bagehot commented sagely on how a politician should approach the public:

> Much argument is not required to guide the public, still less a formal exposition of that argument. What is mostly needed is the manly utterance of clear conclusions; if a statesman gives these in a felicitous way (and if with a few light and humorous illustrations, so much the better), he has done his part. . . . A statesman ought to show his own nature, and talk in a palpable way what is to him important truth. And so he will both guide and benefit the nation.[19]

Could anyone better state Ronald Reagan's own practice? It helps a lot, however, if the "clear conclusions" have popular appeal. Engaging Reagan on Bagehot's terms, Mondale also had only four months to display his "true nature," while Reagan had had four years. Mondale's hopes required that the president "blow it." In their first debate, the president almost did; he seemed aged and confused. Suddenly suspense infused the campaign. But the suspense ended with the second debate, when Reagan again was the Reagan voters thought they knew.

William Schneider of the *National Journal* explained that Mondale's "calculated risk" was aimed at seizing control of the political agenda. If Mondale could force the president to talk about specific policies, then "the campaign [would] move in the direction of the Democrats best issue—fairness."[20] Mondale's strategy temporarily put the president on the defensive. It exacerbated the internal Republican split over taxes in which Jack Kemp and Bob Dole led the rival factions. Critics in the media joined in urging "economic realism" (that is, a tax increase) on the president. Administration representatives hedged.[21] Conservative columnist George Will remarked on the disarray and the threat to Reagan: "The tax issue bothers Reagan because it threatens to blur the sharp outline of his political profile. It has been well said that the way to get across an idea is to wrap it up in a person. Reagan became a political force by embodying clear elemental ideas."[22] Will obviously had read Bagehot.

The Democrats' tactic failed because Reagan righted his ship and took a strong antitax course, which hardly meant that voters believed there would be no tax hike. It meant instead that most voters recognized the truth of Senator Dole's explanation of the difference between the two parties: "With candidate Mondale, a tax increase is a top priority; with President Reagan it is truly a last resort."[23]

The Deficit and the Election

When Mondale lost, carrying only the District of Columbia and his home state of Minnesota, many aspects of Reagan's victory, especially his large margin among eighteen- to twenty-four-year-old voters, suggested that the long-awaited partisan realignment might follow.[24] Except for blacks and Jews (and maybe Norwegians), no group from 1980 swung toward the Democratic column. The Democrats' advantage in party identification narrowed dramatically, as Republicans seized back the advantage (won in 1981, lost in 1982) as the party of prosperity.[25] The themes of 1980's recriminations and of the Yellow and the Blue books—that the party had to embrace new ideas, avoid being tagged as spenders, and emphasize prosperity instead of redistribution—once more echoed across the pages of the nation's press.

The threatened realignment made Democrats so nervous they took the tax hike almost entirely off their public agenda. "If he wants taxes," Tony Coelho summed up their sentiment, "Mr. Reagan will have to plead with the American people for higher taxes." An ironic consequence of the election, therefore, was that the Senate GOP was left more isolated than before; instead of hoping to get the House to join with them against the president, in 1985 they first would have to win over their president, lacking a credible threat to proceed without him. A weak position.

Although most politicians took the election as a mandate *against* something—tax hikes—they did not believe that Reagan had a mandate *for* anything in particular. Polling data analyzed by Warren Miller and Merrill Shanks suggests that the electorate felt Reagan had been too conservative (in giving too little to welfare and too much to defense) but, because times were better, they reelected him anyway.[26] The president's reelection campaign had done nothing to convince politicians that voters who chose Reagan were voting to cut domestic programs. Chief of Staff James Baker declared that "it was a victory for [Reagan's] philosophy and a victory for him personally, but I'm not sitting here claiming it's a big mandate."[27]

Reagan himself did not believe that policy success in a second term required explicitly endorsing those policies. Thus, at the beginning of 1984 he had this exchange with a *Newsweek* interviewer:

Q: What's different about a second term?
A: In the first term [in California] we laid the groundwork for the great comprehensive welfare reforms that were unlike anything that had been done any place in this country before. I never mentioned them in the campaign for reelection. Never made them an issue, never held them up as something to look forward to. I didn't want to politicize it. And

immediately after the election, we went to work on them, and we achieved them.

Q: Is there a parallel here? Do you feel that in a second term you will be able to do something about the runaway cost of entitlements?

A: I believe there have to be some structural changes in our government. . . . And this is part of the getting at the deficit problem over the long haul that I look forward to doing.[28]

Reagan certainly did not campaign on the issue of controlling entitlements. The presidential election sent no message about dealing with the deficit, save that a tax hike would be politically unwise.

If the congressional election sent any message, it was an endorsement of the status quo. To regain control of the House, the GOP needed to regain almost all the twenty-six seats lost in 1982. Instead they won only fifteen, and their ideological gain was more like ten seats. Democrats, moreover, gained two seats in the Senate. Since the development of a stable two-party system, no president had emerged from his election with a smaller portion of partisans among the representatives.[29]

The voters loved Reagan but gave him a Congress that had little desire to endorse his policies. The most probable explanations for this election result include the many advantages of incumbency, good times that eliminate the impulse to "throw the bums out,"[30] and the undoubted advantage that control of state legislatures, especially in California, gave Democrats in creative redistricting. There was also some evidence to back up John Ferejohn and Morris Fiorina's suggestion that "a large majority feels hesitant to trust either party with full control over the government."[31] That is, maybe the public wanted budget and overall political stalemate or at least preferred it to any alternatives.

The public's choice of officeholders maintained the stalemate. Opinion data in 1984 told two other stories: first, the structure of opinion that constrained policy changes remained; second, the deficit, though a concern, did not dominate public opinion the way it dominated policy debate in Washington.

We already know that the public saw budget deficits as very bad, so much so that people overwhelmingly supported the balanced-budget amendment. The political question is the salience of a particular problem—how many people care how deeply about it. One index is Gallup's recurrent polling of what people consider the "most important problem" facing the country. On that subject, the deficit (or excessive spending) figured as a pretty minor item in the polls, never above 5 percent until 1984. For much of this period Reagan's budget cuts were cited by about the same percentage. In February 1984, however, the deficit jumped up to "most important problem" designation for 12 percent of respondents.

Gallup's time series on this question shows that throughout this period citizens' economic problems were far more important than the deficit. As inflation declined and unemployment increased, concern shifted to the latter. As unemployment then began to decline, foreign policy (perhaps spurred by events in Lebanon and elsewhere) sparked concern. The 1984 rise in worry (to still unimpressive levels) about the deficit, therefore, suggests not alarm so much as that slightly more than a tenth of the public felt happy enough with trends on more important issues to see the deficit as the most important problem.

This analysis of the deficit issue's marginality is supported by other data from Gallup's February 1984 poll. When asked if they approved the president's handling of his job, the public did so by a 55 percent to 36 percent margin. Reagan's worst rating—even worse than on Lebanon—was on the deficit. In an April 1984 poll, voters were asked, "Regardless of your own political views, what would you give as the best reason for voting against President Reagan?" The deficits ranked ninth, at 4 percent, far behind foreign policy (21 percent) and fairness (18 percent), less even than his age (8 percent) and distributional concerns about cuts in social programs (5 percent) or excess defense spending (5 percent). In other words, he had botched the deficit, but it did not matter too much.

The next question is, what was the public willing to do about those deficits? Throughout our history we have shown that public opinion expressed skepticism of tax cuts if it meant increasing the deficit. Even in 1983, at the height of a recession, during which people could easily claim they needed help, "narrow majorities," as William Schneider summarizes the data, were "willing to postpone or even cancel the third year of Reagan's income tax cut." But these very same people were unwilling to pay more than they already were. An early 1983 Roper poll had shown, for instance, that five respondents would rather live with the deficit for every three who would pay higher taxes to bring it down.[32] If offered other options, people overwhelmingly chose to avoid tax increases. Indeed, *once they received the final installment of the tax cut, few would willingly give it back.* Just as it is harder to cut benefits than to prevent their improvement, convincing people to forego a tax cut is much easier than persuading them to pay more. The politics of taxes and the deficit therefore passed a crucial threshold on July 1, 1983. Once people had the money, concern about the deficit, absent bad economic conditions tied to the deficit, would not convince them to give it back.

So far public opinion was all good news for Reagan; now comes the bad part. Like Congress, the public was more interested in cutting defense, though not drastically, than in reducing social spending. The public's opinion of domestic spending depended on its description. Support for "maintaining cost-of-living increases in social security benefits" and opposition to cuts in entitlement programs remained overwhelming—around eight to one—throughout this period.[33] At the end of the campaign increased spending for social programs was favored by a three to one margin.[34] Twice as many election-day respondents favored more rather than less spending on the poor (no one asked how much they were personally willing to pay). Yet voters also worried more that some people who did not deserve welfare might get it than that some who deserved it might do without.[35]

Each major political faction, therefore, was out of step with the public in some major way. The public rejected Reagan's desire to reallocate money from social to defense spending, House Democrats' desire to raise taxes, and Senate Republicans' desire to do lots of unpleasant and unpopular things to repair a deficit about which they cared far more than did most people. Yet the overall policy—worry about, but don't take much action on, the deficit—was pretty close to public preference.

Both Reagan's month-to-month job approval rating and his final margin in the election were strongly related to economic conditions. "In short," says Scott Keeter, "Reagan succeeded in accomplishing what most government heads try to do, and that is to have the cyclical upswing of the economy coincide with the latter part of an election year."[36] Election day polls showed that approval of the economy's performance was easily the largest element of Reagan's support. Both improved personal finances and hope for the economy as a whole contributed to Reagan's landslide.[37]

The deficit issue helped Mondale very little. In the end, exit polls showed that between 14 and 25 percent of voters were influenced by the deficit, and that they split fairly evenly between Mondale and Reagan. Thus, the issue helped Mondale but nowhere near enough to justify his effort.[38] In fact, if we combine deficit reduction with the tax issue, Mondale's stance was clearly unpopular. The *Los Angeles Times* poll reported that the 17 percent of voters who named taxes an important issue voted for Reagan by 80 to 20 percent. Although not all people who opposed a tax increase would have voted for Mondale in any case, the tax proposal only hurt his chances at election.

The Democrats were left committed to a position on a fundamentally Republican issue. Both ABC and *Los Angeles Times* polls showed that people who worried about the deficit marginally favored Mondale. But the larger number, who emphasized either taxes or government spending, favored Reagan by more than four to one. Many Democrats, especially politicians, now had reasons to dislike deficits. But the real, visceral deficit haters are in that large group who object to government spending and who share Reagan's belief that deficits mean excessive spending.

"I keep pointing out that that's the problem," said Maine Democratic Senator George J. Mitchell. "There's no pressure on Reagan to do anything [about deficits] because most people who are concerned are Republicans who are going to vote for him anyway."[39]

Mondale tried to make the deficit an argument for unease about the economy. It didn't work because it's hard to convince people to pay something now (e.g., taxes) for an uncertain future reward. The epitaph for the Democrats' use of the deficit in the 1984 presidential campaign was pronounced by a student in Youngstown, Ohio: "I have a personal debt, and I can't afford taxes being raised," he explained. "The national debt might hit me later in life but I've got to put bread on the table right now."[40]

The Deficit and Elite Opinion

The election, at a minimum, suggested that the deficit was not such a great electoral issue. The economics of the deficit were at best obscure. Why, then, one might ask, did the election not cause the issue to begin to fade away? If the public was basically satisfied, and experience suggested it gave no partisan advantage, then why didn't the politicians find something else to worry about?

Error and inertia and the short-run attractiveness of banging on the other side explain some persistence of the deficit issue. We would emphasize another factor as well. Unlike *Time*'s student in Youngstown, the politicians could not so easily separate the nation's debt from their self-esteem. The deficit was their responsibility as the nation's governors and thus a measure of their own worth. True, the public kept returning incumbents to office, seemingly indicating satisfactory performance. Yet within their own group, as well as the realm of opinion formation and debate to which they paid most attention, the deficit became a sign of their own ineptitude.

This intermediate realm of "informed," "elite," or "responsible" opinion is what V. O. Key called the "political stratum." Throughout the budgetary struggles we have seen politicians verbally mortifying themselves over their deficit sin, lamenting their own lack of courage, and prophesying the visitation of the sins of the fathers upon the children and grandchildren unto endless generations. You would think they were discussing the sacking of the Temple of Solomon. We have seen commentators galore, the mass media and academics, holding politicians accountable; the newsweeklies running cover articles on the deficit monster searching for ill effects and, as they stubbornly refused to appear, stubbornly concluding that retribution was inevitable. *The deficit battle has been, in large measure, a panic of responsibility, a panic among the responsible.*

There is a quality of group-think to our story that might best be left to the social psychologists. Politicians are a group, talking to each other, reinforcing their own opinions. And they pay close attention to their peer groups of Washington influentials, the media and policy experts.[41] Yet the tendency to all say the same thing resulted also from some ways politicians relate to the public.

American politicians are entrepreneurs in a market for representation. They are continually insecure, fearful that their market will be raided by a competitor. Worse yet, their customers' preferences are fickle, influenced by other noncompetitive but also uncontrollable actors (the media, academics, etc.) who are not competitors but also cannot be controlled. Politicians can never be sure what the public wants. All of us come to understand other people by associating them with ourselves; politicians similarly expect the public to share their personal fears and values even while suspecting that the public may be different. Fear of both opponents using the deficit and other influencers increasing the marketability of antideficit appeals, encouraged politicians to believe that the public would punish deficit makers. This belief, of course, was fed by many pieces of evidence ranging from poll data to personal contacts. But it was wrong.

Democracy, a wise man (we think Adlai Stevenson) once said, is a political system in which the people get the kind of government they deserve. In a fair world, politicians could tell the public that it should resolve the contradictions within itself. What did it want compared to what it was prepared to pay for? In the real world, politicians could not blame the voters. That is not only a bad way to get reelected (compare Jimmy Carter and his "malaise" to his buttering up the public in 1976), but it also admits politicians' impotence, a denial of responsibility for governing the nation. Politicians of all stripes would take the moral objections to deficits more seriously because, if the deficit signified bad management, they were the bad managers.

When the press blasted politicians, it quoted politicians to do so. Dan Rostenkowski declared that "word of our impotence will precede us"; Warren Rudman described himself and his colleagues as "a bunch of turkeys." The whole complex of moral notions surrounding the deficit— household management, trusteeship, care for future generations, good government—spoke to the self-worth of the nation's governors more than to that of the public. The politics of responsibility was self-imposed by many of our leaders upon their visions of themselves.

In 1980 and 1981, the deficit ostensibly had been so important because it had something to do with the economy. By 1983 and 1984, deficits were much worse, and the economy was somewhat better. If the real concern were the economy, worry about deficits should have diminished.

On balance, worry about the deficit did diminish among the public, but agony over it among politicians increased. The issue remained, but its meaning changed.

The deficit became a symbol of order and legitimacy within the political household. Both its persistence and level of budgetary strife convinced politicians they were failing to govern the nation. Thus, the failure to solve the problem became the problem: the deficit mattered because it proved the politicians were too inept to handle it. Desperate to show they could act, Congress and the president adopted two radical proposals: tax reform and Gramm-Rudman-Hollings.

There are many differences and similarities between the politics of 1985–1986, when GRH and tax reform were adopted, and the politics of 1981, the year of the Omnibus Budget Reconciliation Act and Economic Recovery Tax Act. The most important difference is in the stakes. In 1981 the question was whether the government could command the economy. In 1985–1986 the question was whether the government could control itself.

NINETEEN

Gramm-Rudman-Hollings, or the Institutionalization of Stalemate

It was a new year, 1985, and a new presidential term, Ronald Reagan's second. New leaders also occupied some key positions. And yet in more fundamental ways nothing had changed. Which may explain why the opposing forces thought more of discomforting the other side than of helping themselves.

Politicians under Pressure

James Jones's term as chairman of House Budget expired. Party leaders were happy to see Jones go, but their preferred successor, Leon Panetta, was ineligible. William Gray (D-Pa.) filled the vacuum. A black preacher from Philadelphia, Gray's political style was the antithesis of that other, better-known preacher, Jesse Jackson. The 1984 *Almanac of American Politics* noted that Gray, elected in 1978 and by 1983 a member of both Budget and Appropriations, "seems quietly to be building up influence." Gray got along far better than had Jones with both party leaders and ideological opponents. Combining support from liberals and members of the Appropriations Committee, Gray easily won the post by convincing some conservatives that only a liberal could win liberal votes for spending cuts. Yet, like Jones, Gray had to satisfy House Democrats with little interest in domestic spending cuts.

The two Republican sides of the triangle also had leadership changes. Reagan remained, as did Stockman (temporarily). But Feldstein had gone back to Harvard, not to be replaced for quite a while; his open opposition to administration policy led to some thoughts of abolishing the CEA. Ed Meese was confirmed as attorney general. Mike Deaver went into a private consulting business. The third member of the troika, James Baker, tiring of staff work, had toyed with the idea of becoming commissioner of major league baseball, but he discovered that Don Regan was also tired of his Treasury job. Baker wanted more independence, and Regan wanted to be closer to the president; they switched jobs. Baker brought Darman with him to Treasury as deputy secretary. It was a blockbuster deal.

Howard Baker, meanwhile, had retired from the Senate; after a five-way contest, Bob Dole won the race to succeed Baker as majority leader. Dole's election was generally viewed as a sign that Senate Republicans wanted a strong hand who could, if necessary, lead them against the White House. Dole's successor at Finance, Robert Packwood, was known for his belief in using tax preferences for public purposes.

The net of these changes replaced the previous main link between Senate and White House, a Baker/Baker chain, with Regan/Dole. Regan had far less understanding (and tolerance) of the needs of politicians than had Jim Baker. Dole was far more likely than Howard Baker to push his own agenda.

Although no one could expect much progress in the budget disputes, there was much fanfare about tax reform. The vague talk about reform during the campaign became real when the Treasury, in its promised postelection report, suggested substantial rate reductions, "simplification" (three rates instead of fourteen), and elimination of many tax preferences. Treasury had proposed, with a few modifications, a tax policy technician's bill that zapped all sorts of constituencies, especially business. The scope of "Treasury 1" (as it was called), its surprising content, Regan and Reagan's continued support for reform in general, and support from some Democrats assured that tax reform would stay on the agenda. Yet few would have bet on its passage; the idea ran against the system's grain. There was no mobilized constituency *for* reform; if anything, the public, which hardly trusts politicians, expected it to turn out badly. Any losers, that is, current beneficiaries of preferences, would mobilize heavily to protect themselves. Like deficit reduction, tax reform seemed foreclosed by a balance of political power that preserved the status quo; the sensible prediction was Yogi Berra's phrase: "Déjà vu all over again."

The same ingredients, reheated again, were likely to yield the same flavor of budgetary, or political, stew. The budget process was beginning to resemble not an ordinary pot but a pressure cooker. As the heat steadily built, so did the pressure; without a safety valve, the pressure eventually would blow the top off. Politicians had been fighting so vehemently for so long that the conflict was about to burst its bounds. Who or what would get splattered in the process remained unknown. The explosion was coming because our politicians were not inanimate objects; they had wills of their own. And they hated life in the budgeting pressure cooker.

They were desperate first about the perceived perfidy of their opponents. Each blamed the others for the heat. Reagan saw a pork-barreling Congress that refused to do its duty by cutting wasteful programs. Worse, it manipulated the budget process, making promises in budget resolutions that it refused to keep and using continuing resolutions to impose policies (e.g., forbidding military aid to Nicaraguan Contras by holding national defense hostage).

House leaders saw a president and a Republican party who, after years of bashing Democrats about deficits, had not only doubled the national debt but had the gall to keep blaming Democrats. Senate leaders saw a president and House leaders that continually put partisan and constituency interests ahead of the greater good—responsible fiscal management. The administration kept rigging the numbers, and the House kept playing games on cuts. Neither stuck to the deal in budget resolutions. Grudges festered. The factions grew more interested in coercing than in negotiating with each other. But frustration with their rivals was only part of the story.

The deficits were widely believed to epitomize a failure to govern. Politicians of left, right, and center could agree on that even as they pointed fingers at each other. The foreseeable future held nothing but unending failure, deficits without compensation. Neither was Reagan to get much more defense, nor were Democrats to get more domestic programs. Politicians want to do positive things, but the deficit had turned politics into a totally negative process.

So, in 1985 and then in 1986, two things happened that never could have if the ordinary logic of politics had applied. Tax reform and something called Gramm-Rudman-Hollings (GRH) passed. Both GRH and tax reform were examples of political macho. Each was an attempt to supersede "special interest" politics—the normal clash of contending forces over identifiable benefits—with their version of the "general interest." Each was endorsed by politicians who feared criticism for not going along, yet neither had a positive political constituency dedicated to their terms.

With GRH politicians tried to slash the Gordian knot of budgeting. With tax reform they tried to do good in an era when good could not be done the normal way—spending. Yet the similar origins of GRH and tax reform should not hide their differences.

The 1986 tax reform bill at least did something: when it became law, Congress and the president could say, "We chose. We governed." Tax reform was a surprising policy choice, maybe wise, maybe not; GRH was an impossible promise that only made things worse.

The essence of GRH was budgetary terrorism. House Majority Whip Tom Foley explained that it was "about the kidnapping of the only child of the President's official family that he loves" (meaning the defense budget) "and holding it in a dark basement and sending the President its ear." The other players felt the same way; they just had different ideas of who were the hostages. Democrats could slice defense's ear only by doing the same to their own "children." Supposedly this hostage game would force participants to reduce deficits in the normal legislative process, so the doomsday machine would not go off. If some other set of cuts had been more politically acceptable, they would have been made, thus negating the need for GRH. The process made no sense. In the end, Gramm-Rudman-Hollings not only did not force a solution, but it actually paralyzed the system.

The Road to Gramm-Rudman-Hollings

If we want to show the buildup of frustration over budgeting, we should sample the world as politicians see it: an onslaught of events, day after wearying day, to no evident end. We present events as they might appear in a politician's diary.

Haven't I Met You Before?

BUDGET DIARY, PART 1

February 4, 1985: The president's budget contains more of the same—a 6 percent increase in defense above inflation and deep domestic cuts but not including social security COLAs.[1]

February 5: People widely regard the budget as politically unfeasible. CBO says administration estimates—based on lower interest rates and improved economic conditions, supposedly reducing the deficit to $100 billion by fiscal 1990—are $86 billion too low.[2]

March 14: Senate Budget passes a budget resolution that would reduce CBO's projected deficit by $50 to $60 billion in FY86, thus lowering it to 2 percent of GNP in FY89. Defense would have no real increase in FY86 and 3 percent in FY87 and FY88; the COLA for social security would be canceled for one year. President Reagan is unhappy about defense.[3]

April 4: The president endorses a compromise with Republicans on Senate Budget. Defense would get 3 percent real increases each year. Social security COLAs would be 2 percent less than inflation, with a minimum of 2 percent, for each of the next three years (thus 2 percent if CPI up 3 percent; 3 percent if CPI up 5 percent). The resolution eliminates, or rather assures elimination, of Amtrak, the Job Corps, UDAG, revenue sharing, and other programs. It's "tough medicine for a tough time," says Senator Domenici. Stockman, Dole, and Barry Goldwater all admit that passing this package on the floor will be difficult.[4]

April 15–19: Skepticism abounds as the budget resolution nears the floor. Senator Thad Cochran (R-Miss.) expects Democrats to "create as many unpopular votes for Republicans as possible, to make us look cruel and heartless"; Senator Ernest F. Hollings (D-S.C.) merely predicts "a mess."[5]

Later in April: At dinner in the Appleton, Wisconsin, Elks Club, Senator Bob Kasten (R-Wis.) hears much the "same as other legislators: reduce the deficit but don't cut programs."[6] Representative Robert I. Matsui (D-Calif.) reports that at twenty-four meetings with interest groups in his district he heard much about protecting spending programs but little about their cost. "The deficit would only come up at my prompting. That portends very poorly for the state of the budget process if other members heard what I did."[7]

April 24: In order to gather support for the Senate Republican resolution, President Reagan goes to the nation on television. Key phrases are "endless appetites to spend . . . big spenders in Congress . . . out of your pocket." Public response is sparse and divided.[8]

April 25–26: After it becomes clear that the president's public appeal didn't win sufficient Republican support, Minority Leader Byrd drops his objections and asks for an immediate vote. After conferring with his colleagues, Dole has the Senate adjourn.[9]

May Day: The Senate conditionally approved the Republican budget— and then began voting to undo it, starting with restoration of all COLAs (based on a motion by Senator Dole, 65 to 34). Senator Domenici still claims there might be a majority for a one-year COLA freeze. Why? He doesn't say.[10]

May 2: The Senate votes to hold defense to an inflation adjustment in FY86, 3 percent real growth in FY87–88.

May 3: The Senate vote to slow down defense increases, called a watershed by its advocates, is deemed an "irresponsible act" by President Reagan.[11]

May 10: After two weeks of negotiations, the Senate approves a FY86 budget resolution that would freeze not only COLAs but also defense spending and, to top it off, assumes Congress would wipe out all funding for thirteen domestic programs. The 49 to 49 tie, achieved by wheeling in Senator Pete Wilson (R-Calif.) from his hospital bed, is broken by Vice President Bush.[12] The day belonged to Senator Domenici: "We have done," he crowed, "what many thought was impossible—significant deficit reduction."[13] A Democratic proposal including new revenues lost, 43 to 54, on May 8. The final plan is a lot like Senate Budget's plan from early March.

May 11–16: "The Senate just laid itself open to the charge it has become the latest mass abuser of the elderly," says Claude Pepper. House Republicans, during Budget Committee negotiations, say they'll gladly restore the COLA. The Democrats' plan, hammered out by new Chairman Gray after many meetings—of the leadership, the Budget Committee, and the caucus—also excludes tax increases. There is momentary hope of bipartisan agreement. Democrats have decided any taxes will be offered by their opponents. But the Democrats have frozen defense BA at the FY85 level, without even an inflation adjustment, for FY86. The Republicans cannot accept that.

On May 16 House Budget adopts its resolution, which purports to equal the Senate's deficit cuts in FY86 ($56 billion) but cuts $37 billion less over the next two years. The difference is mainly that the House Budget Committee plan eliminates only one program, General Revenue Sharing. Actually, the House plan matches the Senate for FY86 only by assuming some rather dubious things, for example, $4 billion in extra revenue from offshore oil leases and large savings from reduced government contracting with the private sector.[14]

May 23–24: Rising to the challenge of meeting what Domenici calls the largest deficit reduction in history (even though you can't have a huge reduction without starting from an even huger deficit), the Democratically controlled House passes its own budget resolution (258 to 170). Democratic leaders say there will be no compromise on the COLAs; in fact, "if the Senate were to take another vote on the COLAs," in the Speaker's judgment, "they'd run so fast from it they'd trample all over themselves."[15]

Conservative Democrat Marvin Leath, wanting more deficit reduction, tries to add a COLA cut to the defense nominal freeze. Supporters argue that the elderly will go along if others are visibly sacrificing. Of House members, 56 seemingly agree; 372 do not. "There was an obvious coalition there," says one Leath supporter. "We just didn't hit them at the peak of their courage." The *Congressional Quarterly Weekly Report* sums it up: the "House Centrist Bloc [is] Still Waiting to Happen."[16] The president, of course, protests defense cuts. "I don't know how in the world we can get the Senate and the House together," Domenici laments.[17]

June 22: "I'll repeat it until I'm blue in the face: I will veto any tax increase the Congress sends me," the president says in his weekly radio address.[18]

June 11–25: After two weeks of getting nowhere, Domenici breaks off the budget resolution conference. He blames House intransigence on COLAs. But the polls, and House Republicans, as a consequence, are siding with House Democrats. Why are Senate Republicans so insistent?

Because they've already taken the risk by voting for their own plan; as one puts it, "The political damage has been done."

June 26: Speaker O'Neill says he, personally, favors expanding the tax on social security benefits for people of higher income.

June 27: Domenici recalls the budget resolution conferees, hoping to make something of the Speaker's suggestion. Not wanting to be out front with a tax increase, House Democratic conferees said O'Neill was not speaking for them.[19] Six senators (three Democrats and three Republicans), led by Gorton and Chiles, suggest a plan with $59 billion in new taxes over three years, providing slightly less defense than in the Senate plan. It thus reduces the deficit by more than either the House or the Senate plans. It still eliminates the COLAs but suggests targeting 20 percent of those saving for programs for the needy elderly.

June 28: Heard Budget Director Stockman, in an off-the-record speech, insist that substantial tax increases are the only way to slash the deficit "consistent with fiscal sanity."[20]

July 9: A cocktail hour reception at the White House—including Chiles, Dole, Gorton, Gray, O'Neill, and Representatives Thomas J. Downey (D-N.Y.), and Mike Lowry (D-Wash.). Opening with a sermon against tax increases, President Reagan obviously didn't want to hear from Senators Chiles and Gorton about their compromise tax increases, saying (according to notes kept by Downey) "Dammit, I can't listen to all of this." The chair of the HBC, William Gray, tells Reagan that recurrent presidential attacks on the House Budget Committee are harmful to the process: "I told him to keep the rhetoric to a minimum and to get the facts straight." Reagan came to the meeting ready to abandon the one-year freeze on social security COLAs—linchpin of his agreement with the Senate Republican leadership. The meeting was held to see what the president could get for it. Dole and Gray debate the realism of savings in the House and Senate budget resolutions. Reagan suggests a "framework for agreement."[21] Stockman announces his resignation, effective August 1.

July 10: President Reagan meets with House and Senate budget conferees to outline the framework for agreement. He and the Speaker have agreed to retain the COLAs while giving defense its inflation adjustment on budget authority. To make the numbers sound better, they'll use the House defense outlay figures. Funny numbers. How, one might ask, will they hit the year's informal target of $50 billion in deficit reductions?

Senator Domenici, who had been left out of the cocktail reception and who felt that Reagan had achieved too little in spending cuts, doesn't take seriously the president's call for a bipartisan effort to recover the same $28 billion that would have come from the COLA freeze. Speaker O'Neill professes himself "very happy" with the outcome but disagrees sharply with Majority Leader Dole about what was decided. COLAs were gone for good, not merely, as Dole insisted, pushed toward the edge of the table.[22]

July 11: Republicans are feeling betrayed; Bob Dole charges the president with "surrendering to the deficit." Nor, in Dole's opinion, does Chief of Staff Don Regan seem exactly eager to take on the budget.[23] A frustrated Dole vents the wrath of senators at being dumped after they stood up to make the tough choices. Obviously, the White House has underestimated the reaction (defeat, dismay, anger) of senators to going back on the COLAs. Not every Democrat is overjoyed; many are disgusted with what their conferees gave away on defense. According to Representative Mike Lowry, "O'Neill and Wright . . . would give away the world for COLAs." Lowry thinks that accepting the Senate position on budget authority for defense eventually will force Democrats to cut domestic programs still more.[24]

July 12: Reagan, meeting with the twenty-two Republican senators up for reelection, "apparently fanned the bad feelings," instead of reducing them. " 'If the president can't support us,' Senator Grassley declares, 'he ought to keep his mouth shut.' " In his seriocomic way, Majority Whip Senator Alan Simpson (R-Wy.), said (of the White House bargain) "that was not an agreement by the fifty guys who jumped off a cliff over here."[25]

There is still no budget resolution. Unless House Democrats come up with an offset for the then sacrosanct COLAs, Dole and Domenici say they will not meet. "Nuts," or words to that effect, came from the House conferees, who offered $3 billion at most. If the senators wanted more, let them be the proposers.[26]

July 13: President Reagan undergoes surprise cancer surgery. The attacks on him are muted. "We're not mad at him," says Dole. "We're mad at the deficit."[27]

July 15: White House spokesman Larry Speakes says the president wants a budget resolution "this week." The conference resumes, and Domenici suggests discarding the Reagan/O'Neill framework. House conferees reject the Gorton/Chiles plan, but Gray promises a new spending cut proposal.[28]

July 16: The House votes, 239 to 181, to waive the point of order against considering appropriations without a budget resolution. Chairman Gray offers $24 billion more, over three years, in spending cuts and a compromise figure on defense BA. Domenici says the House defense number violates the framework that, a day before, he had suggested discarding.[29]

July 17: A headline reads: "Talks on Fiscal 1986 Budget Collapse,

Agreement This Summer Seems Unlikely." Senate conferees, led by Domenici, and including Chiles and Hollings, are complaining that domestic cuts proposed by House members are fictitious. Even if it's true, House members say they have already cut below the support in their chamber.[30] Terming the complaint sanctimonious, Gray accuses the senators of "moving the target" to seek ever greater domestic cuts. Not so, Domenici retorts. "I disagree radically with you," Gray snaps back. When Representative Wright suggests that conferees "exorcise the devil of bad feeling" by not preaching, Domenici says, "Don't preach to us." His parting words are "don't call us, we'll call you."[31]

July 18: The president, from his hospital bed, pleads for an item veto, but the Senate fails (57 to 42) to apply cloture (a rule requiring a three-fifths majority). The filibuster is led by the chairmen of Appropriations (Mark Hatfield, R-Oreg.) and Rules (Charles Mathias, R-Md.) who argue that the item veto amounts to usurpation of power.[32] "If the president wants a balanced budget," asks Senator Weicker, "why has he not submitted one?"[33]

July 22–23: Domenici gives Dole a birthday present comprised of the thirty-five plans for budget resolutions the Senate Budget Committee had considered in 1985.[34] "The more we look at it," Dole tells reporters, "the more we're giving up."[35] Dole, meeting with Don Regan, David Stockman, House Minority Leader Robert Michel, and others at the White House, wonders whether perhaps COLAs could be indexed against inflation only every two years.[36]

When the president invites Republican legislators to the White House that week, Dole insists that a range of legislation be discussed. "The primary purpose," he said with some exasperation, "is not to spend 90 percent of the time talking about the budget."[37]

July 24: On a strict party-line vote, 22 to 14, working from the House budget resolution, House Ways and Means met its reconciliation target today by voting revenue increases and spending decreases that are supposed to reduce the deficit by $19 billion over three years. It's fairly typical: medicare providers cut, a scheduled tax decrease (on cigarettes) again postponed, and more money for welfare.[38]

July 25: There they go again: attempting to break the impasse, Republican leaders up the ante; they are proposing a $5 a barrel tax on imported oil, biennial indexing of both COLAs and the tax code that would not take effect until after the 1986 election, and still big cuts in other domestic programs. All the Senate conferees except Jim Sasser (D-Tenn.) support the proposal. They still are trying to make big cuts in one area palatable by cutting in other areas as well. The $338 billion deficit reduction in three years is considerably larger than their earlier biggest reduction and $70 billion more than the House resolution. The

Senate budgeters' strategy still isn't working. Chief of Staff Regan says the administration will study the proposal carefully; but his boss, the president, caught on the way to a cabinet meeting, repeats his war cry: "I'm not for any tax." Speaker O'Neill makes a point of telling reporters that he is "stubbornly opposed" to reducing social security benefits and that Northeasterners like himself were against oil import fees.[39]

July 28: Read in the *New York Times* today that "almost every day some members of Congress express frustration at their failure to reach agreement on a budget plan setting overall spending levels."[40] The House, however, had already passed five of the thirteen regular appropriations bills, all of which freeze spending at 1985 levels. "A freeze is on," notes Representative Neal Smith (D-Iowa), "budget resolution or no budget resolution."[41]

July 29: After meeting with GOP legislative leaders, President Reagan rejects the taxes and COLA reductions in the new Senate proposal. That writes finis to the three-year, $300 billion deficit-reduction package put forward by Republican leaders. Complimenting the conferees for a good try, Reagan advises them to "act with dispatch . . . put aside their differences, get down to business and produce a budget." A little galling, no? Senator Dole is bitter: "There will not be too many Republican senators responding to pleas from the White House." Dole has his hostages, too. He predicts that "there will be no tax reform this year unless there is a budget."[42]

July 30: Senator Dole fails to show up for a meeting with President Reagan.[43] "There won't be any plank-walking anymore," says Senator William Cohen (R-Maine). "Not unless Bob Dole is the one that makes the request." A lot of anger is directed at Donald Regan, who "didn't hurt his relations with Senate Republicans," according to Senator Gorton, "because they weren't any good to begin with." Senators try to back off from anger at the president himself—Gorton moving from "the president has sold us down the river again" (July 30) to "he's the greatest political asset we have and he remains that asset" (August 1).[44] They're still resentful.

August 1: Domenici, Chiles, Gray, and Latta, after two nights of meetings, reveal to their fellow conferees a compromise plan: essentially the House wins. The only big program terminated is revenue sharing. Yet domestic discretionary programs not for the poor take a 20 to 30 percent hit. All budget conferees except Hollings endorse the plan, which then whizzes through House and Senate by large margins before Congress goes home for August. "The one thing we have not done," said Senator William Armstrong (R-Colo.), summing up prevailing feeling, "is solve the underlying problem: the deficit."[45] It is projected at $171.9 billion for FY86. Hollings fumes that, in resisting deficit reduction, "you've got

Tip O'Neill and Jim Wright acting like they work for the White House."[46] Moderate Republican Senator Warren Rudman (N.H.), in frustration, also opposes the conference report.[47]

August 2: Calling the budget resolution "not a giant step—maybe a bunny hop," William Gray put his finger on an aspect of the situation—self-denigration—that has been troubling participants who have struggled so hard to come up with something. The public could hardly appreciate the progress that has been made, he complained, when "the people who participated in it are pooh-poohing it."[48]

August 15: Amid harsh attacks on the budget resolution (as "a limp rag"—David Stockman), CBO Director Rudolph Penner comes up with the surprisingly optimistic conclusion that there has been "enormous progress from the kind of disastrous projections we were making just a year and a half ago." The nonpartisan CBO chief says the projected deficit for FY90 has fallen from 6 percent of GNP (as estimated in 1984) to 2.1 percent (as of August 1985). Shutting down the defense buildup, DEFRA, and the new budget resolution (if enforced) could, by FY87, get the deficit to a level where interest payments would begin to decline. So why the hysteria? Penner says it is due to members expecting the problem to be "solved all in one year."[49] He may be right, but no one is listening.

A Bad Idea Whose Time Has Come

Grumpy and dispirited, congressmen went home for the Labor Day recess. Once again the Senate Republicans had rallied themselves to promote deficit reduction, only to be slapped down by the House and the White House. The final, bipartisan effort of Senate conferees had been similarly thwarted. In form the budget process had survived; a resolution was now in place. But Senator Domenici and his allies had to wonder if a process that did so little and took so long was worth preserving.

At least they were out of Washington—the president at his California ranch, while lobbyists, staffers, and members scattered to districts or any place other than Washington in August. On August 1 David Stockman left for good. But Stockman's former sidekick, Phil Gramm, by now a Republican, hung around.

When John Tower retired in 1984, Gramm easily won the Republican nomination for Tower's Senate seat. Gramm then beat a liberal Democratic opponent, joining the Senate in 1985. As a very junior senator, he had little voice in the budget battles in our diary. But he had kept his contacts with interest groups and the administration, and he still had a lot of ideas as well as an instinct for the political jugular. Where everyone else saw a mess, Gramm saw opportunity; while Congress recessed, he went to work.

Gramm in Congress

Senator Philip Gramm's economics and his politics were but different sides of the same coin. He believed not only in a market economy but also that competitive individualism was the proper basis for social life.

Representative Vin Weber (R-Minn.) commented that "in every conversation I've ever had with him about politics, he's had a vision and a strategy. At the core of that strategy is to permanently rip apart the Democratic coalition."[50] Gramm wanted to weaken Democratic ability to support what he calls its "bought constituencies"—labor unions, farmers, students, the lot. " 'The Democratic Party is the party of Government,' Gramm argues, 'and anything that lessens the power of Government, as against the private sector, is going to hurt them.' "[51] Because the behavior he disapproves is doing what comes naturally for both politicians who get elected and constituents who receive benefits, Gramm set out to make that behavior unprofitable.

Gramm's distrust of institutions that restrain individuals extended to his behavior in Congress. No supporter of established authority, he ignored not only some normal incentives but also the normal authority structure of politicians. Conforming to the expectations of (or even agreements with) others was not his idea of fulfillment. Gramm would defer to neither those with the stature of chairmanships nor those with many years in office. He would not delegate to staff if he thought he could do a job better, however technical or "low-status." Gramm was a competitive individualist, trying to create institutions that encouraged persons like himself.

The new senator had long supported rules changes that would bolster his position, including the balanced budget/spending limitation amendment. Barely two months after assuming office in 1979 as a Democratic representative from Texas, Gramm (with Jones and Latta) tried—unsuccessfully—to add a balanced budget requirement in a bill to raise the debt limit. In 1981 he persuaded Majority Leader Jim Wright (D-Tex.) to join him in sponsoring another, but this time meatier, balanced budget bill. Like its far more famous successor, this 1981 bill required the president to sequester funds through automatic percentage cuts if the budget were not balanced. The bill died.[52] Gramm offered it again in 1982. "I felt then," Gramm recalled, "the time had not come, but it was going to come."[53]

Combining across-the-board cuts with spending limits was hardly without precedent: at least five efforts to do just this had been tried between 1967 and 1972. The 1967 effort, attached to a continuing resolution, provided for percentage cuts while exempting uncontrollable, mostly entitlement, costs. The 1968 attempt was similar, except that six categories of expenditure were exempted: farm price supports, public assistance, social security, debt interest, veterans' benefits, and the costs of the Vietnam War.[54]

From 1983 on, insiders such as Dole, Domenici, Bob Michel, and Trent Lott had more or less ineffectively floated similar proposals for impoundment authority and/or across-the-board cuts. Gramm, by contrast, was in dead earnest. He meant to attach his plan to the next increase in the debt ceiling—an increase particularly vulnerable to a deficit-reduction rider because it would raise the ceiling over $2 trillion. Senators did not want to have to admit voting for a $2 trillion debt; if they could say that simultaneously they had done something about the deficit, the vote would be easier to justify.

Gramm revised his 1981 bill to extend his sequestration procedure in stages over five years rather than to reduce the deficit to zero in one year. Everything, defense as well as social security, was to be in the pot. Exactly how sequestration would work he left vague. It is better to first get people committed to the principle and then work out the details later. By the end of August 1985, Gramm was winning support from his natural allies, such as the Chamber of Commerce. But it soon became apparent that he could not do it alone, for he was far from welcome everywhere. Distrust of him mingled with disbelief that so simple (some would say simple-minded) a solution could work or would pass. So Gramm decided to seek a minimum number of cosponsors—another Republican with better access and a Democrat.

Warren Rudman (R-N.H.), who had openly talked of retiring from the Senate because it seemed incapable of solving major national problems, asked to join Gramm. "This place," Rudman told a reporter, "is 99 percent frustration and 1 percent exhilaration. It's hard to live on that 1 percent."[55] What Rudman lacked—budget expertise—he thought that Gramm, an economist, had. A former state attorney general accustomed to doing his own legal research, Rudman had looked at forty-three state statutes on budget balance in his own search for procedural reforms that would make deficit reduction more likely. And he had what Gramm needed; Rudman himself put it as delicately as possible: "I have five times more experience in the Senate than Phil Gramm has. I have a great working relationship with a wide range of senators on both sides of the aisle. And my work is very well respected. Not that Phil's isn't respected, but it takes time to develop."[56] Rudman believed Gramm's proposal would do the job, though not quite in the way Gramm intended. The prospect of sequestration would be so horrendous, Rudman thought, that it would compel Congress and the president to negotiate a reasonable settlement.[57]

Rudman also recruited Fritz Hollings, former Budget chairman, far more senior than his two colleagues. Hollings's influence was limited by his minority status and his less-than-perfect relationship with his colleagues, but he made the bill look bipartisan. Gramm would have been quite happy to see the sequester actually occur; Rudman thought the sequester was so crazy it would force a bargain on some other terms; and Hollings's preference was never really clear. "One of the great things about Gramm-Rudman-Hollings," a sponsor commented, "is that everybody saw something different in it."[58] Of such stuff are grand coalitions made.

The three worked first on defining a more precise proposal and then selling it to others. They divided up the lobbying task but agreed that none of the three should face the press alone. Gramm would be the outside man, working with the White House, conservative groups, and OMB (where his old friend and colleague James Miller had been nominated to succeed Stockman). Hollings, and especially Rudman, were the inside men, selling it to the senators.

Leaving details aside, their product was a radical revision of the policy base. Gramm-Rudman-Hollings set declining targets for the deficit, from $180 billion in FY86 to $144 billion in FY87, $108 billion in FY88, and so, in $36 billion chunks, to zero in FY91. If, as each fiscal year began, Congress had not yet acted to meet these targets, then an automatic procedure, the sequester, would take effect, reducing budget authority across-the-board by whatever amount was required. "It's one of the rare examples I've seen since I've been here of a truly new idea," Slade Gorton commented. "There's a tremendous inertia under the present system in favor of the status quo. The genius of GRH . . . is that it profoundly changes the consequences of inaction." Unlike previous proposals to grant impoundment authority, GRH would not allow the president either to pick and choose or to refuse to make cuts—or so the sponsors claimed.

No one, but no one, in the Senate wanted to vote for a $2 trillion debt limit; it was obscene. "I frankly don't believe, as the Majority Leader," Senator Dole told a group of business executives, "I have the votes" to pass the new debt limit. This reluctance gave Gramm, Rudman, and Hollings leverage: they had the stick of holding up a vote and forcing their colleagues to vote against budget balance; they offered the carrot of doing something that might actually achieve balance—and that certainly would change things.

There were many technical difficulties. "Senator," a key author of the final package recalls asking Gramm, "how do you cut 10 percent out of medicaid? As a program manager, what do I do? What do I tell the hospitals?" How do you cut budget authority in order to get the needed outlays? Does it mean that a program spending half as quickly must have its budget authority cut twice as much? Do you cut outlays by repealing obligations already entered into, thereby abrogating contracts? The answers to such questions could determine whose priorities were favored by the plan. The administration, however, signed on to the concept without much attention to such details.

The new White House team (Chief of Staff Don Regan brought new people when he changed places with James Baker) was immediately charged with amateurism if not incompetence in comparison to the Stockman-Baker-Darman triumvirate they replaced. Naturally, they weren't pleased. And though they admired the old team's savvy in dealing with Congress, the new group saw itself as far more attuned to the president's desires. Like the man they worked for, the White House staff was appalled by the deficit. Adding a trillion dollars to it in the president's first term did not sound wonderful to them; nor did existing budget process operate to their liking. "After having beaten your head against that rock and it didn't move," a senior staff member explained, "you step back and see if there isn't some other way."[59]

Perhaps some sort of impoundment would work? Staff members recalled that in the Treasury Department in 1984 and sporadically in the White House during winter and spring 1985, there was talk of a "4-3-2-1" approach, ratcheting down the deficit by 1 percent of gross national product per year until it reached zero.

The idea of a staged decline in the deficit was hardly original, but no one had turned a staged reduction into a political commitment. The difficulty was that the practice of simply promising to balance the budget was losing credibility.

While the president was at his California ranch in August, after his operation, further discussions reemphasized the undesirability of accepting gigantic deficits without providing an acceptable path to reducing or eliminating them. President Reagan was thinking also that he did not want to be known as the man who left town with the biggest deficit ever. There must be a way. As he boarded his helicopter on the ranch to start back to the White House, budget documents in briefcase, the president motioned to Don Regan's top aide, Dennis Thomas, and told him that while there was no way to restore balance in one year, something along the lines of 4-3-2-1 might be feasible. Would he work out the numbers?

Chief of Staff Don Regan joined the presidential plane in St. Louis. Thomas briefed him, Regan discussed the matter with the president, and Thomas was asked to work on alternative paths to multiyear balance, without touching social security or increasing taxes. Thomas called in

Joseph Wright (then running OMB until Stockman's replacement was found); the two believed they could make the numbers add up without defense being hit much harder. The missing links were the mechanism to assure compliance and the strategy to secure political support.[60]

On September 12 came the first phone call from Senator Gramm outlining his proposal. It received a cautious welcome; the welcome came because it fit with the 4-3-2-1 scheme pushed back a year; the caution was due to the necessity of checking various bases. One was the Pentagon: Could the five-year proportional cut be merged with 0-3-3 (one year of keeping defense steady in real terms, followed by two years of 3 percent increases)—the agreement that the White House thought it had won in the budget resolution? OMB was asked to supply possible domestic cuts that would add up to the proposed annual deficit reduction. Concern with political acceptability was limited by the new OMB team's lack of experience and the hope that the sequester would change the political dynamic.

Treasury wanted a clean debt ceiling increase.[61] Defense Secretary Weinberger and National Security Advisor Bud McFarlane cared far less about getting domestic cuts than about avoiding defense cuts; GRH just didn't seem like a good deal. But, from Reagan's and Regan's perspectives, the question was not whether defense would be cut—that was already happening—but whether the administration would get anything in return. A "senior White House aide" explained to Kirschten and Rauch that, in 1985 and before, the administration

> had the worst of all possible worlds. Defense cuts were used to pay for the restoration of social programs that you had opposed and with no effect on the deficit. You couldn't get a consultant in to figure out how to mess it up more than that. The difference between current law and what might exist under Gramm-Rudman is that at least here, if there is to be a hit on defense, it will be applied to deficit reduction.[62]

What remained was an idea that could change the strategic environment in the president's favor. If the bill did not pass, it could still score political points: "We were really worried the Democrats were going to kick the blank out of us on the debt ceiling, and boy this came around just at the right time."[63] Gramm's new plan might have pitfalls, but it beat the alternatives.

Challenged to explain why he had vigorously advocated support for GRH despite its admitted imperfections, a member of the White House staff answered with other questions: "Is this imperfect? Relative to what? Is it more or less imperfect than what we have tried for the last five years, the result of which has been a trillion dollars worth of debt?"[64]

On October 4 the president endorsed GRH in a "rousing political speech" delivered in New Jersey.[65]

By that time Dole and Domenici had swung behind the plan, and social security had been taken out of the pot. One might have thought that this would make GRH less attractive to Dole and Domenici; apparently, however, they decided that the threat of the sequester was powerful enough, even so, to force later action. Dole became so eager for GRH to pass that he kept the Senate in session for the entire weekend of October 5–6 to dispose of various proposals. Republicans thought they had Democrats on the spot.

Some Democrats were not so sure. A Reagan official recalled being at Ways and Means "when Gramm-Rudman came over. Gephardt looked at it and said the same thing as Dole and Domenici: he thought 'can this be?'—it's the undoing of the Reagan revolution, ensuring a defense cut and almost certainly a revenue increase." Lawton Chiles didn't like GRH but saw the potential to change it from "a single barrel act with the barrel aimed at Congress and not the President" to a gun pointed both ways. After all, Domenici and his staff had no desire to give Reagan a free hand. While Domenici would not take all of Chiles's changes, agreement was reached on a package of about twenty-five amendments that dealt with some technical and constitutional issues. Carl Levin (D-Mich.), a solid liberal, decided that the sequester would represent a more equal threat if Reagan's discretion could be further limited. On October 9 Levin won passage of an amendment that defined the subdivisions across which cuts had to be uniform, not as broad aggregates of budget "accounts" but at the much more specific level of individual "programs, projects or activities"—in essence, anything mentioned in an appropriations bill or, as it finally developed, committee report or agency submission. To preserve the remnants of presidential discretion, Gramm tried to prevent that amendment but Rudman went along.

Nobody was sure about the bill on its merits. Rudman himself called it "a bad idea whose time has come."[66] When Senator Nancy Kassenbaum (R-Kan.) told Dole she couldn't support GRH because social security had been excluded, Senator Dole responded, in his usual wry way, "Oh, you've read the bill," as if knowledge of its contents would reveal its irrationality.[67] Yet the Senate's leading budgeters still went along. They thought that eventually the sequester would force Reagan to give in on taxes to save defense and force House Democrats to give in on social security to save other domestic programs.

Ronald Reagan had a different view. The president viewed GRH as good because it avoided tax increases while guaranteeing domestic cuts, instead of merely promising them. Some liberals hoped it would force deep cuts in defense. And both liberals and moderates expected to push the chief executive into accepting tax increases.[68]

Nevertheless, many Democrats had doubts. Declaring that "we're buying a pig in the poke," Minority Leader Robert Byrd informed the Senate that "we're not prepared to bring the Sword of Damocles down on the poor, the young, the old, on all the defense and domestic programs."[69] He and Chiles offered a Democratic party substitute: a plan that would balance the budget by 1990. If annual targets were missed, the amount would be made up one-third from taxes and one-third each from domestic and defense programs. Means-tested programs were exempt.[70]

The Byrd-Chiles plan was defeated 59 to 40.[71] With this last gasp, Senate opposition to Gramm-Rudman collapsed. On October 9, almost all Republicans and half of the Democrats, by an overwhelming 75 to 24, voted in favor of the Deficit Reduction and Balanced Budget Act of 1985. Explaining his vote, indeed his cosponsorship of GRH, liberal champion Senator Edward Kennedy (determined to remove the albatross of profligacy from Democratic necks) spoke in institutional terms: "We can no longer afford a deadlock in which the Congress stands its ground and the President refuse[s] to meet us halfway."[72] Phil Gramm, triumphantly anticipating the next step, predicted that "with both [Democratic] senators of Massachusetts voting for it here, with one of them a co-sponsor, it's going to be difficult for Tip O'Neill to sweep this movement under the rug, since it's bigger than the House."[73] Many senators rationalized backing the plan by assuming the House would take the rap for killing it, but House leaders were not at all sure they could do so.

Speaker O'Neill declared that GRH would "subvert the Constitution," that it resulted from an "artificial crisis," and that Gramm and other Republicans were responsible for the "mess the nation is in."[74] Yet his party was split among liberals and older members who wanted to kill the plan, conservatives who would vote for anything that claimed to reduce the deficit, and pragmatists who, like Gephardt, thought they could turn GRH to the party's advantage.[75]

It turned out that they could not beat GRH. As a staff member informed us, "We counted and knew we would lose the southerners."[76] So the issue became whether it was better to let the disaster occur and later blame the Republicans or to try and "fix" GRH. A senior House Democrat recalled:

> I was one who said, let's give it to 'em. They got Teddy Kennedy; all the liberals in the Senate were blowing about the deficit and how responsible they were. I said to Tip, let's give it to 'em. Then [my liaison to the Budget Committee] kept coming in with another terrible consequence. . . . We

changed it from an absolutely asinine piece of legislation to something with the thinnest coating of reason.[77]

In the end, under the leadership of Democratic Caucus Chair Richard Gephardt (D-Mo.) and Whip Thomas P. Foley (D-Wash.), a concerted effort was made not to produce a bill the president would have to veto or that the Senate could not accept but to get one more to the Democrats' liking that would still follow the original model.

When GRH was added to the Senate debt ceiling on October 9 and sent over to the House with that bill, House leaders feared they would lose a vote on the GRH sections. Instead, on October 11, they won approval for a conference on the debt ceiling. Democratic House leaders appointed forty-eight representatives to the conference, determined to build support by thoroughly investigating all issues raised by the sequester proposal. They had some time because on October 9—"much to Dole's disgust"[78]—the Treasury had initiated a complicated maneuver in which it used the Federal Financing Bank to borrow $5 billion, respecting the debt ceiling and enabling the government to function until November 1.

The Senate appointed nine conferees, conspicuously excluding Gramm, Rudman, and Hollings. One reason was personal; Gramm was left out (like Hamlet without the prince) for fear he would enrage members of the House.[79] "This legislation passed probably in spite of him," Representative Trent Lott (R-Miss.) commented, advising Senate Republicans to keep Gramm even out of the House gallery.[80] By excluding all three, the Senate leaders could claim their reasons were impersonal— mainly, seniority. But there was a larger purpose: Finance and Budget leaders themselves wanted to control the Senate position.

Now that Gramm-Rudman-Hollings had reached the conference committee stage, Congress began hearings on the bill. The star witness was a staffer, Steve Bell of the Senate Budget Committee. "The curious thing," an aide recalled, "was, Steve Bell was front and center, and he carried the testimony. . . . He did a superb job of explaining and translating the provisions." Several legislators suggested Bell should be "stapled" to GRH so he would always be there to answer questions. Thousands of staff hours were devoted to investigating issues ranging from determining the bill's constitutionality to sequestering a contract.

After about two weeks, the House conferees broke down into task forces. Whether these were bipartisan efforts to evolve a House position or partisan efforts to develop a Democratic position depended on the participants. Task Force 1 on economic issues, such as whether the targets should be void during a recession, was led by old rivals, David Obey and Jack Kemp. It was not very bipartisan. Task Force 2 on the details of sequester—what to cut, when, how?—had the most participation and staffing: Gephardt, Panetta, Fazio, Waxman, and Whitten for Democrats; Gradison, Tom Loeffler, and Bill Frenzel for Republicans—the budget pros. Task Force 3 investigated how GRH would amend the process itself; that was Rules Committee territory and the key players were Martin Frost (D-Tex.) and Minority Whip Trent Lott. Finally, Task Force 4 covered constitutional issues. Democrats were led by Jack Brooks, the tough, experienced chairman of House Government Operations, and Mike Synar, a young Oklahoman ready to make his mark. Republicans were led by Richard Cheney of Wyoming, leader of the party conference and, as former chief of staff to President Ford, an old hand in executive-legislative relations.

Democrats in Task Force 4 were less interested in resolving constitutional issues than in pointing up its unconstitutionality so that the Supreme Court would void the law. Democrats in Task Force 2 felt that if they could make the terms tough enough for the president, it might force him into a tax hike that, for Democrats, would mean it had "worked." "Working" had two totally contradictory meanings: a sequester that was rational enough to be lived with or one that was crazy enough to force people to make some other deal. Within the latter category, a GRH that worked meant, for each player, something that would force the other guys to deal. Therefore, their positions depended on calculating how the hostage game would play out.

What would happen, for example, if Congress in some future year met its GRH target with a tax hike? Then Reagan could veto the taxes, saying he was not increasing the deficit because GRH would make the automatic cuts. Leon Panetta proposed a rule that sequester authority would lapse if the president vetoed deficit-reduction legislation, but that rule was rejected because it might provoke Reagan to veto GRH itself. Senate leaders wanted GRH to be tough enough to coerce Reagan but not so bad that he would veto it. Democrats decided that, if Reagan were to veto GRH, he should be forced to do so in behalf of his unpopular defense buildup rather than his popular objection to taxes.

On October 22 James Baker announced that, if the ceiling were not raised by November 1, the Treasury would begin dipping into the Social Security Trust Fund. Members of Task Force 2 could not find a Goldilocks solution—provisions that were "just right" (or, in this case, "just wrong" enough). On October 31, Senate leaders formally proposed disbanding the conference. Senate and House Republicans devised a new version of GRH that cleaned up many technical problems. House Democrats would present their own version. If the GOP won on the House floor, the battle was over.

One difference between the two plans reflected the parties' traditional economic positions. Republicans wanted to set deficit targets regardless of economic conditions. Democrats, in Keynesian fashion, wanted the size of the deficit reduction to depend on those conditions. Another issue was who would have authority to determine whether or not the sequester would be triggered and to allocate the cuts. The House gave CBO, not OMB, that power. Giving an arm of Congress such direct power over the executive was probably unconstitutional, which could invalidate the whole law, but Brooks and Synar didn't like the law to begin with so an unconstitutional provision served their purposes. The Republican plan rested final authority with the GAO, also an arm of Congress, but its head, the comptroller general, was appointed by the president. Recent district court cases implied that the comptroller general, as an "officer of the United States," might be deemed able to exercise the sequester authority.

The key issues involved terms of the sequester. Democrats required a sequester for FY86 as well as subsequent years, set a lower deficit target for each year, and aimed to balance the budget in 1990 instead of 1991. They intended to make Republicans, who had twenty-two of the thirty-four senators up for reelection in 1986, pay for the consequences of cuts.

A subtle but vital difficulty was the translation between outlays and budget authority. In order to make outlay cuts of a certain amount how much, and which, budget authority should be sequestered? Democrats believed prior contracts, particularly in defense, could not sensibly be sequestered. That put a greater burden on current and future spending. Republicans either believed or pretended to believe that it was possible. Beyond that were extremely complicated issues on handling new budget authority with widely varying spend-out rates.[81]

The Democrats chose a version that would devastate defense procurement to protect personnel. An aide recalled how, on the morning of November 1, "we got the table from CBO and I started to hand it out, then I looked at it and thought, 'Oh, no, we're not handing this out'—it was called the defense special rule and would have cut about $50 billion in Budget Authority to get $10 billion in outlays." On a matter as complicated as GRH, however, nobody understood everything. In fact, the staffer who wrote the special rule told us, "I *wanted* it that way. The people in Armed Services *wanted* to shift the cuts to procurement." Luckily for the Democrats, they didn't explain it, and nobody noticed; thus, they were able to bring a very hard bargaining position into the second conference.

The policy issue that most divided Democrats was deciding which programs would be excluded from the sequester process. Republicans excluded several dozen small programs (on which there were real technical problems), social security, and interest on the debt. House Democrats, wanting to add a number of other programs, were divided as to how many. The short list included AFDC, food stamps, Women and Infant Children (WIC), SSI, child nutrition, and veterans' pensions and compensation. The long list would have added, among others, education and community health programs.

Caucusing on the evening of October 31, House Democrat negotiators supported the short list but only by twelve to eleven.[82] "Essentially it was a tie," recalled an aide who was there. The next morning, November 1, the Speaker went with the short list, urging Waxman, Rostenkowski, and other holdouts to go along. The Democrats also wrote a rule strictly limiting cuts in medicare. "As an individual," the Speaker said of the short list, "I'm opposed to it." But "I face the facts of life. This bill will pass."[83] Budget Chairman William Gray, who otherwise had been very quiet, persuaded the Black Caucus to go along (we don't say "reluctantly" because that was true of almost everyone). "We're holding our noses," declared the chair of the Black Caucus, Mickey Leland of Texas, "but we're committed, loyalist Democrats."[84] Most Democrats spoke of "damage limitation."[85]

The key was Marvin Leath of Texas, the boll weevils' man on the Budget Committee. Assiduously courted by Gray and other Democratic leaders, he had been made to feel a part of the decision process within the party. They had been especially attentive to his concerns about veterans. Like many of his colleagues, Leath was more worried about the deficit than defense; he had wanted to freeze everything. His policy preferences were probably closer to the Republicans, but there were no pressures to "support the president," no calls from constituencies or Ronald Reagan himself, and no evidence of an electoral realignment. A full-fledged weevil in 1981, Leath led all but two of his colleagues in support of the Democratic plan. On November 1 it passed the House, 249 to 180. On November 6 the Senate adopted the revised, Republican version of GRH.

A new conference began on November 12. Senators now had someone to bargain with: a unified House Democratic contingent that had demonstrated impressive support on the House floor. To the original fifty-seven, nine conferees, including Gramm, Rudman, and Hollings, were added. Rostenkowski, because the debt limit was a Ways and Means matter, chaired the conference; at his suggestion, the real work was done by a smaller group of twenty-nine.[86] It became clear that senators were not trying to make the president a budget czar and that representatives were not out to scuttle the bill.[87]

The second conference was a three-cornered game among House, Senate, and administration. To the extent that both sets of conferees wanted to bind the White House, they were allies. No player was sure whether the sequester would happen. The conferees' words suggested that the sequester would be so bad that everyone would negotiate to keep it from occurring; yet their actions—endless bargaining over the terms—suggested fears that it might indeed occur.

The final terms of Gramm-Rudman would be set by House Democrats and Senate Republicans, the two groups that, as majorities, were responsible for the operation of their chambers and the functioning of government. Since 1982, deficit reduction had required such a coalition of responsible legislative majorities. "Inevitably," Representative Fazio said, "the people who run institutions are going to have to compromise. We're driven together by our responsibilities."[88] His colleague Leon Panetta thought the polarizing effect of elections could be countered by putting "the two elements together that have the most to lose—Senate Republicans and House Democrats. Both have a responsibility to lead their institutions."[89] Against the view that Democrats ought to allow Republicans to fail, House Whip Thomas Foley argued that "there's an incumbent's party as well as a Democratic or Republican party. Bad news falls on the government in general." Nor would Democrats in office lose out, for, Foley concluded, "if there are great events being celebrated, no stage is too small to get everybody in office on to take a bow and take credit."[90]

Its proponents could hope that GRH, by threatening a train wreck in the form of a sequester, would impel the leaders of these responsible majorities both to avoid blame for possible carnage and gain credit for deficit reduction by negotiating a settlement. What made leaders leaders, however, was responsibility to their own constituencies. Foley owed allegiance to House Democrats and the people they represented; if he shirked that, he would be in a very weak position to serve the institution. In the negotiations over GRH, as in all previous budget battles, party leaders tried to serve both areas of responsibility by compromising, but compromising less than the other guys.

When the real bargaining began on November 12, House Democrats had a pretty simple agenda: make GRH as bad as possible for Republicans; maximize the hit on defense; keep as close as possible to the House set of domestic exclusions; and minimize Reagan's discretion. Democrats were divided on whether GRH was a good idea or not; many would have been happy if the whole episode ended with either Reagan vetoing the bill or the Supreme Court outlawing it. In their minds, however, they did not really have to choose between sabotage and salvage. Democrats defined the choices that might provoke a veto merely as good policy.

One complication for the Democrats lay in the chance that the sequester might be activated. Did they really want to clobber defense? Not as much as their proposal would have done. Les Aspin (D-Wis.), elected chair of the Armed Services Committee at the beginning of 1985, wanted to hit procurement more and personnel less; he was a critic of the Pentagon and a leader of the congressional group of military reformers. Yet as chair of a fairly hawkish committee, as well as by his own choice, Aspin did not want to cripple the military, as several years of cumulative cuts under GRH might do. As a leader of those who thought the Pentagon should allocate its resources intelligently, Aspin objected to a plan that would slash resources without even a pretense of logic.

The other complication was how drastically the Democrats wanted to change the budget process in order to accommodate GRH. The whole sequester process would be meaningless, for example, if Congress, after the sequester, could pass supplementals to replace the money. Or Congress might pass no appropriations before the sequester; then there would be nothing from which to sequester. The budgeting schedule would have to be revised to include the new sequester stage. These matters raised difficult issues of relations among committees, particularly Ways and Means, Appropriations, and Budget.

Senate conferees were out to strengthen their Budget Committee at the expense, especially, of Appropriations. Domenici, Chiles, and their staffs already had escalated the battle between those committees in 1985 by trying to hold Appropriations to outlay targets; in GRH they wanted a series of reforms that would bind Appropriations in budget resolution choices.

Senate conferees also had to deal with a sequester's effects on running the government. There was no way to sequester medicaid, but, if that were excluded, the hit on other things would have to be bigger. Each issue interacted with all the others to make the senators' choices particularly difficult.

The administration knew what it wanted—essentially the opposite of what House leaders wanted—but not how to get it. Although Gramm was, more or less, the administration's representative, he was not, as the best-known sponsor, likely to urge a veto that might be in the administration's interests. The Pentagon had a real interest in how defense was treated, but Secretary Weinberger wanted to kill GRH more than to shape its terms. Throughout November and into December, the DOD remained aloof from conference negotiations. At OMB, Jim Miller was new, scrambling to assemble a FY87 budget proposal. Domenici and Packwood were emphatic that the bill now was theirs, not the president's, so OMB's chief lobbyist was excluded from negotiations.[91]

The political dynamic left President Reagan on the spot. Once the Senate and House agreed, they could present him with a take-it-or-leave-it proposition. He could veto, but then he would be in the embarrassing position of not only opposing deficit reduction but also reversing his own stand. Even the pressure from the debt ceiling began to reverse. When the government ran out of money yet again on November 12, Treasury could not repeat its social security maneuver; and Reagan certainly didn't need a fiscal confrontation before his November 14 meeting with Soviet Party Chairman Gorbachev in Geneva. Congress and the administration agreed therefore to a temporary increase in the debt limit, giving negotiators another month to work out their differences.

Before Thanksgiving the core group of negotiators neared settlement on some crucial issues. Over the holiday recess staff made further progress. At 1:00 a.m. on December 10, conferees settled the last outstanding issue. In describing the law as passed we will highlight the meaning of key compromises.

How the Balanced Budget and Deficit Reduction Act of 1985 (GRH) Was Supposed to Work

Following regular budget procedure, failure to agree on a budget as a whole, or on any part of it, merely ratified the status quo. In order to bring the deficit center stage, Gramm-Rudman-Hollings transforms inaction into a form of action for bringing the budget into balance over a five-year period. Perhaps the most important decision was retaining the principle of fixed targets. Congress chose the Gramm targets for FY87–FY91 ($144 billion down to zero), adding a FY86 target of $171.9 billion—the figure in the budget resolution. Keeping a fixed schedule made the targets a clearer promise to public, media, and financial markets; more explicit rules are harder to break.

The sequester for FY86 accommodated the House's desire for a smaller dry run of the procedure; it hoped both to show everybody how senseless the sequester would be and to make Senate Republicans pay in the 1986 election for any pain inflicted. Thus, the sequester was set at a maximum of $11.7 billion to occur on March 1, 1986, because that was roughly the amount by which Domenici and Chiles expected FY86 reconciliation and appropriations action to fall short of the budget resolution targets for deficit reduction.[92]

The sequester, if enforced, would be the last stage in a new budgeting schedule. The president would submit his budget by the first Monday after January 3. Congress would pass its yearly budget resolution by April 15, its reconciliation legislation by June 15, and the House would pass appropriations by June 30. To force budget committees to act and to give appropriations committees a chance, appropriations bills could be considered in the House on May 15, even if no budget resolution had passed. To force House passage of appropriations by June 30, GRH created a point of order against Independence Day recess. But even the *Congressional Quarterly Almanac* called that rule "quixotic," and so it proved—in 1986 a motion to suspend the rule prohibiting adjournment whizzed by in two minutes flat.

THE DEFICIT REDUCTION TIMETABLE

FYs 87–91	*Required Action*
Aug. 15	CBO and OMB take a "snapshot" of the deficit by projecting the level of federal revenues and outlays for the fiscal year that begins Oct. 1.
Aug. 20	CBO and OMB issue their joint report to GAO identifying the deficit excess over the target (if any) and calculating the amounts (budget authority and outlays) to be reduced by program, project, or activity in order to meet the prescribed deficit target.
Aug. 25	GAO submits a report to the president (based on the joint CBO/OMB deficit and outlay reduction estimates) on which the president's order sequestering outlays to meet the deficit is based.
Sept. 1	President issues the *initial* sequester order based on the GAO report.
Sept. 1–30	Congress has opportunity to consider an alternative set of budget reductions to meet GRH prescribed deficit targets.
Oct. 15	President issues *final* sequester order based on the initial order as adjusted for any changes made since issuance of the initial sequester order.[93]

The Gramm-Rudman process would be invoked if, and only if, the preexisting process failed to meet the annual deficit reduction targets—from $171.9 billion in 1986 to $144 billion in 1987 and so on to zero in

1991. Except in the first and last years, a $10 billion cushion is allowed above the target figure before the sequestration procedure is invoked.

On August 15 OMB and CBO would issue a "snapshot" estimating revenue and expenditures—and, also, the gap between them at that moment—for the fiscal year beginning October 1. OMB and CBO would also estimate economic growth for each quarter of the current year and for the last two quarters of the preceding year. Two consecutive quarters of negative growth would allow sequestration's suspension. By August 20, the directors of OMB and CBO would submit their joint report to the comptroller general. It would estimate revenues and expenditures for the fiscal year and state for the record whether the difference plus the allowable $10 billion were larger than the maximum deficit amount (MDA). If the target figure were breached, the joint report would specify the reductions necessary in each Program Project and Activity (PPA) to reach that MDA level.[94]

The comptroller general's authority here was a Senate provision. Congress did not trust OMB; it was clearly unconstitutional for CBO to take such a role; and a joint OMB/CBO role raised the issue of what to do if they disagreed. Some said "split the difference," but sophisticated budgeters realized that meant OMB might skew its numbers to shape the average, and, by having to anticipate OMB's maneuvers, CBO's analytic neutrality, the heart of its position, would be destroyed. The comptroller general, then, would review the OMB/CBO calculations, explain differences between their report and his, and issue his own independent calculations. On August 25 he would issue a report detailing how much authority should be sequestered from each PPA.

The base for sequestration included around 40 percent of total spending. The exclusions were the price of the inclusions; in order to agree on sequential, across-the-board reductions it was necessary to leave out what a majority of Congress cared most about. Some things, as we have said, would not be touched—interest, social security, AFDC, WIC, child nutrition, medicaid, veterans' pensions and compensation, food stamps, the Earned Income Tax Credit (EITC). The list is the House Democrats' short list, plus medicaid and EITC. Senate acquiescence to these exclusions reflected the belief by moderates as well as liberals that it was wrong to subject the poor to automatic cuts. The list was virtually identical to the list of programs protected in the FY86 budget resolution (that was supposedly so unreasonable). Because the decisions had been made by the very same people, this should have surprised no one. But its meaning was missed: GRH had not changed the nature of distributional preferences, even if it stressed concern about the deficit.

After excluding much spending, step one of the sequester allowed small cuts in certain programs. Payments to doctors and other providers—under medicare, community and migrant health centers, and veterans' and Indian health programs—could be cut under sequestration no more than 1 percent the first year or 2 percent for the remaining four years.

Step two was the bulk of the sequestration; half would come from defense and half from domestic programs. This was the key compromise: rather than determining a formula for the cuts and wondering how it would affect defense vis-à-vis domestic, the distributional issue was settled first. If, say, $36 billion was needed, $18 billion would come from defense and $18 billion from domestic. This made conflict over which social programs to exclude simpler: excluding a social program would hurt only other social programs, not the military.[95]

Because the balance of defense spending equaled 60 percent of what was not excluded and because defense would have to take only half the cut, the defense sequester percentage would be smaller than the cut applied to domestic programs. But much of the domestic budget was already excluded.

Conferees resolved the relation between budget authority and outlays in the sequester by inventing a new category, "budgetary resources." The solution compromised between cutting defense procurement and personnel, while giving the president, after the first year, as little discretion as possible.[96] The terms allowed sequestering contracts under conditions that most negotiators thought highly unlikely but on which Gramm, representing the administration, insisted. Judging from our interviews, even the participants were not quite sure what was going on right up to the very last discussions after midnight on December 10. To us, the final terms look pretty clever, but the sequester still seems fraught with trouble. How do you cut 10 percent of an aircraft carrier?

GRH calls for quite possibly dumb, from a program perspective, arbitrary, percentage cuts across many programs. But it would be false to conclude, as many have, that the act is mindless in the sense of lacking a strong sense of priorities. Indeed, in its inclusions and exclusions, *GRH contains the clearest expression of national priorities of any single act ever passed*: clearly, what cannot be cut has priority over what can.

Under GRH the president would issue an initial sequestration report on September 1 telling Congress he had followed the rules; he then could suggest an alternative budget quite outside these rules, providing it met the MDA. If Congress passed that or any other plan in the time between September 1 and October 15, the sequester might not be invoked. But if the sequester did take place, its uniform percentage reductions were calculated at such a detailed level that the president could not choose either to protect what he considered more important programs or to advantage new ones with small bases, compared to large ones with large bases that could better withstand cuts.[97]

GAO's final sequestration report, binding on the president, would be due October 10. This binding character led the Reagan administration to join in the challenge to the constitutionality of the provision, a challenge upheld by the Supreme Court.[98] If Congress and the president had not agreed on an alternative, sequestration would occur on October 15. A month later the comptroller general would issue a report evaluating the degree to which sequestration had been carried out according to statute.

The act provided a backup procedure in case the courts invalidated the GAO's role. This bone, for those who wanted most to ensure that GRH have some effect, if only to force a bargain, balanced another provision allowing an expedited court test of GRH's constitutionality. Special provisions allowed first a special District Court panel and then the Supreme Court to rule on a suit, so the matter would be settled by July 1986. Even supporters had to admit that to have GRH operate for a while and then be ruled unconstitutional would not do much for the legitimacy of the government.

The backup procedure allowed for the joint CBO/OMB report to go to a temporary joint committee on deficit reduction made up of the entire membership of House and Senate budget committees. Within five days this Temporary Joint Committee would report a sequestration proposal to both houses. Then, however, it was subject to tactics of obstruction or, ultimately, to presidential veto. If the GAO oversight role were ruled illegal, seemingly GRH would lose all its force. That, however, was not quite correct; sequestration, not the heretofore unmentioned changes in budgetary procedure, would be lost.

The Importance of Considering Others

Because they survived the court ruling, GRH's process reforms—a mixture of proposals from an old House Rules Committee task force, chaired by Anthony Beilenson (D-Calif.) and proposals pushed by Senate Budget—turned out to be the most important parts of the act. Some provisions were less controversial; thus, credit programs were subjected to much greater annual control. GRH also codified the budget process developments of the 1980s: no Second Resolution, a binding First Resolution, and reconciliation on the First (now the only) Resolution. More significant was a series of new points of order that would make the budget resolution more binding, in terms of both detail and difficulty of breaking the bonds.

The resolution itself had to conform to the MDA. Amendments in the Senate that could increase the deficit were subject to a point of order. At the conference report stage, a point of order in the House on these grounds could be waived only by three-fifths of members present and voting. Until completion of a budget resolution, any legislation on spending revenues, debt, or credit would be out of order—save for appropriations after May 15 in the House.

GRH also changed the 302(b) process that had far-reaching implications for the balance of power among committees in Congress and for the budget process itself. It created a point of order against legislation by any committee that had not yet made its 302(b) allocation. Then, GRH made the 302(b)s binding by creating a point of order against bills, mainly appropriations, that exceeded the allocation made in a committee's 302(b) report. This meant that the Appropriations Committee could not exceed their allocation on early bills by claiming that it would make up the difference on later ones. The 1974 act had provided a point of order only against bills that would cause total spending limits to be exceeded; that is, there were controls only on the very last bills, namely, no real control. Unless the sponsor of such an increase came up with a cut elsewhere or a new tax, under GRH that legislator had to get a three-fifths majority to overcome a point of order. For years budget committees had lusted after a way to object to earlier bills so as to make the process meaningful. Now this "offset" provision was it.

The point of order for the 302(b)s would, however, work very differently in each chamber. That was another compromise, reflecting the much stronger position of the House Appropriations Committee. GRH codified the Fazio rule, under which House Appropriations had to meet its 302(b) targets only for discretionary spending. Supplemental appropriations for mandatory spending, such as payments to the states for medicaid, therefore would not be subject to a point of order and would not require compensating cuts elsewhere. From Appropriations' standpoint, that only made sense: If the budget resolution misjudged the economy and therefore underestimated "mandatory" expenses, why should other programs pay? Republicans objected that the appropriations' argument was, in the words of one House aide, "well and good, but if entitlements force you to hit the wall on appropriations then you will have to take action, whether a reconciliation, or a presto-chango on interest rates, or whatever." This thinking prevailed in the Senate. Even more important, the Senate allowed a 302(b) point of order for outlays. Both appropriations committees resisted controls on outlays, but, while the House committee succeeded, a budget leader in the Senate remarked "we just ran over" the Appropriations Committee.

The new rules, if followed, meant that the Senate Budget Committee, because it calculated the outlay savings for each budget authority cut, could use that power to push Appropriations to make cuts SBC would score as adequate. Unless SBC was willing to fudge on the outlays, it also meant that the classic compromise on budget resolutions, in which outlay estimates were kept low but budget authority estimates were raised, would no longer work. If they actually enforced the outlay figures, they would not be able to use all the budget authority supposedly allowed. Having had a very bad experience on outlay enforcement already in 1985, as Domenici and Chiles challenged bills on the Senate floor, Appropriations leaders resisted stoutly. The budget resolution could cheat them by underestimating both mandatory spending (through optimistic economic projections) and outlays; then Appropriations would have to pay up in the coin of budget authority for discretionary programs.

The Fazio rule, and sticking to BA, meant the House Appropriations Committee could not be cheated. Rather, the new rules might even strengthen Appropriations vis-à-vis the rest of the House. A veteran staffer explained:

> The irony is that the new process changes will make the full committee 302s *the* debate on defense vs. domestic. . . . *Our* committee-generated 302(b)s are now the rule, and can't be changed on the floor. The intent was to stick it to the Appropriations Committee, but over the long haul it would make Appropriations stronger.
> Our guys will use the 302(b) ceilings, load each up to about $85 from the brim, so that any amendment will be subject to a point of order. To add something they will have to cut something, and it will be very hard to have any amendments. We'll control the details.

Was control over details such a prize if the totals were so tight that any choices would only anger large parts of the House? If the final bill had to pass Senate controls on outlays, what good would it do for the House to ignore those same restrictions? Nobody knew.

We have saved the most important provision for last: the points of order in the Senate could be waived only by a three-fifths majority. Because these waivers would have to be bipartisan, they thus were unlikely. All these rules, therefore, probably would hold.

And if they did hold? The rules were meant to force both appropriations to fit a resolution and a resolution to fit deficit-reduction targets. But what if nobody wanted to live with the consequences? Well, then the cuts would occur. But the meat-ax approach in GRH implies that the cuts would be made very inefficiently, significantly more damaging than economical. No doubt. Therefore, a proponent replies, members will be motivated to settle on a deficit-reduction package more variegated and hence more sensible than across-the-board cuts. Unfortunately, being sensible calls for the freedom to choose among the entire panoply of government programs. But because the act eliminates more than half (mostly entitlements and debt interest) from across-the-board cuts, only some 46 percent is available for sequestration. Why should the members who got the rest excluded turn around and cut them?

Rather than force a comprehensive settlement, GRH would force everybody to stall. No negotiation would make sense until the players could compare it to the actual extent of sequestration as determined by the size of the deficit estimated in mid-August. Worse yet, early agreement on any particular program or appropriations bill would not protect it from sequestration; the size of the across-the-board cut depends on not one account but everybody's accounts. Thus, the incentives all worked toward delay. Furthermore, the very same severity of GRH that was supposed to spur negotiation would raise doubts about its workability. If the consequences were all that catastrophic, then some way would be found around it. At some crossover point the cry of catastrophe becomes its own dirge; hence, there is even more reason to stall.

Late one night in December 1985, two loyal Senate aides were drafting final terms of the bill. They had been working nonstop since September. One of them recalled:

> At 4 a.m. I looked at X and said, "This isn't going to work." X is very literal; he said, "I'll fix it." I said, "No, the *whole freaking thing* isn't going to work." I was like Saul on the road to Damascus. I realized suddenly it was going to congeal the whole legislative process. Domenici's notion was that Gramm-Rudman would compel a quick resolution and reconciliation. That it was the only hope to keep the budget process intact. . . . We got all the enforcement that I ever wanted. But I realized at that moment that we will never move a single appropriations bill.

Any action on appropriations meant confronting all those Senate points of order. Congress had constructed a doomsday machine, all right. But instead of forcing action due to the threat of horrible policy consequences, it made inaction the best strategy. The victim would be not the deficit but Congress itself.

Doing the Same and Feeling Worse

Not that things were going very well anyway. While debating GRH, Congress also tied itself in knots about immediate budget choices; the new year brought no relief. To summarize events, let us return to our diary.

BUDGET DIARY, PART 2

September 15, 1985: Rules Committee members Anthony Beilenson (D-Calif.) and Butler Derrick (D-S.C.), who chair the Budget Committee task force on reconciliation, deny Representative Rostenkowski a fast-track rule on the grounds that the proposed Ways and Means reconciliation bill falls $2.4 billion short of what the budget resolution (S.Con.Res. 32) requires. The Ways and Means chairman, who usually avoids such upsets, said he had been "blind-sided."[99]

September 24: Acting in tandem, the chair and ranking minority member of the Senate Budget Committee, Pete Domenici and Lawton Chiles, succeed in delaying and making small cuts on appropriations bills that do not comply with S.Con.Res. 32. The issue—budget authority (spending over time) versus outlays (spending during a fiscal year)—surfaced when Domenici and Chiles got the Senate to cut $139 million in Treasury-Postal outlays because they were over the budget resolution. Appropriations people are livid. Senator Mark Hatfield, Appropriations Committee chair, argued that Congress had never before considered appropriations bills in terms of outlays. That whole issue had been fought with Stockman again and again. If the focus was to be on outlays, then whoever controls outlay estimates controls the bills; it sure looks like a naked power grab by the Budget Committee. Desperate to get some handle on the deficit, Domenici and Chiles made no apologies.[100]

September 25: Congress quickly adopts a CR extending to November 14 to stop the government from being shut down. At least they could agree on something. Also today GRH is introduced in the Senate.[101]

September 29: Former Budget Director David Stockman called for Congress to stop faking and find at least $100 billion in new taxes because "we just can't live with these massive deficits without traumatic economic dislocations." He predicts that "sooner or later" deficits would "bring inflation back."[102] How soon he didn't say.

October 9: The Senate passes the balanced budget (Gramm-Rudman) amendment to the debt ceiling bill.[103]

October 23: Senate Budget and Appropriations go to war over the transportation bill. Faced with the tight targets in the resolution, Subcommittee Chairman Andrews slashes $500 million from the FAA and the Coast Guard. Domenici says nobody believes the House will agree to that in conference; he wants to cut mass transit, Amtrak, and highways instead. Andrews agrees that cutting the FAA and Coast Guard is unrealistic but adds, "if we keep the misery in two categories . . . maybe somehow or another the happy bird of truth will fly in through the window and those who lead the Budget Committee will realize that [the resolution] . . . should have . . . never seen the light of day." Domenici and Chiles win a 1.6 percent across-the-board reduction.

Meanwhile, the subcommittee had left out a $16.3 million road project in New Mexico. Domenici won an amendment to get it back (56 to 40), but most members of Appropriations opposed him. Feelings were not friendly.[104]

October 24: The House passed what it claimed to be a $60.9 billion reconciliation package, while the Senate delayed and OMB—claiming overstated savings and objecting to some policy decisions—threatened a veto.[105]

Extraneous measures ("riders," they used to be called) have multiplied to well over a hundred; so Senators Domenici and Chiles, along with Majority Leader Dole and Minority Leader Byrd, are trying to limit them. Byrd introduces a bill to restrict future amendments to reconciliation bills by requiring a three-fifths vote to overturn a ruling that amendments were not germane. The Byrd amendment, cosponsored by Senators Dole, Domenici, Chiles, and Ted Stevens passed 96 to 0. Apparently no senator approved of what most of them did.[106]

October 29: Alleging that "if [Reagan] can meet with the Russians, he can meet with us," Representative James Jones and other GRH conferees ask for a budget summit conference as a substitute for the GRH proposal's procedures. The president refused.[107]

October 31: The Ways and Means Committee reconciliation (H.R. 3128) has passed. It meets GRH targets by assuming later passage of a superfund cleanup authorization that provides $3.1 billion in new revenues for that trust fund. The biggest savings were in medicare; some increases were made in poverty programs.

The House combined H. R. 3128 with previously approved H. R. 3500 and sent it to the Senate. The two bills have entirely different reforms of the Pension Benefit Guarantee Corporation, one from Education and Labor, and one from Ways and Means; both committees, however, claim savings. There are some real cuts: the bills have abolished synfuels; slowed the filling of the Strategic Petroleum Reserve (maybe not wise, but it saves money); frozen federal pay for FY86; cut spending authority for the Highway Trust Fund and SBA direct loan programs; authorized less housing aid than in the past; put a means test on some veterans' health care and a new one on student loans; and cut about 15 percent from Community Development Block Grant (CDBG) and Urban Development Action Grants (UDAG).

November 1: The House approves its version of Gramm-Rudman.[108]

November 6: The Senate does likewise.

November 8: Senator Dole begins singing "Jingle Bells" to his colleagues to remind them that failure to pass a budget is holding up adjournment for the Christmas holidays.[109]

November 13: The debt limit is extended—again.

November 14: The Senate passes its version of reconciliation, including agriculture and superfund provisions that the House had passed as separate bills.

December 4: By a narrow margin (212 to 208), the House approves a catchall appropriations bill to cover most government spending until the end of the fiscal year (September 30, 1986). The president threatened to veto on the usual grounds.

December 6: The reconciliation conference begins. Chairman Domenici "expressed consternation that despite the potential for 'amazing' savings, 'nobody cares. . . . I think people have just grown used to budget issues being big now.' "[110] No, they have just been listening to Domenici and his allies saying everything is terrible and Congress isn't doing anything.

December 12: President Reagan signs the Gramm-Rudman-Hollings bill committing the government to balance the budget by October 1990 and raising the national debt limit. Also, a new stopgap CR is passed to keep the government going over the weekend.[111]

December 16: Although the interim catchall appropriation will expire at 6:00 p.m., the administration advises federal employees to report for work. After some obstruction by GOP Representatives William E. Dannemeyer (Calif.) and Robert S. Walker (Pa.), the Speaker pushes another short-term CR through the House.[112]

Later, the House defeats the CR recommended by the appropriations conferees, 239 to 170. Republicans oppose it, two to one. Democrats split; liberals are upset because the conferees basically accepted the Senate's defense figures. They feel that gives defense a cushion against GRH.[113]

December 18: The CR conferees try again. They give defense $1.3 billion less in new BA than the Senate's figure and significantly restrict the use of about $6 billion in unobligated prior-year balances, essentially a windfall from lower inflation. While these figures are still closer to the Senate, Senator Stevens says they provide a 2 percent cut in purchasing power; the coming sequester will make the cut more like 7 percent.[114]

However, the Senate and House conferees dealing with reconciliations are deadlocked over financing the superfund cleanup of toxic wastes. The House wants a tax on all manufacturers while the Senate insists on confining the tax to the petrochemical industry. Why the fuss? The broader tax was the equivalent of a value-added tax (VAT), essentially a sales tax at each stage of production, which Republican conservatives opposed because, if extended, it would be a huge money-maker. And as revenue rose, following the children's allowance theory, so would spending, thus making government considerably larger.

At the same time, another disagreement arose over extending the cigarette tax.[115] The process of reconciliation had (as Richard Cohen wrote in the *National Journal*) "run amok."[116] It took up 198 pages in the *Congressional Record* and involved some thirty separate subconferences, running the gamut from straightjacket to Christmas tree, all under the name of deficit reduction.

December 19: By an overwhelming 78 to 1, the Senate approves the conferees' deficit reduction bill, except for the superfund tax provisions, which remain in disagreement.[117] The CR passes the Senate on a voice vote, the House by 261 to 137.

December 20: Reconciliation stalemate: the administration objects to a $6 billion distribution to the states of revenues from coastal oil leases, an import fee to support workers who lost jobs due to foreign competition, and increases for poor people's programs. Senate Democrats fail to win approval for the House version of reconciliation. The Senate refuses to adjourn, which supposedly means the House cannot. With Christmas and a big snowstorm approaching, the House leaves anyway. Reconciliation is dead.

"The whole year has been spent on deficit reduction and without this crowning element . . . all we've done has been for zero," mourns Senator Chafee.[118] Senate Minority Leader Byrd sums up the session as "the worst I've seen since I've been here."[119]

December 21: On his weekly radio broadcast, the president argues that GRH does not require tax increases or that domestic programs be funded by diminishing national defense.[120] Tom Foley tells the *New York Times* that "it's going to get much worse next year."

Early January 1986: OMB must produce a budget that meets the GRH targets, and nobody is going to believe it—but, OMB doesn't believe anybody else's numbers either. Director James Miller declares that the pending reconciliation bill, claiming to reduce the deficit over three years by between $60 and $80 billion, actually amounts to a mere $16.6 billion. Domenici retorts that these OMB figures are "patently absurd."[121]

Later: OMB tries to lighten the mood by parodying the idea that the budget is "Dead on Arrival." An OMB official takes an ambulance, lights flashing, to the Government Printing Office where a group of hospital-gowned attendants tear pages out of the budget to symbolize the economic surgery the president thought necessary. "The 1987 budget lives," declares OMB public relations staff. But Tip O'Neill calls the budget "crazy and nonsensical" because it refuses tax increases, insists on defense increases, and demands cuts in domestic programs, as well as eliminating eighty-one of them—something that will never happen.[122]

Mid-January 1986: The FY86 reconciliation process resumes. Senators from tobacco-growing and offshore-oil states, who had benefits stuck in the moribund reconciliation bill, are urging its resuscitation. The administration now sees it may have erred in helping block reconciliation; it would have made the cuts required in Gramm-Rudman easier. Agreement has been reached to deal with the superfund on its own and to consider dropping those extraneous measures that caused controversy.[123]

February 25: Senate and House leaders confer. Senators agree to prepare an offer. Four months have elapsed since October, reducing by one-third the possible savings for 1986.[124]

March 3–6: The Senate offer meets administration objections—giving states too much oil revenues and expanding medicare, medicaid, and AFDC.[125] The House votes to meet the Senate halfway; it deletes superfund and cuts health costs but stands firm on AFDC.

March 14: Agreeing to delete the superfund provision, the Senate, urged by the administration, also insists upon eliminating some state offshore-oil revenues and increases in health funding. With White House blessing, the Senate scales down the House offer, although Majority Leader Dole and Speaker O'Neill can't quite agree.

March 18: House leaders call the Senate position unacceptable. But House Republicans move to accept the Senate amendments and lose by only twenty-five votes as the House Democratic position erodes.

In Assistant Majority Leader Allan K. Simpson's image, reconciliation was "beginning to lose its feathers and entrails," like a pigeon caught in a badminton game. Stephen Gettinger's dry account cannot be improved upon: "The House returned the bill to the Senate March 18, which sent it back to the House the same day, the ninth time it had crossed the Capitol since . . . December 19."[126]

March 20: Republicans join tobacco and offshore-oil Democrats to pass the March 14 Senate offer, on the second try, 230 to 154.

April 1: The official text of H. R. 3128, the reconciliation law, was sent to the president on this appropriate day. Congressional parliamentarians could not remember a law that had been so frequently amended. Just as the Gramm-Rudman act had been dubbed "Grammbo," in reference to Sylvester Stallone's film *Rambo*, so, in anticipation of his next film, H. R. 3128 has been called COBRA, the Consolidated Omnibus Budget Reconciliation Act.[127]

Budget Director Miller is credited with a triumph. His refusal to compromise paid off more than once. As OMB spokesman Edwin Dale told reporters, Miller "won by hanging tough on it, and Bob Dole did a great job. We're pretty delighted with it, and it will be signed by the president."[128]

How a Bill Becomes a Law (Revised)

Robert B. Dove, the Senate parliamentarian, says he knows of no bill that bounced between the Senate and House as many times as did HR 3128, the fiscal 1986 reconciliation (or deficit-reduction) bill. HR 3128 went back and forth nine times in late 1985 and early 1986 after the conference report was filed.

HOUSE

OCT. 24
House passed HR 3500, containing deficit-reduction proposals from most House committees.

OCT. 31
House passed HR 3128, containing deficit-reduction proposals from the Ways and Means Committee. (HR 3500 was later combined with HR 3128 for conference.)

SENATE

NOV. 14
Senate passed S 1730, containing deficit-reduction proposals from all Senate committees. The bill was renumbered HR 3128.

CONFERENCE

DEC. 19
More than 240 conferees, meeting in 31 groups over two weeks, reached agreement on HR 3128.

DEC. 19
House rejected the conference report, voting to strip off a conference provision establishing a new manufacturers' tax to pay for the "superfund" hazardous-waste cleanup program.

DEC. 19
House rejected the Senate proposal.

MARCH 6
House voted to strip off the superfund tax, but also offered compromises on health care and offshore oil revenues.

MARCH 18
House rejected the latest Senate proposal.

MARCH 20
House accepted March 14 Senate proposal, clearing the bill for the president.

DEC. 19
Senate adopted the conference report.

DEC. 19
Senate voted to reinstate the superfund tax.

DEC. 20
Senate voted again to keep the superfund tax.

MARCH 14
Senate agreed to delete ᴜᴇ superfund tax, but at White House insistence also demanded elimination of welfare and offshore drilling provisions and further cuts in offshore oil revenues for states.

MARCH 18
Senate insisted on its March 14 proposal.

SOURCE: *Congressional Quarterly Weekly Report*, April 5, 1986, p. 753. Reprinted by permission of Congressional Quarterly, Inc. All rights reserved.

Although parliamentary practice usually prohibits amendments beyond the second degree (an amendment of an amendment), passing COBRA required special rules allowing five degrees of amendments. Officially, then, the House would be considering "the Senate amendment to the House amendment to the Senate amendment to the Senate amendment to the House amendment to the Senate amendment."[129] As a monument to this labyrinthian process, the *Congressional Quarterly* prepared a neat, simplified version of how this bill became law.

Unlike Sisyphus, Congress had finally gotten its reconciliation boulder to the top of the hill. Of course, some claimed that in the process the boulder had eroded into a pebble. The budgeters had time neither to quibble nor to celebrate. They had to figure out what to do about Gramm-Rudman-Hollings, the plan they had adopted to (in essence) make budgeting easier by making it harder.

When people continually disagree over the same issues, yet they must try to come to an understanding because some budget must be passed, cooperation can take two forms: they can concentrate on who can hurt the other the most (GRH), or they can discover an integrative solution in which each comes to believe that their otherwise opposing preferences will be served by the same program. That is tax reform.

TWENTY

Counterpoint: The Improbable Triumph of Tax Reform

As Congress finished its budget cycle, a half-year late, another issue reached its crisis point. On April 18, 1986, Chairman Packwood broke off the deliberations of his Senate Finance Committee on a bill to reform the tax system by lowering rates and reducing preferences. The bill, President Reagan's prime domestic priority, was being picked apart by the senators, who kept restoring benefits that Packwood proposed to eliminate.

Because it was "revenue neutral," supposedly neither raising nor lowering the deficit, the Tax Reform Act of 1986 might not seem integral to the battle of the budget. Yet tax reform rearranged the landscape for all future efforts at deficit reduction by eliminating many preferences that might have been targets for the budgeters. As a model of what is conventionally termed the "public interest" (fewer exceptions and lower rates) in battle against "special interests" (holders of preferences), tax reform also poses the major issues about our political system that are raised by the budget battles. Can Congress govern? Can it overcome myriads of private interests by imposing on them its own version of a public interest?

Preferences as Policy

We have seen that tax "breaks" or "loopholes" or, in more neutral tones, "preferences," are both easily criticized and a normal part of government. In addition to (or in place of) raising revenue, tax laws may include provisions providing relief from taxes for people who act in socially desirable ways. Using tax provisions as an instrument of policy, furthermore, may accomplish purposes that other legislation, such as appropriations, cannot. Tax advantages may be used as leverage, attracting investment or providing the margin that allows a family to buy a home. At the same time, use of the tax code rather than direct spending can have strange consequences. It is hard to imagine housing subsidies that increase with a person's income being approved as an appropriation, yet this deduction costs billions and is politically sacrosanct.

The government manifests its preferences through the tax code as one of a number of instruments of public policy. Nothing wrong (slimy, sleazy, even faintly illicit) there. Tax legislation may suffer even more seriously than other policy making from common difficulties of the legislative process: complexity obscures choice from all but the directly interested; committees are "captured" by special interests; politicians help groups in return for groups helping them.

Although some U.S. citizens say that taxes should be levied for revenue purposes only, other countries do not practice this doctrine. Everywhere, taxes are used to regulate behavior—whether through sin taxes on commodities that elites believe bad for the masses or by exemptions, such as those relating to the arts, that elites believe good for themselves. Taxation is a major instrument of public policy.

Many of the tax code's preferences are based on notions of equity. Imagine, if you will, a simple income tax with no preferences. Taxpayer A is a young man with an income of $20,000 living by himself in a rented villa. Taxpayer B is a blind, old-age pensioner who supports his wife and two disabled children in their family home on an income of $20,000 a year—from disability and pensions. In a nonpreferential system, A and B would pay exactly the same tax. Equity would appear to require not simplicity but complexity so that B ends up paying less than A.

Can the amount of tax expenditures be known? Yes and no. Yes, it is possible to estimate roughly the loss of revenue to the Treasury from provisions such as accelerated depreciation, or deductions for medical expenditures, or not counting fringe benefits as income. No, it is not possible to estimate accurately. When tax process provides incentives, motivations are involved. How is one to know whether the taxpaying entities concerned, once blocked in a certain direction by abolishing or reducing a preference, will not take action to counter the expected loss of income? As the common scare story goes, to cut the mortgage interest deduction will reduce home starts, driving the housing industry and the entire economy into a slump that reduces revenues. Exaggerated, perhaps, but some backfire is possible. To estimate the synergistic effects of preferences on incentives may well be beyond existing capabilities.

Most returns—about 60 percent—do not itemize deductions. Yet in 1984 over 38 million did itemize. Over 10 million, most with incomes under $30,000 per year, claimed deductions for medical or dental expenses. Deductions for other taxes were claimed by 38 million; 27 million claimed for home mortgage interest; 35 million for charitable contributions. Out of $359 billion in itemized deductions, about $281 billion, nearly 80 percent, were claimed in those categories. The bulk of tax preferences are for categories that are hard to stigmatize as special interests.[1]

Because preferences are worth more at higher incomes in a progressive tax system, a large part of the deductions goes to a comparatively small number of taxpayers. In 1984, about 12.7 million returns (13 percent) claimed about half of the deductions. They paid a slightly larger share of the taxes.[2]

No instrument of public policy is good for all purposes. The dilemma involved in extensive use of tax preferences is well known to observers: individual and collective rationality are at odds. Though the vast bulk of tax preferences originates in the desire to achieve some self-evident good—locating industry in areas of high unemployment, increasing the supply of vital commodities, fulfilling the dreams of home ownership—the collective consequences of reducing taxes for these items may be undesirable. The number of preferences, the fact that they have been adopted at different times and hence may work at cross-purposes, and their high rate of interaction with each other and with existing provisions have led to a complex code. The large amounts by which preferences reduce the revenue base require higher marginal tax rates. Worst of all, to the taxpayer this combination of complexity and cost leads to delegitimation of the tax process; most people suspect other people of cheating. The very language used—"loopholes" and "gimmicks"—suggests that it has become morally suspect to make legal and proper use of those statutory provisions deliberately designed to encourage such behavior.

What, in fact, was meant by "reform"? Essentially three things: lower rates, fewer brackets, and fewer preferences. The key words were "fairness" and "simplification." "Fairness" is used in the sense that people would be treated, if not equally, then proportionally to their financial condition. The existing system was held to give some people opportunities that others could not enjoy. Why should cattlemen, or oil drillers, or union members (with good health benefits) get special treatment? To those who disliked a progressive tax, the flat tax—one rate for all—seemed fair. Ronald Reagan had long been in that camp; while lecturing for General Electric in the 1950s, he had described the progressive income tax as "created by Karl Marx." "It simply is a penalty on the individual who can improve his own lot; it takes his earnings from him and redistributes them to people who are incapable of earning as much as he can."[3]

Fewer brackets—either one (a flat rate), or three (as in the Bradley-Gephardt proposal), or some number much less than the then-existing fourteen—sounds simpler, as does reducing the number of preferences. Actually, the appearance of simplification was deceptive. In practice, most people calculate their tax from tax tables; and no matter whether the amount owed for a particular taxable income was calculated from three or thirty brackets, the table would look no different. Also, the vast majority of taxpayers were using only a small number of the available preferences, some of which (like nontaxability of fringe benefits) required no individual effort. Yet filling out tax forms was still a bother; people did not like hiring experts to protect them from the IRS. The populist appeal of simplification was power: a simpler system would make people less dependent on experts. Rich people could afford to hire experts; the common man could not. In the same vein, simplification promised openness, a more transparent system. But simplicity and fairness, as tax experts know, are at odds. For fairness requires distinctions that complicate tax returns.

Which was better for economic growth, targeted preferences or lower marginal rates? The theoretical debate—selective versus universal incentives—merged, as usual, into empirical differences: one side found marginal rate reduction to increase individual incentives and the other claimed selective tax preferences to encourage investment to be superior. Tax preferences to aid industry became a contested concept. Some market-oriented politicians began to see tax preferences as subsidies that distinguished unfairly between different industries, a question only market competition should decide. There was no single obvious truth, but multiple truths.

The Origins of Tax Reform

The first step toward radical change is to delegitimate the existing system. A very good job of this was done by all sectors of opinion from the mid-1960s through the mid-1980s. Those who thought domestic government was far too big naturally thought they were paying too much for it. Those who approved in general of various governmental programs protested that the system taxed the poor too heavily and the rich not enough. The criticism's harsh edge developed from the growing feeling that "other people" were not paying their proper share. Between charges that the system was morally corrupt in favoring the well-to-do and economically irrational in encouraging businesses to seek tax losses the existing tax structure had few defenders.

But where were the centrists who usually can be counted on to defend the nation's institutions? Those actively involved in making tax policy, like former Representative Barber Conable, now head of the World Bank, believed that the tax code was complicated for a good reason:

almost every provision existed in response to a cry for equity from some deserving group. But they lost support.

In a heartfelt statement to his Senate colleagues explaining how he became converted to tax reform, Senate Finance Committee Chairman Robert Packwood insisted that tax preferences were moral. In order to appreciate the position of many experienced legislators on tax preferences, as well as to empathize with their moral defensiveness, Packwood's words in describing witnesses at a tax hearing are quoted at length.

> But, indeed, everybody in this country belongs to some special interest. . . .
>
> Blue Cross-Blue Shield, a nonprofit medical insurance group that exists in all of the States. They are, at the moment, not taxed. They very frankly said, "If we are taxed, we are going to have to raise the premiums for all of our subscribers."
>
> Is that greed? Is that evil? Were they malevolently motivated because they did not want to have to increase the premiums that they charged to all of their subscribers? Are they a special interest?
>
> Another witness: Bread for the World. This is a low-income, poverty group interested in feeding the poor throughout the world.
>
> The Children's Defense Fund. An extraordinary organization that has done extraordinary things in this country in the last 10 years. A greedy, special interest?
>
> The Coalition on Smoking and Health. They are trying to alert this country to the continued dangers of smoking.
>
> Common Cause. Of all the groups that, I think, to themselves might deny being a special interest, it would be Common Cause although they often allege that others are guilty of that. They testified.
>
> Environmental Action.
>
> Hale House. That wonderful, wonderful organization in New York that Dr. Lorraine Hale founded that takes care of narcotic-addicted newborn babies that have become addicted and abandoned because their mothers were addicted. She had a problem with the tax bill. Greedy, special interest?
>
> Next is the umbrella group that represents almost all charities in this country. They were worried about charitable contributions. . . .
>
> The solar lobby. A wonderful group of people who are trying to encourage the use of solar energy. We have solar tax credits in the law now, and they were afraid those might disappear.[4]

Preferences, Packwood argued, in our opinion, correctly, were mostly about worthy causes.

This party of balance found its voice drowned out by the cacophony of criticism. Therefore, the very desire of its adherents to legitimize American institutions led the centrists to worry that, whatever the cause, the tax system no longer commanded support.

The idea of a broader-based, lower-rate income tax has been in the air since the end of the Second World War. Among economists and tax lawyers, it had two main sources of support: liberals and libertarians. As tax preferences proliferated, Professor Stanley Surrey, an author and a Treasury official, mounted a campaign to have preferences called by what he considered their right name—tax expenditures.[5] Joseph Pechman and other economists joined in the criticism with calculations showing that tax rates could be much reduced if revenues were not siphoned off through these tax expenditures.[6] They hoped to make support of government programs more sustainable both by requiring a vote on subsidies and by keeping rates down. Pechman and his colleagues (at the Brookings Institution and throughout the liberal academic community) worked during two decades for reform, never suspecting that their most powerful ally would be, of all people, Ronald Reagan.

Preferences, to libertarians, were subsidies that distorted markets and at the same time increased the scope of governmental intervention. Far better to remove preferences so as to lower tax rates and simultaneously to lessen governmental intervention while enhancing the performance of the private sector.

The contemporary story began on August 5, 1982, when Senator Bill Bradley and Representative Richard Gephardt introduced their Fair Tax Act. Just as President Reagan liked to tell about how he cut back his acting schedule when tax rates became nearly confiscatory during the Second World War, Bradley, a basketball star, couldn't quite get used to being a "depreciable asset."[7] He, too, had considered how to reduce his taxes and, on behalf of the players' union, taxes of other athletes as well.[8] Bradley won a seat on the Senate Finance Committee in 1980 and began to immerse himself in tax provisions. At the same time, from his seat on House Ways and Means, Gephardt began to view tax preferences as a means of promoting special interests. The tax system, he thought, had gotten out of hand:

> It is all vivid to you because you see the storm window manufacturer coming and saying, "We've got to have this credit for storm windows in order to have a good energy policy for the country." And you see it go in the code, and you see the regulations written three years later . . . and when you watch all that I think you begin to question what we're doing.[9]

Sometime in 1983, according to David Stockman, Secretary of State George Shultz, also a noted economist, had suggested a flat tax to the president. Perhaps the president was too far out of touch to see that the idea was unfeasible. In any event, he is reported to have scribbled a note to Secretary of the Treasury Don Regan on the back of an article on the flat tax saying the idea was a good one.[10]

Earlier that year, Jack Kemp met with a number of intellectuals identified with supply-side economics—Paul Craig Roberts, an economist with a year in the Treasury;[11] Lewis E. Lehrman, a business man who had narrowly been defeated for governor of New York; Jude Wanniski and Alan Reynolds, economic consultants; and Irving Kristol, professor at New York University, editor of *The Public Interest,* and an intellectual leader among neoconservatives. Kristol suggested that Kemp back the Bradley-Gephardt bill. "We all came to the conclusion," Kemp recalled, "that Kristol was right, that Reagan and Kemp should endorse Bradley-Gephardt. That would have thrown the Democratic Party into a state of real confusion because Mondale was getting ready to talk about a surtax [to reduce the deficit] and Bradley and Gephardt were talking about growth and jobs—just what supply-siders had been talking about in the 1970s."[12] The campaign group in the White House was leery of the proposal. But that was not to be the end of it.

Following the president's lead, and his own distaste for the jumble of preferences in the tax code, Secretary of the Treasury Don Regan wanted the chief executive to come out for a flat tax in the 1984 State of the Union message. Chief of Staff James Baker asked Regan to hold off, however, on the grounds that any precise plan would call needless attention to details, anger some people, and might subject the president to premature, possibly harmful criticism. Mondale's talk about an excise tax was target enough. Don Regan agreed to hold back, but he and the president wanted at least to signal their intent in his State of the Union message on January 25, 1984. They may have laughed when he sat down at the presidential piano, but they sang along when they heard the melody. "For the first time in a generation," Senator Edward Kennedy, hardly a Reagan idolater, boomed out as the Senate was considering tax reform in June 1986, "the impossible dream of tax reform is on the threshold of reality, and it is our responsibility to make it happen."[13] Getting from ironic laughter to a sing-along took two and a half years.

The Politicians Try Tax Reform

The secretary of the Treasury assembled a team of specialists to work out a policy from which to start, a trial balloon to cause reactions that would produce information about budgetary and political feasibility: Is there enough latitude in preferences to allow for lower rates, and, if there is, might there be sufficient support?

Despite the president's decision to postpone the Treasury report until after the 1984 elections, politicians with similar programs were motivated to act. On April 12, Senator Bradley and Representative Gephardt announced a petition drive to mount public support for their fair tax. A few days later, the new Populist Conservative Tax Coalition, chaired by

Richard Viguerie (a political operator who sparked use of mass mailing and computerized telephone techniques) announced a petition drive to garner a million signatures for a 10 percent flat tax.[14] The symbols used—"fair" and "populist conservative"—showed possible signs of political coalition. If fair is populist and populist is conservative, maybe the two sides can get together. But not at 10 percent!

On April 26 Representative Jack Kemp and Senator Robert Kasten introduced their "fast tax." Like Bradley-Gephardt, Kemp-Kasten would have eliminated deduction of state and local taxes, repealed the investment tax credit, raised personal exemptions, and continued the housing deduction. Kemp-Kasten was flatter—24 percent as opposed to 14, 26, and 30 percent—and provided larger preferences for investment.[15]

During the year other proposals emerged. They ranged from a consumption (cash flow) tax, to across-the-board reductions in tax preferences (base-broadening), to a flat tax—essentially, the Hall-Rabushka scheme for a 19 percent flat rate on all business and personal income with a large personal deduction to get poor people off the rolls.[16]

As the presidential campaign warmed up, Senator Bradley tried in vain to convince Walter Mondale that it was essential to increase the perceived fairness of the tax system before trying to raise revenues that would reduce the deficit. Nevertheless, Mondale chose to focus on the deficit, and proposed raising taxes.[17] The Democratic party platform, along with castigating the existing system and criticizing President Reagan for taking from the poor to give to the rich, pledged itself generally to broaden the tax base and shift the tax burden.[18] By contrast, the Republican platform came out for a "modified flat tax."[19] Following its president, the Republican party pledged that "tax reform must not be a guise for a tax increase."[20]

During summer 1984, top Treasury officials met to review tax reform proposals.[21] In response to assertions that wholesale reform "would never fly on the Hill," Secretary of the Treasury Don Regan replied that "I don't want to hear about the politics of it. If we worry about the politics, we'll never get anything done."[22]

The idea of a flat tax was dropped because the rate would have to be too high. A close adviser to the president recalls that at 19 percent, "it would mean a lot of increases for a lot of people." Instead, the Treasury tax staff, trading tax preferences for lower rates, came up with personal rates of 16, 28, and 37 percent and a corporate rate of 28 percent. Ronald Pearlman, who succeeded John "Buck" Chapoton as assistant secretary for tax policy, felt that the disparity between the top rates for individuals and corporations was so large it would encourage the movement of resources, so he lowered the individual and raised the corporate rate. "If we're so close," Don Regan asked and advised, why "can't we get to 15,

25, and 35 percent?" Now the top personal rate, coincidentally, would be just half of the 70 percent rate in force when the Reagan administration took office. Lowering the individual rates meant raising the corporate rate to 33 percent, still substantially below the 46 percent rate when Reagan became president.[23] Following a series of hearings in which House Ways and Means member Charles Rangel (D-N.Y.) provided vivid examples of how large a proportion of income was taken from the working poor, the Treasury plan was modified to keep many of this group from being taxed at all.[24]

The 262-page Treasury report on "Tax Reforms for Fairness, Simplicity, and Economic Growth" that appeared after the November 1984 election pulled few punches: business taxation was "deeply flawed"; its subsidies to favored industries "distorted choices"; tax shelters for the wealthy "undermine confidence in the tax system." What more could tax preferences, with their accompanying high rates, be accused of than discouraging "saving, investment, invention and innovation"?[25]

The price for reducing corporate and personal tax rates was high: eliminating the low rate for capital gains (which, however, would be indexed) and wiping out the investment tax credit, accelerated cost recovery system, state and local income and sales taxes, and parts of fringe benefits. Essentially, personal taxes would be cut by $148 billion while business taxes would rise by $165 billion.[26]

If one picked a bunch of tax economists and lawyers at random, gave them the constraint of revenue neutrality, and told them to come up with a large-scale reform, Treasury 1, as it was called, would be it. Treasury 1 bespoke a commitment to free-market economics, supporting enterprise as a general concept rather than for particular industries.

But not without a struggle. The assistant secretary of the Treasury for economic affairs argued strongly in favor of retaining tax incentives for capital investment. Secretary of the Treasury Regan ruled against him.[27] Indeed, after much debate and not a little soul searching, his other assistants persuaded Regan to go for evenhandedness by having capital gains taxed at the same (now higher) rate as ordinary income. Reagan was told that indexing the original investment against inflation would better protect the investor who saw his stake reduced in value by years of inflation.[28]

Treasury 1 raised howls from the business community and cries of glee from Democrats. After debate within the White House, the president chose to treat the plan as Treasury's, not his, but a good start. On December 7 (perhaps the losers saw it as another Pearl Harbor) President Reagan praised the Treasury plan as among "the best proposals for changing the tax system that have ever occurred in my lifetime." And, in his State of the Union message on February 6, President Reagan sought to get Congress on the move by issuing a call for "historical reform."[29]

Words of caution were heard. Don Regan, who had become chief of staff, said Treasury 1 was written on a word processor and could be changed. Republican members of the House Ways and Means Committee urged the president not to allow tax reform to divert attention from the deficit. Undersecretary of the Treasury Richard Darman agreed.[30] Still, the president, waxing eloquent in his State of the Union speech, had spoken of "restoring fairness to families" by increasing the personal exemption and exempting the poor. Why, Congress could "pass, this year, a bill . . . making this economy the engine of our dreams, and America the investment capital of the world."[31]

There were the usual charges of presidential misunderstanding, only this time from the other side. Despite Reagan's reassurance that capital formation would be protected, Jack Albertine, president of the American Business Council, complained that the man in the White House did not seem to realize that increased taxation of capital gains was part of the Treasury plan.[32] A group of ninety-seven House members wrote to the president protesting against the higher rate for capital gains.[33] Lobbyists for the Independent Sector, representing nonprofit groups, and charitable agencies spread concern about the effects of lower rates on donations. As the chorus of protests swelled, White House efforts to distance the administration from commitments to specific provisions created doubts of its commitment to reform.

Politicians and public officials were full of folk wisdom about why nothing much would be done. California Democrat Fortney H. (Pete) Stark, chair of the House Ways and Means Subcommittee on Select Revenue Measures, observed that "leveling the playing field"—a congressional term for reducing tax breaks, so that individuals and industries were treated alike—meant that "the guys who are going to go down are going to fight like hell." His prediction in November 1984 was that "Congress in the middle of something like that never does anything courageous." Stark was seconded by Representative Gephardt, who observed, "My experience in politics leads me to believe that people who are about to lose something tend to be more effective than people who are about to experience a continuation of the status quo even though they don't like it." As the committee's chief counsel, John J. Salmon put it, "There are only big cats and dogs left and they bite."[34]

No one could be more experienced than Wilbur Mills, chairman of Ways and Means from 1958 to 1974. He summed up the difficulty: "There's no constituency for tax reform. People who've got deductions don't want to give them up, and, while most people might be better off, it's hard to convince the public." Indeed, it is, if only because various segments of the general public want different things. Various polls taken in 1982, for instance, revealed strong support for both a flat tax of 14 percent for everyone, with no preferences, and a progressive income tax. Public opinion analyst William Schneider concluded that, although the public was dissatisfied with the tax system, the people were also reluctant to depart from it.[35] In a more refined analysis of opinion, on particular provisions studied over many years, John Witte (author of the best study of the political aspects of the income tax) concluded that dissatisfaction with the system as a whole is overcome by a lack of support for alternatives. Item by item, Witte finds, contrary to his initial expectations, that the internal revenue code is exquisitely sensitive to whatever public preferences exist.[36]

In mid-1985, starting with the view that paying taxes is hardly a popular activity, Everett Carl Ladd (executive director of the Roper Center for Public Opinion Research) nevertheless found no "populist groundswell" for reform. In a *Los Angeles Times* poll in January 1985, 59 percent agreed that the present system was unfair, but the same proportion believed they had personally paid the right amount of tax; from that Ladd concluded that "there certainly isn't what I would call significant resistance to the present tax structure."[37]

In the face of "instant obituaries" for tax reform in *Business Week* and other publications, Ronald Reagan began to reassert that he was serious. He and his people were "totally dedicated" to tax reform, the president told a reporter at his press conference. Worried that the reform would be used to raise taxes to reduce the deficit, Reagan said also that "we're not sending them [the spending budget and Treasury 1] up there [to Congress] as a package that somehow people can begin trading between one and the other."[38] If tax reform turned out to be a tax increase, he might well lose on both counts as his supporters deserted him on the increase and his opponents raised the ante for taxing high incomes. Accommodation would become impossible.

For months Senator Bradley, whose own proposal resembled Treasury 1, had said he would wait for the State of the Union message before lending his own weight to the enterprise; he wanted to see how strongly the president came out for reform. Praising the speech as a major step, Bradley raised the level of commitment: "He's [Reagan's] got to go directly to the people if he's going to counter the special interests."[39] House Ways and Means Committee Chairman Dan Rostenkowski also told everyone in sight that the president's "got to take the heat with the rest of us. A list of lofty principles is not enough."[40] Rostenkowski's ally on Ways and Means, Don Pease (D-Ohio), made the quid pro quo clear: "We won't get any place unless President Reagan is willing to invest a lot of his personal time, energy and political capital in trying to get it through. If we don't get a signal he's trying to do that, I think the committee will not go through the motions."[41] Democrats and other politicians wanted the "great communicator" to rally the public against the lobbyists.

In spite of what the *New York Times* called "an extraordinary personal effort" by Reagan[42] to generate that support in speeches and in meetings, he failed. The very fact that he kept trying despite lukewarm response, however, meant that it was worthwhile for others to keep trying. Had President Reagan just sat there waiting for others to take the lead, tax reform would have languished.

New Senate Finance Chairman Robert Packwood was no fan of reform: "I do like to use the tax code for incentives," he told anybody who would listen. "I sort of like the tax code the way it is."[43] But other potent people saw promise. Packwood's new chief of staff to the Finance Committee, William M. Diefenderfer III, saw a chance to broaden the appeal of the Republican party. Diefenderfer characterized himself as one of the "many [who] feel we need a major occurrence [like tax reform] to have the average guy say, 'yes, indeed, the Republican Party is my party.'"[44] Similarly, Dan Rostenkowski, the strongest supporter of tax reform among House Democrats, argued strenuously with skeptical colleagues stressing that "our first order of business is to reduce rates for the people. That's a good Democratic position for us to be in. . . . I'm sure Ronald Reagan is going to try to steal that thunder."[45]

Rostenkowski Delivers

In regard to philosophy, Dan Rostenkowski thought it wrong that working people, like his own daughter, had to pay so much in taxes. Aware that a person of his background, who plays politics with such evident relish, might not be thought of as embodying the national interest, Rostenkowski explained that "I want to be a patriot, too. It sounds like corn but, if we get no credit at all on this tax reform bill, my God, we're elected to do what's right."[46] Rosty and Reagan had come a ways since 1981, when they competed for votes with the commodity tax straddle.

Credit or not, the Ways and Means chairman's prestige depended on passage of some sort of tax reform. Rostenkowski had not fared too well in past years. Badly beaten by the across-the-board tax cuts of 1981, having to dodge the House floor to pass TEFRA in 1982, he had eventually consolidated his influence in his committee and on tax policy but not in a way that won him much credit as a leader or innovator. Rostenkowski was looking for a winner. Tip O'Neill had announced his retirement. Would Rosty run for Speaker against James Wright of Texas? "I'd like to see the kind of tax reform plan the House can produce first," he responded. "Winning a big fight over a tax bill can make you do just about anything."[47]

On May 28, President Reagan gave a major address from the Oval Office outlining his revised tax reform proposal. He appealed to common feelings: "Well, how many times have we heard people brag about clever schemes to avoid paying taxes or watched luxuries casually written off to be paid for by somebody else—that somebody being you? I believe that in both spirit and substance, our tax system has come to be un-American."[48] Reagan's appeal could have been dismissed as just more fine words from a master wordsmith. Instead, Rostenkowski, in the Democratic response, echoed the president's rhetoric and laid claim to its Democratic heritage:

> Trying to tax people fairly: That's been the historic Democratic commitment. . . . My parents and grandparents didn't like to pay taxes. Who does? But like most Americans they were willing to pay their fair share as the price for a free country where everyone could make their own breaks.
>
> Every year politicians promise to make the tax code fair and simple, but every year we seem to slip further behind. Now most of us pay taxes with bitterness and frustration. Working families file their tax forms with the nagging feeling that they're the biggest suckers and chumps in the world. . . .
>
> But this time there's a difference in the push for tax reform. This time, it's a Republican president who's bucking his party's tradition as protectors of big business and the wealthy. . . . If the president's plan is everything he says it is, he'll have a great deal of Democratic support.[49]

The chairman ended by asking his audience to "write Rosty"—or their own legislators—to show their support.

Rosty got 75,000 letters and a lot of praise in the media. The public response was not enough to convince other politicians to go along, but it was enough to reinforce Rostenkowski's personal commitment to producing a bill. The two speeches put Reagan and Rostenkowski in a public alliance that ensured tax reform would stay on the agenda, for now politicians would have to take public stands "for" or "against."

Responding to the attacks on Treasury 1, Treasury made a series of compromises in a new plan, dubbed "Treasury 2." It protected oil and gas interests at the insistence of the Texan Treasury Secretary, James Baker. It gave bigger breaks to upper- than middle-income taxpayers. Capital gains rates went down instead of up; state and local taxes no longer would be deductible. But it eliminated taxes for families of four with incomes of $12,000 or less, cut the highest corporate rate to 33 percent, and kept the Treasury 1 individual rate structure (15/25/35).

For Rostenkowski, Treasury 2 was not acceptable, but it was a starting point.

During the summer Ways and Means held voluminous hearings, searching for possible soft spots in group resistance. Public support for the reform effort remained "tepid."[50] "I scheduled five town meetings on tax reform across Arkansas during the August recess," Democratic Senator David Pryor noted. "We averaged 200 to 250 at each meeting and I got no support. All that people wanted to talk about was the $2 trillion debt."[51]

Cross-pressured particularly on state and local taxes (which New York's Governor Cuomo had made a crusade for his state's large delegation) and worried about the deficit, members of the House wondered out loud why they should bother with reform at all. Representative Byron C. Dorgan's (D-N.D.) retort—"no matter what people are hearing from back home" an "outrageously complicated and unfair" tax system had to go—was about the best plug that reform got.[52]

The first stage of Ways and Means' effort reached its climax during markup on October 15. Chairman Rostenkowski was beaten 17 to 13 on an amendment that proposed expanding (by $4.8 billion over five years) the deductions banks can take for reserves to cover bad debts. Here ended revenue neutrality at a time of deficits. Rostenkowski was angry. Bank lobbyists, waiting in droves outside the committee rooms, were so joyous (in poring over a tally of the vote that was not supposed to be released until the next day) that one of them shouted, "We won, we won."[53] That rankled. Were these representatives, servants of the people, really at the beck and call of the monied interests? "If I were a bank," advised Representative Fortney Stark who had been a banker, "I wouldn't start to spend that money."[54]

The Ways and Means chairman decided to wait rather than immediately attempt to reverse the bank amendment.[55] He believed the pressure for tax reform was essentially negative; as columnists Birnbaum and Murray put it, "Anyone who stood in the way of reform would be tagged in the press as having sold out to special interests; that was a harsh label few were eager to accept."[56] Congressmen had to be flogged into action by the press; and failures in public, ironically, might raise press condemnation to a level that would overcome interest-group pressure. So Rostenkowski decided to let the vote "hang there," to "let them stew in it for a while."[57]

The committee worked on other provisions while the members stewed. Rostenkowski was trying to keep within the limits of his informal understanding with Reagan: that if he hit the president's targets for rates and if the bill were revenue neutral, the president would hold fire while retaining the right to suggest changes after the bill left the committee. They shared an interest in establishing that *some* bill was likely to pass; if they could do so, then the changes not made would seem like benefits to the lucky nonvictims. The leaders' timing was everything. If opposition became too vocal, opponents might seek to kill reform then and there. Concessions at the right time, however, would give former opponents a stake in the bill.

On October 21, Rostenkowski made his crucial move. The New York bloc was adamant about preserving the state and local deduction; even representatives of low-tax states opposed its elimination. Tax reform's ideological opponents, like James Jones, a believer in incentives for capital formation, had allied with the New Yorkers in hopes that, with state and local deductions preserved, there was no way to get lower rates and the same revenues. After realizing they could raise revenues by lowering the brackets, so the middle and top rates applied to more income, Rostenkowski and his staff decided to cut a deal on state and local. They secretly gave in to the New Yorkers in return for support on the rest of the bill. Then Rostenkowski used that agreement, and pressure on the amendment's sponsor, Ronnie Flippo (D-Ala.), to compromise on the bank issue. He won 14 to 7.[58]

Treasury would be upset about state and local, so Rostenkowski concealed the deal as long as possible. Because this was a provision his committee Democrats had been particularly loath to lose, however, they were relieved and encouraged.[59] "I was always going to give you state and local taxes," Rostenkowski told a surprised colleague. "If you were," Thomas Downey (D-N.Y.) responded, "you deserve an academy award."[60] Representative W. Henson Moore (R-La.) agreed: "I have seen a master politician at work."[61]

After eight days of meetings, begun November 15, the committee Democrats agreed on a bill. It had a fourth and top bracket (38 percent), a higher top corporate rate (36 percent), and tougher depreciation provisions than in Treasury 2. Some House Republicans particularly objected to a provision that raised the personal exemption for nonitemizers more than itemizers (they called this antifamily; in essence, it favored poorer over richer families). The Ways and Means plan also maintained existing deductions for medical expenses and nontaxability of employer-paid health benefits.[62] For these reasons, the administration was hesitant, hoping that some other bill could emerge from the House. Rostenkowski's version passed Ways and Means (28 to 8) on December 3, 1985; but only five Republicans supported it.[63]

Without endorsing either the majority committee bill or the Republican alternative, President Reagan asked for a "positive vote" in the

House. However, Republicans—feeling cut out as Ways and Means Democrats caucused, believing Baker and Darman had ignored them while attending to Rostenkowski, and opposing reform anyway—were seething. Amid threats about who Ronald Reagan would not campaign for in 1986, James Baker and Richard Darman arranged to shuttle Republican House members over to see the president. "I hope you won't let me down," Reagan told them. He wanted it any way he could get it, whether the final plan was more Republican or more Democratic, and assured legislators that problems would be fixed in the Senate.[64] Minority Leader Robert H. Michel (R-Ill.) found his members strongly opposed— "They don't want to vote for this turkey just to get to conference."[65] "The phrase the 'Senate will fix it up' is the moral equivalent of 'I'll respect you in the morning,'" commented Bill Frenzel (R-Minn.) of Ways and Means.[66]

A number of Democrats also disliked the bill's treatment of federal pensions, including their own. As the rule for the bill came up for debate on December 11, they rose to denounce it. They were joined by oil-state Democrats. Seizing their opportunity, Republican leaders quickly mobilized their whip organization to beat the rule. They succeeded, 223 to 202, as only fourteen Republicans voted to allow consideration of their president's greatest legislative priority.[67]

"If the President really cares about tax reform," Tip O'Neill rubbed it in, "then he will deliver the votes. Otherwise, December 11 at 12 noon will be remembered as the date that Ronald Reagan became a lame duck." Unless the president assured him of at least fifty Republican votes, the Speaker wouldn't bring the bill back to the floor.[68]

With Darman and Baker at his side, President Reagan engaged in a personal lobbying effort. "I just can't accept we would let this historic initiative slip through our fingers," the president told House Republicans.[69] Aside from telling them, personally, he did care about their views, the president gave GOP congressmen written assurance that he would seek to reduce the top 38 percent personal rate voted by Ways and Means (for the incentive faction); increase the personal exemption to $2,000 for everyone (for the family order faction); and provide more generous deductions for business (for the capital formation faction). Reagan succeeded in getting seventy Republicans to vote for the rule bringing up the bill on December 17, whereupon the Ways and Means plan passed on a voice vote.[70]

Speaker O'Neill had his written statement ready when the vote took place: "Democrats tonight have rescued tax reform from the jaws of big business Republicans. We have delivered on our historic commitment to tax fairness. Only the Republican Senate can stop tax reform now."[71]

Like the target bear in a shooting gallery, Richard Darman observed, "It [tax reform] gets hit, it rises, pauses, turns a bit—and then it keeps going."[72]

Packwood's Conversion

In the Republican Senate there was deep concern over shifting huge tax burdens to companies that were already facing hard times. Would the country be better off, senators wondered, if individuals paid lower taxes, but there were no (or ill-paid) jobs?[73]

And what about the deficit? Fifty senators, including seven members of the Finance Committee, wrote to President Reagan on March 4 requesting him to delay the tax bill until there was agreement on reducing the deficit.[74] According to the originator, Senator Rudy Boschwitz (R-Minn.), who, Dole said, spoke for a majority, the Senate would "neither consider nor debate" the tax bill until the second round of Gramm-Rudman had been settled.[75] On April 9 the Senate voted (72 to 24) in a nonbinding resolution to delay the tax bill.[76]

Republican Senator Grassley expressed the sentiment of many when he argued that "the country would be better off if we would pass a one-sentence bill saying we're not going to change the tax law for five years." Yet, without wishing to go forward, Congress couldn't quite get itself to go back. "Tax reform," Grassley continued, "has taken on a life of its own."[77]

Members of the Senate Finance Committee held a private retreat on January 24 and 25. They started by deciding not to begin from the House bill, which most considered put too great a burden on business. "The Ways and Means Committee has always been close to the people," Senator Moynihan explained. "Finance has always been a committee close to industry."[78] Even so, the group agreed that their bill should be revenue neutral and should move tax burdens from individuals to business.[79]

In March, before Finance began its markup, one episode gave meaning to such shadowy terms as "the street" and "the market." The activities of the tax committees are carefully scrutinized by those who will be affected by them. At the request of Baker and Darman, who were convinced that tax-free municipal bonds enable wealthy individuals to escape taxation, Senator Packwood suggested making such bond income subject to a 20 percent minimum tax. At once, trading in municipal bonds stopped. The crisis was overcome by a joint statement from Packwood and Rostenkowski stipulating that such a provision, if enacted, would apply only to new but not to old bonds.[80] That revenue raiser was the first, but not the last, revenue raiser dumped when markup began on March 24.

Discovering that it was not easy to reconcile lower personal and corporate tax rates with the demands for exemptions for specific industries, Senator Packwood proposed eliminating the deduction for excise taxes on many commodities, such as alcohol, tobacco, and telephones. Easy money in the tens of billions, or so it seemed. But soon Democratic party critics of such taxes as unfair to people of low income were joined by the industries involved in forming the (inevitable) Coalition Against Regressive Taxation. It purported to show that the income tax reductions for low- and middle-income taxpayers would be effectively wiped out by higher excise taxes. That proposal and, with it, $62 billion in revenues also evaporated.[81]

After three weeks of bargaining on provisions, Senator Packwood suddenly announced on April 18 that, rather than kill the bill by continuing on as they were, he was suspending his committee's markup.[82] What had happened? Compared with his initial proposal, based on the administration's version, Finance Chairman Packwood had already given up $10 billion in tax preferences over five years. There followed a series of votes on such issues as foreign taxation, private pensions, and tax-exempt bonds, amounting to some $19 billion more.[83] Packwood himself had sought to keep preferences for the lumber industries—so important to the depressed economy in his home state of Oregon. He thought it fair play to allow each committee member to keep his first priority preferences. It turned out, however, that, if these were granted, secondary and tertiary priorities then moved to the top of the list.

When Senator Chafee (R-R.I.)—joined by Moynihan, Bradley, Mitchell (D-Maine), and Assistant Secretary of the Treasury Roger Mentz—tried to delete a preference for builder bonds issued under governmental auspices, Packwood opposed the suggestion as contrary to what he called the "tradition of subsidies for housing." It lost 7 to 10. When Chafee joined the fray by moving to dilute Packwood's proposal to tax trusts established by parents for their children, the latter protested on grounds of revenue loss. "That," Chafee retorted, "hasn't seemed to slow anyone else down. If you can't fight them, join them, and it's a big crowd to join."[84] Chafee also wanted to preserve a preference for federal retirees that would cost an estimated $7 billion in revenue.[85] By then, $25 or $30 billion had been used up.[86] "I think our low point came," recalled Senator Moynihan, "when we solemnly concluded that the depreciable life of an oil refinery was five years, an absurd idea for so permanent a structure."[87] But the final straw came when Senators Durenberger and Moynihan garnered sufficient votes to restore the deductibility of state and local taxes. As Moynihan graphically described the events in a newsletter to his constituents: "Packwood . . . recognized that our amendment would be followed by dozens more. His proposal was in ruins. He banged the gavel and announced there would be no more votes that day, and no more meetings until further notice. Tax reform was promptly pronounced dead."[88]

Although he believed that tax preferences were a creative use of the tax code for worthy causes, Senator Packwood was nonetheless intrigued with the concept of a low-rate, broad-based tax. Back home, as he traveled around Oregon, the senator had begun to ask how far down rates would have to go before the other person lost interest in preferences. Though proposals on rates varied, they centered around 25 percent.

At the same time, Packwood had reviewed a list of witnesses coming before his committee, thinking "they all have a preference and they can't conceive how they can act without that preference."[89] Something was very wrong when business had become addicted to preferences and Congress couldn't stop feeding that addiction.

After adjourning the Finance Committee, Packwood went to lunch with Bill Diefenderfer, who had come to serve as chief of staff in order to help with the tax bill; both were appalled at the way things had gone. The publicity about an orgy of special interests embarrassed them.[90] Packwood's reputation, in both the short-term currency of Washington judgments of influence and the long-term judgment of history, was in danger.[91] Up for reelection, he was not looking good in the newspapers.

Three weeks of exhausting efforts in markup had ended up with more of the same. But what would happen if they seized the ideological high ground with a truly radical proposal, cutting rates to 25 percent, challenging all their colleagues so to speak to give up their preference for preferences? Maybe something would emerge that would credit the Senate and make their work worthwhile. At the worst, Packwood could gain political credit.[92] "We looked at each other," Packwood recounted, "and I said, 'Why not give it a try?' "[93] If they were going to lose, they might as well lose, as Moynihan put it, "in the cause of the most extraordinary tax bill in our history."[94]

That afternoon, Packwood and Diefenderfer called the top tax expert in Congress, staff head of the Joint Committee on Taxation, David H. Brockway, who, if anybody could, would know whether a 25 percent rate was feasible. "Dave," Packwood asked, "draw us a series of tax plans that sets the rate at 25 percent." It developed that 25 percent would work only by eliminating the deduction for state and local taxes. Packwood ruled that out as politically impossible. But a 26 percent or 27 percent rate might make it.[95]

On Tuesday, April 22, Packwood asked the five committee members he had reason to believe would support tax reform—Republicans Chafee and Danforth, and Democrats Bradley, Mitchell, and Moynihan—to meet in his office. (The Chernobyl disaster was in the headlines, so nobody paid any attention to them.) Packwood told the group what they already knew; if everyone promoted his own interests, that was the end. The president wanted a bill. Everyone had given up on reform. What was there to lose? They agreed to try.[96]

Every morning as they met, Moynihan would deliver his "Grace Report," noting that W. R. Grace and Co., whose chairman led a crusade for reducing waste in government, had paid taxes to Quadafi's Libya but received a half-million-dollar refund from Uncle Sam.[97] A couple of tax plans ending up with 26 or 27 percent rates were presented at a private committee meeting on Thursday, April 24. The faithful five told Packwood they liked it. They needed only five more of the committee's twenty members to go ahead.[98]

The "core group," as they called themselves, made three choices. One was to peg the rates at 15 percent for families up to $42,300 in income and 27 percent above that. A second was to adopt the president's proposal for a $2,000-per-person exemption, easing the burden on families, especially low-income families who would not have sufficient taxable income to remain on the tax rolls. The third, suggested to Moynihan by New York tax attorney Donald Shapiro, was to distinguish between "active" and "passive" income (passive meaning essentially paper gains and losses by people who do not personally participate in a business), in order to tax the passive part. This provision alone, by killing most real estate tax shelters, would bring in $50 billion over five years. (Introduced by Moynihan and Chafee in 1983, Moynihan narrowly missed getting the provision into a 1984 tax bill and promptly put it in the hopper for 1986 as S. 956.) Its size gave the core group hope of avoiding an attack on highly popular deductions like mortgage interest.[99] But it would hit up the wealthy who used lots of tax preferences "almost exclusively," thereby making the package as a whole better for the middle class and making up for the big cut in the top rate.[100]

Meeting long into the evening on Saturday, May 3, and finishing on Sunday, May 4 (absent the usual lobbyists), the core group, with Treasury Secretary Baker's encouragement, finished designing its bill.[101] A key to the proceedings was that Chairman Packwood—who, some members felt, had previously taken too much for his state's lumber interests—now was willing to reduce preferences for home builders.[102] "It was like a poker game," Packwood remembered. "Everyone anted up to make the pot worthwhile."[103] Amid the usual senatorial doubts—tax reform was "comatose and in intensive care" (Senator Heinz), "very silly . . . public interest is about zero . . . die on the floor" (Senator Durenberger)—the Finance Committee reconvened.[104]

Between May 5 and May 7, the Finance Committee bargained out a bill. As it met, Finance had an entirely new attitude. First, Russell Long had decided to back the core group's plan, with a few exceptions, and was rallying his allies.[105] Second, Packwood, making a few strategic concessions in advance, won approval for a rule that, during the formal markup, any amendment would have to be revenue neutral.[106] "That," Senator Pryor judged, "was the critical moment in this bill. After that it was a totally different game. Each of us knew that with any amendment, you'd have to find the money to pay for it."[107] Various industries—oil, gas, mining—got some back in return for slightly higher rates and some sleight-of-hand. But the bill remained largely intact.

After the new bill passed unanimously in committee, every member stood up to applaud Chairman Packwood. Although by no means was every member in favor, none felt able to oppose so impressive a measure. Moynihan reports that a large gathering of lobbyists in the basement of the Dirksen Senate Office Building "broke out in hissing."[108]

In a long speech to the Senate explaining how all this had come about, Chairman Packwood gave credit to Bill Bradley and others who had seen the wisdom of returning to the earliest philosophy of the income tax so that America would once again be "a place where people may make investments or may give to charity because they are motivated by the charity or because they think the investment is a good investment."[109] Packwood did not predict a capitalist renaissance, but otherwise the thought could well have come from Ronald Reagan.

The day after the Finance Committee acted, the world looked different; tax reform had gone from "silly" two weeks earlier to now unstoppable. the *Wall Street Journal* spoke of it as an "overwhelming likelihood."[110] "It's the 15% and the 27%," Senator Lloyd Bentsen (D-Tex.) stated. "It's very dramatic. That's what brought me over."[111] "That's the locomotive," Senator David Pryor (D-Ariz.) agreed.[112] Even Senator Boschwitz, who earlier had threatened to hold up the tax bill, was all for it. "What we had then," he explained, "was tax complication. What we have now is tax reform. I am left breathless by this bill."[113]

Obstacles remained. The provision that drew the most criticism from the public, as well as from the mutual fund industry, was the restriction on individual retirement accounts.[114] Was the IRA a spur to saving, a boondoggle for the rich, or both, or neither? Finance Committee Chief of Staff William Diefenderfer said it wouldn't be so easy to amend the bill on the floor because the proposer would have to take over $20 billion from someone else's preferences to replace revenue losses. He'd rather use the money to lower taxes across the board.[115] Governor Cuomo of New York, supported by Republican Senator D'Amato, objected to changes in the sales tax deduction.[116] Senator Dole suggested the transition rules be written to raise revenue in the first two years, reducing the deficit.[117] Such an increase would risk conservative defection. But it, and the sales tax issue, could wait for conference with the House.

Asserting that tax reform was not yet "unstoppable," Dole joined Packwood and White House strategists in calling for a "clean," that is, unamended, bill. Changes should be saved for conference. Packwood claimed that thirty-two senators had agreed on a "no amendment" strategy, and President Reagan seconded that at a breakfast meeting with senators on June 5.[118] Inevitably, some senators objected to being treated like a lesser breed, namely members of the House who traditionally were restricted by closed rules to prevent amendments to revenue bills. Yet the ethos of the clean bill proved so strong that no one wanted to be the first to offer an amendment that would be struck down in the name of reform. In order to break the ice, Senator Robert Stafford offered an amendment, later withdrawn, in which any person who reached age seventy-five and whose hair had not turned white wouldn't have to pay taxes.[119]

The fact that Packwood had thirty-two votes against any amendment helped; just as important was a requirement that reduced revenues had to be "paid for" somewhere else. Where did that offset device come from? Of all places, Gramm-Rudman-Hollings![120] Thus by voice vote the Senate rejected a bid by Senator Alan Dixon (D-Ill.) to retain the sales tax deduction. He lost support because he proposed to pay for the change by disallowing a small percentage of all deductions, including portions of the state and local tax deduction. The leadership did allow the Senate to signal the conference committee by voting 76 to 21 in favor of a nonbinding resolution requesting conferees keep the sales tax deduction.[121]

Another key vote was on IRAs. That was partly a class issue: whether the users were deserving (poorer people) or undeserving (richer people). When evidence from returns (two-thirds were in the $75,000 to $100,000 income bracket compared to one-fourth between $30,000 to $40,000 and little below that[122]) showed that most of the IRA users earned over $75,000 a year, the attractiveness of IRAs waned. The 1981 argument that IRAs increased savings had also been under heavy attack from many economists, who claimed it only attracted money from taxable to tax-free accounts.[123] Yet the users remained a huge and politically very active group. Liberal Senator Dodd (D-Conn.) joined conservative D'Amato to sponsor an amendment to retain IRAs, paid for by a higher corporate minimum tax and individual taxes.[124] The crucial vote to table their amendment was 51 to 48. The intense interest of IRA investors was shown by the fact that all nine Democrats and nine of the eighteen Republicans running for reelection supported retention. Senator Steven D. Symms (R-Idaho) had received more than 900 letters a week, most of which were handwritten and therefore more meaningful than the usual, organized, preprinted postcards.[125] Packwood had secretly to promise to support Senators Gramm, Gorton, and Evans on a sales tax amendment in order to get their votes to beat the IRA amendment.

To mollify IRA backers, a sense-of-the-Senate motion calling for its own conferees to assign the "highest priority to maintaining maximum possible tax benefits for IRAs" was passed 96 to 4. The language of the amendment—the conferees are advised to act "in a manner which does not adversely affect the tax rates or distribution by income class" of the tax bill—explains why IRAs were not rescued.[126]

Another serious challenge to the bill—because it threatened what Dole called the "glue"[127] holding it together, namely the top 27 percent rate—came from a proposal by Senator George Mitchell, a member of the core group, to add a top rate of 35 percent. Despite the fact that Mitchell raised the old battle cry of the liberals, progressivity, the liberal leader in the Senate, Ted Kennedy, stuck to the no-amendment strategy.[128] Senator Packwood won its rejection (71 to 29).

The next day found Packwood hiding from view as the Gramm, Gorton, and Evans sales tax proposal got turned down.[129] Naturally they were furious, but, when the no-amendment strategy showed signs of unraveling a week later, Packwood came up with $1.6 billion in alternatives to pay for a compromise restoring 60 percent of sales tax deductability in states (like Texas and Washington) that had no income tax.[130]

Good sentiments cost little, so the Senate passed a resolution (95 to 1) urging the conference committee to give the middle class a better break.[131] There was no specification of incomes. That provision fit an emerging pattern: amendments came up, they were defeated, and then the Senate adopted position-taking instructions to conferees that they should protect the very interests they were engaged in bashing. As during House debate, the promise was that things would be "fixed in conference." It would be quite a conference. The Senate plan had two brackets instead of four, and its low bracket was much lower than in the House plan. There were differences in many other areas. Yet, compared to the existing code, the similarities between the House and the Senate bills were more dramatic than the differences.

The Senate voted 97 to 3 for tax reform. "Motherhood" could hardly have won more votes. Almost no one, apparently, wanted to be left out of this historic occasion.

Life and Death

Asserting that "those who are waiting for a battle of the tax titans are likely to be disappointed," Dan Rostenkowski and Robert Packwood agreed that they wanted to make reform come true. And President Reagan, speaking at Dothan, Alabama, reminded everyone how he had unswervingly pursued the objective of a big reduction in tax rates paid for by an offsetting decrease in tax preferences, despite public indifference and cynical politicians. "The president's reappearance, center stage, as a main actor in the tax reform drama," *Congressional Quarterly* reporter Eileen Shanahan suggested, together with a supportive press conference by Chief of Staff Regan, augured well.[132] But Reagan was not a conferee.

The House had a much higher top rate (38 percent instead of 27 percent) and higher business taxes. Those two provisions allowed the House to give more tax relief to the broad middle class and not, for example, eliminate deductions for state sales taxes. The House was committed to its distribution, but senators were leery of taxing business more than they already had (the 27 percent top rate had been crucial to Senate passage). What to do? Rostenkowski moved first, announcing on June 27 that he would "be willing to shoot for the Senate's top rate as long as we approach the House's after-tax income distribution."[133] Birnbaum and Murray report that "Rostenkowski's concession set the direction for the conference."[134]

The conference, which began July 17, used revenue estimates by the Joint Tax Committee (JTC). Because these estimates were static, that is, based on current conditions remaining the same, they could be questioned. Yet it was easier to agree on static assumptions than on which way the world would change. By using JTC numbers, conferees could avoid the numbers games that bedeviled budget politics.

Unfortunately, JTC numbers themselves kept changing. On July 24 the staff revealed that the Senate bill actually fell $21.2 billion short of revenue neutrality (the decimal point suggests a spurious precision). Oops. Someone's taxes would have to make up the difference.[135]

The Senate made a couple of attempts to recoup the shortfall, but neither won much support among House conferees. They did, however, accept some of the Senate's individual deduction repeals, particularly the "passive loss" provisions. The House counterproposal then added about $23 billion in business taxes to the Senate bill, thus taking around $142 billion from that sector, a considerable comedown, they said, from their original $160 billion. If senators insisted on further protecting corporate tax preferences, Representative Rostenkowski said, bargaining in public, "their choice is to either shift more of the tax burden to the middle-class income family or to raise the rates for both individuals and corporations." But many senators weren't willing to increase business taxes. "If ever," Senator Malcolm Wallop (R-Wy.) declared, "there was a dead body leaving the morgue, this is it."[136] Such a proposal, Republican John Chafee of Rhode Island insisted, "would be absolutely rejected." Various senators expressed fear of job losses.[137] At the same time, House conferees insisted on maintaining the deduction for state and local sales taxes, as well as for income taxes.[138]

The conference stalemated. Under the headline, "Tax Reform: Last Lap or Last Legs," the *New York Times* asked the conferees to "put national interest first." The paper wondered whether "they understand : . . how much blame they will suffer if the opportunity is lost?"[139]

By August 12 the conferees had made some progress. Searching for revenues, the House had moved toward the Senate's tougher provisions on IRAs and agreed also to eliminate separate, preferential treatment of capital gains. But they still wanted more business taxes and refused to give in on state and local taxes. They rejected Senate claims that $17 billion could be raised by tougher IRS enforcement.[140]

At an impasse, Russell Long convinced the conferees to empower their chairmen to meet privately seeking an agreement. Word of heated exchanges leaked out.[141] "Yelling at each other," "questioning motives," "pretty nasty," were some of the phrases used.[142] Yet the chairmen made considerable progress, moving toward slight increases in the top rates for individuals and businesses.

Fate, or perhaps an unwarranted reliance on estimates, intervened. Economic changes, or rather CBO estimates of future economic growth, had altered sufficiently to suggest an additional $17 billion was necessary to achieve revenue neutrality. "Danny and I looked at each other," Packwood recalled, "and he said 'I wish we could blame each other.' "[143]

Frustrated, the two chairmen considered giving up. Packwood lashed out at the JTC staff, the bearers of bad news. Yet if they gave up before the August recess, the whole package might unravel as members caught flak at home. They tried again. Each threw some items in the pot that mattered greatly to some of their conferees but not to majorities.[144]

Following twenty hours of meetings, Senator Packwood announced in the early hours of Saturday, August 16, that he and Representative Rostenkowski had reached agreement.[145] To agree, Packwood had to abandon one of his strongest backers, Senator Danforth, on a $3.5 billion defense contracting issue. In total, the chairmen made up the missing $17 billion with $10 billion in business taxes and $7 billion more from individuals.[146] Taxing business $124 billion more than current law, it turned out, was very close to President Reagan's original proposal.[147]

House conferees thought the tax cut to people with incomes between

$50,000 and $100,000 (middle class?) was too small. After a day of arguments in meetings and phone calls, both sides agreed to a faster phaseout of certain tax exemptions (i.e., saying people above a certain income would not receive those breaks), which raised the effective, but not nominal, marginal rate in higher brackets ($100,000–$200,000) to 33 percent. Very tricky, but it would do. Senator Wallop, worrying about damage to industry, said, "I think it's [tax reform] become an obsession"; there he had found a critical clue to Congress's ability always to find a way around obstacles. "I want a bill, Packwood wants a bill," Rostenkowski exclaimed. "It's an emotional thing with us."[148]

In the end, only two Senate members (Wallop and Danforth) and one House member (Bill Archer, R-Tex.) voted against the conference report. Members were held until 11:00 p.m. on Saturday, August 16, so there would be a solid conference report to which they could return, rather than promises that might be picked apart by lobbyists. Left for "transition rules" was $5 billion; congressmen, especially conferees, could thus buy local favors.[149] This is either unconscionable (the rules should apply to all or to none) or a modest sop to constituency interests. Take your pick.

Senator Bradley, an original proponent of tax reform, played a unique role in running back and forth between House Democrats and his Senate colleagues. House Republicans appear largely to have been ignored.[150]

Amazement was one reaction: "It simply accomplishes what nobody believed was possible," said Fred Wertheimer, president of Common Cause. "It takes a huge chunk out of special interest after special interest who were not paying their fair share."[151] "They said out there it couldn't be done. Well, well," Rostenkowski cried, "we've done it." The sense of triumph in Congress mingled with a sense of achieving historical change. "None of us," mused John Sherman of Rostenkowski's staff, "will ever work on a piece of legislation that grand again."[152]

Under the heading of "A Reagan-Style Bill," Peter J. Kilborn of the *New York Times* described it as "less Republican than . . . Populist . . . and . . . less traditionally conservative than . . . the expression of the Reagan . . . credo [of] low individual taxes and small government." If this legislation passed, Kilborn concluded, "Ronald Reagan will have earned himself a place among the handful of presidents who have nurtured fundamental change."[153]

Maybe so, but the grandeur of change was little consolation for some of those affected. A series of headlines in the *New York Times* expressed second thoughts: "Realty Woes Seen in Tax Bill: Property Values Could Decline";[154] "Educators See Great Harm";[155] "Danforth Promises Determined Battle";[156] "U.S. Tax Bill May Force New York to Cut Housing and Public Works."[157]

House Republicans sounded ambivalent: Minority Leader Bob Michel said his own feet were "firmly planted in mid-air." Jack Kemp spoke of "a moment of truth for the Republican Party. Is it going to be a party of tax breaks or a party of the people?" Kemp's populist theme did not appeal much to Bill Frenzel, who termed the reform "anti-growth, anti-savings, and anti-capital formation." Representatives from both parties repeatedly observed that their constituents were lukewarm or cynical, believing that no matter what was said, most people would end up paying higher taxes.[158] And yet it was hard to oppose "reform"—the public might be skeptical at heart, but all the voices in public debate and the pressure from the press would mock opponents.

In what was described as the best speech of his career, Richard Gephardt urged House colleagues to remember "the good parts" of tax reform: taking millions of poor people off the rolls, imposing a stiffer minimum tax so the wealthy and the profitable would have to pay, and reducing rates for the middle class. But Majority Leader Jim Wright spoke against the bill saying that its revenue neutrality failed to reduce the deficit. "It's like a big drink of bad whiskey," the Texan told fellow Democrats. "It makes you feel good now, but you wind up with an awful hangover." Wright, however, in deference to O'Neill and perhaps to his own prospects of replacing the Speaker, would not lead a fight against the bill.[159]

On September 18, with release of the final version of the tax bill to be voted on, the transition rules were made public. Although legislators claimed more than a thousand requests had been denied, many were granted. The costliest, at one-half a billion dollars (brought up by Charles Rangel of the House Ways and Means Committee and strongly seconded by Senator Moynihan, an unwavering supporter of reform), provided relief for investors in existing low-income housing projects. Also, colleges, sports stadiums from Buffalo to St. Louis to San Francisco, Chrysler, General Motors, Phillips Petroleum, and other companies were able to hold on to existing tax breaks. No doubt this swayed some votes.[160]

Institutional and party loyalty won out. Representative Bill Archer told a meeting of House Republicans that he planned to offer a motion on the floor to send the tax bill back to conference with instructions to reinstate some popular deductions such as IRAs and sales taxes that had been restricted or diminished in August. Normally, the most senior Republican member of Ways and Means who opposes the bill—the ranking Republican, John Duncan of Tennessee, supported it—would have the right to offer the recommittal motion, and Archer was it. The Republican leadership understood, however, that "it would be very embarrassing, at the least, for this No. 1 domestic priority of the President's to be rejected by House Republicans." So Michel offered a preemptive motion to recommit the bill to the conference committee with no instructions, a motion that, stripped of enticements, was sure to fail. Phillip M. Crane of Illinois wanted to challenge Michel, but Archer refused; "there's no challenge to his leadership. If he wants to offer the motion, more power to him."[161]

After a rare speech from the floor by Speaker O'Neill—he said tax reform was "the decision of a lifetime" to make good the promise of the 1952 national Democratic party platform, when he had first run for office, and that "justice requires the elimination of tax loopholes which favor special interests"—the House first voted against recommittal by 108 votes (Republicans gave a bare 92 to 86 margin) and then provided a decisive 292 to 136 majority.[162] It was, as Secretary of the Treasury James Baker said, a victory for bipartisanship: there were 176 Democrats and 116 Republicans in favor and 74 Democrats and 62 Republicans against.[163]

On September 27, by a vote of 74 to 23, the Senate passed the final bill. "As an unbiased observer," an early political advocate of a low-rate, broad-based tax, Bill Bradley, offered his judgment: "I'd say this is the most significant tax bill since 1954 and maybe since 1913" (when the amendment making the graduated income tax constitutional was passed).[164] Larger effects resulted from 1981's ERTA, but 1986's tax reform was a more dramatic and improbable victory.

If it was a triumph for "the people," the people didn't know it. In CBS-*New York Times* opinion polls of probable voters, a plurality of Republicans and Independents favored the bill, but Democrats were opposed. Just over one-half of Republicans and Independents and over two-thirds of Democrats polled thought people richer than themselves would benefit. Small majorities of all three identifications thought that people poorer than they were would benefit most.[165] These results laid bare the profound public suspicion of politicians and the tax code.

On October 22, 1986, President Reagan signed tax reform into law. He took pride in giving the nation "the lowest marginal tax rates among major industrialized nations." He called it "fair and simple." Now, "fair" is in the eyes of the beholder, but most people did agree; whether it would be simple, even with the qualifier "for most Americans," was doubtful.

An Integrative Solution

When Senator Packwood was asked who deserved credit for passage of tax reform, he replied, "God, I think."[166] Although it will be hard to improve upon this definitive source, the reader will have to put up with some less inspired explanations.

Following a headline that neatly summed up the matter—"How Tax Bill Breezed Past, Despite Wide Doubts"—Stephen V. Roberts of the *New York Times* quite properly began by asking why many legislators voted for it despite their qualms. Representative George E. Brown, Jr., a California Democrat, was typical: "I'm going to vote in favor of the bill. But I have severe reservations about it. I did not find any support for the bill out in my district, and I don't want to make too many of my constituents mad at me."

Speculating on what might have been the strongest factors in resolving these doubts, Roberts emphasized leadership, especially President Reagan's. He argued the president succeeded in defining the issue. "Moreover, Mr. Reagan made tax reform his clear priority for his second term. He 'isolated the one thing he wanted to do,' Mr. Gephardt noted, and did not clog the agenda with other plans. As a result, leaders in both parties felt compelled to support the measure." The Speaker, for example, told House Democrats that if they blocked the bill, they would be giving Mr. Reagan "a club to hit us over the head with from now to November." Roberts also claimed that Rostenkowski's reputation as "a man who remembers his friends and gets even with the rest" did not hurt.[167]

None of this explains, however, why leaders "felt compelled to support" tax reform. The Speaker, for example, did not feel compelled to support aid to the Contras, or the MX, or defense spending. Reagan's insistence that tax reform stay on the agenda obviously was critical. But if he succeeded in defining the issue, why could he do that on tax reform but not on other matters? Because neither Republicans nor the public at large seemed to care about reform, why was it a club to hit Democrats?

Whatever might be said of President Reagan's or Dan Rostenkowski's leadership, or Speaker O'Neill's institutional loyalty, or Senator Packwood's instant conversion—none of it explains why they all differed on so many issues but worked together on tax reform. Nor, whatever their degree of cohesion, can it explain why tax reform struck so responsive a chord among so many otherwise disparate politicians.

Writing in the *Congressional Quarterly*, Eileen Shanahan gave an institutional explanation:

> what really made the legislation happen was the conviction, right across the political spectrum, that both lower rates and cutbacks in special preferences were necessary not just to get a bill through Congress but to deal with a troubling cynicism in the body politic.[168]

Certainly, the devotions of many senators, including Packwood, Moynihan, and Bradley, were based on feeling that the legitimacy of the tax system had been undermined and had to be shored up, by drastic change if necessary.

Yet many good things, supposedly necessary to legitimize the political system, do not come to pass. This book is about one of them: budget balancing. Surely the deficit was as great or greater an institutional concern than the tax system. Why was tax reform easier to manage?

Normal political analysis involves looking and seeing who is helped and who is hurt by a proposal. If it passes, those who were helped must be stronger than those who were hurt; if it fails, then vice versa. Perhaps a proposal will pass after modifications to gain allies. This approach is always useful, but with tax reform we have a problem: the people who ended up doing well—the general public and the working poor—had not been beating down the doors for tax reform. Does this make the standard analysis irrelevant? No, but it is only partially useful.

Answering "who got what" cannot tell us why tax reform got on the agenda or why it would not go away. It can help us understand why tax reform was not stopped: unlike the various "three-legged stools" of deficit reduction, it did not penalize everyone equally; like the successful deficit reductions, it isolated minority voting blocs.

Who Wins and Who Loses: Tax Preferences

Let us begin with what was not cut. Start with the overwhelmingly popular homeowner deductions for mortgage interest. Although this has been criticized on the grounds that richer people with more expensive houses and higher marginal rates benefit more and that tenants are discriminated against, which is true, the will of the people is overwhelmingly in favor. No lobbying effort was needed because no one could imagine antihomeowner legislation. (Second homes, however, are more controversial.) It is politically unfeasible to eliminate the mortgage deduction.

Employer-paid fringe benefits—health plans, insurance, pensions, meals—have been a favorite target of economist reformers. Senator Bradley might argue that "a fringe benefit is not a free good. It leaves all of us paying a higher [tax] rate than we would otherwise."[169] Senator Durenberger might argue that setting a cap on tax-free fringe benefits would make consumers more cost conscious; for example, while tax reform was being debated, medical care costs rose far faster than the low rate of inflation. Durenberger also might hope that the need for revenues would compel his colleagues and "some of the selfish corporate and union interests to abandon this open-ended tax subsidy for the richer corporations."[170] Others might argue that fringe benefits were income-in-kind, no different than other things money could buy. But recipients did not think so.

Just to make sure, the health and life insurance industries launched a massive advertising and lobbying effort against the Treasury's original proposal. More than nine hundred lobbyists reportedly were involved, including the AFL-CIO, NAM, the U.S. Chamber of Commerce, the American Council of Life Insurance, the Business Roundtable, Blue Cross-Blue Shield, and more. Senator Packwood was vehemently opposed to taxing fringe benefits.[171] When Representative William Gradison visited union plants in his Ohio district to drum up support for tax reform, he was told that proposals to tax fringe benefits and to deny deductions for personal safety equipment and union dues made members believe "it would cost them." A union official reported that "it is very difficult to find support for tax reform on the shop floor."[172] Supported by organizations and voters across the political spectrum, fringe benefits remained unscathed.

A centerpiece of the Reagan administration's tax reform, estimated to release $149 billion over five years to pay for lower rates, was an end to deductibility of state and local taxes, taxes most people pay. The Treasury viewed these deductions as a subsidy from low-tax to high-tax states. High-tax, high-services states feared that the end of deductibility would cause richer people to move, thereby lowering state revenues. Governor Mario Cuomo of New York took the view that this reform "punishes states that are trying to provide essential services in the face of massive federal spending cuts."[173] It turned out, however, that low-tax states were not eager to give up their benefits, though smaller, in return for the dubious advantages of such competition. Almost all state and local lobbies united against limiting deductions. That in itself was not enough; they also liked revenue sharing, and it went under in 1986. But voters cared a lot more about taxes than about revenue sharing. Even more important, there was no way to build a majority for tax reform without the big state representatives for whom state income tax deductibility was life or death. If those guys joined with the capital formation types, no bill. Finally, only the sales tax deduction was shaved.

"Don't tax poor people." With this injunction, Joann S. Lublin of the *Wall Street Journal* aptly summed up the prevailing ethos uniting politicians otherwise as far apart as Ronald Reagan and Ted Kennedy. By increasing the personal exemption, the standard deduction, and the earned income tax credit, six million households would be dropped from the rolls. And for good reason. Largely because ten years of inflation had eroded the value of the standard deduction and personal exemption, people with low incomes found themselves paying much higher rates than they could afford. Because Reagan beat the Democrats on the 1981 tax bill, it cut rates rather than raising exemptions, so the poor had received barely any relief. Whereas in 1979 a family of four started paying income tax at $1,200 above the poverty line, by 1984 they began contributing at $1,500 below that line. A single parent with three children who earned $8,000 in 1979, just above the poverty line, paid $481 or 6 percent of income in federal tax. By 1984 that person was earning $11,456, a 43 percent increase in nominal income, but had to pay $1,384 or 12 percent in federal tax.[174]

Tax reform would become the major egalitarian initiative of the Reagan years. Just as exempting poverty entitlements from budget cuts and Gramm-Rudman-Hollings was widely supported, so also redressing the increased tax burden on the poorest elements of the population had wide support in both parties.[175] Here we have not a powerful group but one that had wide sympathy from everyone else. Because recent policy trends were so negative, the norm of "fair shares" required redress. But it was also true that, if poor people had not been helped, no bill would have passed. Liberal Democrats would have defected and combined with business advocates, thereby constituting a majority.

Consideration of reducing tax preferences for business was heavily influenced by the growing perception that it was morally wrong and politically indefensible for large corporations to pay little or no taxes, even though they were using perfectly legal measures designed to enhance economic growth. Parallel with tax reform and urged by mounting deficits was enactment of a stiff minimum tax of 15 or 20 percent that applied after a company had used its tax preferences. Although the data on individual companies had long been available, it took Robert McIntyre to drive home the point with horror stories of huge profits and no tax payments. Trained by Ralph Nader, operating on a modest budget of $150,000 a year or so provided by unions, McIntyre churned out data showing that huge companies—General Dynamics, International Telephone and Telegraph, Transamerica, Boeing, etc.—paid no net tax. "We named names," rather than using aggregate statistics as was common, he said, "and that made all the difference." McIntyre claimed that of 275 firms he studied from 1981 to 1984, 50 paid no net tax. "Despite $568 billion in pre-tax domestic profits," he concluded, "these 50 companies received net tax rebates totaling $72.4 billion." *Fortune* magazine published his blacklist. Congressman Matsui testified that McIntyre "made a big impact, gave us the fuel . . . for tax increases on the business community. I'll bet every member used his statistics in speeches back home."[176]

Real estate developers, syndicators, and investors took the biggest hit from tax reform. In addition to the long-standing view among economists that the triple subsidization of housing—deduction for mortgage interest, local taxes, and artificial tax losses—had led to overinvestment, thereby reducing the prospects for other industries, there was a growing distaste for what was called "passive" investment. Limited partners in real estate syndicates had invested in large part to generate early losses to offset against their other income, without actively participating in the business. Whether the active-participation distinction made economic or moral sense—most investment was passive—it still placed the real estate industry on the defensive. When the Senate proposed to eliminate or severely restrict passive losses, as well as most other aspects of real estate preferences, including long-term depreciation, the reaction of the industry was well conveyed by President Wayne Therenot of the National Realty Committee—"Terror and disbelief," but "at least our people have nice big buildings of their own to jump from."[177]

The attack on the Treasury proposal by the National Association of Realtors, with its 600,000 members, was direct: Reform was "anti-savings, anti-investment, and anti-home ownership."[178] But it wouldn't wash. Before long, real estate lobbyists were scrambling to lengthen the phase-in provisions so as to cut their losses.[179] Sensing the prevailing scheme of values, they also changed their tune. Real estate lobbyists claimed that poor people would suffer; increased rents would overwhelm tax cuts. Why, a mere 2.7 percent increase in rents would wipe out the envisaged tax reductions. Unfortunately for the realtors, those legislators who cared most about the poor were not convinced. "Whatever benefits [poor families] do receive," said the skeptical Representative Rangel, "it's an afterthought of the whole process."[180]

This is one time when it is easy to draw simple conclusions. All preferences used by large numbers of people, with the exception of state and local sales taxes, were retained. The overall package was shaped by the need to isolate the losers; thus, they were limited to many businesses and, essentially, those individuals who had used breaks to pay taxes substantially below the average level for their incomes. The reforming impulse, strongest within Treasury, to create a purist code designed only to raise revenue in a neutral manner was overcome by democracy: tax preferences for large numbers of people evidently are judged equitable; thus, such social purposes may be subsidized through the tax system.

"Equity," however, is not graven in stone. Social forces shape its meaning. In 1986, as in 1984 and 1982, it was widely considered "fair" to increase taxes on business. In 1986, equity demanded reducing taxes on the working poor as well as exempting the poor from automatic spending cuts. In 1980 and 1981, equity mattered less—or meant something different. That should remind us that there is a politics of defining such public interest concepts as fair shares, or how to encourage economic growth—a political trend that ran for business from 1979 to 1981 and against it from 1982 to 1986.

The distributional politics of tax reform was identical to the politics of deficit reduction. Big interests, such as mortgage deductions and untaxed fringe benefits, were protected just like social security, essentially a majority in itself. At the same time, any package that angered the ideological right *and* left would go nowhere. No proposal, for instance, that combined a flat tax with higher business taxes could ever have passed because protectors of both the poor and the corporations would have united against it. Instead, the costs were imposed on business alone.

Business interests were not, however, simply left standing in a game of musical chairs. At first they failed to mobilize. No one anticipated that Treasury 1 would really be the tax specialists' baby, that they would simply be let loose on the Code by Don Regan. Neither the president's commitment nor the legislative elites' desire to do something important was expected by the lobbyists.

In the usual way of the world, that is, accidentally, tax reform proved well crafted to split business interests. First, entrepreneurs as individuals would get lower rates. Second, within industry, Paul Huard, vice president of NAM, said with an evident sigh, "We're like the guy with one foot on each side of a barbed wire"; the fence divided industries that would gain from lower rates from those that would lose from lower tax preferences. The business community, he continued, with admirable foresight, hoped to avoid "degenerating into a pack of wolves tearing at each other's tax." For "if that happens, . . . Congress will walk all over us and pick the bones off the carcass."[181] And so it did.

On the grounds that if you can't beat them, join them, a variety of business groups came together in TRAC (Tax Reform Action Coalition), which proposed to support the president's plan while trying to reshape it to be more helpful for capital accumulation.[182] No one wanted to challenge a popular president, nor did anyone see Reagan as antibusiness. The full-fledged war-against-Reagan tactic tried by the Chamber of Commerce in 1982 on TEFRA was not most businesses' style. Besides, it had not worked.

"Up until four weeks ago," John Malloy, a senior vice president of DuPont noted in June 1986, "we didn't think there was going to be a tax bill."[183] When the politicians moved, they did it for their own reasons, particularly the desire to avoid blame for failure, reasons that businesses could do little about. At that point, a mutual fund lobbyist put it well: "Prayer is our no. 1 strategy. I advise my fellows to go to the church of their choice."[184]

The amazing saga of tax reform should alert us to the possibilities of rapid change. The dean of business lobbyists, Charls Walker, was philosophical about being locked out of tax reform: capital formation might yet come back into fashion; he would have a chance to get his back. With one thing Walker says we could not agree more: "This isn't the last tax bill."[185]

Politicians' ability to turn on business might seem like proof of their independence, thus confirming their ability to deal with the deficit. They do have some independence, important in evaluating our political system. Yet independence from individual interest and independence of mind differ greatly from independence from majority control. Politicians rarely buck aware majorities. On tax reform they did not. By definition, it was revenue neutral; its distributional consequences would be no worse than a wash. By contrast, deficit reduction was a negative-sum game.

Spending and Tax Reform: Two Radical Changes Compared

Such a radical change would not have been possible without Ronald Reagan as president, if only because no one would go to all that trouble only to face a veto. Reagan's role was far more positive than that, but it was not the role normally assigned to him: a "great communicator" with massive popularity. Although Ronald Reagan in the first two years of his second term was the most popular president since the origins of polling in the 1930s, that did not translate into an unbroken series of victories. On the contrary, he continued to be challenged: winning, only by great effort, small sums for his Central American policies; suffering major reverses on South Africa and defense spending; and failing to gain approval for most aspects of his domestic agenda. Whatever political realignment might be in the making, President Reagan was certainly not its beneficiary. How, then, in the midst of substantial dissensus over public policy and acrimony over many things (such as William Rehnquist's nomination for chief justice of the Supreme Court) were majorities, backed by the president, mobilized in favor of radical change in taxing? What did President Reagan do to facilitate radical tax reform?

His most important actions lay in a willingness to impose costs on his own followers in order to achieve a larger objective. Without transferring taxes from individuals to business, tax reform would indeed have been an impossible dream. On one side, such a president must be popular enough with his own followers and strong enough inside his own administration to make his preferences stick. On the other side, the president must be able to envision a larger benefit for which smaller ones might be sacrificed.

The president wanted a limited domestic government supported by a larger economy that operated under market incentives. Though a friend of business, Reagan believed that tax-induced investments, in general, were bad for enterprise. Low rates, on the other hand, were good. He believed as well that it would be very difficult to raise rates again once they had come down. Low tax rates would be seen as—and Reagan surely would present them as—a promise to the American people. He may have realized that, save in wartime, Congress never raised the basic rate. Indexing assured it would not go up by bracket creep. Since 1981 revenues had been raised by eliminating preferences, and that might have continued. But tax reform wiped out most preferences anyone could imagine touching, in return for lower rates. What a deal! Reagan got a tax system that better fit his ideology, one that would be much harder to modify than the one he inherited. He traded short-term dissatisfaction among his constituents for a long-term policy structure that fit and favored his ideals. With revenue increases made even harder to achieve, Reagan's opponents might even be forced to admit the need for spending cuts to deal with the deficit.

Tax reform might have failed if Democrats had shared Reagan's calculation. But many of them, like Bradley and Gephardt and Robert McIntyre and Joseph Pechman, believed the new situation would make revenue increases easier. A broader tax base, they believed, meant more revenues could be raised with smaller rate increases. Smaller increases, if needed, might be easier to get. Maybe. We doubt it. Here, though, as with GRH and the Budget Act of 1974, the parties judged the strategic situation differently, based on differing visions of what the public really wanted.

The immediately preceding years had taught everyone lessons in advanced stultification. GRH and tax reform were designed to do for Congress what tariff and bank reform had done in prior times—restore both the reality and the appearance of effectiveness by reducing the clout of external interests while at the same time simplifying congressional consideration of controversial matters. The struggle over the fairness of the tax code has deflected attention from the main expected beneficiaries of reform—Congress and the president.

Moderates pushed aside severe doubts about the desirability of the policies contained in these reforms in order to defend Congress's capacity to govern. Whatever the results, no one could say that Congress was not in control.

Although reform as a restructuring to reduce overload has its attractions for those who identify with Congress and the presidency as institutions, what was in it for the more policy-minded? How could adherents of a lesser and greater spending role for government, domestic or foreign, or a more or less progressive tax, come together? As the host of a radio talk show asked one of us, is this a "liberal" or "conservative" tax reform?

Tax reform is a classic example of what Mary Parker Follette, early in this century, called an "integrative solution": liberals feel they have helped the poor far more than they have advantaged the rich. Economic conservatives believe they have shored up free enterprise in a way that will compensate for the loss of spurs to investment. Moderates believe that to show Congress is able to govern will reinforce social order sufficiently to cope with the disruption invariably caused by large-scale change.

Now, most policies try to have something for everybody. Tax reform worked in part because of what it gave: distributional benefits to liberals who cared most about distribution; economic incentives to conservatives who cared most about market systems; legitimacy to moderates who cared most about the perceived integrity of the political system.

Because deficit reduction is so heavily minus-sum—each side ends up feeling like losers—there is no way to do much without angering enough interests to block a proposal. One can either think of the problem in terms of organized groups or just look at the polls: either way, $150 or $180 or whatever the current billion in deficit reduction is nowhere to be found. Politicians wanted deficit reduction even more than they wanted tax reform. But the constraints, against spending cuts and tax hikes, were overwhelming. The politicians blamed each other's hypocrisy or lack of courage, and in doing so they missed the point.

In a democracy politicians must balance two roles: exercising their own judgment and representing the public. The dilemma is as old as democracy itself. On many issues it does not arise because either active participants or citizens—or both—pay small attention to the result. When the dilemma does arise, politicians do follow their own judgment more than we or they might believe; but they will not take actions seriously disapproved of by majorities of the American public. In tax reform our governors stretched the boundaries of the constraints set by American democracy in the 1980s. On the deficit, they were locked in by the same constraints. They could not solve the deficit and still represent that huge, contentious, energetic, bewildered, and contradictory "interest group" called the American people.

Because it paid each side in the currency it valued most, tax reform became a positive-sum game; each side thought it ended up better off than it started. The president's insistence on tax reform, Congress's frustration and desire to show that it could govern, and the ability to appeal to the three major ideologies helped overcome the usual obstacles. Gramm-Rudman-Hollings tried to combine similar factors—presidential insistence, congressional concern with governance, and a widespread appeal—to solve the deficit problem; that is why it passed. It failed to work, however, because GRH did not really give anything to anybody.

Each faction's stake in GRH was negative; it would not help them, but it would hurt others. If we ever reach the point where political factions are more eager to hurt each other than to help themselves, then our political system really will be in trouble. When hatred and feuding override self-interest in living together, a polity becomes like Lebanon.

TWENTY-ONE

Budgeting with Gramm-Rudman-Hollings, or "Help Me Make It Through the Night"

The year 1986 began with three signs of hope. A sudden sharp break in oil prices meant lower inflation (and therefore lower COLAs), lower fuel costs for the military, and more dollars in the economy to buy other things. Many economists argued, therefore, that any harm to the economy from higher taxes or lower spending to reduce the deficit would be offset by the oil windfall. The second piece of good news, at least for budgeters, was the March sequester. Those spending reductions were real and, when incorporated into the baseline of current policy, would be replicated in the projections for each subsequent year. This contributed to the third bit of good news: CBO decided that because Congress had actually cut defense BA by 6 percent for FY86 (including the sequester and effect of inflation), the budget office would no longer incorporate defense increases in long-term, baseline projections. The difference between five years of 5 percent growth, compounded, and a year of 6 percent shrinkage followed by stability was huge: $96 billion by FY90.[1] Combining all the good news, CBO's deficit estimate for FY90 fell to $120 billion; the target for FY90 was $36 billion. If Congress could get the extra savings of around $36 billion required by GRH for FY87, and if those compounded on themselves, it might be possible to come very close to the GRH targets in all years. Out of the mess a miracle might yet emerge.

CBO's projections, however, called for no real growth in defense, while the president was demanding (by CBO's estimate) real growth of about $13 billion. Because Reagan was likely to dig in his heels, there would be a struggle over keeping to the CBO baseline. The economic optimism of early 1986, furthermore, could well be as wrong as the optimism about other years.

The president's budget called for a "streamlined federal government" with a deficit of \$143.6 billion, just under the GRH ceiling.[2] The administration had its usual (hopeless) list of domestic programs to be eliminated; only the proposed abolition of the Interstate Commerce Commission was new.[3] "The White House," *Business Week* reported, "has accepted the sharp reduction in the growth of defense spending approved by Congress last year as a fact of life."[4] True, but not the larger reduction Congress and CBO had in mind.[5]

"I hope your numbers are accurate," Representative David Obey (D-Wis.) told the CEA chair, upon hearing his predictions of 4 percent economic growth rather than the 2.2 percent average of the previous five years, "because if they're not, all hell is going to break loose in August."[6]

While the possibility of the sequester encouraged delay, the new system of points of order reduced demands. Lobbyists got the message that for anyone to gain, or even stay even, he had to convince Congress to slash someone else. Awkwardly and reluctantly, the lobbyists tried to play that game. "Gramm-Rudman-Hollings," said a lobbyist for public higher education, is "a new way of thinking, a new mentality."[7] A chorus of senatorial voices affirmed Pete Domenici's observation: "I see less demand by special-interest groups for increases than I have ever seen in my five years of being Budget chairman and in fourteen years of serving as a senator."[8] As Martin A. Corry, who lobbies Congress for the AARP noted, GRH means that "basically, if you want to change something, you have to come up with something else to make it neutral. It establishes a substantial amount of discipline."[9] Unfortunately, this dream of budget reformers through the ages would not help get rid of the \$200 billion deficits already present.

While the lobbyists were wondering how to play this new game that they could not win, both Congress and the White House kept hoping for a miracle. In April and May 1986 the authors of this book interviewed a number of participants all of whom told us that the "other" side would have to give in. "Our judgment is, they will flinch," proclaimed one administration stalwart. And "when the president has to look at sequestering defense as against an option of an omnibus appropriations bill with revenue enhancement [a euphemism for higher taxes]," said one Senate moderate, "I think he'll find a way to accept it. We'll help provide him a face-saving out. The Republican leaders will get up and say, 'Yes, we forced him to do it.' And Walter Mondale will have a party." His prediction of an inevitable tax increase would at last have come true.

Public statements matched private. Senator Slade Gorton, arguing that Reagan would have to accept tax hikes, mused that "I think he's got more at stake in this than we do."[10] Representative Dan Rostenkowski declared, "The president must realize he will not get his way on defense and military foreign aid without participating in a balanced approach, which includes revenues."[11] Senator Bradley included Congress in his prognostications: "When Congress sees how many national parks will have to be closed and how much the cost of transportation will increase, everyone will be considering tax increases."[12]

Administration hopes, however, were based on a fundamental misunderstanding of GRH. A group of people with very disparate preferences cannot be made to "flinch" into a complex, carefully balanced bargain. Moreover, since GRH protected the liberals' greatest priorities, how could the administration do better? A veteran civil servant at OMB commented acidly, "I don't get it. He's [Director Miller] saying to the Democrats, 'If you don't agree to eliminate 81 programs, we'll cut programs 8 percent. And, to really make you miserable, we'll slash defense heavily!' Huh?" We don't get it either.

But the idea that Reagan would flinch was just as shaky. Prevailing opinion, as usual, underestimated the president's aversion to higher taxes and assumed (as he did not) that the strategic situation would stay the same. The president did want both a more balanced budget and higher defense spending. But he did not trust Congress to give him those good things in return for higher taxes. Congress had been rejecting his defense requests for quite a while; why should he knock himself out for something Congress wouldn't give him anyway? At least GRH assured that comparable cuts would take place in domestic programs.

If Democrats and angry Republicans cared only about thwarting the president, they could go on demanding their way on the budget; but there was no such thing as "their way." There was no majority to support the grand compromise that would raise revenues and cut defense, social security, and domestic programs enough to greatly reduce the deficit. GRH (and only GRH) commanded support, which was why it had passed; an omnibus agreement is possible only by fudging the numbers, which makes future agreements that much more difficult. For the same reason—no mutually agreeable alternative—GRH is in a perpetual state of resurrection.

GRH left unchanged Congress's choices and difficulties. The Senate Budget Committee endorsed a resolution with higher taxes and less defense than Reagan wanted; he called it "totally unacceptable." Nevertheless the Senate on May 2 endorsed, 70 to 25, a resolution that raised more revenues ($10.7 billion) and slashed more money ($19 billion) from defense while doing less to cut domestic programs than the president wanted. Once the Senate moved, House leaders were more willing to admit their desire to gain revenues. House Democrats said they wanted to be known not as the party of "tax and spend" but as the party of "tax and save."[13] But saving was hard. In the midst of House votes on the budget resolution, an amendment to take $111 million away from a program for honey producers was passed—and then reversed. "I am ashamed to say this," George Miller (D-Calif.) stated, "but the honey program is stronger [than we are]."[14]

Although severe cuts in defense loomed, Marvin Leath (D-Tex.) was able to persuade members of the Armed Services Committee that the GRH meat ax would be worse. Vic Fazio took the same line with the heads of Appropriations subcommittees: "They were very leery of voting for it. But I told them this is Gramm-Rudman. We've run out of running room."[15] Gramm-Rudman perhaps encouraged compromises within each chamber. The resolution passed on May 15 (245 to 179) included protection of poor people's programs, substantial cuts in defense and in the remaining areas of domestic spending, and came up with the same revenues as had the Senate. But it was only a budget resolution.

"Not only will we not raise taxes before I leave office," the president responded, "but I plan to make sure we have a balanced budget amendment that puts a permanent lid on taxes and doesn't let the government grow any faster than the economy."[16] Domenici's reaction was "nothing new, nothing different." He warned continuously about defense inevitably losing even more unless there was a tax increase.[17] He and Senator Chiles suggested that a fund be set aside from new taxes that could go only to defense.[18] Old wine in new bottles—this was George Miller's old "pay-as-you-go."

Splitting the differences between the two chambers on defense and domestic programs, on June 26, 1986, Congress approved (effortlessly in both houses) a budget resolution for FY87. Perhaps resolutions had become easier to pass because they now meant less.

The ides of August, when Gramm-Rudman might hit, were fast approaching. The political atmosphere was as humid and heavy as the Washington air. *U.S. News and World Report* published a chart on what Gramm-Rudman would mean if it actually happened. The numbers were frightening: What would happen if federal prisons had to be cut from $531 million to $311 million over three years; or the FAA from $2.9 billion to $1.7 billion? People in Washington joked that if you were planning on flying anywhere, you had better do it soon. But if you wanted to smuggle something, wait a while; GRH cuts would cripple the Customs Service. Even the Supreme Court was not immune—it would fall from $13 million to $7 million. But the justices had other ideas.

The Supreme Court and the Separation of Powers: The Comptroller General's Role in Sequestration Ruled Unconstitutional

When President Reagan signed GRH he had expressed doubts about the constitutionality of GAO involvement. Because various people in the

TABLE 12.   Shrinking Government*a* (in dollars)

	1986	1988
Defense	273 bil.	250 bil.
Commodity Credit Corp.	19 bil.	11 bil.
NASA	5.2 bil.	3.0 bil.
Farmers Home Admin.	3.6 bil.	2.1 bil.
IRS	3.2 bil.	1.9 bil.
Federal Aviation Admin.	2.9 bil.	1.7 bil.
Institutes of Health	2.6 bil.	1.5 bil.
Coast Guard	1.5 bil.	892 mil.
College, student aid	1.4 bil.	800 mil.
EPA	1.1 bil.	661 mil.
FBI	1.0 bil.	613 mil.
Congress	1.4 bil.	598 mil.
Aid to schools	814 mil.	477 mil.
Customs Service	796 mil.	466 mil.
National Park Service	595 mil.	348 mil.
Amtrak	588 mil.	344 mil.
Prisons	531 mil.	311 mil.
Food and Drug Admin.	369 mil.	216 mil.
White House	95 mil.	55 mil.
Supreme Court	13 mil.	7 mil.

SOURCES: Table taken from chart in Jeffrey L. Sheler, "Budget Skirmishing Begins," *U.S. News and World Report*, Feb. 3, 1986, pp. 20–21. Basic data found in Office of Management and Budget, Congressional Budget Office, *U.S. News and World Report* economic unit estimates.
*a*Projected changes in federal spending during the next three years if Gramm-Rudman forces automatic reductions in the budget.

White House were of different minds, sometimes on the same day, we cannot say whether Representative Michael Synar (D-Okla.) came entirely to the correct conclusion: "it was very obvious [the administration] wanted a constitutional test to have the whole thing chucked out. They want the courts to do the dirty work for them."[19] In any event, Attorney General Edwin Meese would not defend the constitutionality of GRH. He had already been litigating the same kind of point, against GAO, in other cases.

A lawsuit brought by Representative Synar and other congressmen and joined by the Public Citizen Litigation Group (affiliated with activist Ralph Nader) argued that "Gramm-Rudman tried to insulate Congress from the hard choices our Founding Fathers gave us and expected us to make."[20] This group joined the Justice Department (strange bedfellows!) in challenging GAO's role.

Instead of relying upon the concept of excessive delegation—that Congress could not delegate its powers to one of its chambers or officers, a principle that might also have threatened the legality of independent regulatory commissions—the Supreme Court held that, although such delegation in itself might be proper, it was unconstitutional to give final authority for making cuts to the comptroller general who could conceivably be dismissed by joint resolution of Congress. Asserting that the Framers had provided not merely a separate but a "wholly independent executive branch" (a big surprise to scholars who follow Richard Neustadt's celebrated formulation of "separated institutions sharing powers") the Supreme Court, by a seven to two majority on July 7, "held that the powers vested in the Comptroller General . . . violate the command of the Constitution that the Congress play no direct role in the execution of the laws."[21]

Most students of the political system, we suspect, would agree with Justice White who, dissenting, criticized the majority's "distressingly formalistic view of separation of powers." White argued that the Comptroller General was in fact "one of the most independent officers in the entire federal establishment." He saw no "genuine threat to the basic division between the lawmaking power and the power to execute the law" but a real loss in depriving the president and the Congress of their effort "to counteract ever-mounting deficits." Justice Blackmun dissented that the old provision for removing the comptroller general, "rarely if ever invoked, . . . pales in importance beside . . . an extraordinary, far-reaching response to a deficit problem of unprecedented proportions." Wise or foolish, Blackmun continued, GRH was among the most important laws of recent decades. "I cannot," he concluded, "see the sense of invalidating legislation of this magnitude in order to preserve a cumbersome, 65-year-old removal power that has never been exercized and appears to have been forgotten until this litigation."[22] Whether or not the threat to separated powers was "wholly chimerical," as Justices White and Blackmun claimed,[23] the politicians had to pick up the pieces.

Congress Copes with the Court Decision

To give Congress time to reconsider the $11.7 billion reductions in spending mandated by the March sequester (which would, by the recent decision, become unconstitutional), the Supreme Court stayed its order for sixty days. Although some doubted that Congress would do directly what had come about indirectly under the GRH proportional cuts, repeating cuts that had already happened proved not so hard: agencies had adjusted to having less money; barely two months remained in the fiscal year; and on July 17, without even waiting for formal inception of the fallback procedure, the House voted 339 to 72 to affirm the cuts.

The Senate immediately agreed by voice vote, and the president said he would sign.[24]

The hard part was what to do about FY87, by which time the sequester would be bigger and more painful. The most plausible analysis was made by an administration leader (but Gramm-Rudman skeptic) in April: "Anyone who thinks they'll vote for cuts in September, two months before an election, is smoking dope."

In one way, budgeting has become highly predictable; as soon as Congress does its duty on the deficit, it must face even more insuperable problems. On August 6, almost exactly a month after the vote to reaffirm the March sequester, the OMB FY86 deficit estimate had risen from $203 to $230 billion. The reasons were explicable, albeit after the fact. Corporate profits and personal income had dipped below expectations, thus reducing revenues. Defense outlays had speeded up: either contractors had finally tooled up, or they feared cuts in spending would knock them out. And agricultural price supports had climbed out of sight.[25] Bad news on FY86 meant FY87 would be more difficult.

Congress next had to decide whether to reinstate some constitutionally permissible form of the automatic sequester procedure. On July 23 Senators Gramm, Rudman, and Hollings introduced an amendment that would have given OMB final say in determining the sequester's procedure, but distrust of OMB was too great to permit its passage. Senator Moynihan claimed that an OMB director would be able to choose whether to hit defense or domestic harder and could distort the actual size of the deficit. Despite the sponsors' assurances that their bill hemmed in OMB so severely it had virtually no discretion left, the measure was postponed to seek other means for tying OMB's hands.[26]

On July 30 the Senate, by a comfortable 63 to 36 margin, including 21 Democrats, voted to amend its annual debt-ceiling measure so as to reinstate the automatic sequester. The new version still required OMB and CBO to submit their versions to GAO, so that the Senate could see how far OMB deviated; but final authority for determining and implementing the sequester was left to the director of the budget. In addition, the whole thing was rendered null and void if defense did not take its full cut.[27]

But the House, more distrustful of the Republican administration, and this time not taken by surprise, would not go along. The lower chamber would agree only to raise the short-term ceiling on federal borrowing by $32.3 billion up to $2.111 trillion, enough, according to the Treasury, to last until September 30. Gramm and company tried to attach a one-year extension of sequestration to this short-run bill. The House stripped off sequestration, 175 to 133, and the Senate did not alter that action.[28] As they got closer to sequester and it became more obvious that the hostage game would not work, Senate leaders backed down. The forces of responsibility, after everything, had flinched.

Rigging the Numbers

The sequester was dead, but the rest of Gramm-Rudman remained. OMB and CBO submitted their required "snapshots" of the budget situation on August 15. With CBO estimating the 1987 fiscal year deficit at $170.6 billion and OMB at $156.2 billion, the two were averaged, according to the law, to come to a deficit of $163.4 billion. Because the GRH target deficit for FY87 was $144 billion, with the usual $10 billion leeway, Congress and the president would have to make at least a $9.4 billion reduction to cut the deficit below $154 billion.[29] These estimates were $14 billion below the two organizations' previous baseline forecasts. Since no appropriations had been enacted by mid-August, both CBO and OMB, following the law, projected the deficit by assuming appropriations at the FY86 (1985) levels, after the March GRH cuts. These, of course, were below the inflation-adjusted baseline.[30] Technically this was not cheating.

By now members had the bright idea of using an extra $11 billion in revenue estimated to come from the first year of tax reform to meet the targets, thereby avoiding such horror stories as reducing the armed forces by 400,000 men and women or crumbling air traffic control towers. Of course, the new revenues, if they materialized at all, would be a one-time thing, so the FY87 problem would be alleviated only by making FY88 much more difficult. "If Congress were covered by the criminal law," Senator Rudman summed up a chorus of objections, "it should be indicted."[31] Nevertheless, in view of the alternatives, the feeling grew that any short-term fix was better than the dreaded sequester. Representative Tom Loeffler (R-Tex.) wanted to gain $6.5 billion dollars by selling federal assets.[32] Democrats had their own grab-bag: hiking the cigarette tax, demanding state and local government employees join medicare, raising telephone excise taxes, introducing a gas tax, and the like, presumably adding up to $6.3 billion.[33]

In mid-September, the budget committees agreed that Congress would have to raise revenue or reduce spending by about $15 billion; $5 billion each would come from sales of assets, from appropriation cuts, and from "user fees" (a euphemism, perhaps, for tax increases). If Congress would not do what Gray and Domenici wanted—namely, find substantial revenue increases and spending cuts for long-term budget balancing—temporary measures would have to do. If they could not fix the deficit, budget leaders at least wanted to establish principles of responsible procedure. Therefore, Bill Gray pressed to prevent spending increases within the reconciliation package. He also wanted to delay the continuing resolution until after reconciliation (so Congress could not go home without passing reconciliation first).[34]

The Continuing, Continuing Resolution

While the budgeters tried to salvage reconciliation, the real battle was on the CR. No appropriation had passed the Senate because no one knew what the sequester or its equivalent would look like. The drift of the 1980s then reached its logical conclusion—a CR for everything.

The skirmishing began with the usual "I'll not be moved so you will have to change your position" statements. The president "laid down a line in the sand," insisting that he had to have more for defense and foreign aid and less for domestic programs before he would sign the $520 billion omnibus bill reported by House Appropriations.[35] A trial balloon launched by Rostenkowski on behalf of a new gas tax (presumably on the reconciliation) was quickly shot down as House Democrats decided not to mention a tax increase unless the Republican Senate first initiated it.[36]

Still, any action on the reconciliation would take some pressure off the CR. House, Senate, and OMB negotiators tentatively agreed on a package of (over)estimated asset sales of around $7 billion, especially in rural housing and development loans; $4 billion plus in revenues, more than half supposedly from increased tax enforcement; a billion or so from a variety of user fees; and a third of a billion from increasing the charges on banks to obtain Federal Deposit Insurance. A final $1.5 billion would be raised by accelerating excise tax collections due in fiscal 1988 and moving back the last payment for general revenue sharing so that it applied to the FY86 budget, which was about over.[37] Not much to be proud of in these accounting gimmicks. "Given the choices, which are none," Representative Mike Lowery, a Democratic member of the House Budget Committee, said plaintively, "it's better to do this, given the ridiculous situation we are in." Lowery's comments were kinder than most. Senator Armstrong called it "a package of golden gimmicks." Senator Exon (D-Neb.) described the measure as "perverted, phony, unrealistic." Marvin Leath, member of the House Budget Committee, declared that "we're about to pull the ultimate scam and everybody's included."[38] Nevertheless, the House added a few new wrinkles,[39] voting 309 to 106 on September 24 to approve an estimated $15.1 billion in deficit reduction.

The next day by the narrowest of margins (one vote) the House passed what conservative Republicans called its BOMB (Bloated Omnibus

Money Bill) of $562 billion, containing all thirteen regular appropriation acts. Among the reasons for negative votes were inclusion of aid to the Contras in Nicaragua and exclusion of money to revive revenue sharing. A presidential veto was threatened not only on the old grounds of too little for defense and too much for domestic programs but on a new one—that arms control provisions, including a moratorium on nuclear tests, did not belong there.[40]

In Iceland for a meeting with Soviet party chief Gorbachev, President Reagan on October 11 had to sign the third stop-gap spending bill in ten days. Congressional leaders feared a mass exodus after October 14 when the election would be just three weeks away. With various bills still in conferences, including reconciliation-cum-debt reduction, debt ceiling, and omnibus appropriations, the last-minute jitters again were afflicting Washington.[41] The budget shuffle gave way to the adjournment stagger.

A few hours after a conference agreement on October 15, the House voted a $576 billion omnibus appropriation continuing resolution. Despite reducing $28 billion from his defense request and reiterating veto threats, President Reagan—seeking to preserve a hard-won $100 million in Contra aid and compromises on many other issues—urged House Republicans to support the CR. Nevertheless, still talking veto, the president wanted the Senate to strip two provisions from the House bill.[42]

Aside from the particular items in which they were most interested, few representatives or senators or their staff members claimed to grasp what was in the 1,200-page CR, let alone the language from other appropriations bills and unrelated legislation it incorporated.[43] Nonetheless, the Senate preliminarily approved the omnibus appropriations bill on October 17. By a voice vote, the Senate stripped from the House version a construction trades amendment that would have given unions more leverage over employers. Still in dispute was a House effort to enforce at least a 50 percent "Buy American" provision regarding offshore oil rigs. Then the Senate got hung up in a classic pork-barrel maneuver by Alphonse D'Amato (R-N.Y.), who was up for reelection. An angry Senator Barry Goldwater (R-Ariz.) engineered a 69 to 21 vote against D'Amato's effort to add $151 million for continued production, on Long Island, of the T-46 jet trainer, which the Air Force did not want.

The Senate passed the CR, and Congress adjourned to campaign. On October 17, the minority staff of the Senate Budget Committee issued a "Fiscal Year 1987 Budget Wrap-up." It began by explaining that, while the deficit was "estimated at about $151 billion . . . more realistic budget estimates show the FY87 budget deficit is likely to end up at about $180–190 billion." Out of $31 billion in supposed deficit reductions, they claimed, only $6 billion were real policy changes. "Ever hear that song, 'Help Me Make It Through the Night'?" Bill Gray asked. "That's what we're doing here."[44]

What Hath Gramm-Rudman Wrought?

There were four main provisos to the Balanced Budget and Deficit Reduction Act of 1985: (1) statutory deficit limits starting at $172 billion in FY86 and hopefully ending at zero in FY91; (2) sequester orders that apply if Congress and the president cannot agree on an alternative budget; (3) an accelerated budget timetable; and (4) procedures, such as offsets, to keep Congress honest when it votes on tax and spending bills. Guess what? They missed the targets, did not sequester, did not follow the schedule, and, though the offsets had some effect, were less honest than ever. The reasons were predictable: all the incentives in GRH worked to make delay strategically advisable; too much was taken off the table; the reason the act was passed in the first place—inability to agree on the budget—caused participants to seek their own solutions rather than compromise; and, at the last moment, the only option was to obfuscate. Obviously, GRH did not force the major actors to come together; they merely found it easier to agree on palliatives and gimmicks that might prevent sequester. What is worse, combined factors—anticipating revenue losses from tax reform, meeting the 1987 requirement by pushing costs into the following year, using the $10 billion cushion, and initially deciding to eliminate a huge deficit in just five years—led to an estimated $65 billion to $75 billion deficit-reduction requirement for FY88, a target that no one believed could be met. And it wasn't.

Though GRH made only a modest dent in the deficit, that is not to say it was totally ineffectual. It reinforced norms of spending restraint. GRH's internal controls were generally supported in the House and Senate, except for the Senate's decision to exceed its budget resolution in order to fund the antidrug bill. Such constraint may not have been a great idea. David Rogers reported efforts to increase foreign aid for the Philippines, where the U.S. wanted to aid Corazon Aquino's new democracy, were impeded because of Gramm-Rudman. "Competing foreign policy interests," he wrote, "feared that any increased allocation to the Philippines would hurt their budgets."[45]

Within the executive branch, Budget Director Miller observed:

One of the things that has been very useful to me in dealing with the agencies is to say look, Gramm-Rudman-Hollings requires offsets. So agency X comes up and says, "We need a supplemental [appropriation]—

we forgot that we're going to have more expenditures for this entitlement program." Someone's going to say, "OK—but you know you have to have offsets. Now where are you going to take it out?" So when we send up a supplement [request], we send up a rescission at the same time and try to tie the two together. Or we try to say, "OK, what you do is you go reprogram [funds]." That's been very useful to us.[46]

But surely it has been less useful to the appropriations committees and agencies. Conflict raged over offset requirements particularly in the Senate as these were stronger than in the House. But the offset requirements remained, shaping budget battles in 1987 and 1988, and probably will continue to do so.

The targets, of course, were virtually impossible to hit. In spring 1987 only a few Republicans (such as Bill Gradison) were willing to admit that; thus, Senate Democrats had to resort to disingenuous movements to get a resolution with higher deficits past the three-fifths point of order in that body. They managed to pass a conference agreement that required "only" the original deficit reduction amount of $36 billion, rather than the much larger amount needed to get down to $108 billion. But to no one's suprise, "only" $36 billion was no easier in 1987 than in 1986. In September 1987, therefore, the Democrats put together a new version of Gramm-Rudman that the president, after much public protest, declared himself compelled to sign.

The new bill was another mixture of hostage taking and posturing. It provided a new deficit-reduction schedule that required a $23 billion cut in FY88 and then skipped FY89 (the 1988 election session) before resuming in FY90. It gave OMB sequester authority but under very restrictive rules. The Democrats thought the $23 billion sequester, over half from defense, would force Reagan to raise taxes. Republicans agreed, so the GRH revision had mostly Democratic support. But everything still depended on the base from which the sequester would occur, that is, the terms of the CR. If anything, the president still seemed better off with a sequester than with any negotiated settlement: the sequester did not threaten to undo the most important policies of his administration, the marginal tax cuts.

Thus, nothing much had changed: all roads still led to gridlock. The only difference between 1986 and 1987 was that constraints had become even tighter.[47] The increasing squeeze did have one real victim in 1986. Jamie Whitten's efforts to extend revenue sharing for another year at $3.4 billion raised the question of whether Congress could ever rid itself of a program. Most members were reluctant to risk the ire of local government officials who, especially in oil-dependent regions, were finding it harder to make ends meet; and few wanted to challenge Whitten. But what could be cut instead? Speaker O'Neill rode to the rescue ("I will always remain a man of the House," he said at his retirement farewell when Congress adjourned). The Speaker persuaded the Rules Committee to strip revenue sharing from the Omnibus Appropriation Act.[48]

Deficit pressure could put some very bad ideas into the heads of agency chiefs. Worried about what a GRH sequester would do to his department, Deputy Secretary of Defense William Taft came up with the idea of delaying payments to contractors under the grace period offered up by the (apparently misnamed) Prompt Payment Act; this would "save" $2.8 billion in fiscal 1987 outlays that thereby would go into fiscal 1988—for somebody else to worry about. But the chair of House Government Operations, Jack Brooks (D-Tex.), and its ranking minority member, Frank Horton (R-N.J.), responded in outrage—private vendors already were refusing government business or charging more because of late payments; moreover, they threatened to legislate total removal of the grace period that had been originally intended to help agencies smooth out their payments.[49]

In 1987, as the pressure increased, the appropriations committees finally ran out of room to maneuver. Even the smaller cuts required by the resolution were more than they could manage by their usual techniques of scrimping on administrative expenses, stretching out purchases, and the like. They left whole agencies out of bills in protest against what they considered impossible targets; the prospect of another sequester just made matters worse. The evil day when across-the-board cuts made programs unmanageable was approaching. Yet the deficit persisted.

Black Monday

On October 14, 1987, the Dow Jones average fell by 95 points. It fell 57 points the next day, and 108 points, a new record, the following day. For the week of October 12, *Newsweek* reported, all shares traded on U.S. exchanges dropped by a "staggering" $490 billion. "Is the Party Almost Over?" that magazine asked.[50]

By the time that issue hit the newsstands, the answer seemed obvious. On Monday, October 19, the Dow fell by 508 points, losing in one day 22.6 percent of its value. To give that number perspective, compare it to "Black Tuesday," the market break of October 29, 1929, which to many minds signaled the Great Depression; on Black Tuesday, the Dow fell by only 11.7 percent.[51]

The New York exchange then stabilized or, rather, gyrated wildly from moment to moment only to end up above the nadir of Black Monday. That good news beat the alternative, but hardly would erase fears of a further rerun of 1929 and what followed. As *The Economist* pointed out, the markets recovered in early 1930 as well—"do not be too reassured by a bounce back over the next few weeks."[52]

The panic was worldwide. Tokyo and London also endured record sell-offs. The market fall's possible causes, as is always the case, were far too numerous for anybody to be sure of their relative weights. They ranged from new technology—computer-generated program trading— to old-fashioned market psychology. Some blamed Dan Rostenkowski because he had sponsored a bill to limit corporate takeover actions. Some blamed Treasury Secretary Baker for criticizing the West Germans for not lowering their own interest rates enough. The most obvious explanation for the size of the slump, though not for its one-day occurrence, was that stocks were overpriced. "Two weeks ago," *The Economist* explained, "investors were buying shares at dividend yields averaging only 3% in London, 2.6% in New York, and 0.5% in Tokyo. . . . The gap between cost and yield was double its normal size in the three previous decades."[53] Unless interest rates came down, stock prices would have to, eventually.

Amid all proposed causes, one had prominence: the federal budget deficit. The logic was:

1. Interest rates were high and would probably have to go higher because the dollar was falling on the international markets.
2. The dollar was falling because foreigners had finally gotten tired of trading their goods for America's paper. "They stopped buying dollar-denominated assets, leaving the job of financing America's $78 billion current-account deficit in the first half of 1987 to the leading central banks."[54] This couldn't do it all.
3. The trade deficit would have to come down through combining less American consumption and greater foreign consumption. From policy makers' standpoint, that meant lower federal deficits in the United States and higher deficits abroad.
4. The Germans and Japanese, especially, would not risk inflation by doing their part unless the United States was seen as doing its part.

Thus *The Economist* editorialized that

> Either the budget deficit is slashed, or interest rates will have to rise a lot; the second path leads to recession, the first could just avoid it. . . . Some people have long argued that the White House and Congress would not tackle the deficit until they were faced with a crisis. This week the markets have been shrieking that crisis-time has arrived.[55]

Newsweek added that "to avoid another disaster, the Reagan administration must show progress toward curing its budget deficits."[56] The calls for deficit reduction were very loud.[57] Robert Samuelson pointed out that "blaming the U.S. budget deficit for all the world's economic problems is simplistic." Yet "blaming the stockmarket crash on the budget deficit," he added, "makes the crisis understandable and manageable." It made choices, although unpleasant, obvious. He thus identified the dynamic that directed more attention to the deficits than might be wise.[58]

Donald Regan had been booted out as Chief of Staff due to the Iran-Contra mess. He was replaced by Howard Baker, who now joined with Treasury Secretary Jim Baker in advising the president to agree to negotiate a deficit-reduction package with congressional leaders. Ronald Reagan was dragged there, metaphorically, kicking and screaming, continually expressing doubt of the wisdom of any new taxes. The president was reviled for not taking the crash seriously enough; only a fool, even an inattentive fool, could fail to see the signs of imminent disaster. (Presumably, the doomsayers are still looking.) His Republican allies divided into two groups: those who did not want *any* new taxes (the Kemp faction) and those who would take new taxes as part of a *really big* deficit-reduction package (the Dole faction).[59] Democrats, too, expressed skepticism. "You've got boxers that have been throwing punches at each other for ten rounds," Leon Panetta commented, "and now you expect them to get together?"[60] Amid calls for much bigger deficit cuts than the $23 billion promised by the revised Gramm-Rudman, Tom Foley, chairman of the negotiations, worried that "the best is the enemy of the good"; $23 billion would be hard enough. The crash, after all, did not prove to any one side that it had been wrong. Rather, it showed that the other side's intransigence was just as stupid and dangerous as charged. The crash meant the other guy should give in.

After nearly four weeks of negotiations, the participants announced their agreement on November 23—promptly derided as, among other things, a "budget mouse"[61] to be greeted with a "chorus of Bronx cheers."[62] The "summit agreement between the president and the joint leadership of Congress" promised $30.2 billion in deficit reduction in FY88 and $45.85 billion in FY89, mainly as a result of the first installment. The FY88 figures included $11 billion in new revenues, $5 billion in defense cuts, $6.6 billion in domestic cuts, and $7.6 billion in other categories, mostly asset sales and lower debt service. It allowed repeal of the GRH sequester, which began on November 20.

The summit agreement kept the squeeze on both defense and domestic spending but avoided the more severe Gramm-Rudman cuts. Its "gimmickry," through asset sales, for example, was widely derided. The summit was not, however, a budget solution; it was a truce, and on those terms it may have been a success.

The 1987 summit provided targets for discretionary domestic, defense, and international affairs spending for both FY88 and FY89. Going either above or below those numbers would violate the agreement. It was also assumed that compliance with the package would be shown by wrapping everything together in two big boxes, a CR and a reconciliation, at the end of the 1987 session. The appropriations committees adopted new procedures, redoing their 302(b)s so the House and Senate plans matched, and provided far more information to OMB than was their previous custom, attempting to document compliance with the terms of the agreement. The FY89 targets were enacted in the reconciliation bill, thereby settling the most contentious issue of the FY89 budget resolution process before it ever began.

There would, of course, be plenty of problems. The discretionary targets were too low to accommodate popular increases that the Reagan administration requested (for science research, space, and the war on drugs) without cutting programs Congress wished to protect. Congress resorted to some gimmicks, reclassifying some discretionary accounts as mandatory to make more room for what was left. As summer 1988 began, it was not clear whether the administration would go along. Yet appropriations bills were moving quickly; talk about the budget seemed to have died down; and the media was even consciously deemphasizing the issue. At the beginning of 1988, the *New York Times* chose to pay less attention to the budget.[63]

Was the budget issue gone? No, it still constrained all other issues, and what Lawrence Hass called "The Deficit Culture" was deeply entrenched in Washington. But it was an election year; Ronald Reagan would be gone at its end. The battle could be resumed when there were new players. The presumptive nominees for president—Vice President Bush and Massachusetts Governor Dukakis—agreed that deficits should be reduced. Both were vague about how they would do so. Dukakis's main disagreement with Jackson appeared to be over not whether tax increases were necessary but whether the party platform should say so out loud. Rejecting all tax increases except user fees, desiring at least to maintain the current level of defense spending, and doing a bit more on social welfare, Bush was hardly a model of consistency. Why is the deficit too hard for the politicians?

Confronting Budget Reality

The budget deficit is a no-win issue. The presidential nominating process showed that any candidate who proposed a real solution would lose more votes than he would gain. On the Democratic side, former Arizona Governor Bruce Babbitt kept challenging his opponents to stand up for a tax hike. Journalists and commentators applauded, but opponents stayed in their chairs as Babbitt was quickly eliminated from the race. Among the Republicans, Vice President Bush bounced back from his Iowa defeat by charging that he was more opposed to tax increases than Senator Dole. Bush claimed he would attack the deficit with vetoes and a "flexible freeze" (a nice self-canceling phrase). Democratic nominee Dukakis, meanwhile, emphasized his experience balancing budgets as a governor. Having increased revenues through stricter enforcement efforts in Massachusetts, he would try that before raising taxes. No pain, except for the bad guys. Because Congress had been throwing such provisions into its budget packages for years, while the IRS was having enough trouble devising forms for the new "simplified" tax code, Dukakis's claims for enforcement were dubious. But the approach beat being specific about program cuts and tax hikes.

Jesse Jackson was the exception who proved the rule: by substantially raising taxes on higher incomes and severely cutting defense, he would reduce the deficit by a sizeable amount. Aside from a little fudging on how far down the income ladder he would have to go—most of the people make most of the money—Jackson was on target.[64] Nothing would satisfy a majority, however, so candidates who wished to win said nothing.

Perhaps the candidates were just hiding their budget plans until after the election. Perhaps, but after the election, members of Congress, having to pass a budget deficit fix, would represent the same public; why would it represent the public any differently than before?

Maybe a Democratic president and Congress would, in trying to show they could govern, put party over constituency by enacting a deficit-reducing tax increase and spending-cut package. Gypsy moths did something similar in 1981. Maybe a Republican president would sell out his own side to make a deal with a Democratic Congress. Maybe turmoil in the financial markets would finally force balance, though one would have to wonder what it would take if Black Monday were not enough. Maybe a fairy godmother would appear, empowering the politicians to solve their problems.

This fairy godmother even had a name—the National Economic Commission, established as part of the budget summit agreement, a bipartisan group modeled on the Greenspan Commission that fixed social security. The Commission, consisting of twelve members, six Democrats and six Republicans, was expected to work through the summer and fall. The president-elect would then appoint two final members. This group of (politically) wise men would, sometime between December and March, propose a budget solution.

Republican members were former Transportation Secretary Drew Lewis, Senator Domenici, Casper Weinberger, former Secretary of Defense and White House Chief of Staff Donald Rumsfeld, Representative Bill Frenzel, and the president of the American Farm Bureau Federation, Dean Kleckner. Democrats were Robert Strauss, former party chairman and U.S. Trade Representative, Representative Gray, Senator Moynihan, investment banker Felix Rohatyn, Chrysler chairman Lee Iacocca, and AFL-CIO president Lane Kirkland. Members chose Strauss and Lewis, experienced negotiators with good ties across parties, as co-chairmen. They selected as staff director the top civil servant in OMB, one of Washington's most respected budget professionals, David Matthiasen, whose appointment, as much as the Commission's membership, showed that the NEC would be where the action was in 1988.

Could twelve wise men do for the federal budget what had been done for social security? Could they devise a plan and give politicians political cover to push it through? In Chapter 14 on social security, we argued that the shortfall, proportionately so much smaller, was far easier to correct than the federal deficit. As members of the NEC quietly met through the summer—in informal, small groups so they could exclude the press—and reviewed budget difficulties, they would face, as the rhetoric goes, a hard reality.

At the beginning of 1988, CBO's baseline budget projected a deficit of $157 billion in FY88, followed by $176 billion in FY89 and, successively, $167 billion, $158 billion, $151 billion until $134 billion in FY93. The Balanced Budget Reaffirmation Act, otherwise known as the new Gramm-Rudman, required a $136 billion deficit in FY89, dwindling to zero in FY93. Let us review the conditions and requirements of balance under CBO and GRH.

How bad are those numbers? That depends, first, on the year we choose for comparison: $157 billion in FY88 was expected to be 3.4 percent of GNP; $134 billion in FY93 would be 2.1 percent.[65] Assuming the baseline was accurate, time would reduce the problem.

The baseline might not be accurate. CBO projected moderate economic growth, around 2.6 percent per year, throughout its forecast period. That projection fit historical trends over five-year periods, but it could easily be wrong. CBO estimated there was a two-thirds chance that growth would average between 1.6 percent and 3.6 percent; that is, the deficit in FY93 would be within $125 billion of the estimated $134 billion. The good news was that the error might be virtuous—higher growth and lower deficits. The bad news was a one-sixth chance that the deficit would be $259 billion or higher.

There were two obvious reasons for pessimism. First, if the deficit were such a bad thing, then something bad eventually had to happen to the economy. Otherwise, why reduce it at all? CBO had essentially adopted former Director Rudy Penner's recommendation that budgeters admit they could not predict the economy's swings, escaping the pressures for optimistic or pessimistic forecast manipulation by predicting that the future would look like an average of the past. However, the deficit was uncharted territory where unpleasant surprises seemed more likely than not.

Meeting that baseline, alone, never mind cutting below it, moreover, would require substantial policy sacrifices. The baseline's definition as current policy was deceptive. In a number of policy areas—control of the AIDS epidemic and drug traffic, NASA's space station, modernized air traffic control system—contemplated expenses in future years would rise well above the baseline, the existing level, because projects were in their early stages. The space station was already under fire within House Appropriations because, if it went above the baseline, other projects might have to be reduced. But that meant a battle just to stick to the baseline.

The domestic spending baseline was tough enough; defense figures posed brutal problems. There was no way to maintain the existing military force structure over the next five years if there were no real growth in military spending. That force structure might, some argued, be reduced without diminishing military capability. A 600-ship navy might not be necessary; some hardware, like the Bradley armored vehicle, might work so poorly it should be abandoned; the country's nuclear deterrent might not require either a rail-mobile MX missile or the single-warhead Midgetman missile. Disagreements abounded. Tough choices were required just to keep spending down to the baseline.

Let us be optimistic, however, and say that the baseline is reasonable. How much deficit reduction would be necessary to attain the new Gramm-Rudman target balance in FY93?

We could assume that the extra couple of billion dollars required by the summit agreement, but not included in the baseline, would be saved in the FY89 appropriations. Beyond that, earlier savings are better because they yield greater long-term savings in interest costs. Using moderate assumptions about interest rates, an average of CBO's projected rates for three-month T-bills and ten-year bonds, reducing the deficit by $100 billion in FY90 would eliminate the deficit in FY93.

It's not that simple, of course. A $100 billion deficit reduction in one year would be a nasty, recessionary swing in fiscal policy. Few economists would approve. We also have the old budget authority versus outlays problem: a $100 billion reduction in BA will not provide so much immediately in outlays. That's actually convenient, phasing in any spending cuts and moderating the fiscal contraction. Any slower, more phased deficit reduction, however, would yield lower interest savings and require more policy change. The $100 billion figure for FY90, therefore, is a

minimum estimate of the amount of policy change needed to meet
Gramm-Rudman targets.

Having made our task a little easier at every step, we are left with a
figure roughly equal to the U.S. Navy. Or, for those more concerned
with domestic spending, a figure larger than medicaid, Department of
Education, National Institutes of Health (including cancer and AIDS research), Department of Justice, Department of State, and Federal Highway Administration combined. Would you rather have no deficit and no
navy? Or both? A deficit, or do without those domestic programs? Or
mix and match: eliminate the deficit but have no medicaid, no NIH, no
State Department, and half a navy? The choices may seem extreme; they
are extreme, but there they are. People sometimes assume that a series
of marginal cuts across programs can do the job, thus various freeze
formulas. Yet, if across-the-board cuts à la Gramm-Rudman are as dumb
as claimed, their policy consequences would be greater than those we
are suggesting.

We might get our $100 billion from taxes. Individual income taxes
would only have to be raised by 22 percent, an ironic number, virtually
reversing the 1981 tax cut. Or we could raise individual income taxes
by 10 percent, corporate taxes by 20 percent, and excise taxes by 50
percent. Whether these options are worse or better than spending cuts
depends entirely on one's ideology. Even the most dedicated fan of the
public sector can imagine the political difficulty of such tax hikes.

There are, of course, many more narrow options for deficit reduction.
Each year CBO produces a volume, "Reducing the Deficit: Spending
and Revenue Options." The March 1988 edition included twenty-six
suggestions for defense savings, twenty-six for entitlements, seven for
agriculture, thirty-eight in nondefense discretionary, eight changes in
federal personnel policies, and twenty-five revenue increases. They
ranged from canceling procurement of the F-15 fighter plane to creating
a national value-added tax. Many, as the examples suggest, are controversial. Others, more obscure, may sound less troublesome. The navy
has thirty-seven SSN-688 nuclear attack submarines—twenty-two on order and seven more they would like to order. Why not cancel the last
seven, waiting for the new, improved SSN-21, on which delivery should
begin in 1995? The navy could still maintain its force objectives, assuming
the SSN-21 was not significantly delayed. But if it were, as is common
for new weapons, Congress and the navy would be stuck. Should we put
all our submarine eggs in one basket?[66] Take another CBO option:
counting, as part of income, payments under the Low-Income Home
Energy Assistance Program (LIHEAP) in determining eligibility or benefit levels for AFDC and food stamps would save $255 million in FY90;
it would also eliminate duplication where some recipients of LIHEAP

are better off than nonrecipients who actually earn more. But the change "would particularly penalize families facing large energy bills." Higher bills mean a higher offset against other payments, but what are the recipients to do, shower in the dark? Move south? Even the more harmless sounding proposals turn out to have thorns.[67]

A value-added tax (VAT), one of CBO's alternatives, is the nuclear option of deficit reduction. Even with exemptions for food, housing, and medical care, a 5 percent VAT yields nearly $80 billion in FY93. Economists love a VAT because it taxes only consumption without inhibiting investment as the income tax can. (Except that people might save less if prices are higher.) States, however, do not like a VAT; sales taxes are their territory. Liberals object to a VAT because sales taxes are regressive (encouraging savings and favoring savers who have more money). And conservatives with any knowledge of comparative politics fear the device that largely finances European welfare states. Conservatives fought a minimal VAT in the 1985–1986 dispute over superfund financing because they feared the principle. In short, compared to other deficit reduction options, a VAT looks quite attractive. As a policy in its own right, the VAT's implications for our federal system are more revolutionary than tax reform, potentially as revolutionary as the invention of the income tax.[68] We do not say it cannot happen; we do say that fundamental change in domestic and defense policy is required to achieve balance.

Even Rudolph Penner and Joseph Minarik, self-described as "two economists not far from the center of the ideological spectrum," in the most informed and careful budget reduction proposal we have seen, in their own words, "can arrive at a balanced budget only with some fairly radical—and many people would say politically implausible—changes in tax and spending policy."[69] They suggested taxing social security benefits, deemphasizing naval "forward deployment" in the European theater, cutting medicare providers by $10 billion and raising recipients' premiums by $5 billion, somehow (they're not sure how) chopping price supports, and a "draconian approach" to intergovernmental grants "and other dubious federal government activities." They would double the cigarette and hard liquor taxes, raise beer and wine taxes, raise the motor fuels tax by 12 cents a gallon but not give the revenues to the trust fund. They would adopt a large menu of "base-broadening" measures on the income tax, such as cutting business deductions for entertainment and meals in half, taxing accrued capital gains, and capping the mortgage interest deduction. We can only agree with their own assessment; their figures add up, but it probably can't be done.

Citizens should realize how hard it is to balance the budget; even if they disagree, they should also be aware that others have good reasons for believing balance is unwise. They should also realize how much the politicians have achieved. In 1986 John Palmer of the Urban Institute estimated the effects on the deficit of all budget decisions since the beginning of 1982. Those actions ranged from TEFRA to the February 1986 sequester.

Starting from a baseline that had defense growing by 7 percent per year—the policy Reagan proposed and Congress seemingly endorsed in 1981—Palmer found the politicians had reduced the FY86 deficit by $162 billion, or 3.9 percent of GNP. Unfortunately, nobody could see that they had done so much because a deficit of $208 billion remained.

The politicians seemed to have done little because the problem each year was much, much bigger than it seemed. Yet, if they actually had done nothing, the FY86 deficit would have been $370 billion, 8.8 percent of GNP. Each year they had acted; in most years their efforts were canceled out by revisions in the economic and technical assumptions. Thus, five-year savings of $184 billion from the February 1982 estimates were overwhelmed by $235 billion in larger deficits from changes beyond their control. Only in 1985 did the surprises go the politicians' way.[70]

After 1986, by Palmer's estimates, the decisions to that point would save even more money. Congress more than shut down the defense buildup, saved some in the 1985–1986 reconciliation, raised taxes, and introduced some domestic cuts (mostly medicare) as part of the budget summit. Without a doubt deficit savings have increased in 1987–1988.[71]

Most deficit reductions after 1981 came from winding down the defense buildup and raising taxes. From 1982 to 1986, domestic spending was cut by roughly 5 percent.[72] As background, domestic spending had taken a big hit in 1981, and the 1983 package took social security off the table. CBO estimated outlays for nondefense discretionary spending would be the same in FY88 as in FY85, about $175 billion. In those years it was squeezed by inflation.[73] Between FY81 and FY88, we see substantial effort, for nondefense discretionary spending fell from 5.7 percent of GNP to 3.7 percent. All these numbers add up to one result: politicians have done a great deal about the deficit, but each step is harder than the previous.

The best arguments against deficit panic, in our opinion, are those of experience. Nothing terrible happened. Yet. But "yet" is a long time coming. All the bad things prophesied from the deficit, from depression to inflation to decline in productivity, historically have happened during periods of balance as well. Why, then, go through tremendous trouble to balance the budget?

By 1987 mainstream economists emphasized that deficits should be cut because they reduced national savings and, thus, investment:

> If continued over the long run, large budget deficits would either drive down domestic investment or be financed by increasingly uncertain, and

potentially reversible, capital inflow from abroad. In either case, living standards of U.S. citizens would fall: a reduced level of domestic investment would retard the growth of the economy, and continued heavy foreign investment would send a larger share of U.S. output abroad in payment of debt service or other returns to foreign investors.[74]

They worried about demand management mainly in terms of how fast to move toward balance, that is, "Will Rapid Deficit Reduction Cause Recession?"[75]

By 1988 this concern with savings was causing many economists to argue that the budget should move into surplus. They wanted social security surpluses invested in the economy, not in financing other federal programs. Minarik and Penner argued that for the social security "accumulation to have any economic meaning, the rest of the federal government must not run a deficit." They emphasized that "the main reason for deficit reduction is to increase long-term growth."[76]

The economists' focus on growth returns us to the "productivity crisis" of the 1970s. It is a legitimate concern. We just have a few questions:

1. If investment is so strongly related to productivity growth, why did growth decrease steadily through the 1960s and 1970s while investment remained steady?
2. Growth is a long-term problem, not a short-term crisis. Why is it to be treated as requiring immediate drastic changes in the entire federal government, rather than a slow movement toward less consumption and more investment throughout our economy? That would require attention to the composition of outlays, the type of taxes, and many other complicated issues we might want to think through before acting precipitously.
3. Given that the federal government is about 22 percent of the economy, why exactly is it alone supposed to solve the national savings problem?
4. Could a falloff in savings be due to other factors, such as changes in the life cycle (e.g., baby boomers spending more on education, housing, children, therefore temporarily saving less)?
5. If productivity goes up, savings increase, and manufacturing grows, as all are showing signs of doing, do we still have to balance the budget?
6. You mean we have to find around $230 billion in deficit reduction by FY93, not $135 billion? Are you kidding?

Lower deficits, even surpluses, might, under some conditions, be a good idea. But the kind of drastic budget action required to use the social security surpluses for savings is impossible. We fear that, as in the famous story of the man who looked for an item not where he lost it but where the light is brightest, the government's budget is being asked to solve a problem because the budget is the nearest instrument at hand, even though not entirely appropriate.

There is only one reason to treat the deficit as a crisis: the markets. They remain the great unknown, at the end as at the beginning of our story. With one big difference: then concern focused mainly on American bondholders. Now we worry about foreign investors and foreign central bankers. Might they refuse to invest? Demand higher interest rates? Keep going because there was no other place to take their money? Invest, even more, just as Americans were investing more in Europe, because of continued prosperity? There is every reason to treat foreign investment as a good thing (if foreigners did not want to invest, wouldn't that be a sign of American decay?) signifying that opportunity and stability are found in the United States. Yet any borrower loses some independence; depending on foreign capital is worse than being the lender; nervousness is understandable.

The wolf, sighted so many times during the 1980s, could finally beat on the door. There is no way to tell. Nor could anybody know what would satisfy its appetite: $20 billion a year? $40 billion? $60 billion? If the markets posed the question, politicians could only guess at the answer.

When continued prosperity intersects with talk of economic Armageddon, do you wait and see, as the American public would like, or do you take drastic measures to ward off the worst, as the political stratum demands? That depends on at least two considerations: whether you think there is a better alternative (we present ours in the final chapter) and whether you believe balancing the budget in the short term is more important than maintaining majority rule.

Strange as it may seem, democracy and deficits now go together. The only way to sever that connection is to vote into office majorities dedicated to budget balance. The public interest and the state, as we shall argue in the next chapter, only coincide when public opinion joins together what political life normally keeps apart.

TWENTY-TWO

The Deficit and the Public Interest

The budget deficit as an issue is important both in its own right, although its effects are controversial, and for its impact on other concerns, ranging from caring for the homeless to the national defense. Yet many of us care about the deficit story for another reason: it tells us how, and how well, our political system is working. The deficit is seen as a test of Americans' ability to govern themselves. The myriad battles of deficit politics, from Carter's remade budget in 1980 to the budget summit of 1987, reveal patterns of power and influence that can help us understand how our government works, for better or worse.

In evaluating the system, our judgments inevitably will be shaped by our opinions of the deficit itself. What people think of a procedure depends on what they think of its results. And it should be obvious that White and Wildavsky do not believe the deficit is the end of the world. It is, we think, a regular size, not a giant size, problem. We have emphasized that deficit reducing choices are hard because they require accepting other evils, from a weaker defense to less investment to sicker children and old people, including the very depression balancing the budget is supposed to prevent. When a problem is difficult its resolution is not obvious. We claim that our deviant views help make more sense out of the events of our story than could be made with other presumptions, such as that the evils of the deficit are so overwhelming that any reasonable person would sacrifice much to fix it. In questioning the deficit's horrors, we admit a bias toward a more favorable view of both the political system and our politicians than may be common.

Several readers of early drafts of our book have complained that it lacks villains. With all major players acting to achieve the good as they understand it, the persistent gimmickry and obfuscation are revealed to be as much products of trying to avoid even worse as determinations to mislead. Understandable if not always laudable behavior has been portrayed as due to frustration at endless inability to agree rather than desire to do wrong. We have diffused blame for the deficit to the point where, to some readers, it might indicate lack of character or atrophy of the critical faculties. Surely (SURELY!), they tell us, President Ronald Reagan with his feckless tax cuts, his heedless refusal to compromise, his utter disregard for the consensus of his own staff and of the vast majority of the nation's economists, let alone all our allies abroad, that the deficit was a very bad thing deserves worse than we have given him. And the unexpected criticism we do offer to the political paragons of budget balance, the heroes of losing battles to balance the budget, but heroes nevertheless, seems (to them) inexplicable or perverse. After all, everyone has heard of extremists of the right or of the left, but extremists of the center, never.

Our point is that Ronald Reagan's, Tip O'Neill's, and Pete Domenici's behaviors, different as they were, all made sense given their different values. Political conflict and everyday life make no sense if we think everybody's the same. Political analysis has to start by asking why which values prevail, not by judging a system entirely according to its output along one criterion of evaluation. In the final chapter we will say what we think should and should not be done about the deficit. Here we ask how the deficit story can help us revise standard evaluations of how the American political system works.

Who Rules?

The most obvious question is that of power. Who rules? The battles of the budget, involving all the federal government's choices as to who gets and pays what over a period of years, provide the best possible evidence for answering such a question. At first blush, the answer is simple enough. The candidates are the mass public, elected officials, civil servants (bureaucrats, if you prefer), interest groups in general, business groups in particular. Required to give a short answer, a reader of this book would be compelled to say either "elected officials" or some compound of "elected officials and the mass public."

It is clear that citizen opinion, as recorded in innumerable polls and as reflected in elections—whether indirectly through anticipation, directly through petitioning legislators (e.g., against social security cuts or interest withholding), or through elections—placed limits on what politicians could do. There were to be neither reductions in social security, nor, after income tax cuts were enacted, increases for the bulk of the population. These constraints ruled out the two most obvious (because most ample) sources of deficit reduction: higher income taxes and greater reductions in the rate of increase in entitlements. Within these biting but broad constraints, elected and appointed officials initiated alternatives and made the ultimate decisions. It cannot be said that public opinion demanded either the Kemp-Roth tax cuts or tax reform, but neither did it oppose them. It can be said that mass opinion wanted more defense and less welfare spending than Carter offered in 1980 and the reverse in regard to Reagan after 1982. Although the public clearly disapproved of deficits, it just as clearly objected to doing anything conclusive, therefore drastic, about them—a state of opinion neatly reflected in the actions of elected officials. At any time in this story, the movement of taxing and spending may be said to be reasonably in accord with the preferences of the mass public.

The most decisive statements of opinion and major causes of budgetary behavior were elections themselves. The difference between 1980 and 1981 was the difference between a troubled but basically Democratic Congress and a Congress dominated (barely) by the Republican/boll weevil coalition. The 1982 election ended that coalition.

Civil servants are seldom heard from, apparently speaking only when spoken to. Because there are multiple and competing sources of advice—agencies, OMB, CBO, CRS, private groups—the politicians are able to choose among them. Economic forecasting is the preeminent example of staff unable to dominate with their expertise given the many competing sources. This does not mean staff is without influence; after 1981 the Treasury's tax policy staff successfully pushed a series of revenue-raising initiatives. They succeeded because their political superiors, John Chapaton and Donald Regan, were skeptical of many business tax breaks. Stockman's OMB and Reagan's political agency appointees show the extent to which an administration can bypass civil servants if it wishes. These administrators could appeal on back channels to the appropriations committees, which might reverse the administration's cuts. But such a strategy only reveals the preeminence of elected officials; it takes Congress to defeat the president. Either way, bureaucrats are not in charge.

Interest groups are ubiquitous, but are they dominant? The difficulty in appraisal consists in differentiating them from other actors who want what they want. From the mid-1970s through the first year of the Reagan administration, for instance, the politicians' concern with capital accumulation led to a considerably reduced effective corporate tax rate. Big business could hardly have done better than it did in 1981. How should these events be interpreted in terms of business power?

Look at what followed. In 1982 and 1984, corporate preferences were whittled down. Did business have fewer resources? No, but the politicians wanted to do something about the deficit; business was the target of opportunity. The agendas of business and elected officials had diverged. Tax reform was an example of the president's agenda differing from that of business; there, also, business lost.

Of course, business groups are a force to be reckoned with, and politicians went to great lengths to adjust their packages so as to anger as few groups as possible. Equally clearly, business groups needed allies. When they did well, as in 1980–1981, it was because the agenda of national policy making—"productivity"—favored them. When business did poorly, the agenda—deficit reduction, preferably from those who could afford it and who had fewest votes—was unfavorable. Business groups could try to set this agenda: a lot of publicizing and lobbying went into building a concern with capital formation, just as a campaign put infrastructure on the agenda in 1982. Yet their influence on the issues in debate was limited. Whatever happened to capital formation, anyway?

Other interest groups were able to exploit opportunities or to beat off attacks. Federal employees and retirees won battles against the budgeters in 1980 and 1982. Oil interests—which means whole states—did very nicely in 1981 and not so badly thereafter. But they and their states still suffered badly from the sharp decline in international oil prices. The banks overwhelmed Congress on withholding in 1983. Most important, whenever the deficit dentists went after social security, the elderly lobby chomped down on them. One thing is evident: the more an interest group looks like a whole mass of angry voters—from five million affected by civil service retirement provisions to untold millions interested in interest withholding, and virtually everyone involved, either immediately or potentially, in social security—the more powerful it gets. That makes it difficult to distinguish interest group power from that of the public. If many, many people want something, Congress either supplies it or doesn't take it away. Is this bad?

Sometimes we distinguish interest power from public preference by emphasizing resources (e.g., money) used by groups. When Congress responds to threats or inducements involving campaign contributions, we see a force that differs from citizen opinion. The dairy lobby is a good example of a sophisticated group that poured money into politics; while it lost some battles, some claim it should have lost more. Business in general with its checkered outcomes is another example of a monied interest. The history of revenue policy shows, at the least, that politicians like to please groups that are big contributors (remember the "commodity tax straddle" in 1981). Yet our politicians also are capable of playing monied interests off against each other (as in 1982, 1984, and 1986). There could not be a better example of a policy discombobulating interest groups—who hardly knew what was happening to them, even if it wasn't that bad—than tax reform. In part because there are so many interests, politicians have substantial independence.

Have we come all this way, then, only to repeat elementary school maxims—America is ruled by its people acting through its elected officials? Given the separation of powers, moreover, Congress counts a great deal, so much, in fact, that any theory of rule in America that omits the legislature is hopelessly wrong. Yes, we think these are truer maxims at this time than common alternatives—America is ruled by business or the military-industrial complex or bureaucrats. Yet judgments of relative power do not explain its exercise. Nor does the relative power of voters and elected officials mean that some citizens are not favored over others, that the system is unbiased. Indeed, bias may arise not from the ways interests are aggregated but from the ways people determine their interests.

Evaluation again cannot be separated from values. Bias exists only in reference to some standard; the system is said to favor business, labor, or farmers if it provides benefits to those forces at the expense of the public interest. Such an evaluation depends on what you think the public interest is. If capital formation is necessary to the general welfare, then policies that favor it, even if they aid rich people more directly than poor, cannot be said to show the system's bias.

Many analysts would argue that who wins the battles of the time is not the issue. Accepting those battles as the standard omits fundamental questions. Why are some people rich and others poor, some well organized and others disoriented? Where do the alternatives come from? Not all alternatives are offered. Medicare was a budgetary crisis, but no one suggested socializing medicine as a solution, though that is common in most of the industrialized world. Hardly anyone suggested getting out of NATO, which might save big bucks. Certain kinds of options—challenges to private property, retreat from America's world role—were not considered.

Whether you believe the political process even asks the right questions—never mind gives the right answers—depends on your ideology with its accompanying worldview, which shapes your judgment about both bias and effectiveness. Yes, public officials rule, economic conservatives agree, that is the trouble. For, in order to curry favor with the electorate, they spend too much, thus taxing too much and thereby weakening capitalism. To stop the government from governing too much, they want a balanced budget–spending limit amendment.[1] That's the trouble, say radical democrats (with a small "d"); the state budgets instead of the people. Instead of ordinary people gaining experience in reconciling differences, they are depoliticized in favor of control by corporations and experts.[2] The real trouble, other critics say, is that the state ought to govern but actually does not. Real power is delegated to irresponsible interest groups.[3] Too simple and too nice, Marxists reply. The state rules not in the public interest but on behalf of private, capitalistic interests. Indeed, the state does better by capitalists than they can for themselves, thus perpetuating an unjust system.[4]

Ultimately, for most people, the questions, Who does the system favor? and Does the system work? merge into one: Does the system serve the public interest? An irony of the deficit battles is that observers from across the political spectrum can agree the deficits reveal the system's failure, even as they disagree about the lost public interest and the found bias.

Capitalism, Democracy, and the Budget

Long before Jimmy Carter confronted his budget difficulties, two broad streams of social science analysis argued that a capitalist democracy, such as the United States, faces potentially crippling obstacles in controlling its budget. Both streams, Marxist and conservative, considered the problem in terms of the independence and the strength of "the state."

The term sounds alien to Americans, who are used to referring to the government or city hall and who are likely to find "the state" too pretentious or archaic, a remnant of absolutism or perhaps an insidious effort to impose strange and harmful European doctrines. We Americans do speak of it but in other words. For in the halls of Congress and on main street the same question is being raised ever more insistently: Is there a government that can govern?

During the 1970s, political scientists throughout the industrialized world rediscovered the state. Their interest grew with the politico-economic crisis that began our story. Governments of all the industrialized democracies faced economies that would not function acceptably. Scholars wrote about "strong" (more capable) and "weak" (less capable) states; America's state was viewed as weak because it directed the economy less. Governments felt responsibility for an inability to manage those economies as well as they would have liked. To others, however, these nations' political economies functioned all too well.

Pride of place in resurrecting the state goes to Marxists, for whom the relationship of politics and economics was always primary. They, however, begin not in the 1970s but before, when things were going well. Therefore, their basic question is different. Why, they ask, despite its moral illegitimacy, its political ineptitude, and its economic incapacities, in sum, its systemic irrationality, does capitalism survive, even prosper? Capitalism, Fred Block writes, faces "the twin dangers of economic crisis and radical working-class movements."[5] Market failure, like the Great Depression and/or popular revolt, could overturn the system. Why has it not done so? Like many other Marxists, he argued that the state apparatus acted to save capitalism from itself.

Before it can be appraised, neo-Marxist theory has to be differentiated from the older, classical version, whose conclusions it seeks to validate while altering the causal path through which they are derived. Starting with the words of Marx and Engels's Communist manifesto—the state is a "committee for managing the common affairs of the whole bourgeois"—Lenin and other Marxists developed an instrumental view of the state. In its most mechanical version, government officials carry out orders from capitalists who, through their ownership of the means of production, lord it over the rest of society. While Marx was attracted to this mechanical view, in order to hold capitalists responsible for their crimes, he also recognized that government officials need not be capitalists to do what they wished. The important point was that these administrators had to serve the interests of capital ("objectively," as Marxists say).

Almost from the beginning doubts were voiced: How do capitalists know so well what is good for them? Are they in fact united? Is there some mysterious relationship at work so that whatever policy capitalists need mysteriously appears? Is government necessary if it only carries out orders? Are these instructions part of a capitalist conspiracy? And, if so, why would a ruling class have to mask its power?

Modern Marxists, confronting these questions and researching them, found that public officials were often neither rich nor capitalist. The growth of the welfare state suggested that capitalism might have benevolent aspects. Studies of interest group–government relations, as well as casual observation, revealed continuing divisions within both sides of this relationship. Often it appeared that state organs had different views from those of business and succeeded in imposing them. And so we have found as well. A more adequate account was called for.

Just as Marx and Lenin developed the theory of the vanguard of the proletariat, made up of ideologically conscious intellectuals who better understood the interests of the working class than the workers themselves, there developed among Marxists a theory of what we will call the "capitalist vanguard," a state composed of government officials who know better than industrialists what is good for them.[6] As Stephen Elkin described the analysis, "class lackeys" became "class fiduciaries."[7] Because capitalists are engaged in competition and because they are short-sighted, that is, interested in immediate profits, Marxist scholars began to argue that they are unlikely either to organize in a class conscious way or to take a long-range view of their class interests. Therefore (consciously or not, views vary) capitalists consent to turn over the task of seeing they remain in business to their own government. "Ruling-class members who devote substantial energy to policy formation become atypical of their class," Fred Block explains, "since they are forced to look at the world from the perspective of state managers. They are quite likely to diverge ideologically from politically unengaged ruling-class opinion."[8]

Such a formulation allows for seeming differences between the state and the capitalists, while assuming shared interests. The state managers' problem then becomes one of keeping the public happy with welfare state measures and regulation while retaining the capitalist character of society and support from the capitalist class. Block describes their response in terms that recall Adam Smith's "invisible hand."

> If the state managers decide to respond to pressure with concessions, they are likely to shape their concessions in a manner that will least offend business confidence and will most expand their own power. These two constraints increase the likelihood that the concessions will ultimately serve to rationalize capitalism.[9]

Business confidence matters because, otherwise, businesses will not invest and the economy will collapse. No conspiracy is needed.

The actions of individual entrepreneurs, in putting forth or withholding their resources, the "investment strike" of Marxist lore,[10] guarantees favorable state action.[11] Far from being an impediment to ruling in the interests of capitalists, it turns out that the class struggle helps the vanguard capitalist state persuade the owners of production to adopt far-sighted policies, such as social security and unemployment insurance, to keep them in power.

Marxist analyses pose the right question: How is political legitimacy combined with maintaining the health of the capitalist economy? The tax and budget battles are about that question. A better answer is needed than that the politicians work it out so the capitalists (or, at least, capitalism) always win. If, as Jon Elster pungently puts it, "it is in the political interest of the bourgeoisie that the State should *not* act in the economic interest of the bourgeoisie," such a proposition is essentially "vacuous."[12]

Was it in the long-term interest of capitalism to cut income tax rates across-the-board by 23 percent? The administration, at least the president, thought it was, but there were worriers about deficits, like the budget director and Senator Domenici. Should these cuts have preceded rather than followed equivalent spending cuts on domestic programs? President Reagan thought so and persuaded most members of Congress, but not without acknowledging their strong qualms. Was it better to accept huge deficits, though no one intended them, than to accept larger revenues that might have hampered the economy, encouraged larger domestic spending, and given anticapitalist forces resources with which to expand their clientele? Was it better for capitalism to enact lower income tax rates or rely on tax preferences to directly enhance capital accumulation? Were the majorities who, after 1981, safeguarded the bulk of welfare programs either the better defenders of capitalism because they may have protected its legitimacy or the worse defenders because money was diverted to what some considered less productive uses?

All these disputes occurred within an overwhelming consensus of the political stratum as to the merits of capitalism. Such doubts as the Democrats would display about the market's wonders were always subordinated to claims of loyalty to dominant economic ideology. Media scorn of Richard Gephardt's rather mild protectionism in the 1988 campaign or labeling Jesse Jackson's policies as radical, shows that dominance, what Italian Marxist Antonio Gramsci would call the hegemony of capitalist ideology. In America capitalism is what everyone swears they want; because no one is exactly sure how to maintain it, however, the lot of state managers is not happy.

Can the notion of state managers have much meaning if it does not include the chief executive? If that is so, in what sense can it include Ronald Reagan? Perhaps his willingness to impose costs on businesses, as in the tax reform, so as to improve long-term conditions for market capitalism, fit this scheme. Is President Reagan, then, the epitome of the socially advanced leader of the state apparatus who knows what is good for capitalism even (or especially) when capitalists themselves disagree?

Perhaps we can view politicians as a group, with all their disagreements, as united in commitments to both capitalism and political institutions. The politicians who look most like Block's state managers are the experienced politicians in the legislature, particularly on revenue and appropriations committees. Fair enough, but what kind of state is colonized so easily by less socialized members of the ruling class, such as Stockman, Reagan, and Regan?

Claus Offe expresses the difficulty of the state managers' task well. (Exactly who they are, we will discuss next.) He argues that the state is, at one and the same time, biased, independent, and troubled. The state, defined as the institutions and the norms that regulate relationships between private and public sectors, is biased because it attempts to maintain the dominance of market relationships. It is independent (or relatively so) because it must try to reconcile acceptance of capitalism by the mass public (legitimacy) with capital accumulation (effectiveness). The state is troubled because it must simultaneously try to reconcile conflicts (1) within the capitalist class, (2) between that class and workers, (3) within its own ranks, and (4) between itself and the rest of society.

Offe treats the state as a political body trying to keep sufficient distance between itself and society to avoid being overwhelmed by the problems it is supposed to solve. In this sense, though Offe does not explicitly say so, his detailed analyses of policy formulation suggest that maintaining the image of the state as a neutral arbiter may be a fiction, but necessary, if the state apparatus is to save itself from the system of relationships it is desperately trying to safeguard.[13] Being in the fray, while being above it, budgeters would agree, is neither an easy nor an enviable position.

Déjà vu. Translated into their own vocabulary, participants in the battles of the budget could only assent to Offe's description of them as state actors. Of course, they would not accept his characterization of their dominance. After all, it is hard to square his evocative description of their beleaguered status as dominating anything. Our participants are sensitive to what they consider misunderstanding. In tax reform, they, the governors, tried to show they were not merely a "switchboard state," passive implementers of other people's desires, but also a "switchblade state," ready to attack those who stood in the way of their conception of general interest. They would show "the special interests" who was in charge. And they did. But not without concern, as Offe suggests, about possibly diminishing capital accumulation. They took actions that at least kept the deficit from growing much larger than it otherwise would have been. If a rise in interest rates or some other factor they could not control vitiated their efforts, that was life, frustrating but inevitable. They were biased; they were in charge; and, to complete Offe's portrait, they were also troubled.

There is truth in Evans, Rueschemeyer, and Skocpol's conclusion that "state interventions in socio-economic life can, over time, lead to a diminution of the state and to a reduction of any capacities the state may have for coherent action."[14] Thus, the combination of spending growth (especially on entitlements), rising social security taxes, Kemp-Roth tax cuts, and tax reform, all of which make it politically difficult to raise income tax rates, restricted the range of feasible alternatives for economic management in general and the debt in particular.

Everybody sees the budget squeeze, but what does it mean? The politicians, instead of blaming the system, blame themselves and each other. Their laments and frustration have filled this book. The general feeling of Democrats, for instance, that taking more than one-fifth of GNP in federal taxes would hurt them at the polls, followed by Reagan's 1984 victory, severely constrained their future action.[15] They might be said to have sacrificed their principles to expediency. Yet this, catering to pronounced public opinion, is what politicians think they are supposed to do. In their eyes, the state ought never, never to be more than partially autonomous because that would mean democracy is dead.

Where Marxists see ineluctable contradictions of capitalism, based on the opposed interests of capitalist and other classes, our politicians see the old Burkean dilemma between good government and representative democracy. Marxists suspect that the problem is unsolvable, that politicians cannot maintain both a growing economy and popular support, because the logic of the economic system is to immiserate the masses eventually. Few American politicians would agree. They think (and, so far, they have been right) that capitalism, prosperity, and democracy ought to be self-reinforcing; it is their task to make sure this happens.

Although politicians do not see hopeless contradictions of capitalism, an influential school of commentators take seriously their Burkean dilemma and see possibly catastrophic contradictions of democracy. Ironically, some conservatives who see the state as a source of order in society, and therefore care most for state capacity, moved during the 1970s to a position much like that of Marxists.

Stagflation in America and stagnation in Europe during the 1970s, which accompanied the growth of governmental budgets, led conservatives to wonder whether an excess of democracy was making their societies ungovernable.[16] Because both society's resources and government's ability to solve problems, like reducing crime or dependence on governmental welfare payments, were limited, one felt government was being overloaded. Richard Rose put it simply: "Governments become overloaded when expectations are in excess of national resources, the government institutions, and the impact that its outputs can achieve. Such an overload arises from the decision of citizens individually and in organized groups to ask more of government than it can in total provide."[17] Because people expected more than government could deliver, it would lose legitimacy. "Because of the lack of any widely shared belief in the legitimacy of the present order," according to Samuel Brittan, the pursuit of private self-interest, driven to excess by "the process of political competition," would overwhelm public institutions.[18] Competition for votes led the parties to offer ever more ample subsidies, which would bankrupt government first economically and then politically. Whether a decline in legitimacy would exacerbate governmental incapacity or vice versa, democratic capitalism might be in as bad shape as Marxists claimed it was.

While winning elections required avoiding tax increases, Samuel Huntington wrote, the same forces required expanding benefits. The (familiar sounding) result, he feared, would be perpetual inflation.[19] Ordinarily abstruse mathematical and geometrical modelers had a field day pointing out the democratic road to perdition. Among the earliest was this warning: "Thus from our model we reach the politico-economic conclusion that a pure democracy with all parties seeking to maximise public support is doomed to increasing inflation and political disintegration."[20]

The earlier concern with economic dislocation soon gave way to a profound unease about political collapse. The state was in trouble. Thus, as Michel Crozier puts it, "the more decisions the modern state has to handle, the more helpless it becomes. Decisions do not only bring power; they also bring vulnerability."[21] The more government intrudes into the lives of citizens, that is, the more welfare payments it must offer, the more it is hemmed in by prior commitments—budgetary promises—and becomes less able to meet new and rising expectations. This gap between promise and performance, Huntington feared, "could lead to deep feelings of frustration, a reaction against existing political institutions and practices, and a demand for a new political system that could and would do what had to be done."[22]

Soon enough, given the rooting of causality within an overloaded political system, the call was, in Anthony King's words, for suggestions on "how the number of tasks that governments have come to perform can be reduced."[23] Although this call was certainly not in line with Marxist preferences, it was based on a parallel analysis.

David Stockman's concern with ideology, with finding a way to define some demands as legitimate and others as not, was a practical response to the conservatives' view of the government's dilemma. His "Social Pork Barrel" article argued in 1975 that government's capacity to make policy was limited by old (and bastardized) policies. His answer, a radical market position, was one example of how concern with the capacity to govern has led to renewed discussion about the proper boundaries of political life. "The concept of politics," Offe observes, "turns reflexive; politics centers on the question of what politics is about—and what it is not [he means, we think, ought not to be] about."[24] He accuses contemporary (neo)conservatives of aiming "at a restrictive redefinition of politics, the counterpart of which is looked for in the market, the family, or science."[25] Just this, indeed, is the view taken in Michel Crozier, Samuel Huntington, and Joji Watanuki's *The Crisis of Democracy*.[26] The private realm of family, work, locality is their preferred arena.

In turn, Huntington views with alarm "the prevalence of oppositional political values and ideologies among key elements of the population" who will first overload government and then delegitimize it for its failure.[27] Radicals and conservatives play into one another's fears.

The conservative distrust of democracy has a long pedigree in American political thought. There can be too much of a good thing: democracy must be dammed up and channeled so it cannot overflow its banks and destroy the very society it normally waters. Alexander Hamilton's distrust of the populace ("Your 'people,' sir, is a great beast!") distilled that fear to its essence. His partner in *The Federalist,* James Madison, expressed the fears more powerfully and acceptably than Hamilton, arguing that checks and balances, federalism, and a large country that made it difficult for interests adverse to theirs to form coalitions could preserve freedom from the "tyranny of the majority."

Few of our sainted founders would have described their constitution as a democracy; the whole point was to be a republic, something better. Lincoln's description of a government "of the people, by the people, and for the people" would have seemed, four score and seven years earlier, radical and extreme. Tom Paine might have applauded; others would not.

Yet, by his time, Lincoln's phrase distilled what Americans chose to believe about their government. Something like the Civil War could never have been justified by the kind of lesser-evil arguments made in the *The Federalist.* Certainly the notion that government was the province of an elite of learning and virtue was destroyed in the Jacksonian political revolution of 1828. Andrew Jackson, his allies, and (reluctantly) his Whig opponents built a political system in which the people were the source of legitimacy. Jackson's genius was to make the presidency into the "tribune of the people" by turning it into an opponent of big government, a strategy emulated by Ronald Reagan. Politicians won (and win) office by proclaiming their similarity to the common man.

The fear of democracy lived on in two transmuted forms. First, and weakest, was distrust of government itself. For most people, government seemed a possible threat to liberty. The logical extension, that democracy threatened liberty, was less popular. Reagan maintained his position by saying government was alien and uncontrolled, in essence undemocratic. That meant, however, that if "the people" wanted big government, it was legitimate. For all that Reaganism tapped into deep American values, on that issue he faced a serious difficulty. Democratic practice, the source of his own legitimacy, justified his opponents as well. Democracy, within these limits, is as hegemonic as capitalism, and democracy itself severely limits capitalism's hegemony.[28]

The second repository of fear of democracy was reverence for the Constitution itself. If citizens did not share the attitudes of the Founders, they still had been socialized into respectful awe of their work. Thus, the political structure was very difficult to change, and that structure, by hamstringing government, inhibited the exercise of the public's will (if such a thing existed) through government. Ironically, for conservatives, the separation of powers that limited government by the unruly passions of the public also limited "responsible government" by elites.

Supporters of the welfare state believe it will improve, perhaps preserve, democratic capitalism. Marxists hope, and conservatives fear, that it will not because it will not be able to accommodate all the demands: To Marxists, capitalist failure provokes those demands; to conservatives, democratic failure invites those demands. In either case, the budget crisis seems to prove the excess of demands.

Both Marxist and conservative analyses sound strange in an America where neither democracy nor capitalism is easily challenged. They may sound alien for another reason as well. If something exists, it must have interests; the concept of "state interest," except in certain legal contexts, would make Americans very uncomfortable. We Americans speak instead of the public interest and ask if the state is serving it. Indeed, our political structure and ideology are oriented toward blocking a distinct state interest from arising. It is hard enough to identify the American state, never mind its interests.

The Dis-United State

We have made a case in this book for the (semi)autonomy of government actors, the holders of formal authority. In the 1950s, by contrast, the dominant theory in American political science, a version of what is called "pluralism," emphasized organized groups much more than officials. Reduced to its essence, in Earl Latham's description, politics could be understood by adding up the group pressures on the various sides; the government was a cash register, giving the total, the largest winning.[29] Over time, the empirical work of political scientists who were both self-consciously pluralist and antipluralist—Robert Dahl, Raymond Bauer, Ithiel Poole, Lewis Dexter, Theodore Lowi, James Q. Wilson, and others—modified this emphasis on groups ruling over politicians.[30]

Political scientists who rediscovered the (semi)autonomy of government actors did not, however, find "the state." Unlike in Europe, they could not sense the self-conscious feeling of top officials that they, not others, have the right to rule. When Hugh Heclo studied the federal executive in his evocative *A Government of Strangers,* he found that they may know the members of their "issue network" but they do not personally know (and are unlikely to get to know) most leading members of the executive branch. There is little sense of common identity within the federal executive; loyalties go to the agency (Forest Service, FBI) or profession (law, social work) rather than to the bureaucracy as a whole. There is no elite corps of administrators similar to France's graduates of the École Nationale d'Administration or the OxBridge products who become permanent secretaries in the British ministries. Political appointees make up far more of the top levels of the executive in America, and they are often in and out within eighteen months. For all these reasons the permanent government, in a sense the Europeans or Japanese understand, does not exist in the United States.

In Europe this top level of the bureaucracy (with or without an admixture of politicians frequently found atop key ministries, such as finance) *is* the state. In Europe the state came first; representative democracy is a control on it, not its creator. Marxist talk about "state managers" makes sense; they are a distinct class of people, united by a process of training and selection and rules for relating to each other (as much informal as formal) and to society (business, labor, politicians) that build boundaries—who is allowed to relate to whom—and define roles— who is allowed to do what. But who in these United States could fill such a role?

The Congressional State

If in America the state were not the bureaucracy, where, if anywhere, could it be found? How about political executives? It is rather hard to conceive of Ronald Reagan as "the state" in a European sense. He certainly had a vision for the long-term success of capitalism; yet he surely did not see himself as part of the government. The political executive is easily colonized by people who have few ties to the bureaucracy, little memory, and no ideology of system maintenance. That can change; Stockman is a revolutionary who was won over to a manager's stance. On balance, the political executives do not much look like the state.

The only group that combines power and continuity in a way that allows the efficacy and identity we might call the state is, of all places, in Congress. The idea that this fragmented institution might be the state seems so ludicrous that it has never, to our knowledge, been taken seriously. Yet when Jamie Whitten, chairman of the House Appropriations Subcommittee on Agriculture for nearly forty years, is jokingly referred to as the "Permanent Secretary of Agriculture," we should take notice. The senior members of Congress have been around a long time, sharing responsibility for running a government. Like European state managers, they have their own bailiwicks; they are also a group of people who know each other well and form a community; they train each other. Unlike European legislators, they run things. Congress has far more control of the budget than does any other legislature we can name. They also feel a responsibility to govern, which is manifest throughout our book. Congressmen such as Senators Dole, Domenici, and Chiles have been most exercised over the deficit.

Although Congress is the core of the American state, the system is fragmented. Congress is hardly the sole possessor of legitimate authority. Presidents have some; so do the courts. In a Madisonian system of "ambition opposing ambition," opposing holders of authority clash over policy. It becomes hard to talk of state interest when the president and Congress are at odds. The structure of America's budget stalemate would make no sense in other countries that have more coherent states.

When president and Congress clash, they turn to the twin sources of legitimacy: the people and the Constitution. It sounds trite, but listen to the Iran/Contra hearings, where each tried to invoke these authorities against the other. The budget fights have seen some attempts to create constitutional authority, namely the proposed balanced budget amendment. Mostly, however, they have involved appeals to the public, to notions of the "public interest."

Congressmen feel their legitimacy (and, in European terms, that of the state) is threatened by failure to pursue the public interest in deficit reduction. This threat exists not in their imaginations (though partially there) but in a political process, hard to characterize but palpable. It is the process of debating and creating "respectable opinion," those ideas that the media and experts, as well as politicians, consider responsible.

Any politician could tell you that experts and the media, particularly the major networks, newspapers, and news magazines, are predominant forces in American politics. Accusations of a liberal or conservative bias (earnestly denied by journalists, of course) reflect that power. News is meaningless if it does not influence opinion. Headlines in *Time,* the *Washington Post,* and other "powers that be" tell us what to think about; their stories then tell us what to think about it. The media's role as purveyor of opinion is most evident when major organs differ, as when *Time* and *Newsweek* disagreed on whether President Carter's FY81 budget showed attention to the lessons of Lyndon Johnson's failure to finance the Vietnam War. Less evident, but more telling, was their agreement that Lyndon Johnson's deficit had started an inflationary spiral; the panic about deficits flowed from that supposed fact.

A policy advocate attains nirvana when his position becomes the conventional wisdom: that deficits cause inflation (1973–1983), that deficits cause high interest rates (1983–present), that defense is badly underfunded (1980–1981), that tariffs are bad because they caused the Great Depression (1946–present). As the examples suggest, such wisdoms are neither immutable nor divorced from real world events. People fight to change them. Nor does conventional wisdom always win. It may identify a problem but not a response, as with the deficit. It may not exist; there was no authoritative analysis of stagflation to guide politicians in 1980–1981. Furthermore, there are politicians who, either because of a loyal constituency or their own conviction, can ignore or resist a media consensus. A Ronald Reagan or a Phil Gramm is not interested in other people's judgments, except as a guide to tactics. Reagan had a further advantage: in many ways he was outside the mainstream of policy debate. Donald Regan's memoir provides a telling example of the difference between Reagan, a politician of conviction, and his conservative but more normal vice president. Reagan tended to quote the *Washington Times,* which matched his ideology but was hardly one of the "powers"; George Bush quoted the *New York Times.*

How the movements of opinion within this stratum of experts and journalists favored one political side or another has, of course, been a large part of our story. In defining some opinion as respectable and some as not, some analysis as fact and some as opinion, the experts and journalists are defining, for purposes of mass consumption, public interest and special interest. Thus tax reform—simplification and fewer loopholes—became the public interest even though (perhaps because) there was no public outcry for it. If Bob Packwood had followed his basic instincts and fought reform, he might have been serving his own constituents and even a majority of the public, but he would have lost face in Washington, reported back home as "Senator Hackwood," an opponent of the public good. This pressure for reform was self-consciously nonpartisan, as was the criticism of budget deficits. In fact, both could be seen and were presented as issues of system maintenance, making the system work the way it should.

What outsiders call the establishment does exist as part of our system of government. It also has some attributes of what social scientists call the state.

The Political Stratum

The editors of the *New York Times,* or economists at the Brookings Institution, have a permanence and interest in governance that some elected politicians will not possess. Foundation executives who fund projects on "The Governance of America" or "The Deficit and the Public Interest," as well as the academics who write those books, perform some functions of system maintenance. During summer 1987 every thirty-second television spot about our wonderful Constitution was a reminder that system maintenance occurs outside the formal procedures of state authority.

The processes that form attitudes are as consequential as those by which people resolve differences over the values they have formed. By this logic, Gramsci reminds us, schools and newspapers are as much a part of politics as are legislators and courts. If we follow this path too far, however, we will reidentify the state and society because all life teaches about values. Furthermore, how are we to separate those acts of opinion formation that are system maintenance (thus the state) from those that are antisystem (thus something else)?

The Public Sphere

The phenomenon we are describing has been differentiated from the state by, among others, Jürgen Habermas. Habermas calls it "the public sphere":

> A realm of our social life in which something approaching public opinion can be formed. . . . Newspapers and magazines, radio and television, are the media of the public sphere. We speak of the political public sphere in contrast, for instance, to the literary one, when public discussion deals with objects connected to the activities of the state.

(One sign of such differentiation, he notes, was "the separation of the public budget from the household expenses of the ruler."[31]) In his view, the public sphere should oppose the state. He mournfully argues that the modern public sphere has lost its critical function, as the press became a mainly commercial enterprise. Thus, instead of discussion of the general interest, there is persuasion and propaganda at the service of established authority. Habermas is wrong because welfare policies are extensively debated: their ostensible failures, whether "left" (too little) or "right" (too much), form a virtual cacophony of criticism. Nor is the media much disposed to praise those in authority. Look, read, and see. Nevertheless, he is right in that the participants in public debate are committed to the fundamental outlines of the existing order.

Yet, if these be evils, what political system could be good? In what kind of system are the fundamental aspects of society extensively debated? Only where there is little agreement on them. Then how do people live together? In El Salvador or Lebanon there is fundamental disagreement. There also is not much of a "public sphere"; decision by debate, instead of bullets, presupposes limited stakes. What Gramsci calls hegemony, and Habermas a failing of the public sphere, may be its first requisite.

In any stable system, the people who participate most actively according to the existing rules and come to the top by those rules tend to believe in them. Otherwise they could not justify their power to themselves or others; any system that gave authority to its enemies, as the Weimar Republic did to Hitler, would not be in power very long. Whether the economic system is capitalist, socialist, or something else, is irrelevant. General Secretary Gorbachev, for example, has been very careful not to question one-party rule in the Soviet Union because his power is based on that primacy.

At the same time, no group of people can ever discuss its general interest without participants pursuing their particular interests in the process. People wish to believe that what is good for them is good for the larger society. So we agree with those, like Madison, who doubted politics could ever be free of such "corruptions," hoping instead only to control their effects.

Thus, we would expect the discussion within the public sphere to include construction companies talking about the nation's decaying infrastructure, businesses talking about capital formation, labor unions about keeping America strong by keeping jobs at home, and wealthy doctors about the long lines and impersonality of socialized medicine. For all we know, they may be right.

Permutations of particular interests shaped attention to the general interest in deficit reduction. Democrats jumped on the issue in part because their constituencies had more problems with Reagan's than with previous deficits. Yet neither the deficit panic in its various forms, nor the dominance of debate over tax reform by appeals to the general interest in a simpler tax code, can be explained by particular interests alone. Similarly, the budgetary rhetoric of fair shares—freezes, three-legged stools, and all that—expressed a norm of balance that has no necessary partisan import. The media are suckers for concepts like deficit reduction, tax simplification, and fair shares because they seem like general rather than special interests. None of these concepts challenge the existing order; instead, they are nearly procedural norms that are supposed to help maintain the system as a whole, which is why they command such widespread support. In everyday rhetoric, in *Time, Newsweek,* and the floors of the House and Senate, they are presented as the embodiment of the general interest. Try to remember deficit reduction, a simpler tax code, or fair shares being described as the demands of special interests. It does not happen.

Rather than the general interest being unrepresented in the American public sphere, certain policy preferences are conventionally distinguished as the general interest within that sphere. The difficulty is that these conventional notions of general interest contradict the interests of most people. *In essence, the policy instructions from the public sphere contradict the instructions legislators receive directly from their constituents.* The crisis of budget politics in our time is not a failure to bring the general interest into political debate; on the contrary, it is spoken there ad nauseum. *The crisis lies in the conflict between what is represented in the debate of the public sphere and majority interest* (more precisely, majorities of interests) *in the electoral sphere.*

The State as a State of Mind

We began looking at the public sphere as part of the search for the state as it is commonly discussed—institutionalized in some form that allows one to talk of the state as having its own interests and tasks, under pressure from society's problems, struggling to maintain its independence. In American politics no one entity fits that role. Senators and representatives come closest, but have no monopoly of authority; in some areas, especially foreign and defense policy, they see themselves as outsiders vis-à-vis the president and his minions. Instead of a group of people or formal institutions, the state, in a sense, is a state of mind.

In the budget battles, participants who emphasize balance above other values feel particularly like the Marxists' embattled state managers. When the media raise a clamor against deficits, they are thinking like state managers but, unlike the politicians, they do not have to do anything. They fulfill their obligations to the system by criticizing the politicians, which, neatly enough, allows the press to believe itself both critical and loyal at the same time. Meanwhile, some holders of formal authority (in Congress and the presidency) resist the balancers, though, under the terms of the political debate, they cannot say they are doing so. No one is *for* the deficit, at least not publicly.

We have an extremely vigorous and important public sphere; it shapes the actions of holders of formal authority, at the same time criticizing them and committing itself to system maintenance. The state itself is a category of interest, distinguishable by the way it is discussed and, for a moment in time, defined. The "party of responsibility"[32] consists of politicians who more likely represent that interest than the two other major aggregations: the established coalition of social hierarchy and competitive individualism, which cares more about moral control and freeing capital, and the liberal, egalitarian coalition, which cares more about changing institutions to provide benefits to the less powerful.[33] Thus, we recreate the basic cleavages sensed by both Marxists and conservatives—versions of capitalism and mass politics, both pressuring the state in the middle—into a more appropriate form. This produces a shifting battle of interests; the state has distinct advantages through its validation in the public sphere, but, because it is just one construction of interest, the state need not win the battle.

"Interest," just like "state," is a social construction. When there is widespread agreement on the answer to the stirring question of the old labor song—"Which Side Are You On?"—we have temporarily accepted the latest definition of who are "the interests" and who is "the state." Usually, things are not that clear. That is why the state is often a state of mind. To those who grew up with power in America as a fissiparous construct, so hard to get hold of it slips through your fingers, namely, the pluralists who until recently dominated debate on American politics, the state is not problematic because they do not expect any group or interest or institution to rule.

This understanding of the special nature of the American state and the public interest can be used to make sense of the major cleavage in American political science, between pluralism, best represented by David Truman, and its critics, best represented by Theodore J. Lowi.

Pluralism and the Dilemma of Public Authority

Our description of the governmental process can be incorporated into David Truman's. Truman sees politics as a competition of interests. An interest, to Truman, is simply an attitude. Some interests will be manifest in political organization; some will not. People sharing an interest organize in response to stimuli—perhaps changes in society, perhaps government policy. An interest may be unorganized (thus invisible) not because it is weak but because it is strong, that is, unthreatened.

Truman describes "interests or expectations that are so widely held in society and are so reflected in the behavior of almost all citizens that they are, so to speak, taken for granted." He calls these "widely held but unorganized interests 'rules of the game.' " These interests become, in Truman's model of group competition, "potential groups." These attitudes may be more strongly and precisely held "at the leadership level" than by "the mass of the population," but these "are interests the serious disturbance of which will result in organized interaction and the assertion of fairly explicit claims for conformity." Often these interests do not have to be visible because they have been embedded in the political structure. "As embodied in these institutional forms and in accepted verbal formulations . . . the interests of these potential groups are established expectations concerning not only what the governmental institutions shall do, but more particularly, how they shall operate." Organized groups with other attitudes must attempt not to violate these rules of the game for two reasons: the group's own members tend also to support the rules (Truman calls this overlapping interests), and others will oppose the group on the basis of rules alone. "Violation of the 'rules of the game' normally will weaken a group's cohesion, reduce its status in the community, and expose it to the claims of . . . competing organized groups that more adequately incorporate the 'rules,' or . . . [are] organized on the basis of these broad interests and in response to the violations."

Truman goes on to explain that these attitudes-cum-interests, inculcated in family, schools, and other experiences, are continually reinforced in political combat. Public officials are under particular pressure to conform.

> The strength of these widely held but largely unorganized interests explains the vigor with which propagandists for organized groups attempt to change other attitudes by invoking such interests. Their importance is further evidenced in the recognized function of the means of mass communication, notably the press, in reinforcing widely accepted norms of public morality.

These attitudes are not always and everywhere dominant because they may be substantively ambiguous (e.g., free speech), are not all equally fundamental, must compete with other interests, or their violation may not be visible.

All this fits the story of the budget deficit near perfectly. Balance is a rule of the game, a weapon in fights for other goals, enforced as an evaluative norm by the media and particularly pressed upon politicians. Economic policy making is also shaped by such "rules of the game." Truman goes so far, following Harold Lasswell, as to describe "the state" as a shared attitude, sometimes weaker, sometimes stronger—"the unique mark of the state is the recognition that one belongs to a community with a system of paramount claims and expectations." Truman adds that "the existence of the state, of the polity, depends on widespread, frequent recognition of and conformity to the claims of these unorganized interests and on activity condemning marked deviations from them."[34]

Thus, the state is a state of mind, reproduced by processes of the public sphere that constitute the hegemony of the "rules of the game," meaning the established order. Truman views the legislature as another potential interest, occasionally manifest (lobbying regulation, his example; tax reform and GRH, ours). Although he does not predict when any given interest will dominate, his list of relevant factors is concise but exhaustive.[35]

The more they ask who actually does what to whom, the Marxists' picture looks more like the pluralist Truman's. Yet they give a different meaning to their picture by asking questions about the relationship between politics and society, about who wins and loses and why.

The question of bias—Does the system favor or work against poor people? Business? The national security?—is generally subsumed in a larger critique by scholars who feel the pluralist system is not sufficiently democratic; that is, it does not represent everyone equally.

We have argued that public opinion and the beliefs of public officials were the strongest forces in our budgetary decisions. When money (doctors and hospitals) confronted votes (the elderly) over medicare cost reductions, votes won. But the elderly were not poor, either, and we have seen the advantages of organization: federal employee and retiree organizations work through the Post Office Committee to fend off the budgeters; farmers escape reconciliation with "cuts" designed to *increase* their incomes. All sorts of narrow interests have hitched rides on the continuing resolutions, where they might go unnoticed in the crowd. There are dramatic cases of politicians holding their noses and supporting a group—for example, the oil auction in 1981—because they found themselves in a pivotal position.

We have emphasized that the hegemonic "rules of the game" include prohibitions against certain policies; thus, they are biased. Truman sees those beliefs as an interest like any other; critics such as Murray Edelman see them as a means of deceiving majorities, diverting them from what he views as their real interests.[36] Both Truman and his critics are self-proving. If, like Truman, we say interest is whatever attitudes people have, "deception" has no meaning. If, like his critics, we say people's interests are what they think people should want, then, if the critics lose (which they must, that's why they are critics), the system is automatically undemocratic. These difficulties on both sides do not remove the larger issue: Do the rules of the game systematically favor some people over others?

The same people don't always win. Federal employees beat the budget cutters in 1980, lost in 1981, and fared a bit worse than a draw in 1982. The poor got cut in 1981, escaped afterward, and won big in 1986. These and other swings resulted not from changes in group resources but from changes in how the rules worked. For both the poor and business, the norm of fair shares required that the winners and losers of 1981 be reversed, though not enough to repeal 1981, in subsequent rounds. In many cases the rules required that majorities in separate institutions put first one interest, then another, in the position of being the marginal vote. In 1981 neither side could pass its tax package without support from the oil patch. In 1982 the budgeters could not pass the TEFRA tax hike without support from advocates for the poor.

These and similar examples show that the majority was not some preexisting entity. Instead, there are many possible majorities. To make the possible actual, majorities must be constructed by bargaining and compromising; that is the heart of democratic politics. In none of these instances did the group identified get its way in isolation: lots of other players accepted the package and also got something. Of course, more people are poor than own oil wells; to say either group can cut deals does not mean the system is equitable. If the bias that is revealed in policy changes, however, then it is possible to change results.

Early pluralists emphasized that results change due to a process of stimulus and response. An interest that is hurt organizes and, because it tries harder in the next round, does better. Savings interest withholding is a wonderful example of that process: banks that did not fight hard on TEFRA decided they did not like the new law, mobilized, and overran Congress in 1983. Yet the overall swing against cutting the poor cannot be explained by such a response; liberal groups were neither mobilized in 1981 nor crucial in 1982. It is true that businesses were more mobilized and united in 1981 than in 1982. But that shows the influence of politicians. When they set an agenda of business tax hikes, their stimulus created a different response—fragmentation and demoralization—than had been created in 1981.

If, with the pluralists, we speak of power eliciting countervailing power, we must say that countervailing power is not just out there in society but also in the norms and the actions of the political stratum, especially in Congress. Time and again they intervened to give, maintain, and take away according to two related but distinct notions of fairness: those who were advantaged earlier should make sacrifices later (business, the military); while those who had been hurt earlier (families with children, the working poor) should be recompensed later; and those whose total resource position was low (poor and disabled people) should be protected against further cuts. Not only are these norms openly avowed, but neither the favorable treatment of families and the working poor in the tax reform, nor the exemption of poor people's entitlements from all or most of Gramm-Rudman's proportional cuts, nor the increases in business taxes after 1981, nor the diminishing role of increases in defense after 1983 can be understood without them.

The attitude of "those who did well last time should sacrifice this time" might be called an interest. Indeed, if widely shared, it could be called a public interest. Then we could ask how large it was and whether policy favored other interests at its expense. Yet such bias would have very different meaning for society than would a bias against blacks, or capitalists, or any specific group of people. Here we reach the problem with Truman's notion of interest; it doesn't fit everyday notions. People tend to think of bias in terms of some objective aspect of people's lives, like their race or income, not their attitudes.

For purposes of evaluation, therefore, a distinction between attitudes not clearly associated with concrete groups and attitudes clearly fitting such groups is in order. The former category is particularly the province of the public sphere: attitudes the mass media believe they can invoke without being accused of taking sides. Truman's notion of "rules of the game" captures their sense: anybody in the game cannot object to a reminder of the rules. In this context, antipluralist critiques then take two forms; these values may in fact advantage one group over another in ways that people, precisely because they hold these values, cannot see, and the values themselves are shunted aside too often, that is, are less influential than they should be.

Every Government Would Bribe Business to Bring Prosperity, If Only It Knew How

The first argument—hidden, systemic bias—restates hegemony identified by scholars who do not call themselves Marxists.[37] We have said our piece; here we insist only that "confidence" is not merely a bribe paid by government to business so as to get a good economy. If it were, every government would pay it; "if only," we hear the pols saying, "we knew whom to pay it to!" And if only, to echo a familiar lament about patronage, they would stay bought. Rather, confidence is the product of successful economic management, or good luck, neither of which requires favoring business. Not knowing what to do, of course, there is a tendency to do what businessmen say will make them happy. In a capitalist society, businesses will have some advantages in debate. But if our story is clear on anything, it is that nobody, including the gurus of the markets, is a reliable guide to policy.

Interest Group Liberalism

The second critique, that the rules of the game are not followed, is the burden of the very common rhetoric that the public interest is shunted aside in the pursuit of special interests. Theodore J. Lowi takes the argument a step further. In perhaps the most influential book on the rules of the game in the past quarter century, *The End of Liberalism*, Lowi argues that a new set of rules, "interest-group liberalism," emerged from pluralist analysis and produced rules that cannot be followed if one wishes to govern. The new ideology argued that the endless battle of interest groups was good by denying the existence of a public interest to be contradicted. In thus justifying our politics, Lowi argues, this ideology lost the justification of government. If the state's actions are merely the current balance of interests, why should losers obey? Government is left with no special legitimacy, no authority separate from society. But a government that cannot separate itself from society cannot govern. People must obey because the government decided, not because their interests are served by the decision. Pluralism as an ideology, to Lowi, abdicates authority.[38]

Lowi denies that the state is an attitude or an interest like any other.

Its defining attribute, the legitimate use of coercion, requires special justification.[39] In this he must be right; at the extreme, the attitude of the state is the soldier's willingness to kill another human being at the orders of his government. Preferences about commodity tax straddles are not of the same order.

We need not agree with either Lowi's construction of interest-group liberalism or his opinion of its influence to agree that the legitimacy of the state—citizens' willingness to accept government's decisions—requires believing the political process creates something more than just a bargain reflecting the balance of power among the currently organized. A majority of groups is not enough to justify coercion—state power over a minority. Instead, government in the democratic state must be able to claim that in some way—some characteristic of its decisions or of how they are made—it represents "the people," not some subset of groups.

We might ask why all the people not affected by a policy should be involved in making it. Normally they care little and know less. That is why we have subgovernments, such as the nexus of interest groups, congressional committees, and agencies that make agricultural policy. Some tendency in that direction is unavoidable; if others don't care, it may be justified. But these subgovernments neither raise their own revenues nor pay their own costs. They are funded by taxes, mostly paid by other people. On what basis, other than fear, are citizens to accept this application of government's coercive powers?

When Charles Anderson wrote that "interest group pluralism is simply not a theory of representation," he confronted the essential difficulty.[40] Grant McConnell crystalized the problem in regard to subgovernments and, even more, organizations that have power sanctioned but not directly controlled by the state, such as corporations and unions. "The problem," he wrote, "is authority. What justifies the existence of power; by what principle is it rightful? For if it is not justifiable, power is properly open to attack and, if possible, destruction."[41]

What rules legitimate authority; do they work? A pluralist line of defense emphasizes that procedures provide acceptable outcomes in the long term. Groups left out in one coalition can join another; groups that lose one time win at another. The difficulty with this standard is that it is not a standard at all. It does not say the rules are intrinsically good; they are to be judged by the long-term substantive consequences of group competition. Thus, one is left without a criterion of judgment that is procedural or substantive. Who is to say how long a term is appropriate, or whether the outcome reached at any point is satisfactory? Both our "disappointed Democrats" on the left and our foes of big government (Gramm, Stockman) on the right rejected the bargain and therefore the way it was made. Lowi argues that this pluralist argument fails precisely because it places no special value on the formality of rules.[42] It eliminates the distinction between a law and a bargain.

Effective governance, in Lowi's formal procedural view, requires affected interests see and feel that the state's decisions are based on considerations on which they, the affected interests, have no claim to superior judgment. If the basis of legitimacy lies in democratic forms, then the state, to be powerful, must be visibly democratic. The ostensible rules must be the real rules. Lowi wants to free both the public and the state from the power of private interest groups by committing the government to clear statements of policy objectives embodied in legislation. That is possible only if political debate is phrased in terms of competing ideologies, of arguments about justice, rather than focused on the peculiarities of individual policy domains that few people understand.

Budget stories almost catalog the objections to Lowi's thesis. Two are primary. First, ideology provides only a limited guide to effective policy. Effectiveness depends not only on perceived legitimacy but also on technique. Policies that do not fit ideology may work; policies that fit ideology may not work. Neither competing conception of justice in welfare programs has told us how to reduce poverty. Free-market Republicans have trouble applying their ideology to farmers. Where a Stockman sees a failure of conviction, we point out that the failure is just as plausibly within the ideology itself. In short, what amateurs at OMB or in the public may understand about a policy—is it interventionist or market-oriented, expensive or cheap, better for poor people or rich?—likely is not all we would want to know. There must be some role in the debate for expertise based on experience; and that lets the special interests (recall these are the people immediately affected by decisions, hence, self-interested) back in.

Second, even more important, there may be no majority for any particular conception of justice or the public good in a policy dispute. There obviously is no such majority in the argument over the budget deficit. Then what? What happens when, in effect, Lowi gets his way and rival conceptions of the good budget clash over and over and over again?

Arguments about justice rarely convince one side it was wrong. Both Stockman and the liberal budgeters were disappointed in their hopes that a budget crisis—by posing the issue as "what is right?"—would favor their side. People do not change their judgments of morality very easily. Thus, a politics of justice or ideology leaves little room for persuasion; that is what we mean by a polarized debate. Such a situation leaves no more room for compromise.

Lowi relies on procedure. Yet when issues are posed so that any solution clearly opposes the will of majorities, but procedure requires majority support, the result is stalemate. The budgeting solution has almost parodied what Lowi condemns in other policies: obfuscation, lies, passing the buck, evasion. Where budget politics is most visible, as on budget resolutions (never mind GRH), it is also most dishonest. This results not from a failure to have a politics of principle but from the inability to assemble a majority that way. What Lowi desires to make decisions easier to enforce—clarity based on open discussion of principle—is precisely what makes decision itself most difficult.

"You must first enable the government to control the governed," Lowi quotes James Madison, "and in the next place oblige it to control itself." We would add that, if government is to enforce decisions, it must first be able to decide. In a sense, we have had an experiment in Lowi's style of democracy. New procedures (budget resolutions and reconciliation) and new conditions (the massive deficit) made budget politics far more ideological, more public and less private, than in the bad old days of the 1960s and 1950s. Then the bad old days started looking a lot better.

Public Interests

Just as hypocrisy pays homage to virtue, otherwise there would be no need to dissemble, no one begins political disputation with the phrase "though the policy I recommended is against the public interest, nevertheless, it is to my advantage." Although politics is often about advantage, that is not all it is about, or there would be no common bonds.

If politics were only about public interests, however, opposite but equally great evils would assert themselves. Hypocrisy (saying one thing while meaning another) would become the only rhetoric because people could not admit what they were doing. Interests important to many people, as David Braybrooke and Charles Lindblom demonstrated in a *Strategy of Decision,* would be neglected because no one had a legitimate right to speak up for them.[43]

Opposing "self-interest" to "public interest" misses the political point, for part of self-interest lies in the viability of institutions permitting self-expression. And part of public interest lies explicitly in facilitating the representation of private interests.

Now the budget may be the last place to look for public interests. No one is disinterested. Everyone involved has something specific they want out of spending and taxing decisions. So many values and valuables are at stake for so many people in government and society in such a dis-aggregated manner that parochialism ordinarily prevails. But, then again, a narrow, self-enclosing vision does not explain tax reform, Gramm-Rudman, or panic about deficits.

We have, then, a dilemma. Contrary to Marxist "crisis of democracy" and antipluralist critics, we argue that a politics of the public interest, conducted in the public sphere of debate, is an important factor in the major struggle in current American politics. Unlike classical pluralists, we claim that such politics can be distinguished from and opposed to other kinds of interests. We hold as well, explicitly with Lowi, that whether the state is perceived as acting within the parameters of the public interest as defined within the public sphere is one source of public authority. The attendant bias may be a problem of equity, we have argued, but not a source of instability. The difficulty is that Lowi's explicit politics of the public interest doesn't work. It has become difficult for the government to perform the most elemental of chores—decide how much money to provide for each of its activities—in a timely manner. It gave up on managing the economy long ago; we can't remember the last time we heard a cogent argument that some particular deficit level would have some particular effect on economic variables.

An Immune System out of Control

Every political system is filled with tensions, with what Marxists call contradictions. Preferences that are logically or practically contradictory must both be satisfied. A logical system is invalidated when beset by contradictions. Politics and society, however, are not logical constructs. Rather than killing a system, its contradictions may define it. What Marxists see as a contradiction between legitimation and accumulation is a choice no modern welfare state can make; the whole point is to keep both democracy and capitalism. Contradictions are important not because they will destroy a system but because they explain so much of the politics within it.

The tension between the state as the holder of formal authority and the state as a set of attitudes toward political questions is especially sharp in America. A president, like Reagan, can have great formal authority yet not share both the positive attitude toward institutions and the sense of common enterprise with other officeholders that we generally associate with state managers. The editors of major newspapers and leaders of foundations tend to have the attitude without the authority. We suspect that any modern political system involves some disjunction between these two sides of stateness. But the strength of the private sphere, combined with the separation of powers, probably allows less overlap in the United States than in other nations. The deficit furor is a case of formal outsiders telling the holders of authority to start acting more like the state.

The split between authority and attitude in the United States helps explain the peculiar spirit of budget politics: an establishment that sounds extremist. The government, not some interest group, has defied the rules of the game.

In the ideal world of the political center, everybody would sacrifice equally to reduce the budget deficit. However, in the real world, most people are unwilling to pay their fair share of deficit reduction, for the reasonable reason that they would lose more than they would gain. That is why packages, including Gramm-Rudman-Hollings, have always clipped only portions of the budget. Overstated claims about the deficit's horrors should be understood as attempts to convince people that they have more to gain from deficit reduction, and therefore should gladly sacrifice more than they currently believe.

Although it is not unique, the contradiction at the heart of deficit politics is unusually concrete, visible, and difficult to live with. There is no way to reconcile three rules of the game: budget balance (or an approximation thereof), fair shares, and majority rule. No majority can be built that will substantially reduce the deficit without clobbering the minority—something centrists won't do. The center's dream of equal sacrifice has not been approximated, for the simple reason that the benefits of deficit reduction, for most individuals, are less obvious than the costs of paying a fair share.

Therefore, the two key processes of the democratic state have been turned against each other. The public interest as articulated in the realm of the public sphere has been defined as deficit reduction. That has been the most obvious violation and the easiest criticism, and value enforcement by the media is most commonly negative; politicians and economists have fed the criticism. The deficit provides an easy way to keep score. But this definition of the public interest in the public sphere contradicts majority interest represented through the formal procedures of legislation.

Politicians have responded with continual legislative hostage taking, mythical budget resolutions, and a quest for automatic formulas. At its worst, in Gramm-Rudman-Hollings, the deficit panic created a law that either meant nothing or meant that all other budget laws did not count. Nobody could tell. Clear, however, is the quest for automatic government that GRH epitomizes, rejecting the normal processes of government through assembly of majority preferences.

In pursuit of the public interest, the most fundamental rules of the game, those that structure the legislative process, have been put up for grabs. That has been done as much in the name of system maintenance (for a Rudman or Domenici or Chiles) as in pursuit of a minority ideology (Gramm) or a partisan advantage (most legislators, most of the time). The politicians are telling people to ignore laws: if we pass an appropriation, we don't mean it; we promise to reduce the deficit with a sequester, but we don't really mean that either. At worst, the politicians have abandoned the idea that procedures have any value separate from whether they reduce the deficit. Why, then, should anybody accept any decision, ever? Lowi's fears are being realized in an entirely unexpected fashion: instead of formal authority being reduced by the pursuit of special interests, it is being battered by a panic about the public interest.

We do not worry that the governed will be immediately disaffected. The crisis of congressional procedure described in this book is an inside-the-beltway story that the public will, in the main, tune out. Its relevance to daily life is slow and indirect. Furthermore, as David Truman knew, the system is legitimated by the public sphere's continual repetition of its wonders. Celebration of the Constitution in 1987 was but one example. Attention is directed, not to the difference between the existing equilibrium and some ideal, but to the difference between America and other places. America is seen as both more free and more stable than anywhere else. Basic emotions of nationalism and patriotism are linked, not to a land or a people, but to the system of government. The forces generating popular support for the governmental system are very powerful.

Yet we wonder how the governors themselves will ever decide what to do if they lose, as they seem to be losing, their willingness to accept the outcome of decisions made by established procedures. Government requires obedience to formal rules for settling disputes. However, since the mythical budget resolution of 1983, such obedience has diminished.

The course of budgeting suggests that the elites, not the masses, have lost confidence in the rules of the game. Politicians engage in endless rounds of hostage taking; the media, instead of condemning procedural terrorism, say it is okay so long as the deficit is reduced. Apparently there is room in the public sphere for furor about only one aspect of the public interest; the interest in authoritative procedure is crowded out.

The budget deficit is sometimes portrayed as a cancer, eating away at society without being visible on the surface. So, though we are dubious, it may be. Yet the reaction to the deficit resembles an immune reaction run amuck. The body has no way to defend itself against itself, just as at present there is no one to defend the politicians of the center and all those most concerned with preserving the political system against their own attacks on the system. The crisis is a crisis of their own confidence.

There is much difference between theorists who view democracy as being about procedures enabling people to agree on what they can and those who view democracy as being about the attaining of certain substantive ends. When there is a dominant party or faction, these differences may amuse philosophers, but they need not trouble members of the political stratum who justify the procedures because they agree on substance and accept majority rule on substance by accepting the procedures. The battles of the budget evoke reflection on such hitherto arcane matters precisely because the political stratum is divided and the public has not yet decided. The grand irony is that the people could resolve the state's problem by developing consistent preferences. The people could resolve their governors' dilemma: What could be more democratic than that?

The trouble nowadays is that the voice of the people—reduce the deficit but do not undertake drastic measures which may do more harm than good—has been drowned out by the shouts of catastrophe coming from the political stratum. We think "the people" are right; as part of this political stratum ourselves, we next shall develop a policy rationale and a political strategy that would fit their voice.

TWENTY-THREE

Nobody's Darling, but
No One's Disaster Either:
A Moderate Proposal on the Deficit

"Putting on the agony, putting on the style" would be a good theme song for the deficit. First the agony: inflation, deflation, depression; no one will buy from the United States, and no one will sell to it; catastrophe is the one certainty, partly because of bad economic policy and partly because of bad politicians who would not administer the bitter medicine in time.

Next comes the style. There cannot be good news because the deficit won't allow it. Consequently, the business pages are a scream. Rising unemployment would at once be taken as a sign that we were finally paying the price of our deficit irresponsibility. But lower unemployment (a fourteen-year low in July 1988) is supposedly a sure sign that inflation will follow. Hence, stylish headlines abound, all variants of "Economy Improves; Markets Panic."[1] Lower consumer spending (hence higher savings) could signal recession, but higher consumer spending means inflation, trade deficit, and lack of investment. If both bad news and good news are bad, maybe we can blame that, too, on the deficit.

After all the agony and style about the deficit, the government still needs a policy. Common sense requires, first, that we know how we got where we are and why. Our book has tried to answer these questions. Why weren't Congress and the president able to come close to balancing the budget, which everyone swore they wanted to do? For one thing, the problem was too big. Congress did a lot: stopped the defense buildup, passed two substantial tax hikes (mostly on businesses), created a growing Social Security surplus, cut medicare providers, squeezed and then Gramm-Rudmaned the domestic discretionary budget—and big deficits remained. For another thing, many in and outside Congress who feared deficits feared solutions—tax hikes or social security cuts, for example—even more. That is part of the reason that the cold-turkey budget-balancing faction has never had anything like a majority: we need agreement on a specific solution, not on the need for one. There is also dissensus, disputes over deficit reduction being entwined with issues of distribution and the role of government in society. You might say that the participants in budgeting agree on everything except how much revenue should be raised and who should pay, how much should be spent and which programs should benefit. Whether balance is achieved at low or high levels of spending would determine the future shape of our government, and our politicians quite reasonably act as if that is as important as the deficit itself.

The Two Elderly Irishmen and Other Misleading Explanations

Nevertheless, the belief has persisted that the real obstacles preventing balance were not the factors we have mentioned but willful, perverse, and short-sighted politicians. What might be called the "two elderly Irishmen" thesis has held that the ideological extremism and personal intransigence of the two most influential party and institutional leaders, President Reagan and Speaker O'Neill, confounded and suppressed the underlying consensus. Neither the replacement of Representative O'Neill by Representative Wright, the conduct of the 1988 presidential election, the collapse of the National Economic Commission, nor the early rounds of budgeting in 1989 revealed such previously hidden agreement.

Had "Dutch" Reagan been willing to accept tax increases, or had at least not insisted on deep cuts, while manifesting willingness to reduce defense, accommodation on the budget readily could have been achieved. Had "Tip" O'Neill similarly been willing to reduce future social security benefits, agreement would have been much easier. True enough in both cases, but is this truth relevant?

Asking the Speaker to cut social security was like expecting him and his party to open a vein and spill out their political blood. Aside from their deep concern about elderly recipients, social security was and is the preeminent symbol of all they have accomplished and all they believe they stand for: the positive use of government to better the lot of people needing help. Asking Ronald Reagan to accept tax increases as good for the country was the same as telling him to renounce his political career and office, for his most important belief would be judged false. The implication would be that the government is a better judge than individuals of what they should do with their income. Instead of income being left with those who earned more, the Republican constituency, it would go to government, that is, to the Democratic party constituency, to pay off their supporters. Reagan's seemingly simple-minded children's allowance theory (if they haven't got it, they can't spend it) was aimed at weakening, if not formally splitting, the Democratic party. Taxes are hardball.

Ronald Reagan and Tip O'Neill were not outside the mainstream of their political parties. Neither was seriously challenged from within, and each ended his term in office more popular than he began. Their unchallenged supremacy should give pause to those who think of them as somehow deviant.

There is far more truth to the hypothesis that the deficit problem stems from the unwillingness of Americans to pay for what they want. True enough—witness the gap—but that doesn't explain much. An appropriate answer to this smug contention (implying that you are reckless but I am responsible) is, "So what else is new?" People always want more than they can afford; we need to know why the seemingly inevitable deficit result finally occurred after 190 years.

Partisans would argue that the deficit arose from the sins of their opponents. Democrats blame the dishonesty of "Rosy Scenario" and Reagan's irresponsible tax cuts and excessive defense buildup. Republicans blame Democrats' refusal to cut wasteful, poorly targeted, and ineffective social programs. We try not to take sides, but we should point out the effect of the division. If you blame the deficit on somebody else's error, the deficit should be solved by correcting that error. Democrats who believe the deficit was created by raising defense and cutting taxes think it only fair that the shortfall be eliminated by cutting defense and raising taxes. To eliminate the deficit by cutting domestic spending seems, to them, to endorse the original mistake. Republicans feel a deficit created by social spending should be eliminated by cutting social spending. Thus dissensus about the cause adds to the belief that how we eliminate the deficit is a question of justice, of right and wrong, and thus not easy to compromise.

Again, mathematically, both sets of partisans have a point. Either's approach *would* reduce the deficit. But earlier in this book we argued from data that the magnitude of the likely FY1990 deficit, roughly 3 percent of GNP, was caused by the interaction of (1) long-term policy commitments and (2) widely-held views on both the limits of acceptable taxation and the desirability of more defense (a view shared in 1980 by both parties), with (3) unexpected economic changes that slowed economic activity, abruptly halted inflation, and drove up interest costs. Neither party expected the drop in inflation to reduce revenues so drastically; the difference between Democratic and Republican tax plans was less significant than their joint misjudgment of the economy. The politicians managed to return revenues to their historic plateau around 19 percent of GNP, but the interest costs incurred in the interim, and public support for the vast bulk of federal activity, made further deficit reduction difficult. Now who is responsible for that? Everyone and no one.

Perhaps the difficulty is in our budgeting institutions? Institutions do matter: the spending cuts of 1981 would have been much more difficult without reconciliation, and Senate offset procedures somewhat inhibit measures that would increase the deficit. A constitutional amendment might make unbalancing the budget more difficult. But the present problem is how to eliminate a deficit, not how to prevent one. The only institutional solution that might work is one that would cut some large group of people (the elderly, the poor, business, the military) out of the political process so they could then be cut out of the budget. We hope and believe that solution is not available. Otherwise, Gramm-Rudman proved that as long as the same players have power, we will have the same results.

Or maybe the crisis just isn't clear enough. The budget summit of late 1987 is as good proof as anyone could want that the problem isn't a lack of panic. Indeed, everything in it—the pressure of the market after "Black Monday," the exasperation and obfuscation, the ideological hostility, the unwillingness to go beyond a certain amount of pain, the uncertainty about the reality of the semisolid mass of spending cuts and revenues—can be met again simply by inserting one's thumb anywhere in our account of prior battles. The sheer repetitiveness of these events (Didn't I meet you last year in Aggravation City?) is stunning.

Throughout the past decade, apostles of budget "responsibility" among experts, politicians, and the media wanted to believe that the necessity of budget balance constituted an irresistible force, such that eventually they could force the deficit reductions so obviously needed. Our story is filled with examples of mainstream politicians predicting that all congressional incumbents would suffer if they did not do their duty to fix the deficit. Instead, the 1980s were the best decade for incumbents in our nation's history. Or, the markets would force action. After the shocking stock market decline of Black Monday, Tom Kenworthy, in the *Washington Post,* reported that for budget balancers like Representative Buddy MacKay (D-Fla.), "who have been trying to engineer a fiscal crisis all year in order to force a 'grand compromise' on the budget . . . Wall Street's troubles have arrived in the nick of time."[2] But even Black Monday could not help politicians find a package that would eliminate the deficit at what seemed like a reasonable policy cost.

Thus Ronald Reagan was pragmatic enough to enter into negotiations—he would have looked bad otherwise—but such "pragmatism" did not extend to giving up his principles. If he gave in on taxes and defense, then government, he believed, would be intrusive domestically and weak internationally. In his two-decade political career his side had gone from a mocked minority to the White House; if he had frequently bowed to others' sense of pragmatism, he would not have been in office. In government but not of it, President Reagan felt responsible to his supporters, not the moderate state managers. Speaker Jim Wright, in turn, believed his party's values worth fighting for. In the wake of the crash, he tried to influence the summit held by White House and congressional leaders by forcing a Democratic reconciliation package, featuring $12 billion in new revenues, through the House. It was a bruising battle, "a rowdy, vituperative floor fight and a one-vote victory wrung amid Republican charges of vote manipulation." Republican Whip Trent Lott was so mad at the Democratic leaders, he said, "I don't want to talk to them, let alone negotiate."[3] He also blasted the leadership's "Mussolini instinct."[4] This could do little for the bipartisan spirit necessary to budget compromise, but that was only significant if such a spirit existed in the first place. There was some, but not enough for the "irresistible force" of budget necessity to overcome the "immovable objects" of party leaders defending what their parties stood for.

The problem has not been stubborn leaders, the sins of the partisans, the cowardice of politicians, the flaws in our budgeting institutions (at least, not now), the inherent flaws of democracy, or, of all things, insufficient attention to the deficit. The problem has been in the target itself, the balanced budget, and in the policy and political theories of the forces of responsibility who are its strongest proponents.

Sliding By

No bipartisan agreement on how to eliminate the deficit was (or is) in sight. But by late 1987 the parties could agree, even if they could not quite articulate the point, on one thing: the nation's politicians were tired of fighting. More battles among the same players could only yield the same results. With an election coming up, it made sense to avoid trouble by limiting conflict. Besides, the election, by changing players, might break the budget logjam. Therefore the two parties (Republican and Democrat) and institutions (president and Congress) called an election-year truce over the two crucial issues, priorities and the size of the deficit.

The Balanced Budget Reaffirmation Act of 1987, otherwise known as the revised Gramm-Rudman, called for only small deficit reductions in FY89, and the Summit Agreement at the end of the year purported to meet those targets. As part of that agreement the contending parties also agreed on the totals for both defense and domestic discretionary spending for FY89. Good luck on the economy (it grew faster than expected), some artful posturing by the president (condemning the continuing resolution in his 1988 State of the Union address), congressmen's own disgust with budget chaos,[5] and clever accounting (allowing Congress to exceed the summit's discretionary spending target by about $2 billion by redefining what was discretionary) allowed Congress to meet the targets. The National Economic Commission would report after the election; neither party dared suggest serious deficit reductions in an election year; and the budget struggle was put on hold to await the new president. With the big issues settled in advance, Congress and the president managed to pass all the FY89 appropriations separately and on time: it is easy if you accept existing priorities and do not try to reduce the deficit.

The election, however, did nothing to break the logjam. The new president, George Bush, had most of the same commitments ("Read my lips: no new taxes" and a strong defense) as his predecessor, in addition to a few expensive new ones (a kinder, gentler, better educated and drug-free nation). The House and Senate remained solidly controlled by the Democrats. The Gallup poll just before the election found "reducing the federal budget deficit" to be the public's top priority (though it didn't say how).[6] Meanwhile the National Economic Commission, reported to be at an impasse before the election, would prove unable to overcome the conflicts that had shaped deficit politics for a decade. Former Defense secretaries Caspar Weinberger and Donald Rumsfeld argued the military should not be cut to reduce the deficit; AFL-CIO President Lane Kirkland and other Democrats were reported to object to social insurance cuts; there was little talk about taxes.[7] On March 1, 1989, the NEC submitted its report, really two separate reports, one Republican and one Democratic.[8] The two sides agreed that the budget should be balanced *excluding* social security; that is, that the problem was even bigger, over $100 billion bigger, than Gramm-Rudman.[9] Unfortunately but typically, they agreed on nothing else. As budgeting expert Allen Schick put it, "They agreed you have to cut the deficit by $230 billion. The only trouble is, they couldn't agree on where the first billion should come from!"

The NEC having failed, signs pointed to another budget donnybrook in 1989. There seemed no way to meet the Gramm-Rudman targets and no willingness to admit they wouldn't be met. Nearly a whole new team was in place: Richard Darman back in government as OMB director, Leon Panetta as chairman of the House Budget Committee, Senator Jim Sasser (D-Tenn.) chairing Senate Budget, Senator George Mitchell (D-Maine) the new majority leader, and of course a new president, George Bush. All were men of moderation and compromise. Led by the House majority leader Tom Foley (later Speaker after Wright resigned and left Congress), they began extensive negotiations, but there was no way to resolve their deep, substantive disagreements.

When the going gets tough, however, the tough get creative. The only sensible response to the fakery of Gramm-Rudman is more fakery, and that's what the negotiators agreed to. On April 14 they announced agreement on a "framework" for meeting the Gramm-Rudman targets. CBO was projecting a baseline deficit of $147.3 billion for FY90; the negotiators claimed to get just below $100 billion.[10] They accomplished this feat, however, with a remarkable combination of smoke and mirrors. The smoke, Representative Lee Hamilton (D-Ind.) explained, was "optimistic economic assumptions, or what might be called best case budgeting." The mirrors were various "accounting gimmicks" and false agreements. The 1987 revision of Gramm-Rudman, Hamilton pointed out, had created a neat division of labor. Congress gave OMB final authority over the economic forecast because "it is in our interest" to accept the inevitably optimistic forecast. And, make no mistake, it was optimistic: in the Blue Chip survey of thirty-nine private economic forecasts, *none* was as jolly.[11] In this case, the smoke "saved" $19.9 billion.[12]

The mirrors included nearly $11 billion in extremely dubious savings,[13] at least $2 billion from continuing existing policies that were due to expire,[14] $1.6 billion from the perennial lower interest costs and more efficient tax collection, and $5.3 billion in increased revenues. The latter sounded real but wasn't; the administration assumed the money could be raised by lowering capital gains taxes (memories of 1980!), while the chairmen of Senate Finance and House Ways and Means, Senator Bentsen and Representative Rostenkowski, refused to go along.[15] In short, about $20 billion in the agreement, and the subsequent House and Senate budget resolutions, consisted of mirrors, to go with the $19 billion in smoke. Maybe $8 billion was real, and even that looked difficult.

Therefore, the most good anybody could find in the agreement was that it was better than nothing. "The most significant aspect of this agreement," Senator Mitchell declared, "is its existence. No one should be deluded into thinking that this is the end of the process. It is the beginning of the process."[16] As Leon Panetta put it,

> We are not going to adopt new taxes. We are not suddenly going to put [a] major burden on the spending side. We are not going to adopt [the Gramm-Rudman] sequestered budget. What are we left with? We are left with having to work around the edges as we did here. . . . We basically struggled to come up with what savings we could in order to, in a credible way, try to achieve the Gramm-Rudman targets. . . .
>
> The test of how good this agreement is will be how good the next agreement is. That is really what we are facing in terms of goals that we have outlined in this budget resolution.[17]

In other words, as summarized by a number of congressmen, "Wait till next year."

The obvious question was, "Why should next year be any different?" Well, maybe George Bush would figure his campaign promise not to raise taxes expired after a year. Or, the trust built in sliding by the FY90 Gramm-Rudman target together would help Congress and the president to confront the *really* impossible FY91 target of a $64 billion deficit. If politics only were a matter of politicians who liked each other ignoring principles and constituencies, of course, you wouldn't be reading this book.

It is common to call for tough choices. And choosing is, indeed, required. But a choice is tough only because both sides are equally (un)attractive. Those who call for toughness think only one choice, balance, is acceptable. Would that it were so, for then choice would be easy.

Defending what even Representative Panetta called the "slide-by" FY90 budget resolution, Representative Lynn Martin (R-Ill.), a loyal Republican and hardly a "spender," nicely described the difficulties she and her colleagues faced:

> Mr. Speaker, let's face it. No matter how we make our budgets, somebody is going to feel left out, frustrated, angered, and resentful. In fact, as the former acting ranking Republican on the Budget Committee, I can testify to the thankless task budgeting is. Not only can't you please everybody; you actually manage to anger everybody in one way or another. Either you are spending too much on defense or too little; and you are always slighting the hundreds of underfunded domestic needs programs. When you are slicing up such a limited pie to begin with, everybody goes home hungry and angry.[18]

We have said it before; it must be said again: the deficit is high because reducing it will have serious adverse consequences for virtually everybody, and therefore for the country as a whole. Until that fact is faced; until politicians, the media, and the public admit that the difficulty is not a lack of courage or insidious "special" interests dominating the "public" interest, debate will remain distorted and unproductive.

What Would We Do?

We, like all Americans, are not separate from the participants in the budget war but integral to it, part of the problem. For we are no more agreed on the size and scope of government than are other politically active Americans. But we can suggest a far more productive approach to the deficit dilemma.

We have emphasized throughout this book that a problem cannot be considered separate from its possible solutions. Policy analysis is not just the craft of finding solutions to problems; it is the art of choosing problems that have solutions. Thinking of policy analysis as the art of the solvable, we come closer to a productive approach to the deficit.

Something should be done, we think, for two reasons. In view of all the uncertainty, first, the nation would do well to limit its risk. Bad times may be in store, as in the past, and a lower deficit would make such times easier to handle. Because many people, including many members of the political stratum, consider deficit reduction vital, they should be placated. How? In part by reducing the deficit and in part by redefining reduction. We would set a target for the deficit that (1) reduced economic risks yet (2) could be reached.

Redefining the Deficit

After all the analysis and argument of the last decade, we cannot see that the economic arguments for budget balance justify the losses in either government or private activity that would be imposed by spending cuts and tax hikes big enough to eliminate the deficit in a few years. The short-term economic evils ascribed to the deficit keep failing to appear. In the long term, the deficit is more a symptom than a cause of any dangerous trends. Since 1973 the entire industrialized West has been going through a painful period of adjustment; Americans have had deficits while Europeans have had unemployment. Many other things have been going on: the international debt crisis; declining prices for third world nations' commodities; the challenge of lower wages in newly industrializing countries to American and European basic industries; a monetary system beyond any government's control. We worry about productivity growth when we don't even know how to measure productivity in the expanding service sector of the economy. If the long-term health of our economy is our concern, we should be thinking far more about these problems and far less about the deficit.

All other things being equal, we would be better off without the deficit. National savings, and thus investment and eventually productivity, might be higher.[19] Foreign money managers might be less nervous—if they did not find something else to be nervous about. In this or any other world, however, we would also be better off with a stronger national defense, housing for the homeless, rebuilt bridges and roads and aqueducts and sewers. A balanced budget is just one of many desirable goals. The nation has lived with deficits for most of the postwar era, a time of unprecedented prosperity.

Therefore the real questions are whether there is a level of deficit with which we cannot live, and what we have to do to ensure that we stay below that level. Because the macroeconomics of the deficit are unclear, we turn to ordinary economics.

No household wants to be in a position where its debt feeds on itself, that is, where interest expenses consume a growing portion of household income. Each dollar for interest is a dollar foregone for some useful task. At the national level, a growing interest bill means that each year's tax dollar buys fewer and fewer new services, as more goes to pay for old government. Running deficits that promise growing interest payments later may be justified by a crisis, such as war or depression. In such times, keeping the nation alive to face future burdens is more vital than avoiding those burdens. But we are not in such a crisis now. Therefore, at a minimum, we believe the interest burden should be brought under control, and preferably set on a downward path.

By FY89, according to CBO's January 1989 report, net interest, at $169 billion, was bigger than the deficit itself ($155 billion). It would grow to $203 billion by FY93, while the deficit, if policy stuck to the baseline, would decline to $129 billion. These numbers show why interest is such a problem for the federal household. Even with this growth, however, interest would decline from 3.3 percent of GNP to 3.1 percent. The deficit itself would decline from 3.0 percent to 2.0 percent of GNP.[20] Thus given the mediocre economic performance incorporated into the CBO baseline, neither interest costs nor the deficit seem so horribly out of control.

So where's the problem? The difficulty is that all the uncertainties go the wrong way. The CBO baseline assumes no real growth in discretionary programs. Yet the nation is highly unlikely to go five years with both no real growth in defense and the same force structure and obligations; the dollars and structure don't fit. We don't know which will change—maybe peace will break out all over and maybe not—but we know the baseline won't work. When Republicans talk about "hundreds of underfunded" domestic programs and get elected by promising a "kinder and gentler" nation, we suspect the domestic discretionary baseline may also be tough to maintain. Further, the economic assumptions, while moderate, could still be optimistic. It is always possible that foreigners who have been lending in the United States will start demanding higher interest rates for their money.

Some deficit reduction, therefore, is worthwhile. It should be enough to maintain control of the deficit and interest costs under less favorable economic assumptions than CBO's. If taken, this action might enable prediction of a balanced budget a few years beyond the Gramm-Rudman target, *but it should be neither sold nor conceived in these terms.* Rather, it should be conceived as a way of preventing the worst when we don't know what is best. And *it should be sold as balance, balance between our ability to pay and payments due.*

In Chapter 21 we discussed the difficulty of a $100 billion deficit reduction in FY90, a minimal definition of the policy cost of hitting the Gramm-Rudman targets. What would have happened, however, if we aimed for $50 billion in policy change, $30 billion in FY90, and $20 billion in FY91? We talk in terms of FY90 and FY91 but, at the rate things were going in May 1989, as we wrote, our readers could insert whatever the next two budget years might be. The details will change, but the major consequences should not.

We would phase in the reductions because many policies take time to put into effect and because it is desirable to minimize any fiscal shock to the economy. Assuming there was no such shock, so that the economy performed as projected by CBO at the beginning of 1989, our suggestion would cut the FY93 deficit in half, to just above $60 billion. That would be less than one percent of GNP, well below deficit levels in the 1970s and average for the 1960s. Interest costs, which depend more on old than new debt, would be affected less dramatically, but still would be about $10 billion lower in FY93.

These policy changes would be enough to more than compensate if growth were to be half a percent of GNP lower, per year, than CBO projected, beginning in January of 1989.[21] The deficit in FY93 would still be significantly less than 2 percent of GNP, that is, below the trend line in the CBO baseline. Therefore a $50 billion package would provide a substantial margin of error to protect against economic bad news.

This target will not satisfy those who believe budget deficits should be eliminated, no matter what. It certainly will not satisfy economists who want to run a surplus by balancing the federal funds budget, spending excluding social security. But if our proposal will not satisfy them, neither will anything else they have a snowball's chance in Hades of getting. Their standard would require about $230 billion in deficit reductions in FY93.[22] That is equivalent to 40 percent of all domestic and defense discretionary spending, or nearly a 40 percent increase in income tax receipts. That kind of policy change is impossible, short of revolution. Given reasonable economic assumptions, the federal funds budget cannot be balanced in the foreseeable future.

Some budget sophisticates say privately that the real point of such unrealistic targets is to get as much savings as possible. Deficit-reducers, like program advocates, use the tactic of the high bid. Then if the politicians meet them half way, they might be satisfied. Economists and budgeteers seem especially prone to that tactic these days, as they tend to believe the rhetoric that politicians always compromise the public interest on behalf of special interests. By this logic, politicians must be scared or bamboozled into doing enough.

We disagree. If we want our readers to remember one single thing from this book, it is that such an understanding of politics and politicians, in deficit politics, has done far more harm than good. Politicians have tried very hard to eliminate the deficit. They have been stymied by legitimate disagreements about the national interest and by the overwhelming size of the task. But reductions also are made more difficult because, so long as only an impossible target is considered acceptable, there is no reward for doing less, even if it is real and helpful. As one senator asked, "Why should I go through all this pain and trouble to get the deficit from $175 billion to $150 billion?" Why, indeed? If a $25 billion cut in the deficit is a pittance, leaving us, by the extreme definition of responsibility, over $200 billion away from what is desired, why suffer the policy and political consequences of $25 billion worth of pain? It is better to "game" Gramm-Rudman, claiming to do more (for we are "on the track" of the Gramm-Rudman "plan") but actually doing less.

Centrist politicians have called for deficit reductions in which all parties paid their "fair share." Naturally all the affected interests have resisted, for the policy rewards of deficit reduction seemed too distant and dubious to be worth the immediate pain. Worse yet, giving in once could only be taken as a sign of weakness, making one's priorities a target in the next round. Thus President Reagan could figure that if he gave in on taxes one year, the deficit cutters would be back again the next year—as they were. Tip O'Neill knew the same about social security, Cap Weinberger about the defense budget, federal employees about their pensions, ad infinitum.

People are sometimes willing to end a battle, even on disadvantageous terms, because the struggle itself is so painful. Peace is its own reward. Yet so long as each year's battle has only been one round in a seemingly endless fight, compromise could not provide peace.

Transforming a Futile Budget Politics

We want to brighten budget politics by providing the politicians a reward: if they take the recommended action, a $50 billion, real, no-fooling package, the deficit crisis will be solved. "Do this and we won't bother you again," our refrain would be; "then you can get on to the rest of the task of governing." Interest groups would get a similar reward; increases would still be difficult, but they would be freed from endless battles to protect their programs.

The deficit reductions would have to be enacted in one package—no magic asterisks—and the political leadership, especially the president and the chairman of the Federal Reserve, would have to make very clear that, if the economy did worse than our pessimistic economic scenario, further deficit reductions would not be appropriate. If any deficit reductions were left to later years, participants would lose part of their reward: a clear limit on losses. If nominal deficit figures were made the target, as in Gramm-Rudman, the government would again become hostage to the economy's swings. Politicians could not be sure of their safety.

Immediate action and certainty about goals are the proper response to financial markets' supposed fears. Credibility, if it can be won at all, requires performance. Performance would also encourage foreign governments and central banks to support U.S. policy; they do not want to base their actions (buying dollars, pumping up their own economies) on promises. Clarity of purpose and standards is the best defense against market panics.

Governments should not calibrate their annual budgets to short-term swings of financial markets. It is a bad way to manage agencies and a worse way to manage markets. A government should try to minimize fluctuations by limiting speculation; changing policy frequently only encourages speculation about it. A government must try to sell its interpretation of the world. If it wants allies to agree, it must show that it is sure of its own policies, not about to pull the rug out from under those who go along.

The federal government cannot control the markets, but it can try to create circumstances in which individuals hesitate to bet against the government. A consistent and coherent and practical policy, supported by the Federal Reserve and our allies, is the best defense against such bets.

Any display of resolve behind a policy that most market participants considered a disaster probably would fail. Of course, nobody knows what markets really want. Still, few analysts would choose to risk bigger deficit reductions than we are suggesting in the short term. A $50 billion package would lower the deficit to levels where there is no rational argument for panic. As a display of will it would be impressive, the biggest deficit reduction in memory. The markets might still panic, but you cannot guard against irrationality.

Public opinion may never approve of unbalanced budgets. For this reason, many politicians might be scared to endorse our proposal. Public opinion, however, is not the real cause of the budget deficit panic. The public views the deficit as one of many evils. The general trend of the economy, as both polls and elections show, is far more important. The budget deficit panic is mainly a phenomenon of the public sphere, national experts and news organizations and politicians themselves excoriating our elected representatives for their supposed lack of courage.

This book is our attempt to use reason against that panic of the center. We can do less about the fact that the struggle over deficits involves basic values about the role of government in our society. Believers in less government may never accept a solution that leaves government bigger than they prefer, nor should they be expected to do so. They will invoke any consensual, "public interest" notions they can in support of their beliefs. We ourselves disagree about the proper size of government, so must believe ideological differences are legitimate. But such differences should not be confused with response to a crisis of the economy or of governance.

Only if the public interest is defined as acts that are not in the interest of any substantial segment of the public would the clamor for budget balance above all other values make sense. The untold story of the deficit is that the political stratum has transformed a middle-sized, complicated problem into a moral test, leading to a policy panic that most Americans, by contrast, have had sense enough to avoid. Group-think on the deficit has led economists, editorial writers, and politicians to set impossible standards, demoralizing themselves, delegitimizing their procedures, feeding whatever fears may whip through those mysterious financial markets. Ignoring the policy and political lessons of the past decade, the forces of responsibility unwittingly increase our economic and political risk.

Whatever one thinks of the Reagan era, one thing is clear. The debate and politics of the deficit have been among the most stultifying experiences in our political history. From one year to the next we heard the same arguments, fought the same battles, prophesied the same doom. Nobody seems to have learned anything. Politicians of the right and left have so much fun beating one another over the head with the deficit that they cannot put it down. Besides, their heads hurt too much to think straight. Politicians of the center have come to see the deficit as a symbol of their own inadequacy. Having made elimination of the deficit the test of their ability to govern, they have come to see the deficit as a crisis because they cannot solve it, not because of any harm it causes. If that seems harsh, just listen to how they talk about their failure to eliminate the deficit.

The deficit has become an all-purpose weapon, used to oppose or support virtually any position. This is bad policy and worse analysis; it has paralyzed our political system. Fixated on the deficit, we ignore other questions. Do we want more savings or more job training? Should we forget about full employment, define it as what we have already achieved, or try to lower unemployment further? What is a sensible defense policy—as opposed to a convenient way to fit into Gramm-Rudman? What is, or should be, our place in the world economy?

Until we end the deficit "crisis," we cannot even ask these and other questions. $50 billion will be very difficult, but possible. It should be enough. Let's do it and start thinking about other problems.

NOTES

Chapter One

1. Office of Management and Budget, "Federal Government Finances: 1985 Budget Data," typescript, February 1984, p. 99. This is an unpublished but available to the public summary of historical statistics produced to supplement each year's budget. It has since been replaced by a published volume, *Historical Statistics*.

2. Ibid., pp. 97–99. Estimated as "relatively uncontrollable under present law: open-ended programs and fiscal costs."

3. Donald Axelrod, *Budgeting for Modern Government* (New York: St. Martin's Press, 1988).

4. No. 58, *The Federalist Papers* (New York: New American Library, 1961), p. 359.

5. In the cases the president cited, according to the report on the Agriculture appropriation, the research was in New Jersey, Michigan, Louisiana, and New Mexico.

6. The American revolutionaries insisted on the absolute nature of the power of the purse because they had seen how George III used his personal wealth and patronage to buy members of Parliament, thus corrupting and dominating the legislature. Modern members of Congress may not be aware of that history, but they are well aware of the uses of patronage in state and local political machines, such as Mayor Daley's Chicago. The power of the purse is therefore inextricably mixed with the everyday struggles of low politics. In a talk at the Brookings Institution in 1986, one leader of House liberals, David Obey (D-Wis.), quoted a leading conservative, Mickey Edwards (R-Okla.), on the nonpartisan subject of presidential discretion. "Imagine," Obey quoted Representative Edwards, "Lyndon Johnson with an item veto!" Obey then recounted an imaginary conversation: LBJ explained how thoroughly he understood Obey's desire for a community health clinic in a small northern Wisconsin town and how much that town needed the clinic but how badly he needed Obey's support for administration policy in Vietnam. Most legislators would like to avoid such situations, or at least have the upper hand.

7. The new Gramm-Rudman requires an earlier release, but the earlier release of the budget hasn't happened.

8. Frederick C. Mosher, *A Tale of Two Agencies* (Baton Rouge: Louisiana State University Press, 1984), p. 25.

9. Ibid., pp. 27–32; esp. p. 28.

10. The appropriations committees stayed within the president's totals partly because of a strong norm of economy—if they weren't there to make cuts, why have committees? Richard Fenno's *The Power of the Purse* (Boston: Little, Brown, 1966) is the classic work on appropriations norms. But one also must suspect more informal coordination than was visible—or so veteran staff and members report today.

11. Fenno, *Power of the Purse.* Joseph White's research on the House committee confirms this picture.

12. The foreign aid bill, Foreign Operations, is the exception that proves the rule of legislation passage: it often has to be packaged with something more popular. Nobody outside D.C. cares much about either the District of Columbia or legislative branch bills, but Congress, of course, does.

13. See Aaron Wildavsky, *The Politics of the Budgetary Process,* 1st ed. (Boston: Little, Brown, 1964); the revolution that has overtaken budgeting is described in a successor volume, *The New Politics of the Budgetary Process* (Glenview, Ill.: Scott, Foresman/Little, Brown, 1988).

14. "FY71." The federal government, like many businesses, operates on a fiscal year that differs from the calendar year. Until the Budget Act was passed, the fiscal year ran from July 1 through June 30; that is, fiscal 1971 began on July 1, 1970. The Budget Act began the year three months later, giving Congress and the president three more months to pass the necessary legislation before the year began. Thus, in 1988 they were considering the budget for FY89, beginning October 1, 1988.

15. See, in particular, Allen Schick, *Congress and Money* (Washington, D.C.: Urban Institute, 1980); and Gary Orfield, *Congressional Power: Congress and Social Change* (New York: Harcourt Brace Jovanovich, 1975).

16. Schick, *Congress and Money,* p. 48.

17. Ibid.

18. The new budget process worked as described here until the Supreme Court, in the *Chadha* decision, outlawed the legislative veto mechanism at its heart. If the president wished not to spend appropriated funds, he could propose a *rescission*; if he wished only to delay the spending, he had to propose a *deferral*. For a rescission to take effect, both houses had to pass a bill approving the change within forty-five legislative days of its proposal. If they did not do so, the money would be spent as appropriated. A deferral would take effect automatically, but it would last no longer than through the end of the fiscal year. Either house could reject the deferral with a vote specifically disapproving it. The procedure exploited the difficulty of congressional action. Rescission, the more serious policy change, was made highly unlikely by requiring positive action by both houses; deferral, the lesser change, was allowed to occur, but either house could choose by majority vote to enforce the appropriation legislation. Thus impound-

ment could be used when the need for spending had disappeared or been delayed, but the president could not use it to challenge Congress's priorities.

19. The first year of the new budget process, 1975 for FY76, formally a dry run, was taken surprisingly seriously.

Chapter Two

1. Timothy B. Clark, "Carter's Election-Year Budget—Something for Practically Everyone," *National Journal*, February 2, 1980, p. 187.

2. See Council of Economic Advisers, *Economic Indicators*, February 1981 (Washington, D.C.: U.S. Government Printing Office, 1981).

3. George H. Gallup, *The Gallup Poll: Public Opinion 1979* (Wilmington, Dela.: Scholarly Resources, 1980), pp. 278–79. Gallup publishes a volume each year that summarizes major survey results in chronological order. This was Survey #141-G, reported November 15, 1979.

4. There is no other way to make sense of his choices. For his own testimony, see Jimmy Carter, *Keeping Faith* (New York: Bantam Books, 1982), pp. 21, 73, 77, in which he mentions how he disagreed with liberals when he took office. Also see Steven R. Weisman, "With New Budget Due Today, McIntyre Gains as a Carter Aide," *New York Times*, January 28, 1980, pp. Al, D11.

5. "Post Interviews Kennedy, Brown," *Washington Post*, January 20, 1980, pp. Al, A8.

6. George H. Gallup, *The Gallup Poll: Public Opinion 1980* (Wilmington, Delaware: Scholarly Resources, 1981), Survey #150-G, Reported March 30, 1980, pp. 72–79.

7. *Gallup Poll, 1979*, Survey #142-G, Reported December 16, 1979, pp. 289–90.

8. James Fallows, "Is It All Carter's Fault?" *Atlantic Monthly*, October 1980, p. 47.

9. Albert R. Hunt, "Do Pollsters—and Iowa—Confirm a GOP Tide?" *Wall Street Journal*, January 24, 1980, p. 20.

10. President's message, excerpted in *New York Times*, January 29, 1980, p. B9.

11. Timothy B. Clark, "Carter's Election-Year Budget—Something for Practically Everyone," *National Journal*, February 2, 1980, p. 176; "Learning to Love Stagflation?" p. 16, and "It's a long way to October," pp. 29–30, in *The Economist*, February 2, 1980.

12. John M. Berry, "Creating Economic Slack Cornerstone of Policy," *Washington Post*, January 31, 1980, pp. D9–D10.

13. Robert J. Samuelson, "The CEA's Economic Report Is Filled with Uncertainties," *National Journal*, February 2, 1980, p. 182. See also Berry, "Creating Economic Slack," *Washington Post*, January 31, 1980; and Steven Rattner, "The Risky Politics of Recession," *New York Times Magazine*, May 11, 1980, pp. 20–23, 28, 78–79, 82–83.

14. "Learning to Love Stagflation?" *The Economist*, February 2, 1980, p. 16.

15. "A Budget of Two Big———," *Time*, February 4, 1980, pp. 66–67.

16. "The Unbalanced Budget," *Newsweek*, February 4, 1980, pp. 59–60.

17. "Imprudent and Irresponsible," editorial, *Wall Street Journal,* January 29, 1980, p. 18 (emphasis added).

18. Harry Anderson, with Rich Thomas, "No Economic Miracles," *Newsweek,* February 11, 1980, p. 75.

19. Steven Rattner, "Economists Say Carter's Budget Plans Are Unrealistic," *New York Times,* February 25, 1980, p. A15. Also "The Hesitant Recession," *Time,* February 28, 1980, pp. 76–78.

20. "America's bond market crash," *The Economist,* March 8, 1980, pp. 12–13.

21. Lindley B. Richert, "Yields for Long-Term Obligations of U.S. Rise Decidedly Above 11% for the First Time," *Wall Street Journal,* January 30, 1980, p. 33.

22. "The world feels worse after Doctor Volcker's physic," *The Economist,* February 23, 1980, p. 89.

23. Daniel Hertzberg, "Troubled Houses," *Wall Street Journal,* February 22, 1980, p. 1.

24. Isadore Barmash, "Economists Back Fed's Rate Rise, But Some Worry That Inflation Won't Respond," *New York Times,* February 18, 1980, pp. D1, D3.

25. Steven Rattner, "Volcker Discloses Goals for 1980 Money Growth," *New York Times,* February 20, 1980, pp. D1, D9.

26. Art Pine, "White House Aides Debate Budget Cuts In War on Inflation," *Washington Post,* February 26, 1980, p. A5.

27. Ibid.

28. "A Lever Against Inflation," editorial, *Washington Post,* February 24, 1980, p. B6.

29. "The Case For a New, and Balanced, Budget," editorial, *New York Times,* February 28, 1980, A22.

30. Harry Anderson et al., "Fighting the Inflation 'Crisis,' " *Newsweek,* March 10, 1980, pp. 24–26.

31. Ibid.

32. Steven Rattner, "Anti-Inflation Plan Aims at Psychology," *New York Times,* March 2, 1980, p. L29.

33. Art Pine and John M. Berry, "Carter's Economists Seeking To Balance Budget for 1981," *Washington Post,* March 4, 1980, pp. A1, A4.

34. Richard J. Levine and Robert W. Merry, "Carter's Plan May Calm Markets but Won't Be Quick Fix for Inflation," *Wall Street Journal,* March 10, 1980, p. 1.

35. Ibid., p. 19.

36. Jerry Knight, "U.S. Won't Pay Farmers To Plant Smaller Crops," *Washington Post,* March 1, 1980, p. A6.

37. Harry Anderson et al., "Carter's Attack on Inflation," *Newsweek,* March 24, 1980, pp. 24–30.

38. Steven Rattner, "Carter's Proposal to Curb Inflation Accepts Increase in Rate of Jobless," *New York Times,* March 9, 1980, pp. 1, 31.

39. Martin Tolchin, "Budget Conferees in a Balancing Act," *New York Times,* March 12, 1980, p. A11.

40. Our discussion of these negotiations is based on interviews and articles. See Art Pine, "$11 Billion in Cuts Is Agreed On," March 11, 1980, and "Options

Narrowed as Time to Unveil Inflation Plan Nears," March 12, 1980, *Washington Post*; Steven Rattner, "U.S. Weighs Oil Fee as Aid for Budget," March 11, 1980, and "Group in Congress Hears Budget Cuts of Over $11 Billion," March 13, 1980, *New York Times*; and Martin Tolchin, "Budget Conferees in a Balancing Act," *New York Times*, March 12, 1980, p. A11.

41. Art Pine, "Hill Office Estimates '81 Budget Deficit of $24 Billion or More," *Washington Post*, March 6, 1980, p. A8.

42. Steven Rattner, "Carter Plan is Due Today on Economy; 10¢ Gas Rise Likely," *New York Times*, March 14, 1980, p. Al.

43. See, for example, John Osborne, "Your Friendly Budget," *The New Republic*, February 2, 1980, pp. 7–9; "It's a long way to October," *The Economist*, February 2, 1980, pp. 29–30.

44. See articles by George C. Wilson, "President Sparing the Pentagon From Budget Scissors," March 5, 1980, p. A4, and "Pentagon Budget Is Stretched Out," March 15, 1980, p. Al3, *Washington Post*.

45. Martin Tolchin, "Caution in Congress," *New York Times*, March 15, 1980, p. Al, A35.

46. William Greider, *Secrets of the Temple: How the Federal Reserve Runs the Country* (New York: Simon and Schuster, 1987), p. 183.

47. Ibid., p. 185.

Chapter Three

1. See Martin Tolchin, "O'Neill Attacks Balanced Budget As Other Democrats Pursue Cuts," *New York Times*, March 6, 1980, pp. Al, Al7.

2. Timothy B. Clark, "Carter takes aim at deeper cuts in '81 budget," *National Journal*, March 8, 1980, pp. 409–10.

3. Timothy B. Clark, "Defense Spending: Something Has to Give," *National Journal*, May 17, 1980, p. 805. According to former Defense Secretary Melvin Laird, 60 percent of army recruits in 1979 fell below the national average for intelligence. Moreover, the number of noncommissioned officers who remained in the services plummeted.

4. Timothy Clark and Richard E. Cohen, "Balancing the Budget a Test for Congress—Can It Resist the Pressures to Spend?" *National Journal*, April 12, 1980, pp. 588–91, 593–94; *Congressional Quarterly Almanac 1980*, Vol. 36, 1980 (Washington, D.C.: Congressional Quarterly Inc., 1981), p. 111 (hereafter *CQA 1980*).

5. Giaimo had become very worried about the deficit. After he retired, he founded a lobbying group, the Committee for a Responsible Federal Budget, and throughout 1980 took a hard line against social spending.

6. See Barbara Sinclair, *Majority Leadership in the U.S. House of Representatives* (Baltimore: Johns Hopkins University Press, 1981), p. 182.

7. Clark and Cohen, "Balancing the Budget a Test for Congress," *National Journal*, April 12, 1980.

8. *CQA 1980*, p. 111; Art Pine and Peter Behr, "House Unit Votes To Slash Budget By $16.4 Billion," *Washington Post*, March 21, 1980, pp. Al, A2.

9. *CQA 1980*, p. 110.

10. Ibid., p. 111.

11. Art Pine, "Republicans Seek Sharper Spending Cuts," *Washington Post,* March 30, 1980, p. A7.

12. See Sinclair, *Majority Leadership,* esp. p. 184; *CQA 1980,* p. 114; and Merrill Sheils et al., "Heading for a Classic Bust?" *Newsweek,* April 14, 1980, pp. 77, 83.

13. Sinclair, *Majority Leadership,* p. 184; *CQA 1980,* p. 114.

14. Ibid.

15. *CQA 1980,* pp. 112–14; Helen Dewar, "Price Support for Tobacco Feeds Sacred Senate Cow," April 3, 1980, p. A4, and "Budget Panel Would Slash Bureaucracy," April 4, 1980, pp. A1, A4, *Washington Post.*

16. *CQA 1980,* pp. 108–19.

17. *CQA 1980,* p. 118.

18. Sinclair, *Majority Leadership,* p. 185; *CQA 1980,* p. 118. We will never know whether the contradictory votes occurred because some Democrats went home after the budget resolution was defeated or because members really did not support any resolution. If everybody had been there, the vote on Latta's motion should have been very close; fifty-eight Democrats supported Latta as it was, so he had to have a good chance of winning.

19. Allen Schick, *Reconciliation and the Congressional Budget Process* (Washington, D.C.: American Enterprise Institute, 1981), p. 7.

20. Congressional Budget and Impoundment Control Act of 1974, Section 301(b)(2), as amended.

21. *Congressional Quarterly Almanac 1979,* Vol. 35 (Washington, D.C.: Congressional Quarterly Inc., 1980), p. 181 (hereafter *CQA 1979*).

22. *Congressional Record,* May 7, 1980, p. HR10159.

23. Ibid., pp. HR10157–58.

24. Ibid., p. HR10173.

25. Ibid.

26. Ibid., p. HR10165.

27. Ibid., p. HR10167.

28. Ibid., p. HR10168.

29. Ibid., p. HR10174.

30. Ibid.

31. Ibid., p. HR10176. David Obey argued they should reconcile to call the budget balancers' bluff, showing by example that balance wouldn't help.

32. Sheils, "Heading for a Classic Bust?"

33. "Turmoil on the Money Front," *Time,* March 31, 1980, p. 48.

34. David Pauly et al., "The Credit Crunch Is On," *Newsweek,* March 31, 1980, pp. 52–56. See also "American Cars: Carter's No Help," *The Economist,* July 12, 1980, pp. 70–71.

35. Ibid.

36. Harry Anderson et al., "Gauging the Depth of the Slump," *Newsweek,* May 5, 1980, pp. 75, 77.

37. Ibid.

38. Helen Dewar, "Senate Opens Debate on '81 Spending," *Washington Post,* May 6, 1980, p. A16.

39. "Budget Boilerplate and Restraint," editorial, *Washington Post*, May 5, 1980, p. A20.

40. Joanne Omang, "Welfare Plans in Danger in 1981, Byrd Predicts," *Washington Post*, May 4, 1980, p. A18.

41. Richard J. Levine, Robert W. Merry, and Brooks Jackson, "Slump's Shadow," *Wall Street Journal*, May 2, 1980, pp. 1, 25.

42. *Gallup Poll, 1980*, Survey #151-G, Reported April 8 and April 10, 1980, pp. 83–95.

43. Ibid.; and Allan Mayer et al., "Reagan's Crossovers," *Newsweek*, April 14, 1980, p. 27.

44. *Gallup Poll, 1980*, Chronology Section, pp. l–liii.

45. "The Bad News Gets Worse," *Time*, June 16, 1980, pp. 64–65.

46. Ibid.

47. Helen Dewar, "Recession May Unravel the Budget Congress Forged, Causing New Woes," *Washington Post*, June 15, 1980, p. A14.

48. *Time*, June 16, 1980, p. 18, "Yahoo! Congress bars a gas tax."

49. See Nelson Polsby and Aaron Wildavsky, *Presidential Elections*, 7th ed. (New York: Free Press, 1988).

50. Edwin Warner, "Marketable Baskets of Issues," *Time*, August 25, 1980, pp. 28–29.

51. See Bernard Asbell, *The Senate Nobody Knows* (Baltimore: Johns Hopkins University Press, 1978), various passages, on how Senator Muskie came to oppose jobs spending.

52. "An Unemployment Wallop," *Time*, May 12, 1980, pp. 54–55. See also Asbell, *Senate Nobody Knows*; Harry Anderson et al., "Out of Work: Who's Next?" *Newsweek*, June 16, 1980, pp. 69–70; "The Budget Resolution," editorial, *Washington Post*, June 13, 1980, p. A18 (among many); and the comments of Carter's supposedly most liberal adviser, Stuart Eisenstadt, *National Journal*, May 17, 1980, p. 805.

53. Sinclair, *Majority Leadership*, p. 187.

54. Allan Mayer et al., "Reagan's Tax-Cut Ploy," *Newsweek*, July 7, 1980, p. 20.

55. Art Pine, "Jittery Senate Democrats Rush Own Tax Cut," *Washington Post*, June 27, 1980, pp. A1, A4.

56. Ibid.

57. Ibid.

58. "Opening the Tax Battle," *Time*, July 7, 1980, pp. 8–9.

59. Walter Heller, "Piercing the Budgetary Fog," *Wall Street Journal*, June 30, 1980, p. 12.

60. "Two for the Tax Cut Seesaw," editorial, *Washington Post*, June 7, 1980, p. A14.

61. "Opening the Tax Battle," *Time*, July 7, 1980.

62. Carter, *Keeping Faith*, p. 539.

63. Ibid., pp. 540, 541.

64. John M. Berry, "Surplus Evaporates—$25–30 Billion Deficit Seen," *Washington Post*, July 15, 1980, pp. A1, A6.

65. Carter, *Keeping Faith*, pp. 540–41.

66. John M. Berry, "Recession, Defense Seen Widening '80 Deficit to $61 billion," *Washington Post*, July 22, 1980, pp. F1, F5.

67. *Gallup Poll, 1980*, p. 159.

68. David S. Broder, "A Bleak Projection for the President," *Washington Post*, August 9, 1980, p. A5.

69. Kenneth H. Bacon, "Carter's Programs," *Wall Street Journal*, August 29, 1980, p. 1.

70. Kenneth H. Bacon, "A Big Role for Uncle Sam," *Wall Street Journal*, September 3, 1980, p. 22.

71. See ibid.; "An Economic Dream in Peril," *Newsweek*, September 8, 1980, pp. 50–52; and Herbert Stein, "Beyond the Reagan Tax Cut," *Wall Street Journal*, November 25, 1980, p. 22.

72. Helen Dewar, "Senate Budget Unit Rejects Tax Cut in 1981 Spending Plan," *Washington Post*, August 22, 1980, p. A5. Also, interviews.

73. *CQA 1980*, p. 120.

74. Lindley H. Clarke, Jr., "Recession's End?" *Wall Street Journal*, September 15, 1980, pp. 1, 18.

75. Christopher Byron, "Slow Rebound from Recession," *Time*, Sept. 29, 1980, pp. 56–58.

76. Greider, *Secrets of the Temple*, p. 194.

77. Ibid., p. 204.

78. Ibid., pp. 193–213.

79. "Cautious Optimism: Many Executives Say Slump Is Over, but See Only a Slow Recovery," *Wall Street Journal*, October 22, 1980, pp. 1, 24.

80. Greider, *Secrets of the Temple*, pp. 214–18; and Kenneth H. Bacon, "Ready Reserve: Fed Vowing to Retain 'Tight Money' Policies, Prepares for Criticism," *Wall Street Journal*, August 4, 1980, pp. 1, 11.

81. Kenneth H. Bacon, "Reducing the Heat: Better Economic News Helps Smother Flames of Fed-Carter Dispute," *Wall Street Journal*, October 6, 1980, pp. 1, 17.

82. *CQA 1980*, p. 90.

83. Helen Dewar, "Hill May Put Off Voting On Money Till After Election," *Washington Post*, September 18, 1980, p. A15; and *CQA 1980*, pp. 170–71.

84. Previously the government let employees work and then passed appropriations in time for their payday. Civiletti ruled that work created an obligation and thus spending, before the outlay; hence, appropriations had to precede employment. But he let this new rule slide in areas where immediate consequences might be truly dire (e.g., the military).

85. Helen Dewar, "Abortion Compromise Leads to Restoration of U.S. Spending," *Washington Post*, October 2, 1980, p. A2; and Dewar, "Senate Moving Sluggishly Toward Stop-Gap Funding," *Washington Post*, September 27, 1980, p. A12.

86. Helen Dewar, "Lame-Duck Session on Budget Foreseen," *Washington Post*, August 1, 1980, p. A11. *CQA 1980*, pp. 124–30, tells the reconciliation story in detail.

87. See Helen Dewar, "House Panel Sets Spending Ceiling, Brushes Aside Protests by Republicans," *Washington Post*, November 12, 1980, p. A2; and Dewar, "Tax Cut Bill Squelched," *Washington Post*, November 13, 1980, pp. A1, A2.

88. Robert W. Merry, "GOP Swings Wild In Initial Bout With Budget Champ," *Wall Street Journal*, November 14, 1980, p. 28.

89. Dewar, "Tax Cut Bill Squelched," *Washington Post*, November 13, 1980; *CQA 1980*, p. 123; and Dewar, "$632.4 Billion Budget Cleared," *Washington Post*, November 20, 1980, pp. Al, A17.

90. Helen Dewar, "Hill's Budget Process Grows Stronger With Every Passing Deficit," *Washington Post*, November 23, 1980, p. A6; Richard L. Lyons, "On Capitol Hill: Congress Passes Hastily Drawn Fiscal '81 Budget," *Washington Post*, November 21, 1980, p. Al8; and *CQA 1980*, p. 123.

91. Lyons, "On Capitol Hill"; and *CQA 1980*, p. 123.

92. *CQA 1980*, p. 130.

93. Ibid., p. 124.

94. "Reagan Would Hike Arms Funds 7%," *Washington Post*, October 28, 1980, p. A2.

95. *CQA 1980*, pp. 185–97.

96. Ibid., pp. 210–17.

97. Ibid., pp. 220–21.

98. See Helen Dewar, "Senate Retreats on Pay, Busing," *Washington Post*, December 11, 1980, pp. Al, A4; and *CQA 1980*, pp. 220–21.

99. Helen Dewar and Richard L. Lyons, "U.S. Agencies Run Out of Money as Spending Bill is Deadlocked," *Washington Post*, December 16, 1980, p. A8.

100. *CQA 1980*, p. 222.

101. Dewar and Lyons, "U.S. Agencies Run Out of Money," *Washington Post*, December 16, 1980.

102. George C. Wilson, "Carter, Cutting Pentagon's Budget Request, Grants Extra $6.2 Billion," *Washinton Post*, December 27, 1980, p. A7.

103. The memo, which we discuss in the next chapter, is included as an appendix to William Greider, *The Education of David Stockman and Other Americans* (New York: Dutton, 1982).

104. Kenneth H. Bacon, "Fast Start: Reagan Economic Blitz to Get High Priority Despite Stiff Obstacles," *Wall Street Journal*, November 26, 1980, p. 1.

105. Alexander Taylor, "Waiting for Reaganomics," *Time*, November 24, 1980, pp. 84–85.

Chapter Four

1. V. O. Key, *Politics, Parties and Pressure Groups*, 4th ed. (New York: Thomas Y. Crowell, 1958), pp. 568–69.

2. See Robert A. Dahl, *A Preface to Democratic Theory* (Chicago: University of Chicago Press, 1956).

3. "Tip: 'Give 'Em Enough Rope,'" *Newsweek*, November 24, 1980, p. 47.

4. Charles L. Heatherly, ed., *Mandate for Leadership: Policy Management in a Conservative Administration* (Washington, D.C.: Heritage Foundation, 1982).

5. Neal R. Pierce and Jerry Hagstrom, "The Voters Send Carter a Message: Time For a Change—to Reagan," *National Journal*, November 8, 1980, pp. 1876–78.

6. William Schneider, "The November 4 Vote for President: What Did It

Mean," in Austin Ranney, ed., *The American Elections of 1980* (Washington, D.C.: American Enterprise Institute, 1981), p. 230.

7. Hedrick Smith, Adam Clymer, Leonard Silk, Robert Lindsey, and Richard Burt, *Reagan the Man, the President* (New York: Macmillan, 1980), p. 59.

8. Nov. 22, 1980, p. 34.

9. Smith et al., *Reagan the Man*, p. 60.

10. Kathleen A. Frankovic, "Public Opinion Trends," in Gerald Pomper with Colleagues, *The Election of 1980* (Chatham, N.J.: Chatham House, 1981), p. 107.

11. See Chapter 1, "Rival Theories and a Method for Choosing Among Them," in Aaron Wildavsky, *Leadership in a Small Town* (Totowa, N.J.: Bedminster Press, 1964), pp. 1–13.

12. Laurence I. Barrett, *Gambling with History* (Garden City, N.Y.: Doubleday, 1983), p. 48.

13. Schneider, "November 4 Vote for President," pp. 242–43.

14. Ibid., p. 241.

15. See J. Merrill Shanks and Warren E. Miller, "Policy Direction and Performance Evaluation: Complementary Explanations of the Reagan Elections," Prepared for 1985 Annual Meeting of the American Political Science Association, August 29–Sept. 1, 1985, New Orleans.

16. See Thomas E. Mann and Norman J. Ornstein, "The Republican Surge in Congress," in Austin Ranney, ed., *The American Elections of 1980* (Washington, D.C.: American Enterprise Institute, 1981), pp. 263–302; and Charles E. Jacob, "The Congressional Elections," in Gerald Pomper with Colleagues, *The Election of 1980*, pp. 119–41.

17. Jacob, "The Congressional Elections," p. 132.

18. Smith et al., *Reagan the Man*, p. 4.

19. Barrett, *Gambling with History*, p. 55.

20. Ibid., p. 59.

21. Ibid., p. 24.

22. For a good example, Paul McCracken editorialized in the *Wall Street Journal* that the tax cut first strategy should be tried; an excerpt was used by Martin Anderson, August 22, 1980, Memorandum for Governor Reagan; also in Fact Sheet for September 9 speech.

23. That was not so easy; he was brought into the 1976 Reagan challenge to Gerald Ford when Reagan got in trouble for proposing a shift of $90 billion per year in federal programs to the states—without saying how the states would pay for them. One Reagan aide commented of Anderson's performance that "he could unscramble an egg." Jules Witcover, *Marathon: The Pursuit of the Presidency 1972–76* (New York: Signet/New American Library, 1978), p. 408.

24. As George Shultz reported to Leonard Silk of the *New York Times*, in Smith et al., *Reagan the Man*, p. 56.

25. Fact Sheet for September 9 speech.

26. Barrett, *Gambling with History*, p. 133.

27. Herbert Stein, *Presidential Economics: The Making of Economic Policy from Roosevelt to Reagan and Beyond* (New York: Simon and Schuster, 1984), pp. 259–60.

28. Spending Control, Caspar Weinberger; Tax Policy, Charles E. Walker;

Regulatory Reform, Murray Weidenbaum; Inflation Policy, Paul McCracken; International Money Policy, Arthur F. Burns; Budget, Alan Greenspan; Economic Policy Coordinating Committee, chaired by George Shultz, included Milton Friedman, Jack Kemp, Michael Halburton (an energy specialist), James T. Lynn, William Simon, and Walter Winston.

29. Steven R. Weisman, "Reaganomics and the President's Men," *New York Times Magazine*, October 24, 1982, pp. 26–29, 82–85, 89–92, 109.

30. Text of Reagan's February 5, 1981, speech in *New York Times*, February 6, 1981, p. Al2.

31. Reagan's theory was not as unusual as it may appear. The sense that the availability of funds causes them to be spent was old; in the early 1950s the Republicans in Congress had proposed replacing the social security dedicated tax with general revenue funding, precisely because they believed that having its own trust fund was an invitation to program growth. See Martha Derthick, *Policymaking for Social Security* (Washington, D.C.: Brookings Institution, 1979).

32. David A. Stockman, *The Triumph of Politics: How the Reagan Revolution Failed* (New York: Harper & Row, 1986), p. 35.

33. Michael Barone, Grant Ujifusa, and Douglas Mathews, *Almanac of American Politics 1980* (New York: E. P. Dutton, 1979), p. 426.

34. Ibid., pp. 49–50.

35. Theodore Lowi, *The End of Liberalism* (New York: Norton, 1969), p. 289.

36. Ibid., p. 72.

37. Stockman, *Triumph of Politics*, p. 33.

38. David A. Stockman, "The Social Pork Barrel," *The Public Interest*, No. 39 (Spring 1975), pp. 3–30.

39. Stockman and Reagan had already met in an unusual way. John Anderson, Stockman's mentor, had run for president as an independent, seeking a constituency that would reject both Carter's performance and Reagan's beliefs. After Carter refused to include Anderson in debates, Reagan and Anderson were to debate alone. Reagan's people asked Stockman to play Anderson in mock debates to help prepare their candidate. He did so well that James Baker asked Stockman to play the same role when Reagan debated Carter. Reagan, too, was impressed. When Reagan offered Stockman the job, Stockman reports that Reagan said, "Dave, I've been thinking about how to get even with you for that thrashing you gave me in the debate rehearsals. So I'm going to send you to OMB." Stockman, *Triumph of Politics*, p. 77.

40. David A. Stockman, "Avoiding a GOP Economic Dunkirk," in Greider, *The Education of David Stockman*, pp. 142, 144.

41. Stein, *Presidential Economics*, p. 266.

42. Timothy B. Clark, "Economic Events May Have Overtaken Reagan's 1981 Budget-Cutting Goals," pp. 2152–57; Michael R. Gordon, "Don't Expect Business as Usual From Reagan's Businesslike Cabinet," pp. 2175–79, *National Journal*, December 20, 1980.

43. Dan Rodrigues, "Tanks, Brifts, and Bulls that Quack," typescript, seminar paper, University of California, Berkeley, 1981.

44. Kenneth H. Bacon, "Economic Broker: Donald Regan Will Sell Both Tax,

Budget Cuts as Treasury Secretary," *Wall Street Journal,* December 12, 1980, pp. 1, 20.

45. Barrett, *Gambling with History,* p. 140. A spending increase here, a tax increase there, in the service of maintaining employment, was not what the Reagan administration wanted. They didn't believe in demand management. Microeconomics, based on price theory, is concerned with resource allocation in markets and, in some cases, as with Weidenbaum, in bureaucracies. Thus, microeconomists think in terms of departures from "efficient" markets and distortions caused by interfering with them. Macroeconomists are more likely to view the economy as a system to be manipulated, so on average, "macro" means more and "micro" means less intervention in the economy by government.

46. Weisman, "Reaganomics and the President's Men," p. 85.

47. See the profile in Barrett, *Gambling with History,* pp. 252–61.

48. Ibid., p. 392.

49. Source for the above description of staff is ibid., chapters on Baker, Darman, Meese, Deaver, Gergen; also *National Journal,* special issue, April 25, 1981, "The Decision Makers."

50. Darman made the point strongly in a February 21, 1981, memo to Baker. Barrett, *Gambling with History,* p. 84.

51. Timothy B. Clark, "Economic Events May Have Overtaken Reagan's 1981 Budget-Cutting Goals," *National Journal,* December 20, 1980, pp. 2152–55.

52. Ibid., p. 2152.

53. Albert R. Hunt, "Stockman's Hour," *Wall Street Journal,* February 19, 1981, pp. 1, 18.

54. Dick Kirschten, "Reagan: 'No More Business As Usual,' " *National Journal,* February 21, 1981, pp. 300, 302–3.

55. Elizabeth Drew, "A Reporter at Large: Early Days," *New Yorker,* March 16, 1981, pp. 84–99.

56. Kenneth H. Bacon and Timothy D. Schellhardt, "Reagan Promises His Tax, Spending Cuts Will Reduce Inflation and Increase Growth," *Wall Street Journal,* February 19, 1981, pp. 3–5; and Dick Kirschten, "White House Strategy," pp. 300, 302–3; Linda E. Demkovich, "Assault on Food Stamps," pp. 301, 308–11; and Robert J. Samuelson, "Reagan's Bet," pp. 301, 304–6, all in *National Journal,* February 21, 1981.

57. Barrett, *Gambling with History,* p. 144.

58. Martin Tolchin, "Democrats and the Budget: Liberals as well as Republicans in Congress are Gripped by Fervor to Achieve Balanced Package," *New York Times,* March 10, 1981, p. D8.

59. Gramm was careful to phrase his written promises in a manner that gave him an out. Wright seems to have indulged in some wishful thinking. If he had been really suspicious, he would have noticed Gramm's hedged language.

60. Richard E. Cohen, "They're Still a Majority in the House, But are Democrats Really in Control?" *National Journal,* January 31, 1981, pp. 189–91; and Richard E. Cohen, "Will the Democrats and Republicans Find Happiness in Their New Roles?" *National Journal,* December 6, 1980, pp. 2064–67.

61. Richard E. Cohen, "In the Conservative Politics of the '80s, the South Is Rising Once Again," *National Journal,* February 28, 1981, pp. 350–54.

62. Barrett, *Gambling with History*, p. 168.

63. "The New House Leaders: bipartisan compromisers," *National Journal*, December 13, 1980, pp. 2136–37; Richard E. Cohen, "For the Congressional Budget Process, 1981 Could Be the Make or Break Year," pp. 59–63; and "The House's Budget 'Compromiser,' " p. 61, *National Journal*, January 10, 1981.

64. Richard Cohen, "Will the Democrats and Republicans Find Happiness," *National Journal*, December 6, 1980, pp. 2064–67.

65. Peter Goldman et al., "Bracing for Reagan's Cuts," *Newsweek*, February 23, 1981, pp. 18–20.

66. Cohen, "Will the Democrats and Republicans Find Happiness."

Chapter Five

1. Harry Anderson et al., "The U.S. Economy in Crisis," *Newsweek*, January 19, 1981, pp. 30–34.

2. Elizabeth Drew, "Reporter At Large: 1980: Reagan," *New Yorker*, March 24, 1980, pp. 49-74 passim.

3. "Reagan Readies the Ax," *Newsweek*, February 16, 1981, p. 20.

4. Text of Reagan's February 5, 1981, speech, *New York Times*, February 6, 1981, p. Al2.

5. Barrett, *Gambling with History*, pp. 148–49.

6. Steven Rattner, "Treasury Secretary Rejects Linking Tax Cuts to Budgetary Reductions," *New York Times*, February 4, 1981, p. 1.

7. Stockman, *Triumph of Politics*, p. 164.

8. Thomas C. O'Donnell, "Backing away from the cut that kills," *Forbes Magazine*, February 16, 1981, pp. 31–32.

9. Stockman, *Triumph of Politics*, p. 93.

10. "Carter's Farewell Budget," *Newsweek*, January 26, 1981, pp. 64–65.

11. Harry Anderson, "Stockman's Ladder," *Newsweek*, February 9, 1981, p. 66; Barrett, *Gambling with History*, pp. 139–43.

12. Stockman, *Triumph of Politics*, p. 96.

13. Office of Management and Budget, *Fiscal Year 1982 Budget Revisions* (March 1981), Table 6, p. 13.

14. Barrett, *Gambling with History*, p. 140.

15. Stein, *Presidential Economics*, pp. 269–70.

16. Barrett, *Gambling with History*, p. 141.

17. Paul Craig Roberts, " 'The Stockman Revolution': A Reaganite's Account," *Fortune*, February 22, 1982, pp. 56–58, 62–70.

18. Greider, *Education of David Stockman*, p. 35.

19. Martin Tolchin, "Budget Conferees in a Balancing Act," *New York Times*, March 12, 1980, p. A11.

20. Stockman, *Triumph of Politics*, pp. 116–19.

21. Ibid., pp. 112–13.

22. Greider, *Education of David Stockman*, p. 13. See also Barrett, *Gambling with History*, pp. 196–97.

23. David S. Broder, "Hill, Reagan Aides Eye Painful Cuts," *Washington Post,* January 2, 1981, pp. Al, A3.

24. Pete V. Domenici, "The Ghosts of Deficit Forever," *Washington Post,* January 21, 1986, p. Al5.

25. Stockman, *Triumph of Politics,* p. 181.

26. "I do not need a fight with 35 million Americans right off the bat," Stockman commented. "That would be the litmus of political stupidity." *Newsweek,* January 19, 1981, p. 39.

27. "Bracing for Reagan's Cuts," *Newsweek,* February 23, 1981, pp. 18–20.

28. See Robert G. Kaiser, "Deep Budget Cuts Urged for Popular Federal Programs," *Washington Post,* February 4, 1981, pp. Al, A4.

29. Greider, *Education of David Stockman,* p. 22.

30. Among many studies of the package's tilt, particularly good ones are: Gregory B. Mills, "The Budget: A Failure of Discipline," in John L. Palmer and Isabel V. Sawhill, eds., *The Reagan Record: An Assessment of America's Changing Domestic Priorities* (Cambridge, Mass.: Ballinger, 1984), pp. 107–39; Palmer and Sawhill, eds., *The Reagan Experiment* (Washington, D.C.: Urban Institute Press, 1982); Jack A. Meyer, "Budget Cuts in the Reagan Administration: A Question of Fairness," and Timothy M. Sneeding, "Is the Safety Net Still Intact," in D. Lee Bawden, ed., *The Social Contract Revisited* (Washington, D.C.: Urban Institute Press, 1984); John C. Weicher, "The Reagan Domestic Budget Cuts: Proposals, Outcomes, and Effects," in Phillip Cagan, ed., *The Impact of the Reagan Program* (Washington, D.C.: American Enterprise Institute, 1986). We base our estimate on the proposals as described in the Office of Management and Budget, *Additional Details on Budget Savings* (Washington, D.C.: U.S. Government Printing Office, April 1981), and Congressional Budget Office, *An Analysis of President Reagan's Budget Revisions for Fiscal Year 1982* (Washington, D.C.: U.S. Government Printing Office, March 1981), Staff Working Paper.

31. See Jane Bryant Quinn, "A Middle Class Deal," *Newsweek,* March 2, 1981, p. 66, as one example.

32. George J. Church, "Are There Limits to Compassion?" *Time,* April 6, 1981, pp. 12, 17. The "notch effect," well known to students of poverty programs, is unavoidable no matter where the line is drawn; whether benefits are changed or not, someone out of the program always seems disadvantaged compared to those just below him who get into the program. A good summary of effects and sources is Wendell E. Primus, "Legislative Impact of Poverty Statistics," paper prepared for the annual meeting of the Association for Public Policy Analysis and Management, October 18–20, New Orleans.

33. Adam Clymer, "Rise in U.S. Optimism on Economy Bolsters Reagan Support, Poll Hints," *New York Times,* April 30, 1981, pp. A1, B10.

34. Darman made the point concerning the benefits distribution in a February 10 memo to the troika; Barrett, *Gambling with History,* p. 143. Meese took the issue so seriously that he opposed reduction of the top tax rate on unearned income (dividends, rents, interest) from 70 to 50 percent; Stockman, *Triumph of Politics,* p. 130.

35. Stockman, *Triumph of Politics,* p. 130.

36. Ibid.

37. Martin Anderson, "The Objectives of the Reagan Administration's Social Welfare Policy," in D. Lee Bauden, ed., *The Social Contract Revisited* (Washington, D.C.: Urban Institute Press, 1984), p. 17.

38. "Budget Reform Plan," in *America's New Beginning: A Program for Economic Recovery* (Washington, D.C.: U.S. Government Printing Office, February 18, 1981), p. 13. Also page 10 of "A White House Report" in the same document.

39. See Stockman, *Triumph of Politics*, p. 124.

40. Why were these "Chapter Two" proposals, in particular, dredged up at the end? Stockman doesn't tell us, and some sources don't remember the proposals brought to the cabinet on February 7 as conceptually separate. Most likely these proposals were more from OMB staff work (the "C" list) than from transition teams; because they obviously could meet stiff resistance from business constituencies, Stockman hesitated to present them. Naturally when Stockman was working from his and Gramm's list and those of Weinberger and the Senate Budget staff, the emphasis was more on social spending for Democratic constituencies; OMB staff, looking for additions, was more likely to look on the tax side because its biases were different and the other stuff had been done.

41. Stockman, *Triumph of Politics*, p. 127.

42. Ibid., p. 131.

43. Greider, *Education of David Stockman*, p. 24.

44. Drew, "Reporter at Large: 1980: Reagan," *New Yorker*, March 24, 1980, p. 71.

45. Richard Halloran, "Carter Seeks $180 Billion For 1982 Military Budget," *New York Times*, January 16, 1981, p. B7.

46. Congressional Budget Office, *An Analysis of President Reagan's Budget Revisions for Fiscal Year 1982*, Staff Working Paper (Washington, D.C.: U.S. Government Printing Office, March 1981), p. 74.

47. Richard Halloran, "Weinberger Begins Drive for Big Rise in Defense Budget," *New York Times*, March 5, 1981, pp. A1, B10.

48. Budget documents; "Hitting the Jackpot," *The Economist*, March 14, 1981, pp. 24, 27–28.

49. "Reagan's Defense Buildup," *Newsweek*, March 16, 1981, p. 22.

50. Stockman, *Triumph of Politics*, pp. 106–9.

51. Ibid., pp. 132–33.

52. Greider, *Education of David Stockman*, p. 36.

53. Office of Management and Budget, *Fiscal Year 1982 Budget Revisions*, March 10, 1981 (Washington, D.C.: U.S. Government Printing Office), p. 3.

54. Stockman, *Triumph of Politics*, p. 125.

55. Ibid., p. 128.

56. Reestimates of the current policy base to a higher level of spending later forced Stockman to find another $7.1 billion by March 10 in order to attain the proposed spending ceiling of $695.5 billion in outlays. Text of Reagan's February 18, 1981, speech, and accompanying proposals, were published as *America's New Beginning: A Program for Economic Recovery* (Washington, D.C.: U.S. Government Printing Office, February 18, 1981).

Chapter Six

1. Philip Shabecoff, "Economic Plan Rejected by Labor Chiefs as Unfair," and Bernard Weinraub, "Coalition to Oppose Cuts in Aid to Poor," *New York Times*, February 20, 1981, p. A10.

2. "Labor Department: It's in Business's Hands Now," *National Journal*, April 25, 1981, pp. 726–28.

3. "The Budget-Cutters' Ball," *New Republic*, February 28, 1981, pp. 5–8.

4. George J. Church, "The Unkindest Cuts of All," *Time*, February 23, 1981, pp. 12–14.

5. Judith Miller, "A Liberal Democrat Finds Constituents Demanding Budget Cuts," *New York Times*, February 17, 1981, p. A14.

6. Martin Tolchin, "Democrats to Seek Significant Changes in Tax-Cut Proposal," *New York Times*, February 21, 1981, p. A1.

7. Ibid.

8. Ed Magnuson, "A Bonanza for Defense," *Time*, March 16, 1981, pp. 26, 31.

9. Elizabeth Drew, "A Reporter at Large: The Democrats," *New Yorker*, March 22, 1982, pp. 130–45. For the basic story on Senate reconciliation, see *Congressional Quarterly Almanac 1981*, Vol. 37 (Washington, D.C.: Congressional Quarterly, Inc., 1982), pp. 250–51 (hereafter *CQA 1981*); on Republican unity, see Allen Schick, "How the Budget Was Won and Lost," in Norman J. Ornstein, ed., *President and Congress: Assessing Reagan's First Year* (Washington, D.C.: American Enterprise Institute, 1982), pp. 14–43.

10. Greider, *Education of David Stockman*, pp. 32–33.

11. Richard E. Cohen, "Budget Battle Takes to the Trenches—But Who Ever Said It Would Be Easy?" *National Journal*, April 18, 1981, pp. 645–48.

12. "New Beginnings, Old Anxieties," *Time*, February 2, 1981, pp. 22–23; Adam Clymer, "Public Prefers a Balanced Budget to Large Cut in Taxes, Poll Shows," *New York Times*, February 3, 1981, p. A1.

13. "The Budget: Bumps Ahead," *Newsweek*, March 30, 1981, pp. 23–24.

14. Quoted by Steven S. Smith, "The Congress: Budget Battles of 1981: The Role of the Majority Party Leadership," in Allan P. Sindler, ed., *American Politics and Public Policy* (Washington, D.C.: Congressional Quarterly Press, 1982), pp. 43–78.

15. Steven V. Roberts, "Critical Approach to Reagan's Budget is Urged by Wright," *New York Times*, March 13, 1981, p. A1.

16. Text in *New York Times*, April 9, 1981, p. B12.

17. Smith, "The Congress," p. 54.

18. See Barrett, *Gambling with History*, pp. 107–25.

19. Ed Magnuson, "Six Shots at Nation's Heart," *Time*, April 13, 1981, pp. 14–38; and Barrett, *Gambling with History*, p. 121.

20. Ibid.

21. Barrett, *Gambling with History*, p. 124; also Peter Goldman, "The First Hundred Days," *Newsweek*, May 4, 1981, pp. 22–23.

22. Peter Behr and Caroline Atkinson, "Economic Advisers Set to Give Reagan Grim Projections," *Washington Post*, January 6, 1981, pp. 1A, 4A. See also

Albert R. Hunt, "Stockman's Hour," *Wall Street Journal,* February 19, 1981, pp. 1, 18; and Robert W. Merry, "Changing Ways," *Wall Street Journal,* February 4, 1981, p. 1.

23. Hunt, "Stockman's Hour," *Wall Street Journal.*

24. Robert J. Samuelson, "Reagan's Tax Package—Is a Bill in the Hand Worth Two in the Bush?" *National Journal,* February 28, 1981, pp. 340–45.

25. Barrett, *Gambling with History,* p. 132.

26. Hobart Rowen, "Put Budget-Cutting First, Burns Urges Committee," *Washington Post,* January 22, 1981, pp. B1, B6.

27. Stein, *Presidential Economics,* p. 269.

28. Steven R. Weisman, "Reaganomics and the President's Men," *New York Times,* October 24, 1982, p. 28. See also Elizabeth Drew, "Reporter at Large: First Year," *New Yorker,* January 4, 1982, pp. 38–52.

29. Weisman, "Reaganomics and the President's Men," *New York Times.*

30. Richard E. Cohen, "The Senator from Tennessee May Hold the Key to Reagan's Economic Plans," *National Journal,* April 11, 1981, pp. 596–600.

31. Ibid.

32. "The Democrats Begin to Regroup," *Newsweek,* March 9, 1981, p. 29; Albert R. Hunt and Dennis Farney, "A Consensus to Cut: Budget Paring Mood Spreads on Capitol Hill, Bodes Well for Reagan," *Wall Street Journal,* March 10, 1981, pp. 1, 16.

33. Stockman, *Triumph of Politics,* p. 161.

34. Ibid., p. 162. Our sources convince us that Stockman misunderstood Howard Baker's position.

35. Ibid.

36. Greider, *Education of David Stockman,* pp. 30–31.

37. Martin Tolchin, "Senate Rejects Bid to Restore Welfare Funds," *New York Times,* April 1, 1981, p. A24.

38. Martin Tolchin, "Democrats, Eying Elections, Maneuver on Budget Cuts," *New York Times,* April 2, 1981, p. B1.

39. Daniel Elazar, *American Federalism: A View from the States,* 2d ed. (New York: Crowell, 1972).

40. Louis Dumont, *Homo Hierarchicus: The Caste System and Its Implications* (Chicago: University of Chicago Press, 1980).

41. For a description of the administration's oil policy, see *CQA 1981,* pp. 248–50; Martin Tolchin, "Democrats' Budget Tops Reagan Figure on Social Programs," April 7, 1981, pp. A1, B8; and "Democratic Budget Proposal," April 8, 1981, p. A24, *New York Times.*

42. Harry Anderson et al., "The Remaking of a Budget," *Newsweek,* April 20, 1981, p. 39.

43. Budget Committee Democrats claimed a new technique, Deferred Enrollment, would enforce the reductions on appropriations. The administration was properly skeptical. Robert Reischauer, "The Congressional Budget Process," in Gregory Mills and John Palmer, eds., *Federal Budget Policy in the 1980s* (Washington, D.C.: Urban Institute, 1984), pp. 385–413.

44. Richard E. Cohen, "Democratic Dilemma—No Credit If They Work With

Reagan, Blame If They Don't," *National Journal,* March 21, 1981, pp. 482–86; "What 'Reconciliation' Means," *Newsweek,* March 2, 1981, p. 32.

45. Reischauer, "Congressional Budget Process," p. 399.

46. In April, ninety-one-day T-bills were running about 13.6 percent; for the year to average out at 8.9 percent would require some heroic assumptions, such as an average rate of about 5 percent for the second half of the year. Actually, the final figure was just over 14 percent.

47. Martin Tolchin, "Senate Panel, 12–8, Rejects Own Plan for Budget in 1982," *New York Times,* April 10, 1981, pp. Al, D3; Tolchin, "Facing Up to Budget Reality," *New York Times,* April 11, 1981, pp. 1, 12; Anderson et al., "The Remaking of a Budget."

48. Editorial pages, *New York Times,* April 16, 1981.

49. Stockman, *Triumph of Politics,* p. 166.

50. Martin Tolchin, "Democrats in Congress Weighing a Proposal to Balance the Budget," *New York Times,* April 29, 1981, pp. A1, A23; *CQA 1981,* pp. 249, 252.

51. Greider, *Education of David Stockman,* p. 34; Steven R. Weisman, "Reagan Backs Plan on Budget By Group of House Democrats," *New York Times,* April 22, 1981, p. Al.

52. S. William Green, "In Search of Fairness," reprint from *Congressional Record,* Vol. 128, no. 90, July 14, 1982.

53. Martin Tolchin, "Democrats in House Add Military Funds to Proposed Budget," *New York Times,* April 30, 1981, pp. Al, A26.

54. Steven V. Roberts, "Some Democrats Accuse O'Neill of a Lack of Strong Leadership," *New York Times,* April 30, 1981, p. A26.

55. Ed Magnuson, "Reagan's Big Win," *Time,* May 18, 1981, pp. 14–16; Peter Goldman, "The Second Hundred Days," *Newsweek,* May 11, 1981, pp. 22–24; Barrett, *Gambling with History,* pp. 153–54; and Paul Craig Roberts, "Making Deficits a Scapegoat for Inflation," *New York Times,* p. A31.

56. See Steven V. Roberts, "Congressmen Hear Voters, But Message Is Not Clear," *New York Times,* April 26, 1981, p. 18; and other stories on Jones and Shannon during the month.

57. Adam Clymer, "Rise in U.S. Optimism on Economy Bolsters Reagan Support, Poll Hints," April 30, 1981, pp. A1, B10.

58. "Majority in Poll Support Reagan on Economic Package," *New York Times,* April 25, 1981, Associated Press wire story, p. A6.

59. Steven V. Roberts, "44 Democrats Are Objects of White House Attentions," *New York Times,* May 1, 1981, p. Al9.

60. Ibid.

61. Kenneth H. Bacon, "Reagan's Regan," *Wall Street Journal,* April 30, 1981, pp. 1, 17.

62. Barrett, *Gambling with History,* pp. 153–54; Greider, *Education of David Stockman,* p. 36.

63. Green, "In Search of Fairness."

64. Stockman, *Triumph of Politics,* p. 176.

65. Hedrick Smith, "Second Honeymoon," *New York Times,* April 29, 1981, p. A22.

66. Ibid.

67. Ed Magnuson, "Reagan's Budget Battle," *Time*, May 11, 1981, pp. 16–18; speech transcript, *New York Times*, April 29, 1981, p. A22.

68. Martin Tolchin, "Democrats in House Add Military Funds to Proposed Budget," *New York Times*, April 30, 1981, pp. Al, A26.

69. Terence Smith, "Despite Doubts, Byrd Will Back Reagan's Budget," *New York Times*, May 3, 1981, p. Al; James Kelly, "Now Comes the Hard Part," *Time*, May 4, 1981, pp. 17–18; and George J. Church, "Flying into Trouble," *Time*, May 4, 1981, pp. 14–16.

70. *CQA 1981*, p. 253.

71. Peter Goldman, "The Reagan Steamroller," *Newsweek*, May 18, 1981, p. 39.

72. Peter Goldman, "The Second Hundred Days," *Newsweek*, May 11, 1981, pp. 22–24.

73. Greider, *Education of David Stockman*, p. 35.

74. Kenneth H. Bacon, "Strange Welcome: Wall Street is Greeting President's Program with Jitters, Turmoil," *Wall Street Journal*, May 7, 1981, pp. 1, 13. See also Lindley H. Clark, Jr., "Slowing Down: Analysts See Economy Flattening Out Now, Expanding in 2nd Half," *Wall Street Journal*, April 16, 1981, pp. 1, 19; and Council of Economic Advisers, *Economic Indicators*, various months in 1981.

75. Stockman, *Triumph of Politics*, p. 181.

76. Ibid., pp. 184–85.

77. Ibid., pp. 187–88.

78. In his book, Stockman says the real problem with altering social security policy was making the change effective immediately. He says that "detail got lost in the shuffle." Yet, all the budget-savings figures depended on when that change began; Stockman had long wanted to make it immediate; by his own report, he objected to other packages that did not yield savings fast enough. In short, Stockman is fudging. If he didn't know the exact date of the change, as he insists, he knew that he wanted it soon. Stockman, *Triumph of Politics*, p. 188.

79. Barrett, *Gambling with History*, p. 157.

80. Stockman, *Triumph of Politics*, p. 189.

81. Barrett, *Gambling with History*, p. 157.

82. See Stockman, *Triumph of Politics*, pp. 190–93.

83. James Kelly, "A Slash at Social Security," *Time*, May 25, 1981, pp. 24–25.

84. Tom Morganthau, "The Gipper Loses One," *Newsweek*, June 1, 1981, pp. 22–23.

Chapter Seven

1. Stuart Eizenstat, "The Hill's Budget Stampede," *Washington Post*, June 21, 1981, pp. C1, C3.

2. *CQA 1981*, pp. 257–58.

3. "Crocodile Tears," editorial, *Washington Post*, January 25, 1988, p. A12.

4. Richard E. Cohen, "Democratic Dilemma—No Credit If They Work with Reagan, Blame If They Don't," *National Journal*, March 21, 1981, pp. 482–86.

5. Robert Reischauer, "The Congressional Budget Process," in Gregory B. Mills and John L. Palmer, eds., *Federal Budget Policy in the 1980s* (Washington, D.C.: Urban Institute, 1984), pp. pp. 397–98.

6. Richard E. Cohen, "For the Congressional Budget Process, 1981 Could Be the Make or Break Year," *National Journal,* January 10, 1981, pp. 59–63.

7. See Hugh Heclo and Aaron Wildavsky, *The Private Government of Public Money,* 2d ed. (London: Macmillan, 1981).

8. Greider, *Education of David Stockman,* p. 57.

9. Morganthau, "The Gipper Loses One," *Newsweek,* June 1, 1981, pp. 22–23.

10. Stockman, *Triumph of Politics,* p. 195.

11. Ibid.

12. The budget resolution's reconciliation instructions to the Committee on Ways and Means read as follows:

> (15)(A) the House Committee on Ways and Means shall report changes in laws within the jurisdiction of that committee which provide spending authority as defined in section 401(c)(2)(C) of Public Law 93–344 sufficient to reduce budget authority by $3,699,000,000 and outlays by $8,247,000,000 in fiscal year 1982; to reduce budget authority by $3,660,000,000 and outlays by $9,247,000,000 in fiscal year 1983; and to reduce budget authority by $3,511,000,000 and outlays by $9,573,000,000 in fiscal year 1984; and
>
> (B) the House Committee on Ways and Means shall also report changes in laws within the jurisdiction of that committee sufficient to reduce appropriations for programs authorized by that committee so as to achieve savings in budget authority and outlays as follows: $978,000,000 in budget authority and $994,000,000 in outlays for fiscal year 1982; $1,294,000,000 in budget authority and $1,312,000,000 in outlays for fiscal year 1983; and $1,647,000,000 in budget authority and $1,675,000,000 in outlays for fiscal year 1984. (*United States Statutes At Large,* 1981, p. 1754)

13. The classic case is the Park Service, faced with a cut, declaring it had to cut the hours for tours at the Washington Monument—the most visible cut imaginable. In 1986 the Library of Congress managed a nice version of this: responding to the Gramm-Rudman sequester, it closed its main reading room at 5:00 p.m. instead of 9:00 p.m.; it got more money.

14. For detailed descriptions of these proposals, see Timothy B. Clark, Linda E. Demkovich, Robert J. Samuelson, and others, "Congress Works a Minor Revolution—Making Cuts to Meet Its Budget Goals," *National Journal,* June 20, 1981, pp. 114–25; Helen Dewar, "Hill Panels Meet or Exceed '82 Budget Cut Goals, Estimates Show," *Washington Post,* June 13, 1981, pp. A1, A5; and Dewar, "OMB 'Indicts' Democrats," *Washington Post,* June 15, 1981, pp. A1, A13.

15. Clark et al., "Congress Works a Minor Revolution"; Helen Dewar and Robert G. Kaiser, "Reagan Allies Ready Budget Alternative," *Washington Post,* June 12, 1981, pp. A1, A5.

16. Stockman, *Triumph of Politics,* p. 200.

17. Ibid., p. 203.

18. Ibid., pp. 204–5.

19. Clark et al., "Congress Works a Minor Revolution"; Helen Dewar, "House Democrats Hunker Down For Next Fight on Budget Cuts," *Washington Post,* June 16, 1981, p. A2.

20. Smith, "The Congress," p. 62.

21. Helen Dewar, "House Democrats Try to Cut Losses on Social Programs," *Washington Post,* June 17, 1981, p. A2.

22. *CQA 1981,* p. 262.

23. Barrett, *Gambling with History,* p. 160.

24. Jane Seabury, "Republicans Criticize Democrats' Slow Pace on Budget Legislation," *Washington Post,* June 22, 1981, p. A2.

25. Robert G. Kaiser, "Budget Warriors Improvised, Coddled," *Washington Post,* July 4, 1981, pp. A1, A2.

26. Peter Goldman, "Reagan's Sweet Triumph," *Newsweek,* July 6, 1981, pp. 18–20.

27. "Unfinished Business," *National Journal,* July 11, 1981, p. 1266.

28. Peter Goldman, "The Honeymoon Is Over," *Newsweek,* June 29, 1982, pp. 36–37; and Art Pine, "Whistling Dixie on Tax Bill: Can GOP Rise Again?" *Washington Post,* June 21, 1981, pp. G1, G6.

29. Pine, "Whistling Dixie on Tax Bill," p. G6.

30. Stockman, *Triumph of Politics,* p. 208.

31. S. William Green, "In Search of Fairness," *Congressional Record,* Vol. 128, no. 90, July 14, 1982.

32. Goldman, "The Honeymoon Is Over"; and Kaiser, "Budget Warriors Improvised."

33. Calculations from *National Journal,* July 4, 1981, p. 1218.

34. *CQA 1981,* p. 259.

35. Smith, "The Congress," p. 64.

36. Stockman, *Triumph of Politics,* p. 218.

37. Barrett, *Gambling with History,* p. 160.

38. Lou Cannon and Dan Balz, "Reagan Taking His Economic Plan on Road, Flays Democrats," *Washington Post,* June 25, 1981, p. A3; and *CQA 1981,* pp. 262–63.

39. Ward Sinclair, "Powerhouse," *Washington Post,* June 26, 1981, p. A1.

40. Ward Sinclair and Peter Behr, "Horse Trading," *Washington Post,* June 27, 1981, p. A1.

41. Ibid.

42. Ibid.

43. According to S. William Green (R-N.Y.), ibid.

44. Richard E. Cohen, "Small But Influential," *National Journal,* July 11, 1981, p. 1260.

45. Peter Goldman, "Reagan's Sweet Triumph," *Newsweek,* July 6, 1981, pp. 18–19.

46. Ibid.

47. Dennis Farney, "President's Budget Wins Vote in House on Rules Question, Stunning Democrats," *Wall Street Journal,* June 26, 1981, pp. 3, 14.

48. Ibid.
49. Stockman, *Triumph of Politics,* pp. 221–22.
50. Smith, "The Congress," p. 66.
51. Barrett, *Gambling with History,* p. 163; see also *CQA 1981,* p. 264; Richard A. Cohen, "Reagan's House victory lightens burden for budget conferees," *National Journal,* July 4, 1981, pp. 1218–19; and Cohen, "Small But Influential."
52. *CQA 1981,* pp. 263, 265.
53. Democrats had, at the time, a 242 to 191 margin; 21 of the 242 had opposed the party on both Republican substitute first resolutions in 1980, so might be expected to defect in 1981. Of this group, 3 (Marty Russo, Ill.; Doug Applegate, Ohio; and Bill Boner, Tenn.) were loyal on Gramm-Latta 1. Each was no conservative and, having made his seat safe in 1980, had few electoral worries. Jack Brinkley and Elliot Levitas of Georgia defected on all other budget votes but supported their party on reconciliation, leaving 16 whom, we may safely say, the Democrats had little chance to win. Another 12 Democrats had defected on one of the 1980 Republican substitutes. Of these, Bill Nichols (Ala.), Andy Ireland (Fla.), Bill Lee Evans and Ed Jenkins (Ga.), Eugene Atkinson, and Kent Hance (Tex.) were all pretty conservative. Only Jenkins, whose anger at Gramm was noted above, resisted Reagan's courtship. The other 6 were moderates with histories of party loyalty. There were, therefore, 24 Democrats whose previous budget votes and ideology made them prime suspects to defect. The Democratic leaders' success in holding the three Georgians—Brinkley, Levitas, and Jenkins— was probably the best that could be expected within that group, bringing the basic margin to 221 to 212, if everyone else voted with their party.
54. James A. Miller and James D. Range, "Reconciling An Irreconcilable Budget: The New Politics of the Budget Process," *Harvard Journal of Legislation* 20, no. 4 (1983), pp. 4–30; quote on p. 25.
55. Ibid.
56. Helen Dewar, "Senators Will Prune Budget-Slashing Bill," *Washington Post,* June 23, 1981, p. A5.
57. Reischauer, "The Congressional Budget Process," p. 389.
58. *CQA 1981,* p. 264.
59. Dewar, in the *Post,* wrote that:

> The leaders agreed to strip out provisions to do such things as permit wider trucks on interstate highways, deregulate the amateur radio industry, allow Western Union to enter international telecommunications markets, reauthorize the Older Americans Act and create a new program sponsored by Senator Jeremiah Denton (R-Ala.) to promote adolescent chastity, sources said.
>
> But they disagreed over other items in such areas as further radio deregulation, television licensing, federal controls over community development grants and curtailment of subsidized housing for cities like Washington that practice rent control. ("Senators Will Prune Budget-Slashing Bill")

60. John L. Palmer and Gregory B. Mills, "Budget Policy," in John L. Palmer

and Isabel V. Sawhill, eds., *The Reagan Experiment* (Washington, D.C.: Urban Institute Press, 1982), pp. 59–96; quote on p. 78.

Chapter Eight

1. Steven R. Weisman, "Reaganomics and the President's Men," *New York Times Magazine,* October 24, 1982, pp. 26–29, 82–85, 89–92, 109.

2. Howell Raines, "Reagan Orders Staff to Repudiate Report of Compromise on Tax Cut," *New York Times,* April 14, 1981, pp. A1, D13.

3. For detailed tables, see *National Journal,* July 25, 1981, p. 1349, and August 8, 1981, p. 1410.

4. Inflation was also driving poor people into brackets where they would be taxed when they had not been taxed before.

5. Robert W. Merry, "Rostenkowski and the Tax Bill," *Wall Street Journal,* March 27, 1981, p. 26.

6. Ibid.

7. Robert W. Merry and Burt Schorr, "Pension Pains: Congress, Reagan See Need to Cut Benefits Paid by Social Security," *Wall Street Journal,* May 10, 1981, pp. 1, 12.

8. Peter Goldman, "The Reagan Steamroller," *Newsweek,* May 18, 1981, pp. 38–40.

9. Robert W. Merry, "Mr. Chairman: Senator Robert Dole Plays Major Role in Future of Reagan Tax Bill," *Wall Street Journal,* July 14, 1981, pp. 1, 15.

10. Barrett, *Gambling with History,* pp. 166–67; Stockman, *Triumph of Politics,* pp. 238–40; and Walter Isaacson, "A Less Than Perfect '10–10–10,'" *Time,* June 1, 1981, p. 16, 21.

11. "The Best-Laid Plans . . . : Negotiations toward a bipartisan tax cut go astray," *Time,* June 8, 1981, p. 19.

12. Ibid.

13. Martin Schram, "Leading the Democrats: Rostenkowski Plays 'Palm' to O'Neill's 'Oak,'" *Washington Post,* June 8, 1981, pp. A1, A2.

14. On Rostenkowski, see ibid.; "The Sultan of Swap," *Time,* June 1, 1981, p. 21.

15. Peter Goldman, "Tax Cuts: Reagan Digs In," *Newsweek,* June 15, 1981, pp. 26–27.

16. Ibid.

17. Richard E. Cohen, "A Reagan Victory on His Tax Package Could Be a Costly One Politically," *National Journal,* June 13, 1981, pp. 1058–62.

18. Art Pine and Lou Cannon, "Reagan, Democrats Unable to Agree on Terms for Tax Cut," June 2, 1981, pp. A1, A3; Art Pine and Lee Lescaze, "Democrats Ease Stand On Tax Cut," June 3, 1981, pp. A1, A4; and Art Pine, "Reagan Rejects Plan By Hill Democrats for 15% Tax Cut," June 4, 1981, pp. A1, A4; all in *Washington Post.*

19. Stockman, *Triumph of Politics,* p. 249.

20. Ibid., p. 247.

21. A tax credit allows the payer to deduct from taxes, not from income,

some portion of the cost of an investment. A 10 percent credit on a million-dollar item is worth $100,000. At a tax rate of 40 percent, a 10 percent deduction would be worth 40 percent of that, or $40,000. The combination of tax credits up front with 10–5–3 depreciation is what gave the Reagan plan its negative rates.

22. Caroline Atkinson, "Argument for Tax Cut to Aid Business Weakened by New Statistics," *Washington Post,* February 5, 1981, p. A2.

23. Ibid; Robert R. Samuelson, "Business Tax Cuts—Needed Stimulant or Poorly Conceived Boondoggle?" *National Journal,* April 4, 1981, pp. 556–61. For the pro-10–5–3, see various Martin Feldstein *Wall Street Journal* articles, including July 15, 1981. Details in *CQA 1981,* p. 96.

24. See Lee Lescaze and Art Pine, "President Challenges Democrats," June 5, 1981, pp. A1, A7; John Berry, "Business Tax Break Cut 33% In Revised Depreciation Plan," June 5, 1981, pp. C8, C9; and Art Pine, "Tax Relief Restoration Is Proposed," June 9, 1981, pp. D6, D8; all in *Washington Post.*

25. Cohen, "A Reagan Victory on his Tax Package Could Be a Costly One Politically."

26. Steven R. Weisman, "Reaganomics and the President's Men," *New York Times Magazine,* October 24, 1982, pp. 26–29, 82–85, 89–92, 109; Barrett, *Gambling with History,* pp. 164–65.

27. Barrett, *Gambling with History,* pp. 171–72. Also see Greider, *Education of David Stockman.*

28. Art Pine, " 'Bidding War' Is Seen During Markup of Bills," *Washington Post,* June 6, 1981, pp. A1, A4.

29. Stockman describes both Baker and Regan as deferring to the president's preferences on the tax bill, and our interviews confirm that judgment. See *Triumph of Politics,* pp. 245–46.

30. Peter Goldman, "Tax Cuts: Reagan Digs In," *Newsweek,* June 15, 1981, pp. 26–27; John Berry, "Revised Proposal Offers Lower Federal Deficits," *Washington Post,* June 6, 1981, pp. A1, A4; Pine, " 'Bidding War' Is Seen During Markup of Bills"; Lou Cannon, "White House Expects Long Tax Cut Battle, Readies the 'Hard Sell,' " *Washington Post,* June 7, 1981, p. A5; Peter Behr, "Compromising on Taxes," *Washington Post,* June 8, 1981, pp. A1, A2; Pine, "Tax Relief Restoration Is Proposed"; Art Pine, "Some Hill Democrats Switch on Tax Relief," *Washington Post,* June 10, 1981, p. A3; Art Pine, "Reagan's Tax Plan Gets a Mixed Reception," *Washington Post,* June 11, 1981, p. A6; and Claudia Wallis, "The Marine Has Landed: As the tax-cut battle heats up, Donald Regan warms to his task," *Time,* June 22, 1981, p. 13.

31. Martin Schram, "Leading the Democrats: Rostenkowski Plays 'Palm' to O'Neill's 'Oak,' " *Washington Post,* June 8, 1981, pp. A1, A2.

32. Art Pine, "In Tax Debate, the Democrats Are Where the GOP Used to Be," *Washington Post,* June 12, 1981, p. A3.

33. Michael Kinsley, "Compromising Positions," *New Republic,* June 20, 1981, pp. 9–10.

34. Caroline Atkinson and John Berry, "Senate Panel Backs Reagan Tax Plan," *Washington Post,* June 19, 1981, pp. A1, A5.

35. The details were fuzzy because the committee was in the early stages of

designing a proposal, not in formal markup. Reports were slightly contradictory, e.g., over the timing of various proposals. See *CQA 1981*, pp. 9899; John W. Berry, "Basic Shift on Business Taxes Gains," *Washington Post*, June 18, 1981, pp. A1, A5; "Rival business tax cuts would cost the same," *National Journal*, June 27, 1981, pp. 1174–75.

36. Atkinson and Berry, "Senate Panel Backs Reagan Tax Plan."

37. See ibid.; and John Berry, "Tax-Cut Debate No Longer Over 'Whether' But 'How,' " *Washington Post*, June 21, 1981, p. G1.

38. Peter Behr, "Reagan's Advisers 'Puzzled' by High Rates' Persistence," *Washington Post*, July 15, 1981, p. E1.

39. *CQA 1981*, p. 101.

40. See, for example, the *Congressional Record* for June 23, 1981, pp. S13249–64, in which the Democrats made a record of their support on the floor.

41. Stockman, *Triumph of Politics*, p. 253. See also *CQA 1981*, pp. 97–98; Robert J. Samuelson, "Death and Taxes—An Instructive Tale About How Congress Makes Tax Policy," *National Journal*, July 4, 1981, pp. 1192–96.

42. *Congressional Record* 1980, p. S17138, and comments of Mr. Armstrong, June 26, 1980, p. S17161, pp. S17164–66.

43. Ibid., pp. S17164–65.

44. Stockman, *Triumph of Politics*, p. 254.

45. *Congressional Record*, July 16, 1981, p. S16121.

46. See Tables V-1 and V-3 in "General Explanation of the Economic Recovery Tax Act of 1981," Staff of the United States Congress Joint Committee on Taxation, Committee Print (Washington, D.C.: U.S. Government Printing Office, 1981). Indexing was not as important as the estimates suggested, for inflation turned out to be lower than anyone had anticipated.

47. Walter Isaacson, "Big Battles on Two Fronts," *Time*, June 29, 1981, p. 21.

48. Caroline Atkinson, "Dole Hopes to Pass Tax Bill in 2 Weeks, Beating the House," *Washington Post*, July 3, 1981, p. A7; Caroline Atkinson and Lou Cannon, "White House Quickly Squelches GOP Talk of Tax Compromise," *Washington Post*, July 10, 1981, pp. A1, A7.

49. *CQA 1981*, pp. 98–99.

50. Peter Behr, "Limited Straddle Curbs Voted," *Washington Post*, July 11, 1981, p. D7; Thomas Edsall, "Reagan Goes To the Hill On Tax Bill," *Washington Post*, July 25, 1981, pp. A1, A10.

51. See Robert Prinsky, "Industry Pushes to Persuade Congress To Accept Its Tax-Straddle Proposals," *Wall Street Journal*, July 31, 1981, p. 32, for the industry's side.

52. Margot Hornblower, "A Boll Weevil," *Washington Post*, July 27, 1981, p. A5.

53. Sources for numbers here, which are, as usual, a bit fuzzy, include Samuelson, "Death and Taxes—An Instructive Tale About How Congress Makes Tax Policy"; "Congress Decorates the Christmas Tree a Little Early," *National Journal*, July 4, 1981, p. 1194; *CQA 1981*, pp. 98, 100–2; Robert W. Merry, "Congress Clears Reagan's Tax-Cut Plan, Rejecting Traditional Economic Policies," *Wall Street Journal*, July 30, 1981, pp. 3, 12, 14, 16; Thomas B. Edsall, "Republicans

Control Tax Legislation," *Washington Post,* July 26, 1981, p. A10; Thomas B. Edsall and Caroline Atkinson, "Ways and Means Democrats Bend a Bit on Tax Trims," *Washington Post,* July 22, 1981, p. A2; and Edsall, "Reagan Goes To the Hill On Tax Bill."

54. Who's to say what a windfall profit is? Presumably, if prices and profits plummeted, no one would suggest a subsidy to make up the difference.

55. Thomas B. Edsall and Edward Walsh, "Senate Bargaining on Tax Cut Bill Chokes Oil Bonanza, Ends Filibuster," *Washington Post,* July 23, 1981, p. A4; Thomas B. Edsall, "Oil Is the Issue Snagging House and Senate Tax Bills," *Washington Post,* July 21, 1981, p. A6; Edsall and Atkinson, "Ways and Means Democrats Bend a Bit on Tax Trims"; *CQA 1981,* pp. 101–2.

56. Thomas B. Edsall and Lou Cannon, "Reagan Opens Tax Bill in Bid for House Votes," *Washington Post,* July 24, 1981, pp. A1, A2.

57. Stockman, *Triumph of Politics,* p. 257.

58. Edsall, "Reagan Goes To the Hill On Tax Bill."

59. Ibid.

60. *CQA 1981,* pp. 102–3.

61. Edsall, "Reagan Goes To the Hill On Tax Bill."

62. Ibid.

63. "Christmastime on Capitol Hill," *Time,* July 27, 1981, p. 25.

64. Stockman, *Triumph of Politics,* p. 262.

65. Ibid., pp. 262–63. Barrett, *Gambling with History,* pp. 164–65, tells the same story but dates it to June 4, which seems less likely.

66. "Cutting Loose on Taxes," Editorial, *Washington Post,* July 22, 1981, p. A20.

67. Thomas B. Edsall, "Rostenkowski Aside, House Likes Indexing," *Washington Post,* July 18, 1981, p. A2.

68. "A Wealth of Tax Objections," *Time,* July 20, 1981, p. 23.

69. Thomas B. Edsall, "Panel Democrats Targeting Tax Cuts at Income Below $50,000," *Washington Post,* July 14, 1981, p. A4.

70. Peter Goldman, "Hanging Tough on Taxes," *Newsweek,* July 27, 1981, pp. 22–23.

71. David Broder, "The Gypsy Moths," *Washington Post,* July 27, 1981, pp. A1, A4.

72. David Broder, "Reagan Backs Off Televised Speech on Social Security," *Washington Post,* July 26, 1981, pp. A1, A5.

73. George H. Gallup, *The Gallup Poll: Public Opinion 1981* (Wilmington, Dela.: Scholarly Resources Inc., 1982), pp. 118–19; Survey #173-G.

74. John F. Stacks, "It's Rightward On," *Time,* June 1, 1981, pp. 12–13.

75. *Gallup Poll, 1981,* No. 191, p. 18.

76. Broder, "Reagan Backs Off Televised Speech on Social Security."

77. Barrett, *Gambling with History,* p. 169.

78. Lou Cannon and Thomas B. Edsall, "Reagan Makes Appeal To Voters for Tax Bill," *Washington Post,* July 28, 1981, pp. A1, A6; Barrett, *Gambling with History,* pp. 169–70.

79. Dennis Farney, "Reagan's Mastery of Economic Policies In Congress May Sag on Social Issues," *Wall Street Journal,* July 30, 1981, p. 14.

80. *CQA 1981,* p. 103.

81. Lou Cannon and Kathy Sawyer, "President's Speech Has Hill Switchboards Ablaze," *Washington Post,* July 29, 1981, pp. A1, A2.

82. Ellie McGrath, "Tracking the Great Persuader," *Time,* August 10, 1981, p. 14.

83. Barrett, *Gambling with History,* p. 170.

84. McGrath, "Tracking the Great Persuader"; Cannon and Sawyer, "President's Speech Has Hill Switchboards Ablaze."

85. Ward Sinclair and Richard L. Lyons, "Tactics That Won," *Washington Post,* July 30, 1981, pp. A1, A8; Thomas B. Edsall, "Reagan Triumphant on Tax-Cut Bill," *Washington Post,* July 30, 1981, pp. A1, A9.

86. McGrath, "Tracking the Great Persuader"; Stockman, *Triumph of Politics,* p. 266.

87. Stockman, *Triumph of Politics,* pp. 264–65.

88. Robert W. Merry, "Congress Clears Reagan's Tax Cut Plan, Rejecting Traditional Economic Policies," *Wall Street Journal,* July 30, 1981, p. 3.

89. Ibid.

90. "Seizing the Helm," *National Journal,* August 8, 1981, p. 1404.

91. See Ward Sinclair and Richard L. Lyons, "Tactics That Won," *Washington Post,* July 30, 1981, pp. A1, A8.

92. *Gallup Poll, 1981,* No. 191, p. 20.

93. Walter Isaacson, "Yeas 238—Nays 195," *Time,* August 10, 1981, p. 12.

94. Sinclair and Lyons, "Tactics That Won"; and Edsall, "Reagan Triumphant on Tax-Cut Bill."

95. Broder, "The Gypsy Moths."

96. Greider, *Education of David Stockman,* pp. 59–60.

97. Ibid.

98. See "A White House Report," *Program for Economic Recovery* (Washington, D.C.: U.S. Government Printing Office, February 18, 1981), p. 16; and Joint Committee on Taxation, *General Explanation of the Economic Recovery Tax Act of 1981* (Washington, D.C.: U.S. Government Printing Office, 1981), Tables V-1, V-3.

99. Isaacson, "Yeas 238—Nays 195."

Chapter Nine

1. Charles Alexander, "Making It Work," *Time,* September 21, 1981, pp. 38–40, 45–47, 50–51.

2. See Robert J. Samuelson, "For the Economy, Unanswered Questions," *National Journal,* August 8, 1981, pp. 1405–10; News Roundup, in *Wall Street Journal,* July 31, 1981, p. 1.

3. See John S. DeMott, "Sky-High Interest Rates," *Time,* May 18, 1981, pp. 64–65; Council of Economic Advisers, "Economic Indicators," various months; and Greider, *Secrets of the Temple,* pp. 381–93.

4. See Lindley H. Clark, Jr., "Mixed Picture: Inflation Slows Down, But So

Does Economy; Joblessness May Grow," *Wall Street Journal*, July 1, 1981, pp. 1, 20.

5. Ibid.

6. John M. Berry, "Fed Decides to Lower Key Money-Growth Target," *Washington Post*, July 14, 1981, p. E1.

7. Ibid.

8. Ibid.

9. John M. Berry, "Banking Panel Attacks Volcker on Tight Money," *Washington Post*, July 22, 1981, p. E1; Robert J. Samuelson, "The Narrow Presidency," *National Journal*, August 1, 1981, p. 1387.

10. Stockman, *Triumph of Politics*, p. 272; interviews.

11. Ibid., p. 269; and Barrett, *Gambling with History*, p. 172.

12. Barrett, *Gambling with History*, p. 172, 340.

13. Ibid., pp. 170–72; Peter Goldman, "Budget-Cut Blues Ahead," *Newsweek*, August 17, 1981, p. 28.

14. Stockman, *Triumph of Politics*, p. 277–78.

15. See description in ibid., pp. 279–81.

16. Peter Goldman, "An Ax Over the Pentagon," *Newsweek*, August 31, 1981, pp. 19–20; Kenneth H. Bacon, "Budget Blight," *Wall Street Journal*, August 12, 1981, p. 1.

17. With only a 5 percent tax cut, scheduled payroll tax increases coming on line in January, and the spending cuts, policy was going to be no more stimulative in either a supply- or demand-side sense than in 1981.

18. Barrett, *Gambling with History*, pp. 176–77; Goldman, "An Ax Over the Pentagon"; Stockman, *Triumph of Politics*, pp. 282–88. Our account of most of these internal debates relies heavily on Stockman. Barrett, however, tells essentially the same story, and this was confirmed in our interviews. The reader who would like an extremely vivid account should see *Triumph of Politics*.

19. Barrett, *Gambling with History*, pp. 177–78; Tom Morganthau et al., "Reagan's Confidence Gap," *Newsweek*, September 21, 1981, p. 27.

20. Morganthau et al., "Reagan's Confidence Gap"; Albert R. Hunt and Dennis Farney, "GOP, Upset by High Interest Fees, Returns to Congress with Talk of Credit Controls," *Wall Street Journal*, September 10, 1981, p. 3.

21. Harry Anderson, "Reagan's Ailing Economy," *Newsweek*, September 7, 1981, pp. 18–20.

22. Greider, *Secrets of the Temple*, chap. 11, pp. 351–404; also 405–31.

23. Stockman, *Triumph of Politics*, p. 291.

24. Ibid., pp. 290–92.

25. Barrett, *Gambling with History*, pp. 178–80; "Snipped," *The Economist*, September 19, 1981, p. 21; Morganthau et al., "Reagan's Confidence Gap"; Stockman, *Triumph of Politics*, pp. 295–99.

26. Stockman, *Triumph of Politics*, p. 299.

27. Ibid., pp. 304–6.

28. Ibid.

29. Ibid., p. 316.

30. Ibid.

31. Ibid., p. 323; Barrett, *Gambling with History*, pp. 182–83.

32. Timothy B. Clark, "Reagan's Balanced Budget—One Step Closer, One Step Further Away," *National Journal*, September 26, 1981, pp. 1712–16; "Reagan's budget plans generate tepid support, plenty of confusion," *National Journal*, October 3, 1981, pp. 1751, 1778–89.

33. Tom Morganthau et al., "Running to Stay in Place," *Newsweek*, October 5, 1981, pp. 24–26.

34. "Reagan's budget plans generate tepid support."

35. "A Reagan Retreat," *Time*, October 5, 1981, p. 10.

36. "Things That Go Bump," *The Economist*, October 3, 1981, pp. 11–13.

37. For a good description of gypsy moths at this time, see Richard E. Cohen, "For the Gypsy Moths, the Goal Is to Change GOP Policy, Not Bolt the Party," *National Journal*, October 31, 1981, pp. 1946–49.

38. *CQA 1981*, pp. 332–33, 338–39; Richard E. Cohen, "Reagan's budget plan faces high hurdles, shortage of time," *National Journal*, October 24, 1981, pp. 1887, 1915.

39. These decreases included $40 billion in entitlement cuts, and $30 billion from reductions in other spending and, because of less borrowing, in interest payments. "You Pay Your Money, You Take Your Pick," p. 1997; and Richard E. Cohen, "Lots of Movement, Little Action on Closing the Deficit," pp. 1971, 1997, *National Journal*, November 7, 1981.

40. Michael Reese, "Goodbye Balanced Budget," *Newsweek*, November 16, 1981, p. 34. *Time* reported this as "I didn't come here to balance the budget. I was elected to reduce Government intrusion in the economy." Ed Magnuson, "Bye, Bye, Balanced Budget," *Time*, November 16, 1981, pp. 26, 31.

41. Barrett, *Gambling with History*, p. 185; Magnuson, "Bye, Bye, Balanced Budget."

42. Timothy B. Clark, "The GOP Is Looking Over Its Shoulder At the Specter of High Interest Rates," *National Journal*, November 7, 1981, pp. 1972–77; Kenneth H. Bacon and Dennis Farney, "Embattled GOP: Reagan's Vow To Stick To Economic Program Saps Base in Congress," *Wall Street Journal*, November 17, 1981, pp. 1, 19.

43. Stockman, *Triumph of Politics*, p. 351.

44. We quote Greider's *Education of David Stockman and Other Americans* liberally in our history; it contains the original article plus Greider's description and interpretation of the flap that followed.

45. Tom Morganthau et al., "Et Tu, David Stockman?" *Newsweek*, November 23, 1981, p. 40.

46. For a similar judgment, see "Mr. Stockman's Future," editorial, *Wall Street Journal*, November 16, 1981, p. 22.

47. Stockman, *Triumph of Politics*, p. 5. For the cartoon, see Pat Oliphant, *Ban This Book!* (Kansas City: Andrews and McMeel, 1982), p. 71.

48. Stockman, *Triumph of Politics*, pp. 1–3.

49. Barrett, *Gambling with History*, p. 189.

50. Ed Magnuson, "A Visit to the Woodshed," *Time*, November 23, 1981, pp. 10–13.

51. The bill funded the legislative branch for the entire year.

52. The Defense Department appropriation to be reported by the House

Appropriations Committee; conference reports on the Interior, HUD, and Agriculture appropriations; House-passed bills for Military Construction and Energy and Water; House-passed bills or fiscal 1981 levels, whichever was less, for Commerce, Justice, State and Judiciary, for Transportation, the District of Columbia, and for Labor, Health and Human Services—Education; the House-passed or Senate-reported bill, whichever was less, for Treasury, Postal Service; the fiscal 1981 or budget request levels, whichever was less, for foreign aid. *CQA 1981,* p. 295.

53. Ibid.

54. Ed Magnuson, "After the Lost Weekend," *Time,* December 7, 1981, pp. 16–19.

55. *CQA 1981,* p. 297.

56. "For taxonomy freaks," an OMB official commented on reviewing our manuscript, this "was called a four percent cut with a Baker floor. Our inability to price out this very amendment was the initial impulse leading to the development" of a new OMB budget scorekeeping system.

57. Magnuson, "After the Lost Weekend."

58. *CQA 1981,* pp. 300–301.

59. Magnuson, "After the Lost Weekend."

60. *CQA 1981,* p. 301. Pages 294–301 are the major source of this story.

Chapter Ten

1. John F. Stacks, "America's Fretful Mood," *Time,* December 28, 1981, pp. 22–23.

2. David M. Alpern, "Polarizing the Nation?" *Newsweek,* February 8, 1982, pp. 33–34.

3. Ibid.; and Stacks, "America's Fretful Mood."

4. Data from Council of Economic Advisers, "Economic Indicators," various dates.

5. Yankelovich poll, *Time,* April 5, 1982, pp. 10–12.

6. Adam Clymer, "Reagan Evoking Rising Concern, New Poll Shows," *New York Times,* March 19, 1981, pp. A1, A20.

7. James Kelly, "Challenging the Red Sea," *Time,* February 22, 1982, p. 14.

8. Walter Isaacson, "Caught in the Riptide of Red Ink," *Time,* December 21, 1981, p. 28.

9. Ibid.

10. Harry Anderson et al., "Reagan's Busted Budget," *Newsweek,* December 21, 1981, pp. 63–64.

11. "End of a Jam Session," *The Economist,* December 26, 1981, pp. 18–19.

12. On the economy, Anderson, "Reagan's Busted Budget," and Isaacson, "Caught in the Riptide of Red Ink" provide good summaries.

13. See Allen Schick, *Congress and the President: Reagan's First Year* (Washington, D.C.: American Enterprise Institute, 1982).

14. John Gilmour's forthcoming book manuscript, "A Most Bizarre Way to

Legislate: Reconciliation and the Congressional Budget Process," discusses this in depth.

15. See "Meanwhile, Back in the 1981 Budget, Another Reagan Victory," *National Journal,* May 9, 1981, p. 846; and *CQA 1981,* pp. 281–85.

16. Melinda Beck and Howard Fineman, "The Farm Bloc Tastes Defeat," *Newsweek,* September 28, 1981, pp. 29–30.

17. Ibid.

18. Walter Isaacson, "Mixing Politics with Parity," *Time,* November 2, 1981, p. 22.

19. See "Farm bill conference a test of Reagan's control of spending," *National Journal,* October 31, 1981, pp. 1931, 1957; Isaacson, "Mixing Politics with Parity"; and Beck and Fineman, "Farm Bloc Tastes Defeat."

20. House Budget Committee, "A Review of President Reagan's Budget Recommendations, 1981–85," August 2, 1984, pp. 133–39; Congressional Budget Office, "An Analysis of Congressional Budget Estimates for Fiscal Years 1980–82," June 1984, p. 65.

21. *CQA 1981,* p. 318.

22. Ibid., p. 269.

23. Ibid., pp. 267–70.

24. Congressional Budget Office, "An Analysis of Congressional Budget Estimates," June 1984, pp. 38–39.

25. " 'A Hell of a Crunch' in '82," *Newsweek,* December 28, 1981, between pp. 20–40.

26. "Playing Both Santa and Scrooge," *Time,* December 28, 1981, p. 24.

27. " 'A Hell of a Crunch' in '82," *Newsweek.*

28. Walter Isaacson, " 'The Floor Is My Domain,' " *Time,* April 26, 1982.

29. Michael Barone and Grant Ujifusa, *Almanac of American Politics 1984* (Washington, D.C.: Barone & Co., 1983), p. 430.

30. Barrett, *Gambling with History,* p. 341.

31. Kenneth H. Bacon, "Advice Gap: Reagan Aides Dispute How to Cut Deficit—and How Harmful It Is," *Wall Street Journal,* December 10, 1981, pp. 1, 18.

32. Timothy B. Clark, "A Divided Administration Wonders Whether It's Time for More Taxes," *National Journal,* January 16, 1982, pp. 113–18.

33. Office of Management and Budget, *The President's Budget for Fiscal Year 1983* (Washington, D.C.: U.S. Government Printing Office, 1982), pp. 2–11 to 2–16.

34. Congressional Budget Office, "An Analysis of the President's Budgetary Proposals for Fiscal Year 1983," February 1982, pp. 33–42.

35. Clark, "A Divided Administration Wonders Whether It's Time for More Taxes." See Paul Craig Roberts, *The Supply-Side Revolution: An Insider's Account of Policymaking in Washington* (Cambridge, Mass.: Harvard University Press, 1984).

36. Michael Reese et al., "The Hard Times of Ronald Reagan," *Newsweek,* February 1, 1982, pp. 17–19.

37. Rochelle L. Stanfield, "Turning Back '61 Programs: A Radical Shift of Power," *National Journal,* February 27, 1982, p. 369.

38. For extensive discussion of the federalism plan, see Rochelle L. Stanfield, "New Federalism: A Neatly Wrapped Package with Explosives Inside," *National Journal,* February 27, 1982, pp. 356–83.

39. Peter Goldman, "Reagan's Taxing Problem," *Newsweek,* January 11, 1982, pp. 18–19. The story is repeated in various forms frequently. Barrett has it as "the papers are right. You *are* plotting against me" (*Gambling with History,* p. 343).

40. Clark, "A Divided Administration Wonders Whether It's Time for More Taxes"; Barrett, *Gambling with History,* p. 344.

41. Peter Goldman, "Reagan's New Excise Taxes," *Newsweek,* January 25, 1982, pp. 28–29.

42. Steven R. Weisman, "GOP Senators Bid Reagan Lift Taxes," *New York Times,* January 16, 1982, p. 36; Barrett, *Gambling with History,* p. 344.

43. Barrett, *Gambling with History,* p. 345.

44. Walter Isaacson, "States of the Union," *Time,* February 8, 1982, pp. 16–18; Peter Goldman, "The Reagan Gamble," *Newsweek,* February 8, 1982, pp. 24–27.

45. See Aaron Wildavsky, "Birthday Cake Federalism," in Robert B. Hawkins, Jr., ed., *American Federalism: A New Partnership for the Republic* (San Francisco: Institute for Contemporary Studies, 1982), pp. 181–92; Richard Nathan, "Toward a Theory of Federal Grants," typescript, 1982; and Richard Nathan and Fred C. Doolittle, "The Untold Story of Reagan's 'New Federalism,'" *The Public Interest,* No. 77 (Fall 1984), pp. 96–105.

46. See Karl Weick, *The Social Psychology of Organizing* (Reading, Mass.: Addison Wesley, 1979).

47. In the early days of the Republic, "corruption" was used by Jeffersonians not to mean stealing but rather debt and other legal devices they believed undermined principles of political equality. See James Savage, *Balanced Budgets and American Politics* (Ithaca, N.Y.: Cornell University Press, 1988).

48. Jonathan Fuerbringer, "Volcker Cautions That Big Deficits Imperil Recovery," *New York Times,* January 27, 1981, p. A1.

49. Goldman, "The Reagan Gamble."

50. "'A Hell of a Crunch' in '82."

Chapter Eleven

1. The Congressional Budget Office projected a FY83 deficit, under current policies, of $157 billion, total spending at $809 billion, and spending on programs other than defense, interest, and social security totaling $318 billion. See CBO, "Baseline Budget Projections for Fiscal Years 1983–87," February 1982, pp. 40, 45. For deficit projections, see CBO, "An Analysis of the President's Budgetary Proposals for Fiscal Year 1983," February 1982, p. xiv.

2. Stockman, *Triumph of Politics,* p. 353.

3. Jonathan Fuerbringer, "Stockman Defends Reagan's Proposal and Size of Deficit," *New York Times,* February 8, 1982, pp. A1, B13.

4. Executive Office of the President, Office of Management and Budget,

Budget of the United States Government Fiscal Year 1983 (Washington, D.C.: U.S. Government Printing Office, 1982), pp. 3–4.

5. Ibid., pp. 3–14.

6. Ibid., pp. 3–12.

7. Congressional Budget Office, "An Analysis of the President's Budgetary Proposals for Fiscal Year 1983," p. 7.

8. Martin Tolchin, "Budget Brings Attacks in Congress From Republicans and Democrats," *New York Times,* February 7, 1982, p. 28.

9. Martin Tolchin, "Baker Tries to Quiet Storm Raised by GOP on Deficit," *New York Times,* February 9, 1982, p. B14.

10. Edward Cowan, "Economists Voice Doubts on Budget," *New York Times,* February 9, 1982, p. B14.

11. Charles Alexander, "Roadblocks to Recovery," *Time,* February 22, 1982, pp. 36–38.

12. Peter McGrath et al., "The Deficit Rebellion," *Newsweek,* February 22, 1982, pp. 22–24.

13. Alexander, "Roadblocks to Recovery"; McGrath et al., "Deficit Rebellion"; Martin Tolchin, "Reagan Aides Hear Budget Attacked From Both Parties," *New York Times,* February 10, 1982, p. A1.

14. Steven V. Roberts, "Voters Reported Less Confident of Reagan Plan," *New York Times,* February 21, 1982, p. A1.

15. Social psychologists Daniel Kahneman and Amos Tversky provide two good examples. First, "most respondents in a sample of undergraduates refused to stake $10 on the toss of a coin if they stood to win less than $30." Second, in "a situation in which an individual is forced to choose between an 85 percent chance to lose $1,000 . . . and a sure loss of $800, a large majority of people express a preference for the gamble over the sure loss." Even though, on average, they will do worse that way. See their "Choices, Values, and Frames," *American Psychologist* 39, no. 4 (April 1984), pp. 341–50; quote on p. 342.

16. Seth S. King, "Labor Challenges Reagan on Budget," *New York Times,* February 16, 1982, p. A1.

17. Edward Cowan, "Business Leaders Object to Deficits in Reagan Budget," *New York Times,* March 4, 1982, pp. A1, D15; "Euphoria Ends," *Time,* May 17, 1982, p. 56.

18. "Bubbles in the Red Ink," *Time,* March 8, 1982, p. 17; Martin Tolchin, "G.O.P. Leaders Tell President His Plan on Budget is Dead," *New York Times,* February 24, 1982, pp. A1, A14.

19. James Kelly, "The Zigzag Art of Politics," *Time,* March 15, 1982, pp. 15–16; Barrett, *Gambling with History,* pp. 349–50.

20. Ed Magnuson, "Playing It Cool or Frozen in Ice?" *Time,* March 22, 1982, p. 34.

21. George J. Church, "A Season of Scare Talk," *Time,* March 15, 1982, pp. 12–14.

22. Jane Bryant Quinn, "Reagan Against Himself," *Newsweek,* March 1, 1982, p. 66.

23. See Martin Anderson, *Revolution* (San Diego: Harcourt Brace Jovanovich, 1988), p. 211.

24. Barrett, *Gambling with History*, p. 351.

25. Ibid., pp. 348–53.

26. George J. Church, "Trying to Be Mr. Nice Guy," *Time*, April 5, 1982, pp. 13–14.

27. Descriptions of the "Gang" are based on interviews and on documents made available by staff for a participant, who kept a notebook on these events.

28. COLAs would be limited to 4 percent and occur every fifteen months instead of every twelve. These provisions, according to the estimates used, would yield a 7.5 percent cut in the benefits received by an individual over the period from July 1, 1982, through December 31, 1985.

29. "Domenici Calls Budget Pact Task of O'Neill and Reagan," Associated Press Wire Service, *New York Times*, April 9, 1982, p. A15.

30. Martin Tolchin, "A Month's Budget Talks Finally Came to Naught," *New York Times*, April 30, 1982, p. A17.

31. Howell Raines, "Reagan Optimistic That Budget Talks Will End Impasse," *New York Times*, April 6, 1982, pp. A1, A17.

32. Howell Raines, "White House Hints Accord on Budget by Tax Surcharge," *New York Times*, April 15, 1982, pp. A1, D20; Kenneth Nobel, "Baker Voices Hope of Gaining Accord on Tax Surcharge," *New York Times*, April 19, 1982, pp. A1, A19; Ed Magnuson, "Stumbling to a Showdown," *Time*, April 26, 1982, pp. 10–14; "Nudging the Budget," *Newsweek*, April 26, 1982, p. 35.

33. Transcript, *New York Times*, April 17, 1982, p. A9.

34. Peter McGrath et al., "In Quest of a Pax Reaganomica," *Newsweek*, May 3, 1982, pp. 20–21; Barrett, *Gambling with History*, p. 361.

35. Martin Tolchin, "Reagan to Enter Talks on Budget as Negotiators Reach an Impasse," *New York Times*, April 28, 1982, p. A1; Barrett, *Gambling with History*, pp. 358–61.

36. These numbers are derived from worksheets of participants.

37. Jerry Adler et al., "The 'Extra Mile' to Nowhere," *Newsweek*, May 10, 1982, pp. 38–42.

38. Tolchin, "A Month's Budget Talks Finally Came to Naught."

39. Transcript, *New York Times*, April 30, 1982, p. A16.

40. Transcript of Bolling's reply to Reagan on behalf of Democrats in Congress, *New York Times*, April 30, 1982, p. A18.

41. Steven V. Roberts, "Senate Unit Begins Drafting a Budget," *New York Times*, April 30, 1982, p. A18.

42. Steven V. Roberts, "House Democrats Emphasizing Unity," *New York Times*, May 2, 1982, p. 26.

43. Martin Tolchin, "Domenici Presents Own Budget Plan," *New York Times*, May 5, 1982, Section 2, p. 11.

44. Martin Tolchin, "White House and GOP Leaders Agree on Budget Proposal for '83," *New York Times*, May 6, 1982, pp. A1, B13.

45. Ibid.

46. Martin Tolchin, "President Pledges to Push Campaign for Budget Plan," *New York Times*, May 7, 1982, pp. A1, D18.

47. Ibid.

48. Adam Clymer, "Talk of Social Security Cutbacks Causes Alarm in Ranks

of G.O.P.," *New York Times*, May 8, 1982, p. A10; Martin Tolchin, "Social Security Issue Causing Problems for New Budget," *New York Times*, May 8, 1982, pp. A1, A9.

49. Martin Tolchin, "G.O.P. in House Opposes Budget of Senate Panel," *New York Times*, May 12, 1982, pp. A1, A24.

50. *Congressional Quarterly Almanac 1982*, Vol. 38 (Washington, D.C.: Congressional Quarterly, Inc., 1983), p. 187 (hereafter *CQA 1982*).

51. Tom Morganthau et al., "The Third Rail of Politics," *Newsweek*, May 24, 1982, pp. 24–26.

52. *CQA 1982*, pp. 191–92.

53. "GOP puts aside bipartisan stance on 1983 budget," *National Journal*, May 8, 1982, pp. 799, 826.

54. Jane Perlez, "Moderate Republicans Feel They Control House Passage of Budget," *New York Times*, May 11, 1982, p. A17.

55. *CQA 1982*, pp. 190–91.

56. Richard S. Cohen, "The Fiscal 1983 Budget Equation: Election + Recession = Frustration," *National Journal*, May 29, 1982, pp. 944–48.

57. *CQA 1982*, pp. 192–93.

58. "House Raising on the Hill," *Time*, May 31, 1982, p. 16.

59. George J. Church, "Chaos Aplenty, but No Budget," *Time*, June 7, 1982, p. 18; Tom Morganthau and Gloria Borger, "Anyone for a Budget?" *Newsweek*, June 7, 1982, pp. 31–32.

60. *CQA 1982*, pp. 192–93.

61. "GOP in Best Position to Win on 1983 Budget," *National Journal*, June 5, 1982, p. 1021.

62. *CQA 1982*, p. 193.

63. Church, "Chaos Aplenty."

64. John Herbers, "President Denounces Budget Process," *New York Times*, May 29, 1982, p. 44.

65. See comments by Senator Bill Bradley, *Newsweek*, May 3, 1982, p. 21; comments of Peter G. Peterson and five former secretaries of the Treasury in *Time*, June 7, 1982, p. 18.

66. See Robert J. Samuelson, "The Interest in Rates," *National Journal*, June 5, 1982, p. 1015.

67. Steven V. Roberts, "President Rejects Bipartisan Budget," *New York Times*, June 3, 1982, Section 2, p. 15.

68. Ibid.

69. Martin Tolchin, "GOP Budget Wins Approval in House by Vote of 219–206," *New York Times*, June 11, 1982, p. A1.

70. Ibid.

71. Ibid., and *CQA 1982*, pp. 195–96.

72. Walter Isaacson, "Breaking the Budget Logjam," *Time*, June 21, 1982, p. 37.

73. Martin Tolchin, "Conferees Agree on Budget for '83 Along GOP Lines," *New York Times*, June 18, 1982, pp. A1, D17. For conference details, see *CQA 1982*, pp. 196–99; and Richard E. Cohen, "Congress's 'House of Cards' Budget

May Be Constructed on Quicksand," *National Journal,* June 26, 1982, pp. 1120–26.

74. Steven R. Weisman, "Reagan's Risky Decision," *New York Times,* February 7, 1982, pp. 1, 30.

75. "Business may be victim of congressional drive to increase taxes," *National Journal,* February 27, 1982, pp. 355, 389.

76. Ibid.

77. Timothy B. Clark, "Lobbyists at Work: Tax Lobbyists Scrambling in the Dark to Fight Taxes That Hit Their Clients," *National Journal,* May 22, 1982, pp. 896–901.

78. Ibid.; and Timothy B. Clark, "Tax-Raising Proposals Off and Running But Few Generate Strong Support," *National Journal,* April 3, 1982, pp. 576–80.

79. See *Economist,* "Back on the Ground," April 3, 1982, pp. 79–80.

80. Clark, "Tax-Raising Proposals Off and Running."

81. Ibid.; and *CQA 1982,* p. 34.

82. Clark, "Lobbyists at Work: Tax Lobbyists Scrambling in the Dark."

83. Richard E. Cohen, "Dole's Toughest Test as Finance Chief—Pushing a Tax Hike Through the Senate," *National Journal,* June 19, 1982, pp. 1089–93.

84. The surcharge idea that arose in the Gang of 17 negotiations had been abandoned.

85. *CQA 1982,* pp. 34–35; "GOP tax hike package takes edge off Democrats' thunder," *National Journal,* July 3, 1982, pp. 1203, 1229.

86. Peter McGrath et al., "A No-Fingerprints Tax Bill," *Newsweek,* August 9, 1982, pp. 16–17.

87. See, e.g., Stockman, *Triumph of Politics,* p. 356.

88. See, for example, Donald Regan, *For the Record* (New York: Harcourt, Brace, Jovanovich, 1988), pp. 182–84.

89. Steven R. Weisman, "Reagan Presses for Tax Increase in Western Trip," *New York Times,* August 12, 1982, p. A1.

90. *CQA 1982,* pp. 37–38.

91. Rich Thomas, "Why Reagan Switched," *Newsweek,* August 23, 1982, p. 27.

92. Karen W. Arenson, "Measure Is Reformers' Delight," *New York Times,* August 17, 1982, Section 4, p. 17.

93. "Transcript of the President's Televised Speech on Tax Policy," *New York Times,* August 17, 1982, Section 4, p. 16.

94. Walter Isaacson, "Scoring on a Reverse," *Time,* August 30, 1982, pp. 14–18.

95. Ibid. provides a good summary. The administration and Chamber virtually went to war. Other business lobbyists described the Chamber's anti-TEFRA campaign as "really vicious," while some in the Chamber who opposed TEFRA claim that the administration tried to get the Chamber's board to fire its president.

96. *CQA 1982,* p. 39.

97. See *CQA 1982,* pp. 29–39; Isaacson, "Scoring on a Reverse"; Melinda Beck et al., "Winning One for the Gipper," *Newsweek,* August 30, 1982, pp. 24–28; Karen Arenson, "Congress Approves Bill to Raise $983 Billion in Taxes," pp. A1, D14; Hedrich Smith, "Reagan's Big Victory: Passage of the Tax-Rise

Bill Vindicates Major Political Gamble by President," p. D14; and David Shribman, "How Bill's Momentum Swept House," p. D14; all in *New York Times*, August 20, 1982.

Chapter Twelve

1. We remember a dinner with Frank Levy, professor at the University of Maryland and author of *Dollars and Dreams: The Changing American Income Distribution* (New York: Russell Sage Foundation, 1987), at which he pointed out that, when "productivity" became a big issue in the late 1970s, many causes of slow productivity growth were suggested. They included OPEC, a younger and thus less productive work force as the baby boom entered it, greater government regulation, the uncertainties created by inflation, and many other suspects. By 1985, trends on virtually all the supposed causes were much better, but productivity growth had not improved.

2. Charles Alexander, "Oh, What a Beautiful Rally!" *Time*, August 30, 1982, pp. 19–20.

3. Ibid., and Charles Alexander, "Wall Street's Super Streak," *Time*, September 6, 1982, pp. 38–41, provided good, if rather breathless, accounts of the rally. Basic statistics can be found in the Council of Economic Advisers, *Economic Indicators*, monthly summary of economic statistics.

4. Alexander, "Wall Street's Super Streak."

5. Alexander, "Oh, What a Beautiful Rally!"

6. Ibid.

7. Merrill Shiels et al., "A Break in Interest Rates," *Newsweek*, August 30, 1982, pp. 16–19; John Greenwald, "Spotlight on the Consumer," *Time*, June 7, 1982, pp. 54–56; and John Greenwald, "Come On Big Spender," *Time*, June 28, 1982, pp. 48–49.

8. On July 6 the Organisation for Economic Co-Operation and Development "sharply scaled back its forecast for the world economy" and predicted unemployment in the world's major industrialized nations would reach nine percent in 1983, with U.S. unemployment at 10.25 percent. Steven Rattner, "O.E.C.D. Is Gloomier on Growth," *New York Times*, July 7, 1982, pp. D1, D13.

9. "Executives are fearful of renewed inflation," *Business Week*, August 9, 1982, p. 10.

10. "Adam Smith," *Paper Money* (New York: Dell Publishing, 1982), p. 206. "Smith," George J. W. Goodman, in a highly readable style, provides an extensive recounting of much of the history that follows. By now the international debt crisis may have generated as much literature as the American budget travails.

11. Alexander L. Taylor III, "The Wobbly World of Banking," *Time*, September 6, 1982, pp. 52–53.

12. The growing liquidity and debt worries had already begun to affect the economy. They contributed, for example, to the strength of the dollar relative to the German mark. See Treasury and Federal Reserve Exchange Operations, in *Federal Reserve Bulletin* 68, no. 10 (October 1982), p. 585.

13. Smith, *Paper Money*, pp. 310–11.

14. In testimony to Congress July 28, 1982; March 8, 1983, and as reported in the minutes of the meeting of the Federal Open Market Committee held on July 2, 1982.

15. Alexander, "Oh, What a Beautiful Rally!"

16. Testimony before the House Budget Committee, March 8, 1983, pp. 86–87.

17. Paul Blustein, "Monetary Zeal: How Federal Reserve Under Volcker Finally Slowed Down Inflation," *Wall Street Journal,* December 7, 1982, pp. 1, 16–17.

18. Data from Council of Economic Advisers, *Economic Indicators,* various months.

19. H. Erich Heinemann, "Record U.S. Borrowing Raising Fears on Credit," *New York Times,* Dec. 7, 1982, pp. D1, D4.

20. Greider's reporting in *Secrets of the Temple* documents the Fed's actions and intentions thoroughly.

21. *Federal Reserve Bulletin* 69, no. 3 (March 1983), p. 132.

22. House Budget Committee hearing, March 8, 1983, pp. 117–18.

23. David Vogel, "Why Businessmen Distrust Their State: The Political Consciousness of American Corporate Executives," *British Journal of Political Science* 8, Part 1 (January 1978), pp. 45–78.

24. " 'No Confidence' for Reaganomics," March 29, 1982, p. 40; "Support erodes for the business tax cuts," April 12, 1982, p. 18; and "Executives are fearful of renewed inflation," August 9, 1982, p. 10; all in *Business Week.*

25. Alexander L. Taylor III, "The Long Gray Line," *Time,* May 17, 1982, pp. 54–55.

26. "Washington Outlook: Why the GOP is Wooing Labor," edited by Lee Walczak, *Business Week,* April 26, 1982, p. 139.

27. Stockman, *Triumph of Politics,* pp. 131, 382–83, 145–47, 155.

28. Transcript in *New York Times,* July 29, 1982, p. Al8.

29. See, for instance, Daniel Walker Howe, *The Political Culture of the American Whigs* (Chicago: University of Chicago Press, 1979).

30. See Aaron Wildavsky, "The Runaway Convention, or Proving a Preposterous Negative," paper prepared for the Taxpayers' Foundation, 1983.

31. See U.S. Congress. House. Committee on Rules. "Item Veto: State Experience and Its Application to the Federal Situation." 99th Cong., 2d sess., 1986. Committee Print.

32. *Congressional Record,* October 1, 1982, H8264, quoted by Representative Peter Rodino (D-N.J.).

33. Mark Starr et al., "Business vs. Reagan," *Newsweek,* March 29, 1982, p. 21.

34. "Making Amends," *Time,* April 12, 1982, p. 19.

35. Transcript in *New York Times,* April 30, 1982, p. Al6.

36. "Amendment Drive Now in High Gear," *New York Times,* July 13, 1982, p. A17.

37. James R. Jones, "A Cowardly Out for Reaganomics," editorial, *New York Times,* August 8, 1982, Section 3, p. 2.

38. The president's endorsement, and Alaska's support, changed the stakes at the state level. A convention might actually happen, so doubts about its wisdom

suddenly became relevant. State legislators also had to consider what the federal government would cut if the amendment were passed; grants to state governments clearly would be high on the list. Missouri legislators adjourned on May 2 without considering the call for a convention. Legislators in Iowa began an attempt to reverse that state's endorsements. *New York Times,* May 3, 1982, p. A16; and Howell Raines, "President Seeking Counties' Support," July 14, 1982, p. A18.

39. *CQA 1982,* p. 394.
40. *Congressional Record,* October 1, 1982, pp. H8256–7.
41. Ibid., p. H8257.
42. Ibid., p. H8262.
43. Ibid., p. H8263.
44. Ibid., p. H8265.
45. Ibid., p. H8266.
46. Ibid., pp. H8271–72.
47. Ibid., p. H8329.
48. Edward Cowan, "Washington Watch," *New York Times,* November 18, 1982, p. D2.

Chapter Thirteen

1. David Mathiasen, "Recent Developments in the Composition and Formulation of the United States Federal Budget," *Public Budgeting and Finance* 3, no. 3 (Autumn 1983), pp. 103–15; quote on p. 107.

2. Hale Champion, "Comments," in Gregory Mills and John Palmer, eds., *Federal Budget Policy in the 1980s* (Washington, D.C.: Urban Institute, 1984), p. 292; Champion's comments on Hugh Heclo, "Executive Budget Making," pp. 255–91.

3. U.S. Congress. Senate. Subcommittee of the Committee on Appropriations. *Hearings on Departments of Labor, Health and Human Services, Education, and Related Agencies Appropriations for Fiscal Year 1983.* 97th Cong., 2d sess., part 4, pp. 142–43.

4. "House Raising on the Hill," *Time,* May 31, 1982, p. 16.

5. David Pauley et al., "Battles Over Bailouts," *Newsweek,* June 21, 1982, pp. 53–54.

6. Martin Tolchin, "House in Quandary as Senate Passes New Version of Spending Bill," *New York Times,* June 30, 1982, p. D22.

7. David R. Mayhew, *Congress: The Electoral Connection* (New Haven, Conn.: Yale University Press, 1974), pp. 117–18.

8. See Richard Neustadt, *Presidential Power* (New York: John Wiley & Sons, 1980).

9. Martin Tolchin, "House and Senate Pass $5.5 Billion Spending Bill," *New York Times,* July 16, 1982, p. A16.

10. U.S. Congress. Senate. Subcommittee of the Committee on Appropriations. *Hearings.* 97th Cong., 2d sess., pp. 100, 105.

11. Ibid., pp. 176–81.

12. U.S. Congress. House. Committee on Appropriations. *Hearings on De-*

partment of the Interior and Related Agencies Appropriations for 1983. 97th Cong., 2d sess., part 2, p. 817.

13. *CQA 1982*, p. 224.

14. *Congressional Record*, September 9, 1982, pp. S11249–50.

15. Quoted by Gary Hart in ibid., p. S11252; the Senate debate is on pp. S11249–67.

16. See Senate Appropriations' report on its 302(B) allocations. S Rept. 97–571, July 29, 1982.

17. The dairy portion of the committee's proposal was written by the National Milk Producers Federation. *CQA 1982*, pp. 358–61.

18. *CQA 1982*, p. 515.

19. Leonard M. Apcar, "House Refuses To Limit Climb In Retirees' Pay," *Wall Street Journal*, August 4, 1982, p. 3.

20. See *CQA 1982*, Reconciliation section, also pp. 515–16; and David Shribman, "Conferrees Meet Impasse on Plan to Cut Spending," *New York Times*, August 14, 1982, p. A28.

21. Martin Tolchin, "Congress Leaders Yield to President on Special Session: Budget Will be the Topic," *New York Times*, September 17, 1982, pp. Al, A20.

22. *CQA 1982*, p. 228.

23. On gerrymanders see William Safire, *Safire's Political Dictionary* (New York: Ballantine Books, 1980), pp. 255–56. On California, see Michael Barone and Grant Ujifusa, *The Almanac of American Politics 1984* (Washington, D.C.: National Journal, 1983), pp. 73–74. Hoping to cut their own deal with Mexican-Americans, California Republicans rejected overtures for a bipartisan effort. They thus put themselves at the mercies of Representative Phil Burton of San Francisco, a political gut fighter of the first order, who knew his state inside and out. He took care of the Hispanics and every Democrat is sight, devising a plan that, through some very strangely shaped districts, both met all legal requirements and gave his party a huge advantage. In the 1982 election Democrats won twenty-eight of the forty-five California seats. On Indiana see ibid., p. 382.

24. Mark Shields, "Learning From the Lame Ducks," *Washington Post*, December 24, 1982, p. A13.

25. "Transcript of Reagan's Speech to Nation on G.O.P. Policy and the Economy," p. B14; "Transcript of Riegle's Reply for Democrats to President's Talk on Economy," p. B14, *New York Times*, October 14, 1982.

26. For polls, see George L. Church, "Facing the Jobs Issue," *Time*, October 28, 1982, pp. 18–19. The president's pollster, Richard Wirthlin, reported similar results, *Newsweek*, November 15, 1982, p. 14.

27. Church, "Facing the Jobs Issue"; William Schneider, "Reaganomics Was on the Voters' Minds, But Their Verdict Was Far From Clear," *National Journal*, November 6, 1982, pp. 1892–93; and table on p. 1893.

28. Ed Magnuson, "Interpreting the New Moderation," *Time*, November 22, 1982, p. 74.

29. Walter Isaacson, "Trimming the Sails," *Time*, November 15, 1982, pp. 12–16, 21.

30. *CQA 1982*, p. 321.

31. William F. Clinger (R-Pa.), editorial, *New York Times*, February 4, 1982.

32. Melinda Beck et al., "The Decaying of America," *Newsweek*, August 2, 1982, pp. 12–18.

33. *CQA 1982*, p. 322.

34. Rochelle L. Stanfield, "Jobs Gain Momentum in Wake of Election Returns," *National Journal*, November 20, 1982, p. 1999.

35. Martin Tolchin, "Jobs Legislation is Gaining Support," *New York Times*, November 11, 1982, pp. Al, Al9; also Ed Cowan, "Gas Tax Rise Urged by Rostenkowski for Road Repairs," *New York Times*, November 10, 1982, pp. Al, Dl4.

36. Howell Raines, "G.O.P. Lacks Votes on Early Tax Cut, President is Told," *New York Times*, November 19, 1982, p. Al.

37. *CQA 1982*, p. 322.

38. Stanfield, "Jobs Gain Momentum in Wake of Election Returns."

39. George J. Church, "How to be Santa Claus," *Time*, December 20, 1982, pp. 18, 21.

40. Susan Tifft, "New Roads for the Unemployed," *Time*, December 6, 1982, p. 23; Kenneth Gilpin, "Spending Proposals Criticized," *New York Times*, November 22, 1982, pp. Dl, D7.

41. Walter Isaacson, "Lame Ducks Lay An Egg," *Time*, December 27, 1982, pp. 12–14.

42. *CQA 1982*, p. 285.

43. Ibid.; and Walter S. Mosberg, "Congress Deletes MX Production Funds But Fine Print Will Allow Five to Be Built," *Wall Street Journal*, December 21, 1982, p. 6.

44. *CQA 1982*, p. 547; see also Mike Causey, "The Federal Diary: Top U.S. Aides Get More Pay: Most Live Here," *Washington Post*, December 22, 1982, p. B2.

45. Martin Tolchin, "House Allocates $5 Billion to Jobs," *New York Times*, December 15, 1982, pp. A1, A28.

46. Martin Tolchin, "How Gas Tax Lost in Senate," *New York Times*, December 18, 1982, pp. Al, Al3.

47. Ibid.

48. Steven V. Roberts, "Filibuster Stalls Key Money Bill on Senate Floor," *New York Times*, December 19, 1982, pp. Al, A26; Steven V. Roberts, "Congress Drops Jobs Program and MX from Funding Measure In Compromise to Avoid a Veto," *New York Times*, December 20, 1982, pp. Al, Dll.

49. Roberts, "Congress Drops Jobs Program"; Mosberg, "Congress Deletes MX Production Funds But Fine Print Will Allow Five to be Built"; and Margot Hornblower, "232 Billion Voted for Defense; Reagan Rebuffed on MX Funds," *Washington Post*, December 21, 1982, p. A4.

50. Steven V. Roberts, "President Decides to Sign Funds Bill Despite Loss of MX," *New York Times*, December 21, 1982, pp. Al, D29.

51. Hornblower, "232 Billion Voted for Defense."

52. Helen Dewar, "Congress Sends Spending Bill to the President: U.S. Employees Told To Come In," *Washington Post*, December 21, 1982, pp. Al, A7.

53. Juan Williams, "Funding Measure Signed," *Washington Post*, December 22, 1982, pp. Al, A5.

54. Uncited details on this and the entire appropriations battle are from *CQA*

1982, Budget and Appropriations. Numbers used in making judgments are from ibid. and from the "Brown Book," Senate Document No. 40, 97th Cong., 2d sess., esp. Tables IV, IVA, V, VIII, VIIIa.

55. Douglas B. Feaver and David Maraniss, "Reagan Lobbies For Senate Votes on Gasoline Tax," *Washington Post,* December 23, 1982, pp. Al, A7.

56. David Maraniss, "Senate Passes Gas-Tax Bill, Closes the 97th," *Washington Post,* December 24, 1982, pp. Al, A4.

Chapter Fourteen

1. Thus, the full social security system is OASDHI: Old Age, Survivors, Disability and Health Insurance.

2. Paul Light, *Artful Work: The Politics of Social Security Reform* (New York: Random House, 1985), pp. 136–37.

3. George J. Church, "A Debt-Threatened Dream," *Time,* May 24, 1982, pp. 16–27.

4. Ibid.

5. Light, *Artful Work,* p. 160, and chap. 13, pp. 152–62.

6. A larger explanation of the politics of assumptions may be found in ibid., pp. 45–57. The economic forecasts determined not only the dimension of the problem but also the size of some solutions. Thus, a projection of high inflation meant that freezing or postponing the COLAs would save more money than if inflation were actually low.

7. Ibid., p. 171.

8. Report of the National Commission on Social Security Reform (Washington, D.C.: U.S. Government Printing Office, January 1983), Appendix K, Tables 5A, 5D, 13.

9. Ibid., Table 3A.

10. Ibid., Appendix K, Tables 7C and 11.

11. Peter G. Peterson, "The Salvation of Social Security," *New York Review of Books,* December 16, 1982, pp. 50–57.

12. Quoted in Eric F. Kingson, "Financing Social Security," *Policy Studies Journal* 13, no. 1 (September 1984), p. 139.

13. Harry Anderson, "The Crisis in Social Security," *Newsweek,* June 1, 1981, pp. 25–27.

14. Light, *Artful Work,* p. 66.

15. Harry Anderson et al., "The Social Security Crisis," pp. 18–23; and Tom Morganthau, "Legions of the Old," *Newsweek,* January 24, 1983, p. 23.

16. Out of average costs of 14.09 percent, taxes would exceed benefits into the second decade of the new century. See Table 5 in Appendix J, *National Commission on Social Security*; and Light, *Artful Work,* p. 171.

17. These OASDI figures are calculated under 2B assumptions. National Commission on Social Security, Appendix K, Table 9B.

18. The percentage of taxable payroll poses a whole different set of questions: If wages constitute a lesser proportion of GNP, what is the balance? Are profits and rentier income higher than before? Why? How are workers talked into that?

19. National Commission on Social Security, Appendix K, Tables 7B, 9B.

20. Kingson, "Financing Social Security," p. 145.

21. Light, *Artful Work*, p. 169.

22. Ibid., p. 172. Only newly hired federal employees or those with less than five years service would be included.

23. Because a mere ten years' employment entitles a person to full social security benefits, some people combined thirty-year careers in federal service with ten outside and thus achieved double pensions. Those who advocated including federal employees argued also that the survivors and disability provisions of social security were desirable and that a combination of social security with a supplementary annuity would provide employees much more flexibility in leaving government. Employee unions, however, believed that CSR gave them a better deal. They also preferred to keep policy within a pond—the House Post Office and Civil Service and Senate Government Affairs committees—in which they were the big fish; the social security ocean seemed big and very risky. Finally, CSR, based on the contributions of current employees, was no more self-financing than OASDI; it had big deficits. If new employees did not contribute to the old CSR system, where would benefits come from? The government, of course, but the numbers would be big, and there might be pressure for cuts. The unions' position made sense—so long as the issue was CSR. When the issue became the health of OASDI, however, they got rolled.

24. National Commission on Social Security, Appendix K, p. 21.

25. Light, *Artful Work*, p. 173.

26. Ibid., pp. 173–74.

27. Ibid., p. 179. Why the number for coverage expansions doesn't fit Light's other figures, we cannot say.

28. Ibid., p. 186.

29. Ibid., pp. 184–85.

30. Ibid., p. 187.

31. National Commission on Social Security, pp. 2–10.

32. See Kingson, "Financing Social Security," pp. 149–50.

33. Compare the $18 billion figure to the National Commission's report, Appendix K, sum of Tables C-8 through C-11, to get a sense of why one would be skeptical of the figures.

34. National Commission on Social Security, pp. 2–12 to 2–13.

35. Light, *Artful Work*, pp. 198–99.

36. Susan Tifft, "Assaulted from All Sides," *Time*, January 31, 1983, p. 28.

37. Susan Tifft, "Taking Two Aspirin Won't Do," *Time*, February 28, 1983, p. 21.

38. *Congressional Quarterly Almanac 1983*, Vol. 39 (Washington, D.C.: Congressional Quarterly Inc., 1984), p. 222 (hereafter *CQA 1983*).

39. Light, *Artful Work*, pp. 209–11; *CQA 1983*, p. 223.

40. Light, *Artful Work*, pp. 213–14; and *CQA 1983*, p. 225.

41. Light, *Artful Work*, p. 217.

42. "Congress Acts on Jobs and Social Security," *Newsweek*, April 4, 1983, pp. 22–23.

43. See Light, *Artful Work*, pp. 225–26.

44. Peter J. Ferrara, *Social Security: The Inherent Contradiction* (San Francisco: Cato Institute, 1980). His latest statement is "Social Security Prospects for Real Reform," a paper delivered to the Pacific Forum, Pacific Research Institute for Public Policy, April 29, 1988.

Chapter Fifteen

1. Charles P. Alexander, "That Monster Deficit," *Time*, March 5, 1984, p. 60.

2. Congressional Budget Office, "Reducing the Deficit: Spending and Revenue Options," A Report to the Senate and House Committees on the Budget— Part III, February 1983, p. 1.

3. Congressional Budget Office, "The Economic and Budget Outlook: Fiscal Years 1986–1990," A Report to the Senate and House Committees on the Budget—Part I (Washington, D.C.: U.S. Government Printing Office, February 1985), p. 162.

4. Gregory B. Mills and John L. Palmer, *The Deficit Dilemma* (Washington, D.C.: Urban Institute, 1983), pp. 8–10, give a short summary of the tax increases.

5. For extensive discussion of entitlements, see Jack A. Meyer, "Budget Cuts in the Reagan Administration: A Question of Fairness," in D. Lee Bauden, ed., *The Social Contract Revisited* (Washington, D.C.: Urban Institute, 1984), pp. 33–64.

6. See Congressional Budget Office, "Reducing the Deficit," pp. 98–99.

7. See Congressional Budget Office, "The Economic and Budget Outlook," p. 153.

8. Peter W. Bernstein, "David Stockman: No More Big Budget Cuts," *Fortune*, February 6, 1984, pp. 53–56.

9. Executive Office of the President, Office of Management and Budget, *Budget of the United States Government Fiscal Year 1984* (Washington, D.C.: U.S. Government Printing Office, 1983), pp. 3–9.

10. U.S. Congress. House. Committee on Ways and Means. *Background Material and Data on Programs Within the Jurisdiction of the Committee on Ways and Means.* 99th Cong., 1st sess., February 22, 1985, pp. 55–56. Committee Print.

11. Martha Derthick, *Policymaking for Social Security* (Washington, D.C.: Brookings Institution, 1979), p. 357.

12. The term is Frank Levy's. See his *Dollars and Dreams: The Changing American Income Distribution* (New York: Russell Sage Foundation, 1987).

13. Congressional Budget Office, "The Economic and Budget Outlook," p. 162.

14. Office of Management and Budget, *Budget of the U.S. Government*, pp. 14–16.

15. Ibid.

16. Stockman, *Triumph of Politics*, p. 399.

17. Ibid.

18. Table from Mills and Palmer, *Deficit Dilemma*, p. 22. Any particular snapshot will provide a slightly different picture, due to changes in experienced and

projected economic performance and in congressional action. But this table is close enough to others for our purposes. For comparison, the 1985 CBO Appendix D and its baseline, including indexing of tax rates in 1981, is particularly reasonable. Blaming Reagan for deficits "caused" by not allowing taxes to rise above the level which helped defeat Jimmy Carter seems unreasonable.

19. See Levy, *Dollars and Dreams*, for a splendid analysis on how demography affects outcomes.

20. Charles P. Alexander, "The Elusive Recovery," *Time*, December 27, 1982, pp. 60–62.

21. "A Slow-Motion Recovery May Speed Up Toward Year End," *Business Week*, December 27, 1982, pp. 54–57.

22. Office of Management and Budget, *Budget of the U.S. Government*, pp. 2–9.

23. Stephen B. Shepard, Robert E. Farrell, and Lee Walczak, "Interview with President Reagan," *Business Week*, February 14, 1983, p. 119.

24. Melinda Beck et al., "Playing Politics with Jobs," *Newsweek*, February 14, 1983, p. 20.

25. Charles P. Alexander, "Here Comes the Recovery," *Time*, February 28, 1983, pp. 42–44.

26. Harry Anderson et al., "A Forecast of Sunshine," *Newsweek*, July 4, 1983, p. 40.

27. Charles P. Alexander, "Showing Some Real Muscle," *Time*, July 4, 1983, pp. 40–41.

28. George J. Church, "Going Back to Work," *Time*, August 15, 1983, p. 12.

29. Council of Economic Advisers, *Economic Report of the President 1985* (Washington, D.C.: U.S. Government Printing Office, 1985), pp. 266–67.

30. Ibid., p. 269.

31. Ibid., p. 277.

32. Ibid., pp. 328–29.

33. Ibid., pp. 258–59.

34. U.S. Congress. House. Committee on the Budget. *A Review of President Reagan's Budget Recommendations, 1981–85*. 98th Cong., 2d sess., August 2, 1984, pp. 37–41. Committee Print.

35. Council of Economic Advisers, *Economic Report of the President*, pp. 32–33.

36. Ibid., p. 35.

37. See Kim Foltz et al., "Economic Theory in Reverse," *Newsweek*, July 16, 1984, pp. 47–48.

38. House Budget Committee, *Review of President Reagan's Budget Recommendations*, p. 13.

39. Greider's *Secrets of the Temple* tells the story of Fed policy. A good indicator of Fed policy is its purchases of federal debt. The Fed increased its holding by more than 20 percent from June 1982 through September 1983. Over the next year its holdings didn't grow at all.

40. John Greenwald, "Topic A in the Money World," *Time*, April 25, 1983, pp. 96–97.

41. Harry Anderson et al., "Voting for Volcker to Stay," *Newsweek*, June 20, 1983, pp. 53–54.

42. Greenwald, "Topic A in the Money World"; John S. DeMott, "Down to the Finish Line," *Time,* June 21, 1983, pp. 58–59; Maureen Dowd, "Chairman Volcker Keeps His Job," *Time,* June 27, 1983, pp. 16, 19; Anderson, "Voting for Volcker to Stay"; Harry Anderson et al., "Volcker: Man for the Moment," *Newsweek,* June 27, 1983, pp. 66–68.

43. Walter Isaacson, "Untamed Monster," *Time,* May 23, 1983, pp. 14–15.

44. Richard I. Kirkland, Jr., "The Reaganites' Civil War Over Deficits," *Fortune,* October 17, 1983, pp. 74–80.

45. Ibid., p. 74.

46. Alexander L. Taylor III, "The Administration's Dr. Gloom," *Time,* November 7, 1983, p. 78.

47. Barry Bosworth, "Statement Before the Joint Economic Committee, United States Congress," September 17, 1985, typescript, p. 5.

48. Walter W. Heller and George L. Perry, "U.S. Economic Policy and Outlook," National City Bank of Minneapolis report, October 18, 1985, typescript.

49. Greider, *Secrets of the Temple*; and Thomas B. Edsall, *The New Politics of Inequality* (New York: W. W. Norton, 1984) are good examples of the critique.

50. Joseph Schumpeter, *Capitalism, Socialism, and Democracy* (London: Allen & Unwin, 1976).

51. "Grumbling About Deficits," *Time,* August 15, 1983, p. 13; and Charles P. Alexander, "Surging Up from the Depths," *Time,* September 26, 1983, pp. 50–51.

52. Harry Anderson et al., "Congress: Ducking the Deficits," *Newsweek,* September 26, 1983, pp. 19, 77.

53. Alexander L. Taylor III, "Labor gets a working over," *Time,* December 19, 1983, pp. 48–49.

54. Congressional Budget Office, "The Economic Outlook," A Report to the Senate and House Committees on the Budget, Part 1 (Washington, D.C.: U.S. Government Printing Office, February 1984), p. xxii.

55. Stein, *Presidential Economics,* p. 290.

56. The validity of this analysis depends on the volume of private saving and the extent to which the government itself is performing constructive investment. Thus, cross-national comparisons, e.g., to Japan, might seem to invalidate the argument but do not. Within a given economy, a shift to higher deficits should favor consumption over investment.

57. Savage, *Balanced Budgets.*

Chapter Sixteen

1. See Savage, *Balanced Budgets,* appendix, p. 266.

2. Ibid.

3. George J. Church, "How Reagan Decides," *Time,* December 13, 1982, pp. 12–17.

4. Ibid.

5. "Interview with President Reagan: 'The recovery may just be better than we think,'" *Business Week,* February 14, 1983, pp. 119, 121–122.

6. Ibid.

7. Soma Golden, "Superstar of the New Economists," *New York Times Magazine,* March 23, 1980, pp. 30–33, 91–95.

8. Ibid.

9. Stockman, *Triumph of Politics,* pp. 356–57.

10. Ibid., p. 358. The joke involves a boy who on Christmas morning receives as a present a gigantic pile of horse manure. Rather than being upset, he immediately sets to digging through the pile. Asked why, he replies, "With all this horse manure, there has to be a pony in here somewhere!" Reagan expressed his skepticism of projections publicly many times. That is a convenient stance; therefore reports of private discussions are better evidence of his position.

11. Ibid., pp. 358–60.

12. See George Reedy, *The Twilight of the Presidency* (New York: New American Library, 1987) for a description of the dynamic under a very different president, Lyndon Baines Johnson.

13. Stockman, *Triumph of Politics,* p. 362.

14. Ibid., pp. 362–64.

15. John Berry, "Interest Rates Are Still the Key," *Washington Post,* January 9, 1983, pp. Gl, Gl7; David Hoffman, "Reagan Advisers Consider Tax Rises in Future Budgets," *Washington Post,* January 9, 1983, pp. Al, A9.

16. See "A Bi-Partisan Appeal To Resolve the Budget Crisis," *Washington Post,* January 20, 1983, pp. Al4–15.

17. Table 11, for example, shows only a $39 billion increase in the deficit from policy in FY84, while the Bi-Partisan Appeal required around $100 billion in FY84 contraction. Table from Mills and Palmer, *Deficit Dilemma,* p. 22.

18. George J. Church, " 'A Little Terrifying,' " *Time,* January 17, 1983, p. 10. Ross K. Baker, "Institutional Norms or Party Discipline?: The Punishment of Phil Gramm," typescript, emphasizes the violation of House norms based on interviews with fourteen members of the House Democratic Steering and Policy Committee.

19. Helen Dewar, "Reagan's Program Attacked," *Washington Post,* January 27, 1983, pp. Al, A7.

20. Walter Isaacson, "Mending and Bending," *Time,* February 7, 1983, pp. 12–14.

21. Walter Isaacson, "Clashes and Compromises," *Time,* February 14, 1983, pp. 13–14.

22. "A *Newsweek* Poll: Arms Wrestling," *Newsweek,* January 31, 1983, p. 17.

23. "Why some executives are cooling on Reagan," *Business Week,* February 21, 1983, p. 19.

24. Thomas Edsall and Spencer Rich, "Conable, Dole Oppose Tax Hike Plan," *Washington Post,* January 19, 1983, pp. Al, A4.

25. Thomas Edsall, "Rostenkowski Asks Tax Freeze," *Washington Post,* February 9, 1983, pp. Al, A6; Thomas Edsall, "Rostenkowski Enrages O'Neill on Tax Stance," *Washington Post,* February 10, 1983, p. A4.

26. *CQA 1983,* pp. 261–64; Harry Anderson et al., "The Push for a Jobs Program," *Newsweek,* January 17, 1983, p. 53.

27. Walter Isaacson, "Searching for the Recovery," *Time,* February 21, 1983, pp. 16–17.

28. They reasoned that a separate bill for these would allow the House to attach yet another "jobs" package.

29. The Treasury claimed that the banks wanted to hold onto the money for their own use.

30. Paul Taylor, "Banks Use Psychology to Stoke Savers' Rebellion," *Washington Post,* March 20, 1983, pp. Al, A6.

31. Helen Dewar, "Jobs Bill Imperiled in Senate," *Washington Post,* March 11, 1983, p. Al.

32. Thomas Edsall, "Demos Boost Banks in Tax Battle With Dole," *Washington Post,* March 12, 1983, p. A8.

33. Helen Dewar, "President———Bank Tax Lobbying," *Washington Post,* March 12, 1983, pp. Al, A8; "On and Off," *Time,* March 21, 1983, p. 18.

34. "No Line of Credit," *Time,* March 28, 1983, p. 19; *CQA 1983,* pp. 261–64.

35. *CQA 1983,* pp. 261–64.

36. Jonathan Alter et al., "Behind the Banks' Victory," *Newsweek,* May 2, 1983, p. 28.

37. "Voting the Bankers' Way," *Time,* May 30, 1983, pp. 12–13.

38. Thomas B. Edsall, "Senate Panel Approves Withholding Repeal," *Washington Post,* May 26, 1983, p. A9.

39. "Exercises in Make-Believe," *Time,* June 27, 1983, p. 19.

40. See *CQA 1983,* pp. 435–37; Richard E. Cohen, "What a Difference a Year—and an Election—Make in Producing a Budget," *National Journal,* April 2, 1983, pp. 696–99.

41. Ed Magnuson, "Uproar Over Arms Control," *Time,* January 24, 1983, pp. 16–18.

42. Walter Isaacson, "The Winds of Reform," *Time,* March 7, 1983, pp. 12–16, 23, 26–30. Unattributed quotes below are from that report. See James Fallows, *The National Defense* (New York: Random House, 1981), for the basic critique.

43. Barton Gellman, "Saga of the World's Costliest Plastic Cap," *Washington Post,* August 21, 1983, pp. Al, A6.

44. See Aaron Wildavsky, *The New Politics of the Budgetary Process* (Glenview, Ill./Boston: Scott, Foresman/Little Brown, 1987), chap. 6, for different sides of the story.

45. Walter Isaacson, "Reagan for the Defense," *Time,* April 4, 1983, pp. 8–19.

46. Michael Reese et al., "Reagan on the Defense," *Newsweek,* April 18, 1983, pp. 22–24.

47. Stockman, *Triumph of Politics,* pp. 369–70; *CQA 1983,* p. 439.

48. Reese et al., "Reagan on the Defense."

49. Helen Dewar, "Stockman Issues Blunt Warning: Budget Agreement Called Vital," *Washington Post,* April 19, 1983, pp. Al, A6.

50. Ibid.; Ed Magnuson, "Feuding in the Family," *Time,* May 2, 1983, pp. 12–14.

51. Helen Dewar, "Conservatives Rebuff Reagan on Budget Counter-Offer," *Washington Post,* April 21, 1983, p. A4.

52. Helen Dewar, "Senate Panel Defies Reagan," *Washington Post,* April 22,

1983, pp. A1, A7; Richard E. Cohen, "Political and Fiscal Blood May Flow Before Battle of 1984 Budget Is Over," *National Journal*, April 30, 1983, pp. 898–900; Magnuson, "Feuding in the Family."

53. Howard H. Baker, Jr., "We Will Pass a Budget Resolution," *Washington Post*, May 15, 1983, p. B8; and Scott Matheson and Jim Thompson, "The States Need a Resolution Now," *Washington Post*, May 15, 1983, p. B8.

54. Helen Dewar, "House GOP Vows Help for Reagan's Tax Cuts," *Washington Post*, April 29, 1983, p. A4.

55. Ed Magnuson, "Going Into the Trenches," *Time*, May 30, 1983, pp. 12–14.

56. Votes are all from *Congressional Record*, May 19, 1983.

57. Mark Starr et al., "Congress: Falling on Its Face?" *Newsweek*, June 20, 1983, p. 23.

58. "Budget Deal," *Time*, July 4, 1983, p. 19.

59. *CQA 1983*, p. 447.

60. "Tough Talk from Dole," *Time*, August 15, 1983, p. 13.

61. Timothy B. Clark and Richard E. Cohen, "Coming Up Empty-Handed," *National Journal*, November 26, 1983, pp. 2460–69.

62. Stockman, *Triumph of Politics*, pp. 371–73.

63. Helen Dewar, "Democrats' Tight-Fisted Spending Bill Snags Their Welfare Aims," September 22, 1983, p. A3; Dewar, "Senate Votes to Cut U. N. Contribution," September 23, 1983, pp. A1, A4; Dewar, "Stopgap Funding Bill Is Put on Fast Track," September 28, 1983, p. A4; and Dewar, "Senate, Wooing Reagan, Votes Against More Education Spending," October 5, 1983, p. A2; all in *Washington Post*.

64. Richard E. Cohen, "Plan to curb deficits by capping COLAs could set off a battle royal," *National Journal*, August 13, 1983, pp. 1671, 1699.

65. Starr et al., "Congress: Falling on Its Face?"

66. Thomas W. Lippman, "Regan Says President Would Veto a Reduction of July 1 Tax Cut," *Washington Post*, June 15, 1983, p. A3.

67. Richard E. Cohen, "Senate Republican Control May Be Put to Test by Tough Issues this Fall," *National Journal*, September 10, 1983, pp. 1824–29.

68. Timothy B. Clark, "Cracks Appear in Business's United Front in Opposition to Tax Boosts," *National Journal*, July 16, 1983, pp. 1493–96.

69. Mark Starr, "Doing Nothing About Deficits," *Newsweek*, August 15, 1983, pp. 20–22.

70. Ibid.

71. Richard E. Cohen, "Choosing Their Poison," *National Journal*, October 15, 1983, p. 2121.

72. *CQA 1983*, p. 233.

73. Cohen, "Choosing Their Poison."

74. Ibid.; and Cohen and Clark, "Coming Up Empty-Handed."

75. *CQA 1983*, pp. 235–36.

76. Ibid., pp. 529–30; Clark and Cohen, "Coming Up Empty-Handed"; T. R. Reid, "Leaders Spurned As House Defeats Spending Measure," *Washington Post*, November 9, 1983, p. A8; Susan Tifft, "Cowering Before the Deficit," *Time*, November 21, 1983, pp. 23, 26.

77. Clark and Cohen, "Coming Up Empty-Handed."

78. Helen Dewar and Martha M. Hamilton, "House Refuses to Consider a Tax Increase," *Washington Post*, November 18, 1983, pp. Al, A4; Ed Magnuson, " 'We're Unable to Act,' " *Time*, November 28, 1983, pp. 18–20; Clark and Cohen, "Coming Up Empty-Handed"; *CQA 1983*, p. 236.

79. Clark and Cohen, "Coming Up Empty-Handed."

80. Helen Dewar, "Senate Marks Time As Debt Deadline Nears," *Washington Post*, October 30, 1983, p. A4.

81. Helen Dewar, "Reagan Threatens Veto In Debt Ceiling Battle," *Washington Post*, November 2, 1983, p. A6.

82. Ibid.

83. Helen Dewar, "Deficit-Reduction Plan Torpedoed by Reagan," *Washington Post*, November 4, 1983, p. A2.

84. Helen Dewar, "Senate Presses On in Quest to Cut Deficit," *Washington Post*, November 5, 1983, p. A4.

85. Ibid.

86. Dewar, "Deficit Reduction Plan Torpedoed by Reagan."

87. Harry Anderson et al., "Congress Fiddles, The Deficits Burn," *Newsweek*, November 21, 1983, pp. 81–82.

88. Dewar and Hamilton, "House Refuses to Consider a Tax Increase"; Helen Dewar and David Hoffman, "Deficit-Cutting Drive Resumes," *Washington Post*, November 16, 1983, pp. A1, A10; Magnuson, " 'We're Unable to Act' "; Clark and Cohen, "Coming Up Empty-Handed"; *CQA 1983*, p. 287.

89. *CQA 1983*, p. 241.

90. Magnuson, " 'We're Unable to Act.' "

Chapter Seventeen

1. Susan Dentzer et al., "A Budget for the Election," *Newsweek*, February 13, 1984, pp. 67–68.

2. Juan Williams, "Reagan Defends Plan To Live With Deficit, Without Tax Increase," *Washington Post*, January 22, 1984, p. A4.

3. T. R. Reid and Juan Williams, "Democrats Considering Veto Right," *Washington Post*, January 28, 1984, pp. Al, A8.

4. Eloise Salholz, "Periscope," *Newsweek*, March 5, 1984, p. 19.

5. Walter Shapiro et al., "The Deficit: Out of Control?" *Newsweek*, December 12, 1983, pp. 36–38.

6. George J. Church, "Reagan Gets Ready," *Time*, January 23, 1984, pp. 10–11.

7. Jane Seabury and Martha M. Hamilton, " '85 Budget To Include Tax Plan," *Washington Post*, December 13, 1983, pp. Al, A8.

8. Stockman, *Triumph of Politics*, p. 374; other such quotes following are from this source.

9. Ibid.

10. Shapiro et al., "The Deficit: Out of Control?"

11. On the Grace Commission, see Steve Kelman, "The Grace Commission:

How Much Waste in Government?" *The Public Interest*, No. 78 (Winter 1985), pp. 62–82. Most experienced analysts concluded that the Grace Commission revealed that at least one group of private sector experts knew little about government. For Reagan on entitlements, see interview with Lou Cannon, David Hoffman, and Juan Williams, *Washington Post*, January 22, 1984, p. A9.

12. T. R. Reid and Margaret Shapiro, "Reagan Hails Recovery, Pledges Peace Efforts: Wary Response By Democrats," *Washington Post*, January 26, 1984, pp. A1, A17.

13. Dick Kirschten, "Blueprint for a Campaign," *National Journal*, February 4, 1984, pp. 215–18.

14. Dentzer et al., "A Budget for the Election."

15. Text of President Reagan's State of the Union address, *Washington Post*, January 26, 1984, pp. A16–17.

16. Kirschten, "Blueprint for a Campaign."

17. Helen Dewar, "Reagan Seeks Talks, Vetoes, Tax Changes In Attacking Deficits," *Washington Post*, January 26, 1984, p. A15; Kirschten, "Blueprint for a Campaign."

18. *Congressional Quarterly Almanac 1984*, Vol. 40 (Washington, D.C.: Congressional Quarterly Inc., 1985), p. 131 (hereafter *CQA 1984*).

19. Stockman, *Triumph of Politics*, p. 375.

20. Peter W. Bernstein, "David Stockman: No More Big Budget Cuts," *Fortune*, February 6, 1984, pp. 53–56.

21. For the politics of the analysis, see Timothy B. Clark, "Stiff Tax Hikes Will be Key to Future Efforts to Close the Budget Deficit," *National Journal*, April 21, 1984, pp. 752–57.

22. Susan Tifft, "Playing For Time," *Time*, February 13, 1984, pp. 10–13.

23. *CQA 1984*, p. 131.

24. See John M. Berry, "Bush Denies Staff Disarray Over Deficits," *Washington Post*, February 6, 1984, p. A1.

25. Reid and Shapiro, "Reagan Hails Recovery, Pledges Peace Efforts."

26. Reid and Williams, "Democrats Considering Veto Right."

27. Jeffrey H. Birnbaum, "Some See Budget Gap Shrinking," *Wall Street Journal*, February 14, 1984, p. 56.

28. *CQA 1984*, p. 149.

29. David Hoffman, "Reagan, GOP Senators Converging on Budgets," *Washington Post*, March 10, 1984, p. A8.

30. Helen Dewar, "New Deficit Measures Would Lose Revenue," *Washington Post*, March 15, 1984, pp. B1, B4.

31. As always, there were technical questions. Some proponents of the plan claimed defense growth would be only 5.1 percent, using the FY84 budget resolution defense total as the baseline instead of actual appropriated spending. See "Glimmers of Hope on the Deficit," *Business Week*, April 2, 1984, pp. 26–27.

32. Jeffrey H. Birnbaum, "GOP's Deficit Plan Faces Hurdles in the Senate but Is Likely to Win," *Wall Street Journal*, March 29, 1984, p. 2A.

33. Martha M. Hamilton and Helen Dewar, "Cutting the Budget Not as Easy as It Sounds," *Washington Post*, February 28, 1984, p. A15.

34. Helen Dewar, "Senate Democrats Propose Budget Deferring Income Tax Indexing," *Washington Post*, March 23, 1984, p. A3.

35. *CQA 1984*, p. 156.

36. Details can be found in *CQA 1984*, pp. 155–56.

37. Richard E. Cohen and Timothy B. Clark, "Congress Is Trying to Convince the Voters It Is Really Worried About the Deficit," *National Journal*, April 21, 1984, pp. 758–62.

38. Helen Dewar, "House Votes Plan to Reduce Deficit By $182 Billion," *Washington Post*, April 6, 1984, pp. Al, A9.

39. *CQA 1984*, p. 156.

40. See Dewar, "House Votes Plan to Reduce Deficit"; *CQA 1984*, pp. 155–56; Cohen and Clark, "Congress Is Trying to Convince the Voters."

41. "What Bob Dole's Tax Bill Would Cost Business," *Business Week*, April 9, 1984, p. 29.

42. Jeffrey H. Birnbaum, "Panel Completes Plan to Cut Deficit, Setting Stage for Debate on House Floor," *Wall Street Journal*, March 29, 1984, p. 2.

43. *Federal Budget Report*, April 2, 1984 (a bimonthly report published by Pasha Publications Inc., Arlington, Virginia).

44. Melinda Beck et al., "Deficit Politics: An Election-Year Frenzy," *Newsweek*, April 16, 1984, pp. 31–32.

45. Cohen and Clark, "Congress Is Trying to Convince the Voters."

46. Beck et al., "Deficit Politics."

47. Cohen and Clark, "Congress Is Trying to Convince the Voters."

48. Nancy Landon Kassebaum (R-Kan.), Joseph R. Biden, Jr. (D-Dela.), Charles E. Grassley (R-Iowa), and Max Baucus (D-Mont.), "Freeze Everything," *Washington Post*, April 27, 1984, p. A23.

49. Cohen and Clark, "Congress Is Trying to Convince the Voters."

50. Ibid.

51. Ibid.; *CQA 1984*, pp. 156–57.

52. Dale Tate, "Part of Deficit-Reduction Package Effort to Pass Spending Cuts Off to Torpid Start in Senate," *Congressional Quarterly Weekly Report*, April 28, 1984, p. 951.

53. Helen Dewar, "Senate Nears Showdown on Proposal to Freeze Federal Outlays for Year," *Washington Post*, May 2, 1984, p. A3.

54. Dale Tate, "Two Alternatives Defeated: Senate Poised for Showdown on GOP Deficit-Cutting Plan," *Congressional Quarterly Weekly Report*, May 5, 1984, p. 1005.

55. *CQA 1984*, p. 152.

56. "GOP Moderates Key to Deficit-Cutting Plan," *Congressional Quarterly Weekly Report*, May 19, 1984, p. 1164.

57. *CQA 1984*, p. 158.

58. Ibid., p. 165.

59. Martha M. Hamilton, "Conferees Continue Standoff on Spending Reductions," *Washington Post*, June 15, 1984, p. A5.

60. *Federal Budget Report*, June 25, 1984.

61. Hamilton, "Conferees Continue Standoff."

62. George J. Church, "Slowing the Surge of Red Ink," *Time*, July 9, 1984, pp. 20–21.

63. DEFRA details are from *CQA 1984*, pp. 145–47. In February 1985, CBO

estimated the extra DEFRA revenues at $9 billion in FY85, $16 billion in FY86, $22 billion in FY87, rising to $30 billion in FY90. Congressional Budget Office, *The Economic and Budget Outlook: Fiscal Years 1986–1990,* A report to the Senate and House Committees on the Budget—Part 1, February 1985 (Washington, D.C.: U.S. Government Printing Office), Table D-3, p. 154.

64. Linda E. Demkovich, "For Poor and Elderly, Congress's Cuts In Health Budgets Have Silver Lining," *National Journal,* July 7, 1984, pp. 1309–11.

65. This account is from ibid.; *CQA 1984,* pp. 147–49; Martha M. Hamilton, "Hill Conferees Agree to Trim $11 Billion," *Washington Post,* June 22, 1984, p. A3; Hamilton, "Conferees Strive for Accord on Taxes, Spending," *Washington Post,* June 23, 1984, p. Al; Hamilton, "Conferees Vote $61 Billion in Deficit Reductions," *Washington Post,* June 24, 1984, p. Al; and interviews.

66. *CQA 1984,* p. 155.

67. Helen Dewar, "Senator Stevens Says Administration Can Expect Defense Rise of 5%," *Washington Post,* August 4, 1984, p. A3.

68. *CQA 1984,* pp. 158–60; Helen Dewar, "Accord Ends Hill Logjam on Defense Funds," *Washington Post,* September 21, 1984, pp. Al, A6.

69. Helen Dewar, "House Vote Adds Crime Package to Spending Bill," *Washington Post,* September 26, 1984, pp. Al, A4.

70. Helen Dewar, "Senate Votes to End Rights Debate," *Washington Post,* September 30, 1984, pp. Al, Al4.

71. See *CQA 1984,* p. 446; Helen Dewar, "Fractious Legislators Stall Action on Rights Spending Bills," *Washington Post,* September 22, 1984, p. A4; Dewar, "House Vote Adds Crime Package"; Dewar, "Senate Votes to End Rights Debate"; Helen Dewar and Margaret Shapiro, "Hill Votes Stopgap Funds Bill," *Washington Post,* October 2, 1984, pp. Al, A4; Helen Dewar, "Rights Bill is Shelved In Senate," *Washington Post,* October 3, 1984, pp. Al, A4; Helen Dewar, "Federal Shutdown Readied as Senate Works on Funding," *Washington Post,* October 4, 1984, pp. Al, A4.

72. David Hoffman and Keith B. Richbury, "Government Shut Down By Reagan," *Washington Post,* October 5, 1984, pp. Al, Al4.

73. The big crime bill, supported by both Senator Thurmond and Senator Kennedy—which is another story—was not in dispute.

74. Helen Dewar, "Deadlock Continues on the Hill," *Washington Post,* October 10, 1984, pp. Al, Al2.

75. Helen Dewar, "Conferees Approve '85 Funds," *Washington Post,* October 11, 1984, pp. Al, A4; Helen Dewar and Margaret Shapiro, "Congress Finishing Session," *Washington Post,* October 12, 1984, pp. Al, A4.

76. See *CQA 1984,* pp. 421–25.

77. *CQA 1984,* p. 167; Helen Dewar, "51 Senators Press Measure For Trial of Line-Item Veto," *Washington Post,* September 27, 1984, p. A6.

78. Helen Dewar, "With Eyes on Deficits, GOP Starts New Drive To Amend Constitution," *Washington Post,* August 2, 1984, p. A3; Helen Dewar, "Balanced-Budget Proposal Suffers Pair of Setbacks," *Washington Post,* September 14, 1984, pp. Al, A7; Kevin Klose, "Michigan Lawmaker Stalls Budget-Amendment Drive," *Washington Post,* September 14, 1984, p. A7.

79. David Hoffman and Ward Sinclair, "Reagan, On Eve of Midwest Trip, Unveils Farm Aid," *Washington Post,* September 19, 1984, pp. Al, A8.

Chapter Eighteen

1. Dennis Farney, "Democratic Study Unit in Ferment," *Wall Street Journal,* April 25, 1984, p. 54.

2. Economic arguments about growth could, however, be made. Defense spending can be alleged to be unproductive, with a smaller multiplier than domestic spending, while much spending by the wealthy could be said to be much better spent by the government. If businesses were more interested in paper profits than in productive investment, then raising their taxes would be little loss. And, because a mass productive capitalist economy needs wide markets but tends to create inequality, government efforts to redistribute income add to growth. There are arguments for anything.

3. Timothy B. Clark, "Promises, Promises—the Presidential Candidates and Their Budget Plans," *National Journal,* March 10, 1984, p. 452–57.

4. Special Task Force on Long-Term Economic Policy, Democratic Caucus/United States House of Representatives, *Rebuilding the Road to Opportunity: Turning Point for America's Economy,* September 1982, p. III. Produced by the House Democratic Caucus, this was known as the Yellow Book because of its cover. It was succeeded by the National-House Democratic Caucus, *Renewing America's Promise: A Democratic Blueprint for Our Nation's Future,* January 1984. Published by the National-House Democratic Caucus, this was known as the Blue Book because of its cover.

5. Yellow Book, p. 1.

6. Ibid., p. 9.

7. Ibid.

8. Blue Book, p. 3.

9. Ibid., pp. 12–13.

10. Ibid., p. 13.

11. Ibid., p. 10.

12. David S. Broder, "Mondale Says He'd Increase Business Taxes," *Washington Post,* September 16, 1983, p. Al.

13. Mark Starr with Howard Freeman, "An Early Labor Endorsement?", *Newsweek,* August 15, 1983, p. 21; Tom Morganthau et al., "Fritz Mondale's Triple Play," *Newsweek,* October 10, 1983, p. 28.

14. The best coverage of labor's problems can be found in *The Economist,* for example, "A harvest of trouble in California," August 27, 1983, pp. 15–16; "The de-unionization of America," October 29, 1983, p. 71; "Economy expands, jobs contract," August 25, 1984, p. 57; "Secure our jobs, and the rise can come later," September 22, 1984, pp. 25–26. For a discussion of the various political considerations, see Dom Bonafede, "Labor's Early Endorsement Will Prove a Psychological Boost and Then Some," *National Journal,* September 24, 1983, pp. 1938–41.

15. Clark, "Promises, Promises."

16. David Broder, "Democrats Exchange Brickbats," *Washington Post,* January 16, 1984, pp. A1, A4.

17. Thomas B. Edsall, " '84 Politics: 'New Patriotism' vs. New Class Allegiances," *Washington Post,* February 5, 1984, pp. D1, D4.

18. Dan Balz and Milton Coleman, "Accepting Nomination, Mondale Offers Voters Era of 'New Realism,' " *Washington Post,* July 20, 1984, pp. A1, A15.

19. Walter Bagehot, "Introduction to the Second Edition," *The English Constitution* (Ithaca, N.Y.: Cornell Paperbacks, 1966), p. 276.

20. William Schneider, "Mondale's Gamble on Tax Increase Could Pay Off If Fairness Becomes the Issue," *National Journal,* August 4, 1984, pp. 1494–95.

21. David Alpern, "Jousting Over a Tax Increase," *Newsweek,* August 6, 1984, p. 16; Kurt Andersen, "Scoring Points with Candor," *Time,* August 20, 1984, pp. 20–21; Lou Cannon and David Hoffman, " 'I Have No Plans to Raise Taxes,' President Says," *Washington Post,* July 25, 1984, pp. A1, A11; David Hoffman and John M. Berry, "Reagan, Mondale Tax Brawl Defies Political Convention," *Washington Post,* July 29, 1984, pp. A1, A8; Tom Morganthau et al., "How Good a President?" *Newsweek,* August 27, 1984, pp. 28–31.

22. George F. Will, "The Economy of Leadership," *Newsweek,* August 27, 1984, p. 84.

23. Robert Dole, editorial, *Washington Post,* August 5, 1984, p. C8.

24. See, for instance, Thomas E. Cavanagh and James L. Sundquist, "The New Two-Party System," in John E. Chubb and Paul E. Peterson, *The New Direction in American Politics* (Washington, D.C.: Brookings Institution, 1985), pp. 33–67.

25. Ibid., pp. 43–48; *The Gallup Report,* No. 223, April 1984, p. 18.

26. J. Merrill Shanks and Warren E. Miller, "Policy Direction and Performance Evaluation: Complementary Explanations of the Reagan Elections," paper delivered at the Annual Meeting of The American Political Science Association, New Orleans, August 29–September 1, 1985.

27. David S. Broder and George Lardner, Jr., "Democrats Challenge President's Landslide as Mandate," *Washington Post,* November 8, 1984, pp. A1, A49.

28. Interview with Thomas M. DeFrank and Eleanor Clift, "To Finish What Is Well Started," *Newsweek,* February 6, 1984, pp. 18–19.

29. Authors' calculations from *CQA 1984.*

30. An extensive literature has documented the incumbency advantages in congressional elections.

31. John A. Ferejohn and Morris P. Fiorina, "Incumbency and Realignment in Congressional Elections," in Chubb and Peterson, *New Direction,* pp. 91–115; quote on pp. 114–15.

32. William Schneider, "Mondale's Gamble on Tax Increase Could Pay Off If Fairness Becomes the Issue," *National Journal,* August 4, 1984, pp. 1494–95.

33. George H. Gallup, *The Gallup Poll: Public Opinion 1983* (Wilmington, Dela.: Scholarly Resources, 1984), Survey #207-G, Interviewing date January 14–17, 1983, reported February 13, pp. 25–30.

34. George H. Gallup, *The Gallup Poll: Public Opinion 1984* (Wilmington, Dela.: Scholarly Resources, 1985), Survey #243-G, Interviewing date September 28–October 1, 1984, reported November 18, pp. 243–45.

35. Scott Keeter, "Public Opinion in 1984," in Gerald Pomper with Colleagues, *The Election of 1984: Reports and Interpretations* (Chatham, N.J.: Chatham House, 1985), pp. 91–111.

36. Ibid., p. 99. See also D. Roderick Kiewiet and Douglas Rivers, "The Economic Basis of Reagan's Appeal," in Chubb and Peterson, *New Direction*, pp. 69–90.

37. See William Schneider, "An Uncertain Consensus," *National Journal*, November 10, 1984, pp. 2130–32; Keeter, "Public Opinion in 1984," pp. 98–99.

38. Keeter, "Public Opinion in 1984," p. 95.

39. Helen Dewar, "Legislators See Paradox In Voters' View of Reagan," *Washington Post*, February 21, 1984, pp. Al, A4.

40. Evan Thomas, "The Goal: A Landslide," *Time*, November 5, 1984, pp. 18–20.

41. One reason Reagan had different opinions was that he listened to different voices. In his memoir Donald Regan remarked that the president was most likely to quote from a story in the morning's *Washington Times*, unlike Vice President Bush who, like most Washingtonians, would refer to the *New York Times*; Regan, *For the Record*, p. 275.

Chapter Nineteen

1. "Undue process," *The Economist*, November 9, 1985, p. 32.

2. Pat Towell, "Pentagon Asks $313.7 Billion for Defense Buildup," *Congressional Quarterly Weekly Report*, February 9, 1985, pp. 229–35.

3. Elizabeth Wehr, "Reagan, Senate GOP Reach '86 Budget Accord," *Congressional Quarterly Weekly Report*, April 6, 1985, pp. 627–28.

4. Ibid.

5. Elizabeth Wehr, "FY '86 Budget Struggle Moves to Senate Floor," *Congressional Quarterly Weekly Report*, April 20, 1985, pp. 717–19.

6. Ibid.

7. Ibid.

8. Jacqueline Calmes and Pamela Fessler, "Response Uneven to President's TV Appeal," *Congressional Quarterly Weekly Report*, April 27, 1985, p. 769.

9. Elizabeth Wehr, with Jacqueline Calmes and Pamela Fessler, " '86 Budget Hung Up in Senate Floor Squabble," *Congressional Quarterly Weekly Report*, April 27, 1985, pp. 768–69, 771.

10. Elizabeth Wehr, "Defense Cut, Social Security Boosted: Republican Budget Package Picked Apart on Senate Floor," *Congressional Quarterly Weekly Report*, May 4, 1985, pp. 815, 817–18.

11. Ibid.

12. Elizabeth Wehr, "Budget Speaks Through Senate Floor Vote," *Congressional Quarterly Weekly Report*, May 11, 1985, pp. 871–74.

13. "Undue process," *The Economist*, November 9, 1985, p. 32.

14. Jacqueline Calmes, "House Panel Gives Quick OK to '86 Budget," *Congressional Quarterly Weekly Report*, May 18, 1985, p. 915.

15. Jacqueline Calmes, "House, With Little Difficulty, Passes '86 Budget Resolution," *Congressional Quarterly Weekly Report*, May 25, 1985, p. 975.

16. Elizabeth Wehr, "House Centrist Bloc: Still Waiting to Happen," *Congressional Quarterly Weekly Report*, May 25, 1985, p. 972.

17. Elizabeth Wehr, "Tough Task: Reaching An '86 Budget Accord," *Congressional Quarterly Weekly Report*, June 1, 1985, pp. 1044–45.

18. Jacqueline Calmes, "Budget Negotiations Resume as Senators Offer New Plan," *Congressional Quarterly Weekly Report*, June 29, 1985, p. 1258.

19. Ibid.

20. Ibid.

21. Jacqueline Calmes, "President Fails to Unsnarl Budget Deadlock," *Congressional Quarterly Weekly Report*, July 13, 1985, pp. 1355–58; "Budget is Settled With President, Leaders Declare," *New York Times*, July 10, 1985, pp. A1, A14.

22. Ibid.

23. Jonathan Fuerbringer, "G.O.P. Rift Widens as Dole Criticizes Reagan and House," *New York Times*, July 13, 1985, p. 1.

24. Ibid.; Calmes, "President Fails to Unsnarl Budget Deadlock."

25. Calmes, "President Fails to Unsnarl Budget Deadlock."

26. Jacqueline Calmes, "Budget Negotiations Collapse for Second Time," *Congressional Quarterly Weekly Report*, July 20, 1985, pp. 1413–15.

27. Ibid.

28. Ibid.

29. Ibid.

30. David Rogers, "Talks on Fiscal 1986 Budget Collapse; Agreement This Summer Seems Unlikely," *Wall Street Journal*, July 18, 1985, p. 48.

31. Calmes, "Budget Negotiations Collapse for Second Time."

32. Jonathan Fuerbringer, "New Senate Budget Plan Proposes Oil Import Fee," *New York Times*, July 26, 1985, p. B5.

33. Pamela Fessler, "Filibuster Keeps Item Veto Off Senate Floor," *Congressional Quarterly Weekly Report*, July 20, 1985, p. 1415.

34. Elizabeth Wehr, "Senate Budgeteers Tie Tax Hike to COLA Delay," *Congressional Quarterly Weekly Report*, July 27, 1985, pp. 1467–69.

35. Jonathan Fuerbringer, "Senate Republicans Consider Dropping Attempt at Compromise on Budget," *New York Times*, July 24, 1985, p. A17.

36. Ibid.

37. Ibid.

38. Janet Hook, "Medicare Savings Approved: $19 Billion Deficit-Reduction Package Wins Committee OK," *Congressional Quarterly Weekly Report*, July 27, 1985, pp. 1483–85.

39. Fuerbringer, "New Senate Budget Plan"; Wehr, "Senate Budgeteers Tie Tax Hike to COLA Delay."

40. Robert Pear, "Spending Freeze Gaining in House Despite Deadlock," *New York Times*, July 28, 1985, pp. A1, A25.

41. Ibid.

42. Jonathan Fuerbringer, "Reagan Rebuffs Senate on Budget," *New York Times*, July 30, 1985, pp. A1, A17.

43. Gerald M. Boyd, "Republicans' Ties to Reagan Frayed by Budget Rebuff," *New York Times,* July 31, 1985, pp. A1, A13.

44. Jacqueline Calmes, "Angry Senate Republicans Bear No Grudges," *Congressional Quarterly Weekly Report,* August 3, 1985, p. 1522.

45. Ibid.

46. Elizabeth Wehr, "Congress Cuts Budget by More Than $55 Billion," *Congressional Quarterly Weekly Report,* August 3, 1985, pp. 1520, 1523–24.

47. Warren Rudman prepared a carefully crafted speech explaining his reasoning, on the Senate floor, August 2, 1986.

48. Jonathan Fuerbringer, "Deficit Forecast Too Optimistic, Leaders Report," *New York Times,* August 3, 1985, pp. A1, A8.

49. Elizabeth Wehr, "CBO Sees Hopeful Signs in Deficit Reduction," *Congressional Quarterly Weekly Report,* August 17, 1985, p. 1651.

50. Steven V. Roberts, "Phil Gramm's Crusade Against the Deficit," *New York Times Magazine,* March 30, 1986, pp. 20–23, 40, 57, 60.

51. Ibid.

52. Jacqueline Calmes, "Gramm: Making Waves, Enemies, and History," *Congressional Quarterly Weekly Report,* March 15, 1986, p. 611–15.

53. Ibid., p. 614.

54. Allen Schick, *Congress and Money* (Washington, D. C.: Urban Institute, 1980), pp. 36–43.

55. "The Senate's Anti-Deficit Duo," *U.S. News and World Report,* November 11, 1985, p. 15.

56. Ibid.

57. Interview with Senator Warren Rudman, April 14, 1986, Washington, D.C.

58. Ibid.

59. Dick Kirschten and Jonathan Rauch, "Political Poker Game Over Deficit Bill Calls Bluff of Reagan and Congress," *National Journal,* December 14, 1985, pp. 2857–58.

60. Interviews with Thomas Dawson, Dennis Thomas, and Donald Regan at the White House, March 14 and July 15, 1986. See also Kirschten and Rauch, "Political Poker Game."

61. Interviews with Dawson, Thomas, and Regan.

62. Kirschten and Rauch, "Political Poker Game."

63. "Symposium on Budget Balance: Do Deficits Matter?" New York City, January 9–11, 1986, sponsored by American Association of Retired Persons, American Stock Exchange, Avon Corporation, The Business Roundtable, Committee for a Responsible Federal Budget, General Foods Corporation, GTE Corporation, and the Kerr Foundation. Quote is on p. V-28; reporter Owen Ullman's remarks were made during Session VI discussion.

64. Kirschten and Rauch, "Political Poker Game."

65. Dick Kirschten, "White House Tests Legislative Flair on Risky Deficit-Reduction Measure," *National Journal,* October 19, 1985, pp. 2380–81.

66. *Congressional Quarterly Almanac 1985,* Vol. 41 (Washington, D.C.: Congressional Quarterly Inc., 1986), p. 459 (hereafter *CQA 1985*).

67. Elizabeth Wehr, "Support Grows for Balancing Federal Budget," *Congressional Quarterly Weekly Report,* October 5, 1985, p. 1977.

68. Jonathan Fuerbringer, "Plan to Balance U.S. Budget by '91 Delayed in Senate," *New York Times,* October 5, 1985, pp. 1, 3.

69. Ibid.

70. Ibid.

71. Jonathan Fuerbringer, "Senate Seeks Bar to Deficits By '91 in Bipartisan Vote," *New York Times,* October 10, 1985, pp. A1, B19.

72. Ibid.

73. Ibid.

74. Jonathan Fuerbringer, "Leaders in Senate Reach Compromise On U.S. Debt Limit," *New York Times,* October 9, 1985, p. A1.

75. Jacqueline Calmes, "Senate's Initiative Leaves Democrats Frustrated at Leadership, Republicans," *Congressional Quarterly Weekly Report,* October 12, 1985, pp. 2036–37.

76. Interview in Washington, D.C., April 14, 1986.

77. We wonder what would happen without informed staff!

78. *CQA 1985,* p. 457.

79. *New York Times,* October 24, 1985, p. 14.

80. Calmes, "Gramm: Making Waves, Enemies, and History."

81. Let us say that some authority (GAO?) calculated that outlays were too high and should be cut 5 percent. If 5 percent of new budget authority were sequestered for each program, project, or activity, the resulting outlay cuts would be very small for any slow-spend program (say buying aircraft carriers), and the total outlay cut for that year (though not over time) would be far below target. Alternatively, average translation of budget authority to outlays could be calculated. About two dollars of new budget authority creates one dollar in outlays each year. So 10 percent of all new budget authority could be sequestered, thereby saving the needed 5 percent of outlays. Here there are two problems: the budget authority cut is huge, and it hurts fast-spend programs such as personnel (and what use are tanks without someone to drive them?). That could be avoided by sequestering exactly enough in new budget authority for each account (or P/P/A) to meet the 5 percent outlay reduction target for that account. In personnel, that would be 5 percent of the budget authority, sensible enough. But in a procurement account most of that year's outlays derive from prior contracts. If these are protected on constitutional and practical grounds, saving 5 percent of outlays that year might require eliminating all new budget authority.

82. Richard E. Cohen, "Balanced Budget Plan Forces House Democrats to Get Their Act Together," *National Journal,* November 16, 1985, pp. 2586–88.

83. Jonathan Fuerbringer, "Democrats Would Exempt the Poor From Budget Ax," *New York Times,* October 30, 1985, p. B6.

84. Steven V. Roberts, "Budget Battle: Democrats United Behind Party Plan," *New York Times,* November 2, 1985, p. 9; Cohen, "Balanced Budget Plan Forces House Democrats."

85. Ibid.

86. The most active were Representatives Aspin, Foley, Gephardt, Obey, Pa-

netta, and Republican Trent Lott, together with Senators Chiles, Domenici, Gramm, Packwood, and Rudman.

87. Elizabeth Wehr, "Gramm-Rudman Both Disappoints and Succeeds," *Congressional Quarterly Weekly Report,* November 15, 1987, pp. 2879–82.

88. Elizabeth Wehr, "Bipartisan Budget Agreement Now Seems Likely," *Congressional Quarterly Weekly Report,* May 17, 1986, p. 1082.

89. Elizabeth Wehr, "Bipartisanship vs. Election-Year Politics: Senate Restlessness May Signal Unique Cooperation on Budget," *Congressional Quarterly Weekly Report,* February 22, 1986, pp. 443–45.

90. Ibid.

91. Kirschten and Rauch, "Political Poker Game."

92. The conference agreement explained it very differently: as a $20 billion maximum prorated for the fact that, as of March 1, 1986, only seven months remained in the fiscal year—thus seven-twelfths of $20 billion equals $11.7 billion.

93. The deficit reduction timetable is slightly altered from Alice C. Maroni and Robert E. Foelber, "The Gramm-Rudman-Hollings Deficit Reduction Process (P.L. 99–177) and the Department of Defense: A Summary Review," Report No. 86–7, Congressional Research Service, January 6, 1986.

94. Even more important to the tactics of GRH, appropriations for the coming year might not have been passed. So what do you sequester from? Essentially, from last year's levels; subsequent additions supposedly would be inhibited by points of order.

95. Two complications in sequestration appear: the reductions in health programs were taken off the top (if, in our example, they were $2 billion, other defense and domestic would be cut $17 billion each, or $34 billion total). COLAs for federal retirement could be sequestered (though existing benefits could not), but it was hard to tell whether they were defense or domestic because they consisted of military, Pentagon civilian, and civilian agency retirees. Therefore, they credited any retirement COLA cuts half to the defense and half to the domestic sequester targets.

96. As for the sources of spending, in any year the defense function (050) has at its disposal (1) new budget authority and old budget authority that (2) is obligated and (3) unobligated to be spent. The outlay base consists of outlays from new budget authority due to be spent that year, plus outlays generated from the prior year's obligated balances, plus new spending from previously unobligated balances. Conferees decided to sequester a new category called "budgetary resources"—all new budget authority, together with unobligated balances. (Obligated balances were left out because the government had already signed contracts to spend them.) This meant that all new budget authority (NBA) and unobligated balances would be sequestered, whether or not they caused outlays in that year. The percentage reduction for outlays is calculated as the amount needed, divided by the definition of the outlay base. That percentage is then applied to the budgetary resources, which are what is sequestered. So, in a personnel account, maybe $1.03 billion in budgetary resources exists with $1 billion in projected outlays. If a 10 percent outlay cut were needed, $103 million in resources would be cut. A procurement account with much greater

BA than outlays would have a much larger difference between the BA sequestered and the outlay target, but the savings, though spread over a number of years, might well be less than the outlay target in the first year.

97. After sequestration, however, presidents would retain whatever reprograming authority they had been able to exercise in the past, a practice based mostly on informal understandings with Congress. Gramm-Rudman-Hollings did nothing to change that whole gray area of appropriations law, in which the obligation of the executive to conform to any congressional instructions not engraved in law was very dubious. It remained to be seen whether GRH would drive Congress and the president into battle over a set of old understandings based largely on custom and without legal force. To continue describing the close monitoring of presidential performance: on September 5 the chief executive would submit a list of proposed changes in contracts to the Armed Services and Appropriations committees. At the end of the month, GAO would certify that savings stemming from sequestration of contracts were correct—if they were.

98. Representative Mike Synar, who brought the suit, and his legal advisers, apparently guessed right in accepting the Senate's terms, hoping the district court rulings on which Senate staff relied would not hold.

99. Elizabeth Wehr, "Ways and Means Bill Blocked: Trouble Brewing as Congress Moves to Reduce Spending," *Congressional Quarterly Weekly Report,* September 21, 1985, p. 1863.

100. Stephen Gettinger, "Budget Leaders Force Cuts in Spending Bills," *Congressional Quarterly Weekly Reports,* October 5, 1985, p. 1984.

101. Jonathan Fuerbringer, "Senate Approves Measure on Budget," *New York Times,* September 26, 1985, p. B10.

102. Warren Weaver, "$100 Billion Tax Rise is Urged by Stockman," *New York Times,* September 30, 1985, p. D7.

103. "Undue Process," *The Economist,* November 9, 1985, p. 32.

104. "Conferees OK Legislative Spending," p. 2172; and Stephen Gettinger, "Senate Votes $9.9 Billion Transportation Bill," pp. 2172–73, *Congressional Quarterly Weekly Report,* October 26, 1985.

105. Jacqueline Calmes, "House Passes, Senate Defers Major Deficit-Cutting Bills," *Congressional Quarterly Weekly Report,* October 26, 1985, pp. 2142–43, 2145–46.

106. Jacqueline Calmes, "House Panels Surpass Deficit-Reduction Target," *Congressional Quarterly Weekly Report,* October 5, 1985, p. 1979; Calmes, "House Passes, Senate Defers."

107. Federal Budget Report, October 29, 1985, p. 3.

108. "Undue process."

109. Diane Granat, "Adjournment Date Slips: Congress Hung Up on Deficit as Fiscal Crisis Week Arrives," *Congressional Quarterly Weekly Report,* November 9, 1985, pp. 2263–65.

110. Jacqueline Calmes, "Up to $85 Billion in Savings Projected: Conferees Begin to Reconcile Versions of Deficit-Cutting Bill," *Congressional Quarterly Weekly Report,* December 7, 1985, pp. 2550–51.

111. Jonathan Fuerbringer, "Congress Adopts Stopgap Measure on U.S. Spending," *New York Times,* December 13, 1985, pp. 1, B8; Elizabeth Wehr,

"Congress Enacts Far-Reaching Budget Measure," *Congressional Quarterly Weekly Report,* December 14, 1985, p. 2604.

112. Jonathan Fuerbringer, " '86 Spending Act Rejected in House," *New York Times,* December 17, 1985, p. B11.

113. Ibid.

114. Jonathan Fuerbringer, "Conferees Compromise on an '86 Spending Bill," *New York Times,* December 19, 1985, p. B22; Pat Towell, "Despite Decline in the Budget, Defense Programs Will Survive," *Congressional Quarterly Weekly Report,* December 28, 1985, pp. 2748–50.

115. Fuerbringer, "Conferees Compromise on an '86 Spending Bill"; Jonathan Fuerbringer, "Congress Reaches Impasse on Plan to Reduce Deficit," *New York Times,* December 20, 1985, pp. 1, D6.

116. Here is a brief listing of some of the hundreds of subjects—some controversial and others mundane—the bill addressed, many of which had little to do with deficit reduction; because the House amended the bill and returned it to the Senate, it is technically still alive though perhaps brain-dead.

—routine extension of several housing programs;

—a requirement that the Transportation secretary withhold 10 percent of highway funds starting in fiscal 1989 from states that have not set their minimum drinking age at 21;

—an instruction to build three highway bridges over the Ohio River between designated points in Ohio and Kentucky;

—a plan to allocate to Gulf Coast states billions of dollars from oil and gas drilling on the Outer Continental Shelf;

—extensive overhaul of medicare, including changes in the 1983 law that set up a new prospective reimbursement system for hospital fees to limit costs;

—extension of the right to social security benefits to children adopted by and living with their great-grandparents;

—eligibility of Connecticut state policy for social security;

—an increase in the federal excise tax on domestically mined coal to finance the black lung disability trust fund and a waiver for five years of interest payments on the funds' indebtedness.

Richard E. Cohen, "Congressional Focus," *National Journal,* January 11, 1986, p. 110.

117. Jacqueline Calmes, "Deficit-Reduction Bill Goes Down to the Wire," *Congressional Quarterly Weekly Report,* December 21, 1985, pp. 2669, 2671–72.

118. Steven V. Roberts, "Many in Congress Say Session of '85 Was Unproductive," *New York Times,* December 22, 1985, pp. 1, 26.

119. Ibid.

120. "President Bars a Tax Increase," *New York Times,* December 22, 1985, p. A34.

121. Jonathan Rauch, "Politics of Deficit Reduction Remains Deadlocked Despite Balanced Budget Act," *National Journal,* January 4, 1986, pp. 15–21.

122. Jeffrey L. Sheler, "Budget Skirmishing Begins," *U.S. News and World Report,* February 3, 1986, pp. 20–21.

123. Jacqueline Calmes, "Congress May Revive Deficit-Reduction Bill," *Congressional Quarterly Weekly Report,* January 18, 1986, p. 106.

124. Pat Towell, "Advisory Panel Backs Pentagon Reorganization," *Congressional Quarterly Weekly Report,* March 1, 1986, pp. 495–96.

125. Stephen Gettinger and CQWR staff, "Deficit-Reduction Bill's Tortuous Journey Ends," *Congressional Quarterly Weekly Report,* April 5, 1986, pp. 751–68.

126. Stephen Gettinger, "$18 Billion Deficit-Reduction Measure Clears," *Congressional Quarterly Weekly Report,* March 22, 1986, p. 682; Gettinger et al., "Deficit-Reduction Bill's Tortuous Journey Ends."

127. "Inside Washington," *National Journal,* April 19, 1986, p. 923.

128. Gettinger, "$18 Billion Deficit-Reduction Measure Clears."

129. Gettinger et al., "Deficit-Reduction Bill's Tortuous Journey Ends."

Chapter Twenty

1. Numbers are from Tables 1.2 and 2.1 in *Individual Income Tax Returns: 1984,* Statistics of Income Division, Internal Revenue Service Publication 1304 (Rev. 11–86). These are estimates based on IRS surveys.

2. Ibid. The cutoff line here is adjusted gross incomes of $40,000 or more, hardly a definition of great wealth. See also John Witte, *The Politics and Development of the Federal Income Tax* (Madison: University of Wisconsin Press, 1985).

3. Barrett, *Gambling with History,* p. 55.

4. Eileen Shanahan, "Senate Tax Debate Opens to Raves . . . Mostly," *Congressional Quarterly Weekly Report,* June 7, 1986, p. 1255–57.

5. Paul R. McDaniel and Stanley S. Surrey, *International Aspects of Tax Expenditures: A Comparative Study* (Deventer, The Netherlands: Kluwer Law and Taxation Publishers, 1985); and McDaniel and Surrey, *Tax Expenditures* (Cambridge, Mass.: Harvard University Press, 1985). For opposing views, see Aaron Wildavsky, "Keeping Kosher: The Epistemology of Tax Expenditures," *Journal of Public Policy* 5, no. 3 (1986), pp. 413–31.

6. Joseph Pechman, Henry J. Aaron, Harvey Galper, George L. Perry, Alice M. Rivlin, and Charles L. Schultze, *Economic Choices 1987* (Washington, D.C.: Brookings Institution, 1986).

7. Jeffrey Birnbaum, "Tax Bill Saga: How a Pre-Emptive Political Step Became a Plan to Restructure Taxation in the U.S.," *Wall Street Journal,* June 4, 1986, p. 56. Bill Veeck, the famed owner of baseball teams (Cleveland Indians, St. Louis Browns, Chicago White Sox) appears to be the person who dreamed up depreciating players.

8. Timothy Clark, "Strange Bedfellows," *National Journal,* February 2, 1985, pp. 251–56.

9. Ibid.

10. Birnbaum, "Tax Bill Saga."

11. For Roberts's view of the world, see his *The Supply-Side Revolution* (Cambridge, Mass.: Harvard University Press, 1984).

12. Clark, "Strange Bedfellows."

13. Jeffrey H. Birnbaum, "Senate Opens Debate on Tax Overhaul; Bill's Passage Expected Within 3 Weeks," *Wall Street Journal,* June 5, 1986, p. 3.

14. Pamela Fessler, "Laying the Groundwork: Special Interests Now Working on Next Year's Tax Legislation," *Congressional Quarterly Weekly Report,* April 28, 1984, p. 953.

15. The Kemp-Kasten 24 percent included an exclusion for 20 percent of wages subject to social security tax. For a comparison of proposals, see Ronald Brownstein, "Wagering on Tax Reform," *National Journal,* February 2, 1985, pp. 245–50.

16. Robert Hall and Alvin Rabushka, *Low Tax, Flat Tax* (New York: McGraw-Hill, 1983).

17. Clark, "Strange Bedfellows"; Timothy B. Clark, "GOP platform edges closer to pledging no increase in taxes," *National Journal,* August 18, 1984, p. 1555.

18. Text of 1984 Democratic party platform, *Congressional Quarterly Weekly Report,* July 21, 1984, pp. 1747–80.

19. Nadine Cohodas, "Solidly Conservative Platform Ready for Adoption By GOP," *Congressional Quarterly Weekly Report,* August 18, 1984, p. 2023.

20. Text of 1984 Republican party platform, *Congressional Quarterly Weekly Report,* August 25, 1984, pp. 2096–2117.

21. Clark, "Strange Bedfellows."

22. Birnbaum, "Tax Bill Saga," p. 56.

23. Clark, "Strange Bedfellows."

24. Birnbaum, "Tax Bill Saga."

25. Timothy Clark, "Business Hit Hardest Under Treasury Tax Plan," *National Journal,* December 1, 1984, p. 2312.

26. Ronald Brownstein, "Wagering on Tax Reform," *National Journal,* February 2, 1985, p. 245; Clark, "Business Hit Hardest"; Pamela Fessler, "Members Await Details of Tax Code Revision," *Congressional Quarterly Weekly Report,* February 16, 1985, pp. 301–2.

27. Jeffrey H. Birnbaum and Alan S. Murray, *Showdown at Gucci Gulch: Lawmakers, Lobbyists, and the Unlikely Triumph of Tax Reform* (New York: Random House, 1987), pp. 49–50.

28. Ibid., pp. 48–54.

29. Steven Pressman, "President Scores for Oratory, but Skepticism Remains on Hill," *Congressional Quarterly Weekly Report,* February 9, 1985, pp. 274–75.

30. "Schedule Uncertain for Tax Reform," *Congressional Quarterly Weekly Report,* February 2, 1985, p. 168; Birnbaum, "Tax Bill Saga."

31. "A Call for a 'Second American Revolution': President Reagan's State of the Union Address," *Congressional Quarterly Weekly Report,* February 9, 1985, pp. 267–70.

32. Elder Witt, "Arguments Set for February 19," *Congressional Quarterly Weekly Report,* February 16, 1985, pp. 307, 309.

33. Ibid.

34. Pamela Fessler, "Key is Presidential Backing," *Congressional Quarterly Weekly Report,* October 27, 1984, p. 2788.

35. William Schneider, "Public Reluctant to Drop 'Unfair' Income Tax in

Favor of Unknown Remedy," *National Journal,* December 29, 1984, p. 2462. Other polls show that the public either supports a flat, broader based lower rate tax compared to the present system or opposes it by small margins. Polls taken late in 1984 revealed widespread belief that the rich always escaped their fair share of taxes, that the ordinary person paid too much, and that the system was far too complicated.

36. John Witte, *Federal Income Tax.*

37. Pamela Fessler, "Successful Tax Code Overhaul Dependent on Reagan's Pitch," *Congressional Quarterly Weekly Report,* May 25, 1985, pp. 980–81. Ladd did warn that, because many people (48 percent according to an ABC/*Washington Post* poll in January 1985) had not heard of the Treasury Department's original reform proposal at the time that the public was being asked about hypothetical changes, opinion might alter dramatically.

38. Text of Reagan press conference, *Congressional Quarterly Weekly Report,* January 12, 1985, pp. 88–91.

39. Steven Pressman, "Familiar Themes, Programs: President Scores for Oratory, But Skepticism Remains on Hill," *Congressional Quarterly Weekly Report,* February 9, 1985, pp. 273, 275, 277.

40. Pamela Fessler, "Rostenkowski Makes Pitch for Tax Overhaul," *Congressional Quarterly Weekly Report,* March 2, 1985, p. 399.

41. Pamela Fessler, "Tax Overhaulers' Next Chore is Generating Public Support," *Congressional Quarterly Weekly Report,* March 30, 1985, p. 604.

42. Susan S. Rasky, "Reagan Postpones Tax Push to Focus on Deficit," *New York Times,* July 5, 1985, p. D6.

43. Timothy B. Clark, "Real Estate Industry, Other Corporate Losers Open Fire on Tax Proposals," *National Journal,* December 8, 1984, p. 2333.

44. Pamela Fessler, "Senior Staff Changes at Tax-Writing Committees," *Congressional Quarterly Weekly Report,* January 19, 1985, p. 111; Pamela Fessler, "Fight to Reap the Political Advantage: Successful Tax Code Overhaul Dependent on Reagan's Pitch," *Congressional Quarterly Weekly Report,* May 25, 1985, pp. 980–81.

45. Fessler, "Successful Tax Code Overhaul Dependent on Reagan's Pitch."

46. Elizabeth Wehr, "Rostenkowski: A Firm Grip on Ways and Means," *Congressional Quarterly Weekly Report,* July 6, 1985, p. 1317.

47. Ronald Grover, "Why Rostenkowski and Reagan are Playing Footsie," *Business Week,* September 16, 1985, p. 31.

48. "Reagan's May 28 Address on Tax Reform," *Congressional Quarterly Weekly Report,* June 1, 1985, p. 1074.

49. Birnbaum and Murray, *Showdown at Gucci Gulch,* p. 99.

50. Pamela Fessler, "Tax Bill Markup Schedule Seen as Ambitious," *Congressional Quarterly Weekly Report,* September 14, 1985, pp. 1796–97.

51. Richard E. Cohen, "Despite Misgivings, Finance Committee May Be Forced to Tackle Tax Reform Bill," *National Journal,* October 19, 1985, p. 2360.

52. Pamela Fessler, "Members Find Little Support for 'Reform': Tax Panel Postpones Markup, Still Hopes to Report This fall," *Congressional Quarterly Weekly Report,* September 7, 1985, pp. 1744–45.

53. Pamela Fessler, "Panel Votes Breaks for Banks, Charitable Gifts," *Congressional Quarterly Weekly Report,* October 19, 1985, p. 2102.

54. Ibid., p. 2103.

55. We should point out that the amendment easily could be argued to have preserved the financial integrity of banks. See Birnbaum and Murray, *Showdown at Gucci Gulch,* pp. 127–28.

56. Ibid., p. 127.

57. Ibid., p. 126.

58. Ibid., pp. 126–35.

59. Pamela Fessler, "State, Local Tax Deduction Could Be Retained," *Congressional Quarterly Weekly Report,* October 26, 1985, pp. 2140–41; Fessler, "Markup Nearly Half Finished: Panel Confident of Reporting Tax-Overhaul Measure This Fall," *Congressional Quarterly Weekly Report,* November 2, 1985, pp. 2197–99.

60. Charles P. Alexander, "Trying to Stage a Tax-Reform Rally," *Time,* November 11, 1985, p. 68.

61. Pamela Fessler, "Ways and Means Finishes Tax Code Overhaul," *Congressional Quarterly Weekly Report,* November 30, 1985, pp. 2483, 2485.

62. Pamela Fessler, "Reagan Criticizes 'Waterings Down': Tax Code Rewrite Continues; Panel OKs Pension Revisions," November 9, 1985, pp. 2276–77; Fessler, "Tax Overhaul Measure Faces an Uncertain Future in the House," November 23, 1985, p. 2417; Fessler, "Success of Tax Bill in Doubt Despite Mild Reagan Support," December 7, 1985, p. 2546; all in *Congressional Quarterly Weekly Report.*

63. "At a Glance—A Weekly Checklist of Major Issues," *National Journal,* December 7, 1985, p. 2827.

64. Pamela Fessler, "GOP Defeats Attempt to Consider Tax Bill," *Congressional Quarterly Weekly Report,* December 14, 1985, pp. 2613–16.

65. Pamela Fessler, "GOP Is Opposed, Democrats Are Split: Success for Tax Bill in Doubt Despite Mild Reagan Support," *Congressional Quarterly Weekly Report,* December 7, 1985, pp. 2543–46.

66. Birnbaum and Murray, *Showdown at Gucci Gulch,* p. 160.

67. Fessler, "GOP Defeats Attempt to Consider Tax Bill"; Birnbaum and Murray, *Showdown at Gucci Gulch,* pp. 164–65.

68. Ibid.

69. Pamela Fessler, "House Reverses Self, Passes Major Tax Overhaul," *Congressional Quarterly Weekly Report,* December 21, 1985, p. 2705.

70. "At a Glance—A Weekly Checklist of Major Issues," *National Journal,* December 21, 1985, p. 2935.

71. Fessler, "House Reverses Self."

72. Dick Kirschten, "Tax Reform Dodges Another Bullet, But May Have Winged the GOP," *National Journal,* December 21, 1985, pp. 2918–19.

73. Ibid.

74. Pamela Fessler, "Finance Panel Moves Toward Tax Bill Markup," *Congressional Quarterly Weekly Report,* March 8, 1986, p. 545; and Stephen Gettinger, "Measure's Savings Now $18.1 Billion: Deficit-Cutting Bill Amended, But Future Action is Uncertain," *Congressional Quarterly Weekly Report,* March 8, 1986, pp. 544–45.

75. Elizabeth Wehr, "Budget Puts Congress in a Combative Mood," *Congressional Quarterly Weekly Report,* February 8, 1986, p. 219.

76. David Rosenbaum, "Senate Puts Budget Effort Ahead of Tax Revision," *New York Times,* April 11, 1986, p. A1.

77. David Rosenbaum, "The Senate Seems to be Going Along to Get Along," *New York Times,* February 2, 1986, p. A7.

78. Pamela Fessler, "Finance Markup Completion Target Is May 1," *Congressional Quarterly Weekly Report,* January 25, 1986, pp. 142–44; Fessler, "Finance Panel Moves Toward Tax Bill Markup."

79. Rosenbaum, "Senate Seems to be Going Along to Get Along."

80. David Rosenbaum, "Panel Set to Defeat Bond Tax: Packwood's Plan Opposed by Senators," *New York Times,* March 21, 1986, pp. D1, D5.

81. Timothy Clark, "Divided They Stand," *National Journal,* April 19, 1986, pp. 929–39.

82. Pamela Fessler, "Finance Panel Suspends Markup of Tax Bill," *Congressional Quarterly Weekly Report,* April 19, 1986, p. 840.

83. Ibid.

84. Timothy Clark, "Forget Simplicity: Let's Make a Deal," *National Journal,* April 26, 1986, p. 1008.

85. Jeffrey Birnbaum, "Packwood's Route to Triumph," *Wall Street Journal,* May 9, 1986, p. 54.

86. Pamela Fessler, "Finance Committee Studies Two-Rate Tax Plan," *Congressional Quarterly Weekly Report,* April 26, 1986, p. 900.

87. Daniel P. Moynihan, "Special Report" (newsletter to constituents), June 1986.

88. Ibid.

89. Jacqueline Calmes, "Bob Packwood: A Tax Reform Convert," *Congressional Quarterly Weekly Report,* May 10, 1986, p. 1011.

90. Ibid.

91. Birnbaum and Murray, *Showdown at Gucci Gulch,* p. 205.

92. Ibid., p. 207.

93. Packwood speech, *Congressional Record,* June 4, 1986, p. S6719.

94. Moynihan, "Special Report."

95. Packwood speech, *Congressional Record,* June 4, 1986, p. S6719. See also Robert D. Hershey, Jr., "Tax Bill's Key Numbers Man," *New York Times,* January 3, 1986, p. D1.

96. Moynihan, "Special Report."

97. Birnbaum, "Packwood's Route to Triumph."

98. Packwood speech, *Congressional Record,* June 4, 1986, p. S6719.

99. Moynihan, "Special Report."

100. See Birnbaum and Murray, *Showdown at Gucci Gulch,* p. 219.

101. Pamela Fessler, "Packwood Promises New Plan May 5: Tax Bill Consensus Claimed, But Some Members Skeptical," *Congressional Quarterly Weekly Report,* May 3, 1986, pp. 962–63.

102. Calmes, "Bob Packwood."

103. Eileen Shanahan, "Finance Panel OKs Radical Tax Overhaul Bill," *Congressional Quarterly Weekly Report,* May 10, 1986, p. 1007.

104. Fessler, "Finance Committee Studies Two-Rate Plan."

105. Birnbaum and Murray, *Showdown at Gucci Gulch,* pp. 227–28.

106. Ibid., p. 230.
107. Ibid., p. 129.
108. Moynihan, "Special Report."
109. Packwood speech, *Congressional Record,* June 4, 1986, p. 3.
110. Jeffrey Birnbaum, "Radical Tax Overhaul Now Seems Probable," *Wall Street Journal,* May 8, 1986, pp. 1, 3.
111. Ibid.
112. Ibid.
113. Elizabeth Wehr, "Tax Bill Could Face Procedural Hurdles on Senate Floor," p. 1013; Eileen Shanahan, "Finance Panel OKs Radical Tax Overhaul Bill," pp. 102–13, 1007–10. See also chart, "Evolution of Proposals to Overhaul the Tax Code," *Congressional Quarterly Weekly Report,* August 23, 1986, p. 1948.
114. Eileen Shanahan, "Tax Debate Keys on Economic Consequences," *Congressional Quarterly Weekly Report,* May 17, 1986, pp. 1093, 1095.
115. Timothy Clark and Richard Cohen, "Tax Reform Locomotive," *National Journal,* May 31, 1986, p. 1301.
116. Jeffrey Schwartz, "NY Leaders Split on Tax Bill," *New York Times,* May 7, 1986, pp. 32, 37.
117. David Rosenbaum, "A Linking of Tax Reform to Budget," *New York Times,* May 13, 1986, pp. D1, D11.
118. Jeffrey H. Birnbaum, "Dole Asserts Tax Bill Is 'Unstoppable,' Will Be on Reagan's Desk by Labor Day," *Wall Street Journal,* June 3, 1986, p. 3.
119. Eileen Shanahan, "Senate Nears Tax Bill Passage," *Congresssional Quarterly Weekly Report,* June 14, 1986, p. 1313.
120. GRH said that any amendment to legislation on the floor of the Senate that would raise the deficit would be subject to a point of order. Because there was no budget resolution, there was no "deficit" number to be increased, so the provision was not technically in force. But the norm, far more important than the formal procedure, remained.
121. Jeffrey H. Birnbaum, "Senate, Leaving Tax Plan Intact, Rejects Proposal to Retain Sales-Tax Deduction," *Wall Street Journal,* June 13, 1986, pp. 3, 5.
122. Timothy B. Clark, "Bill's Biggest Boom is to Working Poor," *National Journal,* July 12, 1986, p. 1730.
123. It "looks like a rich man's out," Speaker O'Neill complained. "It's a mighty loophole for the wealthy of America" (Birnbaum, "Senate, Leaving Tax Plan Intact").
124. Shanahan, "Senate Nears Tax Bill Passage"; Timothy B. Clark, "Taxation—Resolving the Differences," *National Journal,* July 5, 1986, pp. 1658–65.
125. Shanahan, "Senate Nears Tax Bill Passage."
126. Here, as elsewhere in matters not central to our story, we are barely able to hint at the complexity of the considerations.
127. Birnbaum, "Senate Opens Debate on Tax Overhaul."
128. David E. Rosenbaum, "Senate Rejects a Tax Amendment to Benefit Middle-Income People," *New York Times,* June 19, 1986, pp. A1, B8.
129. Birnbaum and Murray, *Showdown at Gucci Gulch,* p. 246.
130. Eileen Shanahan, "Christmas Presents Beginning to Pile Up: Panel's Tax

Bill Largely Intact As Senate Nears Final Passage," *Congressional Quarterly Weekly Report,* June 21, 1986, pp. 1377–79; Birnbaum and Murray, *Showdown at Gucci Gulch,* p. 251.

131. Timothy Clark and Richard E. Cohen, "Resolving the Differences," *National Journal,* July 5, 1986, p. 1662.

132. Eileen Shanahan, "Tax Reform Warmup: Harmony on Some Points," *Congressional Quarterly Weekly Report,* July 12, 1986, pp. 1566–68.

133. Birnbaum and Murray, *Showdown at Gucci Gulch,* p. 258.

134. Ibid., p. 259.

135. Shanahan, "Tax Reform Warmup"; David Rosenbaum, "A Tentative Tax-Rate Accord," *New York Times,* July 26, 1986, p. 35.

136. Jeffrey H. Birnbaum, "Senate Tax Conferees React Negatively To House Plan to Lift Corporate Taxes," *Wall Street Journal,* August 1, 1986, p. 3.

137. Eileen Shanahan, "Corporate Hit Could Sidetrack Tax Conference," *Congressional Quarterly Weekly Report,* November 2, 1986, p. 1228.

138. David E. Rosenbaum, "House Team Sets Strategies for Bargaining," *New York Times,* July 31, 1986, p. D1.

139. "Tax Reform, Last Lap or Last Legs," editorial, *New York Times,* August 8, 1986, p. A26.

140. Birnbaum and Murray, *Showdown at Gucci Gulch,* pp. 264–67.

141. Jeffrey H. Birnbaum, "Tax Conferees Reach Impasse on Overhaul," *Wall Street Journal,* August 13, 1986, pp. 3, 14.

142. David Rosenbaum, "Tax Conferees Divided: Chairman Seeks Accord," *New York Times,* August 13, 1986, pp. D1, D6.

143. David Rosenbaum, "Chairmen Hit a Snag on Tax Bill: Face Shortfall of $17 Billion Over 5 Years," *New York Times,* August 15, 1986, pp. D1, D2.

144. Birnbaum and Murray, *Showdown at Gucci Gulch,* pp. 273–76.

145. David Rosenbaum, "Accord on Taxes Has Been Reached, Packwood Says," *New York Times,* August 16, 1986, p. 1.

146. Tom Redburn and Michael Wines, "Tax Accord Achieved, Top Conferee Declares," *Los Angeles Times,* August 16, 1986, pp. 1, 22.

147. Rosenbaum, "Accord on Taxes Has Been Reached"; Redburn and Wines, "Tax Accord Achieved."

148. Robin Toner, "Behind the Scenes in Tax Bill Drama," *New York Times,* August 16, 1986, pp. 35, 37.

149. Jeffrey H. Birnbaum, "What's Next? In Turning to Deficit, Congress May Tinker With the Taxes Again," *Wall Street Journal,* August 18, 1986, pp. 1, 10.

150. Ibid.

151. E. J. Dionne, Jr., "Political Memo: For Richer, for Poorer, in Taxes and Ideology," *New York Times,* August 22, 1986, p. A10.

152. Robin Toner, "Elation and Nostalgia on Capitol Hill," *New York Times,* August 18, 1986, p. B10.

153. Peter J. Kilborn, "A Reagan-Style Bill," *New York Times,* August 18, 1986, p. A1.

154. Albert Scardino, "Realty Woes Seen in Tax Bill," *New York Times,* August 26, 1986, p. D5.

155. Leslie Maitland Werner, "Educators See Great Harm; Large Cut in Gifts Feared," *New York Times,* August 21, 1986, p. D15.

156. Linda Greenhouse, "Danforth Promises Determined Battle," *New York Times,* August 20, 1986, p. D10.

157. "U.S. Tax Bill May Force New York To Cut Housing and Public Works," Bruce Lambert, "Bond Costs Likely to Rise," and Eric N. Berg, "Entrepreneur Curb Seen," all in *New York Times,* August 20, 1986, p. 1.

158. Jeffrey H. Birnbaum, "Tax-Overhaul Vote Represents Moment of Truth for GOP as It Tries to Shed Big Business Image," *Wall Street Journal,* September 12, 1986, p. 50; Eileen Shanahan, "Despite Skeptics, House Eases Way for Tax Bill," *Congressional Quarterly Weekly Report,* September 13, 1986, p. 2118.

159. Eileen Shanahan, "Time and Numbers Work Against It: Discontent Grows Over Tax Bill as House Prepares for Final Vote," *Congressional Quarterly Weekly Report,* September 20, 1986, p. 2183.

160. Douglas Harbrecht, "350 exemptions in final tax accord," *San Francisco Examiner,* September 19, 1986, p. A3.

161. David Rosenbaum, "A G.O.P. Effort to Block Tax Bill Is Frustrated," *New York Times,* September 25, 1986, p. D1.

162. Thomas Oliphant, "House passes tax revision bill," *Boston Globe,* September 26, 1986, pp. 1, 13.

163. Ibid.

164. Ann Swardson, "Senate OKs Tax Overhaul," *Oakland Tribune,* September 28, 1986, pp. 1, 8.

165. *National Journal,* November 22, 1986, p. 2854.

166. Swardson, "Senate OKs Tax Overhaul."

167. Stephen V. Roberts, "How Tax Bill Breezed Past, Despite Wide Doubts," *New York Times,* September 26, 1986, p. A20.

168. Eileen Shanahan, "It May Be Tax Reform, but Will It Last?" *Congressional Quarterly Weekly Report,* August 30, 1986, p. 2053.

169. Julie Kostervitz, "Broad Coalition Prepares to Do Battle on Taxing Employee Fringe Benefits," *National Journal,* May 4, 1985, p. 956.

170. Janet Hook, "Issue of Fringe-Benefit Taxes Only Partly Defused by Reagan," *Congressional Quarterly Weekly Report,* June 8, 1985, pp. 1099–1101.

171. Pamela Fessler and Steven Pressman, "Tax Overhaul: The Crucial Lobby Fight of 1985," *Congressional Quarterly Weekly Report,* March 9, 1985, p. 450.

172. Timothy Clark, "At Grass Roots, Not Much Groundswell of Support for Reagan's Tax Reform," *National Journal,* July 27, 1985, p. 1738.

173. Nadine Cohodas, "Battle Looms Over State, Local Tax Issue," *Congressional Quarterly Weekly Report,* June 1, 1985, p. 1041.

174. Robert Rothman, "Reagan Critics Praise Tax Cut for the Poor," *Congressional Quarterly Weekly Report,* July 6, 1985, p. 1323; Joann S. Lublin, "Amid Debates Over Tax Preferences for the Rich, Lawmakers Agree on Sweeping Relief for the Poor," *Wall Street Journal,* May 23, 1986, p. 40.

175. A word of caution is in order. Most people of modest means pay not income but social security taxes. The percentage reduction in income tax under the tax reform passed by the Senate is substantially but by no means entirely reduced when combined into a grand total with social security. Thus, those who

earn between $10,000 and $20,000 annually see their reduction lowered from 20.1 percent on income tax alone to 12.9 percent when social security is figured in. However, when the earned income tax credit is added in, many working poor will receive rebates that they can subtract from their social security payments.

176. Timothy Clark, "How to Succeed Against Business," *National Journal*, May 3, 1986, p. 1059.

177. Jeffrey H. Birnbaum, "Reborn Bill: Radical Tax Overhaul Now Seems Probable As Senate Panel Acts," *Wall Street Journal*, May 8, 1986, pp. 1, 22.

178. Fessler and Pressman, "Tax Overhaul: The Crucial Lobby Fight of 1985." ·

179. *Inside the Administration*, May 29, 1986. This weekly newspaper is an Inside Washington Publication.

180. Robert Rothman, "Construction Down, Cost Up: Real Estate Industry Predicts Dire Harm From Reagan Plan," *Congressional Quarterly Weekly Report*, August 31, 1985, pp. 1707–10.

181. Nadine Cohodas, "Other Justice-Related Spending Up Slightly; Law Enforcement Spending Remains Level," *Congressional Quarterly Weekly Report*, February 2, 1985, p. 250.

182. Ann Cooper, "New Business Coalition Wants to Keep the Ball Rolling on Reagan's Tax Reform," *National Journal*, July 20, 1985, pp. 1675–79.

183. Jeffrey Birnbaum, "Tax Bill Saga: How a Pre-Emptive Political Step Became a Plan to Restructure Taxation in the U.S.," *Wall Street Journal*, June 4, 1986, p. 56.

184. Brooks Jackson and Monica Langley, "Lobbyists Take Aim at Conference Panel To Get Favors in Final Tax Overhaul Bill," *Wall Street Journal*, June 25, 1986, p. 24.

185. Eileen Shanahan, "Tax Debate Keys on Economic Consequences," *Congressional Quarterly Weekly Report*, May 17, 1986, p. 1095.

Chapter Twenty-One

1. Congressional Budget Office, "Reducing the Deficit: Spending and Revenue Options," Report to the Senate and House Committees on the Budget— Part II, March 1986, pp. 4–7.

2. Stephen Gettinger, "Reagan Budget Projects $143.6 Billion Deficit," *Congressional Quarterly Weekly Report*, February 8, 1985, p. 246.

3. The Reagan administration wanted to eliminate or phase out the following programs: air service subsidies to communities for service lost through deregulation; Agency for International Development housing guarantees— phase out beginning in 1987; Agricultural Stabilization and Conservation Service cost-sharing; Amtrak—end in 1987; Appalachian Regional Commission; Carl Perkins scholarships for high school graduates interested in teaching; categorical aid to migrant health centers, black-lung clinics, and family-planning clinics, to be wrapped into a block grant program; coastal zone management state grant program; college housing loans—phase out beginning in 1987; commercial fishing industry assistance; Community Services Block Grant; crop insurance subsidies—phase out by 1991; Economic Development Administration; energy

conservation grants and state energy planning and extension programs; Environmental Protection Agency loans for asbestos removal; Federal Housing Administration—develop proposals in 1987 to turn agency over to private sector; Farmers Home Administration housing and rural aid programs, wrapped into the Department of Housing and Urban Development (HUD); GI enhanced recruitment bill (PL 98–525); graduate education programs, including fellowships for women and minorities and for law and public service students; HUD grants for rental housing development and rehabilitation, rental rehabilitation loans, and new subsidized housing construction; immigrant education; Impact Aid Part B for schools serving U.S. employees' children; Interstate Commerce Commission; Legal Services Corporation; library aid, for public library research and librarian training; Justice Department grants for juvenile justice, state and local aid; Mariel Cubans and regional information sharing system programs—turned over to states to run with no federal funding; maritime subsidies—ship construction loan guarantees, aid to six state maritime schools, research and development (after 1987), and the cargo preference requirement included in the 1985 farm bill (PL 99–198); National Sea Grant college program; Postal Service subsidy; Public Health Service training grants; railroad rehabilitation loans—phase out beginning in 1987; rail service assistance to states; revenue sharing—end in 1987; Rural Electrification Administration; Soil Conservation Service programs on private lands, including the small watershed program; Small Business Administration credit assistance programs; State Student Incentive Grants; Tennessee Valley Authority regional economic programs; Urban Development Action Grants; U.S. Travel and Tourism Administration; waste treatment construction grants—phase out by 1990; Work Incentive Program (WIN) for adults receiving benefits under Aid to Families with Dependent Children.

4. Stephen H. Wildstron, Richard Fly, and Ronald Grover, "The Budget Has a Fighting Chance," *Business Week,* February 17, 1986, pp. 30–32.

5. Jonathan Rauch, "In Uncharted Waters," *National Journal,* February 8, 1986, pp. 312–17.

6. Pamela Fessler, "Reagan's Economic Forecast Attacked as Excessively Rosy," *Congressional Quarterly Weekly Report,* February 8, 1986, p. 283.

7. Jonathan Rauch, "Zero-Sum Budget Game," *National Journal,* May 10, 1986, p. 1099.

8. Ibid., p. 1097.

9. Ibid.

10. Rauch, "In Uncharted Waters."

11. Stephen Gettinger, "House OKs Democratic Budget for Fiscal 1987," *Congressional Quarterly Weekly Report,* May 17, 1986, pp. 1079–80.

12. Lee Walczak, Stephen H. Wildstrom, Richard Fly et al., "Is a Tax Hike Coming?" *Business Week,* February 3, 1986, pp. 48–53.

13. Stephen Gettinger, "Budget Panel Uses New Taxes to Cut Deficit," *Congressional Quarterly Weekly Report,* May 10, 1986, pp. 1061, 1063–64.

14. "Senate, House Committee FY 1987 Budget Resolutions," *Congressional Quarterly Weekly Report,* May 10, 1986, p. 1062.

15. Gettinger, "House OKs Democratic Budget"; Stephen Gettinger, "The

Making of the Democrats' Budget: A New Conservative-Liberal Coalition," *Congressional Quarterly Weekly Report,* May 17, 1986, pp. 1080–81.

16. Jeffrey H. Birnbaum, "Senate Tax Bill Is Seen Passing Before Friday," *Wall Street Journal,* June 17, 1986, p. 3.

17. David Rogers, "Conferees May Limit Defense Outlays Until Revenues in '87 Budget Are Raised," *Wall Street Journal,* June 11, 1986, p. 22.

18. David Shribman, "Conferees Consider New '87 Budget Plan Limiting Defense Cuts, Adding Revenues," *Wall Street Journal,* June 16, 1986, p. 41.

19. Ronald Grover, "Showdown Time for Gramm-Rudman," *Business Week,* January 10, 1986, p. 22.

20. Elizabeth Wehr, "Court Strikes Down Core of Gramm-Rudman," *Congressional Quarterly Weekly Report,* July 12, 1986, p. 1559, 1562–63.

21. "Supreme Court's Gramm-Rudman Opinion," *Congressional Quarterly Weekly Report,* July 12, 1986, p. 1581–83.

22. Elder Witt, "Court Sees Fatal Gramm-Rudman Flaw in Power Given to Comptroller General," *Congressional Quarterly Weekly Report,* July 12, 1986, pp. 1560–61.

23. "Supreme Court's Gramm-Rudman Opinion."

24. Jonathan Fuerbringer, "Congress Ratifies Spending Cuts," *New York Times,* July 18, 1986, p. A1.

25. Paul Blustein, "White House Raises Deficit Projection For 1986 but Sees Improvement in 1987," *Wall Street Journal,* August 7, 1986, p. 3.

26. Elizabeth Wehr, "Gramm-Rudman Repair Effort Stumbles on Mistrust of OMB," *Congressional Quarterly Weekly Report,* July 26, 1986, p. 1682.

27. David Rogers, "Senate Acts to Change Gramm-Rudman Law to Allow Automatic Spending Cuts," *Wall Street Journal,* July 31, 1986, p. 12.

28. Stephen Gettinger, "Gramm-Rudman Deficit Target Is in Sight," *Congressional Quarterly Weekly Report,* August 23, 1986, pp. 1943–46.

29. Ibid. The major differences between CBO and OMB estimates came from accounting for pay raises and estimates of entitlements. OMB assumed that the Department of Agriculture would not make $5.1 billion of advance price supports in spring 1987 and that spend-out rates for defense would be $5.2 billion slower than CBO thought.

30. Paul Blustein, "Report Shows 1987 Budget Must Shrink By $9.4 Billion to Avoid Automatic Cuts," *Wall Street Journal,* August 20, 1986, p. 5; Symposium on Budget Balance, discussion by Dr. Rudolph Penner, director of CBO, January 9–11, 1986, pp. 10–31.

31. Richard E. Cohen, "Tax Plum Fueling Budget Fight," *National Journal,* August 30, 1986, pp. 2068–69.

32. *Inside the Administration,* August 14, 1986, pp. 1–2.

33. David Shribman, "Across-the-Board Cuts Called Unlikely As Gramm-Rudman Process Is Launched," *Wall Street Journal,* September 12, 1986, p. 21.

34. Memo to Committee for a Responsible Federal Budget, as reported in that committee's memorandum/newsletter to board and members, September 19, 1986. This memorandum/newsletter is mailed periodically to Board and Members of the Committee.

35. Presidential spokesman Larry Speakes quoted in Jonathan Fuerbringer,

"Reagan Threatens Veto of Spending Bills for 1987," *New York Times*, September 17, 1986, p. A22.

36. Jeffrey H. Birnbaum and John E. Yang, "Ways and Means Panel Balks at Raising Taxes to Meet Gramm-Rudman Targets," *Wall Street Journal*, September 17, 1986, p. 3.

37. *Federal Budget Report*, September 9, 1986, pp. 3–4; Jonathan Fuerbringer, "Accord is Tentatively Reached on Cutting Deficit," *New York Times*, September 19, 1986, p. A30.

38. Jonathan Fuerbringer, "Senate Approves $13.3 Billion Plan to Cut '87 Deficit," *New York Times*, September 20, 1986, p. 1.

39. What Jack Brooks called "gimmickry of the worst kind" included a new $1.83 billion customs fee (illegal under the General Agreement on Tariff and Trade because it far exceeded the cost of collection), better enforcement by the IRS, and a $1 billion across-the-board cut to be taken equally from domestic and defense programs. These provisions were ostensibly large enough to compensate for expansion of medicaid coverage and a drop in the previously scheduled increase in medicare deductibles. Jonathan Fuerbringer, "House, 309 to 106, Votes Plan to Cut Deficit $15 Billion," *New York Times*, September 25, 1986, pp. 1, B11.

40. David Rogers, "House Clears $562 Billion Spending Bill; Reagan's Budget for Military Is Slashed," *Wall Street Journal*, September 26, 1986, p. 16.

41. Helen Dewar, "Big Agenda for Congress' Final Days," *Oakland Tribune*, October 12, 1986, p. A3.

42. David Rogers, "House Votes $576 Billion Spending Bill To Fund U.S. for the Rest of Fiscal 1987," *Wall Street Journal*, October 16, 1986, pp. 2, 26; *Inside the Administration*, "Congress Gives Reagan Nearly All He Sought in Continuing Resolutions," October 23, 1986, p. 11.

43. David Rogers, "Senate Votes $576 Billion Spending Bill But GOP Seeks to Strip Two Provisions," *Wall Street Journal*, October 17, 1986, p. 3.

44. David Rogers, "Fiscal '87 Budget of $576 Billion Signed Into Law," *Wall Street Journal*, October 20, 1986, pp. 3, 14.

45. David Rogers, "Senate Rejects Amendment Designating More Economic Aid for the Philippines," *Wall Street Journal*, September 30, 1986, p. 7. Eventually the Senate provided some aid; see *Congressional Quarterly Almanac* (Washington, D.C.: Congressional Quarterly, Inc. 1986), pp. 392–93.

46. Jonathan Rauch, "Playing the Budget Game Under New Rules," *National Journal*, April 12, 1986, p. 898.

47. "Budget Cutting is Still Lonely Work," *Congressional Quarterly Weekly Report*, August 16, 1986, p. 1933.

48. Richard E. Cohen, "House Democracy," *National Journal*, October 18, 1986, p. 2532. Namely, the dismay at the resuscitation of revenue sharing by Gray and Domenici at a breakfast for The Committee for a Responsible Federal Budget, September 8, 1986.

49. *Inside the Administration*, November 6, 1986, pp. 1, 7.

50. Susan Bentzer et al., "Is the Party Almost Over?" *Newsweek*, October 26, 1987, p. 50.

51. "Extraordinary Butchery," *The Economist*, October 24, 1987, pp. 75–76.

52. "As Time Goes By," in ibid., p. 77.

53. "When the bull turned," *The Economist,* October 24, 1987, pp. 11–12. For a typical menu of causes, see Larry Martz et al., "After the Meltdown of '87," *Newsweek,* November 2, 1987, pp. 14–20.

54. "When the bull turned."

55. Ibid.

56. Martz et al., "After the Meltdown of '87."

57. See Bill Powell et al., "Averting a Crisis: What Can Be Done?" *Newsweek,* November 9, 1987, pp. 32–37.

58. Robert J. Samuelson, "The United States Can't Solve the Crisis By Itself," *Newsweek,* November 9, 1987, pp. 38–39.

59. See Dick Kirschten, "White House Notebook," *National Journal,* November 28, 1987, pp. 3046–47.

60. Elizabeth Wehr and John R. Crawford, "Cordial Talks on Deficit Belie Hardball Politics," *Congressional Quarterly Weekly Report,* October 31, 1987, p. 2652.

61. "America's budget mouse," *The Economist,* November 28, 1987, p. 12.

62. Lawrence J. Haas, "Chorus of Bronx Cheers for Budget Pact," *National Journal,* November 28, 1987, p. 3048.

63. Conversations with Susan Rasky, reporter for the *New York Times.*

64. Lawrence J. Haas, "Promises to Keep," *National Journal,* April 2, 1988, pp. 859–67.

65. Congressional Budget Office, *The Economic and Budget Outlook: Fiscal Years 1989–1993,* A Report to the Senate and House Committees on the Budget (Washington, D.C.: U.S. Government Printing Office, February 1988), p. 50.

66. Congressional Budget Office, *Reducing the Deficit: Spending and Revenue Options,* a Report to the Senate and House Committees on the Budget—Part II (Washington, D.C.: U.S. Government Printing Office, March 1988), pp. 44–45.

67. Ibid., pp. 135–36.

68. For discussion of the importance of VAT, see Harold Wilensky, *The Welfare State and Inequality* (Berkeley: University of California Press, 1975); Henry J. Aaron, "The Value-Added Tax, Sorting Through the Practical and Political Problem," *The Brookings Review,* Summer 1988, pp. 10–16; Aaron Wildavsky, "The Unanticipated Consequences of the 1984 Presidential Election," *Tax Notes* 24, no. 2 (July 9, 1984), pp. 193–200.

69. Joseph J. Minarik and Rudolph G. Penner, "Fiscal Choices," in Isabel V. Sawhill, ed., *Challenge to Leadership* (Washington, D.C.: Urban Institute, 1988), pp. 279–316; quote on p. 290.

70. The reader may consult the annual CBO baseline reports, and August/September updates, for further data.

71. Palmer did his calculations for "Should We Worry About the Deficit?" by John Palmer and Stephanie Gould, *The Washington Monthly,* May 1986, pp. 43–46. We are working from background tables and drafts that he kindly provided.

72. Authors' estimates from John Palmer's work tables.

73. Congressional Budget Office, *Economic and Budget Outlook,* Tables II-7 and G-5, G-6.

74. Henry J. Aaron, Harvey Galper, Joseph A. Pechman, George L. Perry, Alice M. Rivlin, Charles L. Schultze, *Economic Choices 1987* (Washington, D.C.: Brookings Institution, 1986), p. 4.

75. Ibid., pp. 8–9.

76. Minarik and Penner, "Fiscal Choices," p. 289.

Chapter Twenty-Two

1. See James M. Buchanan and Richard E. Wagner, *Democracy in Deficit: The Political Legacy of Keynes* (New York: Academic Press, 1977).

2. Sheldon S. Wolin, "The New Public Philosophy," *Democracy* (October 1981), pp. 23–36.

3. Theodore J. Lowi, *The End of Liberalism: The Second Republic of the United States*, 2d ed. (New York: W. W. Norton, 1979).

4. B. Jessop, *The Capitalist State* (London: Martin Robinson, 1982).

5. Fred Block, "The Ruling Class Does Not Rule: Notes on the Marxist Theory of the State," *Socialist Revolution*, Number 33, Vol. 7, No. 3 (May–June 1977), pp. 6–28; quote on pages 7–8.

6. Where Marx emphasized the causal force of the substructure of society as the relations engineered by ownership of production, holding the superstructure of ideas to be determined by it, the capitalist vanguard theory has it at least partly in reverse. What, then, following up the parallel to the proletarian vanguard as the Communist party, would prevent the state apparatus from subordinating industrialists to their own purposes?

7. Stephen L. Elkin, "Between Liberalism and Capitalism: An Introduction to the Democratic State," in Roger Benjamin and Stephen L. Elkin, eds., *The Democratic State* (Lawrence: University Press of Kansas, 1985), p. 5.

8. Block, "Ruling Class Does Not Rule," pp. 13–14.

9. Ibid., pp. 23–24. See also Nicos Poulantzas on the relative autonomy of the state, arguing that the state cuts into the short-term economic advantages of business in order to secure its long-range political dominance. *Contemporary Capitalism* (London: New Left Books, 1974).

10. See Ralph Miliband, *The State in Capitalist Society* (London: Weidenfeld Nicolson, 1969); and G. William Domhoff, "State Autonomy and the Privileged Position of Business: An Empirical Attack on a Theoretical Fantasy," *Journal of Political and Military Sociology* 14, no. 1 (Spring 1986), pp. 149–62.

11. See Block, "Ruling Class Does Not Rule"; and Charles E. Lindblom, *Politics and Markets* (New York: Basic Books, 1977).

12. Jon Elster, "Marxism, Functionalism, and Game Theory: The Case for Methodological Individualism," *Theory and Society* 11, no. 4 (July 1982), pp. 453–82.

13. Claus Offe, "The Capitalist State and the Problem of Policy Formation," in Leon N. Lindberg, Robert Alford, Colin Crouch, and Claus Offe, eds., *Stress and Contradiction in Modern Capitalism* (Lexington, Mass.: D. C. Heath, 1973).

14. Peter B. Evans, Dietrich Rueschemeyer, and Theda Skocpol, "On the Road Toward a More Adequate Understanding of the State," in Evans, Rueschemeyer, and Skocpol, eds., *Bringing the State Back In* (Cambridge: Cambridge University Press, 1985), pp. 347–66; quote on p. 354.

15. In his *The Fiscal Crisis of the State* (New York: St. Martin's Press, 1975) James O'Conner argues that the government, unable to rely on the private sector

to create sufficient employment, subsidizes both worker and capital, thereby depleting its resources while providing insufficiently for each; he carries further the contention that the state has become the arena for class conflicts it cannot contain. Maybe. Just as (or more) likely, the expansion of resource mobilization into the furthest reaches of the population generates pressures to control state spending so as to alleviate taxation. Indeed, tax revolts skip a step by reducing revenue in order to place downward pressure on spending.

16. Apparently the term "ungovernability" was coined by news commentator Eric Severeid in 1974. James Douglas, "Review Article: The Overloaded Crown," *British Journal of Politics* 6 (October 1976), pp. 483–505.

17. Ibid., p. 493.

18. Samuel Brittan, "The Economic Contradictions of Democracy," *British Journal of Politics* 5 (April 1975), pp. 129–59.

19. Samuel P. Huntington, "Postindustrial Politics: How Benign Will It Be?" *Comparative Politics* 6, no. 2 (January 1974), p. 181.

20. Douglas, "Overloaded Crown," p. 484.

21. Quoted in Douglas, "Overloaded Crown," pp. 492–93.

22. Huntington, "Postindustrial Politics," p. 177.

23. Douglas, "Overloaded Crown," p. 494.

24. Claus Offe, "New Social Movements as a Meta-Political Challenge," type-script, 1983, p. 4.

25. Ibid., p. 4.

26. Michel Crozier, Samuel Huntington, and Joji Watanuki, *The Crisis of Democracy* (New York: The Trilateral Commission and New York University Press, 1975).

27. Huntington, "Postindustrial Politics," pp. 189–90ff.

28. See Herb McClosky and John Zaller, *The American Ethos: Public Attitudes toward Capitalism and Democracy* (Cambridge, Mass.: Harvard University Press, 1984).

29. Earl Latham, *The Group Basis of Politics* (Ithaca, N.Y.: Cornell University Press, 1952).

30. Robert Dahl, *Who Governs?* (New Haven: Yale University Press, 1961); Raymond Bauer, Ithiel Poole, and Lewis Dexter, *American Business and Public Policy* (Hawthorne, N.Y.: Aldine Atherton de Gruyter, 1972); Theodore Lowi, "The Welfare State and the State of Welfare," typescript, n.d.; James Q. Wilson, ed., *The Politics of Regulation* (New York: Basic Books, 1980).

31. See Carolyn Webber and Aaron Wildavsky, *A History of Taxation and Expenditure in the Western World* (New York: Simon & Schuster, 1986).

32. See Aaron Wildavsky, "The Three-Party System—1980 and After," *The Public Interest*, No. 64 (Summer 1981), pp. 47–57.

33. For discussion of these categories, see Aaron Wildavsky, "Choosing Preferences by Constructing Institutions: A Cultural Theory of Preference Formation," *American Political Science Review* 81, no. 1 (March 1987), pp. 3–21; Michael Thompson and Aaron Wildavsky, "A Poverty of Distinction: From economic homogeneity to cultural heterogeneity in the classification of poor people," *Policy Sciences* 19 (1986), pp. 163–99; and Mary Douglas, "Cultural Bias," in Douglas, *In the Active Voice* (London: Routledge & Kegan Paul, 1982).

34. David Truman, *Governmental Process* (New York: A. A. Knopf, 1951), all quotes from pp. 512–15.

35. Ibid., pp. 506–7. The battle of the budget can be described only partly in his terms because his book is about preferences, not effectiveness. The whole "nonpolitical" side of our story, the economic crisis and the difficulty of response, requires different terms and questions than Truman provides. He could say, of course, that resource constraints must exacerbate group conflict. But that does not tell us what kind of governance is possible and therefore how much we can demand of our governors. The cognitive difficulties of policymaking and the relationship between the financial markets and the politicians cannot be discussed only as attitudes. They constitute constraints of systematic importance. These resource constraints serve, in effect, as objectives that must be met to secure system maintenance. We judge our representatives, as David Mayhew points out, by whether they represent our preferences; see Mayhew, *Congress: The Electoral Connection* (New Haven, Conn.: Yale University Press, 1974). But we judge our government by its effects; in evaluating our political system and explaining its gyrations, therefore, we have to ask what it can do, not just what it wants to do.

36. Murray Edelman, *The Symbolic Uses of Politics* (Urbana: University of Illinois Press, 1974).

37. See C. E. Lindblom, *Politics and Markets* (New York: Basic Books, 1977); and David Vogel, "Why Businessmen Distrust Their State," *British Journal of Political Science* 8 (January 1978), pp. 45–78, as sources of further argument and evidence.

38. Lowi, *End of Liberalism,* chap. 2.

39. Ibid., p. 50.

40. Charles W. Anderson, "Political Design and the Representation of Interest," *Comparative Political Studies* 10, no. 1 (April 1977), p. 139.

41. Grant McConnell, *Private Power and American Democracy* (New York: Knopf, 1966), pp. 51–52.

42. Lowi, *End of Liberalism,* pp. 50–51, 96–97.

43. No one has ever put this better than John C. Calhoun in his *Disquisition on Government* (New York: Political Science Classics, 1947):

> I have said—if it were possible for man to be so constituted, as to feel what affects others more strongly than what affects himself, or even as strongly—because, it may be well doubted, whether the stronger feeling or affection of individuals for themselves, combined with a feebler and subordinate feeling or affection for others, is not, in beings of limited reason and faculties, a constitution necessary to their preservation and existence. If reversed—if their feelings and affections were stronger for others than for themselves, or even as strong, the necessary result would seem to be, that all individuality would be lost; and boundless and remediless disorder and confusion would ensue. For each, at the same moment, intensely participating in all the conflicting emotions of those around him, would, of course, forget himself and all that concerned him immediately, in his officious intermeddling with the affairs of all others; which, from his limited reason and faculties, he could neither properly understand nor

manage. . . . Government would be impossible; or, if it could by possibility exist, its object would be reversed. Selfishness would have to be encouraged and benevolence discouraged. Individuals would have to be encouraged, by rewards, to become more selfish, and deterred, by punishments, from being too benevolent; and this, too, by a government, administered by those who, on the supposition, would have the greatest aversion for self-ishness and the highest admiration for benevolence.

To the Infinite Being, the Creator of all, belongs exclusively the care and superintendence of the whole. (pp. 5–6)

Chapter Twenty-Three

1. "Robust Economic Figures Indicate Threat of Inflation," *Wall Street Journal,* July 11, 1988, p. 22.

2. Tom Kenworthy, "Hill Sees Opportunity for Progress on Deficit: Market's Dive Yields Wave of Responsibility," *Washington Post,* October 31, 1987, p. A9.

3. Anne Swardson, "House Chaos Provided a Day to Remember," *Washington Post,* October 31, 1987, p. A9.

4. Jeffrey H. Birnbaum, "White House, Top Capitol Hill Democrats Remain Far Apart on Deficit-Curb Plans," *Wall Street Journal,* October 29, 1987, p. 7.

5. See Joseph White, "The Continuing Resolution: A Crazy Way to Govern?" *Brookings Review* 6, no. 3 (Summer 1988): 28–35.

6. George Gallup, Jr., and Alec Gallup, "Deficit is top issue among the electorate," *Oakland Tribune,* November 6, 1988, p. A6.

7. Paul Blustein, "Fractious budget commission at impasse as deadline nears," *Oakland Tribune,* November 6, 1988, p. A6.

8. *Report of the National Economic Commission* (Washington, D.C.: U.S. Government Printing Office, March 1, 1989). The Republicans were joined by former Rep. Thomas Ashley (D-Ohio), one of President Bush's two appointees, who though he had a fairly liberal record in the House was a close friend of George Bush. Therefore, theirs constituted the Majority Report.

9. Ibid., pp. 13, 36, 50, 56.

10. David Rapp, "Negotiators Agree on Outlines of Fiscal 1990 Plan," *Congressional Quarterly Weekly Report,* April 15, 1989, pp. 804–5. See also Elizabeth Wehr, "Budget Plan Entails Tax Bill, but Details Are up in Air," in ibid., p. 806; David Rapp, "Bipartisan Pact Lets Everyone Be A Winner—For Now," *Congressional Quarterly Weekly Report,* April 22, 1989, pp. 880–82; and especially Democratic Study Group, "The FY 1990 Budget Resolution," Fact Sheet no. 101–3 (mimeo), May 1, 1989. The negotiators were Foley, Darman, Panetta, Sasser, Secretary of the Treasury Nicholas F. Brady, and the ranking minority members of the budget committees, Rep. Bill Frenzel and Sen. Pete Domenici.

11. See the speech given by Representative Hamilton during debate on the budget resolution, *Congressional Record,* May 3, 1989, pp. H1553–H1556, especially H1553.

12. Democratic Study Group, "FY1990 Budget Resolution," p. 4.

13. $5.7 billion in asset sales, but specifically not President Bush's proposals

to sell the Elk Hill Naval Petroleum Reserve and federal power marketing administrations; $1.2 billion in extra user fees and offsetting collections from administrative improvements and sale of the right to make chlorofluorocarbons; $850 million from paying some farm costs in FY89 instead of FY90; $477 million from writing off all food stamps not cashed in previous years as an outlay savings in FY90 (??); $496 million from legislation allowing sales of some VA loans; and $2,120 billion from taking the Post Office and a farm credit agency off budget.

14. Maintaining Medicare Part B premiums at 25 percent of program cost; extending National Flood Insurance Fund and VA loan origination fees; and not providing the judicial and legislative branch pay raises that Congress had already rejected.

15. Senator Bentsen didn't even attend the announcement of the agreement; see David Rapp, "Negotiators Agree." Representative Rostenkowski showed his skepticism on the House floor; see *Congressional Record*, May 3, 1989, p. 1533.

16. David Rapp, "Negotiators Agree."

17. Panetta in *Congressional Record*, May 3, 1989, pp. 1523–24.

18. *Congressional Record*, May 3, 1989, p. H1519.

19. This had become, by 1989, the major argument by academic economists for deficit reduction. Indeed, "the crisis," Charles Schultze of Brookings frequently remarked, "is that there is no crisis." He and others therefore feared politicians might ignore the costs to long-term growth from using national savings to finance government consumption. The difficulty is that the consequences of increased savings through reduced deficits are rather murky. CBO reported that running a 2 percent budget surplus after FY93, rather than a balanced budget, would reduce personal consumption for five to ten years, but by the year 2040 would raise personal consumption by between 2 and 14 percent. Neither the scale nor the certainty of benefit involved seems, to us, a convincing argument for an extra $100 billion in policy change now. See Congressional Budget Office, *The Economic and Budget Outlook: Fiscal Years 1990–1994* (Washington, D.C.: U.S. Government Printing Office, January 1989), pp. 93–95.

20. Ibid., pp. xv, 41, 57.

21. This estimate is based on the figures in Table II-4 in ibid., p. 51, for the effect of one percentage-point less real growth.

22. Ibid., Table II-3, p. 47.

INDEX

657

Compositor: J. Jarrett Engineering, Inc.
Text: 10/12 Baskerville
Display: Baskerville
Printer: Edwards Brothers
Binder: Edwards Brothers